Slave Country

Slave Country

American Expansion and the
Origins of the Deep South

Adam Rothman

HARVARD UNIVERSITY PRESS
Cambridge, Massachusetts
London, England

First Harvard University Press paperback edition, 2007

Library of Congress Cataloging-in-Publication Data

Rothman, Adam, 1971–
Slave country : American expansion and the origins of the Deep South /
Adam Rothman
p. cm.
Includes bibliographical references and index.
ISBN-13 978-0-674-01674-3 (cloth: alk. paper)
ISBN-10 0-674-01674-2 (cloth: alk. paper)
ISBN-13 978-0-674-02416-8 (pbk.)
ISBN-10 0-674-02416-8 (pbk.)
1. Slavery—United States—History—19th century.
2. United Sates—Territorial expansion.
3. Slavery—Southern States—History—19th century.
4. Southern States—History—1775–1865.   I. Title.

E446.R67 2005
306.3'62'0973—dc22   2004057658

For my parents

There warn't nothing to do now but to look out sharp for the town, and not pass it without seeing it. He said he'd be mighty sure to see it, because he'd be a free man the minute he seen it, but if he missed it he'd be in a slave country again and no more show for freedom.

—MARK TWAIN,

Adventures of Huckleberry Finn

Contents

Preface

WHY DID SLAVERY expand in the early national United States? This question is central to some of the most important issues in nineteenth-century American history, including the transition from colonial society to independent nation-state; the process of continental expansion and the character of the frontier; and the origins of the Civil War. Yet it is not a question that has been answered convincingly. Many Americans regard slavery as an embarrassment to the revolutionary commitment to liberty, an example of sordid interests temporarily blocking the fulfillment of the country's ideals. Some believe that it is unrealistic to wonder why the revolutionary generation did not abolish slavery or overcome racism in addition to all its other achievements. But why did such an imaginative group of people declare independence from one of the greatest empires on earth and establish a truly novel polity but not get rid of an institution that most of them thought was immoral and dangerous? The question is not merely why the revolutionary generation did not abolish slavery, but why slavery expanded under its watch.

For it cannot be denied that slavery expanded in the United States for fifty years following the American Revolution. These formative years of the republic represent a dynamic but mysterious middle period in the history of American slavery, bridging the colonial slave system and its antebellum descendant. During this middle period, the slave population grew in number, moved across space, and changed in composition. It had taken more than 100 years for the slave population of colonial North America to reach 500,000—a threshold crossed sometime between 1770 and 1790—but by 1820 more than 1.5 million slaves lived in the United States.[1] While slavery contracted in the northern states in the early national era, it expanded geographically to the south and west. Six new slave states joined the Union during the period: Kentucky, Tennessee, Louisiana, Mississippi, Alabama, and Missouri. As slavery expanded in the new United States, slaves forcibly transported to the new plantation areas were put to work cultivating cotton and sugar, which had not been important crops in North America during the colonial era. Thousands of slaves arrived from Africa and the Caribbean during these years, although the United States ultimately divorced itself from transatlantic sources of slave labor by banning the importation of slaves. At the same time, forced migration reappeared within North America as an internal slave trade emerged to satisfy the growing demand for slaves in the country's expanding plantation areas. All these changes molded the slave system of the United States into the distinctive form that it assumed in the decades leading to the Civil War.[2]

Why did this happen, and how? Discovering the origins of the Deep South—the region that became the states of Louisiana, Mississippi, and Alabama—helps to answer the question. In the 1780s, the region was thinly populated by a congeries of peoples subject to the overlapping jurisdictions of several American Indian nations, Spain, and the United States. Plantation slavery was limited to a thin strip of settlement in the lower Mississippi Valley devoted to the cultivation of indigo and tobacco. Compared with other places in the Americas, the region scarcely registered in the roll of slave societies.[3] Everything changed over the next thirty years. As the United States extended its sovereignty—at times by force of arms—thousands of free and enslaved people arrived there and jointly made the region one of the major producers of slave-grown commodities in the world. By the beginning of the 1820s, it was the leading edge of a dynamic, expansive slave regime incorporated politically into the United States and firmly tied to the transatlantic system of commodity exchange. Explaining these developments goes a long way toward understanding the early United States as a "slave country."

Nothing is ingrained more deeply in American ideology than that ours is a free country. Yet freedom and slavery were densely entangled in the early United States. After the American Revolution won independence for most of the British colonies of North America, the United States became a free country in an important sense of the term. Moreover the new country's citizens (and many of its other inhabitants) insisted on their own individual freedom by opposing excessive taxation, extending the franchise, and throwing off habits of deference to social superiors. Nevertheless slavery permeated virtually all human relations in the new country in direct and indirect ways. Slavery was a social reality for millions of people, an important economic institution, and a basic metaphor of power in the prevailing rhetoric of politics that emerged from the Revolution. The entangling of freedom and slavery in the early national era was starkly revealed in the popular claim among slavery's defenders that the legacy of the American Revolution included the right to own other human beings as slaves, and that government-sponsored abolition was a despotic infringement of individual liberty. To identify the early national United States as a "slave country" is thus not merely an epithet. It is also the starting line for an analysis of the new country's most vexing predicament.[4]

Few living in the 1780s could have predicted what lay ahead. Slavery's expansion in the Deep South emerged from contingent global forces, concrete policies pursued by governments, and countless small choices made by thousands of individuals in diverse stations of life. All these are the subject of this book.

Slave Country

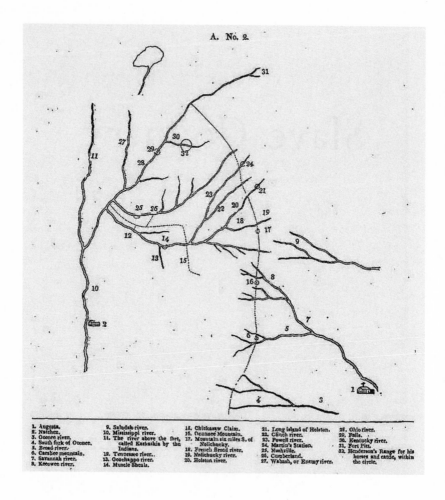

A. No. 2.

A map copied in 1785 from one drawn by Old Tassel, headman of the Cherokee Indians, to clarify the boundaries of the Cherokee nation. It offers an indigenous view of territory and sovereignty in the region that later became the Deep South. Natchez is in the lower left corner of the map and Augusta in the lower right corner. Fort Pitt is located in the upper right corner. Old Tassel was assassinated in 1788. REPRODUCED FROM *AMERICAN STATE PAPERS, INDIAN AFFAIRS* (WASHINGTON, D.C.: GALES AND SEATON, 1832), 1: 40.

CHAPTER I

Jefferson's Horizon

FOR THOMAS JEFFERSON, the cataclysms of history dissolved into the soothing scene of the American landscape. In *Notes on the State of Virginia,* written in the early 1780s, Jefferson described the sensation of gazing at the majestic confluence of the Potomac and Shenandoah Rivers in western Virginia's Blue Ridge Mountains: "The first glance of this scene hurries our senses into the opinion, that this earth has been created in time, that the mountains were formed first, that the rivers began to flow afterwards, that in this place particularly they have been dammed up by the Blue ridge of mountains, and have formed an ocean which filled the whole valley; that continuing to rise they have at length broken over at this spot, and have torn the mountain down from its summit to its base." The agents of nature were historical forces, powerful and catastrophic. They left marks of a tumultuous past all over the landscape. By contrast, the future lay in the "distant finishing" beyond the cloven mountains. There Jefferson found solace in "a small catch of smooth blue horizon, at an infinite distance in the plain country, inviting you, as it were, from the riot and tumult roaring around, to pass through the breach and participate of the calm below. Here the eye ultimately composes itself; and that way too the road happens actually to lead." The full view suggested that beyond the tumultuous landscape of history lay the harmonious landscape of the future, a pleasant scene of agricultural and commercial activity. That future beckoned to Jefferson, who viewed it from a distant promontory.[1]

One aspect of the American vista especially troubled Jefferson, and that aspect was slavery. Jefferson recognized that slavery was the most dangerous and intractable problem that the infant nation confronted. He wrote that slaveholders were despots and slaves were their enemies. Slavery corrupted the manners of slaveowners and threatened to bring the just wrath of God down upon them. Of all the social problems in Virginia that Jefferson identified, only the problem of slavery compelled him to contemplate the kind of cataclysmic forces that had created the Potomac Gap. But just as Jefferson's gaze moved from the valley to the horizon, Jefferson expected that slavery would eventually disappear. "The spirit of the master is abating, that of the slave rising from the dust, his condition mollifying, the way I hope preparing, under the auspices of heaven, for a total emancipation, and that this is disposed, in the order of events, to be with the consent of the masters, rather than by their extirpation."[2] Jefferson's optimism was not entirely unfounded. In the northern United States and in parts of the upper South where slavery was not a dominant social relation, many white people had come to believe that slavery was an obstacle to progress. The presence of slavery in the United States, they argued, inhibited economic development, endangered national security, and undermined the virtue of the people. Private acts of manumission and public acts of emancipation slowly undermined slavery from New England to the northwestern districts of Virginia in the decade following the American Revolution.[3]

At the same time, Jefferson ignored powerful demographic, economic, and political circumstances that strengthened slaveowners' power and set slavery on the road to expansion. The slave population of the new United States was large and growing. In a country of almost 3.9 million people in 1790, nearly 700,000—or 15 percent—

were enslaved. Slaves lived in every state except Massachusetts and Vermont, but they were concentrated in the states south of Pennsylvania. Almost 95 percent of all enslaved people in the United States in 1790 lived in Delaware, Maryland, Virginia, North Carolina, South Carolina, Georgia, and the territory that would become Kentucky. Jefferson's Virginia, the most populous state in the Union, also contained the most slaves—nearly 300,000. One-third of the people living in the southern states were slaves, and about one-third of all households there included slaves. Especially in the southern states, then, slavery was a vital part of society.[4]

Natural reproduction and importation swelled the number of slaves in the southern states. The slave population in the Chesapeake region began to reproduce itself naturally by the 1720s, and that of the Carolina lowcountry by midcentury. Relatively equal numbers of enslaved men and women, and an increasingly native-born slave population, were both features of slavery in British North America that distinguished it from slavery in the Caribbean.[5] Yet the ongoing importation of slaves partly masked the natural growth of the slave population. More than 300,000 enslaved Africans arrived in the British North American colonies between 1700 and 1790. Slave imports peaked in midcentury, then declined until the end of the American Revolution, when they picked up once again.[6] Contemporary observers did not have precise statistical knowledge of the relative importance of natural reproduction and importation, but they generally knew that the slave population was increasing, and that knowledge stoked white Southerners' fears of being overwhelmed by a growing black population in the event of a general emancipation.

Most of all, slavery's contribution to the economy of the new United States militated against emancipation. The crucial export sectors of the southern states—tobacco in the upper South, rice and indigo in the lower South—depended on the labor of enslaved people and had done so for almost a century. Exports from the southern states accounted for almost half of the value of all exports from the United States in 1789–90, with tobacco, rice, and indigo accounting for almost one-third of the value of the country's exports. Planters put slaves to work cultivating the new crops that emerged as profitable commodities in the 1790s—wheat in the upper South, short-staple cotton in the lower South.[7] The phenomenal expansion of short-staple cotton production in the 1790s especially strengthened the connection between slavery and national economic development. South Carolina's governor, John Drayton, declared in 1800 that his state's cotton production had become a "matter of National Joy."[8] To their owners, enslaved people were valuable property, worth on average $200 each. One early nineteenth-century statistician estimated that slaves accounted for 12.5 percent of the country's total wealth in 1800.[9] They were bought and sold, rented out, mortgaged, and inherited. ("Slaves pass by descent and dower as lands do," Jefferson blandly explained in his *Notes*.)[10] Many dreams and a great deal of suffering flowed from these transactions. The routine of economic life frequently disrupted slaves' families and communities, as slaves were sold to pay off debts or distributed among the heirs of an estate.[11]

While their numbers and economic might guaranteed that slaveowners would constitute a formidable political bloc in the new republic, the structure of politics amplified their power. Despite the popular mobilization of the revolutionary era, national office holding remained the province of elites, who were more likely to be slaveowners than were the mass of free people.[12] Added to this elitist bias was a regional accommodation. The new Union could not survive without the participation of the southern states, and the price of the southern states' participation was a guarantee that the national government would refrain from trampling on the rights of slaveowners. Thus, the federal Constitution protected slavery without ever using the word. The three-fifths clause (Article 1, Section 2) gave an advantage in the House of Representatives to states with large slave populations. The slave-trade clause (Article 1, Section 9) prevented the national government from prohibiting the importation of slaves for twenty years. And the fugitive clause (Article 4, Section 2) prevented runaway slaves from finding any legal refuge in "free" states.[13]

Slaveowners dominated the national government from the start. President George Washington was one of the country's largest planters. His secretary of state (Jefferson) and attorney general (Edmund Randolph) were also large slaveowning planters from Virginia. In the first federal Congress, twenty-nine of sixty-five representatives (45 percent) and ten of twenty-six senators (38 percent) were from Maryland, Virginia, North Carolina, South Carolina, and Georgia. Of these, fourteen representatives and eight senators were planters.[14] They threw their weight around Congress early in 1790 when three antislavery groups petitioned Congress to determine the powers of the national government with respect to slavery. No senator came forward to defend the petitions, and the Senate refused to consider them. The petitions got a friendlier reception in the more democratic House, which—over the vehement objections of representatives from Georgia and South Carolina—formed a committee to investigate the issue on the strength of support from the North and the upper South. Composed by six northerners and a Virginian, the committee's report upheld some basic restrictions on the power of the national government to emancipate slaves, outlined some modest powers to regulate the African slave trade, and promised that Congress would pursue the "humane objects" of the abolition societies "so far as can be promoted on the principles of justice, humanity, and good policy." Representatives from the upper South now joined their fellows from the lower South in eviscerating the report's antislavery tone and content. While allowing that Congress had the power to restrain American citizens "from carrying on the African trade, for the purpose of supplying foreigners with slaves," the final report declared that Congress had "no authority to interfere in the emancipation of slaves, or in the treatment of them within any of the States; it remaining with the several States alone to provide any regulations therein, which humanity and true policy may require."[15] Slavery would be a matter for the states, not the national government, to regulate.

The debates over the Constitution and the antislavery petitions reveal regional and ideological fissures in the early national politics of slavery. Many white northerners disliked slavery on philosophical grounds but opposed immediate emancipation even in their own region. Respect for slaveowners' property rights and disdain for black people's capacity for citizenship resulted in laws for gradual rather than immediate emancipation in most of the northern states. Most northerners were reluctant to extend this pattern of gradual emancipation to the southern states. Some were relatively indifferent toward slavery in the southern states, and others were downright hostile to emancipation, believing that it would send hordes of free black people to the North. Slaveowners found a useful ally in the northern states' powerful merchants, who profited from carrying slave-produced agricultural commodities from the southern states to foreign markets. Moreover, northern politicians in Congress needed southern support for their own favorite measures, including the assumption of state debts. Northern antislavery societies could not surmount the low priority accorded to emancipation by their representatives on the national stage.[16]

Elites in the upper South condemned the Atlantic slave trade but staunchly defended the rights of white people to own slaves. Their position flowed directly from the combination of population growth and economic transition that bequeathed a surplus of slave labor to the region.[17] James Madison articulated the anti–slave trade, proslavery position during the Virginia debates over the ratification of the proposed Constitution. He argued that the Constitution improved the odds for an eventual prohibition on the importation of slaves while affording greater protection for slaveowners' special property interests through the fugitive slave clause.[18] Representatives from the upper South reiterated their position in the first Congress during the debates over the antislavery petitions. They joined opponents of slavery in giving the petitions a hearing and in affirming the power of the national government to regulate American citizens' participation in the foreign slave trade, but joined slavery's defenders in strictly prohibiting the national government from interfering with slavery in the states.[19] These developments on the national level coincided with a renewed defense of slavery on the state and local level, exemplified in a series of petitions addressed to the Virginia state legislature in 1784 and 1785 attacking the liberalization of the state's manumission laws and repudiating a Methodist antislavery campaign. Petitioners from Lunenberg County declared that they had "seald with our Blood, a Title to the full, free, and absolute Enjoyment of every species of our Property, whensoever, or however legally acquired." They argued that emancipation would invite poverty, crime, and "final ruin to this once happy, free, and flourishing Country." Others charged that the Methodists' attack on slavery was "unsupported by Scripture," citing chapter and verse to show that the Bible sanctioned slavery.[20]

The most vigorous defense of slavery in all its aspects came from the lowcountry elites of South Carolina and Georgia. It was the delegates from the lower South who had blocked the federal Constitution from immediately prohibiting the importation of slaves, and during the debates over the antislavery petitions in 1790, they were the ones who threatened to leave the Union or resist by force of arms if Congress contemplated emancipation.[21] They did not shirk from defending slavery in forthright language. In a long speech to the House of Representatives in March 1790, South Carolina's William Loughton Smith assaulted the antislavery petitions with the full arsenal of proslavery doctrine. He argued that Congress had no power to emancipate slaves, that the citizens of the southern states would not allow it, and that if it occurred, the freedpeople would "either starve or plunder." He taunted the emancipationists for their racist views, asking if any of the Quakers had "ever married a negro, or would any of them suffer their children to mix their blood with that of a black?" He denied that slavery weakened his part of the country or degraded its citizens. Rather, he insisted, the civilization of the lowcountry depended on slave labor and would not survive without it: "Remove the cultivators of the soil, and the whole of the low country, all the fertile rice and indigo swamps will be deserted, and become a wilderness."[22] While slaveowners in the upper South unanimously opposed slave importation, those in the lower South split on the issue. Following a four-year revival of slave imports after the American Revolution, South Carolina prohibited slave importation in 1787 and—against pressure from the upcountry—maintained the prohibition until 1803. Georgia, which had come late to slavery and was rapidly increasing in population, continued to admit foreign slaves until 1798.[23]

Given its social importance, slavery was bound to have ideological consequences. Fear of enslavement suffused the Americans' revolutionary rhetoric. It was the most potent metaphor of injustice in their vocabulary. No less a figure than George Washington described the war against Great Britain as "a struggle which was begun and has been continued for the purpose of rescuing America from impending Slavery."[24] But a hatred of slavery could easily shade into contempt for slaves. If slavery was degrading, demoralizing, and dishonoring, then did it not follow that enslaved people were degraded, demoralized, and dishonored?[25] And did it not also follow that if emancipated, freedpeople would be unfit for citizenship, and might even try to avenge the horrible wrongs done to them? The structure of the revolutionary antislavery argument thus created a terrible dilemma. Slavery was unjust—so the argument went—but the consequences of its injustice made immediate emancipation untenable. In Query 14 of his *Notes*, Jefferson proposed a way out: a program of gradual emancipation and deportation (euphemistically termed "colonization" by later advocates) of the emancipated. Deportation, he argued, was made necessary by "deep rooted prejudices entertained by the whites; ten thousand recollections, by the blacks, of the injuries they have sustained; new provocations; the real distinctions which nature has made; and many other circumstances."[26] Jefferson's long and infamous rumination on the biological differences between black and white people in his *Notes* was itself a literary eruption of the deep-rooted prejudices against people of African descent that had been produced by slavery and now vexed its abolition. "This unfortunate difference of colour, and perhaps of faculty, is a powerful obstacle to the emancipation of these people," Jefferson concluded.[27]

Thus the newly independent United States entered into history as a slave country. Its population included many slaves. Vital economic sectors depended on slave labor. Elite slaveowners and their allies composed a dominant political coalition. Racism flourished under these conditions. Despite the decline of slavery in the northern states, slavery was deeply woven into a national fabric that had begun to stretch across America.

"beginning the world"

Jefferson's vision for the new country was geographically expansive. It ran all the way to the Mississippi River, which he predicted would become "one of the principal channels of future commerce for the country westward of the Allegheny."[28] Jefferson's prophecy for the Mississippi holds a clue to the kind of country he imagined. The North American interior would be inhabited by commercial farmers whose livelihood depended on their ability to sell their surplus to distant markets. As Jefferson penned his *Notes on the State of Virginia,* white and black Americans were already crossing the mountains into the trans-Appalachian frontier, but contrary to Jefferson's vision of peaceful expansion, mass migration into the North American interior brought the United States into conflict with the indigenous groups already there. It also generated pressure on the United States to secure sovereignty over the interior rivers that carried backcountry commodities to the Gulf of Mexico, their outlet to the world market. These continental struggles coincided with sustained international turmoil caused by the French Revolution and the Napoleonic wars that followed. One result was a vast geographic expansion of the sovereignty of the United States in North America, and the absorption of the region that eventually became the Deep South—the present states of Louisiana, Mississippi, and Alabama—into the Union.[29]

Sovereignty over the North American interior was ambiguous and heterogeneous. The peace settlement between Great Britain and the United States in 1783 had left the southern and western boundaries of the United States in dispute. Spain, Georgia, North Carolina, and the United States all claimed jurisdiction over territory north of the thirty-first parallel and east of the Mississippi River, while most of the lands in dispute were actually occupied by the southern Indian nations—the Creek, Choctaw, Chickasaw, and Cherokee Indians—who also claimed them. An indication of the contested character of the boundaries can be seen in contrasting maps from the period. The nationalist perspective is illustrated in a map of the southeastern region of North America published in *Morse's Geography* in 1792. Morse's map recognized the western land claims of Virginia, North Carolina, and Georgia. It stretched the names of these states all the way to the Mississippi in boldface and large type, overshadowing the names and boundaries of the Indian nations. In contrast, a 1794 map published by Laurie & Whittle in London diminished the jurisdictional claims of the United States while emphasizing the American Indian nations and Spanish dominions. It was more thorough in marking Indian towns and trading paths but did not mark any boundaries between the territorially indeterminate Indian nations. A third map drawn by the Cherokee headman Old Tassel in the 1780s presented an indigenous perspective. Drawn to clarify Cherokee territorial claims, Old Tassel's map emphasized rivers and clearly marked the boundary between Tassel's country and the United States. "I have shown you the bounds of my country on my map," he explained to a delegation of commissioners from the United States.[30]

Men and women from the original states poured into these contested regions. Census takers counted almost 75,000 white and black people in Kentucky in 1790. Ten years later, census takers counted more than 220,000 white and black people in Kentucky and another 105,000 in Tennessee.[31] They came largely from Pennsylvania, Virginia, and North Carolina. Some were pushed out by rural overcrowding, others by soil exhaustion or indebtedness. Others were pulled by the western country's reputation for good, cheap land and the opportunity to get rich or gain status.[32] Levi Todd, one of the first lot holders in the town of Lexington, Kentucky, witnessed the opening of the post–Revolutionary War migration. "Emigrations into this

Country from Virginia and Pennsyl[vani]a have been very great since last Summer," he wrote to a relative in February 1784. "Our Number since then has nearly doubled—and the People who have been confined to Forts are now entering the Woods, beginning the World." Todd's rhetoric offers a key to the mental map of westering migrants. They were not rugged individualists but participants in an act of social creation. "I believe we shall in a few years be a free a rich and happy People," he wrote.[33] Additional pressure against the southern frontier came from Georgia, which grew rapidly after the war. Its free and slave population almost doubled in the 1790s, the largest percentage increase in population of any of the original states. The sense of rejuvenation was echoed here as well. One Savannah merchant observed in 1783 that the inhabitants of Georgia were "settling again and beginning the World anew." He associated population growth with the expansion of commerce and slavery. "Trade will expand here beyond conception," he wrote. "Negros will be in great demand."[34]

White settlers in Kentucky, Tennessee, and Georgia saw two big threats to the progress of the southern frontier. The first was the prospect of war with the Cherokee and Creek Indians, who regarded the migrants as intruders. The violence of the postrevolutionary southern frontier was real, and its consequences were devastating. One observer estimated that 300 Kentuckians were killed between 1783 and 1787.[35] Georgia authorities reported that the Creeks had killed 72 white and 10 black people, and taken 30 white and 110 black prisoners, between 1787 and 1789.[36] More than 100 black and white inhabitants of the Southwest Territory were killed, wounded, or taken prisoner from January 1791 to November 1792.[37] Statistics on Indian casualties were not reported to the authorities, but Creek and Cherokee diplomats made it clear that their people suffered greatly from trespassing, theft, and murder at the hands of the white intruders. As one Cherokee agent protested, "Their flourishing fields of corn and pulse were destroyed and laid waste; some of their wives and children were burnt alive in their town houses, with the most unrelenting barbarity; and to fill up the measure of deception and cruelty, some of their chiefs, who were ever disposed to peace with the white people, were decoyed, unarmed, into their camp, by the hoisting of a white flag, and by repeated declarations of friendship and kindness, and there massacred in cold blood." Among the victims was Old Tassel, the mapmaker, deceitfully assassinated under a white flag of truce.[38]

Reviewing the situation on the southern frontier in 1789, Secretary of War Henry Knox found a Hobbesian world where "the sword of the republic only, is adequate to guard a due administration of justice, and the preservation of the peace."[39] But the sword of the republic had all it could handle north of the Ohio, where a coalition of Shawnee Indians and their allies defeated U.S. armies in 1790 and 1791, diverting the attention of the United States away from the southern frontier. Hoping to mollify the Creeks, Knox invited their mestizo leader Alexander McGillivray to a parley in New York in the summer of 1790, where the two men negotiated a treaty that failed to bring peace.[40] Instead, violence intensified. The Shawnee victories north of the Ohio emboldened militant factions among the Cherokees and Creeks, whose bravado reverberated in the words of White Lieutenant, an Upper Creek war leader. "Your mad men may think they can tear us up branch and root," he wrote to an American official in 1793, "but tell them the woods are large, and the days are not all gone."[41] Some months later when the same official ran into a company of Georgia militiamen, the company commander declared "that he would destroy all Indians he came across, whether friend or foe; and that he was opposed to peace."[42] Indian assaults on frontier settlements provoked severe and unauthorized reprisals by local white militias. The culmination of these reprisals came in September 1794, when more than 500 mounted troops from the Southwest Territory burned Nickajak and Running Water, two strongholds of militant Cherokees. A fragile peace prevailed thereafter for almost twenty years, during which time the United States launched a program to "civilize" the southern Indians and gradually acquire the rest of their land.[43]

Slaveowners on the southern frontier found their human property to be especially vulnerable in this anarchic milieu. Not only did enslaved people run to the Indians, but they also could be victims of violence, along with their owners, at the hands of the Indians. John May discovered the difficulty and complexity of keeping slaves in the wilderness as he surveyed lands at the falls of the Ohio in 1780. Unable to hire labor, May brought one of his slaves with him into the woods. May wrote that the man "fell in with some worthless Negroes who persuaded him to run away & attempt to get with the Indians; however, after ten days absence he thought it prudent to return." The surveyor concluded that the western districts "will be a bad place to bring Slaves to, being so near Indians that they will frequently find their way to them."[44] Slaves were frequently taken captive by Indian raiding parties, adding to the list of white settlers' grievances. Some black people were killed along with their white owners and neighbors, though the official records rarely name them. For example, Michael Cupps testified in 1793 that he saw thirty Indians near the Oconee River "firing upon and massacreing Richard Thresher, two children, and a negro wench."[45] So long as the border wars endangered black people, neither plantation slavery nor African American community life could flourish on the southern frontier.

For white settlers, Spanish control over the rivers—especially the Mississippi—constituted another threat to the progress of their society. Farmers in the Ohio and Tennessee river valleys recognized that the Mississippi offered the cheapest way to get their commodities to lucrative markets. Boatmen floated whiskey, tobacco, hemp, pork, and many other goods down the Mississippi to New Orleans, where the goods were transferred to seafaring vessels and shipped to the eastern states, Spanish America, the West Indies, and Europe. Back-country farmers who could not easily carry their goods to the Mississippi looked to the other rivers that flowed into the Gulf of Mexico—the Apalachicola, Tombigbee, Mobile, and Pearl—which Spain also controlled. American settlers in the trans-Appalachian interior considered the free navigation of these rivers to be a right derived from nature and nature's God. In 1788, a correspondent from Davidson County in western North Carolina (which would later become part of Tennessee) explained that his neighbors believed God had given them the Mississippi River for the use of all mankind, and no European power should have the power to restrict their access to it: "These inhabitants say that Spain has no more right to impede our navigation than to hinder the Sun's shining on our Fields."[46] A few years later, the Democratic-Republican Society of Lexington, Kentucky, insisted that Kentuckians had a "natural right" to the free navigation of the Mississippi. The society expressed a providential view of American geography. "It cannot be believed," declared its members, "that the beneficent God of Nature would have blessed this Country with unparalleled fertility, and furnished it with a number of navigable streams, and that, that fertility should be consumed at home, and those streams should not convey its superabundance to other climes."[47] The delegates to Tennessee's first constitutional convention in 1796 were so committed to this principle that they inscribed the right to free navigation of the Mississippi into their state constitution, declaring, "An equal participation of the free navigation of the Mississippi is one of the inherent rights of the citizens of this State; it cannot, therefore, be conceded to any prince, potentate, person or persons whatever."[48]

Not everyone shared the view that the westerners had a natural right to free navigation of the rivers, nor did everyone think that expansion was good policy. Northeasterners worried about the diminishment of their power, the insecurity of the frontier, and the character of the western emigrants. "Shall we not fill the wilderness with white savages?—and will they not become more formidable to us than the tawny ones which now inhabit it?" asked John Jay.[49] It was Jay, a New Yorker, who most provoked the western settlements when he proposed in 1786 to give up navigation rights on the Mississippi for twenty-five to thirty years in exchange for a favorable commercial treaty with Spain.[50] Detecting a northeastern plot to abandon the west, southern delegates to the Continental Congress vehemently defended free navigation of the Mississippi. "I look upon this as a contest for empire," argued Virginia's William Grayson in 1788. "The Southern States are deeply affected on this subject." Grayson worried that the closing of the Mississippi would stop emigration, prevent the formation of new states to the west, and preserve northeastern power in Congress.[51] The conflict over the Mississippi revealed a widely held assumption that the patterns of internal migration favored the southern states, and that most of the emigrants would end up in the southwest rather than the northwest.[52]

That prospect rather worried Spanish officials in Louisiana. Baron de Carondelet, the Spanish governor of Louisiana, wrote a report in 1794 warning his superiors of powerful expansionary tendencies within the United States. Carondelet saw that the United States had begun to push the trans-Appalachian Indian nations out of their lands and was "attempting to get possession of all the vast continent which those nations are occupying between the Ohio and Mississippi Rivers and the Gulf of Mexico and the Appalachian Mountains." He feared that the United States also had designs on Spanish holdings in North America: the rivers that emptied into the Gulf of Mexico, the fur trade of the Missouri, and, ultimately, the rich mines of New Spain. For Carondolet, one of the most remarkable aspects of this expansionary tendency was the United States' "prodigious and restless population." He feared that the Spanish were going to be overrun: "Their method of spreading themselves and their policy are so much to be feared by Spain as are their arms."[53] Carondelet and other Spanish officials pursued a variety of strategies to protect Louisiana from the United States. They dangled the prospect of navigation rights on the Mississippi in front of western settlers in the hope of divorcing them from the United States. They tried to attract European immigrants to counterbalance the Anglo-Americans. And finally, mired in the European wars, they gave up New Orleans, the Mississippi River, and Louisiana.[54]

While the United States' "restless population" pressed toward Spanish Louisiana, a volatile international context contributed to the country's territorial expansion. In 1793, revolutionary France de-

clared war on Great Britain and Spain. The alliance of those two tra-
ditionally hostile powers ended in the summer of 1795, when Spain
independently made peace with France. Anticipating a clash with
Great Britain, Spain sought to head off an alliance between the British
and the Americans by making an overture to the United States in
the form of concessions concerning territorial claims and navigation
rights on the Mississippi. These concessions were codified in the 1795
Treaty of San Lorenzo, also known as Pinckney's Treaty in honor of
the cosmopolitan South Carolinian Thomas Pinckney, who negotiated
it for the United States. The treaty settled the boundary between the
United States and West Florida at the thirty-first parallel, conceding
the valuable Natchez district to the United States. It also granted citizens of the United States the right of navigation on the Mississippi
River and provided to them a three-year privilege of landing and
transferring cargoes at New Orleans without paying custom duties.
Pinckney's Treaty won broad support and was quickly ratified by the
Senate. Robert Goodloe Harper summed up the attitude of most congressmen. "The Spanish Treaty is very favourable," he wrote to his
constituents in South Carolina.[55]

The Mississippi question remained quiet until 1800, when Spain
secretly ceded Louisiana to France in the Treaty of San Ildefonso,
inaugurating a famous chain of events that led to the Louisiana Purchase.[56] Republicans and Federalists alike considered French possession of New Orleans to be a direct threat to the security and prosperity of the Union. They feared that France would strangle the western
settlers' free navigation of the Mississippi, entice the western states
and territories away from the Union, and block what they had come
to regard as the continental destiny of the United States. Southern
politicians also worried that French officials—in league with the former slaves of St. Domingue—would intrigue with American slaves in
dangerous ways. In 1798, Mississippi's territorial governor Winthrop
Sargent warned Secretary of State Thomas Pickering that if Louisiana
fell into the hands of the French, "a few French Troops with a Cordial
Co-operation of the Spanish Creoles, and arms put into the hands of
the Negroes, would be to us formidable indeed."[57] In 1801, James

Madison predicted that French possession of Louisiana would foster "inquietude . . . among the Southern States, whose numerous slaves [had] been taught to regard the French as patrons of their cause."[58] And speaking in Congress in 1803, Representative Samuel Purviance of North Carolina warned that if the French retained control of Louisiana, "the tomahawk of the savage and the knife of the negro would confederate in the league, and there would be no interval of peace."[59] In fact, the slaveholders of the United States had the rebellious former slaves of St. Domingue and their ally, yellow fever, to thank for helping to deliver Louisiana into their hands by foiling Napoleon's plans for a greater French empire in the Americas. Starved for cash, eager to prevent an Anglo-American alliance, and stripped of his most important colony by the former slaves of St. Domingue, Napoleon sold Louisiana to the United States in 1803.[60]

The Louisiana Purchase was the great triumph of Jefferson's presidency, generating an outpouring of nationalist self-congratulation. Jeffersonian Republicans defended it as a nation-building measure that would strengthen the Union. By guaranteeing Americans the free navigation of the Mississippi, the acquisition secured the prosperity of the western states, which in turn opened up a market for eastern goods. By ridding North America of the French, the Louisiana Purchase eliminated the possibility that westerners might be tempted away from the Union by a powerful European nation. By placing at the government's disposal vast lands in the western regions of North America, it raised the possibility that the United States might resolve its pressing difficulties with the American Indians by removing them to the western side of the Mississippi. Jefferson summed up his view in his annual message to Congress in October 1803: "While the property and sovereignty of the Mississippi and its waters secure an independent outlet for the produce of the western States, and an uncontrolled navigation through their whole course, free from collision with other powers and the dangers to our peace from that source, the fertility of the country, its climate and extent, promise in due season important aids to our treasury, an ample provision for our posterity, and a wide-spread field for the blessings of freedom and equal laws."[61]

With Pinckney's Treaty and the Louisiana Purchase, the United States acquired the region that eventually became the states of Louisiana, Mississippi, and Alabama. It was not empty. About 50,000 white and black people already lived there, as well as 40,000 American Indians of the Choctaw, Chickasaw, and Creek nations. The rapidly increasing white and black population was concentrated along the banks of the Mississippi River from Natchez to New Orleans, while the Indians inhabited the country between the settled Mississippi River districts and the western limits of Georgia. The region's communities were ethnically and linguistically diverse, having been molded during the eighteenth century by indigenous migrations, successive waves of French, Spanish, and British colonists, and the introduction of people of African descent.[62] The economy of the Deep South was varied and changing. Planters and slaves in the plantation districts along the banks of the Mississippi were shifting their energies from indigo and tobacco production to more lucrative cotton and sugar. The raising of livestock—especially cattle and horses—was another important element of economic life, and one gaining acceptance among the Choctaws, Chickasaws, and Creeks.[63] New Orleans was increasingly becoming an entrepôt for agricultural commodities—flour, cotton, tobacco, whiskey, cordage, and peltry, to name a few—originating in the upper country and exported to the Caribbean and Spanish America, the eastern seaboard, and Europe.[64] The Deep South had already begun an enormous demographic, economic, and social transformation under Spanish rule. That transformation would accelerate after the region became a part of the United States, but not until the national government decided on the legal status of slavery in its new possessions.

"extenuate the general evil"

Territorial expansion in the early republic raised the question of slavery in a new context. The Northwest Ordinance passed by the Continental Congress in 1787 famously prohibited slavery in federal territory north of the Ohio River but not in the territories south of the Ohio. Kentucky and Tennessee had been admitted as slave states in the 1790s, and the prospect of even more slave states emerging from the territories acquired in Pinckney's Treaty and the Louisiana Purchase alarmed northern opponents of slavery. Furthermore, expansion intersected with two related developments having to do with slavery. One was white Americans' invigorated fear of slave rebellion and the other was a hardening of national opposition to the importation of slaves. All of these issues fused in the brief but important congressional debates over the legal status of slavery in the Mississippi Territory in 1798 and the Orleans Territory in 1804, which laid a political foundation for the domestication and extension of slavery in the United States.

The concept of "domestication" connects several related elements in the transformation of slavery in the United States during the early national era.[65] It describes the country's fitful withdrawal from the Atlantic slave trade, which made the United States essentially autarkic with respect to slave labor during the nineteenth century. Paradoxically, the process of withdrawal occurred during the same era that the importation of slaves into North America reached its highest levels. One assiduous historian has recently estimated that approximately 170,000 slaves were introduced into North America between 1783 and 1810, with more than 100,000 of these arriving in the first decade of the nineteenth century.[66] But rising slave imports coincided with a hardening political consensus against the Atlantic trade. State after state banned foreign slave importation for reasons of humanitarianism and prudence. By 1807, when Congress finally passed a law banning further slave importation after 1 January 1808, the trade was legal only in South Carolina—and even there it was controversial.[67]

At the same time that they prohibited the importation of foreign slaves, many states tried to regulate the interstate movement of enslaved people. In 1792 the Virginia legislature required immigrants from other states to swear that they did not intend to violate the state's laws preventing the further importation of slaves, and that they had not brought any slaves with them into Virginia "with an intention of selling them." In the same year, South Carolina's legislature banned the importation of African slaves and slaves from other states but permitted settlers to bring their slaves with them. In 1796 Maryland provided for the emancipation of any slave unlawfully admitted into the state but permitted citizens of the United States taking up "*bona fide* residence" in the state to bring their slave property with them. In 1798 Georgia prohibited the importation of slaves for sale from other states but adopted a constitutional provision enabling migrants from other states to bring their slaves with them.[68] After a protracted debate over slavery, Kentucky adopted a constitution that allowed the state legislature to prohibit the importation of slaves as merchandise for sale but not to prohibit migrants from other states from bringing their slaves with them into Kentucky.[69]

Laws banning the importation and interstate transfer of slaves contributed to the evolution of proslavery doctrine by drawing a line between slave trading and slaveholding. That line originated as a useful fiction written by planters in the upper South during the revolutionary era. They contrasted the vicious commercial world of the Atlantic slave trade, which was dominated by British merchants, with the more virtuous agrarian world of the American plantation.[70] Implicit in the contrast were the rudiments of a patriarchal defense of slavery. Slaveowners increasingly argued that their slaves were an integral part of their households—even families—and were bound to them by ligaments of mutual obligation and affection. The patriarchal perspective held that enslaved people were obliged to labor for and submit to their owners in return for their owners' protection and care. A slaveholder was entitled (even required) to punish his slaves for disobedience or poor performance, but he could not treat them sadistically or neglectfully without endangering the peace of the community or risking his honor. The patriarchal outlook endowed slavery with a moral justification, but it also opened slaveowners to charges of hypocrisy when, in time, law and honor failed to prevent the emergence of a sizable interstate slave trade.[71]

A final element in the concept of domestication involves the process by which slaveowners and their allies in the United States tried to protect their country from the most democratic, egalitarian, and terrifying prospect of the Age of Revolution: a generalized slave rebellion. If they were not aware of it before, the American Revolution had made slaveowners acutely aware that enslaved people were a dangerous form of property. Thousands of enslaved men and women fled to the British during the war. Some even took up arms against their former masters. The Revolution did not overthrow the slave system in the American South, but it did engender a new language of liberty and equality among enslaved people.[72] Nobody thereafter could deny that slaves were human beings with the will, passion, and natural desire for freedom common to all people. Many white Americans concluded that slaves were therefore the inveterate enemies of their masters, and if given a chance, would avenge themselves. They could not and would not take part in the national solidarity essential to the new United States, as Jefferson declared in one of the most famous passages in *Notes on the State of Virginia*. Slaves could have no patriotism, he warned, for "if a slave can have a country in this world, it must be any other in preference to that in which he is born to live and labour for another."[73]

White Americans' fears became more acute in the 1790s, when the slaves of St. Domingue rose up in a rebellion that ended with the formation of the first independent black nation-state in the Americas, the Republic of Haiti, in 1804. Letters, newspaper reports, and refugees from the island disseminated information about the ongoing slave rebellion throughout the Atlantic world, where for better or worse, it became a ubiquitous sign of both the universal passion for liberty and slavery's latent dangers. The impact of the events in St. Domingue on the debate over slavery and abolition in the United States cannot be overestimated. The slave revolt penetrated the consciousness of North Americans in every rank and station, which is not to say that they all drew the same lessons from it. It inspired some people and appalled others. It was invoked by slavery's opponents to justify emancipationist measures and by slavery's defenders to head them off. It stiffened southern slaveowners' efforts to curtail the importation of foreign slaves in the 1790s. It also echoed in the behavior of rebellious slaves and in the repression that greeted them. Like ashes from a volcanic eruption, the legacy of the St. Domingue slave revolt was carried throughout the Atlantic world by what the poet William Wordsworth called "the common wind."[74]

The common wind blew through Virginia and North Carolina between 1799 and 1802 in a series of real and alleged slave conspiracies inspired in part by the Atlantic radicalism of the prior decade. The most spectacular occurred in Richmond in the summer of 1800, where an enslaved blacksmith named Gabriel allegedly masterminded a plot to take over the city. One slave informer testified that the rebels planned to march under the banner "Death or Liberty."[75] White Virginians were not willing to applaud this echo of their own revolution. John Randolph of Roanoake observed that the conspirators "exhibited a spirit, which, if it becomes general, must deluge the southern country with blood."[76] But whose blood would it be? Bad weather and frayed nerves undid the plot, and as with so many failed slave conspiracies, it was the authorities rather than the conspirators who performed most of the bloodletting. After seventeen slaves were executed, a mortified Thomas Jefferson warned the governor, "There is a strong sentiment that there has been hanging enough."[77]

As Governor James Monroe and the Virginia General Assembly wrestled with the flurry of violence, they looked to the West for alternative solutions to the crisis. Under an 1801 law passed for the occasion, they sentenced some of the slaves convicted of conspiracy to be transported outside the United States. Nine of the convicts were purchased by the traders John Brown and William Morris for transportation to Spanish territory. The slaves were taken down the Ohio River, where two of them escaped into the Northwest Territory. The traders recaptured the runaways and continued down the Mississippi to Louisiana, where they discovered to their chagrin that "the Crimes Trials & convictions of the s[ai]d Slaves were well known to the inhabitants." Unsuccessfully petitioning the Virginia assembly for relief, Brown and Morris complained that they were unable to sell the convicts "except upon a Considerable credit, and at an Under Value."[78] It is difficult to say what is the most remarkable aspect of this chain of events: the will to freedom of the conspirators, the audacity of the traders, or the willingness of purchasers in New Orleans to buy slaves convicted of capital crimes. More important, though, is the implication that the continental slave trade originated in a marriage of convenience between slaveowners in the upper South who wanted order and slaveowners in the Deep South who needed labor.

Louisiana also figured in another of the Virginia assembly's responses to Gabriel's conspiracy: an inquiry into the possibility of purchasing land in the west or elsewhere to serve as a colony to which "persons obnoxious to the laws or dangerous to the peace of society may be removed." Monroe intimated to Jefferson that the plan for removal might expand beyond the immediate object of getting rid of the Richmond slave conspirators to "vast and interesting objects"—a veiled allusion to Jefferson's pet project of gradual emancipation and the expulsion of people of African descent from Virginia. A proposal of that very nature had recently been published by George Tucker, who recommended locating such a colony in Spanish Louisiana. Jefferson's response to Monroe and his fellow Virginians paired continental expansion with ethnic cleansing (to use a modern phrase). Jefferson doubted whether the citizens of the United States would tolerate a colony of free people of color in or near them, nor did he believe that Great Britain, Spain, or the various Indian nations would be willing to establish one. Again he looked to the horizon of the future. "It is impossible not to look forward to distant times," he predicted, "when our rapid multiplication will expand itself beyond those limits, and cover the whole northern, if not the southern continent with a people speaking the same language, governed in similar forms and by similar laws. Nor can we contemplate with satisfaction either blot or mixture on that surface." Here was Jefferson's fantasy of a geographically extensive and sociopolitically homogeneous America. Neither slavery nor black people plagued Jefferson's fantastic empire.[79]

All of these concerns with the moral, social, and political aspects of slavery surfaced in the contests over the organization of the Mississippi and Orleans Territories. In each case, a minority of northern Federalists led the opposition to the extension of slavery. They were motivated by moral revulsion against slavery and a political interest in blocking the growth of southern power. Opposing them were pro-slavery stalwarts, largely from the lower South, who defended the expansion of slavery as a matter of rights and policy. The stalwarts were convinced that restrictions on the expansion of slavery in the southwest violated the property and constitutional rights of the inhabitants in the territories as well as in the original states. They also believed that restrictions on slavery would prevent the economic and social development of the Deep South. Another source of opposition came from the upper South, where Jeffersonian Republicans advocated a two-pronged policy of prohibiting the importation of foreign slaves into the new southwestern territories while allowing slaveowners from the original states to carry their slaves there. The Jeffersonians hoped that this policy—called "diffusionism" by historians—would diminish the growing strength of the North American slave population and set the stage for gradual abolition. The diffusionist position would ultimately resolve the status of slavery in the Deep South, but contrary to Jefferson's hopes, it did not lead to emancipation or to the disappearance of black people.[80]

In March 1798, Congress began to consider a bill to resolve Georgia's western limits and organize the territory ceded to the United States by Spain in the Treaty of San Lorenzo. Representative George Thacher, a Massachusetts Federalist, "rose and said he should make a motion touching on the rights of man." The motion was to prohibit slavery in the Mississippi Territory. Thacher intended to jab at the Republicans, who had recently been harping on the rights of man, but he was also a committed opponent of slavery. "The existence of slavery in the United States," he declared, was "an evil in direct hostility to the principles of our Government."[81] Thacher had a few allies, including the Republican Albert Gallatin of Pennsylvania, who argued that the principles of the Northwest Territory should apply to Mississippi. Another Republican, Joseph Varnum of Massachusetts, agreed that the prohibition on slavery was responsible for the prosperity of the Northwest Territory, and added that he "looked upon the practice of holding blacks in slavery in this country [the United States] to be equally criminal with that of the Algerines carrying our citizens into slavery."[82] The restrictionists emphasized the moral evil and political hypocrisy of allowing slavery in the new southwestern territories.

Both Federalists and Republicans objected, largely on prudential grounds. The South Carolina Federalist Robert Goodloe Harper argued that the motion "would be a decree of banishment to all the persons settled [in the Territory], and of exclusion to all those intending to go there." Another Carolina Federalist, John Rutledge, warned that debate over restrictions on slavery "lead to more mischief than gentlemen are aware of." Harrison Gray Otis, a Boston Federalist, joined the two South Carolinians. He feared that Thacher's motion would provoke a slave insurrection and the inhabitants of the Natchez district would be "massacred on the spot." Otis also accepted Harper's argument that the Mississippi Territory would be settled by southerners "who cannot cultivate the ground without slaves." Two Virginia Republicans, William Giles and John Nicholas, articulated the diffusionist argument for gradual emancipation. "If the slaves of the Southern States were permitted to go into the Western country," Giles explained, "by lessening the number in those States, and spreading them over a large surface of country, there would be a great probability in ameliorating their condition, which could never be done whilst they were crowded together as they now are in the Southern States." Nicholas asked his colleagues "if it would not be doing a service not only to them [the slaves] but to the whole Union, to open this Western Country, and by that means spread the blacks over a large space, so that in time it might be safe to carry into effect the plan which certain philanthropists have so much at heart, and to which he had no objection, if it could be effected, viz., the emancipation of this class of men?"[83] Confronted with the threat of insurrection and the promise of diffusion, Thacher's motion won only twelve votes in the House and was easily defeated.

Shortly after the debate on Thacher's motion, Robert Goodloe Harper introduced a motion to prohibit the importation of foreign slaves in the Mississippi Territory. Thacher moved to amend Harper's motion to prohibit the introduction of slaves from the rest of the United States, but his amendment was not seconded. Harper's motion, by contrast, was approved by the House without any recorded debate.[84] The act organizing the Mississippi Territory thus codified the basic program of the diffusionists: a prohibition on the importation of foreign slaves combined with an allowance for the introduction of slaves from elsewhere within the United States.[85] It is strange that Harper and the other representatives from the lower South did not have any constitutional scruples against prohibiting the importation of foreign slaves into the Mississippi Territory, which seems on its face to have violated the slave-trade clause of the Constitution. One possible reason is that they understood the geographical location and political situation of the Mississippi Territory made it almost impossible to stop illegal smuggling of foreign slaves from Spanish Louisiana and West Florida. They also may have interpreted the slave-trade clause as not applying to federal territory but only to the original states.

Five years later, the nation again confronted the question of slavery as Congress organized the territories gained in the Louisiana Purchase. New circumstances charged the debate with a vital energy. The slave conspiracy scares between 1799 and 1802 rendered the problem of slave resistance more palpable and acute. Moreover, the election of 1800 had catapulted Thomas Jefferson into the presidency on the strength of slaveowners' constitutionally sanctioned advantage in the electoral college. The specter of new slave territory further augmenting slaveowners' national power was more than the beaten Federalists could bear.[86] The Jeffersonians themselves raised the stakes of the debate by investing the Louisiana Purchase with a profoundly liberal symbolism ("a wide-spread field for the blessings of freedom and equal laws"). The greater the promise of liberty embodied by Louisiana, the more important would be the question of slavery there. The magnitude of the issue resonated in a petition drawn by the American Convention for Promoting the Abolition of Slavery, which called on Congress to recognize its God-given opportunity to prohibit the importation of slaves into Louisiana. "While the Governments of Europe are shaken by civil discord, or surrounded by the incalculable cruelties and horrors of national warfare," the petitioners argued, "a beneficent and overruling Providence has been pleased to preserve for our country the blessings of peace, to grant us new proofs of his goodness, and to place us in a condition of prosperity, unrivalled in the records of history. Does it not become the duty of a nation, so crowned with the blessings of peace, and plenty, and happiness, to manifest its gratitude, to the whole world, by acts of justice and virtue?"[87]

The question of slavery in the vast Louisiana Purchase related to broader issues of continental governance, economic development, and public safety. All these themes were in evidence during the Senate debate on the issue in late January 1804. The proceedings were not preserved in the official records of Congress, but Senator William Plumer, a New Hampshire Federalist, roughly captured his colleagues' arguments in his valuable *Memorandum*.[88] Plumer's record reveals a complex series of alignments without obvious partisan or sectional axes. The senators from the slave states were roughly divided between those willing to accept some federal restrictions on the interstate movement of slaves and those unwilling to accept any restrictions at all. Northern senators were also fragmented. A handful used the slavery debates to register a dissent against the whole enterprise of Louisiana. Others searched for a way to impose a politically tenable restriction on the expansion of slavery. One or two even aligned themselves with slavery's most ardent southern defenders. In this morass of ideals and interests, diffusionism provided enough solid ground to support a majority coalition.

The most vocal supporters of slavery in Louisiana were James Jackson of Georgia and Jonathan Dayton of New Jersey. They argued that the terms of the Louisiana Purchase obliged the United States to respect the rights of the territory's inhabitants, including their right to own slaves. Moreover, Louisiana's climate made slave labor necessary if coffee, cotton, and sugar were to be cultivated. Dayton drew particular attention to the prospect of growing sugar in Louisiana— "That we can do if we have slaves," he contended. Without slavery, Louisiana would relapse into wilderness. As Jackson put it, "Slavery must be established in that country or it must be abandoned."[89] Jackson and Dayton found oblique support from Vermont's two Republican senators, Israel Smith and Stephen Bradley. The two Vermonters thought that restricting the importation of foreign slaves into Louisiana would be ineffective and counterproductive, as it would simply encourage the eastern states to import more slaves and send their worst to Louisiana. The two senators from Massachusetts, John Quincy Adams and Timothy Pickering, opposed any legislation respecting slavery in Louisiana. "I think we are proceeding with too much haste on such an important question," Adams complained.[90]

Opponents of the importation of foreign slaves into Louisiana insisted that the slave trade was a moral evil, that an increasing slave population posed grave dangers to the safety of the country, and that white laborers could tolerate Louisiana's climate. One of the most pointed arguments came from Samuel White, a Federalist from Delaware. Decrying the "disgraceful traffick in *human flesh*," White argued that the treaty of cession did not guarantee to the Louisianians "the *power*, I will not say *right*, of holding slaves." He insisted that Congress had a duty to oppose slavery "& thereby avoid the fate of St. Domingo." He reminded his colleagues that only a thunderstorm had prevented the fulfillment of Gabriel's conspiracy in Richmond, and pointed to the many provisions enacted by slave states to guard against slave rebellion. He also countered the idea that white people were unfit for labor in Louisiana's climate by arguing that it was slaveholding rather than the climate that made white people in the South disdain hard work. "Let white men be accustomed to the culture of that country," he suggested, "& they will, I believe, find they are able to bear the fatigue of it." Prefiguring an argument that would eventually become vital to the political antislavery movement, White concluded that slavery was responsible for the noticeable difference between the eastern states, where the people were "strong, powerful & wealthy," and the southern states, where the people were "poor, weak & feeble." Most southern Senators would have disputed White's critique of slavery, but they joined him in opposing the importation of foreign slaves into Louisiana. Plumer saw self-interest at work in this alignment. The southerners' motives, he wrote in his *Memorandum,* were "to raise the price of their own slaves in the markett—& to encrease the means of disposing of those who are most turbulent & dangerous to them."[91] On 26 January the Senate voted twenty-one to six to prohibit the importation of slaves into Louisiana from outside the United States, and to entitle any slave illegally imported into the territory to receive his or her freedom. Four of the six negatives came from New England, and the other two came from Georgia's pro–slave trade stalwarts.[92]

The debate then turned to the question of regulating the movement of slaves from the United States to Louisiana. Here the diffusionists made their decisive contribution by offering an antislavery rationale for the expansion of slavery. Their leader was John Breckenridge, a Kentucky Republican and a confidant of Thomas Jefferson. Breckenridge had migrated from Virginia to Kentucky in the early 1790s with his family and slaves. He quickly became a leading planter, lawyer, and advocate of southwestern interests. He defended slavery during Kentucky's constitutional debates of 1798 and 1799, publishing a broadside that asked, "Where is the difference whether I am robbed of my horse by a highwayman, or of my slave by a set of people called a Convention?"[93] As a member of Kentucky's House of Representatives in 1798, Breckenridge presented the Kentucky Resolutions, secretly written by Jefferson in opposition to the Alien and Sedition Acts. He was subsequently elected to the United States Senate, where he became one of Jefferson's most trusted lieutenants. It was Breckenridge who shepherded the Louisiana bill through the Senate, and it was Breckenridge who staked out the diffusionist position. He declared that it was "good policy" to send slaves from the eastern states to Louisiana. "This will disperse and weaken that race—& free the southern states from a part of its black population, & of its danger."[94]

Diffusionism bridged the gap between the extensionists and restrictionists. It appeared to provide a way to supply Louisiana with slave labor without necessarily increasing the total population of slaves in the country as a whole. It also appeared to provide a way to diminish the danger posed by slaves, by cutting them off from the sources of transatlantic resistance and dispersing them across a larger territory. Among those who recognized the logic of diffusionism was Lewis Kerr, the well-traveled sheriff of New Orleans. In a remarkable letter written in March 1804, Kerr analyzed the impact of slave migration. If Congress allowed foreign slaves to be admitted to Louisiana, he believed, nothing but trouble could be expected. "It is surely to be dreaded that a considerable share of that importation will be derived from the french islands, and consist principally of such negroes as cannot be retained there with safety to their owners or the public peace," he explained. If foreign slaves were proscribed, however, "the Louisianians could from time to time draw off the slaves now in the western states, and thereby at least extenuate the general evil." Because slaves were more necessary in Louisiana than in Kentucky or Tennessee, Kerr argued, "it would therefore render those states an essential service to open an advantageous foreign market for what is probably their most useless stock: and this province would be at the same time furnished with a race of servants already acquainted with our habits and attached to our country."[95] In short, diffusionism promised to insulate the United States from black Jacobinism while allowing market forces within the country to transplant the native-born slave population into the southwest, where slavery was daily becoming more profitable.

On 30 January, the Senate debated several motions regarding the introduction of slaves into Louisiana from the United States. James Hillhouse, a Federalist from Connecticut, presented a motion that would have emancipated adult slaves taken to Louisiana, but it was defeated by a vote of eleven to seventeen. Hillhouse then introduced a new motion to prevent recently imported slaves from being transported to Louisiana, and to limit the introduction of slaves into Louisiana to "person or persons removing into said territory for actual settlement, and being at the time of such removal *bona fide* owner of such slave or slaves." The motion was intended to prevent the emergence of an internal slave trade while allowing slaveowners to migrate to Louisiana with their human property. On the first of February the Senate approved Hillhouse's restriction by a vote of eighteen to eleven. Eight senators who had opposed Hillhouse's first motion (including five from slave states) supported his second motion. Led by Breckenridge, this group of moderate restrictionists swung the Senate to its diffusionist conclusion. They did so over the objections of the senators from Virginia and Georgia, who considered Hillhouse's second motion to be overly restrictive.[96]

That the restrictions on the internal movement of slaves were supported largely by senators from the northern and western states and opposed largely by senators from the southeastern states suggests that the law had genuine but limited antislavery intentions. In the end, the 1804 act prohibited the importation of foreign slaves into the newly organized Orleans Territory and restricted the introduction of slaves from the United States to those accompanying bona fide owners who intended to settle there. In effect, it nationalized the strategy of domesticating slavery already under way in most of the states.[97]

The law drew criticism from opposite ends of the political spectrum. Many of Louisiana's sugar planters thought the ban on African slave importation was "a serious blow at the Commercial and agricultural interest of the Province."[98] For instance, Joseph Dubreuil complained to Jefferson that a prohibition on the importation of African slaves would turn Louisiana into a "vast swamp unfit for any creatures outside of fishes, reptiles, and insects."[99] The planters sent a memorial to Congress enumerating their grievances. They charged that the United States had violated the treaty rights of inhabitants of Louisiana, accorded preference to using English in public proceedings, and —most important—threatened the economy of Louisiana by closing off the African slave trade. The planters argued that the region's civilization would collapse without African slaves. Not only were Africans naturally and habitually better suited to labor in the climate of the country, they argued, but also their labor was necessary to redeem the land from the forces of nature. "The banks raised to restrain the waters of the Mississippi can only be kept in repair by those whose natural constitutions and habits of labor enable them to resist the combined efforts of a deleterious moisture, and a degree of heat intolerable to whites," the memorial claimed. "This labor is great, it requires many hands, and it is all important to the very existence of our country. If, therefore, this traffic is justifiable anywhere, it is surely in this province, where, unless it is permitted, cultivation must cease, the improvements of a century be destroyed, and the great river resume its empire over our ruined fields and demolished habitations."[100] Like sugar planters throughout the Americas, those in the Orleans Territory unequivocally associated the African slave trade with progress. They discovered to their chagrin that many of their new countrymen in the United States did not share that view. One anonymous poet ridiculed their argument: "Receive us to your arms as Brothers / And grant us *to make slaves of others*."[101]

Another critic was Tom Paine, the cosmopolitan democrat recently returned to America, who published an open letter lambasting the Louisiana planters for seeking to continue the African slave trade. "Dare you put up a petition to Heaven for such a power, without fearing to be struck from the earth by its justice? Why, then, do you ask it of man against man?" he charged.[102] In a private letter to Jefferson a few months later, Paine outlined a plan to encourage American and European migration to Louisiana, focusing especially on the transportation of German redemptioners who would work as bonded laborers until they had paid off the price of their transatlantic passage. Under

Paine's proposal, not only would Congress provide a bounty to ship owners carrying redemptioners to Louisiana, but it would also grant twenty acres of land to each redemptioner once his term of service had expired. By this means Louisiana "would become strong by the increase of citizens," rather than weakened by the increase of slaves. But Paine did not want to exclude black people from Louisiana altogether. Reminding Jefferson of a plan they had discussed years earlier, Paine suggested that Congress also pay for the passage of free people of color to New Orleans, where they could hire themselves out to local planters for one or two years in order to "learn plantation business." The government would then place them on land of their own, just as if they were redemptioners. Though Paine's proposal was politically infeasible, it serves as a useful reminder of a path imagined but not pursued—what might have been if things had not been as they were. There were alternatives to the expansion of slavery.[103]

Still another protest came from outraged Massachusetts Federalists who thought they saw a Virginia-led conspiracy to oppress their section of the Union. They feared that the Louisiana Purchase would revive the slave trade, augment southern power, and eventually lead to the debasement of New England. "Ranked by Virginia as a fit people for hewers of wood and drawers of water," one overheated essayist predicted, "we shall soon find the driver at our back, and our native land become a plantation, with her hardy sons for slaves."[104] The Federalists concentrated their anger against the three-fifths clause of the Constitution, which took the slave population into account in apportioning the House of Representatives. They charged that the clause gave the southern states a political interest in reopening the slave trade and expanding slavery. In the spring of 1804 a congressman named William Ely drafted a constitutional amendment to abolish the three-fifths clause of the Constitution and instead apportion representation according to the free population of each state. Defending the amendment, Josiah Quincy described Louisiana as a "new hot bed of slavery."[105] The Massachusetts legislature endorsed the amendment, but its supporters could hardly have expected to win on the national stage. Instead they hoped to draw attention to the ways slavery skewed the distribution of power among free people in the United States. So deep was the New England Federalists' dissatisfaction that some of them even began to toy with the idea of secession. Their protests foreshadowed more consequential struggles over the expansion of slavery in the decades ahead.[106]

Those who predicted that Congress's restrictions on the introduction of slaves into the Orleans Territory would be ineffectual were prophetic. Congress quickly elevated the Orleans Territory to the second stage of territorial government, which ended the restrictions on the interstate movement of slaves.[107] Hundreds of African slaves imported into South Carolina between 1803 and 1808 were shipped to the Orleans Territory. Others were smuggled in. Thousands of slaves belonging to refugees from the Caribbean were also allowed to enter the Orleans Territory under humanitarian pretexts. But after 1808, when Congress applied the prohibition on slave importation to the whole country, the influx of foreign slaves diminished. The diffusionist pattern that emerged from the debates over the status of slavery in the Mississippi and Orleans territories prevailed over the long run. Unlike Cuba and Brazil, where the nineteenth-century expansion of slavery relied largely on the continued importation of Africans, the expansion of slavery in the United States relied on natural population growth and the forced migration of enslaved people from one part of the country to another. As the slave country began its half-century tilt toward the Deep South, Thomas Jefferson admitted that he had "long since given up the expectation of any early provision for the extinguishment of slavery among us."[108] Jefferson's horizon—a free and white America—appeared more distant than ever.

Territorial expansion tragically dovetailed with new opportunities for slaveowners to profit from slavery in the region that became the Deep South, where two distinct but overlapping economies based on slave labor arose between 1790 and 1812. The first was the cotton frontier, which spread unevenly in the extensive fertile districts from western Georgia through the Indian backcountry to Natchez. The second, more narrowly limited to New Orleans and its neighboring sugar-producing parishes along the Mississippi River, comprised a zone of especially dense commercial activity. The rise of cotton and sugar transformed the region and generated extraordinary tensions among the people who lived there.

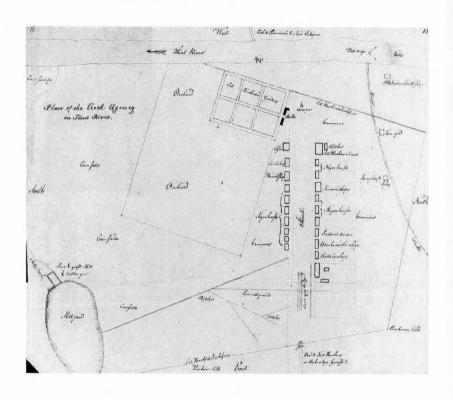

Plan of the Creek Agency on the Flint River, *drawn around 1810. The Creek Agency was the headquarters of the Jeffersonian program for civilizing the southern Indians. Note the twelve "Negro houses" among the double row of buildings. A road on the west bank of the Flint River leads to New Orleans.* COURTESY OF MORAVIAN ARCHIVES, WINSTON-SALEM, NORTH CAROLINA.

CHAPTER 2

Civilizing

the Cotton Frontier

SURVEYING THE BOUNDARY between the Mississippi Territory and Spanish dominion in 1798, Thomas Freeman reported that he and his company were "immersed in an impenetrable Forrest condenced by Cane & cemented by grape vines, so that a dozen trees must be cut before one can fall, & this on the most irregular hilly broken & unfinished part of the globes surface."[1] Freeman's evocative description of a wild landscape signaled the great challenge that lay ahead for advocates of U.S. expansion. Beginning in the late 1790s, a host of public officials, economic entrepreneurs, and evangelical Protestants struggled to "civilize" a region they considered wild and benighted. Their civilizing mission entailed fundamental political, economic, social, and cultural changes intended to create a republican society. Infused with a providential sense of American destiny and supported by the twin pillars of the national government and the transatlantic cotton economy, the civilizers molded the southern frontier in ways that advanced plantation slavery.

New habits of life were not merely imposed on the region by outsiders. Some of the region's inhabitants welcomed change, including tobacco and indigo planters who had already established themselves along the Mississippi River, and who led the transition to a cotton economy. Factions among the southern Indians joined with the civilizers to reform their customs and practices, while others increasingly resented the erosion of native sovereignty that these changes brought about. Many slaves also participated in the civilizing of the Deep South. Their labor supported the cotton economy, and their religious zeal supported the spread of evangelical Protestantism, but at the same time conflict and violence tinged relations between slaves and other people on the cotton frontier. Countless episodes of collaboration, adaptation, and antagonism shaped the slave country in the years leading to the War of 1812.

The Jeffersonian civilizing mission began with an idea about the proper relation between land, people, and self-government. "Cultivators of the earth are the most virtuous and independent citizens," Jefferson wrote in *Notes on the State of Virginia*.[2] That belief colored his vision of westward expansion. The continual addition of new land would allow the United States to remain a nation of industrious, commercially oriented farmers. So long as it did, republicanism would endure. The Jeffersonian vision was conservative in that it intended to keep the country's social structure at an agrarian state of development, delaying its inevitable march toward a more decadent, industrial society.[3] But the Jeffersonian vision was also progressive in that it demanded the transformation of the western "wilderness" into a commercially oriented agricultural society, which involved a broad policy to convert the western lands into saleable property and encourage widespread landownership. Jeffersonians hoped that the creation of a vast market in land would provide the basis for a prosperous economy and a loyal citizenry by attracting migrants from the eastern United States.

From a Jeffersonian perspective, stimulating migration was also the best way to guarantee security without sacrificing liberty. The American grip on the Deep South seemed precarious. The region was distant from the centers of government and inhabited by foreigners and indigenous people who possessed no special loyalty to the country.

The peacetime military establishment was small and ineffective, and, moreover, republican sensibilities viewed standing armies as a threat to liberty. The solution to this predicament was to populate the Deep South as quickly as possible with what one public official in the Mississippi Territory called "real Americans" and to organize them into citizen-militias.[4] Jeffersonians argued that a strong militia would keep the peace while at the same time inculcating habits of discipline and patriotism within the citizenry. As Governor William C. C. Claiborne reminded the people of the Mississippi Territory in 1802, "The Yeomanry of a Country, should constitute its chief defence, against internal commotion, external violence, and that where this Sentiment is not fostered, Liberty must soon cease to dwell."[5]

The Land Ordinance of 1785 provided the template for the settlement of the Deep South. Passed by the Continental Congress under the Articles of Confederation, the Ordinance initiated a system of rectangular survey for the United States' national domain. It imposed an abstract, Cartesian order on the western landscape, which contrasted with the irregular patterns of land ownership that prevailed in districts settled under French, British, and Spanish authority in the eighteenth century. It contrasted even more sharply with the communal patterns of land use and possession that prevailed among indigenous peoples. The rectangular survey was intended to make it easier for purchasers to secure title to land without fraud or conflict, and therefore to facilitate orderly settlement through the mechanism of the market. Once the land was sold to private citizens, the government would retreat into the background, providing invisible support for the natural laws of supply and demand that American officials hoped would create an "empire of liberty."[6]

In the Deep South, however, the national government had to accommodate myriad interests with competing claims to the land. One important group comprised landowners who traced their titles back to the years of French, British, and Spanish dominion. Solicitous treatment of these landed interests would cement their allegiance to the United States and ensure continuity in the region's booming agri-

cultural economy. The national government established several commissions to confirm the validity of extant titles and to protect against
the fraudulent engrossment of land. The commissions also granted
land and preemption rights to claimants who could prove they had
"inhabited and cultivated" their land before the United States took
possession of the region. These policies eventually exempted from
the public domain several million acres of land located in areas colo-
nized by Europeans during the eighteenth century. Colonial patterns
of landownership would thus persist in the established plantation districts—for instance, along the Mississippi River from Natchez to
New Orleans—that would become the core of the slave country.[7]

Another complication originated in Georgia, which claimed sovereignty over lands extending to the Mississippi. Early in 1795 the state
legislature sold 35 million acres of "Yazoo" land (named after one of
the region's rivers) to four private companies for the paltry sum
of $500,000. Outrage spread quickly through Georgia and the rest
of the country. Anti-Yazooists argued that "immense monopolies of
land" threatened democracy, robbed the coffers of the state, and
stifled the progress of the frontier. The offending politicians were
swept out of office and the sale was repealed by a new legislature the
following year, but by that time much of the land had already been
gobbled up (on paper) by northern speculators who contended that
the repeal violated their constitutional rights of contract. In 1802
Georgia ceded its western lands to the United States, which placed
responsibility for resolving the Yazoo claims in the hands of the national government. Another decade of lobbying and litigation (including the landmark 1810 Supreme Court case of *Fletcher v. Peck*) earned
holders of Yazoo stock more than four million dollars in compensation, and ultimately cleared the way for the sale of Georgia's ceded
lands by the national government.[8]

The Creek, Choctaw, and Chickasaw Indians also laid claim to millions of acres between Georgia and the Mississippi River. At the beginning of the nineteenth century, the American Indians of the Deep
South outnumbered the white and black population and possessed

much of the territory that eventually became the states of Mississippi and Alabama. Three or four thousand Chickasaws inhabited what is today northern Mississippi, northwestern Alabama, and western Tennessee.[9] The Choctaws included fifteen thousand people divided into three major geographic districts stretching from the Pearl River in the west to the Tombigbee-Alabama-Mobile river system in the east. Their territory covered much of what is today the heart of Mississippi and western Alabama.[10] The Creek Indians, also numbering fifteen thousand people, occupied the lands from the ambiguous western boundary of Georgia near the Ocmulgee River to the Coosa River in present-day Alabama. The Creek confederacy comprised loosely affiliated towns divided into two major districts. The Upper Creeks, as they were known to American officials, lived along the Coosa-Alabama-Tallapoosa river system, while the Lower Creeks inhabited the lands watered by the Chattahoochee and Flint rivers.[11] Another group, the Seminoles, had emerged in Florida as an offshoot of the Creek Indians but did not include more than three thousand people. Their numbers grew in part from the absorption of runaway and captured slaves from Georgia and East Florida.[12] Small Indian settlements could also be found in lower Louisiana, mostly the scattered remnants of various nations that once predominated in the lower Mississippi Valley, including the Biloxi, Natchez, Tunica, Houma, Chitimacha, Opelousas, Atakapas, and Qapaw Indians. One exception was the Caddo nation, on the Red River beyond Natchitoches, which remained sizable and intact if battered by conflict with the Choctaws to the east and the Osages to the west.[13]

The United States recognized the southern Indians' right to the soil based on prior occupancy, but it was also committed to extinguishing Indian title. Most American policy makers believed that the Indians had too much land and failed to use it productively—that indigenous dependence on hunting amounted to a monopoly that stunted the progress of civilization. In the 1790s the United States began to encourage native peoples to abandon the hunt in favor of settled agriculture and animal husbandry. Government officials hoped that the shift would lead the Indians to discover that they possessed surplus land, which the laws of supply and demand would induce them to sell to the United States. As Jefferson put it in 1803, the civilizing process would create a "coincidence of interests" between the Indians, who had "lands to spare" but needed "other necessaries," and the citizens of the United States, who had other necessaries to spare but needed land. Market exchange rather than conquest would be the instrument of American expansion.[14] Yet from 1795 to 1810 the United States acquired only a small proportion of Choctaw, Chickasaw, and Creek land in the Deep South. One major cession came via the Treaty of Mount Dexter in 1805, in which the Choctaws sold about five million acres of land in the southwestern portion of the Mississippi Territory, but that treaty was an exception to the general pattern of refusal among indigenous peoples to part with their land. Most of what is today Mississippi and Alabama remained in indigenous hands on the eve of the War of 1812.[15]

While the national government sorted through these many and varied claims, its surveyors set the Jeffersonian land machine in motion. They were a vanguard of the republican civilizing mission. Usually expert in astronomy and mathematics, surveyors took the measure of the land and mapped a national domain that could be parceled out and sold to the highest bidder. Isaac Briggs, appointed surveyor general of lands south of Tennessee in 1803, supervised the initial stages of this process in the Deep South. Briggs was the son of Quakers from Haverford, Pennsylvania. He enrolled in Pennsylvania College in 1780, where he earned two degrees and a name for himself in mathematics. After college, Briggs helped Andrew Ellicott lay out the District of Columbia, taught at a Friends' School in Maryland, contributed calculations for almanacs, and finally, in 1799, published his own *Friends' Almanac*. Along the way, he became acquainted with Thomas Jefferson, who praised him as "a Quaker, a sound republican, and of a pure and unspotted character" and one of the best scientists in the country. Pious, precise, and patriotic, Briggs appeared to be the kind of man Jefferson was looking for in a surveyor.[16]

Briggs's brief career in the Deep South reveals some of the physical, psychological, and political difficulties that plagued agents of the Jeffersonian civilizing mission. In the spring of 1803, he left his wife, Hannah, in Maryland and embarked for Natchez to take up his duties as surveyor. Accompanied by his brothers Joseph and Samuel, Briggs arrived in Natchez in late August after an eventful trip down the Ohio and Mississippi rivers from Pittsburgh during which he was attacked by dysentery and had a close encounter with a notorious river bandit. Homesick, he described himself as "a poor strayed sheep in the wilderness!"[17] In the ensuing months, Briggs would often lament the irregularity of the mail, which did not bring letters from his beloved wife often enough. Perhaps this is one reason why Briggs agreed to survey the route for a new post road connecting New Orleans to the eastern states, a difficult task that took him through the Indian country early in 1804.[18] Among his other activities, Briggs became the first president of the Mississippi Society for the Acquirement and Dissemination of Useful Knowledge. Its goals included "Cultivation of social harmony,—Improvement of natural science, primarily Agriculture—and the establishment of a Library." The society's founders hoped it would spread enlightened values through the territory's rude settlements.[19]

Briggs's main task was to survey the public lands and prepare them for sale, but it was not an easy task. The two men Briggs hired as deputies, Charles De France and George Davis, ultimately found the work too difficult and the remuneration too small. Defeated by nature and the high cost of labor, the two men quit in January 1804 after falling into debt. De France complained of "the many insurmountable Difficulties a surveyor had to encounter in this country, (such as lakes, swamps, extremely steep hills, and numerous cane brakes, that in many places are almost impenetrable, and also the extravagant prices of Labor and provisions)."[20] The slow progress of the surveyors led to problems with squatters, as migrants arriving in the Deep South planted themselves on lands that were not yet ready for sale. Many officials feared that the squatter communities would degenerate into lawlessness and impede the sale of the land. "It is a matter of regret that the surveying should have been so long delayed," lamented Albert Gallatin, the secretary of the treasury.[21]

Briggs finally chose his family over his country. As Congress expanded his duties to include both the Mississippi and Orleans Territories, Jefferson and Gallatin stepped up the pressure to complete the surveys, especially of the land district west of the Mississippi. Conscious of security problems on the southern frontier, Jefferson urged Briggs "to use all possible expedition in surveying lands for sale on the western side of the Mississippi . . . that we may be enabled to hasten the settlement in those parts most convenient for the defence of New Orleans."[22] While all this was going on, Briggs asked Hannah to join him in the Mississippi Territory, but she politely, firmly, refused.[23] Briggs's desperation mounted. "I ardently long, for a release from the labyrinth of difficulty and unhappiness into which I have fallen in this Country," he wrote to Jefferson in the fall of 1806, "and to have it in my power to return to the peaceful bosom of my dear family."[24] Briggs soon abandoned his office, left the Mississippi Territory, and returned to Hannah in Maryland. His passage through the "labyrinth of difficulty" suggests that the civilizing of the Deep South depended on public officials who faced considerable challenges in the fulfillment of their duties. If, like Briggs, more of them had given up and gone home—or more of them had paid attention to their wives' wishes— the whole enterprise might have failed.

But others stepped in. Briggs's successors eventually brought the first public lands in the Deep South to market. From 1807 through 1812, the government sold almost half a million acres of public land in the Mississippi Territory for a total of more than one million dollars—about 10 percent of the land-office business up to that point.[25] The opening of the public lands in the Deep South enticed eagle-eyed planters who could spot opportunity at a distance. "You will have discovered that the U.S. Land Office is opened and lands offered on good terms," Leonard Covington wrote to his brother in the Mississippi Territory. (His cousin Levin Wailes served as a deputy surveyor in the territory.) "Will it be possible for all of us to get together upon some of this rich and cheap land?"[26] Alexander Donelson, a nephew of the Tennessee planter Andrew Jackson, could hardly restrain his praise after scouting lands on the Tombigbee River in 1811. "I am much pleased with a great proportion of that country," he reported to his uncle. Its easily navigable river, healthy climate, and extraordinarily fertile soil made it "the most desireable country I have ever seen, if settled by civilized people."[27] Donelson's idea of a civilized people did not include the southern Indians who already inhabited the region. Instead it included free, white, propertied citizens of the United States—many of whom owned slaves.

The Jeffersonian land system did not create a yeoman's paradise in the Deep South. Public land was cheap but not free, and at two dollars per acre, the market favored the wealthy. A memorial to Congress from citizens of the Mississippi Territory in 1803 argued that land should not be sold to the highest bidder but rather granted to actual settlers. If sold, the memorial warned, the land would fall into the hands of "the rich," who are "generally attached a certain species of population, which would endanger the country in proportion to its increase."[28] Yet Congress consistently rejected proposals to donate land to settlers (including a proposal offered by Jefferson himself in 1806) because the public lands were too valuable a resource to give away for free. Important national goals, including the reduction of the country's debt, depended on revenue earned from the sale of public lands. As the petitioners had warned, the sale of public lands allowed rich and well-connected planters like Leonard Covington to get a jump on their poorer competitors in the race for the best land.[29] The public land system—perhaps the most important instrument of the Jeffersonian civilizing mission—thus facilitated the spread of the plantation system in the Deep South just as a burgeoning cotton economy increased the value of the land and the profits to be earned from slave labor.

"we are all mostly in cotton"

In the late eighteenth century, industrial capital began to stride the world in seven-league boots, but it did not leave the same footprint everywhere. In the 1780s, cotton textile manufacturers in England discovered an almost insatiable worldwide demand for cheap calicoes and muslins. Manchester capitalists erected textile mills and employed wage workers in a relentless and ever-expanding quest for profits. After experimenting with various raw cottons from around the world, they found that "upland" cotton, a black-seeded variety of the genus *Gossypium,* which happened to grow astoundingly well in the southern regions of North America, best suited their purposes. Responding to this new opportunity for profit, North American planters, farmers, and slaves began to grow cotton for export to distant markets. By their efforts, North America claimed a rapidly increasing share of the British market—almost 45 percent by 1803—outranking producers in the Caribbean, Brazil, and the East Indies.[30]

The cotton revolution transformed and solidified the Deep South's connections to the world market and induced more of its people to enter into the "civilizing" economy of commercial agriculture. Jeffersonian political economy held that mere subsistence economies were primitive and barbaric, while commercial agriculture stimulated industriousness and wealth, qualities considered essential for a virtuous citizenry.[31] The salutary effect of commercial agriculture was obvious to Ephraim Kirby, an official sent by the United States to resolve land claims in the eastern district of the Mississippi Territory in 1804. Kirby thought that the region was poor and backward, but that once the land titles were settled and the rivers opened to navigation, commerce would civilize the frontier. "Industry and laudable enterprize will find their reward; law and justice, which have been long disregarded, will be properly respected; and honest, virtuous people take the place of the vicious and profligate," he predicted.[32]

Various circumstances had combined to persuade planters and farmers in the lower Mississippi Valley to grow upland cotton for export. In 1790, Spain had opened up its markets to tobacco from the United States and withdrawn its subsidy for Louisiana tobacco, crippling growers there. Around the same time, indigo manufacturers found themselves up against natural pests, declining prices, and foreign competition. In contrast to the gloomy picture in tobacco and indigo, cotton prices in the 1790s were extremely high, consistently above twenty-five cents per pound and reaching a peak of forty-four cents per pound in 1798. Furthermore, versions of Eli Whitney's cotton gin reached the lower Mississippi Valley by 1795, eliminating the most serious technical obstacle to the commercial production of short-staple cotton. Taking advantage of new technology and high prices, planters and farmers from Natchez to Baton Rouge rapidly abandoned tobacco and indigo and adopted cotton.[33] Riding through the Mississippi Territory in 1800, the Presbyterian minister James Hall observed that cotton "is now the staple commodity in the territory."[34] The following year, the New Orleans merchant Shepherd Brown encountered fierce competition when he tried to procure cotton from Natchez planters. "There are not less than twenty persons now here who are engaged by the Orl[ean]s Merch[an]ts to buy for them and are daily riding throu' the Country to contract with the Planters," he complained.[35] The cotton boom was under way.

Soon thereafter, upland cotton from the Deep South appeared on the international stage. James Maury, the United States' consul in Liverpool, registered its entrance in 1802, when he noted that two vessels had arrived from New Orleans with cotton.[36] Around the same time, Liverpool cotton merchants Ewart and Rutson began to worry that the increasing quantities of New Orleans and Mississippi cotton sold in the British market would depress the price of their own West India cotton.[37] They had reason for concern. Green & Wainwright, another Liverpool firm, favorably reported to a Mississippi planter late in 1803, "The Manufacturers have substituted the better kinds of Natchez Cotton for Demerara & We have had the satisfaction of seeing those who have once tried it become constant Customers."[38] Planters in the Deep South had the satisfaction of seeing the value of their foreign exports—mostly cotton—more than double between 1804 and 1807, from about $1.7 million to more than $4.3 million.[39]

Established planters along the Mississippi River led the charge toward cotton in the 1790s, with William Dunbar out in front. A native of Scotland, Dunbar had been educated in Glasgow and London before he traveled to North America in 1771 at the age of twenty-two. Dunbar's mercantile pursuits took him to Spanish Louisiana, where he established a plantation and set his slaves to the business of making staves for the West Indian market. In 1783, he moved to a plantation near Natchez and went into indigo, but he transferred his operations to cotton in the mid-1790s. Dunbar and his slaves experimented with new strains of cotton, improved on the design of the cotton gin, invented a screw press for packing cotton, and pioneered techniques for extracting cottonseed oil. With the help of his London factors Green & Wainwright, he also gained an international reputation for his cotton, an important advantage in a competitive world market. Other large planters followed Dunbar's lead. "We will think ourselves very happy if we can tread in your footsteps," wrote Julian Poydras, an indigo planter. And follow in Dunbar's footsteps he did, declaring some months later, "We are all mostly in cotton."[40]

As established planters like Poydras and Dunbar turned their indigo and tobacco plantations over to cotton, migrants from the eastern seaboard and elsewhere joined them. Thomas Rodney noted a "continuous influx of people" into the Mississippi Territory in 1805.[41] Similarly, the French naturalist Michaux wrote in his 1805 memoir, "The great profits derived from cotton entice an immense number of foreigners into that part."[42] One of these "foreigners" was David Bradford, a leader of the Whiskey Rebellion in Pennsylvania, who fled to Spanish Louisiana and became a cotton planter in the Bayou Sarah district. In 1802 a traveler found Bradford "well Settled" and prosperous in "the Richest Uplands I ever Saw."[43] When John Steele emigrated to the Mississippi Territory in 1799 to take up a commission as secretary of the new territorial government, he stayed at the house of "a very hospitable Irishman" near Natchez. The man was wealthy, Steele reported, and "will send to market very shortly near thirty thousand wt of clean Cotton, like the driving snow as it comes from the Gin."[44]

The territorial government helped planters as a class by regulating the cotton market and cracking down on independent selling by slaves. Officials in the Mississippi Territory established inspections for cotton gins and presses, and graded cotton according to its quality. The regulations were intended "to promote the interests of this territory, by establishing at foreign markets the good reputation of the staple of this country."[45] Another notable reform prohibited slaves from growing and marketing their own cotton, a practice "permitted by some few Planters to the probable injury of most of them," as the governor of the territory put it. The avowed purpose of the law was to prevent slaves from stealing cotton, but it had the additional effect of limiting slaves' independent production and enabling their owners to gain more complete control over their time and labor.[46]

Slave labor was central to the whole enterprise. Cotton planters assumed they needed slave labor just as they needed soil and rain. The Natchez elite made this clear in a 1797 petition urging Congress not to abolish slavery in their territory. Without slaves, claimed the petitioners, "the farms in this District would be but of little more value to the present occupiers than equal quantity of waste land."[47] Migrants identified cotton growing with slave labor as if the relationship were natural. Edward Turner decided "to purchase a plantation not exceeding 1000 Dollars, which in a few years say two or three I am in hopes to be enabled to put 5 or 6 Negroes upon and shortly after my self."[48] Nathaniel Cox urged a friend to sell his lands in Kentucky and come out to the Mississippi Territory: "If you could reconsile it to yourself to bring your negroes to the Miss. Terr, they would certainly make you a hansom fortune in ten years by the cultivation of Cotton."[49] Among those who recognized the profits to be gained from using slaves to grow cotton were agents of the U.S. government. When Hore Browse Trist arrived in Natchez in 1803 to serve as collector of customs, he observed that his new home was a good country "for making money by cultivation" because of the productivity of slave labor, including children and women. "Hands from 10 years old & upwards of both sexes clear upon an average 12 to 1500 weight of clean cotton besides corn & meats for their own consumption," he informed his wife.[50] Garrisoned near New Orleans in the spring of

1811, the young soldier William Hamilton estimated that forty slaves cultivating 200 acres of land could earn a planter $10,000 every year. "If the negroes will follow me I will place myself at their head and march them here with ease & facility," he proposed to his father in North Carolina.[51]

National power and the plantation economy merged in the person of Winthrop Sargent, the first governor of the Mississippi Territory. Sargent was a native of Massachusetts, a Harvard graduate, an accomplished surveyor, and a partisan Federalist. He presided over the establishment of territorial courts, a militia, and a criminal code in the Mississippi Territory between 1798 and 1801.[52] Described by one acquaintance as "a pen and ink man," Sargent carefully observed his new environment.[53] He logged his journey to Natchez in the summer of 1798, recorded meteorological data and the height of the Mississippi River, and published an analysis of the New Madrid earthquakes of 1811 in the journal of the American Academy of Arts and Sciences.[54] Soon after he arrived in Natchez, he married Mary McIntosh Williams, "a very amiable young widow with a considerable fortune," whose property included two large plantations, Grove and Bellemont, and dozens of slaves.[55] The marriage made Sargent one of the territory's biggest cotton planters, and as governor, he looked after the interests of his class. After learning about Gabriel's conspiracy in Virginia, for instance, Sargent instructed militia officers in the territory to regard the enforcement of the slave code as "a point of honor."[56] Sargent placed the power and authority of the national government at the disposal of the territory's slaveowners.

The rising cotton economy generated a brisk demand for slaves among the farmers and planters of the Deep South. John Steele directed his brother in December 1799 to sell his property in Richmond and buy slaves with the proceeds. "I would take two Negros for it," he calculated, "they would here sell for 1,000 or 1200 Dollars."[57] Early in 1801, William McIntosh arrived on Maryland's Eastern Shore only to find the price of slaves "very high, owing to the number of Purchasers." Several other Natchez planters, quicker out of the gate than McIntosh, were heading home with "Eighty or Ninety neagros young & old."[58] Wishing to emigrate to the Mississippi Territory, the Tennessee planter Robert Butler wrote that he would "invest my funds in Negroes, and as I am informed that land can be purchased very low on the west side of the [Mississippi] river, and Negroes bearing a high price then I can make sale of some for that purpose."[59] Around the same time, Leonard Covington sent fifty slaves from his tobacco plantation in Maryland to his new cotton plantation in the Mississippi Territory, which he called "that land of promise."[60] William Rochel floated "twenty likely Virginia born slaves" down the Mississippi in a flat-bottomed boat to Natchez, where he advertised his intention to sell some of the slaves and barter others in exchange for a small farm.[61] John Hutchins, the son of a wealthy Natchez planter, traveled all the way to New York to purchase slaves. The New Yorkers tried to run away in Pittsburgh, but Hutchins foiled their plot and transported them to the Deep South, where he put them to work on his father's plantation.[62] Schemes such as these contributed to the fourfold increase of the slave population of the Mississippi Territory in the first decade of the nineteenth century, from 3,499 slaves in 1801 to 16,703 in 1810.[63]

Masters and slaves collaborated in the creation of a cotton economy but not as equals. They lived and worked together in a hierarchical, coercive relationship. Slaves had little choice but to participate. The plantation economy provided enslaved people with their means of subsistence, and they were subjected to physical punishment and the threat of sale if they resisted their enslavement. On Winthrop Sargent's Grove and Bellemont plantations, the slaves planted a wide variety of food crops, including peas, beans, celery, potatoes, sweet potatoes, carrots, lettuce, parsley, turnips, radishes, artichokes, and corn. They also planted apple, locust, and willow trees; gelded lambs; constructed dams; and cleared new fields. Cotton planting began in late March, and when that was done, the slaves turned their attentions once more to food crops and rye, pausing in mid-June to thin the growing cotton, which was left to grow on its own ("laid by") in early

July. Picking began in late August and continued through the fall, interspersed with the harvesting of corn, pumpkins, potatoes, and other produce. Then the picked cotton had to be dried, ginned, baled, and shipped to market. All of this was accomplished by the slaves, who then prepared for another year of the same tedious work. The labor regime was accompanied by a harsh cycle of birth and death, which Sargent tersely recorded in his journal: "August 13th last night Sophie delivered of mulatto female child alive, but premature birth and it soon died—for the three or four days past Negroes employed in gathering corn blades for fodder."[64]

Collaboration was also the rule on John Palfrey's cotton plantation. A Bostonian who moved to New Orleans around the time of the Louisiana Purchase, Palfrey bought 900 acres of land in Attakapas near the Gulf coast of the Orleans Territory in 1810. He judged the region to be "well calculated for new beginning without much capital." After buying twenty-one slaves, Palfrey moved to his new plantation, aptly named Forlorn Hope.[65] (The significance of Palfrey's naming his plantation Forlorn Hope may be gleaned from Crèvecoeur's famous description of American backwoodsmen: "They are a kind of forlorn hope, preceding by ten or twelve years the most respectable army of veterans which come after them.")[66] Beginning in March 1811, Palfrey's slaves cleared land, built fences and dwellings, and planted cotton, corn, and vegetables. They endured bad weather and sickness. Harry, one of the slaves, occasionally ran away but never got very far. ("Caught Harry in the neighborhood of the cabins in pursuit of provisions nearly famished," Palfrey noted in his journal entry for 7 April 1812. "By his account he has eaten but once since he ran away.") Beginning in September, Palfrey meticulously tallied each day's cotton harvest, noting the weight of cotton picked by every slave. Women and children picked about 80 percent of the cotton. Three women— Phillis, Mimy, and Aimy—picked more than 40 percent of it, and seven children—Tom, Bob, Ephraim, Joe, Ben, Elsey, and Fanny— picked another 40 percent. The adult men—Harry, Sam, Amos, and Daniel—picked less than 15 percent of the cotton. They were more likely to be found engaged in odd jobs elsewhere on the plantation, from splitting and hauling fence rails to chopping firewood. Altogether the slaves picked about 37,000 pounds of cotton in the plantation's first year.[67] Early in 1813 Palfrey's son, Edward, proudly reflected on the household's achievement. "During the two summers that we have been here, notwithstanding we came on a piece of land without fence, house, or any thing of the kind and never had a plough been put to it, we made nearly fifty bales of Cotton, besides an immense stack of Plantation food, such as Corn, Pumpkins, Potatoes etc. etc."[68] Fences, houses, plows, a saleable crop, and an abundance of food—for Edward Palfrey and others of his ilk, these were signs of progress in the civilizing of the southern frontier.

Life on the cotton frontier did not appeal to everyone. A boatman descending the Mississippi River was overhead to declare, "D—n my precious eyes if I would not rather be at allowance of a mouldy biscuit a day, in any part of Old England, or even New York, Pennsylvania, or Maryland, than I would be obliged to live in such a country as this two years, to own the finest cotton plantation, and the greatest gang of negroes in the territory."[69] Slaves also found ways to register their dissatisfaction. A correspondent in Richmond observed in 1807: "There is a very great aversion amongst our Negroes to be carried to distant parts, & particularly to our new countries."[70] Forced migration severed many of them from their families and communities. Writing from Natchez, John Steele observed that his slave George was "extremely uneasy to hear from Millie and his Children" in Virginia.[71] Some enslaved people tried to return home, or at least that is what their owners thought they were attempting to do. In 1807, for instance, Ferdinand L. Claiborne of the Mississippi Territory advertised for the return of two runaway slaves, Sandy and Lewis. Sandy was from the mouth of the Cumberland, and Lewis had been brought from near Nashville the previous spring. "It is supposed that their object will be to return to the state of Tennessee," Claiborne surmised.[72] Samuel Elkins guessed that his runaway slave Nathaniel would "attempt to cross the lake and return to Kentucky, from whence he was brought last spring by Mr. Joseph Miller, of Bourbon county."[73] But these fugitives were exceptional. Under duress, most enslaved people collaborated in the civilizing of the cotton frontier and contributed to its progress.

The Deep South's first cotton boom ended when the national government enacted a countrywide embargo on exports in December 1807. The embargo was intended to force the belligerent nations of Europe, especially Great Britain, to respect the neutral rights of American shipping, and ultimately to open foreign markets for U.S. agriculturalists.[74] The measure received wide support in the Orleans and Mississippi territories even though it battered the region's cotton growers. Unable to export their crop, purchasers of public lands found themselves mired in debt with no means of escape. As a petition from the Mississippi Territory's House of Representatives reminded Congress, "Our produce lies unsold and unsaleable in our Barns."[75] The value of exports from New Orleans and Mobile fell to a mere $540,000 in 1809 and would not return to pre-embargo levels until 1815.[76] Late in 1811 a New Orleans merchant reported to John Palfrey that the cotton market was still depressed. "Business was never perhaps in so great a State of Stagnation," he observed, "nor can we flatter ourselves with any revival unless some understanding should fortunately be effected with the British Government, or some great change take place in Europe."[77] As the merchant suggested, the prospects of the Deep South now rested on distant economic and political forces that the people of the region could not control. They had not yet achieved the kind of independence promised by Jeffersonian republicanism, nor would they so long as their livelihood rested on the unreliable foundation of international trade.

"so many wolves or bares"

The Jeffersonian civilizing mission presented a special challenge to the indigenous inhabitants of the Deep South. Increasing numbers of white and black people, an expanding cotton economy, and an activist

U.S. government all pressured the southern Indians to partake in what one public official called "the sweets of civilization."[78] Jeffersonians hoped that America's native people would abandon hunting, adopt animal husbandry and commercial agriculture, and sell their surplus land to the United States. These changes would prepare the Indians either to be assimilated into civilized, American society or to be removed west of the Mississippi River—an alternative that gained favor among many Jeffersonians after the Louisiana Purchase doubled the country's size. In the Deep South, the Creek, Choctaw, and Chickasaw peoples responded to the Jeffersonian challenge in complex and contradictory ways, ranging from the eager adoption of chattel slavery to the violent repudiation of U.S. expansion.

The southern Indians' geopolitical position steadily declined after the American Revolution. Accustomed to navigating balanced imperial rivalries for much of the eighteenth century, the southern Indians now confronted a hegemonic power in the United States. The expulsion of the British had left Spain as the only major European counterweight to U.S. expansion into the Deep South, and the southern Indians quickly discovered that Spain was an unreliable ally. One Chickasaw leader accused Spanish officials of leaving his people "to the jaws of the Tiger and the bear."[79] Nor did the southern Indians present a united front. Historical animosities between different indigenous groups, disputes over boundaries, and the highly decentralized, consensual character of their internal politics inhibited pan-Indian solidarity. Equally important was American officials' ability to use the considerable financial and diplomatic resources at their disposal (including bribery) to disrupt Indian unity. In 1805 and 1806, for instance, the United States took advantage of disagreements among the southern Indians to acquire lands in what is today central Tennessee and northern Alabama. The twists and turns of the negotiation almost brought the Cherokee and Chickasaw Indians to blows. The southern Indians did not stand together, so they risked falling apart.[80]

The rapidly growing white and black population of the Deep South pressed against the southern Indians' land and sovereignty. Indigenous people considered the immigrants to be intruders. The Creek Indians called them Ecunnaunuxulgee, which one official roughly translated as "people greedily grasping after all their lands."[81] It was an apt term, as many of the intruders did indeed want the Indians out of the way. In 1810, for instance, more than four hundred American squatters living on lands claimed by the Chickasaws petitioned the president and Congress to expel them. The squatters promised to support the government, cultivate the land, and build a civil society. They could not understand why fertile land should be denied to those who would "improve" it, for the sake of "a heathan nation" who seemed content to "saunter about like so many wolves or bares."[82] The squatters' petition echoed a long tradition of Anglo-American political philosophy, expressed most famously in John Locke's *Second Treatise of Government,* which held that land possessed by a savage people could rightfully be claimed by those who would convert the land into property and cultivate it as God intended.[83]

While white migrants clamored for the Indians' land, U.S. officials were busy encouraging the Indians to adopt farming, animal husbandry, and domestic manufactures. The most important and influential of these officials was Benjamin Hawkins, the U.S. agent to the Creek Indians. Born in North Carolina and educated at the College of New Jersey, Hawkins was a man of the American Revolution. He was elected to the North Carolina legislature in 1778, to the Continental Congress in 1784, and to the United States Senate in 1790. He began his thirty-year career among the southern Indians as one of the federal treaty commissioners at Hopewell in 1786, where he developed a keen interest in the Indians' languages. President George Washington sent him to the southern backcountry in 1796, where for twenty years he supervised American efforts to promote agricultural and political reform among the Creek Indians. "This is his hobby horse," Isaac Briggs reported to Jefferson.[84] Like other Indian agents, Hawkins provided material and political support for the civilizing project. He supplied agricultural implements and machinery to those who wanted them. He gave advice and rewarded those who took it. One

of his greatest achievements was the Creek Agency, his headquarters
on the Flint River and an outpost of republican civilization. By 1809
the agency included a large plantation cultivated by slaves, a post office, saw and grist mills, a tanyard, various artisans' shops, two looms,
and a school for Indians. In the unlettered southern backcountry,
Hawkins kept a library of nearly two hundred books covering law,
history, and philosophy, including Jefferson's *Notes on the State of Virginia*.[85]

Hawkins and the other U.S. agents discovered many allies in the
Indian backcountry, especially among those men and women who
wanted to participate in the cotton economy. The Choctaw agent
Samuel Mitchell indicated in 1800 that some of the Choctaws "appear
willing to attempt the raising of cotton." He offered them seed and
lessons in planting, and looked forward to the arrival of a cotton
gin—"a great spur to industry."[86] In 1802 a trader named Abram
Mordecai set up a cotton gin below the junction of the Coosa and
Tallapoosa rivers in south-central Alabama and bought cotton from
the Creeks.[87] That same year, William Claiborne authorized the establishment of a cotton gin in the Choctaw nation and directed the
factor in the Chickasaw nation to buy cotton from the chiefs for cash
or barter.[88] White travelers lauded these developments. The Presbyterian missionary James Hall reported in 1800 that federal agents
were teaching Indian men to farm and the women to spin and weave.
Cotton gins had been raised and, he predicted, "it is probable that in a
few years the cotton trade will be considerable among them."[89] Cotton provided the southern Indians with an alternative to the declining
deerskin economy. It could be exchanged for the European commodities they had become accustomed to acquiring through trade, or
turned into clothing and used at home.[90]

Mestizos made up the vanguard of the cotton economy in the Indian backcountry. Throughout the eighteenth century, the indigenous
peoples of the Deep South absorbed small numbers of European traders who married Indian women and raised their children among the
Indians. These mestizos helped to mediate between the Indians and

the outside world, especially through trade and diplomacy, where multilingual literacy was particularly useful. They often assumed positions of influence within their Indian communities even as they remained socially and culturally distinctive. The Colbert family provides an outstanding example of *mestizaje* among the Chickasaw Indians. The Scottish trader John Logan Colbert established himself among the Chickasaws in 1729, marrying three Chickasaw women in succession. Colbert's sons—William, George, Levi, Samuel, Joseph, and Pittman—became leaders among the Chickasaw people by the late eighteenth century. Levi Colbert became familiar to travelers passing through the Chickasaw country between Tennessee and New Orleans because he managed an inn along the road. "He has at this place a large well cultivated farm, about 30 or 40 likely slaves and a white overseer to superintend them—a good stock of cattle and hogs," observed one traveler. "He keeps a Public house in a large frame building & affords very tolerable accommodations; & as many travellers on their road to and from N. Orleans, Natchez, &c, call on him, he through that medium obtains an ample market for his superfluous produce." Levi Colbert was a friend to travelers, an ally to the U.S. government, and a beneficiary of the Jeffersonian civilizing mission. He was also a slaveowner.[91]

As the description of Levi Colbert's compound indicates, black slavery suffused the mestizo milieu. The African presence among the southern Indians had begun to grow in the latter half of the eighteenth century, when English merchants plying the deerskin trade took slaves into the backcountry to serve as teamsters, drovers, handymen and agricultural laborers at the trading houses. Slaves also fled into the backcountry from the frontier settlements of the Carolinas, Georgia, and Florida, leading British officials to reward Indians for capturing runaways and handing them over to the colonial authorities. During the American Revolution, Indians raiding Anglo-American settlements transported more people of African descent into the backcountry, and when the war ended, refugee Loyalist merchants and traders carried still more slaves to the Indian country, where they settled.[92] Long experience in the backcountry gave some multilingual black people an opportunity to serve as intermediaries between whites and Indians. One of the most notable was Cesar, a slave hired by Governor Winthrop Sargent in 1798 to communicate with the Choctaws who frequented Natchez. Sargent regarded Cesar's work to be "highly important to National Dignity and Interests," but a racist grand jury in Adams County denounced his employment as shameful to "a free and independent people." Cesar eventually accompanied Philip Nolan's ill-fated expedition to Texas in 1801, and was later discovered living with a Spanish military officer in Chihuahua. It was Cesar, more than Nolan, who might aptly have been called a man without a country.[93]

Slaves were already a coveted commodity among the Indians by the 1790s, and the cotton boom made them even more valuable. During negotiations over the return of runaways and captives, a Creek delegation pointed out that the slaves "cause great disputes among us . . . as some are sold, and bartered, from one to another, and the property paid for them consumed."[94] Benjamin Hawkins frequently noted the presence of black slaves in the Indian backcountry. Peter McQueen, a leading man among the Upper Creeks, "has a valuable property in negroes and stock and begins to know their value." Some of the Lower Creeks "have negroes, taken during the revolutionary war," he reported, "and where they live, there is more industry and better farms." Hawkins associated slaveowning with the progress of civilization among the Indians, but he did not think it was enough merely to have slaves. They must be disciplined and put to work in economically productive activities, including the growing and spinning of cotton. One Creek woman possessed eighty slaves, Hawkins reported, but "from bad management they are a heavy burthen to her and to themselves, they are all idle." Early in 1802, the interpreter Alex Cornells brought the old Creek leader Efau Haujo to Hawkins and told him that "the old man had no corn and his negroes were under no government." After supplying Efau Haujo with agricultural tools, Hawkins advised him to shape up: "Put your negros and family to work, make them pen and milk your cattle, let me see your fields enlarged and well fenced." A civilized farmer, he implied, should manage his slaves properly.[95]

Although U.S. officials occasionally worried about a black-Indian alliance endangering the peace of the frontier, the Indian backcountry was no haven for slaves. Runaways fleeing into the Indian country sometimes suffered greatly from cold and hunger. One frostbitten fugitive was captured in the Choctaw nation in 1793.[96] Indians on the west side of the Mississippi River discovered two runaway slaves belonging to Winthrop Sargent "in the woods almost perished" in 1802.[97] As these episodes indicate, the native inhabitants of the Deep South often recovered runaway slaves and delivered them to U.S. officials, who encouraged the practice.[98] There are even records of slaves escaping from Indian owners. For instance, a black woman appeared at Fort Pickering in 1800 with five children. She declared that she had been the property of a white man named Pettigrew who was killed six years earlier on the Tennessee River, and she had been carried into the Cherokee nation by an Indian warrior named White Man Killer, who was now dead. White Man Killer's sons were abusing her and selling her children. She feared, wrote Major Zebulon Pike, that "the Moment the Indians got them in their power a distance in the Wilderness They would kill Her Oldest Son and Daughter."[99] And in 1809, the Chickasaw leader George Colbert requested assistance in the recovery of a slave who had fled into the United States and was allegedly in jail in North Carolina.[100] Whatever their nationality, slaveowners shared a common interest in keeping slaves from running away, and recovering those who fled.

Lethal violence scarred relations between black people and the southern Indians. Some killings occurred in the context of the Indians' retaliatory customs of justice. In 1797, for example, a Creek headman executed two slaves for stealing horses, and warned other slaveholders "that they must take care of their slaves, as he would undoubtedly put the law in force against them."[101] Five years later, the Cusseta Creeks killed an American slave in retaliation for the murder of a Creek man.[102] Acting at the behest of Benjamin Hawkins, who wanted the Creek Indians to formalize their system of justice, the Creek National Council tried a slave for the murder of an Indian woman in 1806. The slave was found guilty and executed in the Creek style, as Hawkins reported to Jefferson. "The warriors took him to a river bank, the brother of the deceased knocked him down with a stake, stabbed him and threw his body into the river." Notwithstanding its gruesome conclusion, Hawkins considered this to be the first fair trial ever conducted by the Creek nation and, hence, another sign of the civilizing of the Indians.[103] Black slaves were also attacked merely for being adjunct to their owners. A particularly dramatic case was reported in 1816 by the U.S. agent to the Chickasaw Indians. "Several negroes in this nation have been murdered in a most cruel, barbarous, and unprovoked manner," he asserted. "One belonging to Mr. Thomas Love was shot by an Indian while in his master's yard riving boards. The only excuse for this murder is, that the Indian says he did not like Mr. Love, and that he would spoil his property."[104] The murder of Love's slave suggests that it is romantic to imagine an alliance between African Americans and the Chickasaw, Choctaw, or Creek Indians in opposition to the expansion of slavery. Formidable obstacles impeded such an alliance. Black people faced economic exploitation, social isolation, and violence at the hands of indigenous people as the slave country expanded into the Indian backcountry. Only among the Seminoles did fugitive slaves find refuge (at least until the 1810s), and that was because neither chattel slavery nor U.S. power had yet spread through Florida.[105]

Contrary to the Jeffersonian hope, the republican program for civilizing the southern Indians did not lead to the peaceful transfer of surplus lands to the United States. The expansion of the plantation complex within indigenous communities increased the market value of the Indians' lands, and stiffened their resolve not to sell out cheaply. If they had to cede land to the United States, they would at least try to bargain for a fair price. Meanwhile, migrants from the United States flocked to the cotton frontier in anticipation of new lands coming to market. Many Indians resented the daily increasing numbers of white intruders who passed through their country, fished in their streams, hunted in their forests, drove livestock on their pastures, cut down their trees, and squatted on their lands. The U.S. government's inability to restrain its citizens undermined the Indians' trust in the intentions and authority of the American agents. Younger warriors wished to prove their manhood by resisting the intruders and attacking their property. Wrote Benjamin Hawkins in the summer of 1811, the Creek leadership was "apprehensive they cannot restrain their young people from committing depredations on property passing thro' their Country, which will involve their Country in ruin."[106] Over time, the civilizing of the southern frontier intensified conflicts within indigenous communities as well as between the Indians and the United States.

"live long in heathen land"

The civilizing of the cotton frontier had a spiritual dimension. "As to every thing Religious," lamented the Quaker surveyor Isaac Briggs, "I am here in a howling wilderness."[107] Where Briggs despaired, others saw a glorious chance to spread the Gospel. Beginning in the late 1790s, missionaries from various evangelical Protestant denominations responded to the scandal of frontier impiety by trolling the Deep South for souls. They handed out Bibles, established congregations, and built churches in the new territories. They carried a message of Christian love that attracted white and black people but not the southern Indians, who eschewed the evangelicals' appeal in the years before the War of 1812. Protestant Christianity on the cotton frontier was thus a biracial collaboration, but at the same time, the demands of chattel slavery inescapably limited the egalitarian potential of religious fellowship across the color line.[108]

Practicing Christians considered the Gospel to be indispensable to the civilizing process. New York Presbyterians asserted the connection in the late 1790s, when they organized a society dedicated to converting the Indians to Christianity. As John Mason announced in his 1797 sermon "Hope for the Heathen": "Instead of waiting till Civilization fit our Indian neighbors for the gospel, let us try whether the gospel will not be the most successful means of civilizing them."[109] The New York Missionary Society appointed Joseph Bullen to begin its work, sending him and his son to the Chickasaw nation in 1799. "You are going to a region which the joyful sound of the gospel has never yet reached," announced the president of the Missionary Society, "where the arts of civilized life are almost unknown—to a people covered with the gloom of ignorance, superstition, and barbarism."[110] Bullen taught English and preached the Gospel among the Chickasaw Indians for four years. He eventually left the Chickasaws and settled down on a small farm in Jefferson County in the Mississippi Territory. There he established the territory's first Presbyterian church in 1804.[111]

Bullen achieved a special rapport with the black slaves living among the Chickasaw Indians. In June of 1799, George Colbert's slaves solicited Bullen to preach to them. He met with twenty of the slaves, read to them from the New Testament, and explained to them that Christ "loves poor blacks as well as others." One week later, Bullen noted in his journal that an elderly black woman owned by William Colbert had traveled thirty miles to hear his sermon. "Me live long in heathen land, am very glad to hear the blessed gospel," she said. During his first summer, Bullen baptized an enslaved man ("a true disciple of Jesus") and his four children. The slaves were owned by James Gunn, who prayed with them and taught them reading and catechism. "It is a blessed thing to have such a master," the slaves told Bullen. The missionary was impressed by the black Christians' zeal. They had been "visited with the outpouring of the spirit of God, inducing them to worship him, to keep the Sabbath day, and to be exemplary, in their lives, while their masters remain in a carnal state." Bullen's experience was not unique. Other missionaries and preachers who came to the cotton frontier were also embraced by black slaves who professed to be Christians. While most southern Indians kept their distance, many black people reached for the Gospel as if it were a rope pulling them from quicksand.[112]

In addition to the Presbyterians, the Baptists and Methodists rooted themselves among the white and black people of the Deep South at the beginning of the nineteenth century. Organized in 1806, the Mississippi Baptist Association included five churches with 196 members in 1807, and eighteen churches with 914 members in 1813.[113] Among the Baptist congregations was an African church, which assembled once a month at Josiah Flower's sawmill on Bayou Pierre, and an African congregation organized in Mobile around 1806.[114] Joseph Willis, a North Carolina–born free man of color, founded a small church on Bayou Chicot in the Orleans Territory. He petitioned the Mississippi Baptist Association in 1810 to ordain him and recognize his church, which it finally did six years later.[115] Methodist church membership increased from 60 people in 1800 to 360 in 1810, when more than one-fourth of the territory's Methodists were black.[116] Their numbers were small, but the congregations carved a niche for evangelical Protestantism on the cotton frontier. Biracial fellowship shaped the contours of Christian civilization in the slave country.

Some clergymen harbored antislavery principles, a legacy of the social radicalism that infused the nascent evangelical movement in the eighteenth century. One example was Tobias Gibson, the first Methodist minister in the Mississippi Territory, who emancipated his slaves before leaving South Carolina to emigrate to the southwest.[117] But strong pressures muted evangelical antislavery. When the Methodists debated slavery at their annual conference held in Tennessee in 1808, recalled the itinerant preacher Jacob Young, "We were sitting here in a slave state, and we had to move with a great deal of caution."[118] Denominational competition compelled clergymen to hold their tongues, lest they lose souls to their rivals. Even more important was a general indifference toward religion among the region's farmers and planters. As the missionaries John Schermerhorn and Samuel Mills reported in 1814, "Most of the emigrants to this country came here for the purpose of amassing wealth, and that object seems to have absorbed their souls."[119] Clergymen had particular trouble getting the inhabitants to keep the Sabbath, or at least to allow the slaves to do so. James Moore, an overseer in the territory, complained that "a man in my Occupation is oblig'd to pay no Regard to Sundays if he pleases his imployer."[120]

The problem of slaves working on the Sabbath symbolized a tension between the economic and religious dimensions of the civilizing process in the Deep South. That tension was resolved in favor of the economic because white evangelicals were restrained by their own dependence on the prevailing social order. For instance, an account book for the Fayette Circuit of the Mississippi Conference reveals that in 1809 Methodist preachers were paid in receipts redeemable for ginned cotton.[121] Thus pious white people in the Deep South turned their attention to improving slaves' conditions instead of attacking slavery. The very first question taken up by the Mississippi Baptist Association was: "What steps would be most advisable to take with members of our society, whose treatment to their slaves is unscriptural?" Their generous answer was to treat such members "with brotherly love according to the rules of doctrine," which apparently meant establishing an investigating committee, demanding repentance from offenders, and inflicting disciplinary sanctions on the unrepentant.[122] This would probably have been a meager consolation to the mistreated slaves, but it may have been better than nothing at all. Evangelicalism did not offer equality or freedom in the corporeal world, but it did provide an alternative to the arrant materialism and social isolation that slaves endured on the cotton frontier.

Innumerable episodes of collaboration and conflict involving white and black people forged the Protestant dimension of the slave country. Most of these episodes are undocumented and have been lost to the past, which makes the few available sources all the more important. One valuable source is the journal of Johann Burckard and Karsten Petersen, two German artisans who lived at Benjamin Hawkins's Creek Agency from 1807 to 1812. The two men had been sent to Hawkins to build looms and spinning wheels, machines coveted by the advocates of civilization. They happened to be Moravians, a central European evangelical sect with missionary outposts around the globe from Ceylon to Dutch Guiana. Moravians had a history of converting people of African descent to Christianity throughout the eighteenth century, and their settlements in Pennsylvania and North Carolina welcomed black people. Once on the cotton frontier, Burckard and Petersen struggled to convey their understanding of Christianity to the slaves who lived and worked at the agency, men and women with their own ideas about the meaning of the Gospel.[123]

The Moravian artisans and the slaves slowly got to know each other. Hawkins's slaves helped transport the two Moravians from Fort Hawkins in Georgia to the Creek Agency, helped erect the Moravians' house there, and from time to time helped to repair it.[124] In April of 1810, Burckard and Petersen bought a slave of their own, but he ran away two weeks later, only to be captured by the authorities in Georgia and hanged for murdering a white man. Hawkins recommended caustically that the two men "confine themselves in future to their gardens and workshops."[125] The two men spent their first Christmas at the Creek Agency in silent prayer, while the slaves "celebrated Christmas, alas, by drinking to excess." During the summer, one of the slaves asked the Moravians to read him the story of creation. He came back several weeks later and listened to Burckard read the story of Maunday Thursday. The following Christmas, some of the slaves dropped in on the two men with holiday greetings and a request for liquor. Burckard and Petersen sadly observed that the slaves "think they know more about Christmas than we can tell them." In the winter of 1811, local black people began to attend Burckard and Petersen's weekly Bible lessons, which were conducted in English. The Moravians altered the schedule of their meetings to accommodate the slaves' work schedule. On 6 April, fourteen people assembled to hear the story of Christ on the way to the Cross. Two days later the congregation reached a high of thirty-one, but then it declined and stabilized at between ten and fifteen congregants, most of whom were African American. The morning of Easter Sunday, twelve black men and women listened to the story of the Resurrection. After the meeting, Burckard and Petersen overheard the slaves saying to each other, "That is the right doctrine. It is the true Word of God."[126]

A slave named Phil became the most devout and most difficult of the Moravians' followers. Phil had shown religious inclinations years earlier, when he had been banned from preaching incendiary sermons to other slaves. Toward the end of March in 1811, Phil passed by the Moravians' hut on his way to draw water from the well. He stopped by the open door to listen to the liturgy and was captivated by what he heard. He began to attend services regularly, becoming a staunch defender of the local church. Inquisitive, intelligent, and independent, Phil plumbed the Moravian doctrines of sin and salvation. One day he asked Burckard "whether the local Negroes who knowingly do wrong in many matters, the evil of which is very evident, could receive forgiveness." Burckard replied that "forgiveness for them was certainly to be had if in their sinful state they turned to the Savior, confessed their sins from the bottom of their hearts and in faith asked His forgiveness." Stimulated perhaps by this conversation, Burckard and Petersen prepared a special sermon for the next liturgy, admonishing the congregation "to turn from the sinful ways and look to the Savior."[127]

In mid-April, the Moravians decided to allow Phil to attend their Sunday liturgy. He claimed to have been baptized twice already, once by the Methodists and once by the Baptists, so Burckard admonished Phil to renew the pledge he gave when he was baptized. Phil responded "that he fully intended diligently to pray to the Savior." With his prophetic yearnings awakened, Phil revealed to the Moravians that he went out to the woods to pray every evening. He began to hear voices. Concerned about these ominous signs, Burckard and Petersen rebuked Phil for "his misleading false sermons and prayers, which are only too well known and which lacked real humility." Phil responded with characteristic bravado, asserting that "he understood the Word of God perfectly and he knew that no one would again be made crazy by his sermons." Phil soon challenged the Moravians' religious authority. In July, Burckard and Petersen agreed to provide sanctuary for a craftsman working at the Creek Agency named Lewis, who was wanted by the authorities in Georgia for murdering a man at a game of cards. Phil instructed the other black Christians at the agency that they should no longer attend the Moravians' services. Murderers were beyond salvation, he insisted, and the Moravians had erred grievously in protecting Lewis. Phil presented himself as the righteous alternative, declaring, "I will preach to you, I know the Bible as well as they." His gambit split the black community. Some stayed with Phil as he "loudly announced Lewis' death sentence late into the night," but others, like a slave named Bob, defied his judgment and allied themselves with the Moravians.[128]

Phil went too far when he tried to turn faith into power. His actions threatened the Creek Agency's social order and had to be punished. With Hawkins temporarily absent, Hawkins's companion Lavinia Downs had Phil and his collaborator, Sam, tied to a tree and whipped. One of the Moravians intervened weakly on the slaves' behalf, but Lavinia insisted on discipline. The slaves had crossed the line and their antics would not be tolerated. To bolster her argument she accused Phil of harboring illicit erotic desires. "You do not know this hypocrite," she charged, "He is haughty and wants to be a preacher and preach in his house where he is able to take the women to his lap, which he is not able to do at your house."[129] Downs thus reiterated the classic conservative indictment that antinomianism led to sexual disorder. Lurking within the Creek Agency, the very model of civilized society, was the specter of a backwoods bacchanal. The whipping of Phil and Sam amounted to the intervention of political authority—indeed, the U.S. government—to suppress a radically subversive flowering of Protestant Christianity in the Indian backcountry.

Yet Phil's rebellious spirit was not quenched by the whipping, nor did the punishment settle all religious questions at the Creek Agency. Some weeks later a slave loyal to the Moravians informed them that

Phil was "washing the feet of some of the Negroes and Negresses as was written in the Scriptures." A symbolic reenactment of John 13, foot washing had been a hallmark of racial egalitarianism in the Moravian communities of North Carolina until 1809, when the Moravian Conference declared that black brothers and sisters might attend the ceremony but could not participate. In the spiritually charged atmosphere of the Creek Agency, the slaves' secret foot washing was an unmistakable gesture of defiance.[130]

Religious conflict again split the Creek Agency during a rash of thefts committed by slaves in March 1812. A slave named Claster (whom the Moravians had described earlier as "badly confused by dreams and visions") came to the Moravians and asked that the slaves be absolved of their crimes. Otherwise their meetings "would be of no value." Seeking forgiveness, some of the slaves broke off into a separate meeting led by Claster. Six or seven remained loyal to the Moravians. Burckard and Petersen complained that many of the slaves were "possessed of the devil and overcome by blindness." A few months later the Creek planter Alex Cornells refused to let Burckard preach to his slaves. He complained that they "had already been made sullen and crazy by those who had preached to them."[131] Clearly, black men and women living among the southern Indians continued to draw subversive lessons from the Gospel, but for Protestant Christianity to grow and flower along with the slave country, its adherents would ultimately have to reconcile themselves to the restraints of chattel slavery. As they did, they laid the foundations of Afro-Protestantism in the Deep South.

The civilizing of the cotton frontier thus advanced on a variety of fronts between 1795 and 1812, and with it marched slavery. Public officials mapped the land and prepared it for sale, hoping to attract migrants and stimulate population growth. They used the resources at their disposal to encourage the southern Indians to adopt a republican way of life and, ultimately, to cede their land to the United States. At the same time, a booming transatlantic cotton economy financed the conversion of a relatively undeveloped region into what Jeffersonians regarded as a more civilized landscape of farms and plantations—like John Palfrey's Forlorn Hope. In a different kind of conversion, Protestant evangelicals toiled among the rough and unchurched people of the southern frontier, where—to their surprise—black slaves welcomed them with special fervor. All these forces and pressures shaped the slave country as it emerged in the Deep South.

At the same time, the civilizing dynamic gave rise to tensions, contradictions, and unfulfilled promises. The Jeffersonian ideal of a society dominated by yeoman farmers was not realized. Difficult terrain, the high cost of labor, legal disputes, and opposition from indigenous groups all delayed the transformation of "wilderness" into saleable property. When the land finally did finally come to market, wealthy planters rather than yeoman farmers got the best of it—increasing the black population along with the white. But even planters were disappointed when Jefferson's embargo cut off access to overseas markets and ended the cotton boom. Many found themselves indebted to the very government that had promised them independence. One petition to Congress summed up circumstances on the cotton frontier in 1811 by describing prospects for the future as "clouded, uncertain, and extremely gloomy."[132]

The transformations taking place on the cotton frontier provoked immense resentments among those indigenous men and women who saw land cessions, intruders, and reformers as a threat to their sovereignty and customs. As the southern Indians experienced "rapid and solicitous advances in civilization," they rippled with conflict over how best to respond to the challenge of American expansion.[133] Traditionalists clashed with the civilizers, and young militants challenged older leaders. Resistance to the United States was emboldened by a mystical movement that originated among the Shawnee Indians north of the Ohio River and swept through the southern Indian backcountry in 1811 and 1812. The Jeffersonians never imagined that their seemingly benign program to civilize the southern frontier would boil into war, but that is precisely what happened.

Christophe Colomb, White Hall Plantation, *ca. 1800. This painting depicts the plantation of Marius Pons Bringier on the Mississippi River. The vitality of the scene illustrates
the dynamism of life in lower Louisiana in an era of change and growth. Note the flatboat
manned by black oarsmen, carrying cotton down the river. Colomb married Bringier's
daughter, Françoise. Reproduced with permission.*

CHAPTER 3

Commerce and Slavery in Lower Louisiana

LOWER LOUISIANA—more precisely defined as New Orleans and its environs—emerged as a distinctive milieu within the Deep South alongside the sprawling cotton frontier. The region had been a colonial backwater through much of the eighteenth century, despite its favorable location at the junction of a vast continental network of rivers and a nearly limitless circum-Atlantic world. Strong currents of change began to flow in the 1790s, initiating an era of commercial reorientation and expansion. Planters along the Mississippi River began to cultivate sugar, while New Orleans turned into the "the great mart of all the wealth of the western world," as one traveler put it.[1] The commercial boom intensified demand for slave labor in the region, which resulted in the arrival of thousands of enslaved people from many different places and the further diversification of an already heterogeneous slave population. As lower Louisiana became part of the United States, it also experienced fundamental transformations in its connections to the broader Atlantic world.

As on the cotton frontier, the extension of U.S. sovereignty over lower Louisiana intersected with the expansion of slavery. The Louisiana Purchase forced the United States government to confront the problems of social order provoked by the sugar boom. One set of problems involved slave importation. Government officials struggled to enforce the national government's laws banning foreign slave importation, while local planters subverted them. Another set of problems involved slave resistance. Government officials struggled to prevent slaves from taking advantage of lower Louisiana's multiplying avenues for escape. They also had to come to grips with New Orleans's increasing population of free people of color, whom many local whites regarded as potentially dangerous. Ultimately all the tensions of commercial and political development in lower Louisiana overflowed in January 1811, when enslaved people in the sugar plantation districts above New Orleans rose in the largest slave rebellion in the history of the United States.

Lower Louisiana's rise to significance began under Spanish rule. The European and African population of Louisiana almost tripled in the first twenty years of Spanish dominion, reaching about 30,000 in 1785, approximately half of whom lived in or near New Orleans.[2] The colony's principal exports—indigo, tobacco, lumber, and fur— reached almost $1.5 million per annum in the late 1780s, a significant increase from twenty years earlier.[3] Several policies adopted by the Spanish Crown contributed to the increase. One was the Crown's decision in the late 1770s to purchase Louisiana tobacco for the Mexican market, which subsidized a boom that lasted until the early 1790s, when Spain withdrew its support and threw Louisiana's tobacco planters into a crisis.[4] Another was its liberalization of trade between New Orleans and the French West Indies, which returned Louisiana to the commercial orbit of the French Caribbean world just as that world was about to fall apart.[5] To stimulate economic development, the Spanish Crown also relaxed its restrictions on the importation of slaves into Louisiana, which boosted the supply of Africans.[6] Among them was Abd al-Rahman Ibrahima, a Muslim prince of the Fulbe nation from West Africa. Captured in battle and sold to an English slave trader on the Gambia River, Ibrahima was transported across the Atlantic Ocean to Dominica, where he was purchased by

Thomas Irwin and shipped to New Orleans, then to Natchez, where he was sold 18 August 1788 to Thomas Foster, who cut off his hair to shame him, then put him to work in a tobacco field.[7]

Events in the French Caribbean colony of St. Domingue initiated a qualitative transformation in Louisiana's development. In 1789 that island had been the leading producer of sugar in the world, exporting almost fifty million pounds of white sugar and more than ninety million pounds of raw sugar, about 30 percent of the world's sugar exports. Then came the French Revolution, the agitation by St. Domingue's free people of color for equal rights, and finally the revolt of the slaves against their owners, which plunged the island into a ten-year war.[8] By 1800–1801, St. Domingue's exports had fallen to less than twenty thousand pounds of white sugar and less than twenty million pounds of raw sugar.[9] Planters elsewhere in the Americas filled the void. In areas where sugarcane was already grown, planters expanded their production; others dedicated new regions to the crop. Jamaica, Cuba, and Brazil won the lion's share of the reshuffled market, but high sugar prices in the latter half of the 1790s and the early 1800s opened up the possibility of profitable sugar production elsewhere.[10] In lower Louisiana, sugar promised to reverse the declining fortunes of indigo growers around New Orleans. "Our planters are founding all their hopes on sugar cane," one of them wrote in 1795.[11]

The slave rebellion in St. Domingue also reorganized world production of sugar by strewing large numbers of what today might be called technical experts around the Greater Caribbean.[12] These people brought useful knowledge and important skills to the places where they ended up, and one of their principal destinations was Louisiana. The Louisiana-born planter Etienne de Boré, who conducted the first successful experiments in the commercial production of sugar in Louisiana in the mid-1790s, worked with Antoine Morin, a sugar maker said to have been a refugee from St. Domingue.[13] Other knowledgeable people from St. Domingue, including skilled slaves, found their way to Louisiana, where a sugar maker lucky enough to be a free person could earn as much as $1,500 a year.[14] Himself one

of the many refugees from St. Domingue who passed through New
Orleans, Pierre-Louis Berquin-Duvallon understood what had happened. Louisiana, he explained in his memoir, "owes its principal advantage to the calamities of St. Domingo, which raised the demand
for sugar from Louisiana, and sent many planters and workmen of
that unhappy island to seek a settlement on the Mississippi."[15]

Louisiana planters adapted the Caribbean sugar complex to their
own local ecology. In tropical climates, sugarcane required at least
fourteen months to mature, but Louisiana's winter frosts shortened
the growing season to eight or nine months and threatened planters
with failure if the cane was planted too early or cut too late. To meet
the challenge of their climate, Louisiana planters imported a new and
hardier strain of cane called Otaheite, which had been introduced to
the Caribbean in the early 1790s by the intrepid William Bligh.[16]
They used advanced irrigation systems to control the water content
of the cane, and invented new ways to protect the cane from freezing
once it had been cut, first covering it with bagasse (the remains of
milled cane), and later adopting the practice of "windrowing," or laying the cane lengthwise in rows with the leaves left on.[17] Breaching
the circadian rhythms of premodern labor, planters ran their mills day
and night in the winter months, racing against time to collect the
juice before it spoiled.[18] They continued to improve their methods of
production for the next half-century, belying the idea that slavery and
technological progress are incompatible.[19]

Large indigo planters led the quick transition to sugar. Their plantations were already protected from the Mississippi by levees maintained by slaves, so they did not have to waste precious labor claiming
land from the swamps.[20] They commanded large forces of enslaved
men and women who could be compelled to perform the difficult
work of raising cane. These two primary advantages of land and labor led to a third: the ability to raise capital. Sugar plantations cost
money, which large planters were able to borrow from factors and
merchants in New Orleans on better terms than could their poorer
and less reputable neighbors. They used that money to erect mills,

where their cane would be crushed and processed into sugar, and to buy more slaves. These investments paid off. The sugar planters "are now generally free of Debt, and many have added considerably to their fortunes," Governor William Claiborne reported to Thomas Jefferson in 1806.[21] Sugar plantations—as many as seventy-five in 1802, producing more than five million pounds of sugar—sprang up along the Mississippi River in lower Louisiana.[22] Their ever-improving big houses, slave cabins, chimneyed mills, neat gardens, orange groves, and cane fields embossed the alluvial landscape with a stamp of civility. Passing up the river from the English Turn to New Orleans in 1801, one traveler thought he saw "a lively picture of a west india settlement."[23] In less than a decade, lower Louisiana became an outpost of the Atlantic sugar plantation complex.

Sugar planters entered a difficult but rewarding business. Bad weather and disease were daily concerns. In August 1807, Henry Brown found himself with a great deal of work to do on his sugar plantation, and only half the number of slaves he needed to do it. Fifteen slaves were sick with a respiratory ailment, and one woman had died. Yet Brown himself prospered. "I grow fat in spite of heat and fatigue," he admitted.[24] Similarly, the grinding season began on William Kenner's Somerset plantation in November 1811 with his overseer and driver ill and Kenner himself "never more completely put to my wits." Still he remained optimistic. "We have been making sugar since the 1st and are making about three Hogsheads of nice stuff pr day and expect soon to make four," Kenner wrote to a friend. "In the midst of all this hard Duty and bustle we (I mean my own family & self) continue thank God to enjoy fine health."[25] It is unlikely that the same could have been said of the enslaved people who lived and died at Somerset.

Although sugar distinguished the economy of lower Louisiana, most free people in the region were not sugar planters. A mixed agricultural economy survived alongside the sugar plantations, and a thriving urban milieu complemented growth in the countryside. Small farmers with and without slaves grew rice, corn, and vegetables. They also raised livestock. Some sold their produce to neighboring plantations, others—especially in St. Bernard and Lafourche—sold to the New Orleans market.[26] In the Opelousas and Attakapas prairies west of the sugar district, ranchers tended vast herds of cattle, which also fed the city and the river plantations.[27] Then there was New Orleans itself, "destined by nature to become one of the principal cities of North America, and perhaps the most important place of commerce in the new world," wrote Berquin-Duvallon, who loathed it.[28] Febrile and motley, New Orleans collected the goods of the increasingly populated North American interior and reshipped them to the Caribbean, South America, the eastern United States, and Europe.[29]

Lower Louisiana's population and economy advanced rapidly. Between 1806 and 1810 alone, the sugar district's population increased by more than 40 percent, from almost 40,000 to more than 55,000. The fastest growth occurred in and around that swelling node of commerce, New Orleans, which increased from 17,000 to 27,000 people, and in Iberville and Baton Rouge, which increased from 2,500 to 4,000. The slave population everywhere increased faster than the white population, and the population of free people of color more than doubled, with most of the increase occurring in New Orleans.[30] Census takers counted ninety-one sugar works in the Orleans Territory in 1810, making almost 10 million pounds of sugar and 180,000 gallons of molasses. There were also seventeen distilleries, making more than 225,000 gallons of low-quality cane liquor known as tafia.[31] River traffic increased despite the restrictive embargo and nonintercourse policies implemented by Jefferson and Madison. The number of vessels arriving in New Orleans from upriver more than doubled, going from 723 in the twelve months beginning April 1806, to 1,624 in the twelve months beginning April 1810.[32] "From the Geographical position of this Territory," Governor Claiborne boasted, "our traders will always be intimately connected with the great Commercial Houses of the Northern and Middle States; and our exporting merchants will have large and extensive dealings, with the Inhabitants of that rich and immense tract of Country West of the Alleghany Mountains, whose various products descend annually to New Orleans, the Great Commercial Depot of the Western World."[33] Nothing seemed more obvious than that New Orleans was destined for greatness.

The profits from sugar and the prospects of New Orleans induced Americans from the eastern seaboard to migrate to lower Louisiana, where, despite cultural differences with the Francophone locals, they insinuated themselves into the local economy and helped to bind the region into the United States.[34] Perhaps the most important migrant was Edward Livingston, a prominent Republican lawyer and politician from one of New York's aristocratic families. In 1803, the same year that his elder brother negotiated with Talleyrand for Louisiana, Livingston served as U.S. attorney for the district of New York and mayor of New York. Shortly after recovering from yellow fever, he learned that one of his clerks had embezzled $40,000 from the U.S. Treasury and fled New York. Livingston took responsibility for the fraud, resigned from both offices, and turned over his property to trustees. Mired in debt, he emigrated to New Orleans, where he hoped to recoup his fortune. Like many others, Livingston saw the city as a promising destination for entrepreneurs.[35]

Livingston quickly established economic, social, and political bonds that made him a leading figure in New Orleans. His law practice blossomed, and a fortuitous choice of clients turned him into a major Louisiana landholder. He married the widow Louise Moreau de Lassy, a refugee from St. Domingue whose father had been a wealthy sugar planter there. The marriage opened doors in New Orleans's French-speaking society, as did Livingston's political commitments. He assumed leadership of a faction in New Orleans that opposed the first governor of the Orleans Territory, William Claiborne. He joined the French-speaking planters who challenged Congress's ban on the importation of African slaves. Livingston's political standing would suffer from his unpopular effort to claim ownership over disputed riverfront property, but he rescued his reputation during the Battle of

New Orleans, when he served informally as an aide-de-camp for Andrew Jackson.[36]

In addition to his diverse economic activities in New Orleans, Livingston became an absentee rice planter.[37] He hired Francis O'Duhigg to operate a rice farm in Plaquemines Parish, and early in 1805 O'Duhigg began the work of surveying the land, clearing it, and preparing it for planting rice.[38] Estimating that each arpent (about five-sixths of an acre) of rice would earn 100 dollars, O'Duhigg wrote to Livingston: "If you send me till the month of May only twelve good task negroes you will make money and defray your expences this year."[39] But O'Duhigg began to have trouble with the slaves. Cudjo complained of a stomach ailment and asserted that he had been poisoned. "I am afraid to see him die in my hands," O'Duhigg wrote, "and if you are answerable to for him, I would advise you to give him up, for he is of no service." Three other slaves who had been hired for the year "are good for nothing," he asserted; "it is stealing your money to hire such negroes."[40] Despite sickness and *marronage* (running away) throughout the spring, the slaves planted fifty arpents of rice along with twelve arpents of corn. O'Duhigg was pleased with the crop. The rice, he wrote in August, "flatters the eyes of every one that sees it."[41]

The harvest commenced in early September and with it, more work for the slaves and headaches for O'Duhigg. Four of the slaves fell sick and had to be sent to town to recover their health. O'Duhigg hired slaves from his neighbors to replace the sick hands, but dismissed them after "finding they did not work to my liking." Desperate for more labor, O'Duhigg decided to pay his own slaves fifty cents a day to work on Sundays. "You'll have a long account to settle with them," he warned Livingston.[42] Two aspects of O'Duhigg's managerial strategies are worth emphasizing, because they do not fit the stereotype of plantation slavery. One is the routine hiring of slaves during seasons of peak labor, a practice that appears to have been widespread in the Deep South if not very effective for O'Duhigg. Another is the direct payment of slaves for extra work, one of the many alternatives to torture that managers used to elicit labor from their slaves.[43]

Francis O'Duhigg had dreams of his own. He understood his arrangement with Livingston as a stepping-stone to better things, financed in part by the profits from slavery. Exasperated with the shortage of labor and the unreliability of his neighbors' slaves, O'Duhigg proposed to Livingston a slave-buying junket to the North. "I am a good Judge of Negroes. I am born among them," he wrote. "I will go there [to the North] by the next opportunity, and buy any quantity you chuse. I'll be back in the winter and ready for the crop. I won't charge no commission but my passage." O'Duhigg represented the junket as a way to express his gratitude to Livingston. He also wanted to purchase a few slaves for himself. He yearned for gentility. "I have bought a beautiful tract of land . . . there is on it forty acres of cleared land & fit for plough in the middle of which is a Hill twenty five feet high, forty feet Broad, and ninety long, that Hill is fit to set a house upon, and in future, I hope to be able to have it settled in a genteel manner."[44] For O'Duhigg and other free men in his position, slaveholding afforded passage from deference to independence.

Livingston's concerns were not merely local. While he inserted himself into Louisiana's Francophone society and local economy, he also maintained connections to his native New York that helped to facilitate Louisiana's integration into the Union. Ambitious emigrants arriving in New Orleans carried letters of introduction to Livingston. New York merchants wrote to him, eager to procure New Orleans sugar and cotton.[45] And when Robert Fulton and Robert Livingston plotted to introduce the steamboat to the lower Mississippi, they turned to Edward for valuable information and political assistance.[46] After the *New Orleans* paddled into the city for which it was named early in 1812, one of Livingston's many correspondents lauded its arrival: "I am happy to find that the Steamboat is so well addapted to the trade of the Mississippi & so admerably calculated for the accommodation of passengers."[47] Over time the steamboat lowered shipping costs, increased capacity, and accelerated the circulation of goods and people around North America.[48]

Other entrepreneurs hoped to use steam power on dry land. The planter Evan Jones ordered a steam engine from Samuel Briggs (Isaac Briggs's inventive brother) in 1805, but the engine was lost in a ship-wreck on its way from Philadelphia to New Orleans.[49] In 1809 the architect and engineer Benjamin Latrobe (who had recently designed a Custom House for New Orleans) proposed to use a steam engine to deliver water to the residents of New Orleans. "Perhaps the whole is a Castle in the air," he wrote secretly to his brother-in-law, "but it is a good looking one."[50] The arrival of the *New Orleans* in 1812 inspired Governor Claiborne to think about using steam power to increase sugar production. "If the force of Steam, could be applied to Sugar Mills, & in a manner simple & not attended with great expence," he mused, "the invention would greatly conduce to the welfare of this Territory, & to the private Interests of the inventor."[51] Other beneficiaries were eastern manufacturers, who would eventually find a market for steam engines among the sugar planters of lower Louisiana.[52]

A vast waterwheel of commerce thus began accelerate in the first decade of the nineteenth century. It powered an extensive national economy involving different sections of the expanding United States. The French naturalist Michaux witnessed its revolutions during a tour through the trans-Appalachian West. In an 1805 memoir, he reported that agents of Philadelphia mercantile houses arranged for corn, pork, whiskey, linen, bar iron, and other commodities to be floated down the Ohio and Mississippi rivers from Pittsburgh to New Orleans. Brokers in New Orleans would then sell the goods locally or reexport them to the Caribbean in exchange for indigo, cotton, and sugar, which they would then ship back to Philadelphia.[53] Louisiana's contribution to the national economy, and vice versa, was a central theme of the *Louisiana Gazette,* which boasted the slogan "America, Commerce and Freedom" on its masthead. In an 1806 editorial, the newspaper argued that Louisiana's growing population would provide a market for goods from the western states, while the shipping of its cotton and sugar would profit eastern mercantile interests. Echoing the Jeffersonian idea of diffusion, the *Gazette* also reminded residents of the "middle and southern states" that Louisiana offered "an outlet for the superabundance of their black population, and an extravagant price for what will shortly be to them, an incumbrance instead of an advantage."[54] With the commercial expansion of New Orleans and its hinterlands came a proliferating slave trade.

"confounded with other nations"

The sugar boom intensified demand for slave labor and turned New Orleans into one of the principal slave markets in North America. Between 1790 and 1810, the transatlantic currents of commerce and politics carried almost eighteen thousand slaves from Africa, the Caribbean, and the United States into lower Louisiana.[55] Their arrival helped to create the most dynamic, heterogeneous, and tumultuous plantation region in North America. Yet the slave rebellion in St. Domingue that made these developments possible also made them problematic. Public officials, whose concern was safety as well as profit, struggled to regulate slave importation to prevent Louisiana from becoming another St. Domingue. After the Louisiana Purchase, U.S. officials in the Orleans Territory took up the difficult task of suppressing slave smuggling while trying to win the allegiance of local planters eager to import slaves.

Local authorities had tried to control the flow of foreign slaves into Spanish Louisiana even before the slave rebellion broke out in St. Domingue. In 1786, Louisiana governor Esteban Miró prohibited the introduction of slaves born in the Caribbean, although he continued to allow traders to reexport African-born slaves *(bozales)* from the Caribbean to Louisiana. Then, fearful of Jacobin influences, the Spanish Crown issued a royal order in 1790 prohibiting the entry of slaves or black refugees from the French islands into Spanish colonies. The New Orleans Cabildo, or city council, issued its own edict two years later banning the importation of slaves from the Caribbean, receiving the support of the Spanish Crown the following year. After a conspiracy among the slaves of Pointe Coupee was uncovered in 1795, the Cabildo and the governor, Héctor Baron de Carondelet clashed over the proper measures for policing slaves, with Carondelet finally banning the importation of all slaves into Louisiana in 1796. Then, bolstered by the sugar boom, a substantial faction of planters petitioned for a reopening of the trade in 1800, inaugurating a new wave of debate. The members of the Cabildo were divided, while the leading Spanish colonial officials in Louisiana, the Marquis de Casa Calvo and Nicolás María Vidal, supported the reopening of the African trade in order to promote economic development. A clash between the governor and the council complicated the disagreement over slave importation and prevented any coherent and undisputed policy from being enacted. In the confusion, African slaves began to arrive in New Orleans after 1800.[56]

The slave trade to Louisiana was thriving at the very moment of the Louisiana Purchase. Arriving in the Orleans Territory late in 1803, the Quaker surveyor Isaac Briggs discovered to his dismay that "the number of slaves in this country is already great, and the infatuated inhabitants are in the habit of increasing it, by large importations."[57] Three French vessels carrying nearly 500 Africans had recently been admitted to the port.[58] Africans continued to arrive in 1804. The schooner *Josephine* arrived in late May 1804 from Kingston with 40 Africans, and returned again in August—this time from Havana—with another 56. Another vessel, the *Diana,* also arrived from Havana in August with 77 "New Negroes." The *Margaret* arrived in July from Angola with 207 "New Negroes." And the *Sarah* arrived in August with 205 African slaves procured in Angola and Nassau. Henry Kennedy advertised them in the *Louisiana Gazette* as "choice healthy young Negroes."[59] Although Governor Claiborne regarded the importation of foreign slaves as inhumane and dangerous, he did not believe that he had any legal authority to block the trade until Congress banned it.[60]

In contrast to Claiborne, most local planters wanted to continue African slave importation. One reason was that they believed Africans were more industrious and less dangerous than enslaved people born into the revolutionary world of the Americas. In 1804 the New Orleans City Council received a series of petitions protesting that the arrival of slaves and free people of color from the Caribbean had exacerbated *marronage* around New Orleans. One petition warned that slaves from St. Domingue "with their hands still reddened with the blood of our unfortunate fellow countrymen are arriving daily in great number in our midst and that perhaps tomorrow their smoking torches will be lighted again to set fire to our peaceful homes." The council drafted a resolution declaring that "any slave not absolutely recognized to be uncivilized cannot be admitted under any pretext, not even as a servant of the captain or of some passenger, unless he belongs to some resident of the Colony who had taken him along on a sea voyage."[61] According to the New Orleans City Council, a civilized slave society could not function with civilized slaves, which meant slaves born and raised in North America or the Caribbean. Many planters agreed that "uncivilized" African slaves, being uncontaminated with the revolutionary ideas of liberty and equality, were less dangerous. In his memoir of Louisiana in 1802, the St. Domingue refugee planter Berquin-Duvallon explained to his readers that slaves born in the Americas were more intelligent and healthier than slaves brought from Africa, but that they were "the most indolent, vicious and debauched." Slaves from Guinea were less skilled in domestic service and trades and more prone to weaknesses of body and mind, he believed, but these disadvantages were offset by the fact that they were "more robust, more laborious, more adapted to the labours of the field, less deceitful and libertine than others."[62]

Congress's initial ban on the importation of foreign slaves into the Orleans Territory fell short of its goal. South Carolina circumvented the ban by reopening the African slave trade in 1803. Many of the almost forty thousand African slaves imported into Charleston from the beginning of 1804 to the end of 1807 were shipped to New Orleans. Late in 1806, two agents for the Rhode Island firm of Gardner and Dean reported that sales of African slaves in Charleston were brisk. "Our market is at this moment extremely favorable for the sale of Africans," they wrote. "They are now worth $300–320 and the probability that they will maintain the prices all the approaching winter and spring as the demand from the back country and New Orleans is very considerable."[63] Slave traders in that city openly advertised the sale of African slaves brought from Charleston. The firm of Kenner and Henderson advertised the sale of "74 prime slaves of the Fantee nation on board the schooner *Reliance* . . . from Charleston" in the *Louisiana Gazette* on 4 July 1806.[64] The following winter, Patton and Mossy advertised the sale of "140 Prime Congo Negroes . . . the first choice from a cargo of four hundred" shipped from Charleston on the *Ethiopian*.[65] These Africans were among the last human beings legally imported into the United States as slaves and among the first to be shipped from the eastern seaboard to the Deep South through the coastal trade.

Enslaved Africans faced death, piracy, and shipwreck on their way to New Orleans. Already weakened by an Atlantic crossing that generally killed one of every seven of them, African slaves kept on dying on their way to Louisiana.[66] In 1806 the *Charleston Courier* reported that the brig *Three Sisters,* bound from Charleston to New Orleans with slaves, had put in at Havana in distress, "30 of the slaves having died on the passage." The *Lucy* departed from Charleston on 4 July 1806, carrying thirty slaves insured from Charleston to Natchez and eleven slaves insured from Charleston to Havana, but was captured en route to Havana and sent to Nassau. At Nassau, the eleven slaves insured to Havana were removed as a lawful prize, but several others had died. The remaining slaves were sent on to New Orleans.[67] Slaves transported from Charleston to New Orleans also faced the danger—and opportunity—of shipwreck. In March 1806 the *Atalanta* was wrecked off Abaco Island. "On the vessel striking," reported the *Charleston Courier,* "two seamen (foreigners) and three slaves took to the boat, and have not since been heard of." The following year, the

Sally was also wrecked off Abaco, but her cargo of slaves was recovered by another vessel and carried on to New Orleans for sale.[68] Forced transatlantic migration entailed a concatenation of traumas that weakened those who survived and made it easier for them to be abused at the end of the journey. This, perhaps, was an unspoken reason why Louisiana planters wanted to keep importing African slaves. Plus they were cheap.

The forces of supply and demand together dictated the shape of lower Louisiana's slave market. One way to perceive the shape of that market is by tracing fluctuations in the price of slaves and comparing the prices of different groups of slaves—all of which can now be done with some reliability using the historian Gwendolyn Hall's *Louisiana Slave Database*. The mean price of a male slave between the ages of fifteen and forty-five more than doubled from 1792 to 1802, probably in response to the rising demand for slaves linked to the sugar and cotton booms, along with episodic restrictions on their importation. Prices declined by about 40 percent from 1802 to 1805, reflecting the reopening of the slave trade, which eased pressure on the market. Prices then stabilized from 1805 to 1814. Buyers paid higher prices for men than women, and higher prices for adults than children. Although the prices of slaves of different origins generally rose and fell together, buyers always paid more for Louisiana born "creole" slaves than for slaves from Africa, the Caribbean, or the United States. Buyers did not pay consistently higher prices for slaves of any particular African region, indicating that they did not really care where on the continent African slaves came from.[69]

Nevertheless the regional origins of African slaves appear in newspaper advertisements for their sale as if their ethnic and national origins mattered to purchasers. In 1806 Henry Molier & Co. advertised the sale of "12 Young Brute Negroes of the Mandingo and Congo nations, fit for a sugar estate."[70] E. Frazier & Co. advertised the sale of twenty-five "Congo Negroes" at Port Gibson in 1807.[71] One advertisement in 1808 enticed planters with news of a public auction of sixty-two slaves, some of whom were "New Negroes of the Mandango Nation" who had been in the country for two years.[72] In 1810 John McDonough purchased thirteen Congo slaves from the Maryland Louisiana Company for a total of $6,050. The slaves included Jean Louis, a "first rate negro of the Congo Nation, being acquainted with the use of the axe, hoe, spade, [?], basket making and other kinds of plantation work having been 3 years in the country"; his wife, Rose, a "good field wench in the country since three years" and their son William; Clarissa and her child Sally; François and his wife, Henrietta; Antielle and his wife, Jannaton; Atys; Nancy; and Pauline, a "strong wench in the country since 3 years acquainted with house & plantation work," and her son Hardtime.[73] Even when they recognized differences of national origin among enslaved people, slave-owners lumped all slaves together under the racist category "Negro." In 1806, for instance, a slaveowner advertised in the *Moniteur de Louisiane* for the recovery of "three Negro men, one of the Congo nation and another of the Bambara, and another from a nation whose name I have forgotten."[74] Time, distance, and the homogenizing force of slavery began to efface the national identities of enslaved men and women in the minds of their owners.

One planter who did pay attention to the African origins of the slaves he purchased was William Dunbar. In 1807 he requested that the Charleston firm of Tunno & Price purchase £3,000 worth of African slaves and ship them to his factors in New Orleans, specifically instructing the merchants to procure Africans between the ages of twelve and twenty-one, "well formed & robust," with one-quarter to one-half being girls or women. He preferred slaves from certain parts of Africa over others but understood that he was unlikely to receive the kind of Africans he wanted: "The Iboa nation lies under a prejudice here & may be excluded. There are certain nations from the interior of africa, the individuals of which I have always found more Civilized, at least better disposed than those nearer the Coast, such as Bornon, Houssa, Zanfara, Zegzeg, Kapina, Tombootoo, all or near the river Niger, but I suppose they do not arrive in any considerable numbers and [are] always confounded with other nations who have made them prisoners."[75] Dunbar knew that Atlantic slave traders drew from vast slave-supplying hinterlands in Africa, gathering slaves from many different ethnic groups and nations and cramming them together—confounding them, as he put it—in the slave ships that crossed the Atlantic. And after collecting their cargo, Atlantic slave traders sailed to many different ports in the Americas, where the slaves were sold and dispersed. In the context of the slave trade as a whole, New Orleans was a minor destination for Atlantic slavers, even during the years of peak importation at the beginning of the sugar boom. The broader patterns of the transatlantic and intra-Caribbean slave trade, not the preferences of local planters, dictated which Africans would end up in the lower Mississippi Valley.[76]

Local planters connived with smugglers and privateers to bring African slaves into the Orleans Territory. "These abuses are seen and regretted," Claiborne complained to Jefferson, "but (under existing circumstances) cannot be prevented."[77] The smugglers were not engaged in a systematic program of slave smuggling but were ad hoc and opportunistic entrepreneurs. They were mostly privateers who preyed on Spanish shipping in the Caribbean, and most of the slaves they smuggled into the United States were captured from slavers sailing for Havana and other Spanish American ports.[78] The privateers' operations mixed adventure with legal wrangling. For instance, Luis Aury captured the *Mossavito,* a Portuguese slaver, off the coast of Cuba in 1810. He put a prize crew on board the vessel and instructed them to take it to St. Bartholemews. After being chased by a British cruiser for three days, the *Mossavito* sailed to New Orleans for provisions then to "long island," about twenty leagues from New Orleans in La Fourche. There the crew burned the ship and sold the slaves, 100 in all, to a Mr. Fortier for $17,000. All of this was attested to by Louis Crispin, a free man of color who described himself as a "subject of the Empire of Hayti." After sailing out of Aux Cayes in a shallop, Crispin had encountered Aury's corsair the *Guillaume* and joined its crew. When the *Guillaume* captured the *Mossavito,* Crispin boarded the slaver as part of the prize crew and ended up in New Orleans, where Aury paid him $126. Slave smuggling had its rewards, even for a free man of color from Haiti.[79]

The laws against slave smuggling did not liberate smuggled slaves.[80] In February 1810 the *Alerta* sailed from the coast of Africa laden with 153 slaves. Four months later, it was captured about thirty miles south of Havana by the French privateer *L'Epine,* which transferred its crew to the slaver and headed for New Orleans "with the intention, as the Captain frequently said, of smuggling the slaves into the Territory and selling them." But the *Alerta* was wrecked in shallow water off the coast of Louisiana, which is where the vessel's desperate crew were discovered "endeavoring to pick up a miserable and precarious subsistence by catching pelicans for their food." After extensive litigation, 145 slaves from the *Alerta* (60 men, 52 boys—including 1 who was very sick—and 33 women and girls) were sold in New Orleans for a total of $44,975.[81]

The lawless tides of Atlantic commerce also swept up a young Brazilian man named Candido Gomez, the son of a slave woman and her owner from Salvador, Brazil. He was supposed to have been a shoemaker. Sometime around 1810, Gomez's father "placed him on board of a vessel bound for the coast of Guinea," allegedly as a punishment for drunkenness. His vessel, the *Falcon,* was captured by privateers near Havana and taken to Louisiana, where he was sold with other Africans at the smugglers' roost of Grande Terre. Several years later, Gomez sued for his freedom in a New Orleans court, but ultimately lost his case because he could not prove he had been free in Brazil, nor did the laws prohibiting the illegal importation of slaves into Louisiana allow for his emancipation. The severe judgment of the Louisiana Supreme Court was that the plaintiff "cannot be listened to in a court of justice."[82]

Federal officials in New Orleans complained to their superiors about the ineffectiveness of laws prohibiting the importation of slaves. Worried that African slaves imported into Mobile were being transported from Spanish Florida to the United States, Governor Claiborne urged Commodore John Shaw to patrol the Gulf Coast as far as the Perdido River and to capture "any Vessel from a Foreign Port, with Slaves on board, that you may find hovering on our Coast or attempting to enter the Bay of Mobile."[83] After the annexation of West Florida, smuggling through Barataria became the bigger problem. Collector of Customs Thomas Williams contended that slave smuggling could not be prevented without "a vigilant cooperation of the Navy," but he complained that the Navy lacked the requisite vessels and manpower to enforce the laws.[84] Over the next two years, the Baratarian smugglers (including Jean Lafitte) became bolder and better organized, preying on Spanish vessels at will, smuggling slaves into the territory with impunity, and clashing with local militias and customs officials. The Baratarian smugglers and the U.S. government famously made their peace when the British invaded Louisiana in December of 1814, but when peace resumed so did the illegal slave trade. The crannied coast, local planters' demand for Africans, and a feeble naval presence made it difficult to stop slave smuggling.

International politics brought still more Caribbean slaves to New Orleans. Thousands of the refugees who had fled St. Domingue in the 1790s ended up in Cuba, where they made important contributions to the development of coffee and sugar. When Napoleon removed Ferdinand VII from the throne of Spain and replaced him with Joseph Bonaparte in 1808, Cuban loyalists began to attack the French-speaking refugee communities on the island. After riots erupted in Havana in March of 1809, the Francophone refugees from St. Domingue began to abandon Cuba. Ten thousand of them fled to New Orleans over the following year, including more than three thousand free people of color and another three thousand slaves. "We are in a fair way of being over run with french people & Negroes from St. Iago, Havana & other ports in Cuba," complained James Sterrett, a former U.S. army officer living in New Orleans.[85] The refugees' arrival was part of the long shadow cast over Louisiana by the slave rebellion in St. Domingue.

The slaves and free black migrants were allowed entry as a humanitarian gesture toward the white refugees, whom Claiborne described

as "persons of good character . . . industrious mechanics and planters." He did not expect the blacks to pose a threat to the safety of the
territory, but he wanted to prevent too many from arriving in New
Orleans at once.[86] Anticipating that no more than three hundred
slaves would arrive with the white refugees, he intended to consider
each case on its own merits.[87] In the meantime, the New Orleans
City Council established a relief committee and welfare fund to provide the white refugees with clothing, shelter, and medical care. The
French-language newspapers exhorted the citizens to contribute to
the philanthropic project.[88] In addition, Francophone Louisianans and
their allies lobbied to allow the refugees to bring their slaves into
Louisiana, insisting that the slaves were "faithful domestics" and no
threat to the territory.[89] The claim was plausible because more than
two-thirds of the refugees' slaves were women and children, who
were not considered dangerous.[90] Mayor James Mather explained to
Claiborne that the refugees' slaves were "trained up to the habits
of strict discipline and consist wholly of affricans bought up from
Guineamen in the Island of Cuba, or of faithful slaves who have fled
with their masters from St. Domingo as early as the year 1803."[91]
Claiborne finally allowed the slave-owning refugees to retain their
slaves after posting security. Congress ultimately settled the matter by
remitting the penalties that refugees from Cuba had incurred in the
effort to bring their slaves into the United States but instructing
Claiborne to divert further immigration away from Louisiana.[92]

Unsatiated by the flow of Africans and Caribbean slaves to the
Deep South, planters and merchants began to transplant slaves from
the eastern United States to the sugar districts of the Orleans Territory. In 1807 P. F. Dubourg & Company advertised the sale of 103
slaves from Maryland "accustomed to plantation work," to be sold in
families forming two large gangs.[93] In 1809 the Louisiana planter
Daniel Clark suggested to his business partner in Philadelphia that the
two men enter into a venture to bring slaves from Virginia to the Orleans Territory. Clark planned to sell some of the slaves immediately
upon their arrival, to pay for initial costs of the venture, while the re-

mainder of the slaves would either be set to work on Clark's lands or be sold in small groups "either to emigrants who daily flock here, or to people desirous of bettering there situation by becoming plant- ers."[94] In May 1811 the New Orleans firm of Fortier & Son advertised the sale of fifteen slaves, all from the same plantation in South Caro- lina. They were being sold "to extinguish a mortgage," according to the advertisement. The slaves included two families: George (a wag- goner), his wife, Priscilla, and their two children, Dinah and Christ- mas; and Isaac (a sawyer), his wife, Nancy, and their two children, Jack and Monday. The remaining slaves included two women, Corry and Rose, and five men, Jacque, Jack, Thom, Mouzon, and March. The family affiliations of these seven slaves were not recorded.[95] The mercantile correspondence, newspaper advertisements, and business records that document the nascent internal slave trade do not reveal very much about enslaved people's own consciousness, but when the Louisiana sugar planter John McDonough, Jr., requested that his fa- ther send him some slaves from Baltimore early in 1804, the elder McDonough wrote back, "There is no Negroes to be got hear that would be willing to go to your countree."[96] Already, it seems, the cane fields had earned a bad reputation among slaves in the eastern United States.

Transatlantic currents of commerce and politics thus swelled Loui- siana's slave population and changed its composition in the two dec- ades following the outbreak of civil war in St. Domingue. Estate in- ventories from the period 1790 to 1794 reveal that almost half (47 percent) of the slave population was born in Louisiana. The African population was heterogeneous, with 13 percent of the slaves coming from the Bight of Benin, 12 percent from Senegambia, 7 percent from Central Africa, 5 percent from Sierra Leone, and 4 percent from the Bight of Biafra. Slaves from the British mainland of North America and the Caribbean accounted for less than 6 percent of the slave population. The remaining slaves included people from the Gold Coast and Mozambique, and American Indians. Two decades of com- mercial development produced a new ethnic pattern. Estate inventories for 1810 to 1814 reveal a substantial increase in the proportion of slaves from West-Central Africa, British North America, and the Caribbean. Enslaved people born in Louisiana remained the most numerous group, but their proportion declined to 40 percent of the slave population. West-Central Africans became the second most numerous group, accounting for 16 percent of the slave population, with British North American slaves increased to 10 percent. Slaves from the Bight of Benin and Senegambia together declined to 15 percent of the slave population, while slaves from the Caribbean increased to 5 percent. Slaves from Sierra Leone slightly increased, while those from the Bight of Biafra slightly decreased. In short, the proportion of the slave population from West-Central Africa, British North America, and the Caribbean increased from 12 percent to 31 percent, while almost every other group's share declined.[97] It appears that John Mills, a planter in Bayou Sara, was basically correct when he reported to a New York cousin in 1807, "Great numbers of Affricans has been brought to this country lately, as well as great numbers brought down the River from Kentucky, Cumberland Virginia, Maryland &."[98] The amalgamation of these disparate newcomers with the extant slave population would become a central dynamic of the region's African American cultural formation throughout the first half of the nineteenth century.

The growing slave population troubled many white observers. Charles Robin observed that the white inhabitants of Pointe Coupee, surrounded by their slaves, lived in a constant state of fear. "One can see how gnawing is the anxiety," he wrote, "which far from diminishing with time, is growing, because the colored population is growing faster than that of the whites."[99] Fearing that the scenes of rebellion in St. Domingue would replay themselves in Louisiana, Isaac Briggs blasted the importation of slaves into the Orleans Territory as a "crying, dangerous, national Sin," and warned Thomas Jefferson that the slaves were "already discontented and disposed to throw off their yoke—on the least prospect of success."[100] John Mills agreed. "The great numbers [of slaves] daily imported is alarming to the thinking part of the people," he wrote to his cousin. "I am fearful that unless a stop is soon put to the increasing of the number, that the day is fast approaching when the Whites will fall a sacrifice to the Blacks."[101] The same commercial expansion that brought economic opportunity to New Orleans and its hinterland now appeared to threaten the region with the catastrophe of slave rebellion.

"order and subordination"

Every slave society has been the scene of constant struggle between enslaved people and their owners, but the balance of power between them—and hence the forms their struggles take—has varied at different times and in different places.[102] During the early years of the sugar boom in lower Louisiana, commercial development and political turmoil increased opportunities for individual and collective resistance by slaves, which in turn provoked new responses from local authorities. Moreover, the region was home to a large and growing population of free people of color whose sympathies and allegiances were complex. Determining their rights and responsibilities was another major challenge facing U.S. officials after the Louisiana Purchase. From the booming port of New Orleans to the borderland of Natchitoches, authorities in lower Louisiana struggled to keep the peace in a country Isaac Briggs called a "Pandemonium."[103]

The first line of defense was the plantation itself. Enslaved people were put to work, kept under close watch, and punished within its confines. John Mills observed the system in all its brutality. Louisiana slaves were "always under the eye of their Master or Overseer, or what is sometimes more unfortunate for them, under a *Driver*," he explained in his letter to his cousin. Slaves who violated the rules of the plantation were whipped by the driver or overseer: "three stakes is drove into the ground in a triangular manner, about 6 feet apart. the culprit is told to lie down, (which they will do without a murmur), flat on the belly. the Arms is then extended out, side ways, and each hand tied to a stake hard and fast. The feet is both tied to the third stake, all stretched tight, the overseer, or driver then steps back 7, 8 or ten feet and with a raw hide whip about 7 feet long well plaited, fixed to a handle about 18 inches long, lays on with great force and address across the Buttocks, and if they please to assert themselves, they cut 7 or 8 inches long at every stroke." Aware that his northern relation would be shocked at such bloodletting, Mills condemned and defended slavery at the same time. "You must know," he reasoned, "that unless there is order and subordination kept up, amongst negroes, they would soon be masters, instead of Slaves, for tho they are black, they have as great a propensity to command and be tyrants as white people generally has."[104] The cruelty of slavery became its own justification.

Slaveowners tried to maintain personal dominion over their own slaves, but the daily routine of commerce removed slaves from their oversight. Many owners allowed their slaves to trade with *caboteurs* who peddled goods from canoes and pirogues on the region's many waterways, and even to sell produce and goods in the New Orleans and Natchez markets. Public authority stepped in to quash slaves' independent economic activity and to curtail their geographic mobility.[105] One of Governor William Claiborne's first directives to local commandants in the Orleans Territory, for instance, was to "to prevent slaves from wandering about either day or night, without passes, or from trading among themselves, or with free people without permission from their owners."[106] The local patrols that policed the countryside performed a double service for slaveowners. They compensated for the owners' inability to control their own slaves while at the same time driving the slaves back to their owners for protection.[107] Pierre-Louis Berquin-Duvallon observed that slaves traveling through the woods at night in Louisiana "frequently meet a patrole of the whites, who tie them up and flog them, and then send them home."[108]

Some slaves took advantage of the commercial pathways in and out of New Orleans to escape from slavery, but not all who tried succeeded. Local officials suspected the boatmen who plied the waters around New Orleans of assisting runaway slaves. In 1808, the commander of Fort St. John complained to the mayor of New Orleans about the movement of slaves across Lake Pontchartrain. "Continually a multitude of negroes and mulattoes come and go by canoe, calling themselves fishermen," explained Lieutenant Marshall, and "under this pretext run-away negroes go through who from then on are lost to their masters."[109] Two years later, the City Council decreed that men going from New Orleans to Lake Pontchartrain to fish must have a pass that included their name and description.[110] Local authorities also suspected that New Orleans's physical expansion was creating new hiding places where slaves and free people could drink, gamble, and trade beyond the reach of the law. "The establishment of the Faubourgs without number around the City adds a large surface of land in the quarters already existing," the City Council argued in 1808. "These new Faubourgs will be for a long time yet without inhabitants, they will serve as a harbor of thieves, to people who receive stolen goods and to run-away negroes."[111] And in 1812 the council complained that "a number of slaves, among whom runaways are even found, frequently indulge in games of chance at various places in the City and especially in the Faubourg St. Marie, which incite them to rob their masters and commit thefts elsewhere."[112]

Slaves escaped New Orleans on ships bound for foreign ports. In 1804 Claiborne directed the commander of the station at Belize to inspect all vessels departing from the mouth of the Mississippi because "Negroes belonging to persons residing in this city and its vicinity often escape from the service of their Masters and by concealing themselves on board of Vessels (sometimes by the connivance of the Captain or Crew) pass out of the province."[113] One advertisement for a fugitive slave in 1805 cautioned that the man would "pretend to be free and try to get employment on board a ship and get a berth to go abroad."[114] Similarly, Elijah Smith of Natchez wrote to Nathaniel Evans in 1810 seeking two runaways, one of whom "is something of a Sailor which induses us to suppose that he may attempt to go to New Orleans and get on Board a Vessel."[115] The Black Code adopted by the

Louisiana legislature in 1806 to regulate the behavior of slaves and free people of color permitted slaveowners to sue ship captains for hiring a slave without permission from the slave's owner. The legislature strengthened this provision in 1816, making ship captains liable to criminal prosecution and civil penalties for hiring black men without the permission of their owners if they were slaves, or without free papers if they claimed to be free.[116]

With or without the permission of their masters, some slaves shipped out to sea. Several incidents reveal the travail of slaves who attempted to escape from New Orleans by that route. In June 1804, George Morgan wrote to David Rees from New Orleans, explaining that he had found Rees's slave Dick concealed on board the ship *Augusta*. The ship steward had betrayed the runaway to Morgan, thereupon claiming a reward. Morgan refused to pay, however, believing that the steward had concocted the entire scheme "with the hope of gain." He took Dick to the New Orleans jail, "where I ordered him a dozen [lashes] which were sufficient to make him remember," and placed him in irons to be shipped back to Rees. Morgan concluded the story with a warning: "[Dick] says that Adam & the other boy of yours advised him to run off. I hope you have not had any trouble with them yet but I think you will have to look sharp after them."[117]

Other slaves got farther before being captured. One New Orleans slaveowner petitioned Governor Claiborne for a passport to travel to the Mexican port of Campeche, where his slave Isidore had been imprisoned after escaping from New Orleans on the *San Francisco de Borghe*. Isidore had been discovered by the captain while at sea and incarcerated once the vessel arrived in port.[118] Though Isidore traveled far, he did not get so far as a man named John Wild. On the first of May 1807, the *Thomas Jefferson* sailed from New Orleans bound for Liverpool. According to the deposition of the ship's second mate, Francis Whitmill, the entire crew was surprised when "a dark mulattoe who called himself John Wild appeared on deck from his concealment in the forecastle." Wild declared himself to be "a freeman born" but had been taken from Charleston to New Orleans by a captain who "sold him along with some slaves." When the *Thomas Jefferson* arrived in Liverpool, the captain had Wild "secured on deck with a watch over him" while he went ashore to consult with the American consul. Before the captain returned, Wild and several of the crew deserted the vessel. But Wild did not breathe the free air of England for long. According to Whitmill, he was impressed into His Brittanic Majesty's Navy. Back in New Orleans, the Reverend Philemon Chase sued the captain of the *Thomas Jefferson* for the loss of his slave "Jack."[119]

Runaways taken up in New Orleans were thrown in jail and—after the New Orleans City Council established a chain gang in 1805—compelled to join other slaves laboring on public works. Slavery and municipal progress were thus conjoined in New Orleans, where chained slaves kept up the levee, demolished and erected public buildings, cleaned the streets, and expanded the city beyond its colonial boundaries.[120] City officials tinkered with the regulations governing the use of slave labor on public works. They instituted and revoked compensation for owners of chained slaves, haggled over the proper rations of food and clothing, and disputed claims for slaves injured or lost while working on the public account. They even extended the chain-gang system to female slaves held in the city jail. Rather than allow the jailed women "to lie around idle and lazy," Major Nicholas Girod argued in 1813 that "the shame and humiliation they would experience in seeing themselves led to these laborious duties, would serve as a greater punishment, more keenly felt than even the prison or the lash."[121] An unequivocal public endorsement of slavery, the chain-gang system provided slaveowners with another instrument for disciplining their slaves while, at the same time, affording the city a cheap source of labor for civic improvement, which had become an important measure of progress in the United States. Local officials' experience using slave labor on public works would prepare them well for the dangerous winter of 1814–15, when a veritable legion of slaves was compelled to dig the ditches and erect the fortifications that stood between the British and the city of New Orleans.

A new political as well as commercial geography created opportunities for some slaves to escape. Just as slaves had often fled from Carolina and Georgia to Florida in the colonial era, so too did they run to Spanish territory once the Louisiana Purchase redrew the lines of sovereignty in the Deep South.[122] In the summer of 1804 the American civil and military commandant of the district of Natchitoches, Edward Turner, reported to Governor Claiborne that planters in his district were "extremely and justly alarmed" at rumors that Spanish authorities had issued a decree declaring all slaves entering their jurisdiction to be free.[123] Months later Turner reported that Spanish emissaries were "mediating mischief" in Natchitoches. Nine slaves had already run off to Nacogdoches; thirty in all were embroiled in the conspiracy. Four runaways had dared to return "to rouse and stimulate their confederates."[124] The enraged slaveowners in Natchitoches were prepared to march on Nacogdoches to retrieve their slaves. "If something is not immediately done, they will not have a Slave left in three months," warned Turner.[125] Casa Calvo, Louisiana's last Spanish governor, assured Claiborne that the Spanish had no intention of freeing any slaves, and he promised that any fugitive slave found in Spanish territory would be returned to his or her owner—if the owner pledged not to injure, maltreat, or abuse the slave on account of the flight.[126]

After the establishment of the "Neutral Ground" between Louisiana and Texas in the fall of 1806, enslaved men and women continued to seek refuge across the border, but they did not always find it. "The evil Cannot be born & Something Must be done about it," protested John Sibley from Natchitoches in 1807.[127] Claiborne pressed the Spanish authorities to stop giving asylum to slaves and to return those who had crossed over. Among them, Claiborne asserted in 1809, was a band of thirty slaves who "were furnished all with Spanish Cockades at Nacogdoches, a dance given them, and since have been marched off to the Trinity River, singing Long live Ferdinand the Seventh."[128] Their brief freedom ended some months later when the governor of Texas, Manuel de Salcedo, restored the slaves to their saber-rattling owners.[129] Whether they successfully escaped from slavery or not, slaves who ran to Nacogdoches and New Orleans, or who stowed away on vessels bound for foreign ports, or who returned through the wilderness to the eastern seaboard, challenged their owners' power over them. One unintended but inevitable consequence of their persistent efforts to escape from slavery was the perpetual reinvention of punitive institutions—the whip, the patrol, and the jail, to name a few—that kept enslaved people in their places.[130]

Lower Louisiana's conspicuous and growing number of free people of color complicated the problem of controlling the slave population. Neither slaves nor citizens, free people of color occupied an intermediate social position, which Louisiana's public officials struggled to understand and define. Were free people of color subversive or merely subaltern? Would they endanger or defend plantation society? These were the questions that lay behind Benjamin Morgan's query to Chandler Price shortly before the United States took over Louisiana. "Upon what footing will the free quadroon mulatto & black people stand; will they be entitled to the rights of citizens or not?" he asked. Morgan argued that the attitude of the free people of color toward the United States depended on the policy of the government toward them: "They may be made good citizens or formidable abettors of the black people."[131]

Louisiana's free colored population in the early nineteenth century was large, diverse, and increasing. A census in 1806 counted 3,350 free people of color in the Orleans Territory, or about 6.5 percent of the total population. More than two-thirds lived in or near New Orleans, where they made up about 13.5 percent of the city's population.[132] Most had gained their freedom under Spanish rule, either through manumission or self-purchase, a right guaranteed to slaves under Spanish law. Almost two-thirds of all slaves emancipated in New Orleans during the Spanish era were women, reflecting the disproportionate number of women in the slave population of New Orleans, where opportunities to earn money were greater than in the countryside.[133] The influx of refugees from Cuba in 1809 brought another 3,000 free people of color to Louisiana (including more than 2,600 women and children), with most of these ending up in New Orleans.[134] By 1810 the number of free people of color in the Orleans Territory had more than doubled to over 7,500, of whom almost 6,000 lived in or near New Orleans. Free people of color made up 10 percent of the total population in the Orleans Territory and more than 18 percent of all free people. They made up 20 percent of the total population in or near New Orleans and almost 40 percent of the free population there, which made New Orleans home to the largest proportion of free people of color in any city in the United States.[135]

Meaningful entitlements distinguished free people of color from slaves. The law allowed free people to enter into civil contracts, marry, accumulate property, and pass it to their heirs.[136] Some even owned slaves. An 1805 census of New Orleans revealed 278 households headed by free people of color, of which 112 (40.3 percent) included slaves.[137] One property-owning man of color in New Orleans was James Johnson, who had once been the slave of Henry Clay's parents. Writing to the senator in 1807, Johnson reported that he owned a small grocery and livery stable and was "doing something for myself." He had earned enough money to purchase the freedom of his brother Daniel, then in the possession of Henry Clay's brother John, a merchant in New Orleans. Later that year, John Clay sold Daniel to James Bristow, who then sold him to Henry Clay, who emancipated him at Johnson's behest.[138] A small number of free men of color became substantial planters. When Louis Dusuau of Conti Street died in 1814, for instance, he owned a sugar plantation at Bonnet Carré with thirty-seven slaves, a farm in Metairie with three slaves, a city lot, and a tract of land in Attakapas.[139] Free men and women of color were a vital part of the urban economy.

The law enlisted free people of color to help manage and control the slave population. The 1806 Black Code required every plantation to have "a white or free colored man as manager or overseer."[140] One such overseer was Jacob, a free black man, who managed a plantation owned by an order of Ursuline nuns. From 1796 until his death in 1811, he supervised "a very fine gang of negroes" who produced milk, vegetables, rice, corn, and fuel for the Ursulines.[141] In 1805 the New Orleans City Council decreed that night patrols should be composed of a captain, eight subaltern officers, and twenty-four men, including six free men of color. Five years later, a new regulation authorized "colored men" to serve on night patrols, "provided that the said colored men are free landowners and well known" in their communities.[142] Similarly, in 1812 the council decided to form two companies of firemen from "free colored men, well known and property owners."[143] In all these instances, the council limited the enlistment of free men of color to the wealthiest and most respectable elements of the population—men who were presumed to have a stake in the social order and could be trusted in its defense.

At the same time, free people of color suffered under legal and social disabilities that subordinated them as a group to white people. Spanish authorities adopted sumptuary clothing laws for free women of color, restricted the ability of free people of color to carry guns and ride horses, and required them to show deference to white men and women. They also prohibited free people of color from marrying white people.[144] (This last restriction did not prevent sexual relations between free people of color and whites, which were frequently acknowledged in legal documents.)[145] The 1806 Black Code retained most of the Spanish discriminations and eliminated the right of self-purchase that had been so important in the growth of the free population of color.[146] The exclusion of free people of color from the political "people" became complete in 1811, when the U.S. Congress excluded them from participating in the creation of the new state government for Louisiana.[147] Neither slaves nor citizens, free people of color lived in a legal limbo.

They had expected better. Early in 1804, free men of color "universally mounted the Eagle in their Hats" and declared their loyalty to the United States.[148] Fifty-four men of color calling themselves "free Citizens" avowed "a lively Joy" that Louisiana had joined the United

States, and in a petition to Governor Claiborne, they expressed confidence in the justice of their new government. Having fought in the colonial militia under Spanish rule, the petitioners reminded Claiborne of their record and offered to serve the United States "with fidelity and zeal" as a volunteer corps.[149] The petition inaugurated a decade-long contest between friends and foes of the free colored militia over whether they would be commissioned, or, in other words, whether the government and white Louisianians would formally enlist free people of color in the defense of plantation society and treat them as citizens. To do so would violate slavery's racist justifications; to fail to do so would alienate a large class of people and possibly throw them into an alliance with the slaves.[150]

The militia issue was complicated by international tension, local conflict between free people of color and whites, and the influx of St. Domingue refugees. In the spring of 1806, as tensions between Spain and the United States escalated on the Louisiana-Texas border, some officials in New Orleans suspected that disaffected free men of color might form a fifth column.[151] Reports of a conspiracy among the free men of color led Claiborne to conclude that they had been "tamper'd with" by Spanish agents, but he did not take any direct action other than ordering nightly patrols in New Orleans.[152] In 1808 city councilors in New Orleans discovered that a free man of color had been offering fencing lessons to other men of color and urged the mayor to stop him. One official complained that "mulattoes have the insolence to challenge whites to a duel" and warned that the fencing lessons might have "very disastrous consequences." White Louisianians must have been relieved when the mayor banned free men of color from teaching the martial arts to their brethren. In New Orleans, it seems, good fencers did not make good neighbors—especially when they were colored.[153]

The free colored population of Louisiana included men who had fought in St. Domingue. In 1804 a slave named Marseille was arrested on suspicion of having served with the "insurgent armies" in St. Domingue. The City Council ordered him deported, but allowed him to remain when his owner posted a $500 bond for his good behavior.[154] A few months later, "a colored man named Dutaque, accused of having taken a very active part in the revolt of St. Domingo," was discovered on board a vessel in the river. The City Council demanded that the governor apprehend the man "so that the city may be protected from such a dangerous character."[155] In 1811 authorities in New Orleans arrested a Congolese man who had been emancipated by the French government in St. Domingue in return for his military service, before coming to New Orleans.[156] More notable was Charles Savary, who had been the mayor of Saint-Marc in St. Domingue. He was alleged to have been the brother of Vincent Ogé, the pioneering spokesmen for the rights of free people of color in St. Domingue. When Saint-Marc was under British occupation, Savary had commanded a colonial infantry corps known as the Prince de Galles. He eventually abandoned St. Domingue and ended up in Louisiana.[157]

The presence of such men troubled local officials. Governor Claiborne estimated that there were at least eight hundred free men of color capable of bearing arms in New Orleans in 1810. "Their conduct hitherto has been correct," Claiborne warned, but "in a country like this, where the negro population is so considerable, they should be carefully watched."[158] The Louisiana state legislature finally organized a free colored militia in 1812, but it restricted enrollment to a small number of propertied, native-born men and required them to serve under white officers. The poor and alien were excluded. The act was a grudging acknowledgment of the colored Creoles' place above slaves—but below whites. It was adopted with war looming and Louisiana widely believed to be a prime British target, which suggests that the legislators might have seen it as a merely temporary measure.[159]

The commercial dynamism and political turbulence in lower Louisiana brought new prospects for social disorder. Public officials believed that there were too many "unfortunate strangers" arriving in the region, too many slaves toiling in the plantation districts, too many fugitives absconding from their owners, too many armed free men of color, and that there was too much communication among all these groups.[160] In response to the nettlesome realities of an expanding slave country, the authorities tried to curb foreign slave importation to keep out dangerous elements. They tried to regulate the movement of slaves along the river and between town and country. They tried to enlist the most reputable free people of color in defense of slavery. These policies were plainly motivated by the fear of slave insurrection, which, as it turns out, was well grounded.

"colours displayed and full of arrogance"

Few people today have ever heard of it, but the largest slave rebellion in the history of the United States took place in the sugar parishes above New Orleans early in 1811. The rebellion was an important event because it dramatically expressed the deep discontent among enslaved people who endured the first phase of the sugar boom in lower Louisiana, and also because it starkly exposed the overwhelming military force that always buttressed slavery but was rarely apparent. As with so many other instances of slave conspiracy and rebellion, evidence concerning the rebellion is fragmentary, and most of it was produced by people directly involved in the suppression of the rebellion. Inevitably the sources (which include correspondence among government officials, court records and trial transcripts, and newspaper articles) reveal more about how the rebellion ended than why it began. These gaps and biases should be regarded not merely as a problem but as a symptom of the imbalance of power that sustained slavery and allowed it to spread.[161]

The rebellion took place on the Mississippi River's "German Coast," St. John the Baptist and St. Charles Parishes, a district that was making the bittersweet transition to sugar. In the 1780s and 1790s, the German Coast had been a district of midsize plantations and farms. Its principal crops were indigo and rice, and a majority of its population was enslaved.[162] Then came the sugar boom. From 1785 to 1810, the population of the German Coast almost doubled, from 3,203 to 6,281, while the proportion of slaves in the district increased slightly from about 58 percent to 61 percent of the population. The year of the Louisiana Purchase, planters in St. Charles produced more than 1.3 million pounds of sugar, with a handful of big planters leading the way. The Meullion, Destréhan, and Labranche plantations together accounted for more than half of the sugar produced in the parish.[163] Francophone planters dominated the early sugar economy on the German Coast, but a few Anglo-American capitalists had joined them by 1810. Among them were William Kenner, James Brown, and Richard Butler. Kenner had migrated to the Natchez district of Mississippi in the 1790s and had married the daughter of one of the region's biggest planters. He moved to New Orleans and established a mercantile business in partnership with Stephen Henderson. The partners' varied economic pursuits included sugar planting and the importation of African slaves via Charleston.[164] James Brown, another Virginian, had especially close ties to political leadership in Kentucky, where his brother served as a U.S. senator. Brown himself served as the U.S. attorney general in the Orleans Territory and was elected to represent the German Coast in the convention that drafted Louisiana's first state constitution. In 1812 he became one of the state's first two senators.[165] Richard Butler was one of many former U.S. military officers who established themselves in the lower Mississippi Valley. Like Kenner, Butler married the daughter of a wealthy Natchez-district planter, whose local ties brought him into good standing with the established planter elite of lower Louisiana.[166] The appearance of such men among the planters of the German Coast helped to integrate lower Louisiana's sugar districts into the United States.

The slave rebellion ran its course along the eastern bank of the Mississippi River, where a ribbon of particularly large plantations ornamented the landscape. Here lived one of the densest concentrations of slaves in North America, comparable to that in the rice districts of the Carolina lowcountry. According to the 1810 census, 274 whites, 89 free persons of color, and 1,480 slaves inhabited the households from Manuel Andry's plantation, where the rebellion began, to Zenon Trudeau's plantation, the southernmost plantation in St. Charles Parish. Eighty-six percent of households included slaves, and the average number of slaves in those households was 43. As the rebels marched down the river toward New Orleans, the plantations they challenged—Picou, Brown, Trépagnier, Bernoudy, Destréhan, Fortier, Labranche, Piseros, Meuillon, Trudeau—were larger and were home to more slaves.[167]

The German Coast slave population was diverse, not monolithic. An analysis of estate inventories from the first decade of the nineteenth century suggests that more than half of the enslaved people in the region had been born outside of Louisiana. These foreigners included substantial proportions of people from Central Africa, Sierra Leone, the Bight of Benin, and Senegambia. Roughly one in every twenty slaves had been in the Caribbean or the eastern United States, and some of the Africans had probably lived in the Caribbean before arriving in Louisiana. The diversity of the slave population was an obstacle to collective resistance, though obviously not an insurmountable one.[168]

Enslaved people had not been dormant before the rebellion. In 1796 local authorities foiled what they believed to be a large-scale plot by slaves to revolt during the Easter mass, but as the details of the plot were extracted by the lash, the extent and even existence of an actual conspiracy cannot be presumed. Slaveowners sometimes concocted rebellions out of rumors.[169] It is more certain that fugitive bands lurked in the swamps. In 1805 a patrol headed by Louis Planchard arrested four runaway slaves, three men and one woman, and recovered some stolen property in their possession. The woman, Celeste, disclosed that she had run away from her owner about two months earlier and joined a group of thirteen runaways, many of whom were women.[170] In 1808 Charles Paquet, a free Negro, was found guilty of harboring runaway slaves and was forced to pay a considerable fine. The slaves—Honoré, Lindor, and Gabriel, who belonged to prominent planters in St. Charles Parish—had maintained clandestine ties to their neighborhood even as they hid out in the cypress swamp. Armed and dangerous, they procured food from a slave woman named Rosette on Delhomme's plantation, killed livestock on Piseros's and Reine's plantations, joined and left other bands of fugitives, and roamed the countryside. Honoré was discovered in Adélard Fortier's slave quarters, and Lindor, hiding in Paquet's chimney. Gabriel remained abroad.[171] Slaves known to have been runaways participated in the 1811 rebellion. Early in 1810, for instance, two slaves, Mandingo Charles and an Ibo man named Cracker, ran away. A year later, Cracker (or Croaker) was killed in the combat between the rebels and the authorities, and Charles was executed in the sanguinary judicial proceedings that followed.[172] These patterns of *marronage* were not unusual in slave societies, nor did they usually lead to rebellion. Something more must explain the outbreak of a full-blown slave revolt early in 1811.

Political turmoil may well have influenced the timing of the slaves' revolt. A popular insurgency led by the priest Miguel Hidalgo y Costilla had broken out in Dolores, New Spain, in September 1810. Carrying the banner of the Virgin of Guadaloupe, Ferdinand VII, and independence, the Hidalgo revolt swept through the Mexican Bajío. Within weeks an enormous rebel army had sacked Guanajuato, a city twice as large as New Orleans. Hidalgo advanced a radical social agenda, calling for an end to the tribute system and a reduction in taxes. He also proclaimed the abolition of slavery, and death to slaveowners who refused to free their chattel. The rebellion was not thwarted until mid-January, when royalist forces won a decisive victory outside of Mexico City. Hidalgo and the other rebel leaders were eventually captured and executed, their heads sent to Guanajuato for a grisly display.[173] News of the Hidalgo revolt quickly reached Texas and crossed into Louisiana, carried by rebel agents and frightened refugees. It is possible that slaves on the German Coast learned of the revolt, and even of Hidalgo's call for the abolition of slavery, through the clandestine channels of communication available to them.[174]

Simultaneous turbulence in West Florida might also have inspired the rebellion. In September, a group of Anglo-Americans seized Baton Rouge, declared independence from Spain, and requested admission into the United States, to which President James Madison promptly acceded. In December, Governor Claiborne traveled to West Florida to organize the territory. He returned to New Orleans just after Christmas, having asserted American sovereignty from Baton Rouge to the Pearl River.[175] News of the West Florida takeover—and the rhetoric of liberty that accompanied it—may well have been communicated to the slaves in Louisiana by the *caboteurs* and slave rivermen who navigated the Mississippi and Lake Pontchartrain, or even unwittingly by the slaves' owners themselves. It was a risk considered by David Holmes, the governor of the Mississippi Territory, who wrote in late September, "At present I do not apprehend danger from any possible occurrence, except that of an insurrection of the Slaves."[176] Enslaved people on the German Coast might have seen the coup in West Florida as marking a propitious moment for their own uprising.

The historical record does not reveal exactly when or where or how the slaves formed their plot to rebel—perhaps at a New Year's revel or back in the swamp, sealed in oaths of blood and magic. Or it may have begun at the house of Charles Paquet, the free man of color convicted of harboring runaway slaves some years earlier. A suspected rebel, interrogated by the authorities on 14 January accused one Joseph the Spaniard of "having called the brigands to the levee before the habitation of Charles Paquet, free man of color, saying to them—Comrades come drink from the tap."[177] If true (and here it should be recalled that everything the slaves said under interrogation was probably extracted from them by torture), it is still not clear what this gesture meant, or when it was made, or who Joseph the Spaniard was. Perhaps this is the evidence that convinced General Wade Hampton that the rebellion was "of Spanish origin."[178] What is known is that sometime in the first week of January 1811 it dawned on local authorities that something was amiss, for on 7 January Governor

Claiborne warned Hampton to provide an escort for the post rider "who carries the Mail thro' such part of the Territory, as you suppose may be infested by the Brigands."[179]

The following evening in St. John the Baptist Parish, rebellious slaves attacked the plantation of Colonel Manuel Andry, one of the leading men on the German Coast. The rebels wounded Andry, killed his son Gilbert ("Gone to a better and a happier world!" mourned the Governor), and seized a cache of public arms stored on the plantation. Ironically, the weapons had been distributed as a caution against unrest among the slaves.[180] Fortified by liquor and well armed, the slaves proceeded downriver—some on horses—toward New Orleans. After marching five leagues, the rebel band reached Fortier's sugar plantation in Orleans Parish around four o'clock on Wednesday afternoon, where they paused to eat, drink, revel, and rest. The most precise estimates placed the rebels' numbers between 200 and 300 people. Never in the history of North America had as many slaves taken up arms against their masters. One slave allegedly confessed that their goal was to "go to the city to kill whites."[181] In fact, they burned down three plantations and killed one other planter, Jean-Francois Trépagnier, whom local folklore holds was hacked to death by a trusted slave.[182]

Trial records and declarations for compensation submitted by the planters after the rebellion make it possible to identify some of the slaves who participated. Most of the leaders appear to have been Creoles and mulattoes. One leader was Charles, a mulatto slave owned by the widow of Jean-Baptiste Deslondes. He had been working on Andry's plantation when the rebellion broke out. Other "chiefs" included Amar, owned by Widow Charbonnet; Cupidon, a Creole owned by the Labranche brothers; Gilbert, a mulatto slave owned by Andry; Dagobert, a Creole slave driver owned by Delhomme; Guamana, owned by James Brown; and Harry, a mulatto slave owned by Kenner and Henderson.[183] The rebellion drew foot soldiers, like its leadership, from the several plantations spread along the river. Of the 115 slaves killed, jailed, or missing as of 18 January, 15 were

from Andry's plantation, 13 from the Meuillon estate, 11 from
Kenner and Henderson's plantation, 8 from Daniel Clark's, 7 from
Achille Trouard's, 7 from George Wenprender's, 6 from Widow
Trépagnier's, and 6 from the widow of George Deslondes, in addition
to others from more than twenty plantations.[184] They comprised a diverse lot of Creoles and Africans, domestic servants and field hands.
Two of the slaves from the Meuillon estate, Apollon and Henri, were
Congolese, as was Acara of Joseph Delhomme's plantation and Hip-
polite of Etienne Trépagnier's. Louis, also of Etienne Trépagnier's,
was from Guinea. Quamley and Cook of James Brown's plantation,
Joseph of Widow Trépagnier's, and Charlot of Etienne Trépagnier's
are all recorded to have been "African." Some of the rebels, like the
leaders Charles and Dagobert, held positions of authority on their
plantations. A few—like Butler and McCutcheon's cook Daniel—
served as domestics, but most worked around the sugar plantations as
field laborers or artisans. There may have been women involved in the
rebellion, but only one appears in the official record, Marie Rose,
owned by Lewis de Feriet. Sentenced to perpetual imprisonment in
the parish of Orleans, she might have been seen in the years to come
shoveling muck from the city's fetid streets.[185] The German Coast
slave rebellion fits into a general pattern of growing Creole leadership
in American slave revolts (at least outside of Brazil) but it also demonstrates that a diverse group of enslaved people could join together
in an effort to liberate themselves by force of arms.

As the revolt began, terrified white inhabitants spread the alarm
from the German Coast to New Orleans, and local authorities scrambled into action. Several groups of armed men converged on the rebels. The first was an assemblage of roughly eighty volunteers from
the German Coast's west bank, organized by Charles Perret and the
wounded, bereaved Manuel Andry, who had escaped from his assailants and crossed the river. Perret's band included several free men of
color, whom he would later praise for their "tireless zeal, & a daunt-
less courage."[186] The second, dispatched from New Orleans by Governor Claiborne on the morning of the ninth, comprised a detach-

ment of army regulars and two companies of city volunteers serving under General Wade Hampton. John Shaw, the naval commander in New Orleans, dispatched a group of several naval officers and forty sailors who joined Hampton's band as they marched up the river "through roads half leg deep in Mud." A third force of light artillery and dragoons under Major Homer Milton had been ascending the river on their way to Baton Rouge; they turned around when they caught wind of the rebellion and headed for the German Coast. Another ragtag group of about a hundred volunteers congregated near Fortier's plantation on the evening of the ninth. As they prepared to attack, Hampton arrived ahead of his troops and cautioned the volunteers to wait for reinforcements. Later that evening a band of hotheads rashly advanced on the plantation, inadvertently alerting the rebels to the encircling danger. The rest of Hampton's force arrived around four o'clock in the morning and they immediately prepared to attack, but in the crepuscular predawn light the rebels spotted them, rang an alarm, "and with a degree of extraordinary silence for such a rabble" retreated up the coast. The next morning the rebels reached Bernard Bernoudy's plantation and made their stand (as Manuel Andry observed) with "colours displayed and full of arrogance."[187]

The rebellion ended at Bernoudy's plantation, where Andry's volunteers routed the slaves. Dozens were killed, many others wounded and captured, and the rest chased into the woods. "We made considerable slaughter," boasted Andry.[188] Patrols scoured the countryside for another week.[189] Hampton ordered a company of light artillery and one of dragoons to descend from Baton Rouge and "touch at Every Settlement of Consequence," crushing any remaining pockets of rebellion.[190] Special mounted and foot patrols policed New Orleans, where taverns had been closed and weapons dealers had been prohibited from selling to Negroes. Claiborne even called out a company of free men of color to help patrol the city.[191] When news of the rebellion reached the Mississippi Territory on 17 January, public officials and private citizens there also took precautionary measures. Governor David Holmes immediately called out the militia and ordered a distribution of arms.[192] The inveterate scribbler Winthrop Sargent noted in his journal, "Intelligence this day of an Insurrection of the negroes near Orleans but not the particulars—have directed Vigilance upon my own Plantations."[193] These deployments kept the rebellion from reigniting or spreading elsewhere in the Deep South.

As the jails in and around New Orleans filled with suspected rebels, local authorities began to decide who should live and who should die. Judge Pierre Bauchet St. Martin and a tribunal of five prominent planters constituted a court on Jean Noel Destrehan's plantation in St. Charles Parish, which, after three days of interrogations and trials, sentenced twenty-one slaves to death.[194] One week after the battle at Bernoudy's, St. Martin reported that sixty-six slaves had been killed or executed, with another twenty-two in jail and twenty-seven still missing and "supposed generally to be dead in the woods."[195] Local authorities orchestrated the rebels' executions to magnify the degrading and terrorizing effects of their punishments. St. Martin's court directed that the condemned slaves be taken to the plantations of their owners, shot to death without torture, and their heads placed on stakes "as a terrible example to all who would disturb the public tranquility in the future."[196]

Other slaves were tried in New Orleans before a jury composed of leading planters: Etienne de Bore, Daniel Clark, Charles Jumonville, Denis de la Ronde, and Jacques Villeré. They sentenced John Janvier to hang on the plantation of his owner, Israel Trask, "in the presence of the whole gang where his body shall remain exposed." Hector was sentenced to hang "between the plantations of Mr. Villerai and Norbert Boudusquie, where his body shall remain exposed." Louis was sentenced to hang "on the levee in front of the Powder magazine on the left bank of the River Mississippi . . . where his body shall remain exposed."[197] The proceedings made an impression on white people in New Orleans. John Shaw reported that "executions by hanging and beheading, are going on daily."[198] Another witness, young Edward Palfrey, described the grisly proceedings to his brother in Massachusetts: "Poor wretches! They are now suffering the punishment of their foolish wickedness. Government has hung one everyday since their trial commenced. They hung one yesterday and one today. After they have hung the negroes, they cut off their heads and stick it on a pole, and set it up in the street."[199] Some three months after the rebellion, a journal-keeping traveler descending the Mississippi to sell flour in New Orleans observed "a number of Negro heads sticking in poles on the levee."[200]

A few slaves received less severe punishments or clemency on account of special circumstances. Gilbert, one of Manuel Andry's slaves and alleged to have been one of the leaders, was found guilty of insurrection and sentenced to death, but "on account of the good and exemplary conduct of Louis Meilleur the uncle of the prisoner who delivered him to justice," he was merely ordered to be shot in Fort St. Ferdinand and his body delivered to the family for a decent burial. Jean, a teenager, was convicted of insurrection but the court spared his life on account of his youth; he was sentenced to thirty lashes and compelled to witness the execution of his comrade Jerry. Theodore, also convicted of insurrection, was eventually pardoned by the governor for having fully confessed his crimes and being "of fair character, and a most faithful Domestic."[201] Still other slaves were commended for their loyalty. Dominique, a slave owned by Bernard Bernoudy, had warned Etienne Trépagnier and several other planters of the approaching rebels on the morning of 9 January. Hermogene Labranche praised his slave driver Pierre, who after learning of the rebellion from slaves fleeing the Delhomme plantation, rushed to his master's room to warn him. Labranche also praised his slave François, whom he sent to spy on the rebels.[202] And the heirs of Meuillon petitioned the legislature to allow them to emancipate the mulatto slave Bazile "in consideration of his good conduct and zeal with which he has extinguished the fire which the brigands had set to the principal house of the plantation . . . and of the courageous resistance which he has solely opposed to many of those brigands, who endeavoured to hinder his good action."[203] Evidently the rebellion had not won universal support among the enslaved; some actively helped to defeat it.

Public officials in the Orleans Territory grappled with thorny issues in the wake of the rebellion. Several planters had lost property,
including slaves killed during the rebellion or executed afterward.
Whether those planters should be compensated was "a delicate, interesting and novel question," admitted the members of the territorial
House of Representatives.[204] In an act that revealed the planters' influence on public policy, the Orleans Territory ultimately awarded
$300 for each slave killed or executed, as well as one-third of the ap-
praised value of dwelling houses burned by the rebels, at a cost of
$29,000 to the government.[205] Governor Claiborne also urged the
legislature to strengthen the militia laws and to prohibit the "indiscriminate importation of slaves," which endangered the territory in
ways that no longer needed to be spelled out.[206] The legislature did
revise and reform the territorial militia, but it did not act on the matter of slave importation. The sugar planters' need for slave labor continued to trump other considerations, especially because they now
knew that the United States military would protect them in the event
of an insurrection.[207]

The slaves' rebellion failed because the rebels were outmanned and
outgunned. It would have been difficult enough for them to overcome
the local patrols and militias, but they also had to face the U.S. Army
and Navy. About 1,500 soldiers and sailors, or 30 percent of the regular peacetime military establishment, were stationed in lower Louisiana when the rebellion broke out. This military presence reflected
the national government's concern over the vulnerability of the country's southwestern frontier and its strategic prize, New Orleans.[208]
Whatever doubt the sugar planters may have harbored about the commitment of the U.S. government to the protection of slavery was alle-
viated by what Wade Hampton called the "prompt display & exhibition" of national military power along the bloodied banks of the
Mississippi River in January 1811.[209] Indeed, the very next month
the legislature of the Orleans Territory invited President James Monroe to increase the number of regular troops permanently stationed
around New Orleans.[210] For slaveowners in lower Louisiana, the

United States offered security, an essential precondition for the expansion of slavery.

In the end the rebellion exposed the lurking tension between commercial development and social order in lower Louisiana, but it did not swamp the slave country. "All the negro difficulties have subsided and gentle peace once more prevails," wrote one observer less than a month after the rebellion ended.[211] Planters carried on the business of making sugar. Flatboats and barges floated downriver in record numbers. New Orleans thrived. General Hampton signaled his confidence by purchasing several large plantations along the Mississippi and transferring gangs of slaves from South Carolina to his new holdings. A soldier wrote that Hampton regarded Louisiana as "the paradise of the new world."[212] But the memory of slave rebellion lingered. When the journalist Henry Marie Brackenridge descended the Mississippi River on a tour of the western United States late in 1811, he delighted in the sugar planters' elegant houses, tasteful gardens, and beautiful orange groves, until he remembered that these coexisted with the evils of slavery, including the threat of rebellion. Sadly he mused, "It is not in this world we are to expect a paradise."[213]

Political turmoil and economic growth beginning in the 1790s fundamentally transformed the region that became the Deep South. Jeffersonian efforts to civilize the southern wilderness and its peoples led to the expansion of slavery on the southwestern cotton frontier, while the rise of a sugar plantation complex in lower Louisiana forced the United States to confront the contradictory legacies emanating from St. Domingue. The slave country survived its own slave rebellion in January 1811, but more serious dangers loomed ahead.

Benjamin Latrobe, View of the New Orleans Battleground, *1819. Latrobe was one of America's most influential architects and civil engineers. He worked on several projects in New Orleans, including the city's waterworks and the Louisiana State Bank. Latrobe died of yellow fever in New Orleans in 1820. Compare the desolation in Latrobe's watercolor with the vitality in Colomb's painting of White Hall Plantation (see Chapter 3).* COURTESY OF THE MARYLAND HISTORICAL SOCIETY, BALTIMORE.

CHAPTER 4

The Wartime Challenge

THE WAR OF 1812 represented an opportunity and a crisis for the budding slave country of the Deep South. Many white inhabitants embraced war against Great Britain because it gave them a chance to realize long-standing nationalist goals of loosening foreign restrictions on American commerce, shattering indigenous power, and eradicating foreign influence in their region. William C. C. Claiborne, now governor of the state of Louisiana, called the war "the only measure that could preserve the Independence of the Nation."[1] But the war also threatened the new society that had been established in the Deep South in the previous two decades. It stopped the influx of migrants, depressed the plantation economy, and shrouded the region in violence. Many white people feared that slaves, free people of color, and Indians would join with foreign powers to strike a blow against the United States' remote southwestern frontier. Whether they could protect themselves and their way of life against such a formidable coalition was an open question at the beginning of the war. Galvanized by the Tennessee planter Andrew Jackson, the citizens of the slave country confronted a fundamental challenge to U.S. sovereignty in the Deep South between 1812 and 1815.[2]

The United States declared war against Great Britain to vindicate the Jeffersonian republican vision of a virtuous agrarian-commercial republic, which could prosper only if the country's agriculturalists were freely able to sell their produce in foreign markets. The Napoleonic Wars had jeopardized that vision. French and especially British efforts to control the flow of Atlantic trade were hurting the United States. American vessels were intercepted, cargoes seized, and sailors impressed into foreign service. In response, the United States implemented a series of retaliatory commercial policies—the embargo and nonintercourse acts—intended to force the warring European powers to stop interfering with American shipping. The republican strategy, however, overestimated British and French reliance on American goods while further crippling American export-oriented interests. The failure of the republicans' strategy for peaceful economic coercion drove the United States to war in 1812.[3]

Most of the citizens of the Deep South, and certainly their political leaders, supported the war. The region's export-oriented farmers and planters had basic economic interests at stake. Cotton planters blamed the British for the declining price of their staple, which had fallen from twenty-three cents per pound in 1805 to less than nine cents per pound in 1811. They viewed war as a last resort to open restricted European markets and increase the price of cotton.[4] A more transcendent principle—the defense of American honor—also animated the citizenry's enthusiasm for war. The country had to choose between "base submission & manly resistance," wrote a resident of the Orleans Territory.[5] Five hundred citizens turned out for a public meeting in Woodville in the Mississippi Territory to support the Madison administration's war measures in July of 1812. The crisis with Great Britain "calls on our free and Independent Government either to proudly assert its inalienable rights, or dastardly submit to the humiliating impositions of our overbearing foe," they declared. In the town of Washington, another meeting of citizens resolved that the United States "has been ultimately compelled to vindicate the rights essential to the sovereignty and Independence of our Country against the unjust pretensions and aggressions of the British Government."⁶ These declarations announced the patriotism of the territories' republican citizenry, and asserted a national unity that stretched even to the remote and vulnerable southwestern frontier.

Some ardent nationalists seized on war as an opportunity to strengthen and extend U.S. sovereignty on the southwestern frontier. Their champion was Andrew Jackson, a Tennessee cotton planter and politician. Jackson was born in the Carolina backcountry in 1767 and orphaned during the Revolution, when he developed a bitter hatred for the British. After studying law in Charleston, Jackson migrated to Tennessee, where he became a lawyer, land speculator, slaveowner, planter, and politician. Strong willed and possessed of a keen sense of personal honor, Jackson fought several duels in his lifetime, including one in 1806 in which he killed a rival. Like other Tennessee planters, Jackson had many connections to the Deep South. He often visited Natchez, a popular destination for horseracing and gambling. It was there that he married Rachel Robards in 1791. He sent cotton, staves, and other goods down the Mississippi and sold goods sent up in exchange. His business dealings entangled him in the slave trade.⁷ When the war broke out, Jackson laid out an expansionist vision in an address to Tennessee volunteers. He wanted to seize West Florida for the United States. Its conquest would improve southwesterners' commercial access to the Gulf of Mexico and deprive the Spanish and British of an "asylum" from which to incite the southern Indians to "rapine and bloodshed."⁸

Preoccupied with the war on the country's Canadian border, the Madison administration kept Jackson and the southwestern expansionists at bay until the fall of 1812, when it authorized Tennessee's governor to send 1,500 Tennessee volunteers to New Orleans to help defend the city against a rumored British invasion. Placed in command of the volunteers, Jackson believed that he would finally secure U.S. sovereignty in Florida and have his revenge against the hated British. "I hope the government will permit us to traverse the Southern coast and aid in planting the American eagles on the ramparts of

Mobile, Pensacola and Fort St. Augustine," he admitted to Louisiana's governor, William Claiborne. "British influence must be destroyed, or we will have the whole Southern tribe of Indians to fight and insurrections to quell in all the Southern states."[9] Here Jackson revealed the southern citizenry's ultimate nightmare: a triple alliance of British soldiers, Indian warriors, and slave rebels. But the rumored invasion did not materialize, and the administration called off Jackson's expedition. He halted his army in Natchez and returned to Tennessee in mid-March. During the spring and summer of 1813, Jackson chafed at the Madison administration's apparent indifference to the southwestern frontier.[10]

Economic depression intensified the wartime sense of crisis. The number of vessels arriving in New Orleans from upriver declined from 1,680 in 1811 to 513 in 1814.[11] The value of exports from New Orleans and Mobile dropped from more than $2.5 million in 1811 to less than $500,000 in 1814.[12] Distress was widespread. John Palfrey found himself mired in debt with no hope of escape. "Altho' my crops have been good & even great they procure me nothing," he complained.[13] George Foote found the wartime conditions difficult to endure. "Indeed it is a hard struggle with me, to pay my rent and keep clear of debt," he groused in 1812.[14] A year later, Foote's health and cotton were ruined, and he ached to return to Virginia. "I find it impossible for me to remain in this climate much longer, if I do it will be under ground."[15] The pressure of the times caused many purchasers of public lands to fear that they would have to default on their payments to the government. In January of 1814, Mississippi's territorial legislature implored Congress to protect purchasers of public lands from "the rude grasp of the Merciless Speculator." Many citizens worried that they would be pauperized as the region fell back into mere subsistence production and a war for national independence drove them deeper into debt.[16]

The territorial legislature's petition hinted that as moneyed men bought up land from distressed farmers, slaves would replace free men and the territory would become less secure. The legislature thus raised the unsettling question of whether a slave society could defend itself in a crisis. Others on the national stage asked the same question. John Randolph of Virginia, a fierce opponent of the war, cautioned the House of Representatives in 1 8 1 1 that twenty years of French radicalism had left their mark on the country's slave population. "God forbid, sir, that the Southern States should ever see an enemy on their shores, with these infernal principles of French fraternity in the van!" he stormed.[17] Even so staunch a supporter of the war as Thomas Jefferson allowed himself to imagine its revolutionary potential on the slave population. Emancipation "will come," he wrote in a famous letter to Edward Coles in the summer of 1 8 1 4, "and whether brought on by the generous energy of our own minds; or by the bloody process of St Domingo, excited and conducted by the power of our present enemy, if once stationed permanently within our Country, and offering asylum & arms to the oppressed, is a leaf of our history not yet turned over."[18] In other words, a British invasion might have an electric effect on American slaves.

Following soon after the German Coast rebellion of 1 8 1 1, war rekindled the white citizenry's deep anxieties about the loyalty of enslaved people.[19] Days after news of the declaration of war reached the Deep South, local authorities discovered a conspiracy among the slaves of Mississippi's Second Creek. "The Negroes were making Every preparation a few Days ago to Rise and Destroy the white inhabitants of this Territory, Women & Children Excepted," reported the overseer James Moore.[20] David Holmes, the governor of the territory, used the occasion to petition General James Wilkinson for guns, powder, and shot. "I am impressed with the belief that real danger exists, and that it is my duty to loose [*sic*] no time in procuring arms for the defence of the Country," he insisted.[21] When Wilkinson ordered Holmes to send territorial militia to Baton Rouge in October, the governor protested that the move would leave the inhabitants defenseless against their domestic enemies. "Nearly one half of the entire population are Slaves and the frontier Counties are thinly inhabited," he reminded Wilkinson. "In Slave Countries the Danger of insurrection always exists, and the Inhabitants should be prepared to meet the event."[22] Real and alleged slave conspiracies plagued lower Louisiana after the declaration of war against Great Britain. Several slaves in New Orleans were hanged or shot for plotting an insurrection in the fall of 1812, and the City Council took the opportunity to prohibit slaves from gaming and dancing.[23] In the spring of 1813, the city's mayor reported that "the negroes intend to hatch a new plot against the safety of the public."[24] Later that year, the commander of the Louisiana militia, Jacques Villeré, was reminded to watch out for slave insurrection: "The rumors might be true or false, but in the present circumstance one must always be 'en garde.'"[25] War placed the civil and military officials in the Deep South on a heightened alert for signs of conspiracy and rebellion among the slaves.

Along with economic distress and fears of slave rebellion came a ripening conflict in the Indian backcountry, where the Jeffersonian program of civilization and the expansion of the cotton plantation system had polarized indigenous communities. The sharpest struggle took place among the Upper Creeks, who occupied what is today western Georgia and eastern Alabama. Essentially the Creek nation split between those who were willing to accommodate the increasing influence of the United States in their lives and those who were not.[26] The Shawnee leader Tecumseh, who was organizing a pan-Indian revolt against the United States in the northwest, visited the southern Indians in the fall of 1811 to bring them into an alliance with their northern brethren. Tecumseh failed in his mission, but he did inspire some of the southerners to take a more militant stance against the Anglo-American intruders and those who collaborated with them. At the same time, a spiritual revival infused the indigenous militants with a religious ardor. Several of the Creek shamans spent time in the Shawnee country, where they were exposed to the traditionalist teachings of Tenskwatawa, Tecumseh's mystic brother, whose lessons included the dangerous promise that Indians could not be harmed by bullets.[27]

The southwestern backcountry broke out in violence during the winter of 1812–13 when a delegation led by Little Warrior, a Creek Indian familiar with the Shawnees, returned to the land of his nativity after visiting Tecumseh. Sympathetic to Tecumseh's appeal for pan-Indian solidarity, Little Warrior fought in the Battle of River Raisin near Detroit before heading south in February of 1813. Tecumseh cautioned him to delay any military action south of the Ohio until the northern Indians and the British could come to his aid, but on their way home, Little Warrior's band killed seven white people near the mouth of the Ohio River. Benjamin Hawkins, the U.S. agent to the Creeks and the champion of Jefferson's civilizing program, urged the Upper Creek leadership to deliver Little Warrior and his followers to the United States; instead the Upper Creeks took matters into their own hands. Led by Big Warrior (Tustunnuggee Thlucco) and assisted by a party of Lower Creeks, they hunted down Little Warrior and his fellows in late April and killed them.[28] Outraged dissidents among the Creeks—called Red Sticks because of their vermilion-stained war clubs—began to retaliate against those responsible for the executions. They killed a pro-American Creek shaman along with his family. They wrecked looms, killed livestock, and assassinated Creek leaders hostile to their cause. They besieged Big Warrior at Tuckabatchie until he and his followers were rescued by William McIntosh and a party of warriors from the Lower Creek towns of Kasihta and Coweta.[29] What began as a cycle of killing and retribution quickly widened into a civil war within the Creek nation.

The Red Sticks targeted the new forms of property and commerce associated with the Jeffersonian program of civilization, including cotton production. The Scottish-born Robert Grierson, a cotton planter living among the Creeks and one of Benjamin Hawkins's allies, "had all his negroes (73) and every eatable living thing taken from him." Grierson's daughter-in-law, who had taught many Creek women in the town of Hillaubee to spin and weave, "had much of her stock, her loom and bolt of cloth destroyed." Adding insult to injury, the Red Sticks humiliated her by stripping her of her clothing "except the shift and petticoat on her back." Assaults such as these convinced Hawkins that his campaign to civilize the southern Indians stood in danger. "The declaration of their prophets is to destroy every thing received from the Americans, all Chiefs and their adherents who are friendly to the customs and ways of the white people, and to put to death every man who will not join them," he reported to the U.S. secretary of war. Hawkins concluded that the Red Sticks' campaign dovetailed with a larger plot "to unite the [Creek] nation in aid of the British and Indians of the Lakes, against their white neighbors as soon as their friends the British will be ready for them."[30] He believed that the outbreak of violence on the southwestern frontier was part of a larger, unscrupulous British strategy to win the war.

As the fighting intensified in the Mississippi Territory, white settlers and their slaves, along with their Indian allies, scrambled into makeshift palisades and prepared for battle. "The clouds thicken around us," wrote a concerned correspondent from Fort Stoddert. He observed that the inhabitants had abandoned their homesteads: "Some are in swamps, some are retired to places of more imagined security."[31] Margaret Austill's family took refuge in a stockade built by "all hands, negroes and whites." Austill described her first days there as "confusion and dismay, expecting at any moment to be scalped or tomahawked." Hannah, an enslaved woman owned by Margaret's father, tended to the Austill homestead while the family huddled inside the pickets. "She made the garden, milked the cows, churned the butter, raised chickens, and came every other day to the Fort with a large basket on her head," Austill recalled.[32] On 27 July at Burnt Corn Creek, a group of American settlers and Creek warriors under the command of James Caller skirmished with a party of Red Sticks led by Peter McQueen, who was returning to the Upper Creek country from Pensacola. Caller's company lost five men, the Red Sticks two.[33] A slave was shot while running from McQueen's party to Caller's.[34] After the battle, Caller's party retreated to a fortification on the site of Samuel Mims's plantation near the confluence of the Tombigbee and Alabama rivers. There, at Fort Mims, came the cloudburst.

As many as 500 men, women, and children of all complexions crowded into Fort Mims in the summer of 1813.[35] About 140 American and Creek volunteers under the command of Major Daniel Beasley and Dixon Bailey defended the post. On 29 August in the evening, two slaves who had been sent out to tend cattle came back to the fort and reported that they had seen hostile Indians in the vicinity. Beasley sent out an armed party to investigate, and when it returned at sundown having found no sign of danger, Beasley had the two slaves whipped for lying. The next morning, 700 Red Sticks attacked, led by the Creek planter William Weatherford (Red Eagle). They rushed through gates that Beasley had carelessly left opened, set fire to the wooden buildings with burning arrows, and slaughtered many of the people they found inside, including women and children. At least 250 of the inhabitants and 200 of the attackers were killed in the battle.[36] "Indians, negroes, white men, women and children, lay in one promiscuous ruin," observed Major Joseph Kennedy, who helped to bury the dead. "All were scalped, and the females, of every age, were butchered in a manner which neither decency nor language will permit me to describe." War came to the Deep South with a vengeance.[37]

Events at Fort Mims demonstrate how slavery shaped the social terrain on which the Creek War raged. Slaves helped to build the American stockades and feed the inhabitants. Captive slaves guided the Red Sticks to Fort Mims. Slaves owned by the Red Stick leaders William Weatherford and Alexander McGillivray helped to overrun the fort. The Creek chronicler George Stiggins claimed that when the attack faltered in the face of fierce resistance from Fort Mims's defenders, the black Red Sticks "would not cease" and urged their fellow warriors to destroy the fort. And although the Red Sticks killed most of the whites and mestizos in Fort Mims, they spared most of the black people, taking more than 200 of them as prizes of war—a customary practice among the southern Indians.[38] One anonymous slave reported that he had been hiding in Mims's house when an Indian told him to come out, saying, "The Master of Breath has ordered us not to kill any but white people and half breeds." He managed to escape to the Creek town of Coweta, whence his description of the fall of Fort Mims was forwarded to Benjamin Hawkins, who sent it to the secretary of war.[39] Hester, another slave who escaped from Fort

Mims, swam across the Alabama and Tombigbee rivers and made her way to Mount Vernon in the Mississippi Territory, where she reported the massacre to Ferdinand Claiborne, brigadier general of the territorial militia.[40] More than half a century later, there were still black people living in the Deep South who claimed to have experienced the events at Fort Mims.[41] Some black people joined the Red Sticks and others fought against them, and most tried as best they could to come out of the conflict alive if not unscathed.

As news of the fall of Fort Mims spread, American outrage at the massacre combined with anxiety over the possibility that the Red Sticks might find an ally in the territory's black population. One territorial official worried that "many of the Negroes will run off to the enemy."[42] Another reported that the slaves had "excited considerable uneasiness, many have gone off with arms, one or more have been tried for saying that the Indians were to pass through this and the Mississippi countries, when the blacks were to join them." He feared that the slaveowners were unwittingly endangering themselves with loose talk: "There are many unwary fools who are in the habit of speaking of these things before their own slaves, acknowledging an inferiority in the whites to withstand the blacks and the reds."[43] Writing shortly after the fall of Fort Mims, Washington County resident Edmund Andrews sensed a crisis. With the whole frontier "left to the ravages of the enemy," he explained to a correspondent in distant New Hampshire, "it is at present very doubtful weather the Chacktaws will remain friendly with us—this added to the danger amongst ourselves—namely the revolt of the negroes whenever opportunity offers, makes our situation rather critical. Property is now out of the question, those who have the least to lose are best off."[44] Once regarded as necessary for the civilization of the southern frontier, slavery now seemed to be a dangerous weakness in the social order.

"no frolic War"

The Fort Mims massacre brought the United States into the Creek civil war and opened one of the worst episodes of violence in the tragic history of antagonism between the people of the United States and the indigenous inhabitants of North America. The Americans intervened to avenge the massacre and crush the hostile Creeks, and to seize West Florida from Spain, but it would not be easy. The Red Stick revolt tested the military resources and organization of the citizenry in the Mississippi Territory, Georgia, and especially Tennessee. The Tennessee planter Andrew Jackson led the campaign against the Red Sticks and was principally responsible for its outcome. His most difficult challenge was not defeating the Red Sticks but keeping an army together to accomplish the task.[45]

Preparations for war were frenzied. The country was "again in arms & in motion," observed John Reid, one of Andrew Jackson's aides in Tennessee.[46] The United States intended to strike against the Creeks from several angles. One force, led by Ferdinand Claiborne, included regulars from the U.S. Army and militiamen from the western portions of the Mississippi Territory. Another, led by General John Floyd, was to enter the Creek nation from Georgia. The third army, from eastern Tennessee under General John Cocke, and the fourth, from western Tennessee under General Andrew Jackson, were supposed to merge in northern Alabama and march south into the Red Sticks' stronghold, where they would unite with the other American forces and stamp out the rebellion. Pro-American Creek, Cherokee, Chickasaw, and Choctaw warriors also joined with the United States to crush the dissidents. Some calculated that the Red Sticks' strategy of direct armed confrontation with the American hegemon was suicidal, while others must have believed that helping the United States to suppress the revolt would win them gratitude and breathing space once the war ended.[47]

In late September, Tennessee's governor ordered Andrew Jackson to organize 2,000 volunteers and militiamen from western Tennessee. He summoned the volunteers who had served with him on the Natchez expedition, and whom he had never formally released from service. Appealing to their sense of manhood, he warned them that the Red Sticks would "advance towards your frontier with their scalping knife unsheathed, to butcher your wives, your children, and your helpless babes."[48] Jackson's volunteers assembled at Fayetteville and marched south, arriving at Ten Islands on the Coosa River in late October, where they erected Fort Strother. They believed that they could whip the Red Sticks if hunger did not block their path. The land on the way to the Creek country was not yet thickly settled, and the war had eroded its agricultural surplus. Provisions in Tennessee were not cheap, nor was it easy for Jackson's contractors to get supplies to the army, owing to poor roads and low water in the rivers.[49] "All I dread is a famine," John Reid wrote to his wife.[50]

The western Tennesseans scored two victories against the Red Sticks in early November but could not conquer hunger. On 2 November John Coffee led 900 volunteers and a force of Cherokee and Creek warriors against the Red Stick town of Tallasahatchee. Coffee established what would become a familiar pattern. His men killed 186 Red Sticks and took 84 prisoners, while losing only 6 men and suffering 41 wounded. A week later Jackson attacked the town of Talladega, killing more than 300 Red Sticks while losing 17 of his own men and suffering 85 wounded.[51] Jackson saw the destruction of Talladega as both a resounding success and a missed opportunity. General Hugh White, in command of the eastern Tennessee army, had refused to rendezvous with the western Tennesseans, and Jackson faced a critical shortage of provisions. Instead of pressing his advantage at Talladega, an anguished Jackson explained to his wife, he was forced to return to Ten Islands to await supplies.[52] With food scarce and hunger mounting, Jackson's soldiers began to grumble. Petitions poured in to Jackson requesting that he allow the men to move north where they could procure supplies. Many threatened to desert if Jackson would not let them go.[53] "You have no conception of our privations, or of the ungovernable spirit of the men," complained John Reid.[54]

The combination of victory and distress was not unique to Jackson's soldiers. The eastern Tennessee and Georgia armies also lacked provisions and suffered from disease, but they still managed to kill Red Sticks.[55] Hugh White's eastern Tennesseans destroyed the town of Little Ocfuskee, then on 18 November laid waste to the Hillabees, who were negotiating terms of surrender with Jackson at the time.[56] The Georgians, along with a large party of Creeks under the command of William McIntosh, routed the Red Stick stronghold of Autossee on the Tallapoosa River in late November.[57] Ferdinand Claiborne tried to engage the Red Sticks in mid-October but could not draw them out. His men, too, suffered from serious privations. After returning from a foray in late October, David Ker wrote that the officers and soldiers in Claiborne's camp were "pretty much tired of the service." They discovered that pursuing the Indians through swamps was difficult work. They lacked tents, slept poorly, and resented the high price of buttermilk. But Ker himself was stalwart. "Do not think however that I am one of those who are going to desert the Standard of their Country," he assured his mother. "I expected no party of pleasure no frolic War."[58] Indeed the Creek War was no frolic for any who fought in it, but it was particularly bad for the Red Sticks.

The Mississippians enjoyed two morale-lifting successes. In a famous skirmish in November, Captain Sam Dale and a small band of soldiers waged hand-to-hand combat with a Red Stick war party, in canoes in the middle of the Alabama River. Paddling Dale's canoe was a black man named Caesar, whom subsequent accounts of the "canoe fight" always mentioned.[59] A more important victory came at the Red Sticks' Holy Ground, or Econochaka, on the upper Alabama. The Holy Ground was the retreat of Josiah Francis, one of the Red Stick prophets, who claimed to have endowed the site with a magical invulnerability. A sizable number of black runaways were reported to count themselves among its defenders.[60] Claiborne attacked the Holy Ground on 23 December with more than 650 Mississippi volunteers, militia, and Choctaw warriors. As they overran the town, most of the Red Sticks escaped, including William Weatherford. Approximately thirty Red Sticks were killed at the Holy Ground, including several black people. Only one of Claiborne's soldiers was killed.[61] The contrast between Caesar at the canoe fight and the black Red Sticks at the Holy Ground reflects the diversity of slave experiences during the

Creek War. But while Caesar was commemorated in white Alabamians' folklore of the Creek War, the black Red Sticks were later reviled—even by Creeks themselves. Kinnie Hadjo, a Creek warrior who had fought at the Holy Ground, later told the historians Halbert and Ball "that the proud and warlike Muscogees on this occasion had compromised the dignity of their nation in stooping so low as to call to their aid the services of such a servile and degraded race as negroes to assist them in fighting the battles of their country."[62] Chattel slavery turned Indians into racists, too.

As 1813 drew to a gory close, Andrew Jackson's army began to abandon him. First the militiamen threatened to leave, then the volunteers. Jackson and his soldiers had differing views of what patriotism required of them. Although the western Tennesseans disliked the Indians and wished them expelled from the frontier, they had enrolled for specified terms of service and were unwilling to fight any longer than legally required. Nor did they believe that the interests of the United States compelled them to starve in the field or altogether abandon their homes and families. They had private obligations as well as public ones. Colonel William Martin, the commander of one of the regiments of volunteers, explained their position to Jackson. He argued that the men were rushed into service and lacked proper clothing for cold weather. Many were persuaded to muster only after being assured that their term of service would expire on 10 December and thus had not prepared for a long campaign. They honored Jackson, but "having devoted [a] considerable portion of their time to the service of their Country, by which their domestic concerns are much deranged: they wish to return & attend to their own affairs."[63]

Jackson's more demanding view of the soldiers' obligations drew from his deeply felt patriotism and sense of personal honor. He could not believe that the men would put a narrow construction on their contractual obligations at a moment of national crisis. In his address to the First Brigade of the Tennessee Volunteer Infantry on 13 December, Jackson demanded to know how they would face their families and friends when they returned to Tennessee: "Will you tell them that you abandoned your General & y[our] late associates in arms, within fifty miles of an assemblage of a savage enemy, that as much delights in sheding the blood of the innocent female & her sleeping babe as that of the warrior contending in battle?"[64] Jackson (who had one legally adopted son) considered himself as a father to his soldiers, and consequently saw the soldiers' mutiny as a childish rebellion. Recounting his standoff with the volunteers to his wife, Jackson wrote that he "felt the pangs of an affectionate parent, compelled from duty, to chastise his child—to prevent him from destruction & disgrace."[65] But the western Tennessee soldiers were not children; they were full-grown men and American citizens with children of their own, and not even Andrew Jackson or hatred of Indians could keep them in the field when they felt within their rights and obliged to go home.

The two different understandings of patriotic duty reflect the different class positions of Jackson and his men. Most of the Tennessee volunteers were farmers who had few slaves or none at all. Many of them were poor. A long campaign would have kept them from their farms and deprived them of their livelihood for another year. It was less the hardships the soldiers encountered in the Creek country than those they imagined awaiting them in Tennessee that sent them home. Jackson, in contrast, was a cotton planter with more than twelve hundred acres of land and at least twenty slaves.[66] In mid-October, as his soldiers' grievances mounted, Jackson directed his wife to hire an overseer to manage the plantation and gather the year's cotton, which she did.[67] His wealth put Jackson in a position to endure a long and difficult campaign away from home, and prevented him from grasping the true cause of his soldiers' unhappiness. He called them cowards. He accused their officers of sowing discontent. In a startling turn, he even blamed the Red Stick prophets, whose "Phisic," he suggested to Rachel, had addled them.[68] By rhetoric and force Jackson staved off his troops' departure as long as possible, but he had to relent in the end. The western Tennessee volunteers left Fort Strother on 14 December, embittered by their experience.[69]

Jackson's army crumbled. Another fifteen hundred eastern Tennessee volunteers had arrived in Jackson's camp on 12 December, but they, too, expected to complete their term of service within a matter of weeks. Jackson sent half of them home, and instructed their commander to raise fresh troops to finish the campaign and to prod the army contractors in Tennessee. John Coffee's cavalry, which had been temporarily dismissed to allow the men to refresh their supplies and horses, reassembled at Huntsville in diminished numbers. As they marched toward Fort Strother in mid-December, they ran into the disgruntled volunteers and caught the spreading homesickness. Shamefaced, Coffee wrote of his brigade, "I don't believe they'll ever do any thing right again."[70] Finally, the remaining Tennessee militiamen concluded that their term of service ended on 4 January rather than three months later, as Jackson insisted. They, too, went home, leaving fewer than 150 men huddled in Fort Strother, and the bulk of those men determined to leave within two weeks. "I am left almost destitute of an army," Jackson raged.[71] If the Red Sticks had fallen on Fort Strother at that moment, the course of southern and even American history might have been different, but that is not what happened.

The first months of 1814 brought thousands of fresh citizen-soldiers to Fort Strother, as Jackson's strident letters to various government officials and the frenzied recruiting efforts of his officers finally bore fruit. Undeterred by cold weather and rain, one Tennessee volunteer later recalled, "We never yet murmured the Least we was going out on liberty's caus to subdue the indians."[72] First to Jackson's rescue was William Carroll, who arrived at Fort Strother on 14 January with more than eight hundred volunteers. As Carroll's men had enlisted for a meager sixty days, Jackson immediately put them in the field. Joining with two hundred Cherokee and Creek soldiers, the troops marched against the Red Stick town of Emuckfau on the Tallapoosa River, which they destroyed on 22 January. On their march back to Fort Strother, they skirmished further with the Red Sticks at Enotochopco Creek and routed them. Jackson's troops killed almost two hundred Red Sticks and lost only twenty of their own men, including Jackson's nephew Alexander Donelson. The victories boosted Jackson's morale after an exceptionally difficult two months. "When I move again," the newly optimistic general assured his wife, "I shall soon put an end to the creek war, carry into effect the ulterior objects of my government and then return to your arms to live & love together thro life."[73] Throughout the Creek War, the tenderness of Andrew Jackson's letters to Rachel contrasts sharply with his harshness toward his own soldiers and, of course, his Red Stick foes.

A lack of troop discipline and supply shortages continued to plague Jackson through February and mid-March. He even executed one unfortunate soldier, John Wood, for mutiny. But as increasing numbers of new troops gathered at Fort Strother, Jackson readied them for a final push against the Red Sticks. He marched out on 14 March—the day of Wood's execution—with approximately 4,000 men under his command. The army moved south to the recently built Fort Williams on the Coosa River, and from there Jackson marched on to Emuckfau with a slightly smaller force composed of 2,000 infantry, 700 cavalry, and 600 Cherokee and Creek Indians. Their ultimate destination was a horseshoe-shaped bend in the Tallapoosa River called Tohopeka, where more than one thousand Red Stick men, women, and children braced themselves behind an impressive barricade.[74]

On 27 March 1814, Tohopeka became a death trap for the Red Sticks. Jackson's army encircled the encampment, set fire to the wooden dwellings, and killed all those who tried to escape. When the slaughter finally ceased, Jackson's troops had killed nine hundred people, including three hundred shot as they swam across the river. "The *Carnage* was *dreadfull*," Jackson wrote to his wife after the battle.[75] In contrast, the U.S. forces suffered only fifty casualties, including twenty-three allied Cherokee and Creek soldiers. The Tohopeka massacre, known afterward as the Battle of Horseshoe Bend, was the bloodiest battle in the long history of conflict between American Indians and the United States. It may also have been one of the most consequential, for it shattered the Red Sticks' rebellion and put the southern Indians at the mercy of the U.S. government. As Andrew

Jackson explained to Thomas Pinckney, "The power of the creeks is I think forever broken."[76]

Jackson praised his troops as the vanguard of progress and Providence. He predicted that civilization would rise from the ruins of hellish barbarism. "The weapons of warfare will be exchanged for the utensils of husbandry," he declared, and "the wilderness which now withers in sterility & seems to mourn the desolation which overspreads it, will blossom as the rose, & become the nursery of the arts." Jackson warned that "other chastisements remain to be inflicted" before the task of securing the foundations of civilization was complete. He vowed to punish the remaining Red Sticks until they completely abandoned their prophets and atoned for their crimes. He revealed to the soldiers that they were agents of divine justice: "How lamentable it is that the path to peace should lead through blood & over the carcass of the slain!! But it is in the dispensations of that providence which inflicts partial evil, to produce general good."[77] It would not be the last time Andrew Jackson recognized the hand of God at work in behalf of the United States and its republican civilization.

Over the next few months, U.S. troops scoured the Creek country, burning Red Sticks' towns, building fortifications, and collecting refugees. One frustrated North Carolina soldier stationed at the newly erected Fort Jackson on the Coosa and Tallapoosa rivers reported in June that 1,500 Indians had come into the camp. "It appears to me that we came to feed more than to fight them," he complained.[78] Many other Red Sticks fled to Florida, where they hoped to find refuge and aid from the Spanish. One of the first people to inform Jackson of the situation in Pensacola was a black woman captured at Fooshatchee on the thirteenth or fourteenth of April. Claiming to have run away from Pensacola, she told Jackson that the Red Sticks had been furnished with ammunition by a clerk with the mercantile firm of Panton & Leslie.[79] Slaves taken by the Red Sticks at Fort Mims and elsewhere also began to trickle in.[80] Many of their owners were dead or missing, making their legal status uncertain. Jackson person-

ally took control of some of the slaves. He sent several to his plantation in Tennessee, where they were put to work.[81] In August, W. C.
Middleton wrote to Andrew Jackson from Natchez to claim a boy
named Ambrose owned by Middleton's brother Captain Hattan Middleton, slain at Fort Mims.[82] In September, Theophilus Powell sold
Jackson five slaves—Seller, Jack, Hannah, Sam, and Amey—whom he
claimed "by virtue of his intermarriage with one of the daughters and
legal heirs of Wm. Dwyer who was killed at the siege and destruction
of Fort Mimms."[83] Lemuel Early wrote to Jackson in 1815 looking for
twenty-five or thirty slaves belonging to his wife's family; Early's
mother-in-law, six brothers-in-law, and a sister-in-law had all died at
Fort Mims.[84] In 1818 a slave named Eliza, captured by the Red Sticks
at Fort Mims, ended an odyssey nearly five years long when Jackson shipped her to Fort Montgomery to be united with her owner,
Susannah Stiggins.[85] For these enslaved men and women, the Creek
War wrote a new chapter in their personal experiences of forced migration.

All of this was a sidelight to the main task of securing a peace
treaty with the Red Sticks. Jackson and many other political leaders in
the Deep South demanded a wholesale expropriation of the Red
Sticks' land. In a letter dated 18 May, Jackson laid out his vision of a
proper settlement. He believed that the Upper Creek country belonged to the United States by right of conquest, and that territorial
contiguity and population were the keys to security. "The grand policy of the government," he explained to John Williams, "ought to be
to connect the settlements of Georgia with that of the Territory and
Tennessee, which at once forms a bulwark against foreign invasion,
and prevents the introduction of foreign influence to corrupt the
minds of the Indians." He recommended that the government "ought
to adopt every means to populate speedily this section of the Union,
and perhaps if she would give a preference right to those that con-
quered it at two dollars per acre of three hundred and twenty acres, it
would be settled by a hardy race that would defend it."[86] Jackson's vision carried forward the Jeffersonian idea that converting Indian land

into private property would invite migration, strengthen security, and ultimately guarantee U.S. sovereignty in the Deep South, but the war had ruined Jefferson's naive hope that republican expansion would occur without bloodshed and with the free consent of all aboriginal peoples.

The Creek War introduced many American soldiers to the Upper Creeks' attractive and fertile lands, which they immediately coveted. Howell Tatum, Andrew Jackson's topographical engineer, was one of those who kept an eye out for marketable lands. Coming across one "elegant red bluff" on the Alabama River, he recorded in his journal that it was "the handsomest situation for a town of any to be found on the river," owing to its proximity to fertile land and its easy access to Mobile.[87] Early in 1814, George Strother Gaines wrote from St. Stephens to James Taylor Gaines in Tennessee: "Should the Alabama lands fall into the hands of our Govt & I will not doubt it, you must come out & select you a tract of land & bring all our friends with you if possible. The Alabama will be the garden of America ere many years."[88] And writing from Fort Jackson in May, William McCauley of North Carolina reported to his brother, "I have been down the Alabama nearly as far as Mobille—some fine lands below here."[89] Observations such as McCauley's helped to fuel the popular clamor for dispossessing the Upper Creeks of their territory.

Over the summer Jackson himself negotiated the terms of peace with the Creek Indians—terms far more punitive than those stipulated by the secretary of war.[90] It was a curious parley, because most of the Red Stick leaders had escaped to Florida and did not participate. Thirty-four of the thirty-five Creek leaders who signed the treaty of surrender had supported the United States during the war, and they were understandably astonished and embittered to find themselves stripped of much of their land. The treaty delivered more than twenty-three million acres of Creek land to the United States, including most of what is today southwest Georgia and central Alabama.[91] After concluding the treaty on 9 August, Jackson descended the Alabama River to Mobile, where he penned a rapturous letter to his wife describing the country he had seen. "I have no doubt but in a few years, the Banks of the allabama will present a beautiful view of elegant mansions, and extensive rich & productive farms," he predicted.[92] Implicit in this vision of elegant mansions and wealth was the advance of plantation slavery rather than Jefferson's hardy yeomanry. Yet those elegant mansions would have to wait, for just as Jackson was mopping up the Creek country, an old enemy appeared on the Gulf Coast.

"a Black Regiment on their Coast"

The war in the North was not going particularly well for the British. They had lost both Tecumseh and Lake Erie in the fall of 1813 and had failed to dislodge the United States from the Canadian border. When Napoleon began to retreat in the face of the allied European monarchs, Britain prepared to widen the war in America. As early as 1812, British commanders thought about encouraging the southern Indians—as well as southern slaves—to rebel against the United States. By 1814, opening a southern front seemed an excellent way to divert the attention and resources of the United States away from the Canadian front and perhaps to undermine southern support for the war. In March the commander of the North American station, Admiral Cochrane, dispatched Captain Hugh Pigot to contact the Creek Indians. Pigot arrived at Apalachicola Bay in Florida in May with arms and ammunition—too late to prevent the Tohopeka massacre. Pigot sent George Woodbine to reconnoiter the region, gather the Indians to the British standard, and train them. Learning of the Red Sticks' perilous situation, Woodbine sailed with provisions to Pensacola, where more than two thousand hungry refugees (including many African Americans) pressed him for assistance.[93]

News of the British presence in Florida once more kindled the Americans' fears of a slave insurrection, especially as that presence was rumored to include black soldiers. In June 1814, Brigadier General Thomas Flournoy notified the secretary of war that an English force had landed at Apalachicola. He supposed that its purpose was "to give fresh vigor to the Creeks, & to encourage & give countenance to insurrection among the negroes of the southern states."[94] Around the same time, George Strother Gaines heard that "several thousand black troops were on their way from the W. Indies" to Apalachicola.[95] Mississippi's territorial judge Harry Toulmin warned Jackson that a British schooner had recently left Pensacola "for the purpose of bringing from Jamaica a body of black troops to some part of the Shores of the gulph of Mexico."[96] Jackson's fears were confirmed in late July, when a new British musket given to the Indians at Apalachicola fell into his hands. He warned Louisiana governor William Claiborne that the British probably intended to strike against Mobile or New Orleans. "I have no doubt these will be their objects," he concluded, "combined with that of exciting the black population to insurrection & massacre."[97] This fear weighed heavily on Jackson as he stripped the Creeks of their land and scurried to Mobile.[98]

American anxieties were not entirely hysterical. The British had black troops and intended to use them in the South. Early in 1813 Senator William Hunter of Rhode Island reminded his colleagues that Spain and England both employed black soldiers. "That unhappy species of population which prevails on our Southern country," he said, "aroused to reflection by the sight of black soldiers and black officers, may suspect themselves to be fellow-men, and fondly dream they likewise could be soldiers and officers. The bloody tragedy of St. Domingo may be acted over again in this devoted country."[99] The West India Regiments, as Britain's black troops came to be known, grew out of the experience of the British military during the American Revolution and the Caribbean disasters of the 1790s. The wars for St. Domingue particularly accelerated the incorporation of African and African American soldiers in Britain's colonial military establishment. British officers found that people of African descent could be worked at military labor and were well suited to guerilla warfare. The astonishing mortality rates of European-born soldiers in the Caribbean convinced the British command to employ soldiers of African descent, whom they considered less vulnerable to tropical diseases.

Over the vehement objections of colonial slaveowners, the British began to organize the West India Regiments in 1795.[100]

Composed mostly of African-born men, the West India Regiments performed useful services under difficult conditions throughout the British Caribbean. They helped to police the local slave populations wherever they were garrisoned, and they occasionally saw combat. But they faced discrimination and prejudice that hampered their effectiveness. Until 1807 most of the soldiers in the regiments were slaves themselves, and colonial authorities sought jurisdiction over them according to local slave codes. Their ambiguous legal status occasionally led to problems of morale. In 1802, for instance, black soldiers of the Eighth West India mutinied at St. Rupert's Bluff in Dominica, apparently fearing that they were about to be sold as field hands. The Mutiny Act of 1807 finally settled the legal status of Afro-British soldiers by effectively emancipating all slaves in British military service. The act freed about ten thousand slaves in the largest act of emancipation in the British West Indies before 1833.[101]

Even after the soldiers were freed, the West India Regiments continued to suffer from poor morale and bad discipline. Because many of the soldiers did not speak English or spoke it poorly, a language barrier separated them from their commissioned officers. Also, few of the black noncommissioned officers could read or write.[102] Moreover, the regiments were generally divided and dispersed throughout the colonies to guarantee that black soldiers did not outnumber white soldiers at any one station. Even when it was not dispersed, a regiment might be sent to a remote location and find itself all but forgotten. After several years in British Honduras, for instance, the Fifth West India Regiment was found by an inspecting officer to be "in a very poor State of Discipline." The officer reported in 1808 that "both Officers & men have become so domesticated, that they almost seem to have forgotten that they are Soldiers, except that Guards are mounted."[103] The West India Regiments also suffered from chronic shortages of clothing, which would hamper their effectiveness in the cold Louisiana winter of 1814–15.[104]

British military officials were well aware of the impact the West In-

dia Regiments might have in the American South—especially in Louisiana. Early in 1813 Captain James Lucas Yeo asserted, "The Population of Slaves in the Southern Provinces of America is so great, that
the People of Landed Property would be Panic-struck at the sight of a
Black Regiment on their Coast and nothing would more effectually
tend to make the War with this Country unpopular than the knowledge of such a measure being in contemplation."[105] A few weeks later
Captain James Stirling wrote a long memorandum to Lord Viscount
Melville detailing the strategic significance and tactical vulnerabili-
ties of New Orleans. He reported that Louisiana's black population
outnumbered its white and that blacks recently had been "very troublesome." Stirling drew the obvious conclusion. "A body of Black
Troops," he suggested, "would consequently do much mischief in an
attack upon this country if it should not be thought improper to exas-
perate the white inhabitants by employing them."[106]

In fact the British command did not intend to use the West India
Regiments to provoke slave insurrections in the South. It was thought
that such a tactic might be counterproductive, although the threat of
it could be useful. As he set out for Louisiana, the British commander
in chief, Lieutenant General Sir Edward Pakenham, was specifically
instructed neither to incite a slave insurrection nor to quiet the slaveowners' fears that he might. "There is nothing so calculated to unite
the Inhabitants against you as an attempt of this description," explained Lord Bathurst, "while the apprehension of your being obliged
to resort to such a measure for your own Protection may be made to
act as an additional inducement with them to make no resistance to
His Majesty's Troops."[107] But there were other reasons to send the
West India Regiments to the Gulf Coast. One was that the British
hoped to recruit men from the American slave population to replen-
ish the ranks of the West India Regiments, whose strength had been
declining ever since the abolition of the slave trade in 1808.[108] It also
appears that soldiers from the West India Regiments were to garrison
New Orleans if the British took it—a plan consistent with the basic
purpose of the regiments, which was to spare European soldiers the
unhealthiest assignments.[109]

These strategies were enacted in the Chesapeake region and in Florida in the summer and fall of 1814. In late August a British expeditionary force that included one of the West India Regiments entered Washington and burned the capital's public buildings. It did not incite a slave insurrection, but did invite hundreds of slaves to run away from their owners and, ultimately, to escape from the United States. Three hundred were convinced to enter British military service as a battalion of the Royal Colonial Marines.[110] When Louisiana governor William Claiborne reported the sack of Washington to Andrew Jackson, he added a note of local concern. "Louisiana has at this moment much to apprehend from Domestic Insurrection," he warned. "We have every reason to believe that the Enemy has been intriguing with *our slaves,* and from a variety of circumstances, we have much cause to suspect that *they* on their part, meditate mischief."[111] The fear of slave insurrection ran like a red thread through Claiborne's correspondence as he readied Louisiana for the expected British invasion.

Meanwhile in Pensacola, George Woodbine and Major Edward Nicolls, a young but esteemed officer of the Royal Marines, recruited Red Sticks, Seminoles, and black people to the British standard. Their activities infuriated slaveowners in Pensacola and alarmed Benjamin Hawkins and other U.S. officials.[112] Jackson criticized the governor of Pensacola, Mateo González Manrique, for harboring Britain's agents. Using undiplomatic language, he warned González Manrique that he would hold him personally responsible for any depredations committed against citizens of the United States, and that he would exact an Indian vengeance: "An Eye for an Eye, Toothe for Toothe, and Scalp for Scalp."[113] Nicolls organized an attack on Fort Bowyer in Mobile Bay in mid-September, but the attack failed and Nicolls (who lost an eye in the battle) retreated to Pensacola, where he continued to attract disgruntled Indians and runaway slaves.[114] Five of Benjamin Hawkins's own slaves ran off in late October. "The business must be put a stop to," Hawkins cautioned the governor of Georgia, "or the evil will soon become highly alarming to the citizens throughout your state."[115] Finally Jackson had had enough. Acting without authority from the president, he marched to Pensacola in early November and drove Nicolls and Woodbine out. "Thus Sir I have broken up the hot bed of the Indian war," he boasted to James Monroe.[116]

Even as he attended to the hornet's nest in Florida, Jackson did not forget New Orleans. He corresponded frequently with William Claiborne, who was coordinating the effort to fortify and defend the city from both foreign and domestic enemies. Louisiana planters freely acknowledged their vulnerability. In September a Committee of Safety formed in New Orleans to help defend the city. In a report sent to Jackson in mid-September, the committee admitted that a society dependent on plantation slavery could not defend itself. "This Country is strong by Nature," the committee asserted, "but extremely weak from the nature of its population." According to the committee, the high ratio of slaves to white inhabitants on the sugar plantations along the Mississippi and the mixed population in the city made Louisiana vulnerable to a slave rebellion, which it expected the British to foment.[117] In mid-October, Jacques Villeré personally implored Louisiana senator Eligius Fromentin for assistance. "We are determined to defend ourselves to the last extremity," he pleaded, "but you know very well the population of this part of the country. You know how much we have to fear about the 'domestic enemy,' and you know very well how limited is our defense in case of invasion. To that horror will our wives, our children as well as ourselves be exposed? Add to this agents of the English Government found everywhere, and who by the most infamous methods incite our slaves to revolt, murder, pilfering, and you will have an idea of our anxiety."[118]

One of the thorniest questions Jackson and Claiborne considered was whether to make use of Louisiana's free men of color as soldiers. Their deliberations echoed those leading to the formation of the West India Regiments. After years of stonewalling, the first Louisiana state legislature had grudgingly authorized the establishment of a militia corps composed of free men of color in 1812. The legislature limited the corps to four companies of sixty-four men each, restricted enlistment to native-born men (and their sons) who had paid a state tax and owned landed property worth at least $200 for at least two years before enlistment, and put the battalion under the command of white officers. The terms were obviously intended to restrict military service to the most privileged and established free men of color. The large group of recent migrants from the Caribbean was excluded, as was the majority of free men of color, who did not meet the property qualification. Command of the battalion was given to Michael Fortier and Pierre Lacoste, both wealthy Creole planters.

In early August Claiborne met with the officers of the free colored battalion, who urged him to extend the privilege of military service to all native-born free men of color in and around New Orleans. Claiborne stalled for time, authorizing a census of the free men of color to be taken and writing to Jackson for further instructions. Claiborne recommended in favor of the men of color. "These men for the most part sustain good characters," he explained, "many of them have extensive connections and much property to defend, and all seem attached to Arms." He argued that their constitutions and habits would make them useful in the event of an invasion, and that if they were not allowed to serve, the British would "be encouraged to entrigue & to corrupt them." Claiborne suggested that another three or four hundred men could be recruited for six-month terms of service, so long as they were assured of serving in Louisiana and not out of the state.[119] Jackson accepted Claiborne's recommendation and replied with instructions to expand each company to 100 men, but he did not promise to keep them in Louisiana.[120]

Claiborne expected that the local planter elite would oppose Jackson's decision to expand the free colored battalion, which had not been popular among them in the first place. In mid-October he reported to Jackson that two "Gentlemen of Influence" had suggested that the planters would accept the arming of free black soldiers if Jackson guaranteed that the soldiers would be removed permanently from Louisiana at the end of the war. If the men were allowed to return to Louisiana after the war "with a Knowledge of the use of arms, & *that pride of Distinction,* which a soldier's pursuits so naturally inspires," the gentlemen insisted, "they would prove dangerous."[121] Jackson acknowledged the planters' concern but insisted that it was better for the free men of color to be enrolled in the service of their country and subject to military discipline than not. "If their pride and merit entitle them to confidence, they can be employed against the Enemy," he explained to Claiborne. "If not they can be kept from uniting with him."[122] Buoyed by Jackson's support, the governor continued to recruit, organize, and arm the free men of color, who rallied to the American standard despite the prejudice and discrimination they endured.

Throughout the slave societies of the circum-Caribbean world, the wartime pressures of a revolutionary age forced military authorities to arm people of African descent, despite slaveowners' objections. Consequently, soldiers of African descent confronted each other as enemy combatants at the Battle of New Orleans.

"my body it shall remain here"

More than six thousand British soldiers gathered in Jamaica's Negril Bay and embarked for Louisiana in late November 1814.[123] After two weeks at sea, the fleet anchored off the Gulf Coast, where a sharp frost and driving rain greeted them. The vanguard of the British troops packed into barges on the morning of 22 December and rowed across a windswept Lake Borgne, reaching the boggy coast in the dark of night. Wending their way through Bayou Bienvenue and Bayou Mazant, they reached a canal leading through the cypress swamp to Jacques Villeré's plantation—a route probably taken by countless smugglers before them. Concealed by tall reeds, the soldiers slogged through the canal until morning, when they broke into the open clearing that marked the left bank of the Mississippi River. An advance company seized Villeré's plantation, which became the British headquarters for the duration of their ill-fated stab at New Orleans.[124]

Beautifully rendered in Benjamin Latrobe's 1819 watercolor of the

New Orleans battleground, the agrarian civility of the sugar plantation landscape impressed the British, particularly as it contrasted sharply with the quagmire they had just traversed. Several aspects of the terrain stand out from the various descriptions recorded by other British soldiers and officers: the levee guarding the river; the ditches and fences crisscrossing the cane fields; the formal gardens and orange groves; and the scattered big houses, outbuildings, and slave cabins rising from the alluvial flatness. The artillery officer Alexander Dickson described the view in his journal: "The cleared land on the left bank of the Mississippi at this point is from 1000 to 1500 Yards wide, being a flat Cultivated plain principally Sugar plantations, fenced by high and strong railings, and much intersected by Ditches, bounded on one side by the Artificial bank of the river against inundations, and on the other by the wood which is every where thick, Marshy, and nearly impenetrable."[125] The day after Christmas, Alexander Dickson commandeered one of the Villeré slave cabins that had the luxury of a fireplace. "The Weather Continuing to be piercing Cold the fire is most agreeable," he wrote in his journal. He did not indicate what had happened to the cabin's previous inhabitants.[126]

The plantations below New Orleans were full of people, and most of them were slaves. According to the 1810 census, almost fifteen hundred people lived on the plantations on the left bank below New Orleans within the Seventh District of Orleans Parish, and of these, almost three-quarters were slaves. The 1810 census lists twenty-five slaves on the Lacoste plantation, forty-seven on the Villeré plantation, and fifty-three on the Jumonville plantation.[127] In his memoir, the British officer Benson Earl Hill recalled a memorable encounter with a slave on the Villeré plantation. While wandering around the plantation, Hill met a young black boy named George, who was wearing a spiked iron collar. In perfect French, George told Hill that the collar was a punishment from his master for trying to run away. It prevented him from sleeping. Hill took George to a blacksmith, who removed this "ingenious symbol of a land of liberty." In exchange for the favor, George pledged to work as Hill's servant and was employed making marmalade from Villeré's oranges. The story may be apocryphal, but it is a plausible introduction to the problem of slavery at the Battle of New Orleans.[128]

The Battle of New Orleans unfolded in one of the richest districts in North America, amid sugar plantations that had been carved out and built up and worked over by thousands of enslaved men and women. Plantation slavery shaped the physical, psychological, and political terrain of the battle even if it did not decide its outcome. As the British approached, U.S. officials took steps to keep the enslaved population under control. They deployed thousands of slaves in military labor, turning potential weakness into strength. Soldiers of African descent fought on both sides, but their presence did not incite a slave revolt as many people feared it would. Instead, as the confrontation between American and British forces dragged on, conflicts over labor tainted relations between Andrew Jackson, local planters, and the free soldiers of color. And when the British finally retreated from the Gulf Coast, several hundred enslaved Louisianians went with them in a bold rejection of life in the slave country.

As usual in moments of crisis, public authorities stepped up their surveillance of enslaved people. City officials in New Orleans took special precautionary measures covering slaves, free people of color, and other suspicious persons.[129] Governor William Claiborne issued general militia orders in early September mandating nightly patrols and recommending "the strictest discipline" among the slaves.[130] The legislature allowed armed men to stay behind to guard the slaves in plantation districts away from New Orleans and granted them unusually broad authority to search slave cabins for arms, ammunition, and signs of rebellion. Evidence from Attakapas demonstrates the vigilance of local authorities. In September 1814, the Attakapas planter David Rees received a circular from Governor Claiborne advising that British agents were "busily engaged in enciting our negroes to insurrection." Rees was instructed to organize a regular patrol with the power to search "all negro cabins and other places where Arms are most likely to be concealed," and to arrest everybody "whose conduct, and character, should furnish reasonable ground of suspicion, of his or their intrigues with the negroes, or being in any manner connected with the Enemy."[131] Claiborne redoubled vigilance measures in Attakapas in early November, asking Rees to raise a company of one hundred "minute men" capable of repelling a British force ascending the Bayou Teche, or for use "in the case of insurrection among the Negroes, whether in St. Mary, in Attakapas or Opelousas."[132] After the British landing, the patrol was again reinforced. Claiborne ordered Rees to maintain "strict & vigilant Patrols night and day," and to "have organized all the exempt from Militia Duty within the bounds of your Regiment, and order that they Perform Patrol Duty." Rees was to guard against a slave insurrection and a British invasion.[133]

Slaves were put to work to defend New Orleans. From December 1814 to March 1815, thousands of slaves (mostly men) were sent to strategic locations and forced to perform the arduous work of military fortification. They helped to dig the trenches, raise the breastworks, and erect the batteries that stood between the British forces and New Orleans. Years of bickering between city officials and local slaveowners had produced a workable system of conscription and compensation for slaves employed on public works in New Orleans, and several of the engineers who directed fortifications under Jackson, including Latour, had previously managed slaves on public and private projects in New Orleans. Moreover, military labor resembled the kind of hard work that enslaved adult men had always performed on sugar plantations. The capacity of Louisiana's officials to mobilize slave labor in defense of New Orleans counteracted to some degree the military disadvantages of plantation society.

Andrew Jackson's first task upon arriving in New Orleans was to scout the American defenses and shore up vulnerable spots. Several batteries were needed to protect the city, and Jackson concluded that only slave labor could build them. "It will require considerable labour to erect the various Batteries contemplated," Jackson instructed Governor William Claiborne, "and this Labour in a great measure must at this rainy season be performed by your Slaves."[134] Louisiana's legislature allocated funds to fortify the city, and requested that Claiborne solicit slaveowners in and around New Orleans to provide slaves for the work.[135] Claiborne sent a circular to slaveowners in the parishes around New Orleans, asking that they send male slaves to Fort St. Charles or to English Turn.[136] Jackson also authorized Jacques Villeré to requisition "negroes, Horses, Oxen, Carts, &c. as he may deem necessary."[137]

Jackson's army relied heavily on slave labor. In late December Howell Tatum noted in his journal that slaves had been procured "to ease the labour of the soldiery and preserve their health and activity for more important service."[138] Many of the slaves were dispersed to corps on the front lines, while others found themselves in large gangs working on specific projects. On Christmas Day, Edward Livingston (now Jackson's aide-de-camp) instructed one officer to "take all the negroes you can collect from the plantations" and cut the levee below the British lines.[139] One hundred fifty slaves worked to construct a line of defense at "Madame Dupree's Mill & Canal" about one mile in the rear of the principal line, under the guidance of Benjamin Latrobe's son, Henry. Another 150 slaves under engineer Lefevre completed a parapet along Boisgervais's Canal on the right bank of the Mississippi, three miles from New Orleans.[140] The commander at Fort St. Leon had almost 200 slaves working on the fort in early January, but these were not enough.[141] "I have had a party of men out every day since I took command of the fort pressing the negroes within my reach," he reported to Jackson.[142] One slave caught up in the dragnet was Archy, a "smart able negro man" hired out to a barge heading down the Mississippi to New Orleans in November 1814. When the barge reached the city, Archy was drafted into military labor and forced to cut timber in the swamps for almost a month. After laboring "incessantly in the water & mud," he took sick and died. Slaves, too, became casualties of war.[143]

After the Battle of New Orleans, the Louisiana legislature praised the state's planters, who "furnished thousands of their slaves, and sent them to every particular place where labour was thought necessary."[144] Slaveowners profited, because they were paid for their slaves' labor. Moreover, some owners surely calculated that their property was more secure under the watchful eye of Jackson's army than on undefended and vulnerable plantations. A few weeks after the decisive battle, Robert Hilliard Barrow wrote to his uncle Bennett Barrow, "The negroes about New Orleans were very serviceable in throwing up breastworks, and thereby kept out of mischief."[145] But military labor did not entirely prevent slaves from getting into mischief themselves. Edward Livingston's son, Lewis, who was stationed at Camp Macarty, reported on 9 January that most of the slaves at work there had run away during the previous day's battle.[146] Similarly, the commanding officer at Fort St. Leon reported at the end of the January that the number of slaves at the fort "diminishes every day." Some were ordered elsewhere, but others ran away.[147]

While slaves labored, free men of color fought on both sides in the Battle of New Orleans. About one in every ten soldiers was of African descent—probably the largest concentration of black soldiers in the United States before the Civil War.[148] On the British side were the First and Fifth West India Regiments, numbering around one thousand soldiers, most of them African-born. The poorly equipped soldiers suffered greatly from the cold Louisiana winter and the arduous labor they were compelled to perform.[149] One British officer recalled seeing soldiers from the West India Regiments enlarging a canal. "Poor wretches!" he wrote, "They worked awkwardly and groaned incessantly, under an occupation which inflicted deadly suffering, and sent numbers to the hospital, and most likely to their graves."[150] When the Fifth West India Regiment returned to the Caribbean, the wear of the campaign showed on the soldiers' bodies. Their commander reported that "a good many man arrived sick on the return of the Corps" and that some of them had to be transferred to garrison duty "having their feet injured by the Frost on the Expedition." Even the regimental surgeon had died from exposure.[151]

The West India Regiments also suffered casualties from combat. Five privates from the First West India and 9 privates from the Fifth

West India were killed in action between 25 December and 8 January.[152] Another 160 men from the First and Fifth West India Regiments died in hospital or at sea between 25 December 1814 and 24 March 1815.[153] British military records afford the merest glimpse of these men. Private James Augustine, for instance, was born in Cape Nicholas Mole in St. Domingue. An upholsterer by trade, he joined the British service on May first, 1801. At five feet ten inches, he was taller than most of his fellow soldiers. He is listed in the records as having black hair, a long face, and black eyes. He would have been eligible for an increase in pay had he survived through May of 1815, but he was killed in action on 28 December 1814. The four other Fifth West India privates killed in action were George Byng, Robert Corbet, William Pattin, and Robert Pegan. They were all "Eboe" men, probably bought by the British specifically to serve as soldiers. Byng's African origins were etched on his face; according to the Description and Succession Book, he had "country marks on his forehead." Byng and Corbet had been enrolled in the regiment on 25 January 1802, while Pattin and Pegan were enrolled on 25 March 1804. All served in the British military for more than a decade before giving their lives on the battlefield below New Orleans. They lived Atlantic odysseys but never made it home.[154]

An American soldier may have gotten a glimpse of one of these men. When the smoke of the battlefield had cleared, reported an anonymous private from Kentucky, the carpet of prostrate, red-coated bodies made the battlefield look like "a sea of blood." Some British soldiers had taken cover among the piles of dead and dying, and as the gunfire ceased, they began to run away or surrender. To the Kentuckian they appeared to rise from the dead. One man in particular caught the attention of the private and his comrades. "Among those that were running off, we observed one stout looking fellow, in a red coat," he wrote, "who would every now and then stop and display some gestures toward us, that were rather the opposite of complimentary." Though many shots were fired at the disrespectful soldier, none hit the mark. A cry went up for the company sharpshooter, a "cadaverous looking Tennessean" nicknamed Paleface: "Hurra, Paleface! load quick and give him a shot. The infernal rascal is patting his butt at us!" Paleface "rammed home his bullet, and taking a long sight, he let drive" at the rascal, who was by now "two to three hundred yards off." The soldier staggered and fell and one of Paleface's company ran across the corpse-littered field to his body. Rolling the man onto his back, the American discovered that the British soldier "was a mulatto and was quite dead."[155]

Two distinct groups of free men of color served on the American side. One group comprised the native-born militiamen under Michael Fortier, and the other, recent migrants from the Caribbean who responded enthusiastically to Jackson's call to arms. The foreign-born were placed under the command of Louis Daquin, a white refugee from St. Domingue. One of their leaders was Charles Savary, a free man of color with long military and political experience in St. Domingue, whose son Joseph served as a captain in the battalion. The men of color performed admirably, especially in the aftermath of the decisive battle on 8 January, when Captain Savary's men sallied onto the field to protect those gathering up the wounded.[156] During that afternoon, the soldiers of color suffered fourteen casualties, including the death of Savary's brother. The thirteen wounded African American soldiers on the day constituted one-third of all American casualties, a higher proportion than in any other confrontation during the defense of New Orleans.[157] American officials praised the soldiers of color. Adjutant General Robert Butler declared that the colored companies "have not disappointed the hopes that were formed of their courage and perseverance in the performance of their duty," and the Louisiana legislature lauded "brave Savary."[158] The men of color were proud of their accomplishments. Reporting on his activities in early February, the native-born Captain Louis Simon declared, "I think however to have done more than my duty serving one's country is a thing which every man of honor glories in."[159]

The British forces retreated to the Gulf Coast in mid-January but remained within striking distance of New Orleans through March.

News of the peace treaty with Britain (which had been signed at Ghent on Christmas Eve) reached the city in early February, but Andrew Jackson refused to relax until he received official notification in mid-March that the Senate had ratified it.[160] In this twilight of the war, Jackson struggled to fortify the American position in the face of intensifying discontent within his own ranks. The central issue was Jackson's continuation of martial law, which some of Louisiana's more prominent citizens believed to be unnecessary, heavy-handed, and even despotic.[161] But contributing to this very public controversy were other less publicized tensions connected to the ramifications of war in a slave country.

After the decisive battle of 8 January, Jackson redoubled his efforts to fortify New Orleans, but his officers found it more and more difficult to procure slaves for the work. Local planters believed the danger from the British had passed and wanted their slaves back on the plantations.[162] Facing a labor shortage, Governor Claiborne proposed paying planters one dollar a day for each slave, but Jackson thought that rate of hire was "extravagantly expensive."[163] Claiborne defended the cost, arguing that a dollar a day was usually allowed for short-term labor, even though the United States generally hired slave labor at $20 per month. The planters, he told Jackson, were "not as ready to meet our requisitions as formerly, attributable I presume to the necessity of preparing their farms for the crop of the present year, & which have for some months been neglected."[164] The sugar planters' determination to make money brought them into conflict with Jackson, who was more concerned with the public good. As the planters returned to business as usual, the work of fortifying New Orleans proceeded haltingly.[165] It was not until the British finally departed from the Gulf Coast that the conflict between the security imperatives of the state and the labor needs of the planters evaporated in the dry air of peace.

The shortage of slave labor impinged on the soldiers of color, eventually provoking a serious conflict between them and the officers directing the defense of New Orleans. Many soldiers eager to return to their homes—including a good number of the soldiers of color—began to abandon their posts.[166] On January 19, Michael Fortier reported to Jackson that Louis Daquin had sent out a party "with an order to arrest & confine all the deserters" from his battalion.[167] The colored soldiers' dissatisfaction intensified in February, when Jackson called on them to perform military labor. He ordered Louis Daquin's battalion to Chef Menteur in the middle of February, but many of the soldiers refused to go. Daquin explained to Brigadier General Robert McCausland that his soldiers were willing to sacrifice their lives in combat but preferred to die rather than be subjected to the degradation of military labor. They did not want to be treated like slaves.[168] Savary refused to march his company to Chef Menteur, and soldiers already there deserted in droves. On 24 February, McCausland sent Jackson a list of deserters, warning him that without "rigid steps," Daquin would soon "be left without a private to command."[169] Jackson began to suspect that British agents were sowing discord among the colored troops. "The Enemy is still near us, and no doubt remains upon my mind that his emissaries have for some weeks been busily engaged amongst us," he explained to a subordinate. A "speedy corrective" was required.[170]

Amid the controversy, Savary and fifteen other colored officers in Daquin's Battalion of St. Domingue Volunteers appealed to Jackson for help. The men asserted that they were loyal to the United States and "ready to fly to any post which may be asigned to them to defend a contry which has given them an asylum." Hoping to enjoy the benefits of peace, they called on Jackson to protect them from the "future insult" of discriminatory laws and prejudice.[171] The soldiers' plea contrasts sharply with the language of the petition submitted to William Claiborne a decade earlier by Louisiana's Creoles of color, who had expressed "the fullest confidence in the Justice and Liberality of the Government towards every Class of Citizens."[172] Savary and his fellow officers lacked that confidence. Their protest was cautious and limited. They trusted neither the government of Louisiana nor the people of the United States but instead sought shelter under Jackson's "paternal care." They appear to have been speaking only for themselves and not for free people of color in general. Along the same lines, Charles Savary, Captain Joseph Savary's father, wrote a personal letter to Jackson pleading for "that succour which his age, infirmities and indigent family so urgently demand." Jackson endorsed the plea and recommended that Congress provide for his support in recognition of the great service father and son had performed. "It is Just to do so," he noted on the back of the letter.[173] Congress never acted, but the Louisiana legislature did grant Joseph Savary a generous pension of $30 per month in 1819 and again in 1823.[174]

In addition to disgruntled planters and free people of color, troublesome slaves continued to preoccupy Andrew Jackson. Fears of slave unrest prompted several anxious communications from Attakapas. Southwest of New Orleans, the region along the coast of Louisiana was particularly vulnerable to a British incursion. In January four state legislators urged Jackson to allow the militias of St. Mary and St. Martin to remain in their parishes to guard against a slave uprising. Their coastal location, they explained, exposed them to a British raid, and the danger "is much increased at the moment, by the great disproportion between the white & black Population." Even in time of peace, "serious apprehensions have been felt from the great number of Slaves in said Parishes, as there is scarcely white Men sufficient at any time to form the necessary Patrols & keep the Blacks in order."[175]

Fear of slave insurrection persisted in Attakapas after the fighting had ended. The longer Jackson kept the Louisiana militiamen in the field, the greater the danger from slaves. In early February Jackson received a letter that confirmed the planters' fears. Writing from Camp Jackson in the parish of St. Mary's, Joshua Baker relayed some chilling news: "There has been a grate alarm amongst the inhabitants of Opelousas, And St. Martin, owing to a rebellion amongst the negroes of these Parishes." According to Baker, seventeen "neagroes" had been jailed, and although the men had not yet been tried, "sum of the neagroes confessed to the fact." According to the testimony of the alleged conspirators, "the signal of the attack was to be the fireing of the British Cannon." The slaves' confessions may have been coerced; indeed the entire story may have been concocted to induce Jackson to allow the Attakapas militiamen to return home. Like so many similar episodes in the history of the American South, it may have been the figment of a fevered collective imagination. Still, that collective imagination grew from real conditions and palpable anxieties.[176]

Runaway slaves were another matter, and a very real one at that. Eyewitness accounts and narratives of the Battle of New Orleans written by American participants or observers asserted that the retreating British forces kidnapped two or three hundred slaves from the plantations that they had occupied during the invasion of Louisiana. On 20 January the Chevalier de Tousard complained to his son-in-law that the British "took with them the harvest of three plantations and more than two hundred negroes."[177] The national press repeated the claim. In February, *Niles' Weekly Register* celebrated the American victory at New Orleans but added a melancholy note: "The English have destroyed the plantations below their camp, and carried away the slaves and behaved generally like vandals."[178] Lacarrière Latour acknowledged that some of the slaves "were very willing" to follow the British but argued that most of the slaves—especially the women—were "carried off by force."[179] The story that the British had kidnapped the slaves strengthened the widely held belief that the American victory prevented a wholesale disruption of the plantation economy. It also implied that slaves would have preferred to remain in the febrile swamps of Louisiana.

In fact the slaves who left with the British freely chose to abandon the plantations, and everyone knew it. According to Alexander Dickson, the retreating British had neither expected nor wanted the slaves to accompany them. "A good many Negroes, both Men, Women and Children have taken the opportunity of the night to accompany the Army down to the Huts," he noted in his journal, "which Genl. Lambert was extremely displeased at."[180] John Lambert, who had inherited command of the British troops in Louisiana after the deaths of

Packenham and Gibbs, subsequently apprised Andrew Jackson of the slaves' activities. "To my great surprise," he wrote, "I found upon reaching my Head Quarters, that a considerable number of Slaves had assembled there under the idea of embarking with the army." He assured Jackson that his men had tried to convince the slaves to remain at home but they came anyway.[181] In the 1820s a series of depositions were taken in preparation for an adjudication of claims for compensation submitted by Americans who suffered loss of property at the hands of the British in the War of 1812. These depositions contain detailed information about the Louisiana slave refugees and their erstwhile owners' attempts to recover them. They reveal that the refugees were not kidnapped but, rather, chose to abandon Louisiana.[182]

Who were these refugees? Louisiana planters submitted claims for the value of 163 slaves.[183] Most were owned by the planters whose estates had been taken over by the British forces—Jacques Villeré alone owned more than 50 of them—but some may have fled to British lines from Jackson's camp. Considered property by their owners, they were valued at a total of $182,050. The slaves ran the gamut of plantation occupations. The men had been drivers, sugar makers, coachmen, carpenters, bricklayers, cartmen, and field hands. The women had worked as field hands and house servants. Without their labor, Latour observed, "the masters could not cultivate their plantations."[184] Most were adult men, and among those whose nativity was recorded, most were native-born Louisianians. One of the most remarkable of the refugees was a thirty-six-year old Louisianian named Osman, described in the depositions as "a good carter, carpenter, and negro-driver, of uncommon intelligence." He was spotted in December of 1814 on a plantation near the Pearl River, where he was procuring oxen and other provisions for the British. A witness contended that the British were "very much attached to *Osman* because he was not only a very smart, active & cunning fellow, but could speak with the indians whose language he understood very well."[185]

The slaves' flight provoked two months of intricate negotiations. Their owners wanted their slaves back, and it briefly appeared that they might get them. Lambert assured Jackson in mid-January that the British intended to return the slaves "to any proprietors that may claim them & sending a Person who may have influence with them as soon as possible."[186] Representing the interests of the planters, Governor Claiborne pressed Jackson to send agents to the British camp to retrieve the slaves, but Jackson resisted. "Would it not be a degradation of that national character of which we boast to condescend to solicit the restoration of stolen property from an enemy who avows plunder & burning to be legitimate modes of warfare?" he asked the governor.[187] Interest eventually trumped honor, as Jackson authorized a delegation to recover the slaves from the British. By mid-February, Jackson concluded that the delegation would obtain nothing but "fallacious promises," but he continued to bicker with the British commanders over the fate of the runaways.[188] The sticking point was that the British commanders refused to force the slaves to return to their owners. As Lambert explained to Jackson, "I shall be *very happy,* if they can be persuaded all to return, but to compel them is what I cannot do."[189] When an American officer arrived at the British camp at Dauphin Island in Mobile Bay, Lambert informed him that he would not comply with the articles of the treaty having to do with slaves, "as it was totally incompatible with the spirit and constitution of his government to recognize *slavery* at all."[190] Lambert certainly knew that the British government had no difficulty recognizing slavery in its overseas colonies and would continue to do so for another generation, but he was in no mood to do the bidding of Louisiana's planters.

Several slaveowners visited the British camp at Dauphin Island hoping to retrieve their slaves. When Hugues Lavergne arrived there at the end of February, Lambert gave orders to have the slaves assemble "in order that they could be seen & spoken to." About two hundred slaves gathered to hear Lavergne's appeal, but most rejected his assurances of good faith and refused to return.[191] Jacques Loutant sailed to Dauphin Island to recover the slaves of Antonio Méndez and Louis Reggio. James, a slave belonging to Reggio, agreed to return, but three other Reggio slaves and four Mendez slaves refused.

Loutant blamed the British officers for turning them against their owners. He was "sorry to say that those slaves were more induced by the English to stay with them than to return to their masters."[192] By the end of March, those slaves still bivouacked on Dauphin Island had tired of the planters' speeches. When Chevalier Delacroix and Michael Fortier arrived there on 29 March, they found that the slaves had "concealed themselves in the tents" and would not come out.[193]

After commanding a regiment of free men of color in the defense of New Orleans, Colonel Pierre Lacoste returned home to discover that thirteen of his own slaves had fled with the British. When he reached Dauphin Island in an attempt to recover them, he encountered a slave named Jean-Baptiste, owned by Louisiana planter Jean Canon. Canon had hired out Jean-Baptiste to Jacques Villeré prior to the British invasion, receiving $15 a month for his labor. According to Canon, the thirty-five-year-old Jean-Baptiste was a "Carter & good servant," and worth $1,200 in the slave market. In January 1815, Jean-Baptiste had retreated with the British in the company of the other Villeré slaves. Lacoste failed to persuade him to return to New Orleans. He testified that Jean-Baptiste was "very insolent" and told him "you may carry my head along with you but as to my body it shall remain here."[194] And so Jean-Baptiste, like several thousand other enslaved people throughout the southern United States, seized the opportunity of war to take his leave from the slave country. Many of these refugees ended up in Trinidad, where British authorities gave them land, freedom, and a new beginning "on Canaan's happy shore."[195]

The Battle of New Orleans ultimately reinforced the Americans' providential view of their country's destiny. The famous battle of 8 January resulted in almost 200 British soldiers killed and more than 1,200 wounded, as against only 13 Americans killed and 13 wounded.[196] Among the British casualties was the commander in chief, Lieutenant General Sir Edward Pakenham, brother of the Duke of Wellington. Rumor had it that his body was packed in a pipe of rum and returned to England (as Henry Palfrey joked) in "high spirits."[197] There had been no major slave rebellion, no plunder of New Orleans, no loss of American honor. Many observers saw the hand of God in the outcome. "The Almighty was pleased to Crown us victorious," Ensign David Weller wrote to his brother on 1 3 January.[198] Andrew Jackson agreed. "If ever there was an occasion on which providence interfered, immediately, in the affairs of men it seems to have been on this," he mused. "What but such an interposition could have saved this Country?"[199]

The idea of freedom rippled through the deluge of nationalist propaganda that followed the Battle of New Orleans. Letters, orations, sermons, plays, poems, and toasts all praised Jackson's victory over the British as a victory for freedom. A young North Carolina congressman named Israel Pickens told his constituents that events on the southwestern frontier proved "a free republic is capable of self-preservation, and of standing the shock of war."[200] One dramatist titled his play *The triumph of liberty, or, Louisiana preserved: a national drama, in five acts*.[201] No propagandist identified the Battle of New Orleans more fully with the cause of freedom than an anonymous poet in Boston, whose verse symbolically abolished slavery.

> Let Britain in sackcloth and ashes deplore,
> That her PACKINGHAM, KEAN, and her GIBBS are no more;
> Where the wide *Mississippi* her waters now lave,
> Shall ne'er be defil'd by the foot of a *slave!*
> Our heroes shall conquer by land and by sea,
> No despot enslaving,
> Our strip'd flag still waving,
> And proves to the world that America's free.[202]

The propagandistic representation of Jackson's victories in the Creek War and the Battle of New Orleans not only suppressed the tensions over slave resistance that had plagued the nation during the war but also denied that the United States was a slave country. At an extreme, the rhetoric of freedom obliterated the reality of slavery.

Contrary to expectation, the Deep South became the arena for the United States' greatest wartime triumphs. Under Andrew Jackson's indomitable leadership, the citizens of the region stamped out the Red Stick revolt and expropriated millions of acres of Indian land. Then they beat back the British at the Battle of New Orleans, redeeming the honor of a country humiliated by the burning of its national capital. Jackson's victories were a balm for a troubled country. "Old Hickory" became a hero, and a nationalist self-confidence buoyed the Deep South. John Reid described the general's triumphal procession up the Mississippi in April 1815. "He is everywhere hailed as the saviour of the Country," Reid reported to his mother. "All the way up the Coast (which is really a town for more than a hundred miles) he has been feasted, caressed, & I may say idolised. They look upon him as a strange prodigy; & women, children, & old men line the road to look at him as they would at the Elephant."[203] A naval officer witnessed the resurgence of commerce and pleasure in New Orleans. "Now Every one is in bustle & commotion," he observed in April, "the wharves crowded with merchantmen continuously pouring in—carts rattling through the streets—& beautiful Girls to be seen in all directions."[204] Writing from the nation's capital, Louisiana's senator James Brown rejoiced in the victory. "Property in Louisiana will rapidly appreciate," he wrote to Edward Livingston, "Every body talks of either visiting that country or settling there."[205] And Henry Johnson of Donaldsonville, Louisiana, wanted to know, "What is the price of negroes in Kentucky?"[206]

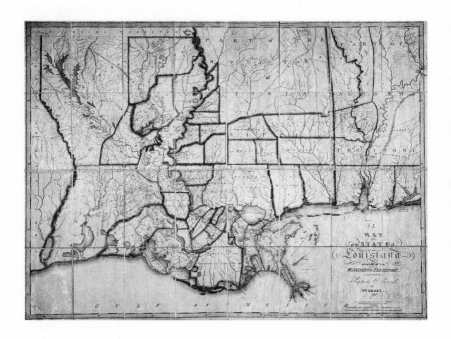

William Darby, Map of Louisiana, *1816. A onetime surveyor, Darby was a leading geographer of the southwestern United States in the early nineteenth century. His maps and books encouraged people to migrate to the Deep South after the War of 1812. Note the differences between Darby's map and the one drawn by Old Tassel three decades earlier (see Chapter 1).* COURTESY OF THE LOUISIANA STATE MUSEUM.

CHAPTER 5

Fulfilling
the Slave Country

WHILE IN THE nation's capital in the fall of 1815, Andrew Jackson often dined with North Carolina's young congressman Israel Pickens, whom he convinced to visit the new lands coming to market in the Deep South.[1] Pickens scouted the Mississippi Territory in the summer of 1816, sold his plantation in North Carolina at the end of the year, and sent most of his slaves to the southwest under the supervision of his brother James.[2] His prospects brightened when President Monroe appointed him as register of the land office east of Pearl River, a position of considerable influence in the rapidly growing territory. Accompanied by his wife, Martha, and their two young children, Pickens settled into a log cabin in St. Stephens in January 1818, where he hoped to "take a fair start with that new world which promises so much to industry & enterprize."[3] By the end of 1819, Pickens had purchased more than a thousand acres of land and was the proud owner of a cotton plantation on the Tombigbee River worked by a large gang of slaves. He helped to draft Alabama's first state constitution, and in 1821 the state's voters made him their governor.[4]

It hardly needs to be said that the Deep South was not a "new world" but an old and inhabited one when Pickens settled there. Calling it a new world was part of the ideological justification for U.S. expansion. (Indeed the idea of its newness was one of the aspects of its history that was not new at all.) But Pickens was right in the sense that the region was about to enter a new phase of its history, namely, a profound and prolonged expansion of plantation society. He and thousands of other people participated in that remarkable expansion; their individual decisions contributed to it. At the same time, those decisions were shaped by deeper, structural pressures that shaped the postwar world. Slaveowners benefited from vigorous policies of nation building pursued by the U.S. government—especially the conversion of millions of acres of Indian land into marketable real estate—as the country worked to thicken its sovereignty in the Deep South. The end of the Napoleonic Wars also brought rising commodity prices and invigorated opportunities to profit from the use of slave labor. Free migrants to the Deep South, as well as planters and farmers already living in the region, responded by expanding their cultivation of cotton and sugar. Taking advantage of opportunities created by American nationalism and the transatlantic economy, southern slaveholders and their allies created a contiguous plantation system stretching from Georgia to Texas.

These developments were catastrophic for American slaves. Forced migration uprooted thousands from their long-standing communities, friends, and kin in the older states and transplanted them in the cotton and sugar fields of the Deep South, where they were subjected to more difficult kinds of work and more lethal disease environments. The swollen slave markets in Huntsville, Mobile, Natchez, and New Orleans boosted slave prices throughout the South and gave slaveowners a potent new weapon in the ongoing struggle to control their human property. As Americans of all stripes confronted the many dilemmas of the market revolution—the quantitative and qualitative transformations of American life associated with the expansion of commerce—developments in the Deep South and the increasing visibility of forced migration provoked both opponents and defenders of slavery to think anew about this American institution. While slavery's opponents realized that slavery was not going to die a slow and natural death, its defenders wrestled with the social, political, and moral consequences of expansion. The Missouri crisis of 1819 crystallized these tensions in the cauldron of national politics and ultimately distilled a solution acceptable to the slave country (though not to the slaves themselves) for another generation.

Early in 1817 a Senate committee on public lands issued an influential report that described the area between the Mississippi River and the Appalachian Mountains as an "irregular frontier" with isolated American settlements scattered in and around Indian country. Its irregularity compromised American sovereignty and had nearly led to disaster during the War of 1812. The committee recommended that the Indians living east of the Mississippi River should be relocated to the west, and the frontier settlements should be integrated as quickly as possible into the economic, social, and political life of the country. Over the long run, it predicted, migration would create a compact, dense, and contiguous population of citizens in the trans-Appalachian West, strengthening American sovereignty there and guaranteeing that the Indian risings of the previous war would not recur. The report spelled out the logic of western expansion and nation building already at work in the Deep South, where the destruction of the Red Sticks and the elimination of British influence had shifted the balance of power further toward the United States.[5]

One expression of that underlying logic was the acquisition of Florida—a goal long sought by Jeffersonian Republicans. So long as Florida remained in Spanish hands, southwestern settlers feared for their access to the Gulf of Mexico and, thus, the world market. Moreover, a weak Spanish government in Florida allowed the coastal region to become a haven for all kinds of dissidents and outlaws.[6] The U.S. ran roughshod over Spanish sovereignty in Florida in the years after the end of the war. American troops invaded Florida three times between 1815 and 1820: first to destroy the so-called Negro Fort established by the British at the end of the War of 1812, then to suppress an ersatz republic of privateers, and finally to crush Seminole and fu-

gitive slave resistance in the colony. Neither wholly endorsed nor decried by the national government, these controversial interventions
assisted the United States in its negotiations with Spain, which increasingly understood that it could not keep Florida out of the Americans' grasp forever. The Adams-Onís Treaty, signed in 1819 and
ratified in 1821, secured Florida for the United States and further
eroded the already vulnerable position of the remaining Indians and
fugitive slaves on the Gulf Coast. The editor of the *Mississippi State Gazette* praised the treaty in 1819. "It rounds off our southern possessions," the newspaper argued, "and for ever precludes foreign emissaries from stirring up Indians to war and negroes to rebellion, whilst
it gives the southern country important outlets to the sea."[7] Still, it
took twenty years and another nasty little war to quell resistance in
Florida's swamps.

The United States acquired vast amounts of Indian land in the five
years after the defeat of the Red Sticks, establishing in the process the
pattern for Indian removal west of the Mississippi. The Treaty of Fort
Jackson, negotiated by Andrew Jackson after the defeat of the Red
Sticks at Horseshoe Bend, wrested twenty-three million acres of land
from the Creek nation in the Mississippi Territory and Georgia. Following the Treaty of Fort Jackson, the United States negotiated three
additional cessions from the Creeks, Chickasaws, and Choctaws in the
fall of 1816, acquiring millions more acres of land in the north-cen-
tral region of the Mississippi Territory. The crowning moment in this
postwar flurry of land acquisition was the Treaty of Doak's Stand,
which Jackson negotiated with the Choctaw nation in the fall of 1820.
The Choctaws ceded five million acres of the most fertile land in the
United States in exchange for almost thirteen million acres of inferior
land in what later became southern Oklahoma and southwestern Ar-
kansas. These postwar treaties did not wholly eliminate Indian sovereignty in the Deep South, but they went a long way to consolidating
U.S. sovereignty in the region and laid the groundwork for the expulsion of the Indians in the 1830s.[8]

The new land had to be surveyed and sold—and the sooner the

better. A rapid distribution of these public lands would bring greater security to the southern frontier and precious revenue into the public coffers.[9] Andrew Jackson constantly reminded the national government of the benefits to be gained by turning the land into real estate. "We will now have good roads, kept up and supplied by the industry of our own citizens, and our frontier defended by a strong population," he explained to James Monroe after completing negotiations with the Chickasaw and Cherokee Indians.[10] But familiar complications prolonged the surveys. Thomas Freeman, the surveyor general for the southern lands, was swamped with applications from aspiring surveyors, few of whom (he suspected) had any idea of the "difficulties, privations, & hardships, unavoidably connected with the Surveying of Public Lands in a wilderness."[11] At the same time he found it difficult to hire and retain sufficient numbers of laborers. Rough terrain, the high price of provisions, Indian harassment, and disease also slowed his work.[12] The delays allowed thousands of squatters to plant themselves on unsold public lands, where they clashed with government officials.[13]

The squatters' defenders argued that they were good if poor citizens whose industry increased the value of the public domain. Settlers in Amite County in the Mississippi Territory pointed out that their "little improvements add so much to the value of the lands." They also reminded the government that it owed them money "for services rendered both in the indian & British wars some of whom laid down their lives while in the service of their Country whose widows & orphan children are now dependent on their friends and a grateful Country for subsistence."[14] Judge Harry Toulmin agreed that squatters should be protected because they aided the development of the frontier. "Men of capital do not like to vest their active property in a wilderness,—where it will take two or three years before they can raise provisions enough to enable them to carry on a plantation on an extensive scale," he explained to the Mississippi Territory's delegate to Congress. "But if 'pioneers' had gone ahead to clear and farm the land, facilitating travel and selling provisions to those coming later, those same men of capital would give fifty percent more for the same land.[15] Such arguments from economy ultimately convinced Congress to grant preemption rights to selected groups of white squatters, although it did not establish a general right of preemption for settlers until 1830.[16]

Land officers fought an uphill battle against illegal manipulations of the land sales by squatters intent on preserving their holdings and speculators hoping to reap windfall profits on undervalued lands. In December of 1815, the surveyor general warned Lewis Sewall at St. Stephens that "intruders" in possession of public lands had threatened to assassinate any person who dared to bid for their lands, so Sewall employed a marshal to keep order at the sale.[17] In 1818 John Coffee and James Jackson ran across a private company that had been organized to monopolize the purchase of lands at Huntsville. James Jackson refused to take part, as he informed Andrew Jackson, "first because there was too much illiberality in the rich combining to push out of market those who were unfortunate enough not to have [. . .] funds, second because I dislike those large combinations and thirdly because I had no confidence in the greater part of those concerned." The company's scheme collapsed as the best lands sold for high prices. "The handsomest game of sink pocket you ever seen was played on them," wrote Jackson, "& you never seen a set of great purs proud gentry so compleatly foiled, vexed & mad."[18] Such combinations sometimes exerted considerable influence. In 1819 land officers postponed a public sale because they detected the operation of a "combination of land speculators."[19] In 1820 land sales at Big Spring in northern Alabama were suspended "from the supposition that the lots were purchased by a company of gentlemen who were determined not to bid against each other."[20]

Despite all these difficulties, the federal government sold plenty of land in the Deep South, almost five million acres by October 1819. Land officers in the region sold just over one-quarter of all the land sold by the United States but generated 40 percent of the revenues earned from the sale of all public lands in the United States. Huntsville's land office by itself sold almost $8.5 million of public land, more than any other office.[21] The best lands rarely sold for the minimum price, and land in the Deep South generally sold higher than elsewhere. The high prices paid for lands were inflated by competition among purchasers, easy credit practices, and the influx of "Mississippi scrip," a notorious currency paid to claimants in the Yazoo speculation, redeemable only for federal land. But these circumstances only augmented the root cause of the Deep South's land mania: high cotton prices.[22] The average price of cotton in New Orleans rose from seventeen cents per pound in 1814 to twenty-seven cents per pound in 1815 to almost thirty cents per pound in 1817, before declining rapidly starting in late 1818.[23] Small wonder, then, that one Baptist preacher wishing to give his congregation a better idea of Heaven called it "a fair Alabama of a place."[24]

While the national government's land policy gave indirect support to the cotton economy, sugar planters enjoyed a more direct encouragement. Before the war, Louisiana's sugar planters benefited from a two-and-a-half-cent tariff on brown sugar, which was increased to five cents during the war. Early in 1815 the sugar planters petitioned Congress to maintain the wartime tariff. Drawing on nationalist rhetoric, they argued that "the interests of the Union loudly demand that this distant State should be assisted in securing to herself, and, consequently, to the nation, the vast advantages which its climate and situation promise." Louisiana would be able to supply the rest of the country with sugar, rum, and molasses, and would in return consume the other states' produce and manufactures. Support for the sugar industry would increase Louisiana's population and strengthen a "distant and frontier State."[25] Louisiana's representative Thomas Robertson forcefully opposed a motion to reduce the tariff to its prewar levels in 1816. "It is as important to the interests of the nation to protect the cultivation of the cane and the manufacture of sugar, as any other merchandise whatever," he declared.[26] The Baltimore newspaper editor Hezekiah Niles supported the protective tariff on sugar, even though he recognized that it made the sugar planters the wealthiest of men. "Everything that tends to relieve my country of its dependence on others," he rhapsodized, "is to me like the beams of the morning to the wearied traveller, who had wandered the night in search of a place of repose."[27] Congress ultimately approved a compromise three-cent tariff on brown sugar, which was lower than what the sugar planters wanted but higher than many sweet-toothed Americans thought they deserved.[28]

The national government also sponsored infrastructural development designed to "bind this Republic together," as South Carolina's ambitious John Calhoun put it.[29] The government concentrated its efforts in the Deep South on cutting a road from Nashville, Tennessee, to Madisonville, Louisiana, appropriating $10,000 for the object in 1816.[30] Colonel A. P. Haynie predicted, "In a national, commercial and military point of view, this road will be of utmost importance."[31] Brewster Jayne, who lived at the southern terminus of the road, thought it would "open a fine communication to the upper Country, and facilitate the progress of the People of Pen & Ohio, Indiana, Illinois Ter., Kentucky & Tennessee in their return to their families after having disposed of their produce in N. Orleans, which they convey there in flat boats."[32] The route was surveyed in the winter of 1816–17 (it partly followed established Indian trails), and construction began in 1817 under Andrew Jackson's supervision. Several hundred soldiers labored on the road for three years, completing it in 1820. When it was finished, Jackson signaled the road's public purpose by telling the secretary of war that the government "can, if it pleases, run the mail stages from the seat of general government to New Orleans in 17 days."[33] A decade later Jackson soured on what he called the "scramble for appropriations" that attended federal support for internal improvements, but in the palmy postwar era, he and other southern nationalists scrambled as well as anyone.[34]

The national government encouraged political as well as economic development. Louisiana was already a state, but Congress still had to decide the fate of the Mississippi Territory—particularly the question of whether it should enter the Union as one or two states. This was a question with significant consequences for the citizens of the territory and for the country as a whole. Before the war, citizens living in the western portions of the territory generally wanted it to be admitted as one state, while those living in the eastern districts wanted to split off and form their own state. When Madison County and the other eastern districts rapidly increased in population after the war, the two groups swapped positions, with the westerners favoring division and the easterners preferring that the territory remain intact in the transition to statehood. The regional clash was tinged with a whiff of class conflict, with the westerners representing the wealthy plantation districts along the Mississippi River and the easterners speaking for a poorer population of yeomen farmers and smallish planters. Congress split the territory in 1817, authorizing the citizens of the western half to form a constitution and government for the state of Mississippi, and organizing the eastern half into the Alabama Territory, which became a state in 1819. At Mississippi's constitutional convention in 1817, William Lattimore explained why he had supported the splitting of the territory. "Division," he told the assembled delegates, "would give to this section of the union an additional state, and of course two additional senators, and two additional electors of President, to maintain its political influence and rights." Lattimore's reasoning would prove its merit during the Missouri crisis.[35]

A comparison of the first state constitutions of Louisiana, Mississippi, and Alabama suggests that the stronger a state's planter class was, the more conservative was the structure of its politics. Louisiana's 1812 constitution was the most conservative of the three. Its stated purpose was "to secure to all the citizens thereof the enjoyments of the rights of life, liberty and property." A skewed system of representation favored the established plantation districts at the expense of New Orleans and the rural districts, which were filling with migrants from the eastern states, while steep property qualifications for office holding made the state government a rich man's club. Suffrage was limited to free white male citizens who paid a state tax and met a residency requirement. The governor—a strong executive with extensive powers to appoint local officials—was selected by the legislature from the two candidates receiving the most popular votes. Louisiana's constitution omitted any mention of slavery, perhaps because the overtly undemocratic structure of its political life rendered unnecessary any explicit guarantees of the rights of slaveowners.[36] The first postwar governor of Louisiana after William Claiborne (who died in 1816) was Jacques Philippe Villeré, who appears to have recovered nicely from the loss of his slaves during the Battle of New Orleans. "What other people can flatter themselves, fellow citizens, to enjoy, under the sole government of laws, an extent of liberty and happiness comparable to ours?" he asked the legislature in 1818.[37]

At Mississippi's constitutional convention in 1817, representatives of the established plantation districts in the southwestern part of the state held sway but had to reckon with delegates from the newer counties, which contained a greater proportion of yeoman farmers. The convention generally rejected the most conservative proposals on representation and suffrage, including motions for viva voce voting and apportionment in the lower house according to the federal ratio (all white people plus three-fifths of all others). The constitution established militia service and taxpaying requirements for suffrage that in practice did not exclude many white men from voting, and its property qualifications for office holding were comparable to Louisiana's. Mississippi's governor was relatively weak, and many local offices were subject to election. Copying Kentucky's constitution, the legislature was prohibited from emancipating slaves without the consent of their owners except when a slave had performed distinguished service for the state, in which case the owner had to be compensated for the value of the slave. The legislature was also permitted to prohibit the importation of slaves as merchandise as well as the introduction of criminal slaves, but it was not allowed to prevent immigrants to Mississippi from bringing their slaves with them into the state.[38]

Forty-four delegates to Alabama's constitutional convention met in Huntsville in July 1819. Their number included a former president of Transylvania University, a onetime trustee of South Carolina College, and three former congressmen (including Israel Pickens). The secretary of the convention, John Campbell, boasted of the delegates' "urbanity and intelligence."[39] The Alabama Territory was divided politically between the northern, yeoman-dominated counties and the southern, planter-dominated counties. The northerners outnumbered the southerners at the convention, which goes a long way to explaining why Alabama's first constitution was the most liberal of those of the three southwestern states. Indeed, as far as white men were concerned, it was one of the most liberal in the entire country. The constitution established free white male suffrage, eliminated property qualifications for office holding, and apportioned representation according to the free white population. The Alabamians adopted Mississippi's provisions on emancipation and the slave trade while authorizing the legislature to pass laws obliging the owners of slaves "to treat them with humanity."[40]

Paradoxically, the country's nation-building efforts in the Deep South—especially the selling of the public lands and the formation of state governments—diminished the importance of the national government in the daily lives of citizens. This diminution was just as well for slaveowners in the Deep South, who immediately adopted the doctrine of state sovereignty to inoculate themselves from federal interference with slavery. The country got an early hint of this tactic in 1818, when a congressman from New Jersey called for an inquiry into the expediency of passing a federal law prohibiting the migration or transportation of slaves from one state to another in cases where the laws of each state already prohibited that transportation. Mississippi's George Poindexter objected. "Any man, he said, had a right to remove his property from one State to another, and slaves as well as any other property, if not prohibited from doing so by the State laws," he asserted. Moreover, the United States had "no right to interfere" with the operation of state laws.[41] And so as the nation consolidated its sovereignty in the Deep South, slaveowners placed firm limits on the power of the national government to regulate slavery in the states where it existed. At the same time, the original constitutions of Louisiana, Mississippi, and Alabama all but guaranteed that slavery could not be challenged on the state level either. This impregnable position was achieved in Louisiana through a skewed political structure that implicitly protected slaveowners' interests, and in Mississippi and Alabama by explicit restrictions on the power of their more popular legislatures to violate the rights of slaveowners. Most important of all, slaves and free people of color were necessarily denied democratic rights and were excluded from the political "people." Slavery placed inescapable limits on democracy.

James Birney's career exemplifies the impossibility of challenging slavery in the Deep South through internal political channels. Birney was a member of Alabama's constitutional convention and a representative in its first General Assembly, where he helped to enact a provision guaranteeing the right of trial by jury to slaves accused of crimes worse than petty larceny. He advocated the humanitarian treatment of slaves and restricting the migration of slaves into the state. In the 1820s he became the principal agent in the Deep South for the American Colonization Society, which he genuinely believed could pave the way for a general abolition and removal of all black people from the country. Birney soon became frustrated by slaveowners' intransigence and began to doubt the efficacy and justice of colonization. He abandoned Alabama, manumitted his slaves, and publicly repudiated colonization in 1834. Moving first to Kentucky and then to Ohio, Birney became active in the antislavery movement, and when an antiabolitionist mob in Cincinnati heaved his printing press into the Ohio River, he became one of the movement's celebrities. Running for president as the candidate of the newly formed Liberty Party in 1840, he won a mere 7,059 votes but gained a foothold for the antislavery movement in Jacksonian politics. Like other southern abolitionists, ranging from Frederick Douglass to the Grimke sisters, Birney had to leave the slave states to fight against slavery.[42]

"bustle and business"

The postwar boom launched the hopes and ambitions of merchants, lawyers, surveyors, farmers, and planters in the Deep South. Scouting lands in northern Alabama, John Campbell promised to take advantage "of every opportunity I see presented to make me independent of the world."[43] Abraham Inskeep thought his prospects as a grocer in New Orleans were very encouraging and in a few years "will lead to an independence."[44] Brewster Jayne of Covington, Louisiana, observed that "every brand of business appears to succeed well, and every prudent man may in a few years obtain a competency."[45] And when Andrew Collins traveled to Louisiana to collect on debts owed to his father, a merchant in Rhode Island, he decided to stay—"as this is the most promising Country for a young man in my circumstance or for any one that has a living to get in this world." Collins partnered with a man aptly named Cash and opened a store in St. Francisville, where the two entrepreneurs expected to "do as much business as any one of the Merchants in this Town."[46] The entrepreneurial energies of men such as these contributed to the fulfillment of the slave country.

The fortunes of the Deep South rested on cotton and sugar. The cotton crop almost tripled, from 54,000 bales in 1814–15 to 159,500 bales in 1819–20, increasing in the same period from 15 percent of the country's cotton production to more than 25 percent.[47] Statistics from Liverpool provide another index of the rising significance of cotton from the Deep South. Between 1816 and 1819, the Atlantic states provided almost 39 percent of Liverpool's cotton. Brazil was second at almost 30 percent, followed by India at 13 percent. New Orleans cotton ranked fourth, but its share of the Liverpool market steadily increased from 6.5 percent in 1816 to 12.2 percent in 1819—a signal for the future.[48] Cotton planters prospered. "My crop on my plantation has a very promising appearance & should Cotton continue at its present price my income from it will be very handsome the ensuing year," predicted John Palfrey.[49] In 1814 James Magruder's slaves picked 25,909 pounds of cotton on his Mississippi Territory plantation, but in 1817 they picked more than 42,000 pounds.[50] After selling his employer's cotton crop in 1816, the overseer James Moore boasted, "I don't know what it is of late to be without cash." Moore purchased three slaves and his own cotton farm three years later. He even hired an overseer. In the spring of 1822, Moore happily reported that he had eight slaves working on sixty acres of cotton land and would soon "live quite easy and above the frowns of the world, and buy 2 or three Negroes."[51]

Although U.S. slavery became increasingly regional in the nineteenth century, its fruits were national. Northern merchants and industrialists purchased one-third of the cotton shipped out of New Orleans in 1822, and while much of this was reshipped to Europe, northern textile manufacturers purchased the rest and spun it in their factories.[52] The political economist Tench Coxe warned his countrymen to pay attention to the cotton economy. "So important, in a direct and indirect view, is cotton wool to the landholders and cultivators of the whole union," he asserted in 1818, "that the right system for its production, its commerce, and its manufacture, is of incalculable value to the United States."[53] Coxe worried that increasing worldwide production would eventually ruin cotton planters in the United States, and he argued that only protecting the domestic cotton textile manufacturing could ensure the long-run profitability of cotton growing. Coxe predicted the fall in cotton prices that began in 1818 but not the recovery that followed, nor did he imagine that U.S. cotton planters would dominate the world market for fifty years.

Unlike their fellows in cotton, Louisiana's sugar planters could not compete in the world market, but the tariff protected them like a levee. Sugar cultivation increased moderately after 1815 as established planters improved their productivity and new ones broadened Louisiana's sugar bowl to the north and southwest.[54] One tally of domestic produce arriving in New Orleans indicated that the sugar crop increased from 12,000 hogsheads in 1814–15 to 20,000 in 1816–17, while molasses increased from 500,000 gallons to one million, and tafia increased from 150,000 gallons to 400,000.[55] The *Louisiana Gazette* reported in April 1818 that the year's sugar crop would exceed thirty thousand hogsheads, and in 1820 the New Orleans merchant John Clay informed his more famous brother that the sugar and cotton crop would exceed the previous year's by 25 percent if the weather remained favorable.[56] At a time when the annual production of sugar did not exceed thirty million pounds, the geographer William Darby predicted that Louisiana's annual sugar production would eventually reach two hundred million pounds (which it did in the 1840s).[57] Already the sugar planters were earning a reputation for wealth. The first rank of sugar planters included Wade Hampton, whose 400-slave plantation in Ascension Parish was one of the largest in North America. One traveler observed that Hampton's estate equaled "that of almost any English nobleman."[58] In 1821 a tour of the plantations along the river convinced Henry Palfrey that "the Mississippi Planters (from the distance of 250 miles from its mouth) are the happiest & most independent class of people in the Union, & generally speaking, theirs is the most profitable business."[59]

The postwar prosperity enlivened New Orleans—"a scene of bustle and business," boasted the *Louisiana Gazette*.[60] In a commentary on the new peacetime priorities, the New Orleans City Council urged Congress to move the arsenal, military hospital, and barracks outside the city and to demolish Fort St. Charles, because the buildings were "particularly injurious to commerce and navigation."[61] Cotton, sugar, tobacco, corn, flour, pork, hemp, fur, whiskey, staves, and many other products arrived daily from upriver and were shipped out of New Orleans in ever-increasing quantities.[62] By 1819 Louisiana's exports ranked third highest of any state in the country, trailing only New York and Massachusetts, and accounted for 14 percent of the value of all goods exported from the United States.[63] People also flooded into the city, and its population increased from about 25,000 in 1810 to more than 40,000 in 1820, including 15,000 slaves and 7,000 free people of color.[64] When Benjamin Latrobe landed there in 1819, he found a city "doing so much & such fast-increasing business that no man can be said to have a moment's leisure." In his journal he noted that everyone had money on his mind. "Their limbs, their heads, & their hearts move to that sole subject. Cotton & tobacco, buying & selling, and all the rest of the occupation of a money-making community fills their time, & gives the habit of their minds."[65]

Nothing symbolized the postwar boom better than the growing number of steamboats plying the rivers of the Deep South. While the number of all river vessels arriving in New Orleans more than tripled from 1814 to 1817, the number of steamboats jumped from fewer than 20 in 1815 to more than 200 in 1820. A negligible proportion of river traffic during the war years, by the end of the decade steamboats accounted for more than one-fifth of all river vessels arriving in New Orleans.[66] They lowered the cost of transportation and altered the natural flow of commerce. After Henry Shreve's successful ascent of the river in his aptly named steamboat *Enterprise* in 1815, steamboats began to carry goods and passengers upriver to Natchez, St. Stephens, Huntsville, Memphis, St. Louis, and Cincinnati. Shreve then challenged the Fulton-Livingston steamboat monopoly, winning a decision in Louisiana court in 1817 that effectively destroyed its exclusive hold on steamboat navigation on the river. Many of Shreve's countrymen credited him with overcoming both the natural and human obstacles to "free" navigation of their waters.[67]

The steamboat meant different things to different people. To Israel Pickens it signified the broader spirit of progress and enterprise. "This country is advancing fast in settlement & improvement," Pickens crowed. "St. Stephens looks every day more like a town. It contains a great number of active intelligent citizens, perhaps so many as any town on the continent of the same numbers. The general morals of the people are the reverse of what they were two years ago. We have a large steam boat which has passed every few days between this & Mobile. Another is proposed to be built to run from here to the falls of the Black Warrior. We expect to be made a State next session of Congress. Our new bank is beginning business here."[68] To other inhabitants of the Alabama Territory, the steamboat was a spectacle. The surveyors James Cathcart and John Landreth ascended the Tombigbee River aboard the steamboat *Mobile* in April 1819. When they passed two barges laden with cotton, the bargemen "exclaimed a Steam boat by G-d & then complimented us in the stile of the Kentucky boat men on the Mississippi." And when they arrived in St. Stephens, Landreth noted that "a great many people came down to the Landing to see the steam boat both white and black and Indians."[69] Some of the black people may have taken a special interest, as the advent of steamboat traffic opened a new escape route for them. James Williams attested to the phenomenon in an 1819 letter written on behalf of his neighbor, who requested to have a runaway slave captured in Natchez, "where he thinks he has gone in a steam boat."[70]

The opportunities available in the Deep South were publicized through the country by word of mouth, letters, gazetteers, travelogues, and newspapers. The military officer Gilbert Russell reported to James Monroe that he was "delighted" with the lands ceded by the Creek Indians and intended "to concentrate what interest I have in the world and locate myself on the Alabama River."[71] Andrew Jackson tantalized Israel Pickens with dinnertime stories about the same lands that caught Russell's eye. A Major Thomas returned to Tennessee in the summer of 1818 after surveying lands in the Alabama Territory. "I have seen his map of the country," wrote James Campbell, "and from his description of it it must be one of the richest spots in the whole southern country."[72] John Sims instructed his cousin not to visit the southwest unless he was in a position to move there. "If you was to see this country you never would be satisfied where you are," he warned.[73] James Wilkinson urged his friend Stephen Van Renssalaer to join him in Louisiana, where a $30,000 investment would earn $5,000 in the first year and $10,000 in the third. "Will you sell, pack up and embark and land at New Orleans where I will meet you and carry you home in a Steam boat?" asked the general.[74] A voluminous travel literature regaled readers with tales of flatboat voyages down the Mississippi, stories of Indian manners and habits, and certification of the astonishing productivity of the southwestern lands.[75] Eastern newspapers published articles and essays documenting the opportunities available in the southwest. *Niles' Weekly Register* enticed "the Planters of Maryland and Virginia" with a long description of the extraordinary profits to be earned from slave labor in the Opelousas and Attakapas districts of Louisiana. Among the examples cited was that of Andrew Jackson and Donelson Caffery, whose twenty-seven hands together produced 72 hogsheads of sugar from 54 acres of cane, ten bales of cotton, 3,000 gallons of molasses, and 1,000 barrels of corn, earning $465 per hand besides provisions. "Is not this the country for the slaveholder?" the article concluded.[76]

Knowledgeable geographers mapped the Deep South for the English-reading world, binding the republic with the printed word. The most renowned geographer of the Deep South was William Darby, a man whose career tracked the early history of U.S. involvement in the region. Darby was born in Pennsylvania in 1775 to parents who were continually moving west. When he was twenty-four, Darby traveled down the Ohio and Mississippi rivers and settled in Natchez, where he married Elizabeth Boardman, the widow of a wealthy slaveowner. Darby quickly became a cotton planter, an officer in the local militia, and his district's tax assessor. After suffering losses in a fire and clashing with the Boardman family, William and Elizabeth abandoned Natchez for Opelousas, recently incorporated into the United States. There his work as a private surveyor came to the attention of Isaac Briggs, and Darby was appointed deputy surveyor for the western district of the Orleans Territory in 1806. While surveying southwestern Louisiana, Darby hit on the idea of writing a geography of Louisiana. He quit his position in 1811 and explored the region for the next three years, rushing to New Orleans in the fall of 1814, where he participated in the Battle of New Orleans as a "topographical advisor" and supervisor of slave labor. After the war, Darby traveled to Philadelphia, the center of geographical knowledge in the United States. His *Geographical Description of Louisiana* came out to acclaim in the spring of 1816 and was shortly followed by a second edition and an *Emigrant's Guide to the Western and Southwestern States and Territories* in 1818. Darby never returned to the Deep South but his publications helped many others who moved there.[77]

And many did. The population of the region that became Louisiana, Mississippi, and Alabama more than doubled between 1810 and 1820, increasing from natural reproduction, the addition of new ter-

ritory, and, above all, migration. The white population increased to
2 1 0,000, and the slave population to 143,000. The population of free
people of color grew more slowly, to 1 1,5 00. Even presuming a high
natural-growth rate of 2.5 percent per year, no fewer than 1 2 5,000
people migrated to the Deep South in the 1 8 1 0s, including at least
7 5,000 white people and 5 0,000 slaves, and the actual numbers were
probably a good deal higher.[78] "I never saw such a Migration in my
life," Philip Foote reported to his father from a crowded Huntsville in
1 8 1 6.[79] Helen Toulmin limned the international parade that passed
through Fort Stoddard the following year. "We have, French, English,
Spanish, Germans, & from every part of the United States, particularly the New England States," she wrote. "The English appear amused
at everything they see, and if they are pleased, it is because *we* are not
as much like savages as they expected. The Spaniards always remind
me of some mysterious novel characters. The Germans are fine
healthy looking people, but their dialect is perfectly unintelligible to
me, and their dress bears a striking resemblance to the Choctaws."[80]
Conspicuously excluded from Toulmin's catalog were people of African descent, even though they also passed through Fort Stoddard in
large numbers.

As the public lands came to market, emigration to the Deep South
seemed to reach epidemic proportions. John Little of North Carolina
observed in the fall of 1 8 1 7, "The *Alabama* Country is all the rage in
this quarter now—Many of our people are moving to it, & more
would go, if they could sell their Land."[81] Samuel McDonald reported
to his sister that the "Alabama Fever" had struck in Georgia. "Scarce
any of those who are attacked by it ever recover," he noted, "it sooner
or later carries them off to the westward."[82] Another North Carolinian, James Graham, was astonished to see some of his oldest and
wealthiest neighbors succumbing to the epidemic. "The *Alabama Feaver*
rages here with great violence and has *carried off* vast numbers of our
Citizens," he wrote to a friend, "for as soon as one neighbour visits another who has just returned from the Alabama, he immediately dis-
covers the same symptoms which are exhibited by the person who has

seen the allureing Alabama."[83] Graham feared that, if unchecked, the rush to the new country might depopulate the old. Such anxieties became a major theme among southeastern agricultural reformers beginning in the 1830s, but in the early days of the postwar boom they seemed the grumblings of a curmudgeon.[84]

The irony in the rhetoric of migration fever was that many migrants to the Deep South suffered from all-too-real fevers when they got there. The danger was especially acute in New Orleans and Natchez, which were prone to outbreaks of yellow fever. The appearance of yellow fever in Natchez "swept off great numbers and put a stop to all business whatever," reported Thomas Gale in 1817, "perhaps no disease has ever been so fatal in any of the seaports of the U.S."[85] Edward Palfrey succumbed to yellow fever in New Orleans in 1817. His brother mourned him as "a very promising, noble hearted young man, affectionate Brother & beloved by all his acquaintances, possessed of the best disposition & every good quality that adorns the Human soul."[86] The yellow fever also killed Henry and Benjamin Latrobe, whose scheme to supply water to New Orleans ultimately led them to their graves.[87] Deep South boosters, including William Darby, insisted that the risk of disease could be minimized by caution and proper habits. Migrants should move to Louisiana in the fall to allow themselves to acclimate before the "fervid heats of summer," wrote Darby. He also suggested that the richest lands were not the healthiest, and that migrants would do well to settle on "land of second quality," where they would not make a fortune but would not die trying.[88]

Despite the risk of disease and failure, wealthy planters grasped the new opportunities available in the Deep South. Isaac Lewis Baker informed Andrew Jackson that Louisiana was "daily receiving large accessions of rich, respectable inhabitants from Maryland Virginia & the Carolinas."[89] Thomas Lewis witnessed the same phenomenon. "Ouachita is looking up at last," he wrote to Edward Livingston in 1819. "Many respectable planters from the Mississippi—Florida—

Rapide Tennessee, N & S Carolina, Georgia & Virginia have visited us this last fall & winter all appear pleased with the Country, some have purchased, others have expressed their intentions."[90] John Read, register of the land office at Huntsville, reported that "many gentlemen from the Eastern States (very considerable capitalists too) have arrivd in this Country."[91] Among them were John and James Campbell, Virginians who visited northern Alabama in December of 1817. In a gushing letter home, John reported that the town was "full of gentlemen from Virginia Kentucky and the Carolina's who like ourselves have been exploring the country." The excitement of the moment produced an esprit de corps among the explorers. "Today I accidentally stept into a Tavern and found a number of young Virginians with whom I am intimately acquainted," John admitted. "We had a most cordial salutation Some of them swore I must settle in the Territory and not think of Tennessee."[92]

Superior resources and connections allowed men of wealth and standing to make the most of their opportunities. They could depend on government surveyors for reliable information—at a price. John Coffee, the surveyor general of the Alabama Territory, contracted with his clerks for half of the proceeds they earned "for purchasing, locating, or giving information" to land seekers.[93] A confidant of Andrew Jackson and one of his lieutenants in the Creek War, Coffee was also a founding member of the Cypress Land Company and a prolific speculator in Alabama land. He eventually became one of the leading planters in northern Alabama.[94] Wealthy men also had the luxury of sending advance parties to scout out the best lands or appointing knowledgeable agents to make their purchases for them. Georgia's one-legged senator, Charles Tait, sent his son James with three slaves to Wilcox County, Alabama, in 1817 to build the new Tait homestead. The four men squatted on public land, raised a crop of corn, and waited for the government auction, when James could buy the land for his family.[95] Similarly, Israel Pickens sent his slaves to Alabama under the supervision of his brother before emigrating himself with his wife and children. Wealthier migrants could also afford better land and more of it. They generally purchased bottom lands with easy access to river transportation, relegating poorer migrants to the hill country or piney woods farther from the main routes of commerce.[96]

The spatial distribution of the slave population within the Deep South reflected the power of the wealthy to monopolize the most profitable land. In Mississippi, for instance, the four counties with slave majorities—Adams, Wilkinson, Jefferson, and Claiborne—all lined the Mississippi River. The seven counties whose slave populations amounted to less than one-quarter of the population—Perry, Pike, Lawrence, Hancock, Monroe, Jackson, and Covington—comprised pine barrens. The 1815 tax lists for Alabama's Madison County reveal a differentiation between plantation and yeoman districts at the local level. Slaveowning households were a majority in two of Madison County's fourteen militia districts, while in six districts, fewer than one-third of households owned slaves.[97] But there was no rigid segregation of planters and yeomen. Wealthy planters always had modest farmers as neighbors, and yeoman-oriented districts always contained some wealthy planters. Moreover, the majority of counties and parishes in the Deep South in 1820 (thirty-seven of sixty-nine) were middling districts, where slaves made up between one-quarter and one-half of the population.

The growth of Mississippi's Jefferson County between 1810 and 1820 reveals the expansion and enrichment of a plantation district. The county's total population increased by 75 percent in the decade, from about 4,000 people to about 7,000, but its slave population increased more than twice as fast as its free population, and the proportion of slaves in the population increased from 43 percent to 53 percent. The number and proportion of non–slave-owning households declined, while the number and proportion of households with larger slaveholdings more than doubled. Leading the pack was Isaac Ross, the county's largest slaveowner, who increased his holdings from 78

to 158 enslaved people over the decade. Almost half of all the enslaved people in Jefferson lived in households with at least 20 other
slaves. Still, even with this expansion in slaveowning, almost two-
thirds of the county's households contained 5 or fewer slaves in 1820.
Most free people in Jefferson County lived on farms, while slaves
were more likely to live on plantations.[98]

The postwar bubble burst at the end of the decade. The price of
cotton in New Orleans began to fall in 1818 and kept falling until the
mid-1820s, when it bottomed out below ten cents per pound. The
value of the Deep South's exports declined from $13 million in 1818
to $7.7 million in 1820. After increasing every year from 1814 to
1818, the average price of an adult male slave in Louisiana also fell.[99]
"We have seldom seen our market so much depressed as it has been
during the present week," wrote John Minor's factors in New Orleans
in the fall of 1819: "The numerous failures to the Eastward have
caused great alarm among those who generally buy here, & we know
none who are willing to do business to any extent for the present."[100]
Debtors despaired. Purchasers of public lands in Alabama alone owed
the national government more than $11 million dollars.[101] Worried
that they would have to forfeit their lands to the government, debtors
flooded Congress with petitions for relief. Along with other western
politicians, Senator John Walker and Representative John Crowell of
Alabama championed their cause in Washington. Congress eventually
passed a law in 1821 allowing purchasers of public lands to relinquish
the unpaid portion of their lands and retain the rest.[102]

Yet exposure to the boom-and-bust cycle of nineteenth-century
capitalism did not scare the Deep South's farmers and planters away
from the market. Burdened with debt, they involved themselves even
further in the cotton and sugar economies, and production of both
staples climbed throughout the 1820s. As John McRea wrote to Andrew Jackson in the spring of 1819, "Such an impetus has aledy been
given to the settlement of the Lands in alebama on the Tennessee
River, that nothing can permanently retard the growth of that section

of our Country."[103] The Panic of 1819 ended the postwar boom, but the great nineteenth-century expansion of slavery in the Deep South had been set in motion.

"everyone will go without a murmur"

The expansion of cotton and sugar generated an unrelenting demand for slaves in the Deep South. "The value of Negroes has enhanced to a surprizing degree within a short time past & all sorts meet a speedy & brisk sale," observed Henry Palfrey, whose vantage in a New Orleans merchant house made him a reliable witness of the postwar boom.[104] Slaves' labor was needed everywhere: in cotton fields and kitchens, in sugar mills and on steamboats, even in the stinking streets of New Orleans. To meet that demand, thousands of black people were forcibly transported to the Deep South. Some were smuggled in from Texas and Florida. Others were kidnapped from more northerly states. An increasing number were ensnared in the burgeoning—and legal—internal slave trade. As the postwar boom invigorated the buying and selling of human beings, white and black Americans both struggled with the consequences. For conscientious white people, no aspect of the postwar boom contradicted their identification of economic progress with moral progress as fully as the revival of the slave trade. Their disquiet is amply recorded in their letters, speeches, and laws. The enslaved people, who were most directly affected by the trade, faced the terror of disease, the rigor of new kinds of work, and the challenge of rebuilding their families and communities. Most adjusted to their circumstances as best they could, while others registered their discontent through flight, rebellion, and even suicide.

"Money Negroes Sugar and cotton and Land Seems to engross all their time and attention," John Landreth wrote of the citizens of St. Mary's Parish in Louisiana.[105] This is clear to all who read the correspondence of planters from the era. Their ability to amass and command slaves made the difference between mere subsistence and wealth—something Israel Pickens knew very well as he scratched away in the Alabama Territory. "I have made a settlement in the Sunflower Bend of the Tombickbe R. 15 miles below here, on a tract I bought in September 1817 at about $4 per acre," he boasted. "About 50 acres are cleared & every rod of the ballance a stiff cane break; the hands are busily cutting cane . . . I think I can make a good crop there if my hands have health."[106] The economy of the Deep South called for many different kinds of labor. There was the work of clearing, ditching, sawing, and hauling; the work of planting, weeding, cutting, and picking; and the work of gardening, cooking, washing, and cleaning. When Michael Fortier's sugar plantation was put up for sale in 1820, the advertisement in the *Louisiana Gazette* indicated that 40 of the 100 slaves being sold "have callings, such as carpenters, coopers, bricklayers, cabinet makers, plain cooks & pastry cooks &c and among the wenches good washers, ironers, pleaters and cooks."[107]

Enslaved people did not work only on sugar and cotton plantations. They worked just about everywhere there was manual labor to be done. In 1815, the Creek Trading House recorded a payment of $120 "for two negro slaves James & George for beating out the insects from the skins for the last six months."[108] Several slaves helped the Congregationalist missionary Cyrus Kingsbury erect buildings for his mission in the Choctaw nation in 1818.[109] Slave women peddled dry goods in the streets of New Orleans.[110] Those same streets were cleaned by gangs of chained slaves from the city jail, who never failed to attract the notice of visitors. "The clanking of their chains, which being fixed round the ankle are brought up along the leg and fastened to the waist, is a distressing sound," observed Benjamin Latrobe early in 1819. "They are now employed in leveling the dirt in the unpaved & cut up streets, in making stages from the levee to the ships in the harbor, & other works of mere labor, about all which they seem to go very much at their leisure."[111] In August 1820 the city leased out twenty or thirty of its chain-gang slaves to dig a ditch for Latrobe's waterworks.[112]

Like free migrants, slaves suffered from disease. They were subjected to illnesses endemic to the lowland environments where they were concentrated. "We lost a negro girl Chainy a daughter of old Esther, since coming here. Her complaint was consumption," Israel Pickens noted shortly after moving to the Alabama Territory.[113] John Minor reported to his sister that illness had struck the plantation: "20 hands are down besides a number of Children with the hooping cough." Two slaves had died and Old Roy, a skilled artisan, had contracted a hip ailment that threatened to prevent him from ever working again.[114] Twelve of Major Thomas's twenty slaves died after he transported them to Louisiana.[115] Israel Trask, the owner of a cotton textile factory in Massachusetts and a cotton plantation in Mississippi, painted a glowing portrait of his southern operations in an 1819 letter to his wife. "I have been moving our hands from 2nd Creek to Wilkinson. I spent four or five days at the lower plantation—things go on very well," he related. "The negroes are very well contented with their new habitations. They say the land is very good & they will prefer cultivating it to the 2nd Creek place . . . William has got his house whitewashed inside & out and his house makes a great show. Harriet keeps the inside very neat, but they move next week to Woodville."[116] Trask may have been doing a little whitewashing of his own. The following year James Trask reported to Israel that the slaves at the river plantation were sickly and the corn harvest poor: "The clearing, fencing, Building, and furnishing provisions &c. have been troublesome."[117]

The notoriety of the Deep South among enslaved people and their understandable reluctance to leave their homes and communities presented a problem for migrating planters who wished to move them. Before sending his people from Georgia to Alabama under the supervision of his son, Charles Tait wrote that he hoped "every one will go without a murmur." He reminded his son to treat the slaves well, especially Hercules, whose "noble & disinterested example" helped convince the others to acquiesce in their removal.[118] Another planter, James Hollyday of Mississippi's Adams County, recognized that slaves who formed their own judgments about the propriety of migration could endanger the whole enterprise. Hollyday worried about allowing his slave Emanuel to visit family back in Maryland, "as he certainly has it in his power to speak many things against the country and a word from one of their own colour will be very apt to outweigh all the persuasion that can be used by a master." Despite the risk, Hollyday seems to have leaned toward letting Emanuel go. "He is generally cautious and as he means to come back will probably be guarded. The people will I dare say give him a hearty welcome and rejoice in the opportunity of getting accurate information of their relatives & connexions here," Hollyday predicted.[119] Travel and correspondence allowed slaveowners to maintain connections to their family and friends across long distances, but most enslaved people lacked basic means of maintaining the human ties sundered by forced migration.

Farmers and planters already in the Deep South tapped distant markets for their slaves. Some looked to the North, where unscrupulous men danced around laws protecting people of color from being kidnapped or exported to the Deep South. Others bought from privateers smuggling African slaves through Texas and Florida. But even the slave country had its rules, and kidnapping and smuggling violated these. Most slave seekers turned to the upper South, especially the Chesapeake, which was quickly becoming the great fountain of forced migration. As entrepreneurs began to apply their savvy to the business of ripping families apart and dispersing them across half a continent, a regular interstate commerce in slaves began to take shape. "Should the price of negroes fall to the North," Israel Pickens plotted in 1819, "I shall wish to send to Maryland for a few next season."[120]

In 1815, slavery was legal but waning in New Jersey and New York, and all the mid-Atlantic states had substantial black populations. As demand for slave labor intensified in the South, slaveowners began to prey on black communities in the North, often with the connivance of northern authorities. It was not a new problem, but public controversy over the practice intensified.[121] In 1818 a sordid affair in New Jersey brought to light the semilegal trade in black slaves and servants.[122] A conspiracy to export black people from New Jersey appears to have been organized by Jacob Van Wickle, a judge in New

Jersey's Middlesex County, and Van Wickle's brother-in-law, a Louisiana cotton planter named Charles Morgan, who had moved from New Jersey to Louisiana in 1800. In early June, a Middlesex Country grand jury charged Charles Morgan with violating New Jersey's antiexportation law by removing sixteen black children without their consent, and one adult by force. The grand jury indicted Jacob Van Wickle's son and several other men for conveying nine black children to Morgan with intent to send them out of the state. The charges shocked local opinion, especially the accusation that the traders attempted to remove free black children to the South where, presumably, they would have been enslaved. In the end, nobody indicted in the affair was convicted. Nevertheless, responding to petitions from Middlesex, Essex, and Somerset counties and the publicity surrounding the matter, the New Jersey legislature revised and strengthened its antiexportation laws in November 1818.

Neither the publicity nor the laws deterred Morgan's associates. After passage of the new law, Lewis Compton (who had been among those indicted and acquitted) tried to remove a group of people from New Jersey for whom Jacob Van Wickle had previously signed certificates of removal. Compton took them to Pennsylvania on 7 November, three days after the law was passed. Two of his accomplices were stopped in Lebanon, where they faced trial for violating New Jersey's antiexportation laws. The judge ordered the people of color freed and placed in the custody of the Pennsylvania Abolition Society. When Compton arrived in Philadelphia to retrieve them, he was thrown in jail. In early December William Stone, Compton's frustrated partner, reported that some of Philadelphia's "straight Coat Gentry" had tried to recover one of the disputed slaves. "I ordered them out of the house," he boasted, "and told them if they ever Came to it again pimping for Negroes to spoil them I would send them out faster than they came in."[123] Though it may seem odd for Louisiana planters to have traveled all the way to New Jersey to procure slaves, the economic rationale was clear enough. Sam Steer, one of the many agents involved in the Van Wickle affair, reported having bought eighty slaves in New York at an average price of $300 each. "I think this is doing pretty well," he explained, "when even fresh imported Guinia Negroes were lately sold in NOrleans at $1500."[124]

While some planters in the Deep South looked to the North for slaves, others tapped into illegal sources of African slaves, the "fresh imported Guinea negroes" whom Sam Steer referred to. Privateers attacking Spanish shipping in the Caribbean smuggled Africans into the United States through Galveston in Texas and Amelia Island in East Florida.[125] These entrepôts drew the attention of the U.S. Navy beginning in 1817, when the captain of the U.S. frigate *Congress* reported that several hundred slaves were being held in Galveston, awaiting purchase by planters in New Orleans. They would be smuggled into Louisiana through the state's innumerable western waterways. "Every exertion will be made to intercept them," he promised, "but I have little hope of success."[126] Later that summer, the collector of customs at New Orleans, Beverly Chew, complained about Luis Aury's "motley mixture of freebooters and smugglers" operating out of Galveston. Chew reported that a New York schooner had arrived in Galveston with 287 slaves on board, all of whom were sold "to the Lafittes, Sauvinet, and other speculators in this place, who have or will resell to the planters."[127] The navy ran Aury out of Galveston in September 1817, but he reappeared on Amelia Island, just south of Georgia on the Atlantic coast in East Florida. During his two months' sojourn at Amelia, Aury managed to smuggle approximately $500,000 worth of contraband goods into Georgia, including as many as one thousand slaves.[128]

Slaveowners weighed the benefits of smuggling against its moral and social dangers. It was widely reported that Aury relied on black mercenaries and sailors. One nervous Georgian described them as "about one hundred thirty brigand negroes—a set of desperate bloody dogs." He warned the secretary of the treasury that their presence on the Gulf Coast was dangerous to the southern states: "I am told that the language of the slaves in Florida is already such as is extremely alarming."[129] Upon arriving in Amelia Island in December

1817 with the express purpose of dislodging Aury, the U.S. officers in charge took special pains to ensure that "all his black soldiers" left the island first.[130] Southern planters also worried about the Gulf Coast smugglers' indiscriminate piracy. In 1817 many of the prominent merchants of New Orleans petitioned the navy to protect their shipping from Spanish privateers. They complained that the insecurity of commerce had raised their insurance premiums to intolerably high levels.[131]

A few years later, former Louisiana congressman Thomas Bolling Robertson complained that the navy had been sent off to the coast of Africa to interdict illegal slave trading "whilst our Coast and the adjoining seas are exposed to the most daring depredations that the world has witnessed since the days of the celebrated Morgan." Although seventeen or eighteen pirates had been tried and convicted in New Orleans and condemned to death, the display of justice did not reassure Robertson. "Threats of an alarming nature thrown out by their numerous confederates have kept the inhabitants of the neighborhood and the City in a state of much anxiety and uneasiness," he informed the secretary of war. In a remarkable synthesis of all the fears of southern slaveowners, Robertson connected these local alarms with the long-standing fear of slave resistance as well as the antislavery sentiment provoked by the Missouri controversy: "I confess I do not think they will carry their audacity so far, but when I reflect on the nature of our population compounded as it is of all nations & colors, of a vast disproportion of Slaves and gangs of Pirates & desperadoes, when I observe the spreading influence of the new born black colored sympathy of our Northern and Eastern brethren, I cannot but consider our situation somewhat dangerous."[132] Southern planters wanted slaves, but they also wanted to be safe. They determined, therefore, to suppress the illegal slave trade with all its dangers.

Even after Aury's expulsion, smugglers continued to send slaves into the southern United States through Texas and Florida. Government authorities scored only a few victories against illegal slave trading, but the cases were highly publicized. The most controversial slave-smuggling case featured David Mitchell, the United States' agent to the Creeks. Mitchell was accused of conspiring to smuggle slaves from Amelia Island into Creek territory, and from there to sell slaves to planters in Georgia, Mississippi, and the Alabama Territory. Though Mitchell was never convicted of violating the laws of the United States, he was removed from his position as Creek agent under a cloud of controversy.[133] Mitchell's disgrace reflected the national consensus hostile to the importation of foreign slaves. Even Andrew Jackson called smuggling a "dreaded evil."[134] By the end of 1821, the federal government had revised the slave trade laws to provide greater incentives for enforcement and harsher penalties for violation. These laws were not completely effective, but they raised the economic and political costs of smuggling and, consequently, helped to domesticate the North American slave trade. The efforts to suppress slave smuggling rank among the various nation-building measures adopted in the Deep South during the postwar boom.[135]

Yet even in the fight against smuggling, where the constitutional authority of the U.S. government was indisputable, the southern states successfully retained their ability to control the laws' enforcement. Smuggled Africans captured by American authorities were not returned to Africa or liberated in the United States. Instead—usually after extensive litigation—they were sold in public auctions and the proceeds distributed to the state that conducted the auction and various other interested parties. After one of these auctions in Louisiana, a local newspaper bragged, "Were any proof wanting to show the riches of our state, the enormous price offered for these rude children of Africa, would be of itself sufficient."[136] One smuggling case went all the way to the Supreme Court of the United States. In June of 1818, during one of the Andrew Jackson's invasions of Florida, American naval officials near Pensacola captured three vessels (the *Louisa,* the *Merino,* and the *Constitution*) carrying more than one hundred slaves. All three vessels had embarked from Havana and were allegedly bound for New Orleans.[137] The case was heard before Judge

Charles Tait in the federal district court in the Alabama Territory, and was appealed to the U.S. Supreme Court. While the case worked its way through the courts, ten of the Africans disappeared under disputed circumstances. "No doubt they will all have new names given them," one official predicted.[138] In the end, most of the Africans were restored to the Spanish trader who had sued for them. Fifteen who were determined to have been illegally introduced into the country were ultimately auctioned by the Court of the Southern District of Alabama in front of the Mobile Hotel on 19 April 1825. They sold for a total of $8,223.[139]

In addition to grappling with the kidnapping of northern black people and the smuggling of foreign slaves, slaveowners in the Deep South also worried about the introduction of criminal and dangerous slaves from the eastern states. Proslavery reformers in the upper South had long envisioned the west and the Deep South as outlets for the most recalcitrant and dangerous slaves. In his *Arator* essays published in 1818, John Taylor argued that slave states should pass laws "compelling the sale of every negro who should run way or be convicted of theft, out of the state, or at a considerable distance from his place of residence."[140] It was customary to sell runaway slaves who had been incarcerated but not claimed by an owner, and many appear to have been bought up by slave traders. Even free blacks incarcerated in the jails of Washington, D.C., were being sold into slavery, declared John Randolph, who demanded a congressional investigation.[141] When a vessel carrying black convicts from New York arrived in New Orleans, the City Council petitioned the legislature to prevent criminal slaves from entering the state, which it did.[142] "Louisiana appears alarmed at being made the depot of the very worst class of slaves, vomitings of the jails and penitentiaries and the refuse of all the rest of the states," observed *Niles' Weekly Register*.[143] But slave traders continued to pluck slaves from eastern jails. On board the *Clio*, en route from Baltimore to New Orleans, Benjamin Latrobe encountered several slaves belonging to "the notorious slave dealer Anderson." One of these, a man named Tom, was purchased from the Baltimore jail where he had been incarcerated. Anderson paid $800 for Tom in the expectation that he would sell for $1,000 to $1,200 in New Orleans, but Tom's death on board the *Clio* cancelled the expected profit.[144]

Slaveowners used sale and the threat of sale to discipline their slaves without resorting to physical torture.[145] "Big Nance's conduct last winter caused me to determine that I should sell her," wrote Thomas Lenoir of North Carolina in 1816, "and in June last I did sell her and her two youngest children (the youngest about 6 or 8 weeks old, both girls) for 637 1/2 Dollars in bank paper."[146] James Monroe instructed his overseer in 1819 to tell a "worthless scoundrel" named Daniel "that you are authorized to sell him to the New Orleans Purchasers, and that you will do it, for the next offense."[147] Slaveowners in the Deep South also used the slave market as a means of discipline. In the summer of 1819 Henry Palfrey sent two of his slaves, Scott and Jack, to his father to be sold in Attakapas. Palfrey described the formidable Scott as "about 24 years old, a first rate Cooper, a good Blacksmith Carpenter Bricklayer Cartman & [?], can handle almost any kind of tools, is of an ingenious disposition, has been accustomed to plantation work & I will venture to say hasn't his match in Attakapas for mauling rails & chopping, speaks French English & Spanish has been in the Country about 12 years & cost me 1000$ Cash in Sept last, was once enticed away from me by a white man & was absent a month, will steal but seldom gets drunk." Jack, who was about the same age as Scott, was "a good Servant Drayman & Field Hand has been accustomed to House work & taking care of Horses, never runs away but steals & drinks sometimes has been a long time in the Country cost 700$." Palfrey wanted to sell them because they were "too unmanageable" and kept bad company in New Orleans. Hard work and a tough master would improve their character, he believed. He advised his father to sell them at the first auction "but not let them know any thing about it until the sale."[148] Louisiana's civil code gave purchasers some protection against those who would fob off difficult or diseased slaves, but in the postwar rage for labor, some purchasers did not really care whom they were buying. So Jacques Charlot purchased an African man named Bombara in January 1818 knowing full well that he was "a drunkard and has many other vices."[149]

Slaves were brought to the Deep South over land, down river, and by sea. Of all these routes, the coastal trade route is the best documented—a consequence of regulations adopted to prevent smuggling. United States Custom Service records provide some evidence as to the organization and scale of the coastal slave trade from the eastern seaboard to New Orleans. From January 1819 through December 1821, at least seventy vessels arrived at the port of New Orleans, carrying more than 3,000 slaves from the eastern seaboard. More than 850 slaves landed in New Orleans in 1819, but owing to the economic panic that gripped the Deep South late in that year, the number dropped almost by half in 1820. As the economy recovered, the slave trade rebounded vigorously in 1821, when more than 1,700 slaves were shipped to New Orleans. Just over 60 percent of the slaves shipped on these vessels were described as fifteen years old or older, and just under 60 percent of the adults were men—a reflection of the sugar planters' preference for adult male slaves. The slaves under the age of fifteen were divided almost equally between boys and girls.[150]

Most of the slaves transported by sea embarked from the Chesapeake. The Custom Service data for 1819 to 1821 reveal that almost 40 percent of the slaves embarked from Norfolk, the leading port of embarkation. Just over 25 percent of the slaves sailed from Baltimore, almost 14 percent from Richmond, and 10 percent from Petersburg and Alexandria. Another 8 percent, more than 225 slaves, sailed from Charleston, while small numbers of slaves were also shipped from Savannah and Mobile. Addressing an audience of abolitionists on the Fourth of July in 1852, Frederick Douglass recalled the dark days of his youth in Baltimore, when he "watched from the wharves the slave ships in the Basin, anchored from the shore, with their cargoes of human flesh, waiting for favorable winds to waft them down the Chesapeake."[151] In all, almost 90 percent of the slaves transported to New Orleans via the coastal trade during these years came from the Chesapeake region. What was it about the political economy of the region that made it so prodigal with slaves? Certainly the answer lies in the ongoing transition from tobacco to wheat production and the remarkable fecundity of the slave population, but dovetailing with these economic and demographic patterns was a lurking desire on the part of some white people not to be—as Spencer Roane put it—"dammed up in a land of slaves."[152]

Although some of the slaves transported on these vessels traveled with migrating owners; many others were shipped by merchants who recognized an opportunity for profit. In 1817 Abner Robinson started to send shipments of slaves from Richmond to New Orleans. In 1818 and 1819 the firm of Allan and Spann sold South Carolina slaves to Alabama. Between 1817 and 1820 Francis Everod Rives sent at least 53 slaves (28 men and 25 women) from Virginia to the slave market in Natchez, earning a profit of more than $10,000.[153] David Anderson, the "notorious slave dealer" described by Latrobe, sent at least 175 slaves from Baltimore to New Orleans from 1819 to 1821. The Anderson slaves were consigned to Hector McLean, a New Orleans merchant, who sold them in the New Orleans market. One hundred ten of the slaves that Anderson sent to New Orleans were adults, and of these, 70 were men. Among the 65 slaves under the age of fifteen that Anderson sent to McLean, 34 were girls and 31 were boys. Perhaps some of the Anderson slaves were included in McLean's July 1819 advertisement in the *Louisiana Gazette*: "We have just received from Maryland new young NEGRO MEN, which we will sell low for Cash."[154] Other merchants active in the slave trade were John Isnard and Dutillet & Sagory of New Orleans, Edwin Lee and James Tabb of Norfolk, and Samuel Woolfolk of Charleston.

Planters sometimes traveled to the upper South themselves and returned with slaves. In the spring of 1820 the Attakapas planter David Rees went to Maryland in search of slaves. He carried a letter of introduction from a fellow planter from Attakapas that identified him as a "gentleman" rather than a "*speculator* or *trader*."[155] When he arrived in Maryland, however, Rees changed his spots. Writing to a friend back home, he reported that "prime fellows" could be purchased for $350, women and boys aged twelve to sixteen could be purchased for $250, and girls for $200. At these prices, Rees suggested, investors could reap 100 percent net profits by reselling the slaves in Louisiana. "I have thought you might perhaps wish to purchase some more Negroes yourself for your plantations or that perhaps some of your friends might be willing to adventure in a speculation of that kind."[156] When Rees returned to Louisiana in November, he advertised the sale of sixteen "likely young negroes of both sexes, among which are two young women, one with four & the other with three fine children, a young creole girl &c."[157] For the right price, a man could be a respectable planter one day and a slave trader the next.[158]

Undocumented by customs officials, the interior slave trade from Kentucky and Tennessee to the Deep South also flourished. Responding to an inquiry from Edward Livingston in 1816, a merchant in Shippingport, Kentucky, discovered that his state's cupboard was momentarily bare. "We find that within the last three or four months there has been four or five persons purchasing for the New Orleans Market," he reported, "they have been all over the State and have purchased every Negro (good or bad) that has been offered for sale within that time."[159] On his way from Virginia to the Alabama Territory in November 1818, John Owen and his family found themselves "pestered with travelers & negro drivers" in Tennessee.[160] That same year, Henry Bradshaw Fearon claimed to have seen fourteen flatboats loaded with slaves floating down the Mississippi River from Kentucky.[161] Traders already had a bad reputation, as one resident of Nashville indicated when he advertised a slave for sale in the Nashville *Whig.* The notice stipulated that the man "will not be sold to those who buy to carry down the river."[162] Further evidence of the interior slave trade comes from advertisements for runaways. Harry, a slave incarcerated in the jail of Ascension Parish, told the sheriff that "he lately came from Baltimore to Kentucky, and was brought thence to this country by one Mr. John Denney, with a drove of horses."[163]

Becca, an "artful" twelve-year-old girl with dimples, ran away from J. Metcalfe in March 1819. "She came from Kentucky in December last, where she was bought by Mr Ross Prather, of Mason County," he noted.[164]

Like kidnapping, smuggling, and the transportation of criminals, the interstate slave trade became controversial. Northern visitors were horrified at the trade, which treated human beings no better than animals. Aghast at the sight of a slave auction in Huntsville, the missionary Elias Cornelius noted in his journal, "The miserable objects of this traffic are bought in the old states and driven like cattle to the western market where they are sold & bought with as little compunction of conscience as if they were so many hogs or sheep."[165] After witnessing the slave markets of Natchez and New Orleans in 1818, the New Hampshire native Estwick Evans lamented in his memoir, "How deplorable is the condition of our country! So many bullocks, so many swine, and so many human beings in our market!"[166] But it was not just northerners who decried the internal slave trade. Mississippi governor David Holmes warned the state legislature in 1817 that "great numbers [of slaves] will be brought to this State, and principally those of the most vicious character, unless by some means we can render the trade at least precarious to those who engage in it."[167] The state legislature went so far as to pass a law in 1819 regulating the importation of slaves into the state. The law required all persons bringing a slave into Mississippi to register the slave with local authorities and to swear that the slave had not been guilty of murder, burglary, arson, rape, or grand larceny, according to the knowledge or belief of the owner. Furthermore, each slave brought into the state for sale as merchandise would be subject to a $20 tax, and if the tax was not paid, the slave could be seized and sold at public auction. Pursuant to the state's constitution, the law did not apply to residents of the state who imported a slave from another state or territory "for their own use."[168]

Mississippi's law was quickly challenged by a group of slaveowners and struck down by the state's High Court, which—in a remarkable concession to national sovereignty—held that the law violated the interstate commerce clause of the U.S. Constitution. Chief Justice John Taylor "would not say, because it was not before him, how far the state might go in prohibiting the importation or introduction of slaves from other states in the regulations of its intercourse with them, but that we had no power to *permit* the introduction and raise a *revenue* from it he was clear."[169] The interstate slave trade defied statutory regulation for another fifty years, despite sporadic attempts by legislatures in the Deep South to rein in the trade. It is hardly surprising that the trade was not curtailed, since this could not have been done in any serious way without trampling southern slaveowners' cherished rights of property. The fact that legislatures in the Deep South even considered the problem indicates white southerners' lingering dissatisfaction with the slave trade.[170]

Forced migration took a terrible toll on black people. At Mitchell's Stand in the Choctaw nation, the missionary Elias Cornelius came across a black man named Aaron who declared himself to be a member of a Baptist church near Frankfort, Kentucky. In a drunken rage, Aaron's former owner had sold him to a slave trader heading down the river, severing the unfortunate man from his wife and two children. The trader abandoned Aaron in New Orleans, where yellow fever was raging. He tried to return to Kentucky but was captured by the trader and sold to Mitchell in the Choctaw nation, which is where Cornelius met him. Aaron informed the clergyman that he had refused to take another black woman for his wife "on the ground of Christian principle." The story moved Cornelius, who recorded it in his journal. "It was very affecting to my heart to hear the poor creature lament his absence from his wife & children whom he said he loved," Cornelius wrote. "His last request was that I would pray for him."[171]

Most transplanted slaves appear to have resigned themselves to their fate, but at least some fought back by running away. Southwestern slaveowners' own advertisements for runaway slaves attest to the dislocations and discontent caused by the transplantation system.[172] E. E. Parker advertised a reward for the return of his slave David, "only a short time come from Washington County, Kentucky, where he probably intends returning."[173] Dick, another Kentucky slave, was brought to New Orleans toward the end of June 1818 and entrusted to the slave-trading firm of DuBourg and Baron. The company hired Dick out as a cook and a shoemaker "to be assured of his capacity," then sold him to Giuseppe Jourdani on 31 July, but he ran away while working on the levee in Faubourg St. Mary.[174] Charles "alias Seymour" arrived in New Orleans from Baltimore on the *Clio* in the spring of 1818 and soon ran away. He was discovered on board the *Eagle* bound for Liverpool and was returned to his owner.[175] That same year Peter Isler, a Natchez slaveowner, advertised a $100 reward for Nace, a mulatto slave in his late teens who was "accustomed to riding races, is fond of that sport, and boasts of his talent as a rider." Nace had been born in Maryland, had traveled to Tennessee with a new owner in 1812 or 1813, and was purchased by Isler in Natchez in late 1817 but had run away soon afterward. Isler supposed that Nace would be "lurking" in New Orleans, but suggested that he might have gone to New York "in order to be remote and avoid apprehension."[176] Although New Orleans was a locus of the slave trade, its maritime milieu offered opportunities for escape and more violent resistance.

A few enslaved people took great risks and committed heinous acts to prevent themselves from ending up in the Deep South. Early in 1820, thirty Virginia slaves on a vessel sailing to New Orleans plotted "to murder all the passengers and crew except two sailors who was to steer them to St. Domingo." A woman belonging to Henry Blanchard exposed the plot, and the conspirators were put in irons.[177] The following year, *Niles' Weekly Register* reported that a Baltimore man had cut his own throat rather than board a ship bound for New Orleans.[178] Episodes such as these were very rare—slavery would not have survived if they had been common—but their occurrence reveals the deep despair of those at the bottom of the market revolution.

"everything at stake"

The postwar boom forced white people in the United States to reckon with slavery in a new and urgent way. One side recognized that American slavery would not die a natural death; the other feared that it might be legislated into oblivion. The Deep South had a part to play in this reckoning. The expansion of slavery there—accompanied as it was by reports of slave smuggling, kidnapping of free people of color, and slave coffles trekking across the country—contributed to the growth of antislavery opinion in the North. At the same time, the emergence of the Deep South bolstered the strength of what would later be known in the North as the "slave power." Slaveowners in the Deep South believed in the need for slavery and in their own benevolence as masters. The region's proslavery representatives in Congress gave the slave power added leverage during the Missouri crisis, an important moment in American political history and the history of American slavery.[179]

When Ethan Allen's grandson Henry Hitchcock arrived in the Alabama Territory from the Green Mountains of Vermont, he was still enough of a Yankee to believe that slavery was unnecessary. "White men can work here as well as elsewhere," he wrote to a friend in 1817.[180] Hitchcock was right. Nonslaveholding free white men and women managed to grow corn and cotton on their farms in Alabama and Mississippi, as they did elsewhere in the South, generally for household consumption and local markets.[181] (And after emancipation, cotton production in the southern United States would far surpass antebellum levels.) But Hitchcock succumbed to the relentless social pressure to buy slaves and get rich. By 1820 he had come to believe that slaves were "the most profitable species of property" and that people of African descent were better off enslaved.[182]

The Louisiana planter and former general James Wilkinson explained why southwestern cotton and sugar planters relied so heavily on slave labor. Although all men "of virtue & Intelligence" believed slavery was a curse, he admitted in 1821, slaveowners yielded to "habit, indolence & ease."[183] Each term in Wilkinson's frank and pithy self-indictment merits elaboration. Slavery had been a dominant relation in the southern regions of North America for more than a century, and even longer in the Caribbean and elsewhere. Antislavery, rather than slavery, was the world-historical innovation of the era. This was essentially the position taken by the Louisiana Supreme Court in an 1817 case. "Slavery," it asserted, "notwithstanding all that may have been said and written against it, as being unjust, arbitrary, and contrary to the laws of human nature, we find, in history, to have existed from the earliest ages of the world, down to the present day."[184] The argument from habit sloughed off slaveowners' moral responsibility for slavery like dead skin.

But the expansion of slavery in the Deep South was not merely the continuation of a conventional social relation. It was also the specific response of southwestern planters to the difficulty of exploiting free people in a system dedicated to the production of agricultural commodities for the world market. Slaveowners argued that people of African descent were better suited for hard labor in the southern climate than were white people. This racist libel masked a deeper truth about power. Free people demanded exorbitant wages, resented close supervision, and struck off on their own as soon as they were able. Whatever their national origin or racial designation, free people chafed at working in other people's fields, and they could avail themselves of local, regional, and national resources—especially access to land—to fend off exploitation. Slaves, in contrast, lacked these resources, and as a result, they could be forced to labor under the most severe climatic and epidemiological conditions. Slaves could be forced to perform tasks that free people would not accept and had the capacity to refuse. The disrupted character of their communal networks and their exclusion from the political "people" rendered them exploitable.[185]

When planters actually expressed a preference for white or black workers, they invariably preferred the black. In March 1818 Henry Palfrey suggested to his father that he expand his labor force, which was small compared with the extent of his arable lands. "I might be able to get a few hands either white or black," he wrote.[186] His father replied that he did not need any more workers for the present year, and he especially did not need any of the recently arrived German immigrants. "I do not think they would at any time answer as labourers to depend on to make a crop," he wrote, "several of them have been brought to Attakapas within a month or two past, they are very apt to run away & besides being natives of a northern climate they would not be able to stand the heat of a vertical sun & I should from motives of humanity be unwilling to expose them to it."[187] Palfrey thus tangled together the various logics that underpinned the racism of slavery. White workers were harder to capture if they ran away. They were less accustomed to work in a hot climate. And finally, principles of "humanity" applied to them and, presumably, not to people of African descent. Edward Livingston's overseer also compared Germans unfavorably with black slaves. The German workers employed on Livingston's plantation were very hard to please, he complained, and "the work that can be got from them is about half the work that Cold be got out of the same number of Negros."[188] In 1821 Robert Cary Nicholas invited a friend to join him as an overseer on a new plantation in Mississippi. All he needed was ten laborers and a woman to cook and wash. "The hands may be black or white," he wrote, "black much to be preferred."[189] The preference for slave over free labor had even infiltrated the national government by 1820. Federal contractors fortifying the Deep South appealed to Secretary of War John Calhoun for funds to hire or purchase slave laborers. Calhoun agreed that, in the climate of Louisiana, "the employment of slaves to work on the fortifications has many advantages over that of white men, drawn from the northern States."[190]

Wilkinson's third and last rationale for slavery was ease, meaning affluence or wealth, one of the unmistakable benefits of slave-owning. "A man's estate consists in the number of his slaves, which here vary from 5 to 50," Henry Hitchcock observed in the Alabama Territory.[191] A planter's income was largely determined by the size of his crop, which was in turn determined by amount of labor—or "hands"—he commanded. "All the farmers in this country are clearing between four and five hundred dollars to the hand. I am told from the best authority that there has not been a single instance of any person settling in this country who has had anything of a capital who has not become wealthy in a few years," wrote John Campbell.[192] Visiting a large plantation on the Bayou Teche, John Landreth learned that it produced "one hundred and twenty hogs heads of Sugar and Eighty Bales of Cotton from the labour of Sixty hands and corn more than sufficient for home consumption which will leave for Sale produce which from the present prices will amount to twenty two thousand dollars."[193] Chattel slavery was at bottom a class relationship enforced by physical coercion in which some people lived off the labor of others.

Some slaveholders, particularly those with religious scruples, tried to infuse the master-slave relationship with ethical content.[194] The effort was not unique to the Deep South, but the evident commercialism of slavery there made it a more difficult and more crucial task. Some masters prided themselves on their benevolence. Thus Fulwar Skipwith, a Louisiana planter, bragged to his kinswoman Lelia Tucker about his treatment of his slaves. Even though his slaves had started out as "stiff labourers" and "awkward pickers," Skipwith wrote, "I have succeeded in bringing them to a sense of duty and subordination, surpassed by none, and with less severity, than I have ever witnessed elsewhere."[195] In a similar vein, John Coffee required his overseers "to keep the Negroes in good order and subjection at all times, as well as on Sundays and nights as when they are at work, to correct them when it is necessary, and at the same time treat them humanely, as much so as their conduct merit."[196] Edward Livingston braided together interest and humanity in an offer to purchase thirty slaves from Andrew Jackson. He promised to keep the slaves on his own plantation, where "they will be sure of good treatment, which from your humanity I know will be a considerable inducement."[197] It may have been exchanges such as these that compelled Timothy Flint to assert that slaveowners in the Deep South "have finally become impressed, that humanity is their best interest, that cheerful, well-fed, and clothed slaves, perform so much more productive labour as to unite speculation and kindness in the same calculation."[198]

Evangelical leaders in the Deep South looked to Scripture to defend slavery and reform it at the same time. Thomas Griffin, a Vir-
ginia-born Methodist who had risen to prominence in Mississippi,
criticized antislavery Methodists from the North at the Methodist
General Conference in 1820. "If it be offensive and sinful to own
slaves," Griffin remarked, "I wish someone would just put his finger
on the place in Holy Writ."[199] Griffin urged Methodists to do more to
convert slaves to Christianity, which he thought would be a great
boon to the slave regime. Like the Methodists, the Mississippi Baptists
did not oppose slavery but urged instead a more godly form of it. In
an 1819 circular letter titled "Duty of Masters and Servants," the Mississippi Baptist Association urged masters to be just, kind, and prudent in their treatment of slaves, and to attend to the slaves' food,
clothing, and religion. In turn, they instructed slaves to accept that
their position was ordained by God. They should be "industrious,
honest, faithful, submissive and humble," and should "obey your
earthly masters with fear and trembling, whether they are perverse
and wicked, or pious and gentle."[200] These efforts laid the groundwork for the maturation and elaboration of proslavery Christianity
later in the nineteenth century, when Deep South clergymen rou-
tinely championed the duties of masters and slaves, emphasizing especially the duties of slaves.

There were white people in the Deep South who deprecated slavery, but finding them is not easy. The Mississippi slaveowner William
Johnson petitioned the state legislature in 1820 to allow him to free a
slave. The act of manumission, he explained, would "extend the hand
of humanity to a rational creature, on whom unfortunate complexion
custom & even Law in this Land of freedom, has conspired to rivet
the fetters of Slavery."[201] During the Missouri debates, the editor of a
Natchez newspaper argued that slavery would ruin the West as large
capitalists engrossed the land and slaves wore out the soil. He even
expressed regret over "the singular anomaly of a nation boasting of its
freedom, asserting itself the champion of the rights of man, and establishing a constitution, securing those rights, and at the same time pos-

sessing no power to prevent, but on the contrary, by that very constitution recognizing the perpetuation of bondage."[202] Yet even as he deplored slavery, the newspaper's editor advocated the strictest possible policing of Mississippi's slave population. "If slavery must be kept up at all," he insisted, "no half way measures will answer."[203]

It was easier to criticize from afar. William Darby's migration to Pennsylvania appears to have loosened his tongue with respect to slavery. In his otherwise laudatory 1817 treatise on Louisiana, Darby charged that slaveholding demoralized and debauched white people. "No country where negro slavery is established," he argued, "but must bear in part the wounds inflicted on nature and justice."[204] An Alabamian studying medicine in London in 1818 wrote a long letter to a friend suggesting a plan of (very) gradual emancipation. The further introduction of slaves into Alabama should be prohibited, he proposed, and the offspring of slaves already in the state emancipated at the age of twenty, with their owners obligated to educate them. The white population would eventually overwhelm the black, which would "soon be amalgamated and lost in the map." The medical student (and future delegate to the Confederate Provisional Congress) anticipated that his friend might consider him a "fanatical enthusiast" and allowed, if that was the case, to "let the subject rest in silence." But he also warned, "It cannot sleep eternally."[205] And having returned from the wilds of Mississippi to the comforts of Delaware, the Quaker surveyor Isaac Briggs implored John Calhoun to find an antidote to the "moral and political poison" of slavery.[206]

In his 1825 memoir, the former overseer James Pearse authored probably the harshest critique of slavery in the Deep South to appear in the first quarter of the nineteenth century. A Massachusetts native, Pearse moved to Mississippi in the winter of 1818–19 with his wife and children. Once there, the family struggled with disease—one of his daughters died from a fever. He got a job as an overseer but clashed with the slaves he managed and the planter who employed him. Pearse finally gave up on the Deep South and returned his family to the North, where he wrote his memoir "to shew the evil of emigrating from free, to slave states." He argued that the Deep South was no place for poor white people. The climate wrecked their health and morals: "I have known many of this class, who have died in a few years; others become broken in health and spirits, fall into dissipation, and become lost to themselves, and to the world." Pearse further argued that slavery bred habits of cruelty and arrogance among slaveowners—not just toward black people but toward everyone of inferior status. And then there were the special terrors inflicted on enslaved people, including the whip and the threat of sale. Pearse knew these well; he had handled a whip himself. Reflecting on his experience, Pearse concluded that slavery was "a moral evil" and should be abolished.[207]

Controversy over slavery came to a national head early in 1819, with what became known as the Missouri crisis. Missouri applied for admission into the Union with a state constitution that resembled Alabama's, including an article protecting slaveowners' right to hold slave property. Representative James Tallmadge of New York, leading those opposed to the expansion of slavery, moved to amend the bill for Missouri's statehood to prohibit the further introduction of slaves into Missouri and to provide for the freedom of the children of slaves already there.[208] Northern supporters of the Tallmadge amendment launched a fierce, unprecedented volley of opinion against expanding slavery into the new state. Slavery was cruel and immoral, they contended, and had to be stopped. It retarded economic and social progress. It vivified the domestic market for slaves, which would stimulate illegal smuggling and kidnapping. And it augmented the slave power—the political strength of slaveowners in Congress. None of these arguments was new, but they were tied to a novel political tactic and advanced with a new urgency. The novel tactic was Tallmadge's attaching a restrictive condition to Missouri's admission as a state, rather than to its organization as a territory. The new urgency derived from the weakness of diffusionist logic in the face of the slave population's evident natural increase. As the Baltimore political economist Daniel Raymond charged, diffusion was "about as effectual a remedy for slavery as it would be for the smallpox."[209]

That Tallmadge did not demand the same restrictions on slavery in Alabama as he did in Missouri suggests how deeply rooted slavery had already become in the Deep South. Alabama unequivocally belonged to the slaveholding section of the country. The 1818 census of the Alabama Territory had already disclosed a slave population exceeding 21,000 people, or more than 30 percent of the territory's population.[210] They lived adjacent to the slave states of Georgia, Tennessee, and Mississippi, and Tallmadge acknowledged the danger of mixing emancipated black people with slaves. "I had learned from southern gentlemen the difficulties and dangers of having free blacks intermingling with slaves," he told the House of Representatives, "and, on that account, and with a view to the safety of the white population of the adjoining states, I would not even advocate the prohibition of slavery in the Alabama territory; because, surrounded as it was by slave-holding states, and with only imaginary lines of division, the intercourse between slaves and free blacks could not be prevented, and a servile war might be the result."[211] But Missouri was differently situated. It belonged to the West, not the South. White people could tolerate the climate, so slavery was not necessary. Few slaves already lived there, so emancipation would not threaten its neighbors. If the march of slavery across North America was going to be halted, opponents of slavery had to hold the line in Missouri.

Tallmadge's amendment and its accompanying antislavery polemics threatened slaveowners' power and insulted their way of life. Slavery's defenders in the Deep South felt no less a sense of urgency than their northern opponents. "We have everything at stake," wrote Charles Tait, "not only political power & consideration, but domestic tranquility & social repose."[212] Writing to his wife during a break in the debate, Louisiana representative Thomas Butler insisted that the Missouri question was "of immense importance to the Southern section of the union & it is absolutely necessary that every southern member should be at his post."[213] Leading planter-politicians in the Deep South considered the proposed prohibition on slavery in Missouri a harbinger. "It is believed by some, & feared by others, that [Tallmadge's amendment] is merely the entering wedge," reported Ala-

bama senator John Walker, "and that it points already to a total emancipation of the blacks."[214] Mississippi representative Christopher
Rankin was one of those who saw a dangerous precedent in the re-
strictionist position. "These doctrines lead to an unlimited exercise of
power," he asserted, "to a declaration that slavery does not exist
within the United States; but if it does, that congress may abolish it,
or confine it to narrow limits." Rankin warned supporters of the
Tallmadge Amendment: "You conduct us to an awful precipice, and
hold us over it."[215] The urgent tone of these warnings and Tait's allusion to "domestic tranquility" hint at slaveowners' fear that the agitation over slavery in Missouri might provoke a slave rebellion. Andrew
Jackson was explicit on the point. The Missouri question, he wrote to
his nephew, "will excite those who is the subject of discussion to insinuation & massacre."[216] Such fears were not entirely irrational. In
1816 Barbadian planters had blamed a large slave rebellion on a debate in Parliament over the registration of slaves in the West Indies.
The insurrection and its alleged causes were reported in American
newspapers, and slaveowners were surely aware of it.[217]

Opponents of the Tallmadge amendment devoted most of their attention to the constitutional argument that the restriction violated
state sovereignty. They argued that requiring Missourians to accept a
restriction that had not been required of any other state violated the
principle of equality between the states. It also violated the terms of
the treaty with France that guaranteed to Missouri's inhabitants the
same rights enjoyed by citizens of the United States. All that the
Constitution required of a new state was that it should exceed a certain threshold of population and extent, and its form of government
should be "republican." Slavery, moreover, belonged to Missouri's domestic affairs and was not a proper object for regulation by the national government. The constitutional authority to prohibit the importation of slaves did not extend to the migration of slaves from one
state to another, argued opponents of restriction. Among the many
debaters who articulated the sovereignty argument was Mississippi
senator Walter Leake, who contended that because "the power to

hold, possess, and regulate this property, has not been delegated to the United States, nor prohibited to the States; then a State, within the meaning of the Constitution, possesses sole control over it, and the United States possess none."[218]

Some of the more ardent defenders of slavery were not content to let the argument rest on constitutional grounds. They also felt compelled to answer for the morality and policy of slavery, and in particular, for slavery's expansion. Representative William Pinckney of South Carolina boldly stated the proslavery case. "The great body of slaves are happier in their present situation than they could be in any other," he declared on the floor of the House, "and the man or men who would attempt to give them freedom, would be their greatest enemies."[219] Some white southerners, including Thomas Jefferson, clung to the fiction that the dispersal of the slave population would lead to gradual emancipation, but the diffusionist argument shifted in a subtle and important way. Its advocates shied away from gradual emancipation and toward the amelioration of slaves' conditions. In its rehabilitated form, diffusionism yoked the new proslavery humanitarianism to the expansion of slavery. It would be cruel, charged diffusionists, to confine slaves to the southeastern states, where increasing poverty and repression would be their fate. As Christopher Rankin bluntly argued, "No man has passed through the States of Kentucky, Tennessee, Mississippi and Alabama, who does not know that [the slaves'] condition is much better there than in the old States."[220]

The Missouri question tested slaveowners' strength in Congress, where all the demographic, social, and political developments of the previous three decades had changed the balance of power between the free and slave portions of the country. The most important development was that the population in states where slavery did not exist or was dying out had increased faster than the population in states where slavery did exist and was expanding. This demographic trend widened the free states' advantage in the House of Representatives despite the three-fifths clause, which more and more slaveowners recognized was not the bulwark they had once anticipated. The first House vote on the Tallmadge Amendment in 1819 demonstrated the dominance of the nonslaveholding states. Representatives from the slave states voted sixty-six to one against the Tallmadge Amendment, but it passed on the strength a vote of eighty-six to ten in its favor by representatives from the nonslaveholding states. Southern representatives were nearly unanimous in opposing the restriction, and a small but significant number of northern representatives sided with them.[221]

Losing ground in the House of Representatives, slaveowners fell back on the Senate, where the addition of five slave states between 1789 and 1819—Kentucky, Tennessee, Louisiana, Mississippi, and Alabama—allowed them to maintain their power. In particular, the division of the Mississippi Territory and the recent admission of Alabama had solidified the slave power just in time to confront the Missouri challenge. The six votes of Louisiana, Alabama, and Mississippi weighed more in the Senate than did their three votes in the House. Charles Tait, who had been so instrumental in dividing the Mississippi Territory and ushering Alabama into statehood, congratulated himself on his own foresight in 1820, explaining to John Walker that the gambit "has given us more strength in the Senate."[222] Indeed, the Senate rejected the restriction on slavery in Missouri and pressured the House to relent. As in the House, in the Senate slaveowners' power benefited from the support of a few northerners. During the Missouri debates, the two senators from Illinois, Ninian Edwards and Jesse Thomas, as well as Harrison Gray Otis of Massachusetts, Abner Lacock of Pennsylvania, and William Palmer of Vermont, opposed restriction, along with every southern senator.[223]

In the end, the Missouri Compromise famously admitted Missouri as a slave state and—in a measure proposed by Illinois's Jesse Thomas —prohibited slavery in all other territories of the Louisiana Purchase above the thirty-sixth parallel. Maine was also admitted, but as a free state, preserving the sectional balance in the Senate. The Deep South largely supported the compromise. Missouri's admission as a slave state passed in the House by three votes—coincidentally, the number of votes cast by representatives from Louisiana (Thomas Butler), Mississippi (Christopher Rankin), and Alabama (John Crowell). Rankin and Crowell joined the compromisers who voted for the Thomas proviso, while Butler joined the southern radicals who opposed it. All six senators from the Deep South states voted for the admission of Missouri as a slave state, and five of the six supported the Thomas proviso. The Deep South's support for the Missouri compromise distinguished it from the old centers of the slave power, where opposition to the Thomas proviso was strong. (Seven of eight senators and thirty-two of forty-nine representatives from Virginia, North Carolina, South Carolina, and Georgia voted against the Thomas proviso.) Though direct evidence is lacking, there are several possible explanations for the strong support for the Missouri Compromise in the Deep South. One is the powerful postwar nationalism of its leaders. They owed much to the United States. Another is that the future of the Deep South depended on attracting slaveowning migrants from the southeastern states, and so its leaders had little incentive to see the whole, vast Louisiana territory opened up to them. Finally it must be remembered that the citizens of the Deep South were concerned about securing relief for the purchasers of public lands in the wake of declining cotton prices, and their political representatives may have been trying to forge a western alliance to accomplish that goal.[224]

The controversy surrounding the admission of Missouri signaled to leading nationalist politicians in the United States that the slavery issue could break the Union and should be removed from national debate. James Monroe, for instance, concluded that "the further acquisition of territory to the west & South, involves difficulties of an internal nature, which menace the union itself."[225] By the end of 1821, the two major controversies over slavery—the slave trade and geographic expansion—were settled for a generation. Revisions in the slave trade laws quelled agitation over smuggling, while the slave power blocked any consideration of further federal regulation or prohibition of the internal slave trade. The Adams-Onís Treaty secured Florida to the United States and abandoned U.S. claims to Texas and northern Mexico. In tandem with the Missouri Compromise, the treaty effectively resolved the explosive question of slavery's territorial expansion for a generation. No new states were added to the Union for fifteen years. So far as slaveowners in the Deep South were concerned, these arrangements inaugurated a golden age, which lasted twenty-five years. The white and black population steadily increased, cotton and sugar production expanded, and the remaining southern Indians were either expelled or brought under the jurisdiction of state laws. Not until the various settlements of 1819 to 1821 collapsed following the Mexican War did the slave country again face a serious challenge from its northern foes.[226]

Epilogue

JOHN EADIS'S ODYSSEY spanned an epoch in the history of American slavery. Born around 1790 in Africa, he was transported across the Atlantic Ocean and ended up as a slave in Virginia. He was later taken to the Mississippi Territory "for sale." There (he claimed) he served as a drummer with Jackson's army. In the summer of 1818, he shipped out from New Orleans on the *Mary* but was captured at the mouth of the Mississippi and thrown in jail. A sparse account of his travels appeared in a notice published in the *Louisiana Gazette* requesting that his legal owner come to get him. There is a bitter irony in the fact that Eadis's life in the slave country was documented only because of his failed attempt to escape it.[1] This book has tried to map John Eadis's vast world of captivity and movement, paying special attention to the topography of power, and it has explored one part of that world in great detail, the region that became the Deep South of the United States in the decades following the American Revolution.

A unique conjunction created the Deep South between the 1780s and 1820s and shaped it in distinctive ways. Two new crops, each with its own geographic, economic, and demographic characteristics, took root in the Deep South. The takeoff of industrial production in the cotton-textile manufactories of Great Britain increased demand for short-staple cotton, which flourished in the soil and climate of the Deep South. Meanwhile the slave rebellion in St. Domingue reshuffled sugar production throughout the Americas and made it possible for planters around New Orleans to profit from the commercial cultivation of sugar, which was sold largely to North American consumers. The rise of cotton and sugar renewed, intensified, and enlarged the region's connections to the North American, Caribbean, and transatlantic economies. For better or for worse, the slave-owning farmers and planters of the Deep South placed themselves in the transatlantic division of labor as producers of agricultural commodities, which left them dependent on outside market forces largely beyond their control. "We only breathe by commerce," explained a New Orleans merchant.[2]

New economic opportunities drew people to the Deep South by the thousands. Free and enslaved migrants arrived from the United States, the Caribbean, and Africa, swelling the population to roughly 400,000 by 1820. Migrants' adjustment to life in the Deep South was often difficult, and the attempt was occasionally fatal, especially for the downtrodden. "A stranger without money need have no surer passport to his grave than to be taken with a fever any where along the banks of the Mississippi," observed a military officer.[3] Relations between newcomers and the prior inhabitants defied simple generalizations. The pattern of interaction ranged from violent conflict in the Indian backcountry to casual intermingling on the New Orleans levee, where Benjamin Latrobe observed "white men and women, & all hues of brown, & all classes of faces, from round Yankees, to drisly & lean Spaniards, black negroes & negresses, filthy Indians half naked, mulattoes, curly & straight-haired, quarteroons of all shades, long-haired & frizzled, the women dressed in the most flaring yellow & scarlet gowns, men capped & hatted."[4] The influx of diverse peoples enriched what was already one of the most culturally diverse corners of the world.

The extension of U.S. sovereignty shaped the Deep South in important ways. The United States absorbed the region through diplomacy and conquest, administered its territorial governments, and then incorporated it into the federal structure of the American Union as the three states of Louisiana, Mississippi, and Alabama. The national government encouraged economic development in its new acquisitions through nation-building measures that included the survey and sale of public lands, the improvement of the transportation infrastructure, and the imposition of a tariff on foreign sugar. It eventually restricted the importation of foreign slaves but allowed the transfer of slaves into the region from elsewhere in the United States in a policy of domestication and diffusion that reflected proslavery economic interests and national concerns over the safety of the slave country. Slaveowners and their allies successfully harnessed the resources of the new United States to defend and extend plantation slavery in the early national era. By the time that antislavery forces took a firm stand against the introduction of Missouri as a slave state in 1819, the phenomenal expansion of slavery in the southwestern states was well under way.

The whole enterprise involved terror and violence. An epoch of war and revolution throughout the Atlantic world brought the Deep South into the United States and carried many thousands of people to its shores. The American Revolution, the slave rebellion and civil wars in St. Domingue, the Napoleonic Wars and their North American adjunct, the War of 1812, all contributed to the rise of the Deep South. The Creek War allowed the United States to wrest millions of acres of fertile land from the southern Indian nations, which were left immeasurably weakened as a result. The expansion of slavery spread violence throughout everyday life in forms ranging from individual struggles between masters and slaves to the once-in-a-lifetime slave rebellion on the Mississippi River's German Coast in 1811. In the words of Alexander Meek, one of Alabama's first historians, the region was "wrought and consecrated through a bitter sacrament of blood."[5] The violence that accompanied American expansion in the Deep South tragically followed from Jefferson's utopian vision of an empire of liberty moving peacefully across the continent.

Though the expansion of slavery in the Deep South may seem inevitable in hindsight, it did not go unchallenged at the time. Isaac Briggs and Tom Paine registered their dissent in eloquent, futile letters to Thomas Jefferson. Small numbers of congressmen actively opposed slavery's expansion in the Deep South, but they did not prevail. Dissident Indians tried to prevent the United States from gobbling up their lands. Enslaved people ran away from their owners, and some even rebelled. It is tempting to wonder what might have happened if the German Coast slave rebellion, the Creek War, and the British invasion had all occurred at the same time. Would the citizens of the Deep South have been able to respond to these crises all at once, or would the combination have overwhelmed them? At the very least the disruption to plantation slavery in the Deep South would have been deeper and more enduring. But that is not what happened. Each challenge followed its own historical rhythm and, consequently, the citizens of the slave country were able to beat them back, one after the other. These victories gave powerful material and ideological support to the expansion of slavery in the subsequent generation. Slavery marched together with Jacksonian nationalism.

From the 1820s to the 1850s, the demographic, economic, and political weight of plantation slavery in the United States continued to shift to the south and west. A few statistics demonstrate the point. The population of Alabama, Mississippi, and Louisiana increased from about 400,000 people in 1820 to almost 2.5 million in 1860, evenly divided between white and black. The three states accounted for 20 percent of the population of the southern states and 8 percent of the whole country's population in 1860. Almost one in three slaves in the United States lived in the Deep South on the eve of the Civil War.[6] As the Deep South grew in population, the region was drawn more closely into the cultural orbit of the southeastern United States. English-speaking, Protestant migrants came to outnumber the original inhabitants. More than half of all white people in the Deep South in 1850 were born outside the region, and about one-third came from the southeastern states.[7] The slave population was also augmented by migrants. Historians estimate that more than 1.1 million enslaved people moved from slave-exporting to slave-importing states during these years, and more than half of them went to the Deep South. Forced migration was central to their experience.[8]

The plantation complex of the Deep South advanced along with the population. Alabama, Mississippi, and Louisiana produced just over 600,000 bales of cotton in 1819–20, which accounted for about one-fourth of the country's cotton production. By 1859–60, they were the top three cotton-producing states in the Union, generating almost five million bales annually, or more than 60 percent of the country's cotton.[9] Louisiana's sugar growers, the technological vanguard of southern agriculture, increased their output tenfold from the 1820s to the 1850s. During the peak years in the 1850s, Louisianians annually produced about four hundred million pounds of sugar.[10] More than half of all U.S. plantations with 100 or more slaves were located in the Deep South in 1860. At the same time, New Orleans rose nearly to the prominence that all its early nineteenth-century boosters had imagined. The average annual receipts at New Orleans increased from $16 million in the years 1823 to 1825 to $165 million in 1856 to 1860. The dollar value of its exports far exceeded that of any other southern port and was second only to New York, which processed a substantial share of the cotton shipped from New Orleans. Along with its other distinctions, New Orleans became the biggest slave market in the United States.[11]

National integration crowded out the Deep South's marginal social groups. The southern Indians could not fend off the expansion of the slave country, especially after Andrew Jackson's victory in the presidential election of 1828 threw the power of the federal government behind Indian removal. Forty-two thousand Creeks, Choctaws, and Chickasaws were expelled from the Deep South in the 1830s and transported to land west of the Mississippi River. Their deportation sparked a new frenzy of speculation and development that further advanced plantation interests.[12] The region's free people of color also suffered, but in more subtle ways. As the number of free white and enslaved people grew, the proportion of free people of color fell to just 1 percent of the Deep South's population in 1860. The number of free people of color in Louisiana and Mississippi actually declined in the two decades before the Civil War. They were subjected to intensifying pressures, ranging from public insult to the threat of deportation and reenslavement.[13]

The Deep South's political power reached its apogee during Andrew Jackson's presidency. No national political leader had been more closely associated with the region's slaveowners than Jackson, who was linked to them by blood, interest, and sentiment. The citizens of the Deep South supported Jackson when South Carolina's planter elite challenged the authority of the national government to impose a protective tariff, and Jackson helped the citizens of the Deep South to deport the remaining southern Indians in the 1830s. But as the Deep South increased its influence within the southern bloc through the antebellum era, that bloc suffered a relative decline with respect to national political power. The trend was most conspicuous in the House of Representatives, where the Deep South increased its presence from 8 percent of the southern representation in 1820 to 19 percent in 1860 while the proportion of southern representatives overall in the House declined from 42 percent to 35 percent in the same period. The southern bloc struggled to hold on to power as the national government's most democratic branch slipped from its grasp.[14]

Southern slaveowners owed their political predicament to the southern states' failure to match the rapidly growing free population of the rest of the country, which left them at a disadvantage in the struggle against the rise of a popular antislavery movement in the North. That failure was most pronounced in the original southeastern states, which did not attract nearly as many foreigners as did the northeastern and mid-Atlantic states in the antebellum era. But it also shaped the demography of the new, western states. The total population of Louisiana, Mississippi, and Alabama was less than half that of Ohio, Indiana, and Illinois throughout the first half of the nineteenth century. Was slavery responsible for the difference? Did free people prefer to move to free states rather than to slave states? Many critics of slavery thought so. This book has argued that the expansion of slavery was crucial to the origins of the Deep South as it actually emerged, but it is also possible that the expansion of slavery blocked the emergence of a very different Deep South where—if he had chosen to go there—John Eadis might have lived in peace and freedom.

The Deep South presents a leading example of the general increase in forced labor in many parts of the world during the first half of the nineteenth century. The process differed from place to place according to geographic, economic, demographic, and political circumstances. The expansion of slavery in Cuba and Brazil depended on the continued importation of African slaves, which had a profound and still-palpable impact on Cuban and Brazilian culture. In West Africa, by contrast, the increased use of slave labor in "legitimate trade" accompanied British efforts to end slave exportation. Forced labor also expanded to the east. Omani and Swahili planters built up a plantation system in Zanzibar that encompassed more than 100,000 slaves by the 1830s. The use of convict labor proliferated all along the Indian Ocean and in Southeast Asia. Serfdom deepened in Russia. Notwithstanding local differences, forced labor was propelled wherever it expanded by increased demand for agricultural commodities, including cotton, sugar, coffee, cloves, peanuts, grain, and palm oil, linked to new patterns of production and consumption associated with the Industrial Revolution. Forced labor did not merely precede transnational capitalist networks of commodity exchange. It was also enmeshed in those networks as they proliferated around the world in the nineteenth century. That forced labor gradually became discredited at the same time as it expanded is surely one of the great paradoxes of world history in the nineteenth century.[15]

Some of the basic issues that roiled the Deep South in the early national era are still relevant today. The expansion of slavery was part of the history of "globalization," which is a euphemism for the ongoing integration of all humanity into a capitalist world-system. That process continues to have disparate effects on many groups of people.

Not all benefit equally, and some suffer. Slavery also created a hetero-geneous population at the same time that it stratified that population along new contours of race and class. Few travelers who visited New Orleans in the early nineteenth century failed to note its astonishing diversity, but the experience of living in a diverse society did not au-tomatically lead to tolerance of others, let alone mutual respect. In the context of inequality and economic exploitation, it led instead to deepening antipathy and horrible violence. Nationalism, racism, and other toxic prejudices likewise corrode our own global society. We live in a world in which slavery has not been eradicated and, if we are not vigilant, may again flourish under a new dispensation of global in-equality.[16]

Abbreviations

Notes

Acknowledgments

Index

Abbreviations

ADAH   Alabama Department of Archives and History, Montgomery

AJP   Andrew Jackson Papers, Library of Congress

BH   *Letters, Journals and Writings of Benjamin Hawkins,* ed. C. L. Grant, 2 vols. (Savannah, GA: Beehive Press, 1980)

BSP   Briggs-Stabler Papers, 1793–1910, MS 147, H. Furlong Baldwin Library, Maryland Historical Society, Baltimore

CAJ   John Spencer Bassett, ed., *Correspondence of Andrew Jackson,* 7 vols. (Washington, DC: Carnegie Institution of Washington, 1926–1935)

CVMM   *New Orleans (La.) Conseil de Ville, Messages from the Mayor, 1805–1836* (trans.), Louisiana Division, New Orleans Public Library

CVOP   *New Orleans (La.) Conseil de Ville, Official Proceedings, 1803–1829* (trans.), Louisiana Division, New Orleans Public Library

DU   Special Collections, Perkins Library, Duke University

ELP   Edward Livingston Papers (CO280), Manuscripts Division, Department of Rare Books and Special Collections, Princeton University Library; published with permission of the Princeton University Library

LBC   Dunbar Rowland, ed., *Official Letter Books of W. C. C. Claiborne, 1801–1816,* 6 vols. (Jackson, MS: State Department of Archives and History, 1917)

LC   Library of Congress

NA   National Archives, Washington, DC

PAJ   Harold D. Moser, Sharon McPherson, and Charles F. Bryan, Jr., eds., *The Papers of Andrew Jackson,* 6 vols. (Knoxville: University of Tennessee Press, 1980–)

PFP   Palfrey Family Papers, Houghton Library, Harvard University; by permission of the Houghton Library, Harvard University

PRO   The National Archives of the UK: Public Record Office, London

RASP   Kenneth N. Stampp, ed., *Records of Ante-Bellum Southern Plantations from the Revolution through the Civil War* (Frederick, MD: University Publications of America, 1985–)

TPUS   Clarence Carter, ed., *Territorial Papers of the United States,* 26 vols. (Washington, DC: Government Printing Office, 1934)

UNC   Southern Historical Collection, Wilson Library, The University of North Carolina at Chapel Hill

Notes

Preface

1. Ira Berlin, *Many Thousands Gone: The First Two Centuries of Slavery in North America* (Cambridge, MA: Harvard University Press, 1999), 370; Inter-University Consortium for Political and Social Research (ICPSR), *Study 00003: Historical Demographic, Economic, and Social Data: U.S., 1790–1970* (Ann Arbor: ICPSR).
2. Brilliantly described in Eugene Genovese, *Roll, Jordan, Roll: The World the Slaves Made* (New York: Pantheon Books, 1974).
3. Daniel H. Usner, Jr., *Indians, Settlers, and Slaves in a Frontier Exchange Economy: The Lower Mississippi Valley before 1783* (Chapel Hill: University of North Carolina Press, 1992).
4. For a seminal analysis of the corelation between freedom and slavery in the early United States, see Edmund Morgan, "Slavery and Freedom: The American Paradox," *Journal of American History* 59 (June 1972): 5–29. A recent challenge to the so-called Morgan thesis can be found in David Eltis, *The Rise of African Slavery in the Americas* (New York: Cambridge University Press, 2000).

1. Jefferson's Horizon

1. Thomas Jefferson, *Notes on the State of Virginia,* in *Writings,* ed. Merrill D. Peterson (New York: Library of America, 1984), 143; Richard Slotkin, *Regeneration through Violence: The Mythology of the American Frontier, 1600–1800* (Middletown, CT: Wesleyan University Press, 1973), 245–247.
2. Jefferson, *Writings,* 289.
3. Ira Berlin, *Many Thousands Gone: The First Two Centuries of Slavery in North America* (Cambridge, MA: Harvard University Press, 1998), chaps. 9–10.
4. Census data for 1790 drawn from Inter-university Consortium for Political and Social Research, *Historical, Demographic, Economic, and Social Data: The United States, 1790–1970* (computer file) (Ann Arbor, MI: Inter-university Consortium for Political and Social Research [producer and distributor], 197?). Data on slave-owning households is for Maryland, North Carolina, and South Carolina.
5. Philip Morgan, *Slave Counterpoint: Black Culture in the Eighteenth-Century Chesa-*

peake and Lowcountry (Chapel Hill: University of North Carolina Press, 1998), 79–95.

6. Herbert S. Klein, *The Atlantic Slave Trade* (New York: Cambridge University Press, 1999), 210–211.

7. *American State Papers: Commerce and Navigation,* 1:24–33, 322. On the transition to new agricultural commodities, see Joyce Chaplin, "Creating a Cotton South in Georgia and South Carolina, 1760–1815," *Journal of Southern History* 57, no. 2 (May 1991): 171–200; Richard Dunn, "After Tobacco: The Slave Labour Pattern on a Large Chesapeake Grain-and-Livestock Plantation in the Early Nineteenth Century," in *The Early Modern Atlantic Economy,* ed. John J. McCusker and Kenneth Morgan (New York: Cambridge University Press, 2000), 344–363.

8. Rachel N. Klein, *The Unification of a Slave State: The Rise of the Planter Class in the South Carolina Backcountry, 1760–1808* (Chapel Hill: University of North Carolina Press, 1990), 247.

9. Lee Soltow, *Distribution of Wealth and Income in the United States in 1798* (Pittsburgh: University of Pittsburgh Press, 1989), 180.

10. Jefferson, *Writings,* 260.

11. Thomas D. Morris, *Southern Slavery and the Law 1619–1860* (Chapel Hill: University of North Carolina Press, 1996), part 2.

12. Paul Goodman, "Social Status of Party Leadership: The House of Representatives, 1797–1804," *William and Mary Quarterly,* 3rd ser., 25 (July 1968): 470, 471; Sidney H. Aronson, *Status and Kinship in the Higher Civil Service: Standards of Selection in the Administrations of John Adams, Thomas Jefferson, and Andrew Jackson* (Cambridge, MA: Harvard University Press, 1964), 89, 115.

13. Eric Foner, "Blacks and the U.S. Constitution," *New Left Review* 183 (1990): 63–74; Jack N. Rakove, *Original Meanings: Politics and Ideas in the Making of the Constitution* (New York: Knopf, 1996), chap. 4. For a somewhat different view, see Don E. Fehrenbacher, *The Slaveholding Republic: An Account of the United States Government's Relations to Slavery,* completed and ed. Ward M. McAfee (New York: Oxford University Press, 2001), 37–47.

14. Kenneth C. Martis and Gregory A. Elmes, *The Historical Atlas of State Power in Congress, 1790–1990* (Washington, DC: Congressional Quarterly, 1993), 6–7. The numbers of planters in the House and Senate were supplied to me by Chuck diGiacomantonio of the First Federal Congress Project, who combed the biographies collected in Linda Grant De Pauw, ed., *Documentary History of the First Federal Congress of the United States of America, March 4, 1789–March 3, 1791,* vol. 14 (Baltimore: Johns Hopkins University Press, 1985). The three-fifths clause did not apply to the first Congress.

15. *Annals of Congress,* 1st Cong., 2nd sess., 1523–1525. For the petition controversy, see William C. diGiacomantonio, "'For the Gratification of a Volunteering Society': Antislavery and Pressure Group Politics in the First Federal Congress," *Journal of the Early Republic* 15 (Summer 1999): 169–197; Richard

S. Newman, "Prelude to the Gag Rule: Southern Reaction to Antislavery Petitions in the First Federal Congress," *Journal of the Early Republic* 16 (Winter 1996): 571–599; Howard A. Ohline, "Slavery, Economics, and Congressional Politics, 1790," *Journal of Southern History* 46 (August 1980): 335–360.

16. Ohline, "Slavery, Economics, and Congressional Politics, 1790." On the gradualism of emancipation in the North, see Berlin, *Many Thousands Gone,* 232–239.

17. Berlin, *Many Thousands Gone,* 264; Richard S. Dunn, "Black Society in the Chesapeake, 1776–1810," in *Slavery and Freedom in the Age of the American Revolution,* ed. Ira Berlin and Ronald Hoffman (Charlottesville: University Press of Virginia, 1983), 49–82.

18. Bernard Bailyn, ed., *The Debate on the Constitution* (New York: The Library of America, 1993), 2: 706–708.

19. Newman, "Prelude to the Gag Rule," 591–595.

20. Frederika Teute Schmidt and Barbara Ripel Wilheml, "Early Proslavery Petitions in Virginia," *William and Mary Quarterly,* 3rd ser., 30 (January 1973): 133–146, quotations on 139, 141. See also David W. Robson, "'An Important Question Answered': William Graham's Defense of Slavery in Post-Revolutionary Virginia," *William and Mary Quarterly,* 3rd ser., 37 (October 1980): 644–652.

21. Newman, "Prelude to the Gag Rule," 585. William Freehling distinguishes sharply between the Chesapeake gentry who wished for the "conditional termination" of slavery, and the Carolina planters who were "perpetuationist" from the start. See William Freehling, *The Road to Disunion: Secessionists at Bay, 1770–1854* (New York: Oxford University Press, 1990), 121–143.

22. *Annals of Congress,* 1st Cong., 2nd sess., 1503–1514.

23. Patrick S. Brady, "The Slave Trade and Sectionalism in South Carolina, 1787–1808," *Journal of Southern History* 38 (November 1972): 601–620; For the debate over slave importation in the South Carolina legislature, see Elizabeth Donnan, *Documents Illustrative of the History of the Slave Trade to America* (Washington, DC: Carnegie Institution of Washington, 1930–35), 4: 480–489, 494–494. For Georgia, see Ruth Scarborough, *The Opposition to Slavery in Georgia Prior to 1860* (New York: Negro Universities Press, 1968), 108–110.

24. George Washington to Francois Jean, Chevalier de Chastellux, 7 May 1781, The George Washington Papers at the Library of Congress, 1741–1799: Series 3h Varick Transcripts.

25. François Furstenberg, "Beyond Freedom and Slavery: Autonomy, Virtue, and Resistance in Early American Political Discourse," *Journal of American History* 89 (March 2003): 1295–1330.

26. Jefferson, *Writings,* 264.

27. Ibid., 270. On Jefferson and slavery, see Peter S. Onuf, "'To Declare Them a Free and Independant People': Race, Slavery, and National Identity in Jefferson's Thought," *Journal of the Early Republic* 18 (Spring 1998): 1–46.

28. Jefferson, *Writings*, 131.

29. D. W. Meinig, *The Shaping of America: A Geographical Perspective on 500 Years of History*, vol. 1: *Atlantic America, 1492–1800* (New Haven: Yale University Press, 1986), 284–288, 290–295.

30. "New map of the states of Georgia South and North Carolina, Virginia and Maryland, including the Spanish provinces of West and East Florida" (Joseph Purcell, 1788), Hargrett Rare Book and Manuscript Library, University of Georgia; "A new & general map of the Southern Dominions belonging to the United States of America" (Laurie & Whittle, 1794), Hargrett Rare Book and Manuscript Library, University of Georgia. For Old Tassel's map and quotation, see *American State Papers: Indian Affairs*, 1:40, 43.

31. For source of data, see n. 4.

32. Eric Hinderaker, *Elusive Empires: Constructing Colonialism in the Ohio Valley, 1673–1800* (New York: Cambridge University Press, 1997), 245–260; Bayly Ellen Marks, "The Rage for Kentucky: Emigration from St. Mary's County, 1790–1810," in *Geographical Perspectives on Maryland's Past*, ed. Robert D. Mitchell and Edward K. Muller, University of Maryland Occasional Papers in Geography 4 (College Park, MD: Department of Geography, University of Maryland, 1979), 108–128; Edward C. Papenfuse, Jr., "Planter Behavior and Economic Opportunity in a Staple Economy," *Agricultural History* 46 (1972): 297–311.

33. Richard J. Cox, ed., "'A touch of Kentucky News & State of Politicks': Two Letters of Levi Todd, 1784 and 1788," *Register of the Kentucky Historical Society* 76, no. 3 (July 1978): 219.

34. "Letters of Joseph Clay, Merchant of Savannah 1776–1793," *Collections of the Georgia Historical Society* 8 (1913): 191–192. See also Joyce Chaplin, *An Anxious Pursuit: Agricultural Innovation and Modernity in the Lower South, 1730–1815* (Chapel Hill: University of North Carolina Press, 1993), 277–280.

35. Stephen Aron, *How the West Was Lost: The Transformation of Kentucky from Daniel Boone to Henry Clay* (Baltimore: Johns Hopkins University Press, 1996), 48.

36. *American State Papers: Indian Affairs*, 1:77.

37. Ibid., 329–331.

38. Ibid., 56.

39. Ibid., 55.

40. Thomas D. Watson, "Strivings for Sovereignty: Alexander McGillivray, Creek Warfare and Diplomacy, 1783–1790," *Florida Historical Quarterly* 58 (April 1980): 400–414. For the Treaty of New York, see *American State Papers: Indian Affairs*, 1:81–82.

41. *American State Papers: Indian Affairs*, 1:401.

42. Ibid., 411.

43. John R. Finger, *Tennessee Frontiers: Three Regions in Transition* (Bloomington: Indiana University Press, 2001), 146–147; *American State Papers: Indian Affairs*, 1:529–542.

44. John May to Samuel [Bell?], 9 December 1780, Beall-Booth Family Papers, Filson Historical Society, Louisville, KY.

45. *American State Papers: Indian Affairs,* 1:369.

46. Abstract from a letter to Benjamin Hawkins, Davidson County [1787?], in "Papers from the Spanish Archives Relating to Tennessee and the Old Southwest, 1783–1800," *East Tennessee Historical Society Publications* 13 (1941): 119.

47. "Proceedings of a Meeting, October 12, 1793," in *The Democratic-Republican Societies, 1790–1800: A Documentary Sourcebook of Constitutions, Declarations, and Toasts,* ed. Philip S. Foner (Westport, CT: Greenwood Press, 1976), 360.

48. Julius W. Pratt, *Expansionists of 1812* (New York: Peter Smith, 1949), 64n13.

49. Michael Allen, "The Mississippi River Debate, 1785–1787," *Tennessee Historical Quarterly* 36 (Winter 1977): 461. On Federalist objections to westward expansion, see Reginald Horsman, "The Dimensions of an 'Empire for Liberty': Expansion and Republicanism, 1775–1825," *Journal of the Early Republic* 9 (Spring 1898): 1–20.

50. Samuel Flagg Bemis, *Pinckney's Treaty: America's Advantage from Europe's Distress, 1783–1800* (New Haven: Yale University Press, 1960), 87–88.

51. Arthur Preston Whitaker, *The Spanish-American Frontier: 1783–1795: The Westward Movement and the Spanish Retreat in the Mississippi Valley* (New York: Houghton Mifflin, 1927), 75.

52. Drew McCoy, "James Madison and Visions of American Nationality in the Confederation Period: A Regional Perspective," in *Beyond Confederation: Origins of the Constitution and American National Identity,* ed. Richard Beeman, Stephen Botein, and Edward C. Carter III (Chapel Hill: University of North Carolina Press, 1987), 226–258.

53. Baron de Carondelet, "Military Report on Louisiana and West Florida," in *Louisiana under the Rule of Spain, France, and the United States 1785–1807,* ed. James Alexander Robertson (Freeport, NY: Books for Libraries Press, 1969), 1: 298.

54. Gilbert Din, "Spain's Immigration Policy in Louisiana and the American Penetration, 1792–1803," *Southwestern Historical Quarterly* 76 (January 1973): 255–276; Arthur Preston Whitaker, *The Mississippi Question 1795–1803: A Study in Trade, Politics, and Diplomacy* (New York: D. Appleton-Century Company, 1934).

55. *Circular Letters of Congressmen to Their Constituents 1789–1829,* ed. Noble E. Cunningham (Chapel Hill: University of North Carolina Press, 1978), 1: 44.

56. Whitaker, *The Mississippi Question,* chaps. 11–15; Drew McCoy, *The Elusive Republic: Political Economy in Jeffersonian America* (New York: W. W. Norton, 1980), 196–203; James E. Lewis, Jr., *The American Union and the Problem of Neighborhood* (Chapel Hill: University of North Carolina Press, 1998), 25–31.

57. Winthrop Sargent to Thomas Pickering, 18 September 1798, in *The Mississippi Territorial Archives 1798–1803,* ed. Dunbar Rowland (Nashville: Press of Brandon Printing Company, 1905), 1: 48.

58. Lewis, *The American Union and the Problem of Neighborhood,* 26.

59. Peter Onuf, "The Expanding Union," in *Devising Liberty: Preserving and Creating Freedom in the New American Republic,* ed. David Thomas Konig (Stanford: Stanford University Press, 1995), 53.

60. Ronald D. Smith, "Napoleon and Louisiana: Failure of the Proposed Expedition to Occupy and Defend Louisiana, 1801–1803," *Louisiana History* 12 (Winter 1971), 36–39.

61. Jefferson, *Writings,* 512.

62. A description of Louisiana at the time of the purchase can be found in *Annals of Congress,* 8th Cong., 2nd sess., 1498–1578. For an estimate of the American Indian population, see Peter H. Wood, "The Changing Population of the Colonial South: An Overview by Race and Region, 1685–1790," in *Powhatan's Mantle: Indians in the Colonial Southeast,* ed. Peter H. Wood, Gregory A. Waselkov, and M. Thomas Hatley (Lincoln: University of Nebraska Press, 1989), 38–39.

63. Claudio Saunt, *A New Order of Things: Property, Power, and the Transformation of the Creek Indians, 1733–1810* (New York: Cambridge University Press, 1999), chap. 7; Daniel H. Usner, Jr., "American Indians on the Cotton Frontier: Changing Economic Relations with Citizens and Slaves in the Mississippi Territory," *Journal of American History* 72, no. 2 (September 1985): 297–317.

64. Whitaker, *The Mississippi Question,* chap. 8; John G. Clark, *New Orleans, 1718–1812: An Economic History* (Baton Rouge: Louisiana State University Press, 1970).

65. Willie Lee Rose, "The Domestication of Domestic Slavery," in *Slavery and Freedom,* ed. William Freehling (New York: Oxford University Press, 1982), 18–36. See also Jeffrey Robert Young, *Domesticating Slavery: the Master Class in Georgia and South Carolina, 1670–1837* (Chapel Hill: University of North Carolina Press, 1999).

66. James McMillin, "The Final Victims: The Demography, Atlantic Origins, Merchants, and Nature of the Post-Revolutionary Foreign Slave Trade to North America, 1783–1810," PhD diss., Duke University, 1999, 40–98.

67. Matthew E. Mason, "Slavery Overshadowed: Congress Debates Prohibiting the Atlantic Slave Trade to the United States, 1806–1807," *Journal of the Early Republic* 20 (Spring 2000): 59–81. A compilation of state and federal legislation pertaining to the importation of foreign slaves can be found in W. E. B. Du Bois, *The Suppression of the African Slave Trade to the United States of America 1638–1870,* with a foreword by John Hope Franklin (1896; Baton Rouge: Louisiana State University Press, 1969), appendix B.

68. Du Bois, *Suppression of the African Slave Trade,* 235–239.

69. Oscar B. Chamberlain, "The Evolution of State Constitutions in the Antebellum United States: Michigan, Kentucky, and Mississippi" PhD diss., University of South Carolina, 1996, 45–50, 56–59; Ivan E. McDougle, *Slavery in Kentucky 1792–1865* (Westport, CT: Negro Universities Press, 1970), 43–45.

70. Steven Deyle, "The Irony of Liberty: Origins of the Domestic Slave Trade," *Journal of the Early Republic* 12 (Spring 1992): 59–61.

71. Eugene Genovese, *Roll, Jordan, Roll: The World the Slave Made* (New York: Vintage Books, 1972), 49–75.

72. Sylvia Frey, *Water from the Rock: Black Resistance in a Revolutionary Age* (Princeton: Princeton University Press, 1991).

73. Jefferson, *Writings*, 288.

74. Julius Sherard Scott III, "The Common Wind: Currents of Afro-American Communication in the Era of the Haitian Revolution," PhD diss, Duke University, 1986.

75. Douglas R. Egerton, *Gabriel's Rebellion: The Virginia Slave Conspiracies of 1800 and 1802* (Chapel Hill: University of North Carolina Press, 1993), 51.

76. Russell Kirk, *John Randolph of Roanoke* (Indianapolis: LibertyPress, 1978), 162.

77. Egerton, *Gabriel's Rebellion*, 93.

78. Accession #11680102, December 1801, in Loren Schweninger, ed., *Race, Slavery, and Free Blacks: Series 1, Petitions to Southern Legislatures, 1777–1867* (Bethesda, MD: University Publications of America, 1998), Reel 16. On transportation as punishment, see Philip J. Schwarz, "The Transportation of Slaves from Virginia, 1801–1865," *Slavery and Abolition* 7, no. 3 (1986): 215–239.

79. *Annals of Congress*, 9th Cong., Appendix, 994–1000. See also Egerton, *Gabriel's Rebellion*, 148–162.

80. Howard Albert Ohline, "Politics and Slavery: The Issue of Slavery in National Politics, 1787–1815," PhD diss., University of Missouri, 1969, 298–303, 353–398; Donald L. Robinson, *Slavery in the Structure of American Politics 1765–1820* (New York: Harcourt Brace Jovanovich, 1971), 386–400.

81. *Annals of Congress*, 5th Cong., 2nd Sess., 1306, 1310.

82. Ibid., 1307.

83. Ibid., 1306, 1307, 1308, 1309, 1310.

84. Ibid., 1313.

85. For the prohibition on the importation of foreign slaves, see section seven of "An Act for the amicable settlement of limits with the state of Georgia, and authorizing the establishment of a government in the Mississippi territory," *Statutes at Large*, 5th Cong., 2nd sess., 550. The act provided for the emancipation of any slave illegally imported into the territory.

86. Leonard L. Richards, *The Slave Power: The Free North and Southern Domination, 1780–1860* (Baton Rouge: Louisiana State University Press, 2000), 40–43.

87. *American State Papers: Miscellaneous*, 1:386.

88. Everett Somerville Brown, ed., *William Plumer's Memorandum of Proceedings in the United States Senate 1803–1807* (New York: Macmillan Co., 1923).

89. Ibid., 111–112, 114–115, 118–121; quotations on 118, 119.

90. Ibid., 117, 119, 126.

91. Ibid., 115–116, 130.

92. *Annals of Congress,* 8th Cong., 1st sess., 240.

93. Jeffrey Brooke Allen, "The Origin of Proslavery Thought in Kentucky, 1792–1799," *Register of the Kentucky Historical Society* 77, no. 2 (Spring 1979): 87.

94. Brown, *William Plumer's Memorandum,* 129. On Breckenridge, see Lowell H. Harrison, *John Breckenridge: Jeffersonian Republican* (Louisville, KY: Filson Club, 1969).

95. Lewis Kerr to Isaac Briggs, 24 March 1804, Box 13, BSP. On Kerr, see Jared William Bradley, ed., *Interim Appointment: W. C. C. Claiborne Letter Book, 1804–1805* (Baton Rouge: Louisiana University Press, 2002), 415–437.

96. *Annals of Congress,* 8th Cong., 1st sess., 244.

97. *U.S. Statutes at Large,* 8th Cong., 1st Sess., 283–289.

98. William C. C. Claiborne to James Madison, 10 March 1804, *LBC,* 2: 25–26. See also "Dr. Watkin's Report," 4 February 1804, ibid., 2: 10; Stuart O. Landry, Jr., ed. and trans., *Voyage to Louisiana by C. C. Robin 1803–1805* (New Orleans: Pelican Publishing Co., 1966), 177.

99. Sarah P. Russell, "Cultural Conflicts and Common Interests: The Making of the Sugar Planter Class in Louisiana, 1795–1853," PhD diss., University of Maryland, College Park, 2000, 93.

100. *Annals of Congress,* 8th Cong., 2nd sess., 1597–1608, quotation on 1606.

101. Junius Peter Rodriguez, Jr., "Ripe for Revolt: Louisiana and the Tradition of Slave Insurrection, 1803–1865," PhD diss., Auburn University, 1992, 73; emphasis in original. On Congress's response to the Louisiana memorial, see George Dargo, *Jefferson's Louisiana: Politics and the Clash of Legal Traditions* (Cambridge, MA: Harvard University Press, 1975), 118–120; Ohline, "Politics and Slavery," 380–384.

102. Moncure Daniel Conway, ed., *The Writings of Thomas Paine* (New York: G. P. Putnam's Sons, 1895), 3: 435–436.

103. Tom Paine to Thomas Jefferson, 25 January 1805, Jefferson Papers, LC. See also Bernard Vincent, "Thomas Paine, the Louisiana Purchase, and the Rights of Man," *Plantation Society in the Americas* 3, no. 2 (Summer 1993): 63–72.

104. *Boston Repertory,* 1 May 1804.

105. *Boston Repertory,* 21 September 1804, 23 September 1804.

106. On the Ely amendment, see Linda Kerber, *Federalists in Dissent: Imagery and Ideology in Jeffersonian America* (Ithaca: Cornell University Press, 1970), 36–40.

107. Ohline, "Politics and Slavery," 390–392.

108. Thomas Jefferson to William Burwell, 28 January 1805, Jefferson Papers, LC.

2. Civilizing the Cotton Frontier

1. Todd Ashley Herring, "Natchez, 1795–1830: Life and Death on the Slavery Frontier," PhD diss., Mississippi State University, 2000, 64.

2. In Thomas Jefferson, *Writings,* ed. Merrill D. Peterson (New York: Library of America, 1984), 301.

3. Drew McCoy, *The Elusive Republic: Political Economy in Jeffersonian America* (New York: W. W. Norton, 1980).

4. Harry Toulmin to Isaac Briggs, 17 December 1806, BSP.

5. "Address to the Freemen of the Territory," 1 March 1802, *Mississippi Territorial Archives,* (Nashville: Brandon Printing Co., 1905), 1: 385. See also Mark Pitcavage, "Ropes of Sand: Territorial Militias, 1801–1812," *Journal of the Early Republic* 13 (Winter 1993): 481–500.

6. William D. Pattison, *Beginnings of the American Rectangular Land Survey System, 1784–1800* (Columbus: The Ohio Historical Society, 1970); Malcolm J. Rohrbough, *The Land Office Business: The Settlement and Administration of the Public Lands, 1789–1837* (New York: Oxford University Press, 1968). Andro Linklater, *Measuring America: How an Untamed Wilderness Shaped the United States and Fulfilled the Promise of American Democracy* (New York: Walker and Co., 2002).

7. Alan V. Briceland, "Land, Law and Politics on the Tombigbee Frontier, 1804," *Alabama Review* 33, no. 2 (April 1980): 92–124; R. S. Cotterill, "The National Land System in the South, 1803–1812," *Mississippi Valley Historical Review* 16 (March 1930): 495–506; Harry L. Coles, Jr., "Applicability of the Public Land System to Louisiana," *Mississippi Valley Historical Review* 43, no. 1 (June 1956): 39–58.

8. C. Peter Magrath, *Yazoo: Law and Politics in the New Republic* (Providence: Brown University Press, 1966), quotation on 129; Joyce Chaplin, *An Anxious Pursuit: Agricultural Innovation and Modernity in the Lower South, 1730–1815* (Chapel Hill: University of North Carolina Press, 1993), 171–178.

9. Arrell M. Gibson, *The Chickasaws* (Norman: University of Oklahoma Press, 1971), 4–5, 62–63.

10. Richard White, *The Roots of Dependency: Subsistence, Environment, and Social Change among the Choctaws, Pawnees, and Navajos* (Lincoln: University of Nebraska Press, 1983), 1–15; James Taylor Carson, "Searching for the Bright Path: The Mississippi Choctaws from Prehistory to Removal," PhD diss., University of Kentucky, 1996.

11. J. Leitch Wright, Jr., *Creeks and Seminoles: The Destruction and Regeneration of the Muscogulge People* (Lincoln: University of Nebraska Press, 1986), 1–18; Kathryn E. Holland Braund, *Deerskins and Duffels: The Creek Indian Trade with Anglo-America 1685–1815* (Lincoln: University of Nebraska Press, 1993), 3–9; Claudio Saunt, *A New Order of Things: Property, Power, and the Transformation of the Creek Indians, 1733–1816* (New York: Cambridge University Press, 1999).

12. James W. Covington, *The Seminoles of Florida* (Gainesville: University Press of Florida, 1993), chap. 1.

13. Eron Rowland, *Life, Letters and Papers of William Dunbar* (Jackson: Press of the Mississippi Historical Society, 1930), 209–210; *Annals of Congress,* 14: 1510–

1514. See also Daniel H. Usner, Jr., "American Indians in Colonial New Orleans," in *Powhatan's Mantle,* 104–127.

14. Thomas Jefferson to Benjamin Hawkins, 18 February 1803, in Jefferson, *Writings,* 1125; Reginald Horsman, "The Indian Policy of an 'Empire for Liberty,'" in *Native Americans and the Early Republic,* ed. Frederick E. Hoxie, Ronald Hoffman, and Peter J. Albert (Charlottesville: University Press of Virginia, 1999), 37–61.

15. Samuel J. Wells, "International Causes of the Treaty of Mount Dexter, 1805," *Journal of Mississippi History* 48, no. 3 (August 1986): 177–186.

16. Ella Kent Barnard, "Isaac Briggs, A.M., F.A.P.S. (1763–1825)," *Maryland Historical Magazine* 7 (December 1912): 409–412, quotations on 412.

17. Isaac Briggs to Hannah Briggs, 24 August 1803, Box 13, BSP.

18. Isaac Briggs to Gideon Granger, 8 September 1803, Box 13; Isaac Briggs to Gideon Granger, 28 January 1805, Box IIIc, BSP.

19. Isaac Briggs to Thomas Moore, 8 December 1803, Box 13, BSP.

20. Charles De France to Isaac Briggs, 30 January 1804, Box 13, BSP.

21. Rohrbough, *The Land Office Business,* 35–36.

22. Thomas Jefferson to Isaac Briggs, 26 April 1806, Isaac Briggs Letterbook, Box IIIc, BSP.

23. Isaac Briggs to Hannah Briggs, 10 August 1805, Box 13; Hannah Briggs to Isaac Briggs, 24 October 1805, Box 13; Isaac Briggs to Hannah Briggs, 25 November 1805, Box 13, BSP.

24. Isaac Briggs to Thomas Jefferson, 27 September 1806, Isaac Briggs Letterbook, Box IIIc, BSP.

25. *American State Papers: Public Lands,* 2:734; R. S. Cotterill, "The National Land System in the South, 1803–1812," *Mississippi Valley Historical Review* 16 (March 1930): 495–506.

26. Leonard Covington to Alexander Covington and James T. Magruder, 6 March 1809, in B. L. C. Wailes, *Memoir of Leonard Covington,* ed. Nellie Wailes Brandon and W. M. Drake (Natchez, MS: Natchez Printing and Stationary Co., 1928), 56.

27. Alexander Donelson to Andrew Jackson, 9 October 1811, *PAJ,* 2: 266–267.

28. Memorial to Congress, 25 November 1803, *TPUS,* 5: 280–281.

29. David F. Weiman, "People the Land by Lottery? The Market in Public Lands and the Regional Differentiation of Territory on the Georgia Frontier," *Journal of Economic History* 51 (December 1991): 835–860.

30. Seymour Drescher, *Econocide: British Slavery in the Age of Abolition* (Pittsburgh: University of Pittsburgh Press, 1977), 84–85.

31. McCoy, *The Elusive Republic,* chap. 3.

32. Ephraim Kirby to Albert Gallatin, 1 July 1804, Box 15, Ephraim Kirby Papers, MS 3041, DU.

33. Brian E. Coutts, "Boom and Bust: The Rise and Fall of the Tobacco Industry

in Spanish Louisiana, 1770–1790," *The Americas* 52 (January 1986): 289–309; Lewis Cecil Gray, assisted by Esther Katharine Thompson, *History of Agriculture in the Southern United States to 1860* (Washington, DC: Carnegie Institution of Washington, 1933), 1: 72, 74, 2: 680–683, 687–689. Jack D. L. Holmes, "Cotton Gins in the Spanish Natchez District, 1795–1800," *Journal of Mississippi History* 31, no. 3 (August 1969): 159–171.

34. James Hall, "A Brief History of the Mississippi Territory, To which is prefixed, A Summary view of the Country between the Settlements on Cumberland River & the Territory," *Publications of the Mississippi Historical Society* 8 (1906): 554.

35. Shepherd Brown to John McDonough, 23 November 1801, John McDonough Papers, *RASP,* Series H, Reel 3.

36. James Maury to the secretary of state, 10 November 1802, Reel 2, Despatches from U.S. Consuls in Liverpool, England, 1790–1906, M141, RG 59, National Archives, College Park, MD.

37. Michael M. Edwards, *The Growth of the British Cotton Trade 1780–1815* (New York: Augustus M. Kelly, 1967), 93.

38. Green & Wainwright to Winthrop Sargent, 19 November 1803, Reel 6, Winthrop Sargent Papers, LC.

39. *American State Papers: Commerce and Navigation,* 1:588–591, 668–672, 693–697, 718–723.

40. Julian Poydras to William Dunbar, 30 June 1799; Poydras to Dulcide Barran, 12 October 1799, "Private and Commercial Correspondance of an Indigo and Cotton Planter, 1794 to 1800," *RASP,* Series H, Reel 1. On Dunbar, see Rowland, *Life, Letters and Papers of William Dunbar.*

41. Thomas Rodney to Cesar Rodney, Washington Mississippi Territory, 10 July 1805, Box 2, Rodney Family Papers, Manuscript Division, LC.

42. Reuben Gold Thwaites, ed., *Early Western Travels 1748–1846* (Cleveland: Arthur H. Clark Co., 1904), 3: 254.

43. G. P. Whittington, ed., "The Journal of Dr. John Sibley, July–October, 1802," *Louisiana Historical Quarterly* 10 (October 1927): 493.

44. John Steele to Samuel Steele, 24 May 1799, Samuel Steele Papers, Mss. 5047, DU.

45. "Copies of Laws Enacted by the Governor and Judges of the Mississippi Territory, from the 30th of June until the 31st of December 1799," 13, Reel 5, Winthrop Sargent Papers, LC. See also Herring, "Natchez, 1795–1830," 177–179.

46. Circular to the Judges of the Mississippi Territory, 5 May 1800, *Mississippi Territorial Archives,* 1: 230–232. See also Daniel H. Usner, Jr., "American Indians on the Cotton Frontier: Changing Economic Relations with Citizens and Slaves in the Mississippi Territory," *Journal of American History* 72 (September 1985): 309–311.

47. Memorial to Congress, 23 October 1797, *TPUS,* 5: 10–11.

48. Edw[ard]. D. Turner to Winthrop Sargent, 4 October 1800, Reel 5, Winthrop Sargent Papers, LC.

49. Robert E. Roeder, "New Orleans Merchants, 1790–1837," PhD diss., Harvard University, 1959, 121.

50. Hore Browse Trist to Mary Brown Trist, 7 January 1803, Nicholas Philip Trist Papers, MS 2104, UNC.

51. William Hamilton to John Hamilton, 15 April 1811, William Southerland Hamilton Papers, MS 1471-C, UNC.

52. John Wunder, "American Law and Order Comes to the Mississippi Territory: The Making of Sargent's Code, 1798–1800," *Journal of Mississippi History* 38, no. 2 (May 1976): 131–155.

53. Francis Xavier Martin Letter, 22 March 1811, typescript, M1032, Louisiana Collection, Jones Library, Tulane University.

54. Logbook of voyage down the Mississippi River, July 17, 1798–August 12, 1798, Winthrop Sargent Papers, LC. Winthrop Sargent, "Account of Several Shocks of an Earthquake in the Southern and Western Parts of the United States," *Memoirs of the American Academy of Arts and Sciences* 3, 550–560. See also Charles S. Sydnor, *A Gentleman of the Old Natchez Region, Benjamin L. C. Wailes* (Durham, NC: Duke University Press, 1938), 122–123.

55. Daniel Coker and Jack D. L. Holmes, "Daniel Clark's Letter on the Mississippi Territory," *Journal of Mississippi History* 32 (May 1970): 164. For Sargent's marriage to Williams, see 164n26.

56. Winthrop Sargent, "Address to Militia Officers," 12 January 1801, in *The Mississippi Territorial Archives 1798–1803*, ed. Dunbar Rowland (Nashville, TN: Press of Brandon Printing Company, 1905), 1: 325.

57. John Steele to Samuel Steele, 12 December 1799, Samuel Steele Papers, MS 5047, DU.

58. William McIntosh to Winthrop Sargent, 4 October 1801, Reel 6, Winthrop Sargent Papers, LC.

59. Robert Butler to Thomas Butler, 12 November 1808, Folder 4, Box 2, Butler Family Papers, MS 1026, Hill Memorial Library, Louisiana State University.

60. Leonard Covington to Alexander Covington, 25 April 1809, in Wailes, *Memoir of Leonard Covington*, 57.

61. Ulrich B. Phillips, *American Negro Slavery*, with foreword by Eugene D. Genovese (Baton Rouge: Louisiana State University Press, 1969), 189–190.

62. "Autobiography of John Hutchins [1844]," 20–28, typescript, Breckenridge Family Papers, Southern Historical Collection, University of North Carolina–Chapel Hill.

63. Census of the Mississippi Territory 1801, Reel 2, Record Group 2, Mississippi Department of Archives and History; Census of the Mississippi Territory 1810, Reel 2, Record Group 2, Mississippi Department of Archives and History.

64. "Agricultural Memorandams," 15 November 1798 through 31 December

1800, Reel 1, Winthrop Sargent Papers, LC. On cotton cultivation in Mississippi, see John Hebron Moore, "Two Cotton Kingdoms," *Agricultural History* 60, no. 4 (Fall 1986): 1–16.

65. John Palfrey to Mark Pickard, 11 October 1810, Palfrey Family Papers, *RASP;* Bill of Sale, 9 March 1811, ibid.; Edward Palfrey to John Gorham Palfrey, 11 March 1811, bMS Am 1704 (669), PFP.

66. J. Hector St. John de Crèvecoeur, *Letters from an American Farmer* (New York: Penguin Books, 1986), 72–73.

67. See John Palfrey Plantation Journal, Attakapas, La., 1 Sep. 1807–1825, bMS Am 1704.16 (37), PFP. Data on cotton picking compiled from Palfrey's tallies at the back of the journal.

68. Edward Palfrey to John Gorham Palfrey, 17 January 1813, in *A Legacy of New England: Letters of the Palfrey Family,* ed. Hannah Palfrey Ayer, vol. 1 (Portland, ME: The Anthoensen Press, 1950), 20.

69. Fortescue Cuming, "Sketches of a Tour to the Western Country," in *Early Western Travels 1748–1846,* ed. Reuben Gold Thwaites (Cleveland: Arthur H. Clark Co., 1904), 4: 310.

70. E. Carrington to Samuel Hodgdon, 22 August 1807, Reel 4, Winthrop Sargent Papers, LC.

71. John Steele to Samuel Steele, 2 May 1799, Samuel Steele Papers, MS 5047, DU.

72. *Mississippi Herald and Natchez Gazette,* 21 October 1807.

73. *Louisiana Gazette,* 2 October 1810.

74. McCoy, *Elusive Republic,* 216–223.

75. "Memorial to the President and Congress," 19 September 1808, *TPUS,* 5: 638.

76. *American State Papers: Commerce and Navigation,* 1:812–817, 866–871, 889–894.

77. John P. Sanderson to John Palfrey, 27 December 1811, bMS Am 1704.7 (104), PFP.

78. Saunt, *A New Order of Things,* 164.

79. Colin Calloway, *The American Revolution in Indian Country: Crisis and Diversity in Native American Communities* (New York: Cambridge University Press, 1995), 241.

80. William G. McLoughlin, *Cherokee Renascence in the New Republic* (Princeton: Princeton University Press, 1986), chap. 4.

81. Benjamin Hawkins to William Faulkener, 25 November 1797, *BH,* 1: 162.

82. Petition to the President, 5 September 1810, *TPUS,* 6: 107.

83. Barbara Arneil, *John Locke and America: The Defence of English Colonialism* (Oxford: Clarendon Press, 1996), chap. 6.

84. Isaac Briggs to Thomas Jefferson, 5 May 1805, Box IIIc, BSP.

85. Florette Henri, *The Southern Indians and Benjamin Hawkins 1796–1816* (Norman: University of Oklahoma Press, 1986).

86. Samuel Mitchell to David Henley, 17 January 1800, David Henley Papers, MS 2486, DU.

87. *American State Papers: Indian Affairs,* 1:647, 700; Gilbert C. Fite, "Development of the Cotton Industry by the Five Civilized Tribes in Indian Territory," *Journal of Southern History* 15 (August 1949): 342–344.

88. John D. W. Guice, "Face to Face in Mississippi Territory, 1798–1817," in *The Choctaw before Removal,* ed. Carolyn Keller Reeves (Jackson: University Press of Mississippi, 1985), 172.

89. James Hall, "A Brief History of the Mississippi Territory, To which is prefixed, A Summary view of the Country between the Settlements on Cumberland River & the Territory," *Publications of the Mississippi Historical Society* 8 (1906): 542.

90. Saunt, *A New Order of Things,* 158.

91. Peyton Short, "Tour to Mobile, Pensacola, &c., by Peyton Short of Kentucky, in 1809. Account enclosed in a letter to Hon. Henry Clay," *Quarterly Publication of the Historical and Philosophical Society of Ohio* 5 (January–March 1910), 6–7. On the Colberts, see Ronald Eugene Craig, "The Colberts in Chickasaw History, 1783–1818: A Study in Internal Tribal Dynamics," PhD diss., University of New Mexico, 1998.

92. Kathryn E. Holland Braund, "The Creek Indians, Blacks, and Slavery," *Journal of Southern History* 57 (November 1991): 606–636; Saunt, *A New Order of Things,* chap. 5.

93. *Mississippi Territorial Archives,* 1: 200; Presentments of the Grand Jury of Adams County, 6 June 1799, *TPUS,* 5: 63. "Some Undistinguished Negroes," *Journal of Negro History* 6 (January 1921): 113–116; Maurine T. Wilson and Jack Jackson, *Philip Nolan and Texas: Expeditions to the Unknown Land, 1791–1801* (Waco: Texian Press, 1987), 100.

94. *American State Papers: Indian Affairs,* 1:603.

95. *BH,* 1: 24, 290, 316; 2: 410–11.

96. Juan de la Villebeuve to Carondelet, 27 February 1793, in "Papers from the Spanish Archives Relating to Tennessee and the Old Southwest, 1783–1800," *East Tennessee Historical Society Publications* 29 (1957): 157.

97. Darnell to Sargent, 22 April 1802, Reel 6, Winthrop Sargent Papers, LC.

98. "Letters of Benjamin Hawkins, 1796–1806," *Collections of the Georgia Historical Society* (Savannah: Georgia Historical Society, 1916), 9: 325, 326, 328, 331, 334.

99. Maj. Zebulon Pike, 6 July 1800, Reel 5, Winthrop Sargent Papers, LC.

100. Joseph Coleman to Samuel Goodwin, 24 December 1809, Cameron Family Papers, *RASP,* Series J, Part 1, Reel 10.

101. "Letters of Benjamin Hawkins," 259.

102. *American State Papers: Indian Affairs,* 1:675.

103. Benjamin Hawkins to Thomas Jefferson, 13 September 1806, *BH,* 2: 508.

104. *American State Papers: Indian Affairs,* 2:107.

105. Eugene Genovese, *From Rebellion to Revolution: Afro-American Slave Revolts in the Making of the Modern World* (Baton Rouge: Louisiana State University Press, 1979), 68–76.

106. Benjamin Hawkins to Wade Hampton, 26 August 1811, *BH*, 2: 590; J. Leitch Wright, Jr., *Creeks and Seminoles: The Destruction and Regeneration of the Muscogulge People* (Lincoln: University of Nebraska Press, 1986), 156–172.

107. Isaac Briggs to Hannah Briggs, 25 November 1805, Box 13, BSP. The phrase "howling wilderness" is an allusion to Deuteronomy 32:10, "He found him in a desert land, and in the waste howling wilderness; he led him about, he instructed him, he kept him as the apple of his eye."

108. On the spread of biracial Protestantism in the early nineteenth century, see Sylvia R. Frey and Betty Wood, *Come Shouting to Zion: African American Protestantism in the American South and British Caribbean to 1830* (Chapel Hill: University of North Carolina Press, 1998), chap. 6.

109. Robert F. Berkhofer, *Salvation and the Savage: An Analysis of Protestant Missions and American Indian Response, 1787–1862* (Lexington: University of Kentucky Press, 1965), 5.

110. *New York Missionary Magazine* 1 (1800): 26.

111. For Bullen's career, see Dawson A. Phelps, ed., "Excerpts from the Journal of the Reverend Joseph Bullen, 1799 and 1800," *Journal of Mississippi History* 17 (January–October 1955): 254–259, and Percy L. Rainwater, "Indian Missions and Missionaries," *Journal of Mississippi History* 28 (February 1966): 20–26.

112. Quotations from Phelps, "Excerpts from the Journal of the Reverend Joseph Bullen," 268, 271, 276, 278.

113. Randy J. Sparks, "Religion in Amite County, Mississippi, 1800–1861," in *Masters and Slaves in the House of the Lord: Race and Religion in the American South 1740–1870,* ed. John Boles (Lexington: University Press of Kentucky 1988), 60; *A Republication of the Minutes of the Mississippi Baptist Association, from Its Organization in 1806 to the Present Time* (New Orleans: Hinton and Co., 1849), n.p.

114. Margaret DesChamps Moore, "Protestantism in the Mississippi Territory," *Journal of Mississippi History* 29 (November 1967): 362; Mechal Sobel, *Trabelin' On: The Slave Journey to an Afro-Baptist Faith* (Westport, CT: Greenwood Press, 1979), 353.

115. Sobel, *Trabelin' On,* 193–194, 345–346.

116. David T. Bailey, *Shadow on the Church: Southwestern Evangelical Religion and the Issue of Slavery, 1783–1860* (Ithaca: Cornell University Press, 1985), 117–118.

117. Ray Holder, *The Mississippi Methodists 1799–1983: A Moral People "Born of Conviction"* (Jackson, MS: Maverick Prints, 1984), 3. On evangelical opposition to slavery, see David Brion Davis, *The Problem of Slavery in Western Culture* (Ithaca, NY: Cornell University Press, 1966), 382–390.

118. Jacob Young, *Autobiography of a Pioneer: or, The Nativity, Experience, Travels, and*

Ministerial Labors of Rev. Jacob Young, with Incidents, Observations, and Reflections (Cincinnati: L. Swormstedt and A. Poe, 1859), 249–250.

119. John F. Schermerhorn and Samuel J. Mills, "A Correct View of That Part of the United States Which Lies West of the Allegheny Mountains, with regard to Religion And Morals (1814)," in *To Win The West: Missionary Viewpoints 1814–1815* (New York: Arno Press, 1972), 30.

120. Herring, "Natchez, 1795–1830," 341. See also "Documentary Material Relating to the Early History of the Presbyterian Church in Mississippi," *Journal of the Presbyterian Historical Society* 21, no. 4 (December 1943): 189–191.

121. John G. Jones, *A Concise History of the Introduction of Protestantism into Mississippi and the Southwest* (St. Louis: P. M. Pinckard, 1866), 112–113.

122. Sparks, "Religion in Amite County," 63; *Republication of the Minutes of the Mississippi Baptist Association,* 13.

123. Carl Mauelshagen and Gerald H. Davis, trans. and eds., *Partners in the Lord's Work: The Diary of Two Moravian Missionaries in the Creek Indian Country 1807–1813,* Georgia State College, Research Paper 21, February 1969. On the Moravians, see Jon F. Sensbach, *A Separate Canaan: The Making of an Afro-Moravian World in North Carolina, 1763–1840* (Chapel Hill: University of North Carolina Press, 1998).

124. Mauelshagen and Davis, *Partners in the Lord's Work,* 15, 17, 19, 30.

125. *BH,* 2: 569; Mauelshagen and Davis, *Partners in the Lord's Work,* 28–29.

126. Quotations from Mauelshagen and Davis, *Partners in the Lord's Work,* 17, 19–20, 21, 36–37.

127. Ibid., 38–39.

128. Ibid., 39, 52–56.

129. Ibid., 59.

130. Ibid., 58–61; Sensbach, *A Separate Canaan,* 201.

131. Mauelshagen and Davis, *Partners in the Lord's Work,* 61, 69, 73.

132. "Petition to Congress by Inhabitants of the Territory," September 1811, *TPUS,* 6: 226.

133. Stacy R. Hathorn and Robin Sabino, "Views and Vistas: Traveling through the Choctaw, Chickasaw, and Cherokee Nations in 1803," *Alabama Review* 53, no. 3 (2001): 218.

3. Commerce and Slavery in Lower Louisiana

1. Amos Stoddard, *Sketches, Historical and Descriptive of Louisiana* (New York: AMS Press, 1973), 151.

2. A census of Spanish Louisiana taken in 1785 found 30,471 Europeans and Africans in Spanish Louisiana, of whom 14,853 people (4,433 whites, 9,513 slaves, and 907 free people of color) lived in the districts of the Chapitoulas Coast, New Orleans, Bayou St. John, and below the city. Daniel H. Usner, Jr., *Indians, Settlers, and Slaves in a Frontier Exchange Economy: The Lower Mississippi*

Valley before 1783 (Chapel Hill: University of North Carolina Press, 1992), 114–115; Thomas Neil Ingersoll, *Mammon and Manon in Early New Orleans: The First Slave Society in the Deep South, 1718–1819* (Knoxville: University of Tennessee Press, 1999), 155.

3. John G. Clark, *New Orleans 1718–1812: An Economic History* (Baton Rouge: Louisiana State University Press, 1970), 201.

4. Brian E. Coutts, "Boom and Bust: The Rise and Fall of the Tobacco Industry in Spanish Louisiana, 1770–1790," *The Americas* 52 (January 1986): 289–309.

5. Clark, *New Orleans 1718–1812*, 188–191, 222–232.

6. Gilbert Din, *Spaniards, Planters, and Slaves: The Spanish Regulation of Slavery in Louisiana, 1763–1803* (College Station: Texas A&M Press, 1999), 122–124; Gwendolyn Midlo Hall, *Africans in Colonial Louisiana: The Development of Afro-Creole Culture in the Eighteenth Century* (Baton Rouge: Louisiana State University Press, 1992), 277–281; Thomas Ingersoll, "The Slave Trade and the Ethnic Diversity of Louisiana's Slave Community," *Louisiana History* 37, no. 2 (1996): 144–148.

7. Terry Alford, *Prince among Slaves: The True Story of an African Prince Sold into Slavery in the American South* (New York: Oxford University Press, 1977).

8. C. L. R. James, *The Black Jacobins* (New York: Vintage Books, 1963).

9. Robin Blackburn, *The Overthrow of Colonial Slavery 1776–1848* (London: Verso, 1988), 241.

10. Dale W. Tomich, *Slavery in the Circuit of Sugar: Martinique and the World Economy, 1830–1848* (Baltimore: Johns Hopkins University Press, 1990), 15, 21–31.

11. Rene J. LeGardeur, Jr., "The Origins of the Sugar Industry in Louisiana," in *Green Fields: Two Hundred Years of Louisiana Sugar* (Lafayette: Center for Louisiana Studies, University of Southwest Louisiana, 1980), 10.

12. Gabriel Debien, "The Saint-Domingue Refugees in Cuba, 1793–1815," trans. David Cheramie, in *The Road to Louisiana: The Saint-Domingue Refugees 1792–1809,* ed. Carl A. Brasseaux and Glenn R. Conrad (Lafayette: Center for Louisiana Studies, University of Southwestern Louisiana), 57–89.

13. LeGardeur, Jr., "The Origins of the Sugar Industry in Louisiana," 18–22; J. Carlyle Sitterson, *Sugar Country: The Cane Sugar Industry in the South, 1753–1950* (Lexington: University of Kentucky Press, 1953), 4–5. Bore's contemporaries considered him to be the founder of Louisiana's sugar industry. See W. C. C. Claiborne to Thomas Jefferson, 10 July 1806, *LBC*, 3: 361–365.

14. Sitterson, *Sugar Country*, 10; V. Alton Moody, *Slavery on Louisiana Sugar Plantations* (New York: AMS Press, 1976), 57; Stuart O. Landry, Jr., trans., *Voyage to Louisiana by C. C. Robin 1803–1805* (New Orleans: Pelican Publishing Co., 1966), 107–111.

15. [Berquin-Duvallon], *Travels in Louisiana and the Floridas, in the Year 1802, Giving a Correct Picture of Those Countries,* trans. John Davis (New York: Printed by and for I. Riley and Co., 1806), 128.

16. Noel Deerr, *The History of Sugar* (London: Chapman and Hall Ltd., 1949), 19.

17. LeGardeur, Jr., "The Origins of the Sugar Industry in Louisiana," 13, 26n65. On irrigation, see Pierre Clément de Laussat, *Memoirs of My Life*, trans. Agnes-Josephine Pastwa, ed. Robert D. Bush (Baton Rouge: Louisiana State University Press, 1978), 124n1; Benjamin Silliman, *Manual on the Cultivation of the Sugar Cane, and the Fabrication and Refinement of Sugar* (Washington, DC: Francis Preston Blair, 1833), 10–11.

18. Landry, *Voyage to Louisiana by C. C. Robin*, 107–111; Berquin-Duvallon, *Travels in Louisiana*, 84–85; "Extract from the Journal of a Trip from Philadelphia to New Orleans by Way of the Mississippi and Ohio 1799," trans. Jane F. Kauffman, 1994, 21–22, Louis Tarascon Journal, Filson Historical Society, Louisville, KY.

19. Richard Follett, "Slavery and Plantation Capitalism in Louisiana's Sugar Country," *American Nineteenth-Century History* 1, no. 3 (Autumn 2000): 1–27.

20. Jeffrey Alan Owens, "Holding Back the Waters: Land Development and the Origins of the Levees on the Mississippi, 1720–1845," PhD diss., Louisiana State University, 1999, especially chap. 3.

21. William Claiborne to Thomas Jefferson, 10 July 1806, *LBC*, 3: 361–365.

22. G. P. Whittington, ed., "The Journal of Dr. John Sibley, July–October, 1802," *Louisiana Historical Quarterly* 10 (October 1927): 483; Landry, *Voyage to Louisiana by C. C. Robin*, 107–111.

23. David Lee Stirling, ed., "New Orleans, 1801: An Account by John Pintard," *Louisiana Historical Quarterly* 34 (July 1951): 221.

24. Henry Brown to [E. Trist?], 14 August 1807, Nicholas Philip Trist Papers, MS 2104, UNC.

25. William Kenner to Stephen Minor, 7 November 1811, William Kenner Papers, *RASP*, Series I, Part 3, Reel 12.

26. Paul Alliot, "Historical and Political Reflections on Louisiana," in James Alexander Robertson, ed., *Louisiana under the Rule of Spain, France, and the United States 1785–1807* (Freeport, NY: Books for Libraries Press, 1969), 1: 97; Landry, *Voyage to Louisiana by C. C. Robin*, 112–114; Amos Stoddard, *Sketches, Historical and Descriptive of Louisiana* (New York: AMS Press, 1973), 161; Claiborne to Jefferson, 5 July 1806, *LBC*, 3: 350–351; Moody, *Slavery on Louisiana Sugar Plantations*, 4–7.

27. Landry, *Voyage to Louisiana by C. C. Robin*, 195; Stoddard, *Sketches, Historical and Descriptive of Louisiana*, 182–3.

28. Berquin-Duvallon, *Travels in Louisiana*, 34.

29. Robert E. Roeder, "New Orleans Merchants, 1790–1837," PhD diss., Harvard University, 1959, 31–36.

30. Compiled from *TPUS*, 9: 702, and the Census for the Territory of Orleans, Roll 10, M252, NA.

31. *Louisiana Gazette*, 11 April 1811.

32. Compiled from "Registers of Flatboats, Barges, Rafts and Steamboats in the

Port of New Orleans, 1806–1823," vol. 1: April 1806 through April 1812, QN420, City Archives, New Orleans Public Library.

33. Message to the Legislative Council and House of Representatives, 30 April 1811, *LBC,* 5: 228–230.

34. Sarah Russell, "Ethnicity, Commerce, and Community on Lower Louisiana's Plantation Frontier, 1803–1828," *Louisiana History* 40 (Fall 1999): 389–405.

35. Edward Livingston to Catherine Garretson, 27 May 1804. Box 49, Folder 1, ELP. On Livingston's career, see William B. Hatcher, *Edward Livingston, Jeffersonian Republican and Jacksonian Democrat* (University: Louisiana State University Press, 1940.)

36. Ari Kelman, "A River and Its City: Critical Episodes in the Environmental History of New Orleans," PhD diss., Brown University, 1998, chap. 1.

37. Edward Livingston to Janet Livingston Montgomery, 1 January 1805. Box 55, Folder 3, ELP.

38. "Articles d'un agreement entre Francis O'Duhigg d'une part, et Edward Livingston de l'autre," 20 November 1804, Box 31, Folder 45, ELP.

39. Francis O'Duhigg to Edward Livingston, 10 January 1805, Box 31, Folder 45, ELP.

40. Francis O'Duhigg to Edward Livingston, 4 February 1805, ibid.

41. Francis O'Duhigg to Edward Livingston, 12 August 1805, ibid.

42. Francis O'Duhigg to Edward Livingston, 19 September 1805, ibid.

43. Roderick A. McDonald, "Independent Economic Production by Slaves on Antebellum Louisiana Sugar Plantations," *Slavery and Abolition* 12 (May 1991): 190–191.

44. Francis O'Duhigg to Edward Livingston, 12 August 1805, Box 31, Folder 45, ELP.

45. The Livingston papers are full of letters of introduction. Two good examples are Aaron Burr to Edward Livingston, New York, 15 June 1804, Box 5, Folder 53, and W[illiam] S[tephens] Smith to Edward Livingston, New York, 24 March 1805, Box 38, Folder 22, ELP. For a letter from a New York merchant eager to secure Livingston's business, see Abijah Hart to Edward Livingston, New York, 27 October 1804, Box 21, Folder 3, ELP.

46. Robert Fulton to Edward Livingston, New York, 24 March 1809 and 27 June 1810, Box 17, Folder 36, ELP.

47. Reuben Kemper to Edward Livingston, 21 January 1812, Box 24, Folder 50, ELP.

48. George R. Taylor, *The Transportation Revolution, 1815–1860* (New York: Rinehart, 1951).

49. Isaac Briggs to Albert Gallatin, 9 December 1805, Letters Received by the Secretary of the Treasury and the General Land Office from the Surveyors General for Mississippi 1 April 1803–4 November 1831, M1329, RG 49, NA. Samuel Briggs had patented a rotary steam engine in 1802. John C. Van Horne and Lee W. Formwalt, eds., *The Correspondence and Miscellaneous Papers*

of Benjamin Henry Latrobe (New Haven: Yale University Press, 1984–8), 1: 313n13.

50. Benjamin Latrobe to Samuel Hazlehurst, 7 December 1809, *Benjamin Henry Latrobe*, 2: 790. For a summary of the New Orleans Water Works project, see ibid., 808–811.

51. William Claiborne to Robert Livingston, 26 January 1812, *LBC*, 6: 40–41.

52. Richard J. Follett, "The Sugar Masters: Slavery, Economic Development, and Modernization on Louisiana Sugar Plantations, 1820–1860," PhD diss., Louisiana State University, 1997, 84–87.

53. Francois Andre Michaux, "Travels to the West of the Allegheny Mountains," in Reuben Gold Thwaites, ed., *Early Western Travels 1748–1846* (Cleveland: Arthur H. Clark Co., 1904), 3: 158–160.

54. *Louisiana Gazette,* 8 August 1806.

55. James McMillin, "The Final Victims: The Demography, Atlantic Origins, Merchants, and Nature of the Post-Revolutionary Foreign Slave Trade to North America, 1783–1810," PhD diss., Duke University, 1999, 60.

56. Gilbert C. Din and John E. Harkins, *The New Orleans Cabildo: Colonial Louisiana's First City Government 1769–1803* (Baton Rouge: Louisiana State University Press, 1996), 175–180; Ingersoll, "The Slave Trade and the Ethnic Diversity of Louisiana's Slave Community," 145–150; Paul F. Lachance, "The Politics of Fear: French Louisianans and the Slave Trade, 1786–1809," *Plantation Society* 1, no. 2 (June 1979): 162–197.

57. Isaac Briggs to Thomas Jefferson, 2 January 1804, *TPUS,* 9: 148.

58. Gilbert Leonard to William Claiborne, 25 January 1804, *TPUS,* 9: 172.

59. Inward Manifests, April 1804–July 1804, Records of the Bureau of Customs, Records of the Customhouses in the Gulf States, New Orleans: Inward and Outward Foreign and Coastwise Manifests, Entry 1631, RG 36, NA; *Louisiana Gazette,* 28 August 1804.

60. William Claiborne to James Madison, 31 January 1804, *LBC,* 1: 352–353.

61. 30 June 1804, *CVOP.*

62. Berquin-Duvallon, *Travels in Louisiana and the Floridas,* 81.

63. Ronald William Bailey, "The Slave Trade and the Development of Capitalism in the United States: A Critical Reappraisal of Theory and Method in Afro-American Studies," PhD diss., Stanford University, 1979, 240.

64. Lachance, "Politics of Fear," 181.

65. *Louisiana Gazette,* 6 February 1807.

66. Mortality statistics derived from David Eltis et al., *The Trans-Atlantic Slave Trade: A Database on CD-ROM* (New York: Cambridge University Press, 1999).

67. Elizabeth Donnan, *Documents Illustrative of the History of the Slave Trade to America,* vol. 4: *The Border Colonies and the Southern Colonies* (New York: Octagon Books, 1969), 513.

68. Ibid., 665.

69. Price statistics compiled using SPSS 11.0.1, from Gwendolyn Midlo Hall,

ed., *Louisiana Slave Database, 1719–1820* (Baton Rouge: Louisiana State University Press, 2000).

70. *Louisiana Gazette,* 8 October 1806.

71. *Mississippi Messenger,* 12 November 1807.

72. Moody, *Slavery on Louisiana Sugar Plantations,* 55–56.

73. Bill of sale, 22 September 1810, in John McDonough Papers, *RASP,* Series H, Reel 10.

74. Michael A. Gomez, *Exchanging Our Country Marks: The Transformation of African Identities in the Colonial and Antebellum South* (Chapel Hill: University of North Carolina Press, 1998), 42.

75. William Dunbar to Tunno & Price, 1 February 1807, in Eron Rowland, *Life, Letters and Papers of William Dunbar of Elgin, Morayshire, Scotland, and Natchez, Mississippi, Pioneer Scientist of the United States* (Jackson: Press of the Mississippi Historical Society, 1930), 351–352.

76. Philip Morgan, "The Cultural Implications of the Atlantic Slave Trade: African Regional Origins, American Destinations and New World Developments," *Slavery and Abolition* 18 (1997): 122–145.

77. William Claiborne to Thomas Jefferson, 25 March 1805, in Jared William Bradley, ed., *Interim Appointment: W. C. C. Claiborne Letter Book, 1804–1805* (Baton Rouge: Louisiana State University Press, 2002), 204.

78. Gene A. Smith, "U.S. Navy Gunboats and the Slave Trade in Louisiana Waters, 1808–1811," *Military History of the West* 23, no. 2 (Fall 1993): 135–147.

79. Case 376, Reel 9, Records of the U.S. District Court for the Eastern District of Louisiana, 1806–1814, M1082, Louisiana Division, New Orleans Public Library.

80. Judith Kelleher Schafer, *Slavery, the Civil Law, and the Supreme Court of Louisiana* (Baton Rouge: Louisiana State University Press, 1994), 150–2.

81. Cases 378–381, 401–403, Reel 9, Records of the U.S. District Court for the Eastern District of Louisiana; Jane Lucas de Grummond, *Renato Beluche: Smuggler, Privateer and Patriot 1780–1860* (Baton Rouge: Louisiana State University Press, 1983), 168–169.

82. *Gomez v. Bonneval,* Eastern District, Louisiana, June Term 1819, #364, Supreme Court of Louisiana Collection of Legal Archives, Accession No. 106, Louisiana Collection, Earl K. Long Library, University of New Orleans. The case is reported as 6 *Mart.* (o.s.) 656.

83. William Claiborne to John Shaw, 11 June 1811, *LBC,* 5: 273

84. Thomas Williams to the secretary of the treasury, 12 August 1810, Correspondence of the Secretary of the Treasury with Collectors of Customs, 1789–1833, Roll 16: Letters to and from the Collector of Customs at New Orleans, 11 October 1803–11 April 1833, National Archives Microfilm Publications, Microcopy No. 178, NA.

85. James Sterrett to Nathaniel Evans, 24 June 1809 [typescript], Nathaniel Evans and Family Papers, *RASP,* Series I, Part 2, Reel 4. On the St. Domingue

refugees, see Debien, "The Saint-Domingue Refugees in Cuba," 31–112; Thomas Fiehrer, "Saint-Domingue/Haiti: Louisiana's Caribbean Connection," *Louisiana History* 30 (1989): 419–437; Paul Lachance, "The 1809 Immigration of Saint-Domingue Refugees in New Orleans: Reception, Integration and Impact," *Louisiana History* 29 (1988): 109–141.

86. William Claiborne to Robert Smith, 10 May 1809, *LBC*, 4: 363–366.

87. William Claiborne to Robert Smith, 15 May 1809, *LBC*, 4: 354–355.

88. Lachance, "The 1809 Immigration," 112–113.

89. Lachance, "Politics of Fear," 188, 192. See also William Claiborne to Robert Smith, 10 May 1809, *LBC*, 4: 363–366; Edward Livingston to John Cauthen, 14 June 1809, Folder 1, Edward Livingston Letters, MS 68, Williams Research Center, Historic New Orleans Collection.

90. Lachance, "The 1809 Immigration," 111.

91. James Mather to William Claiborne, 18 July 1809, *LBC*, 4:387–389.

92. Lachance, "Politics of Fear," 191; Lachance, "The 1809 Immigration," 119, 121–122.

93. *Louisiana Gazette*, 27 January 1807.

94. Roeder, "The New Orleans Merchant," 79–80.

95. *Louisiana Gazette*, 7 May 1811.

96. John McDonough to John McDonough, Jr., 15 April 1804, in John Minor Wisdom Collection (John McDonough Series), *RASP*, Series H, Reel 12.

97. Calculated from Hall, *Louisiana Slave Database,* using SPSS 11.0.1.

98. John Mills to Gilbert Jackson, 19 May 1807, Mills (John) Letters, MS 1375, Hill Memorial Library, Louisiana State University.

99. Landry, *Voyage to Louisiana by C. C. Robin,* 115–117.

100. Isaac Briggs to Thomas Jefferson, 2 January 1804, *TPUS*, 9: 148.

101. John Mills to Gilbert Jackson, 19 May 1807.

102. For a review of some of the most important factors shaping the likelihood of slave revolts, see Eugene Genovese, *From Rebellion to Revolution: Afro-American Slave Revolts in the Making of the Modern World* (Baton Rouge: Louisiana State University Press, 1979), chap. 1.

103. Isaac Briggs to Thomas Jefferson, 2 January 1804, *TPUS*, 9: 148.

104. John Mills to Gilbert Jackson, 19 May 1807. See also Landry, *Voyage to Louisiana by C. C. Robin,* 239–240.

105. Landry, *Voyage to Louisiana by C. C. Robin,* 118–119.

106. Circular to the Commandants of Districts, 30 March 1804, *LBC*, 2: 72.

107. Eugene Genovese, *Roll, Jordan, Roll: The World the Slaves Made* (New York: Pantheon Books, 1974), 617–619.

108. Berquin-Duvallon, *Travels in Louisiana,* 88.

109. 2 March 1808, *CVMM.*

110. 3 October 1810, *CVOP.*

111. 3 February 1808, *CVOP.*

112. 18 July 1812, *CVOP.*

113. William Claiborne to Captain Johnson, 18 January 1804, *LBC*, 2: 256–257.

114. *Louisiana Gazette,* 14 May 1805.

115. Elijah Smith to Nathaniel Evans, 8 February 1810, Evans (Nathaniel and Family) Papers, MS 670, 913, Folder 3, Box 1, Hill Memorial Library, Louisiana State University.

116. Schafer, *Slavery, the Civil Law, and the Supreme Court of Louisiana,* 99–100.

117. George Morgan to David Rees, 19 June 1804, David Rees Papers, *RASP,* Series H, Reel 29.

118. Acting Mayor C. Trudeau to William Claiborne, 29 November 1811, New Orleans (La.) Office of the Mayor, Letter Books, 1811–1820, Volume 1: 16 January 11–22 November 1827, Microfilm Reel 90–144, Louisiana Division, New Orleans Public Library.

119. Deposition of Francis Whitmill, 28 November 1807, Folder 4, James Brown Papers (MS 44), Hill Memorial Library, Louisiana State University.

120. 22 May 1805, 14 June 1805, 21 January 1806, *CVOP.* For a good example of the corvée system at work, see 17 May 1809, *CVOP,* and 17 May 1809, *CVMM.* For slave labor on public works in New Orleans, see 15 February 1804, 8 March 1808, 7 August 1811, 11 September 1811, 16 October 1811, 30 November 1811, 2 May 1812, 9 May 1812, 22 January 1814, *CVOP.*

121. 8 May 1813, *CVMM.* For further debate over the employment of women on the chain gang, see 15 May 1813, 22 May 1813, 3 June 1820, *CVOP;* 22 May 1813, 12 March 1814, *CVMM.*

122. Villasana Haggard, "The Neutral Ground between Louisiana and Texas, 1806–1821," *Louisiana Historical Quarterly* 28 (October 1945): 1069–1073.

123. Edward Turner to William Claiborne, 30 July 1804, *TPUS,* 9: 271–272.

124. Edward Turner to James Wilkinson, 15 October 1804, *Annals of Congress,* 15: 1204.

125. Edward Turner to William Claiborne, 17 October 1804, *LBC,* 2: 385–386.

126. Marquis de Casa Calvo to William Claiborne, 6 November 1804, *TPUS,* 9: 323–324. For further material on the 1804 Natchitoches fugitives, see *TPUS,* 9: 325–326; *LBC,* 3: 5–6, 6–7, 8–9, 30–31, 32–33, 155.

127. Penny S. Brandt, "A Letter of Dr. John Sibley, Indian Agent," *Louisiana History* 29 (Fall 1988): 381.

128. William Claiborne to James Madison, 1 January 1809, *LBC,* 4: 283–284.

129. William Claiborne to James Madison, 15 January 1809, *LBC,* 4: 299; Message to the Legislature, 20 January 1809, *LBC,* 4: 306; William Claiborne to Judge Carr, 26 March 1809, *LBC,* 4: 336.

130. John Hope Franklin and Loren Schweninger, *Runaway Slaves: Rebels on the Plantation* (New York: Oxford University Press, 1999).

131. Benjamin Morgan to Chandler Price, 7 August 1803, *TPUS,* 9: 7. Two good introductions to the history of colonial Louisiana's free people of color are Kimberly S. Hanger, *Bounded Lives, Bounded Places: Free Black Society in Colonial New Orleans, 1769–1803* (Durham: Duke University Press,

1997), and Thomas N. Ingersoll, "Free Blacks in a Slave Society: New Orleans, 1718–1812," *William and Mary Quarterly* 3rd ser., 48, no. 2 (1991): 173–200.

132. "General Return of the Census of the Territory of Orleans taken for the year 1806," *TPUS,* 9: 702.

133. Ingersoll, *Mammon and Manon,* 222–232.

134. Lachance, "The 1809 Immigration," 111.

135. Compiled from the U.S. Census for 1810, Microfilm M-252, NA. Statistics for New Orleans include the city and suburbs of New Orleans, the precincts of New Orleans, and Plaquemines and St. Bernard parishes. I include all four for the sake of comparison with the 1806 figures for Orleans Parish. Baltimore had the second highest proportion of free people of color (12.2 percent). Philadelphia (9.5 percent) and New York (8.1 percent) both had more free people of color than did New Orleans in 1810, but because the populations of these cities was so much larger than in New Orleans, the proportion of free people of color was smaller.

136. Kimberly S. Hanger, "Patronage, Property, and Persistence: The Emergence of a Free Black Elite in Spanish New Orleans," *Slavery and Abolition* 17 (April 1996): 44–64; Paul Lachance, "The Limits of Privilege: Where Free Persons of Colour Stood in the Hierarchy of Wealth in Antebellum New Orleans," ibid., 65–84.

137. Compiled from Charles L. Thompson, ed., *New Orleans in 1805: A Directory and a Census* (New Orleans: Pelican Gallery, 1936).

138. James Johnson to Henry Clay, 5 February 1807, *The Papers of Henry Clay,* ed. James F. Hopkins (Lexington: University of Kentucky Press, 1959), 1: 276–277, 304, 370.

139. Ingersoll, *Mammon and Manon,* 326.

140. Moody, *Slavery on Louisiana Sugar Plantations,* 20.

141. *Jacob et al. v. Ursuline Nuns,* 2 Martin La. 269.

142. 5 October 1805, 3 October 1810, *CVOP.*

143. 31 October 1812, *CVOP.*

144. Thomas N. Ingersoll, "Slave Codes and Judicial Practice in New Orleans, 1718–1807," *Law and History Review* 13, no. 1 (Spring 1995): 23–62.

145. Paul F. Lachance, "The Formation of a Three-Caste Society: Evidence from Wills in Antebellum New Orleans," *Social Science History* 18, no. 2 (Summer 1994): 211–242.

146. Schafer, *Slavery, the Civil Law, and the Supreme Court of Louisiana,* 4–6.

147. For the brief debate over allowing only whites to vote for delegates to the state constitutional convention, see *Annals of Congress,* House of Representatives, 11th Cong., 3rd sess., 107, 131, 151–152, 937–938, 960, 963–964; *Louisiana Gazette,* 18 March 1811.

148. James Wilkinson to Henry Dearborn, 11 January 1804, *TPUS,* 9: 159–60.

149. Petition to William Claiborne, 17 January 1804, *TPUS,* 9: 174–5.

150. Ira Berlin, *Slaves without Masters: The Free Negro in the Antebellum South* (New York: The New Press, 1974), 118–125.

151. James Brown to Albert Gallatin, 7 January 1806, *TPUS,* 9: 559; William Claiborne to James Madison, 7 January 1806, *TPUS,* 9: 561.

152. William Claiborne to James Madison, 24 January 1806 and 29 January 1806, *LBC,* 3: 248, 253.

153. On the problem of free fencers of color, see 20 April 1808, 30 April 1808, 18 May 1808, *CVOP;* 25 May 1808, *CVMM.*

154. 13 June, 18 June, 27 June, 1 August, 4 August 1804, *CVOP.* For Paimbeouf's petitions to the City Council, see New Orleans (La.) City Council, Letters, Petitions, and Reports, 1804–1835, #505 and #514, Louisiana Division, New Orleans Public Library. Marseille appears again in the proceedings on 27 April 1805, when Paimbeouf petitioned the council for permission to sell him. See 27 April 1805, *CVOP.*

155. 8 August 1804, *CVOP.*

156. Affadavit of Mayor James Mather, 5 February 1811, in New Orleans (La.) Office of the Mayor, Letter Books, 1811–1820. Volume 1: January 16, 1811– November 22, 1827. Microfilm Reel 90–144. Louisiana Division, New Orleans Public Library.

157. On Savary, see Debien, "The Saint-Domingue Refugees in Cuba," 174.

158. Charles Gayarre, *History of Louisiana* (New Orleans: F. F. Hansell and Bro., Ltd., 1903), 4: 226–227.

159. Donald E. Everett, "Emigres and Militiamen: Free Persons of Color in New Orleans, 1803–1815," *Journal of Negro History* 38 (October 1953): 394–395.

160. Quotation from William Claiborne to Julian Poydras, 4 June 1809, *TPUS,* 9: 843.

161. James Dormon, "The Persistent Specter: Slave Rebellion in Territorial Louisiana," *Louisiana History* 18 (Fall 1977): 389–404; Junius Peter Rodriguez, Jr., "Ripe for Revolt: Louisiana and the Tradition of Slave Insurrection, 1803–1865," PhD diss., Auburn University, 1992, 93–112; Thomas Marshall Thompson, "National Newspaper and Legislative Reactions to Louisiana's Deslondes Slave Revolt of 1811," *Louisiana History* 33 (1992): 5–29; and Tommy R. Young III, "The United States Army and the Institution of Slavery in Louisiana, 1803–1815," *Louisiana Studies* 13 (Fall 1974): 201–222. Most of the relevant primary sources pertaining to the rebellion are compiled in Albert Thrasher, *On to New Orleans! Louisiana's Heroic 1811 Slave Revolt* (New Orleans: Cypress Press, 1995).

162. Helmut Blume, *The German Coast during the Colonial Era 1722–1803,* trans. and ed. Ellen C. Merrill (Desrehan, LA: German-Acadian Coast Historical and Genealogical Society, 1990), part 3.

163. Ibid.

164. Craig A. Bauer, "From Burnt Canes to Budding City: A History of the City of Kenner, Louisiana," *Louisiana History* 23, no. 4 (Fall 1982): 358–360. For

Kenner & Henderson's slave trading, see *Louisiana Gazette*, 31 October 1806, 2 December 1806, 5 June 1807, 10 May 1808.

165. Bradley, *Interim Appointment*, 258–263.

166. Sarah Paradise Russell, "Cultural Conflicts and Common Interests: The Making of the Sugar Planter Class in Louisiana, 1795–1853," PhD diss., University of Maryland, College Park, 2000, 107.

167. Population and slaveholding statistics drawn from Robert Bruce L. Ardoin, comp., *Louisiana Census Records Volume III* (New Orleans: Polyanthios, 1977), 121–124, 163–167. Sugar statistics from Glenn R. Conrad, *The German Coast: Abstracts of the Civil Records of St. Charles and St. John the Baptist Parishes 1804–1812* (Lafayette: Center for Louisiana Studies, University of Southwestern Louisiana, 1981), 5.

168. Calculated from a sample of estate inventories from St. Charles and St. John the Baptist Parishes in Hall, *Louisiana Slave Database,* using SPSS 11.0.1.

169. Thrasher, *On to New Orleans!* 136–137. On rumor and slave conspiracy, see Michael P. Johnson, "Denmark Vesey and His Co-Conspirators," *The William and Mary Quarterly* 3rd ser., 58 (October 2001): 915–976; and the responses in ibid., 59 (January 2002).

170. Conrad, *The German Coast,* 21.

171. Ibid., 65–66.

172. John Palfrey to James Johnston, 1 February 1810, Palfrey Family Papers, *RASP,* Series I, Part 1, Reel 1. Declaration of Kenner & Henderson, 7 March 1811, Act #21, St. Charles Parish Original Acts, Book 41, 1810–1811, 141–143. See Thrasher, *On to New Orleans!* 68, for other examples of runaways who participated in the rebellion.

173. Hugh M. Hamill, Jr., *The Hidalgo Revolt: Prelude to Mexican Independence* (Gainesville: University of Florida Press, 1966); John Tutino, *From Insurrection to Revolution in Mexico: Social Bases of Agrarian Violence, 1750–1940* (Princeton: Princeton University Press, 1986).

174. Félix D. Almaráz, Jr., *Tragic Cavalier: Governor Manuel Salcedo of Texas, 1808–1813* (Austin: University of Texas Press, 1971), chap. 5.

175. Isaac Joslin Cox, *The West Florida Controversy, 1798–1813: A Study in American Diplomacy* (Baltimore: Johns Hopkins University Press, 1918). For a recent reassessment of the West Florida rebellion, see Andrew McMichael, "The Kemper 'Rebellion': Filibustering and Resident Anglo-American Loyalty in Spanish West Florida," *Louisiana History* 43, no. 2 (2002): 133–165.

176. David Holmes to Thomas Cushing, 28 September 1810, *TPUS,* 6: 121–122.

177. St. Charles Parish Original Acts, 14 January 1811, "Interrogation of Jean," St. Charles Parish Colonial Record Books, Book 41, University of Southwestern Louisiana Library.

178. Wade Hampton to William Claiborne, 12 January 1811, *TPUS,* 9: 916–917.

179. William Claiborne to Wade Hampton, 7 January 1811, *LBC,* 5: 94.

180. William Claiborne to Colonel Andre, 13 January 1811, *LBC, 5*: 97; Thompson, "Louisiana's Deslondes Slave Revolt," 7.

181. Act #17, 20 February 1811, St. Charles Parish Original Acts, Book 41, 1810–1811, in Thrasher, *On to New Orleans!* 216.

182. *Louisiana Gazette,* 10 January 1811; *Louisiana Gazette,* 17 January 1811. The legend of Trépagnier's death is reprinted in Thrasher, *On to New Orleans!* 54. Commodore John Shaw estimated the number of rebels at 200 to 300. John Shaw to Paul Hamilton, 18 January 1811, Papers of John Shaw, LC. John Nancarrow estimated their number at 300. John Nancarrow to Edward Livingston, 20 January 1811, Folder 19, Box 31, ELP.

183. These men were identified as principal leaders during the interrogations of 13–14 January. Many historians indicate that Charles was from St. Domingue, but I have found no evidence supporting this claim.

184. "Statement of the slaves killed, arrested, and missing after the insurrection," 18 January 1811, Act #2, St. Charles Parish Original Acts, Book 1810–11, 3–4.

185. Declarations, Act #24, 7 March 1811, St. Charles Parish Original Acts, Book 1810–1811, 149–162. All the available declarations for compensation are translated and published in Thrasher, *On to New Orleans!* 216–224. For Marie Rose, see *Acts Passed at the Second Session of the Third Legislature of the Territory of Orleans 1811,* 18, in Thrasher, *On to New Orleans!* 277.

186. *Moniteur de la Louisiane,* 17 January 1811, in Thrasher, *On to New Orleans!* 63.

187. William Claiborne to Robert Smith, 9 January 1811, *TPUS, 9*: 915–916; Wade Hampton to William Eustis, 16 January 1811, *TPUS, 9*: 917–918; Thrasher, *On to New Orleans!* 59; Shaw to Hamilton, 18 January 1811; *Louisiana Gazette,* 17 January 1811; Manuel Andry to William Claiborne, 11 January 1811, *TPUS, 9*: 915–916.

188. Manuel Andry to William Claiborne, 11 January 1811, *TPUS, 9*: 915–916; *Louisiana Gazette,* 11 January 1811; Hampton to Eustis, 16 January 1811, *TPUS, 9*: 917–918; *Moniteur de la Louisiane,* 12 January 1811, in Thrasher, *On to New Orleans!* 282. Quotations from Andry's letter to Claiborne.

189. *Louisiana Gazette,* 12 January 1811; William Claiborne to Robert Smith, 14 January 1811, *LBC, 5*: 100; William Claiborne to Col. Villeré, 16 January 1811, *LBC, 5*: 101.

190. Wade Hampton to William Claiborne, 12 January 1811, *TPUS, 9*: 916–917.

191. Shaw to Hamilton, 18 January 1811, Papers of John Shaw, LC; 12 January 1811, *CVOP;* 12 January 1811, *CVMM;* William Claiborne to Robert Smith, 14 January 1811, *LBC, 5*: 100.

192. Governor David Holmes to Col. John Wood, 17 January 1811, Executive Journal of David Holmes, 1810–1814, Record Group 2, Mississippi Department of Archives and History.

193. Entry for 17 January 1811, "Winthrop Sargent's Diary, January 1, 1810 through December 31, 1813," Reel 2, Winthrop Sargent Papers, LC; David

Holmes to Thomas Butler, 18 January 1811 and 19 January 1811, in Thrasher, *On to New Orleans!* 272.

194. Act #2, 13 January 1811, St. Charles Parish Original Acts, Book 41, 1810–1811, 17–20. St. Martin's summary of the trial proceedings has been translated and published as "Summary of Trial Proceedings of Those Accused of Participating in the Slave Uprising of January 9, 1811," *Louisiana History* 18 (Fall 1977): 472–473.

195. "Statement of the slaves killed, arrested, and missing after the insurrection," 18 January 1811, Act #2, St. Charles Parish Original Acts, Book 1810–1811, 3–4. Quotation from *Louisiana Gazette,* 21 January 1811.

196. "Summary of Trial Proceedings," 471.

197. Cases 184, 189, 190, in City Court (1807–1817), Criminal Records, Louisiana Division, New Orleans Public Library. Most of the records from the City Court trials have been published in Thrasher, *On to New Orleans!* 229–247.

198. Shaw to Hamilton, 18 January 1811, Papers of John Shaw, LC.

199. Edward Palfrey to John Gorham Palfrey, New Orleans, 23 January 1811, in Hannah Palfrey Ayer, ed., *A Legacy of New England: Letters of the Palfrey Family* (Portland, ME: Anthoensen Press, 1950), 1: 19.

200. Anonymous, "Trip to New Orleans 1811," 34, MMC-1796, LC.

201. Cases 193, 187, 192, City Court; Proclamation by William Claiborne, 12 February 1811, *LBC,* 5: 150; *TPUS,* 9: 982.

202. Act #18, n.d., St. Charles Parish Original Acts, Book 41, 1810–1811, 129–130. These depositions were taken in consequence of a resolution passed by the territorial legislature on 5 February 1811 "for the purpose of ascertaining the number and names of the slaves who have distinguished themselves during the late insurrection by saving the life of their master or of some other white person." *Acts Passed at the Second Session of the Third Legislature of the Territory of Orleans 1811,* 196. Reprinted in Thrasher, *On to New Orleans!* 278.

203. Thrasher, *On To New Orleans!* 224.

204. "Answer of the House of Representatives of the Orleans Territory to Governor Claiborne," 31 January 1811, *LBC,* 5: 130–131.

205. *Acts Passed at the Second Session of the Third Legislature of the Territory of Orleans 1811,* 132; William Claiborne, Message to the Legislative Council and House of Representatives, *LBC,* 5: 218–219. See also Thompson, "National Newspaper and Legislative Reactions," 26–27.

206. William Claiborne, Speech to Both Houses of the Territorial Legislature, 29 January 1811, *LBC,* 5: 123.

207. Thompson, "National Newspaper and Legislative Reactions," 24–26.

208. *American State Papers: Military Affairs,* 1:320.

209. Hampton to Eustis, 16 January 1811, *TPUS,* 9: 917–918.

210. *Louisiana Gazette,* 28 February 1811.

211. D. Holliday to Nathaniel Evans, 26 January 1811, Evans (Nathaniel and Family) Papers, Hill Memorial Library, Louisiana State University.

212. William Hamilton to John Hamilton, 12 April 1811, William Southerland Hamilton Papers, MS 1471-C, Southern Historical Collection, University of North Carolina. See also Ronald Edward Bridwell, "The South's Wealthiest Planter: Wade Hampton I of South Carolina, 1754–1835," PhD diss., University of South Carolina, 1980, 388–404, 770.

213. Henry Marie Brackenridge, *Views of Louisiana together with A Journal of a Voyage up the Missouri River, in 1811* (Chicago: Quadrangle Books, 1962), 175.

4. The Wartime Challenge

1. Robert V. Haynes, "The Southwest and the War of 1812," *Louisiana History* 5 (1964): 51.

2. On the War of 1812 in the Deep South, see especially Thomas D. Clark and John D. W. Guice, *The Old Southwest, 1795–1830: Frontiers in Conflict* (Norman: University of Oklahoma Press, 1989), chaps. 7–8; Frank Lawrence Owsley, Jr., *The Struggle for the Gulf Borderlands: The Creek War and the Battle of New Orleans 1812–1815* (Gainesville: University Press of Florida, 1981).

3. On the causes of the War of 1812, see Reginald Horsman, *The Causes of the War of 1812* (Philadelphia: University of Pennsylvania Press, 1962); Drew McCoy, *The Elusive Republic: Political Economy in Jeffersonian America* (New York: W. W. Norton, 1980), 216–223; J. C. A. Stagg, *Mr. Madison's War: Politics, Diplomacy, and Warfare in the Early American Republic, 1783–1830* (Princeton: Princeton University Press, 1983).

4. George Rogers Taylor, "Agrarian Discontent in the Mississippi Valley preceding the War of 1812," *Journal of Political Economy* 39 (August 1931): 491–492, 496–497; Stuart Bruchey, ed., *Cotton and the Growth of the American Economy: 1790–1860* (New York: Harcourt, Brace and World, 1967), table 3P.

5. Haynes, "The Southwest and the War of 1812," 49.

6. "Resolutions of Citizens of Wilkinson County," 25 July 1812, *TPUS* 5: 302; "Resolutions of Citizens of Washington," 28 July 1812, *TPUS*, 5: 303.

7. Robert W. Remini, *Andrew Jackson and the Course of American Empire 1767–1821* (New York: Harper and Row, 1977), chaps. 1–10. For Jackson's slave trading, see *PAJ*, 2: 261–262.

8. To the Tennessee Volunteers, 31 July 1812, *PAJ*, 2: 317–318.

9. Andrew Jackson to William Claiborne, 5 January 1813, *PAJ*, 2: 352.

10. Remini, *Andrew Jackson*, 173–186.

11. Compiled from "Registers of Flatboats, Barges, Rafts, and Steamboats in the Port of New Orleans, 1806–1823" vol. 2: May 1812–March 1823, QN420, City Archives, New Orleans Public Library.

12. *American State Papers: Commerce and Navigation*, 1:889–894, 1021–1024.

13. John Palfrey to John Gorham Palfrey, 20 March 1813, bMS Am 1704 (677), PFP.

14. George Foote to William Foote, 23 April 1812, Foote Family Papers, 1759–1987, Filson Historical Society, Louisville, KY.

15. George Foote to William Foote, 23 August 1813, ibid.

16. Memorial to Congress by the Territorial Legislature, 11 January 1814, *TPUS*, 5: 409.

17. *Annals of Congress,* House of Representatives, 12th Cong., 1st sess., 451.

18. Thomas Jefferson to Edward Coles, 25 August 1814, in Thomas Jefferson, *Writings,* ed. Merrill D. Peterson (New York: Library Classics of the United States, 1984), 1345. On fears of slave insurrection during the War of 1812, see Merton L. Dillon, *Slavery Attacked: Southern Slaves and Their Allies 1619–1865* (Baton Rouge: Louisiana State University Press, 1990), 77–80.

19. Junius Peter Rodriguez, Jr., "Ripe for Revolt: Louisiana and the Tradition of Slave Insurrection, 1803–1865," PhD diss., Auburn University, 1992, 122–140.

20. Todd Ashley Herring, "Natchez, 1795–1830: Life and Death on the Slavery Frontier," PhD diss., Mississippi State University, 2000, 243.

21. David Holmes to James Wilkinson, 22 July 1812, *TPUS*, 6: 298–300.

22. David Holmes to James Wilkinson, 19 October 1812, *TPUS*, 6: 328–329.

23. Folder 228, New Orleans City Court (1807–1817), Criminal Records, Louisiana Division, New Orleans Public Library; 2 November 1812, *CVOP.*

24. 5 June 1813, *CVMM.*

25. A. La Neville to Maj. Gen. Villeré, 12 September 1813, Folder 1, Jacques Philippe Villeré Papers, 1813–1815, MS 14, Williams Research Center, Historic New Orleans Collection, New Orleans.

26. J. Leitch Wright, Jr., *Creeks and Seminoles: The Destruction and Regeneration of the Muscogulge People* (Lincoln: University of Nebraska Press, 1986), 156–172.

27. Benjamin Hawkins to John Armstrong, 11 October 1813, *BH,* 2: 672. On the spiritual revival among the southern Indians, see Joel Martin, *Sacred Revolt: The Muskogees' Struggle for a New World* (Boston: Beacon Press, 1991).

28. Benjamin Hawkins to Alexander Cornells, 25 March 1811; Benjamin Hawkins to Upper Creek chiefs, 25 March 1811; Benjamin Hawkins to John Armstrong, 29 March 1813; Benjamin Hawkins to David Mitchell, 26 April 1813, *BH,* 630–634; *American State Papers: Indian Affairs,* 1:841, 843–84.

29. Benjamin Hawkins to John Armstrong, 22 June 1813; Hawkins to Armstrong, 28 June 1813; Hawkins to David Mitchell, 11 July 1813; Hawkins to David Mitchell, 22 July 1813; Hawkins to Armstrong, 26 July 1813; Hawkins to Armstrong, 28 July 1813, *BH,* 2: 641–649, 651.

30. Benjamin Hawkins to John Armstrong, 28 July 1813, *BH,* 2: 651–652. For the Red Sticks' opposition to new property relations, see Claudio Saunt, *A New Order of Things: Property, Power, and the Transformation of the Creek Indians, 1733–1816* (New York: Cambridge University Press, 1999), chap. 11.

31. Reed McC. B. Adams, "New Orleans and the War of 1812, Part II," *Louisiana Historical Quarterly* 16 (July 1933): 498.

32. Margaret (Eades) Austill, "Memories of Journeying through Creek Country and of Childhood in Clarke County, 1811–1814," *Alabama Historical Quarterly* 6 (Spring 1944): 95–96.

33. Owsley, *Struggle for the Gulf Borderlands,* 30–33.

34. George Stiggins, *Creek Indian History: A Historical Narrative of the Genealogy, Traditions and Downfall of the Ispocoga or Creek Indian Tribe of Indians,* introduction and notes by William Stokes Wyman, ed. by Virginia Pounds Brown (Birmingham: Birmingham Public Library Press, 1989), 100–101.

35. Owsley, *Struggle for the Gulf Borderlands,* 34–41.

36. "Memoir of Thomas C. Holmes," Notes upon History of Alabama, Section 4, Pickett Collection, ADAH; David Beasley to General F. L. Claiborne, 30 August 1813, Mississippi Territory, Military Correspondence, 1806–1813, SG3112, ADAH.

37. John Buchanan, *Jackson's Way: Andrew Jackson and the People of the Western Waters* (New York: John Wiley and Sons, 2001), 224. For the causes of the Fort Mims massacre, see Karl Davis, "'Remember Fort Mims:' Reinterpreting the Origins of the Creek War," *Journal of the Early Republic* 22 (Winter 2002): 611–636.

38. Stiggins, *Creek Indian History,* 111–112; Thomas S. Woodward, *Woodward's Reminiscences of the Creek, or Muscogee Indians, Contained in Letters to Friends in Georgia and Alabama* (Montgomery, AL: Barrett and Wimbish, 1859; repr. Tuscaloosa: Alabama Book Store, 1939), 100.

39. Benjamin Hawkins to John Armstrong, 21 September 1813, *BH,* 2: 664–666.

40. "Memoir of Thomas C. Holmes."

41. Henry Sale Halbert and Timothy Horton Ball, *The Creek War of 1813 and 1814,* ed. Frank L. Owsley, Jr. (University, AL: University of Alabama Press, 1969), 161; "Incidents of the Creek War of 1813 by H. S. Halbert, Crawfordsville, Lowndes County, Mississippi. November 1, 1883," Reel 119: 10 YY 91, Draper Manuscripts, State Historical Society of Wisconsin, Madison; George P. Rawick, ed., *The American Slave: A Composite Autobiography, Supplement* (Westport, CT: Greenwood Press, 1977), ser. 1, 1: 471–474.

42. Ferdinand Claiborne, 3 September 1813, Mississippi Territory: Military Correspondence, 1806–1813, SG 3112, ADAH.

43. W. C. Mead to F. L. Claiborne, 20 September 1813, Mississippi Territory: Military Correspondence, 1806–1813, SG3112, ADAH.

44. Edmund O. W. Andrews to [unknown], 19 September 1813, Andrews Family Papers, Mississippi Department of Archives and History, Jackson MS.

45. Robert S. Quimby, *The U.S. Army in the War of 1812: An Operational and Command Study* (East Lansing: Michigan State University Press, 1997), chaps. 13–14; Remini, *Andrew Jackson,* chaps. 13–14. For southerners' war aims, see Willie Blount to Thomas Flournoy, 15 October 1813, *American State Papers: Indian Affairs,* 1:855–856.

46. John Reid to Nathan Reid, 3 October 1813, John Reid Papers, LC.

47. Halbert and Ball, *The Creek War,* 211–218; Arrell M. Gibson, *The Chicka-saws* (Norman: University of Oklahoma Press, 1971), 97–98; William G. McLoughlin, *Cherokee Renascence in the New Republic* (Princeton: Princeton University Press, 1986), 188–194.

48. To the Tennessee Volunteers, 24 September 1813, *PAJ,* 2: 428.

49. Read, Mitchell, and Company to Jackson, 18 October 1813, *CAJ,* 1: 333.

50. John Reid to Betsy Reid, 24 October 1813, John Reid Papers, LC. For Jackson's concerns over food, see Andrew Jackson to Col. Pope, Col. Perkins, Maj. Brahan, and Mssrs. Burrows, Allen, and Bibb, Dr. Manning and Col. Thompson, 23 October 1813, *CAJ,* 1: 335.

51. Quimby, *The U.S. Army in the War of 1812,* 1: 407–410.

52. Andrew Jackson to Rachel Jackson, 12 November 1813, *PAJ,* 2: 448–449.

53. Andrew Jackson to Willie Blount, 14 November 1813, *PAJ,* 2: 453–454.

54. John Reid to Abram Maury, 21 November 1813, John Reid Papers, LC.

55. Quimby, *The U.S. Army in the War of 1812,* 1: 413–414, 427.

56. Ibid., 415–416.

57. Ibid., 427–429.

58. David Ker to Mary Ker, 25 October 1813, Ker Family Papers, MS 4656, UNC.

59. Quimby, *The U.S. Army in the War of 1812,* 1: 400–402. For a typical account of the canoe fight that mentions Caesar, see "Jeremiah Austill," *Alabama Historical Quarterly* 6 (Spring 1944): 85.

60. Stiggins, *Creek Indian History,* 117–121.

61. Ibid., 118–119; Saunt, *A New Order of Things,* 269–270.

62. Halbert and Ball, *The Creek War,* 258–259.

63. William Martin to Andrew Jackson, 4 December 1813, *PAJ,* 2: 469.

64. Address to the First Brigade, Tennessee Volunteer Infantry, 13 December 1813, *PAJ,* 2: 484.

65. Andrew Jackson to Rachel Jackson, 29 December 1813, *PAJ,* 2: 515; Michael Paul Rogin, *Fathers and Children: Andrew Jackson and the Subjugation of the American Indian* (New Brunswick, NJ: Transaction Publishers, 1991), 154–156.

66. List of Jackson's Taxable Property, *CAJ,* 1: 212.

67. Andrew Jackson to Rachel Jackson, 11 October 1813, *PAJ,* 2: 436.

68. Andrew Jackson to Rachel Jackson, 19 December 1813, *PAJ,* 2: 494.

69. Quimby, *The U.S. Army in the War of 1812,* 1: 422.

70. John Coffee to Andrew Jackson, 20 December 1813, *CAJ,* 1: 401; Quimby, *The U.S. Army in the War of 1812,* 1: 423–424.

71. Andrew Jackson to John Williams, 7 January 1814, *CAJ,* 1: 438; Quimby, *The U.S. Army in the War of 1812,* 1: 424–425; Owsley, *Struggle for the Gulf Borderlands,* 70.

72. Levi Lee Diary, 1813–1830, pp. 7–8, ADAH.

73. Andrew Jackson to Rachel Jackson, 1 February 1814, *PAJ,* 2: 23–24. See also Quimby, *The U.S. Army in the War of 1812,* 2: 451–455; Andrew Jackson to Rachel Jackson, 28 January 1814, *PAJ,* 3: 17–21.

74. Owsley, *Struggle for the Gulf Borderlands,* 72–85; Remini, *Andrew Jackson,* 213–217; Quimby, *The U.S. Army in the War of 1812,* 2: 467–470.

75. Andrew Jackson to Rachel Jackson, 1 April 1814, *PAJ,* 3: 54.

76. Andrew Jackson to Thomas Pinckney, 28 March 1814, *PAJ,* 3: 53.

77. To Tennessee Troops in Mississippi Territory, 2 April 1814, *PAJ,* 3: 58.

78. William McCauley to John McCauley, 10 June 1814, Andrew McCauley Papers, MS 4059, UNC.

79. Andrew Jackson to Thomas Pinckney, 14 April 1814, *CAJ,* 1: 500. On the Red Sticks' flight to Florida, see also Jackson to Pinckney, 14 April 1814, *PAJ,* 3: 62. Jackson to Willie Blount, 18 April 1814, *PAJ,* 3: 64; Benjamin Hawkins to Pinckney, 17 May 1814, *BH,* 2: 680–681.

80. Andrew Jackson to David Holmes, 18 April 1814, *CAJ,* 1: 504–505; Jackson to Willie Blount, 18 April 1814, *PAJ,* 3: 64; Joseph Graham to [unknown], 7 June 1814, Joseph Graham: Mississippi Territory Military Records: typed transcript, SPR 368, ADAH.

81. Andrew Jackson to Rachel Jackson, 8 May 1814, *PAJ,* 3: 71.

82. W. C. Middleton to Andrew Jackson, 22 August 1814, Reel 11, AJP.

83. Theophilus Powell Bill of Sale, 7 September 1814, Reel 12, AJP.

84. Lemuel Early to Andrew Jackson, 22 June 1815, Reel 18, AJP.

85. Receipt for the delivery of a slave to David Tate, 2 June 1818, Reel 25, AJP.

86. Andrew Jackson to John Williams, 18 May 1814, *PAJ,* 3: 74.

87. John Spencer Bassett, ed., "Major Howell Tatum's Journal while acting Topographical Engineer to General Jackson Commanding the 7th Military District," *Smith College Studies in History* 7, nos. 1–3 (October 1921–April 1922), 26.

88. George Strother Gaines to James Taylor Gaines, 8 February 1814, in "Letters from George Strother Gaines Relating to Events in South Alabama, 1805–1814," *Publications of the Alabama Historical Society, Transactions* 3 (1898–1899): 188–189.

89. William McCauley to John McCauley, 8 May 1814, Andrew McCauley Papers, MS 4059, UNC.

90. *American State Papers: Indian Affairs,* 1: 836–837.

91. Ibid., 826–827; Owsley, *Struggle for the Gulf Borderlands,* chap. 8.

92. Andrew Jackson to Rachel Jackson, 23 August 1814, *PAJ,* 3: 117.

93. John K. Mahon, *The War of 1812* (Gainesville: University of Florida Press, 1972), 340–341; Owsley, *Struggle for the Gulf Borderlands,* 98–100; Saunt, *A New Order of Things,* 274–277.

94. Thomas Flournoy to John Armstrong, 20 June 1814, Reel 61, M221, RG 107, NA.

95. George Strother Gaines to James Taylor Gaines, 11 June 1814, in "Letters from George Strother Gaines," 189–192.

96. Harry Toulmin to Andrew Jackson, 22 June 1814, *CAJ,* 2: 10.

97. Andrew Jackson to William Claiborne, 21 July 1814, *PAJ,* 3: 91.

98. Andrew Jackson to John Coffee, 10 August 1814, *PAJ,* 3: 113.

99. *Annals of Congress,* Senate, 12th Cong., 2nd sess., 527.

100. Roger Norman Buckley, *Slaves in Red Coats: The British West India Regiments, 1795–1815* (New Haven: Yale University Press, 1979); Peter Voelz, *Slave and Soldier: The Military Impact of Blacks in the Colonial Americas* (New York: Garland Publishing, 1993), 161–192.

101. Buckley, *Slaves in Red Coats,* 63–81.

102. Ibid., 111–113.

103. PRO, WO 1/95, pp. 274–275.

104. Buckley, *Slaves in Red Coats,* 121–122. On clothing shortages, see PRO, WO 27/89, "Inspecting Officer's Report, Detachment of His Majesty's 1st West India Regiment, Frenada, 19 July 1805"; WO 27/90, "1st West India Regiment, Inspecting Officers Return Dominica January 1806, Six Companies Dominica," 22 January 1806; "1st West India Regt. 3 Companies Trinidad," 25 February 1806; "Inspecting Officers Report, Detachment 1st West India Regiment, One Company Tobago," 8 March 1806; WO 27/99, Part One, "5th West India Regiment, Inspection Report, Brigdier General Farley," 28 April 1810; WO 27/103, Part One, O'Meara to Morrison, 7 June 1811.

105. "Observations Relative to New Orleans," Captain James Lucas Yeo, 19 February 1813, Folder 40, Box 3E480, Edward Alexander Parsons Collection, Center for American History, University of Texas—Austin.

106. James Stirling Memorandum, MS 194, Williams Research Center, Historic New Orleans Collection, New Orleans.

107. Bathurst to Packenham, 24 October 1814, PRO, WO 6/2, p. 28.

108. Buckley, *Slaves in Red Coats,* 130–134.

109. See PRO, WO 1/141, pp. 12–13; Owsley, *The Struggle for the Gulf Borderlands,* 98; Mahon, *The War of 1812,* 340.

110. Christopher George, "Mirage of Freedom: African Americans in the War of 1812," *Maryland Historical Magazine* 91 (Winter 1996): 427–450; Frank A. Cassell, "Slaves of the Chesapeake Bay Area and the War of 1812," *Journal of Negro History* 57 (April 1972): 144–155; Mahon, *The War of 1812,* 312–315.

111. William Claiborne to Andrew Jackson, 20 September 1814, *PAJ,* 3: 143.

112. Owsley, *Struggle for the Gulf Borderlands,* 107; Saunt, *A New Order of Things,* 278–279. For reports of British activity in Pensacola, see Benjamin Hawkins to John Armstrong, 16 August 1814, *BH,* 2: 693; Hawkins to Andrew Jackson, 30 August 1814, *BH,* 2: 694; Big Warrior to Hawkins, 25 August 1814, *CAJ,* 2: 36n1; Statement by Micco Auchule, 29 August 1814, Reel 11, AJP; William Wootton to Jackson, 3 November 1814, *CAJ,* 2: 89.

113. Andrew Jackson to Mateo González Manrique, 24 August 1814, *PAJ,* 3: 121.

114. Owsley, *Struggle for the Gulf Borderlands,* 109–116.

115. Benjamin Hawkins to Peter Early, 5 November 1814, *BH,* 2: 703. For Hawkins's slaves, see Hawkins to Early, 30 October 1814, *BH,* 2: 698.

116. Andrew Jackson to James Monroe, *CAJ,* 2: 97. For Jackson's invasion of

Pensacola, see Remini, *Andrew Jackson*, 239–244; Quimby, *The U.S. Army in the War of 1812*, 2: 791–799.

117. Committee of Safety to Andrew Jackson, 18 September 1814, *CAJ*, 2: 51–4.

118. Villeré to Fromentin, 19 October 1814, Villeré Papers, Williams Research Center, Historic New Orleans Collection, New Orleans.

119. William Claiborne to Andrew Jackson, 12 August 1814, *PAJ*, 3: 115–116.

120. Andrew Jackson to William Claiborne, 22 August 1814, *CAJ*, 2: 27. See Jackson to Claiborne, 21 September 1814, *PAJ*, 3: 144.

121. William Claiborne to Andrew Jackson, 17 October 1814, *PAJ*, 3: 165. Italics in original.

122. Andrew Jackson to William Claiborne, 31 October 1814, *CAJ*, 2: 88.

123. Quimby, *The U.S. Army in the War of 1812*, 2: 816.

124. Robert Gleig, *A Subaltern in America; comprising his narrative of the campaigns of the British Army at Baltimore, Washington, &c. &c. during the late war* (Philadelphia: E. L. Carey & A. Hart, Chestnut Street, 1833), 194–216; Charles Ramus Forrest, "Journal of the Operations against New Orleans in 1814 and 1815," *Louisiana Historical Quarterly* 44, nos. 3 and 4 (July–October 1961), 112–117.

125. Alexander Dickson, "Journal of Operations in Louisiana," *Louisiana Historical Quarterly* 44, nos. 3 & 4 (July–October 1961), 12.

126. Ibid., 15.

127. 1810 Federal Census, Orleans Parish, M252–10, NA.

128. Benson Earle Hill, *Recollections of an Artillery Officer: Including Scenes and Adventures in Ireland, America, Flanders, and France* (London: Richard Bentley, 1836), 1: 318–319.

129. 24 September 1814, 17 December 1814, *CVOP*; Rodriguez, "Ripe for Revolt," 134–135. On slave patrols in Virginia and the Carolinas during the War of 1812, see Sally E. Hadden, *Slave Patrols: Law and Violence in Virginia and the Carolinas* (Cambridge, MA: Harvard University Press, 2001), 162–165.

130. Arsène Lacarrière Latour, *Historical Memoir of the War in West Florida and Louisiana in 1814–15, with an Atlas*, ed. Gene A. Smith (Gainesville: Historic New Orleans Collection and University Press of Florida, 1999), 199.

131. William Claiborne Circular to Alexander Declouet, 19 September 1814, David Rees Papers, *RASP*, Series H, Reel 29.

132. William Claiborne to David Rees, 3 November 1814, ibid.

133. Joshua Baker to David Rees, 27 December 1814, ibid.

134. Andrew Jackson to William Claiborne, 10 December 1814, *PAJ*, 3: 201–203. See also Jackson to James Monroe, 10 December 1814, *CAJ*, 2: 111.

135. Reed McC. B. Adams, "New Orleans and the War of 1812, Part 4," *Louisiana Historical Quarterly* 17 (January–July 1934): 170–171.

136. Latour, *Historical Memoir of the War*, 49–50.

137. General Orders, 19 December 1814, *PAJ*, 3: 210–211.

138. John Spencer Bassett, ed., "Major Howell Tatum's Journal while Acting Top-

ographical Engineer to General Jackson Commanding the 7th Military District," *Smith College Studies in History* 7 (October 1921–April 1922): 119.

139. Edward Livingston to Gen. Morgan, 25 December 1814, Folder 35, Box 3E480, Edward Alexander Parsons Collection, Center for American History, University of Texas–Austin.

140. Latour, *Historical Memoir of the War,* 90.

141. Gen. David B. Morgan to Maj. James Gordon, Doctor Flood's Plantation, 2 January 1815, Folder 12, Box 3E482, Edward Alexander Parsons Collection, Center for American History, University of Texas–Austin.

142. James Gordon to Andrew Jackson, January 4 1815, Reel 15, AJP.

143. Matthew Lyon to Andrew Jackson, 10 August 1818, Reel 25, AJP; *Annals of Congress,* House of Representatives, 16th Cong., 1st sess., 878–9; *American State Papers: Claims,* 668–669, 679.

144. Latour, *Historical Memoir of the War,* 294.

145. Robert Hilliard Barrow to Bennett Barrow, 28 January 1815, in Robert Ruffin Barrow Papers, *RASP,* Series H, Reel 18.

146. Lewis Livingston to Villeré, 9 January 1815, Folder 34, Villeré Papers, Williams Research Center, Historic New Orleans Collection, New Orleans.

147. Capt. Penne to David B. Morgan, 29 January 1815, Folder 8, Box 3E483, Edward Alexander Parsons Collection, Center for American History, University of Texas–Austin.

148. Quimby, *The U.S. Army in the War of 1812,* 2: 889–892.

149. Dickson, "Journal of Operations in Louisiana," 18–19.

150. George Laval Chesterton, *Peace, War, and Adventure: An Autobiographical Memoir of George Laval Chesterton . . . ,* (London: Longman, Brown, Green, and Longmans, 1853), 205.

151. PRO, WO 27/133, Part Two, O'Meara to Fuller, 22 June 1815.

152. PRO, WO 1/141, pp. 172, 179, 219–220.

153. See PRO, WO 25/2259, for the Fifth West India casualty returns, and WO 12/11247 for the casualties listed on the paylist for the First West India.

154. Derived from the casualty returns for the Fifth West India Regiment in PRO, WO 25/2259, and the Fifth West India Description and Succession Book, WO 25/656.

155. "A Contemporary Account of the Battle of New Orleans by a Soldier in the Ranks," *Louisiana Historical Quarterly* 9 (January 1926): 14–15.

156. Bassett, ed., "Major Howell Tatum's Journal," 130.

157. "Report of the Killed, wounded and missing of the army under the command of Major General Andrew Jackson in the actions of the 23rd, and 28th December 1814 and 1st and 8th January 1815 with the enemy," Reel 67, AJP.

158. Latour, *Historical Memoir of the War,* 295, 341.

159. "Captain Louis Simon's Journal during the Expedition of 1814 (December)," Letters Received by the Secretary of War, Registered Series, 1801–1860, Roll 66, May 1814–December 1815 (S-T), RG107, M221, NA.

160. Robert Remini, *The Battle of New Orleans: Andrew Jackson and America's First Military Victory* (New York: Viking, 1999), 194.

161. Matthew Marshauer, "The Battle of New Orleans Reconsidered: Andrew Jackson and Martial Law," *Louisiana History* 39 (Summer 1998): 261–291.

162. Robert Butler to Villeré, 20 January 1815, Entry 72, Vol. 1, RG94, Records of the United States Army Commands, 1784–1821, NA; Thomas Butler to William Darby, 2 February 1815, William Darby to Andrew Jackson, 5 February 1815, and [Jacques?] Tanesse to Andrew Jackson, 20 February 1815, Reel 16, AJP.

163. Andrew Jackson to William Claiborne, 6 February 1815, Reel 16, AJP.

164. William Claiborne to Andrew Jackson, 6 February 1815 and 7 February 1815, Reel 16, AJP.

165. [Jacques?] Tanesse to Andrew Jackson, 20 February 1815, Reel 16, AJP; Jackson to Charles Woolstonecraft, 26 February 1815, Reel 62, AJP; Stephen Hopkins to L. Bourgeois, 20 February 1815, and Bourgeois to Hopkins, 22 February 1815, Reel 16, AJP.

166. Warshauer, "The Battle of New Orleans reconsidered," 275–277.

167. Col. Fortier to Andrew Jackson, 19 January 1815, Reel 15, AJP.

168. Louis Daquin to Robert McCausland, 15 February 1815, *CAJ*, 2: 171. See also McCausland to Andrew Jackson, 16 February 1815, Reel 16, AJP.

169. Robert McCausland to Andrew Jackson, 24 February 1815, *PAJ*, 3: 287.

170. Andrew Jackson to Mathew Arbuckle, 5 March 1815, *CAJ*, 2: 183.

171. Petition to Andrew Jackson from Joseph Savary et al., 16 March 1815, *PAJ*, 3: 315–316.

172. For the 1804 petition, see *TPUS*, 9: 174–175.

173. Charles Savary to Andrew Jackson, 31 March 1815, Folder 43, Box 23, ELP.

174. Carolyn Cossae Bell, *Revolution, Romanticism, and the Afro-Creole Protest Tradition in Louisiana, 1718–1868* (Baton Rouge: Louisiana State University Press, 1997), 64.

175. "Representation from the Members of the Legislature of the county of Attakapas," January 1815, Reel 16, AJP.

176. Joshua Baker to Andrew Jackson, 2 February 1815, *PAJ*, 3: 264.

177. Norman B. Wilkinson, ed., "The Assaults on New Orleans, 1814–1815," *Louisiana History* 3 (Winter 1962): 51.

178. *Niles' Weekly Register*, 11 February 1815, 379.

179. Latour, *Historical Memoir of the War*, 136.

180. Dickson, "Journal of Operations in Louisiana," 82.

181. John Lambert to Andrew Jackson, 20 January 1815, *PAJ*, 3: 253.

182. Deposition of Bartholemew Macarty, 19 May 1821, "Slave Evaluation Report," MS 199, Williams Research Center, Historic New Orleans Collection, New Orleans (henceforth cited as "Slave Evaluation Report").

183. I have compiled the information contained in this collective biography from the depositions found in "Slave Evaluation Report." The information in the

depositions includes the names of the 163 slaves, the names of their owners, and their sex, age, birth status indicating nationality or color (not available for all the slaves), skills or occupation, and valuation.

184. Latour, *Historical Memoir of the War,* 137.

185. Deposition of Antonio Sadice, 21 August 1821, "Slave Evaluation Report"; emphasis in original.

186. John Lambert to Andrew Jackson, 20 January 1815, *PAJ,* 3: 253.

187. Andrew Jackson to William Claiborne, 5 February 1815, *PAJ,* 3: 270–271.

188. Andrew Jackson to Hugues Lavergne, 20 February 1815, *PAJ,* 3: 283.

189. John Lambert to Andrew Jackson, 27 February 1815, *PAJ,* 3: 290.

190. Joseph Woodruff to Andrew Jackson, 23 March 1815, in Latour, *Historical Memoir of the War,* 289.

191. Deposition of Hugues Lavergne, 26 November 1824, "Slave Evaluation Report."

192. Deposition of Jacques Loutant, 22 June 1821, "Slave Evaluation Report."

193. Deposition of Chevalier Delacroix and Michel Fortier, 27 November 1825, "Slave Evaluation Report."

194. Deposition of Pierre Lacoste, 28 July 1821, "Slave Evaluation Report."

195. Lorna McDaniel, "Memory Spirituals of the Liberated American Soldiers in Trinidad's 'Company Villages,'" *Caribbean Quarterly* 40 (March 1994): 51; John McNish Weiss, *Free Black American Settlers in Trinidad 1815–1816* (London: John Weiss, 1995).

196. Mahon, *The War of 1812,* 368.

197. Henry Palfrey to John Palfrey, 20 January 1815, bMS Am 1704.7 (73), PFP.

198. David Weller to Samuel Weller, 13 January 1815, Samuel Weller Letters, Filson Historical Society, Louisville, KY.

199. Andrew Jackson to David Holmes, 18 January 1815, *PAJ,* 3: 249–250.

200. Israel Pickens' Address to his Constituents, 20 February 1815, Bryan and Leventhorpe Family Papers, Mss. 3994, UNC.

201. John Blake White, *The triumph of liberty, or, Louisiana preserved: a national drama, in five acts* (Charleston, S.C.: Printed for the author by J. Hoff, 1819).

202. *Unparralleled victory* (Boston: Printed by Nathaniel Coverly, Jun., [1815]).

203. John Reid to Sophia Reid, 20 April 1815, John Reid Papers, LC.

204. L. C. Hardy to William M. Reid, 3 April 1815, War of 1812 Series, Collection 541, Howard-Tilton Memorial Library, Tulane University.

205. James Brown to Edward Livingston, 14 February 1815, Box 5, Folder 23, ELP.

206. Henry Johnson to William Johnson, 1 April 1815, Folder 2, William Johnson Papers, Mississippi Department of Archives and History, Jackson.

5. Fulfilling the Slave Country

1. Israel Pickens to Thomas Lenoir, 2 January 1816, Lenoir Family Papers, MS 426, UNC.

2. Israel Pickens to William Lenoir, 8 December 1816, Chiliab Smith Howe Papers, *RASP,* Series J, Part 6, Reel 20; Edm. Jones to William B. Lenoir, 23 October 1816; Israel Pickens to Martha Pickens, 16 February 1817, Lenoir Family Papers, MS 426, UNC.

3. Israel Pickens to Thomas Lenoir, 1 May 1817, Lenoir Family Papers, MS 426, UNC. For life in the log cabin, see Israel Pickens to William Lenoir, 18 January 1818, ibid.

4. On Pickens's career, see Hugh C. Bailey, "Israel Pickens, Peoples' Politician," *Alabama Review* 17, no. 2 (April 1964): 83–101.

5. *American State Papers: Indian Affairs,* 2:123–124.

6. D. W. Meinig, *The Shaping of America: A Geographical Perspective on 500 Years of History,* vol. 2: *Continental America, 1800–1867* (New Haven: Yale University Press, 1993), 25–32; Frank Lawrence Owsley, Jr., and Gene A. Smith, *Filibusters and Expansionists: Jeffersonian Manifest Destiny, 1800–1821* (Tuscaloosa: University of Alabama Press, 1997), 22–26.

7. *Mississippi State Gazette,* 24 March 1819. On the United States and Florida between 1815 and 1821, see James E. Lewis, Jr., *The American Union and the Problem of Neighborhood: The United States and the Collapse of the Spanish Empire, 1783–1829* (Chapel Hill: University of North Carolina Press, 1998), 69–125; Owsley and Smith, *Filibusters and Expansionists,* chaps. 6–8; Robert Remini, *Andrew Jackson and the Course of American Empire, 1767–1821* (New York: Harper and Row, 1977), chaps. 22–24.

8. Thomas D. Clark and John D. W. Guice, *The Old Southwest, 1795–1830: Frontiers in Conflict,* with a foreword by Howard R. Lamar (Norman: University of Oklahoma Press, 1996), 237–243.

9. James Monroe to Andrew Jackson, 14 December 1816, *CAJ,* 2: 266.

10. Andrew Jackson to James Monroe, 23 October 1816, *PAJ,* 4: 69–70. See also Jackson to Monroe, 4 March 1817, *PAJ,* 4: 93–94.

11. Thomas Freeman to Josiah Meigs, 7 October 1815, Letters Received by the Secretary of the Treasury and the General Land Office from the Surveyors General for Mississippi 1 April 1803–4 November 1831, M1329, RG 49, NA.

12. Malcolm J. Rohrbough, *The Land Office Business: The Settlement and Administration of American Public Lands, 1789–1836* (New York: Oxford University Press, 1968), 96–100.

13. William Barnett to the Acting Secretary of War, 12 March 1817, *TPUS,* 18: 70–72.

14. "Memorial to Congress by Inhabitants of Amite Country," 22 March 1816, *TPUS,* 6: 670–671. See also Claborn Harris to Andrew Jackson, 14 January 1816, Reel 20, AJP.

15. Harry Toulmin to William Lattimore, 28 December 1815, *TPUS,* 6: 631–632.

16. Rohrbough, *The Land Office Business,* 92–96.

17. Lewis Sewall to Josiah Meigs, 8 December 1815, *TPUS*, 6: 598–599.

18. James Jackson to Andrew Jackson, 12 February 1818, *PAJ*, 4: 177–178.

19. *Niles' Weekly Register*, 29 May 1819; Rohrbough, *The Land Office Business*, 126–127.

20. *Alabama Republican*, 16 June 1820.

21. *American State Papers: Public Lands*, 3:420, 460.

22. Daniel Dupre, *Transforming the Cotton Frontier: Madison County, Alabama, 1800–1840* (Baton Rouge: Louisiana State University Press, 1997), 41–46; Paul W. Gates, *The Farmer's Age: Agriculture, 1815–1860* (New York: Holt, Rinehart, and Winston, 1960; repr., Armonk, NY: M. E. Sharpe, 1989), 59–63; Rohrbough, *The Land Office Business*, 109–127.

23. Stuart Bruchey, *Cotton and the Growth of the American Economy: 1790–1860 Sources and Readings* (New York: Harcourt, Brace and World, 1967), table 3P.

24. Milton B. Newton, Jr., ed., *The Journal of John Landreth, Surveyor* (Baton Rouge: Louisiana State University, 1985), 168.

25. *Annals of Congress*, 14th Cong., 1st sess., Appendix, 1658.

26. Ibid., House of Representatives, 14th Cong., 1st sess., 1261.

27. *Niles' Weekly Register*, 20 January 1816.

28. Joseph George Tregle, Jr., "Louisiana and the Tariff, 1816–1846," *Louisiana Historical Quarterly* 25 (January 1942): 29–33.

29. Robert L. Meriweather, ed., *The Papers of John C. Calhoun* (Columbia: University of South Carolina Press, 1959), 1: 401.

30. Yancey M. Quinn, "Jackson's Military Road," *Journal of Mississippi History* 41 (1979): 335–350.

31. Ibid., 345.

32. Brewster Jayne to Selah Strong, 28 July 1817, Jayne (Brewster H.) Letter, M242, Louisiana Collection, Jones Library, Tulane University.

33. Quinn, "Jackson's Military Road," 347.

34. Thomas Perkins Abernethy, *The South in the New Nation 1789–1819* (Baton Rouge: Louisiana State University Press, 1961), 423–433. The phrase "scramble for appropriations" comes from Jackson's 1830 Maysville Road veto.

35. *Mississippi Republican*, 17 September 1817. On the division of the Mississippi Territory, see Thomas Perkins Abernethy, *The Formative Period in Alabama 1815–1828*, with an introduction by David T. Morgan (Tuscaloosa: University of Alabama Press, 1990), 44–50, 52–53.

36. Cecil Morgan, ed., *The First Constitution of the State of Louisiana* (Baton Rouge: Louisiana State University Press, 1975); Joseph G. Tregle, Jr., *Louisiana in the Age of Jackson: A Clash of Cultures and Personalities* (Baton Rouge: Louisiana State University Press, 1999), 55–62.

37. Sidney Louis Villeré, *Jacques Philippe Villeré: First Native-Born Governor of Louisiana 1816–1820* (New Orleans: Historic New Orleans Collection, 1981), 85.

38. Oscar B. Chamberlain, "The Evolution of State Constitutions in the Antebel-

lum United States: Michigan, Kentucky and Mississippi," PhD diss., University of South Carolina, 1996, 79–87; Winbourne Magruder Drake, "The Framing of Mississippi's First Constitution," *Journal of Mississippi History* 29, no. 4 (November 1967): 301–327.

39. John Campbell to John Campbell, Sr., 10 July 1819, Box 4, Campbell Family Papers, MS 872, DU.

40. Malcolm Cook McMillan, "The Alabama Constitution of 1819: A Study of Constitution-Making on the Frontier," *Alabama Review* 3 (October 1950): 263–285; J. Mills Thornton III, *Politics and Power in a Slave Society: Alabama 1800–1860* (Baton Rouge: Louisiana State University Press, 1978), 10–14.

41. *Annals of Congress,* House of Representatives, 15th Cong., 2nd sess., 336.

42. On Birney's career, see William Birney, *James G. Birney and His Times* (New York: Negro Universities Press, 1969); Betty Fladeland, *James Gillespie Birney: Slaveholder to Abolitionist* (New York: Greenwood Press, 1969).

43. John Campbell to Robert Campbell, 29 December 1817, Box 3, Campbell Family Papers, MS 872, DU.

44. Abraham H. Inskeep to James Giles, 17 February 1819, Fanny Leverich Eshleman Craig Collection, Collection 225, Howard-Tilton Memorial Library, Tulane University.

45. Jayne (Brewster H.) Letter, M242, Louisiana Collection, Jones Library, Tulane University.

46. Andrew Collins to John Collins, 10 January 1819 and 6 November 1820, Collins Family Papers, Collection 467, Howard-Tilton Memorial Library, Tulane University.

47. James L. Watkins, *King Cotton: A Historical and Statistical Review 1790 to 1908* (James L. Watkins & Sons, 1908; repr., New York: Negro Universities Press, 1969), 29, 138–139, 166, 191.

48. These statistics are derived from printed tabulations found in the William Minor Papers, UNC. See also Lewis Cecil Gray, assisted by Esther Katharine Thompson, *Agriculture in the Southern United States to 1860* (Washington, DC: Carnegie Institution of Washington, 1933), 2: 693.

49. John Palfrey to William Palfrey, 22 April 1816, bMS Am 1704.8 (19), PFP.

50. James Trueman Madgruder Journal, 1812–1818, Mississippi Department of Archives and History, Jackson.

51. Todd Ashley Herring, "Natchez, 1795–1830: Life and Death on the Slavery Frontier," PhD diss., Mississippi State University, 2000, 155–156.

52. Robert Greenhalgh Albion, *The Rise of New York Port 1815–1860* (New York: Scribner, 1939; repr., Boston: Northeastern University Press, 1984), 100–101.

53. Tench Coxe, *An Addition, of December 1818, to the Memoir, of February and August 1817, on the Subject of the Cotton Culture, the Cotton Commerce, and the Cotton Manufacture of the United States* . . . (Philadelphia: n.p., 1818), 13. See also Gray, *History of Agriculture in the Southern United States,* 693.

54. Richard J. Follett, "The Sugar Masters: Slavery, Economic Development, and Modernization on Louisiana Sugar Plantations, 1820–1860," PhD diss., Louisiana State University, 1997, 94–109; Sarah Paradise Russell, "Cultural Conflicts and Common Interests: The Making of the Sugar Planter Class in Louisiana, 1795–1853," PhD diss., University of Maryland, College Park, 2000, chaps. 3 and 4; J. Carlyle Sitterson, *Sugar Country: The Cane Sugar Industry in the South, 1753–1950* (Lexington: University of Kentucky Press, 1953), 29.

55. *Increase of trade of New-Orleans: Comparative Statement of the internal produce and articles of domestic growth which have come to this port in the years 1815, 1816, and 1817,* Prices Current in Process, New Orleans—General 1815–1860, Baker Business Library, Harvard University. A hogshead equals 1,000 pounds.

56. *Louisiana Gazette,* 30 April 1818; John Clay to Henry Clay, 31 October 1820, *The Papers of Henry Clay,* ed. James F. Hopkins (Lexington: University of Kentucky Press, 1959), 2: 899.

57. William Darby, *A Geographical Description of the State of Louisiana, the southern part of the State of Mississippi, and Territory of Alabama . . .* (New York, James Olmstead, 1817), 225; Sitterson, *Sugar Country,* 30.

58. Russell, "Cultural Conflicts and Common Interests," 168. See also Ronald Edward Bridwell, "The South's Wealthiest Planter: Wade Hampton I of South Carolina, 1754–1835," PhD diss., University of South Carolina, 1980, 770.

59. Henry Palfrey to John Palfrey, 3 September 1821, bMS Am 1704.7 (76), PFP.

60. *Louisiana Gazette,* 19 August 1815.

61. 21 June 1815, *CVOP.*

62. Gates, *The Farmer's Age,* 174–178.

63. *American State Papers: Commerce and Navigation,* 2:389.

64. For 1810 population statistics of New Orleans, I have combined the figures for the "City and Suburbs of New Orleans" and "Precincts of New Orleans" from *Third Census of the United States,* M252, Roll 10, pp. 468–469, NA. This covers the same area as the figures for "Orleans Parish" from *Fourth Census of the United States,* M33, Roll 31, p. 193, NA.

65. Benjamin Henry Boneval Latrobe, *Impressions respecting New Orleans: Diary & Sketches 1818–1820,* ed. and with an introduction and notes by Samuel Wilson, Jr. (New York: Columbia University Press, 1951), 32. On New Orleans after the War of 1812, see Thomas Ingersoll, *Mammon and Manon in Early New Orleans: The First Slave Society in the Deep South, 1718–1819* (Knoxville: University of Tennessee Press, 1999), part 3.

66. Compiled from "Registers of Flatboats, Barges, Rafts, and Steamboats in the Port of New Orleans, 1806–1823" vol. 2: May 1812 through March 1823, QN420, City Archives, New Orleans Public Library.

67. Ari Kelman, "A River and Its City: Critical Episodes in the Environmental History of New Orleans," PhD diss., Brown University, 1998, 67–77; Edith McCall, *Conquering the Rivers: Henry Miller Shreve and the Navigation of America's Inland Waterways* (Baton Rouge: Louisiana State University Press, 1984), 30–

32, 148–158; Alfred R. Maass, "The Right of Unrestricted Navigation on the Mississippi, 1812–1818," *American Neptune* 60 (2000): 49–59.

68. Israel Pickens to Walter R. Lenoir, 2 September 1818, Lenoir Family Papers, MS 426, UNC.

69. Walter Prichard, Fred B. Kniffen, and Clair A. Brown, "Southern Louisiana and Southern Alabama in 1819: The Journal of James Leander Cathcart," *Louisiana Historical Quarterly* 28 (July 1945): 858; Newton, *The Journal of John Landreth*, 161.

70. James Williams to James Wilkins, 17 November 1819, Folder 6, Box 2E548, James Campbell Wilkins Papers, Natchez Trace Collection, Center for American History, University of Texas–Austin. On runaway slaves and the Mississippi River, see Thomas C. Buchanan, "The Slave Mississippi: African-American Steamboatworkers, Networks of Resistance, and the Commercial World of the Western Rivers, 1811–1880," PhD diss., Carnegie Mellon University, 1998, chap. 4.

71. Gilbert Russell to James Monroe, 9 July 1815, *TPUS*, 6: 540.

72. James Campbell to David Campbell, 15 July 1818, Box 3, Campbell Family Papers, MS 872, DU.

73. John H. Sims to William Sims, 9 October 1819, William Sims Papers, *RASP*, Series F, Part 2, Reel 9.

74. Thomas Robson Hay, "General James Wilkinson—The Last Phase," *Louisiana Historical Quarterly* 19 (April 1936): 416.

75. For example, see Estwick Evans, *A Pedestrious Tour, of Four Thousand Miles, through the Western States and Territories, during the Winter and Spring of 1818* (Concord, NH: Joseph C. Spear, 1819); Henry Ker, *Travels through the western interior of the United States, from the year 1808 up to the year 1816* . . . (Elizabethtown, NJ: published for the author, 1816); William Richardson, *Travel diary of William Richardson from Boston to New Orleans by land in 1815* (New York: n.p., 1938).

76. *Niles' Weekly Register*, 13 September 1817.

77. J. Gerald Kennedy, *The Astonished Traveler: William Darby, Frontier Geographer and Man of Letters* (Baton Rouge: Louisiana State University Press, 1981). For Darby's supervision of slaves at the Battle of New Orleans, see Thomas Butler to William Darby, 2 February 1815, and William Darby to Andrew Jackson, 5 February 1815, Reel 16, AJP.

78. Population estimates derived from Inter-university Consortium for Political and Social Research, *Historical Demographic, Economic, and Social Data: U.S., 1790–1970* (Ann Arbor, MI: Inter-university Consortium for Political and Social Research, 197?). For estimates of the rates of natural increase in the nineteenth century, see Peter D. McClelland and Richard J. Zeckhauser, *Demographic Dimensions of the New Republic: American Interregional Migration, Vital Statistics, and Manumissions, 1800–1860* (Cambridge, MA: Cambridge University Press, 1982).

79. Philip Foote to William Foote, 20 November 1816, Foote Family Papers, 1759–1987, Filson Historical Society, Louisville, KY.

80. Helen Toulmin to Mildred Ann Fry, 9 December 1817, Bullitt-Chenoweth Family Papers, Filson Historical Society, Louisville, KY; emphasis in original.

81. John Little to John Hamilton, 15 September 1817, William Southerland Hamilton Papers, Mss. 1471-C, UNC; emphasis in original.

82. James David Miller, "South by Southwest: Planter Emigration and Elite Ideology in the Deep South, 1815–1861," PhD diss., Emory University, 1996, 34.

83. James Graham to Thomas Ruffin, 9 November 1817, in *The Papers of Thomas Ruffin*, ed. J. G. de Roulhac Hamilton (Raleigh: Ewards and Broughton Printing Co., 1918), 1: 198.

84. Steven Stoll, *Larding the Lean Earth: Soil and Society in Nineteenth Century America* (New York: Hill and Wang, 2002), 143–150.

85. Thomas Gale to Benjamin Johns, 25 October 1817, Gale and Polk Family Papers, MS 266, UNC.

86. Henry Palfrey to John Gorham Palfrey, 11 September 1817, bMS Am 1704 (675), PFP.

87. John C. Van Horne and Lee W. Formwalt, eds., *The Correspondence and Miscellaneous Papers of Benjamin Henry Latrobe* (New Haven: Yale University Press, 1988), 3: 945–947, 951–952, 1065–1068.

88. Darby, *Geographical Description of the State of Louisiana*, 257–260.

89. Isaac Lewis Baker to Andrew Jackson, 7 April 1819, *PAJ*, 4: 281–282.

90. Thomas C. Lewis to Edward Livingston, 28 January 1819, Box 27, Folder 23, ELP.

91. Rohrbough, *The Land Office Business*, 121.

92. John Campbell to David Campbell, 16 December 1817, Box 3, Campbell Family Papers, MS 872, DU.

93. Contract between John S. Boxey, James H. Weakley and James W. Exum and John Coffee, 10 January 1818 (typescript), Container 5, Folder 6, John Coffee Papers, 1796–1887, LPR27, ADAH.

94. Gordon T. Chappell, "John Coffee: Land Speculator and Planter," *Alabama Review* 23 (January 1969): 25–33.

95. Elizabeth Tait to Charles Tait, 29 December 29, Container 1, Folder 7, Tait Family Papers, 1786–1899, LPR35, ADAH.

96. John M. Allman, "Yeoman Regions in the Antebellum Deep South: Settlement and Economy in Northern Alabama, 1815–1860," PhD diss., University of Maryland, 1979.

97. Dupre, *Transforming the Cotton Frontier*, 32, 34. See also Paul Horton, "The Culture, Social Structure and Political Economy of Antebellum Lawrence County, Alabama," *Alabama Review* 41, no. 4 (October 1988): 243–270.

98. For census returns in 1805, see RG 2, Microfilm Reel 2, Mississippi Department of Archives and History, Jackson. For Jefferson County in 1820, see

Hobbs Freeman et al., eds., *Early Jefferson County, MS Records,* vol. 1 (Vicksburg: Vicksburg Genealogical Society, 1991).

99. Cotton prices from Bruchey, *Cotton and the Growth of the American Economy,* table 3P. Export statistics from *American State Papers: Commerce and Navigation,* 2:155–160, 385–390, 466–471. Slave prices were compiled using SPSS 11.0.1, from Gwendolyn Midlo Hall, ed., *Louisiana Slave Database, 1719–1820* (Baton Rouge: Louisiana State University Press, 2000).

100. William Kenner & Co. to John Minor, 5 June 1819, William Kenner Papers, *RASP,* Series I, Part 3, Reel 13.

101. Hugh C. Bailey, *John Williams Walker: A Study in the Political, Social, and Cultural Life of the Old Southwest* (University: University of Alabama Press, 1964), 151.

102. Murray N. Rothbard, *The Panic of 1819: Reactions and Policies* (New York: Columbia University Press, 1962), 24–32.

103. John McRea to Andrew Jackson, 15 April 1819, *PAJ,* 4: 285. On the effect of the Panic of 1819, see Dupre, *Transforming the Cotton Frontier,* 49–77; Rohrbough, *The Land Office Business,* 137–156; Bailey, *John Williams Walker,* 151–167.

104. Henry Palfrey to John Palfrey, 8 December 1815, bMS Am 1704.7 (76), PFP.

105. Newton, *Journal of John Landreth,* 22.

106. Israel Pickens to William Lenoir, 27 December 1818, Container 1, Folder 5, Pickens Family Papers, ADAH.

107. *Louisiana Gazette,* 25 January 1820.

108. Daniel Hughes to John Mason, 2 October 1815, Records of the Creek Trading House, Letterbook, 1795–1816, M227, ADAH.

109. Cyrus Kingsbury to Jeremiah Evarts, 10 November 1818, Reel 755, Papers of the American Board of Commissioners for Foreign Missions, Houghton Library, Harvard University.

110. Latrobe, *Impressions respecting New Orleans,* 101–102.

111. Ibid., 57.

112. 16 August 1820, *CVOP.*

113. Israel Pickens to William B. Lenoir, 27 April 1818, Lenoir Family Papers, MS 426, UNC.

114. John Minor to Kitty [Minor?], 27 May 1815, Minor Family Papers, *RASP,* Series J, Part 6, Reel 2.

115. James Campbell to David Campbell, 28 October 1819, Box 4, Campbell Family Papers, MS 872, DU.

116. Israel Trask to Eliza Trask, 18 January 1819, vol. 1, Trask Papers, MS 899 (1807–1861) T775, Baker Business Library, Harvard University.

117. James Trask to Israel Trask, 16 August 1820, ibid.

118. Charles Tait to James Tait, undated, Container 3, Folder 5, Tait Family Papers, ADAH.

119. James Hollyday to Mrs. James Hollyday, 26 April 1819, Hollyday Family Papers, *RASP*, Series D, Reel 4.

120. Israel Pickens to William Lenoir, 5 June 1819, Container 1, Folder 5, Pickens Family Papers, ADAH.

121. Carol Wilson, *Freedom at Risk: The Kidnapping of Free Blacks in America, 1780–1865* (Lexington: The University Press of Kentucky, 1994).

122. Frances D. Pingeon, "An Abominable Business: The New Jersey Slave Trade, 1818," *New Jersey History* 109, nos. 3–4 (Fall/Winter 1991): 15–35.

123. William Stone to John Marsh, 1 December 1818, in Avery Family Papers, *RASP*, Series J, Part 5, Reel 10.

124. Joe Gray Taylor, *Negro Slavery in Louisiana* (Baton Rouge: Louisiana Historical Association, 1963), 37–38.

125. W. E. B. Du Bois, *The Suppression of the African Slave-Trade to the United States of America* (Baton Rouge: Louisiana State University Press, 1969 [1896]), 109–130; Frances J. Stafford, "Illegal Importations: Enforcement of the Slave Trade Laws along the Florida Coast, 1810–1828," *Florida Historical Quarterly* 46, no. 2 (October 1967): 124–133.

126. Charles Morris to the secretary of the navy, 10 June 1817, in *Niles' Weekly Register,* 22 January 1820.

127. Beverly Chew to William H. Crawford, 1 August 1817, in *Niles' Weekly Register,* 27 December 1817.

128. Owsley and Smith, *Filibusters and Expansionists,* 136–140; Stafford, "Illegal Importations," 126.

129. McIntosh to William Crawford, 30 October 1817, in *Niles' Weekly Register,* 3 January 1818. See also *Annals of Congress,* House of Representatives, 16th Cong., 1st sess., 905.

130. Bankhead to Graham, 24 December 1817, in *Niles' Weekly Register,* 24 January 1818. See also J. D. Healey to D. W. Crowinshield, 24 December 1817, in ibid.

131. "Memorial of merchants of New Orleans to Com. Patterson, of the 28th July 1817," in *Niles' Weekly Register,* 27 December 1817.

132. Thomas Bolling Robertson to John Calhoun, 24 April 1820, in Meriweather, *Papers of John Calhoun,* 5: 74–75.

133. Royce Gordon Shingleton, "David Byrdie Mitchell and the African Importation Case of 1820," *Journal of Negro History* 58, no. 3 (1973): 327–340.

134. Stafford, "Illegal Importations," 128.

135. Judd Scott Harmon, "Suppress and Protect: The United States Navy, the African Slave Trade, and Maritime Commerce, 1794–1862," PhD diss., College of William and Mary, 1977, 71; Du Bois, *Suppression of the African Slave Trade,* 119–123.

136. *Louisiana Gazette,* 31 July 1818.

137. George Mercer Brooke to Andrew Jackson, 2 July 1818, *PAJ,* 4: 218. The case is recorded as *The Merino. The Constitution. The Louisa.,* 9 Wheaton 391–408.

138. *Alabama Republican,* 4 May 1821.

139. "An Account of the Sales of Fifteen African Slaves Sold on the 19th of April 1825," Folder G, *United States of America v. Schooners Constitution, Merino, Louisa, and 84 Slaves,* Case #230, U.S. District Court, Southern District of Alabama, National Archives and Records Administration, Southeast Region, East Point, Georgia.

140. John Taylor, *Arator, Being a Series of Agricultural Essays, Practical and Political: in Sixty-Four Numbers,* ed. M. E. Bradford (Indianapolis: Liberty Classics, 1977), 358.

141. *Annals of Congress,* House of Representatives, 14th Cong., 1st sess., 1115–1117. See also Wilson, *Freedom at Risk,* 69–70.

142. 23 November 1816, *CVOP; Louisiana Gazette,* 27 November 1816; *Acts of the First Session of the Third Legislature of the State of Louisiana* (New Orleans, 1817), 44–48.

143. *Niles' Weekly Register,* 8 February 1817.

144. Latrobe, *Impressions respecting New Orleans,* 9–10.

145. Norrece T. Jones, *Born a Child of Freedom, Yet a Slave: Mechanisms of Control and Strategies of Resistance in Antebellum South Carolina* (Hanover, NH: Wesleyan University Press, 1990), 37–63.

146. Thomas Lenoir to William Lenoir, 11 August 1816, Lenoir Family Papers, MS 426, UNC.

147. Brenda Stevenson, *Life in Black and White: Family and Community in the Slave South* (New York: Oxford University Press, 1996), 159.

148. Henry Palfrey to John Palfrey, 21 July 1819, bMS Am 1704.7 (76), PFP. See also Henry Palfrey to John Palfrey, 16 June 1819; Henry Palfrey to John Palfrey, 5 January 1820, PFP.

149. Thomas Morris, *Southern Slavery and the Law, 1619–1860* (Chapel Hill: University of North Carolina Press, 1996), 111.

150. The statistics on the coastal slave trade are based on a compilation and analysis of inward slave manifests for the port of New Orleans for 1819, 1820, and 1821. The manifests are drawn from U.S. Customs Service, Port of New Orleans, Louisiana, Inward Slave Manifests, Reel 1: 1807, 1819–1821, Record Group 36, NA.

151. Frederick Douglass, "The Meaning of July Fourth for the Negro," in *The Life and Writings of Frederick Douglass,* ed. Philip S. Foner (New York: International Publishers, 1950), 2: 194.

152. Drew McCoy, *The Last of the Fathers: James Madison and the Republican Legacy* (New York: Cambridge University Press, 1989), 272–273.

153. Michael Tadman, *Speculators and Slaves: Masters, Traders and Slaves in the Old South* (Madison: University of Wisconsin Press, 1989), 21, 24, 205.

154. *Louisiana Gazette,* 1 July 1819.

155. [William?] Brent to George Brent, 3 May 1820, in David Rees Papers, *RASP,* Series H, Reel 29, emphasis in original.

156. Rees to unidentified correspondent, 16 July 1820, David Rees Papers, *RASP,* Series H, Reel 29.

157. Advertisement, 4 November 1820, David Rees Papers, *RASP,* Series H, Reel 29.

158. See also Michael Tadman, "The Hidden History of Slave Trading in Antebellum South Carolina: John Springs III and Other 'Gentlemen Dealing in Slaves,'" *South Carolina Historical Magazine* 97 (January 1996): 6–29.

159. J. Berthoud & Son to Edward Livingston, 9 October 1816, Box 3, Folder 27, ELP.

160. "John Owen's Journal of His Removal from Virginia to Alabama in 1818," *Publications of the Southern History Association* 1, no. 2 (April 1897), 95.

161. T. D. Clark, "The Slave Trade between Kentucky and the Cotton Kingdom," *Mississippi Valley Historical Review* 21, no. 3 (December 1934): 332.

162. Robert Gudmestad, "A Troublesome Commerce: The Interstate Slave Trade, 1808–1840," PhD diss., Louisiana State University, 1999, 119.

163. *Louisiana Gazette,* 26 June 1817.

164. *Mississippi State Gazette,* 24 March 1819.

165. Entry for 12 November 1817, "Missionary Journal to Indian Nations Nov 8 Dec 1817," Elias Cornelius Papers, DU.

166. Estwick Evans, *A Pedestrious Tour, of Four Thousand Miles, through the Western States and Territories, during the Winter and Spring of 1818* (Concord, NH: Joseph C. Spear, 1819), in *Early Western Travels 1748–1846,* ed. Reuben Gold Thwaites (Cleveland: Arthur H. Clark Company, 1904), 8: 320.

167. For Holmes's speech, see *Journal of the Mississippi Senate, 1818,* 16.

168. "An Act to amend the act entitled, 'An act regulating the importation of slaves, and for other purposes,'" *Acts Passed and the First Session of the Second General Assembly of the State of Mississippi* (Natchez: Marschalk and Evans— State Printer, 1819), 4–8.

169. *Mississippi Republican,* 27 July 1819, emphasis in the original.

170. Gudmestad, "A Troublesome Commerce," 160–216.

171. Entry for 23 November 1817, "Missionary Journal to Indian Nations," Elias Cornelius Papers, DU.

172. Steven Deyle, "The Irony of Liberty: Origins of the Domestic Slave Trade," *Journal of the Early Republic* 12 (Spring 1992): 54–57.

173. *Louisiana Gazette,* 25 July 1818.

174. Ibid., 15 September 1818.

175. Ibid., 11 June 1818, 13 June 1818.

176. Ibid., 23 April 1818.

177. M. W. de Bree to John B. de Bree, 29 January 1820, Slave Insurrection Letter, MS 10930, Special Collections, University of Virginia.

178. Gudmestad, "A Troublesome Commerce," 280.

179. On the slave power, see Leonard L. Richards, *The Slave Power: The Free North and Southern Domination 1780–1860* (Baton Rouge: Louisiana State University Press, 2000), esp. chap. 3.

180. Darrel E. Bigham, "From the Green Mountains to the Tombigbee: Henry Hitchcock in Territorial Alabama, 1817–1819," *Alabama Review* 26, no. 3 (July 1973): 216.

181. Gray, *History of Agriculture in the Southern United States to 1860*, 695–696.

182. Bigham, "From the Green Mountains to the Tombigbee," 223.

183. Hay, "General James Wilkinson," 419.

184. *Seville v. Chretien*, 5 Martin 275, September 1817.

185. Barbara J. Fields, "Slavery, Race and Ideology in the United States of America," *New Left Review* 181 (May/June 1990): 103–108.

186. Henry Palfrey to John Palfrey, 18 March 1818, bMS Am 1704.7 (76), PFP.

187. John Palfrey to Henry Palfrey, 7 April 1818, Palfrey Family Papers, *RASP*, Series I, Part 1, Reel 1.

188. William Chidester to Edward Livingston, 3 March 1820, Box 7, Folder 14, ELP.

189. Robert C. Nicholas to Lewis Sanders, 16 September 1821, Sanders Family Papers, Filson Historical Society Louisville, KY.

190. John Calhoun to Jacques Philippe Villeré, 25 November 1820, in Meriweather, *Papers of John C. Calhoun*, 5: 453. For requests from government contractors to purchase slave labor, see ibid., 3: 631, 5: 407.

191. Bigham, "From the Green Mountains to the Tombigbee," 215.

192. John Campbell to David Campbell, 16 December 1817, Campbell Family Papers, MS 872, DU.

193. Newton, *The Journal of John Landreth*, 21.

194. Eugene Genovese, *Roll, Jordan, Roll: The World the Slaves Made* (New York: Pantheon Books, 1974), 49–70.

195. Phillip Hamilton, "Revolutionary Principles and Family Loyalties: Slavery's Transformation in the St. George Tucker Household of Early National Virginia," *William and Mary Quarterly*, 3rd series, 55, no. 4 (October 1998): 549.

196. Chappell, "John Coffee," 34–35.

197. Edward Livingston to Andrew Jackson, 2 February 1816, Reel 71, AJP.

198. Russell, "Cultural Conflicts and Common Interests," 158.

199. David T. Bailey, *Shadow on the Church: Southwestern Evangelical Religion and the Issue of Slavery, 1783–1860* (Ithaca: Cornell University Press, 1985), 140. See also Bishop Charles B. Galloway, "Thomas Griffin: A Boanerges of the Early Southwest," *Publications of the Mississippi Historical Society* 7 (1903): 163–164.

200. *A Republication of the Minutes of the Mississippi Baptist Association, from Its Organization in 1806 to the Present Time* (New Orleans: Hinton & Co., 1849), 72–4. See also Bailey, *Shadow on the Church*, 141.

201. Accession #11085913, 21 January 1820, in *Race, Slavery, and Free Blacks: Series 1, Petitions to Southern Legislatures, 1777–1867*, ed. Loren Schweninger (Bethesda, MD: University Publications of America, 1998), Reel 3.

202. *Mississippi Republican*, 11 January 1820, 18 February 1820.

203. Ibid., 17 August 1819.

204. Darby, *Geographical Description of the State of Louisiana,* 275. Darby defended slavery in the 1830s. See Kennedy, *The Astonished Traveler,* 91.

205. Thomas Fearn to Clement Comer Clay, 29 July 1818, MS 692, UNC.

206. Isaac Briggs to John Calhoun, 19 December 1816, in Meriweather, *Papers of John Calhoun,* 1: 371.

207. James Pearse, *A Narrative of the Life of James Pearse . . .* (Rutland, VT, 1825; repr., Chicago: Quadrangle Books, 1962). For quotations see 10, 54, 79.

208. For Tallmadge's amendment, see *Annals of Congress,* House of Representatives, 15th Cong., 2nd sess., 1170. On the Missouri crisis, see Glover Moore, *The Missouri Controversy, 1819–1821* (Lexington: University of Kentucky Press, 1966).

209. Moore, *The Missouri Controversy,* 293.

210. "Abstract of the Territorial Census," *TPUS,* 18: 462.

211. *Annals of Congress,* House of Representatives, 15th Cong., 2nd sess., 1203.

212. Charles Tait to John Williams Walker, 5 February 1820, Container 1, Folder 2, Walker Family Papers, ADAH. See also Hugh C. Bailey, "Alabama Political Leaders and the Missouri Compromise," *Alabama Review* 9, no. 2 (April 1956): 120–134.

213. Thomas Butler to Ann Butler, 7 February 1820, Folder 46, Box 2, Butler Family Papers, MS 1026, Hill Memorial Library, Louisiana State University.

214. John Walker to Charles Tait, 8 December 1819, Container 1, Folder 9, Tait Family Papers, ADAH.

215. *Annals of Congress,* House of Representatives, 16th Cong., 1st sess., 1344.

216. Andrew Jackson to Andrew Jackson Donelson, 16 April 1820, *PAJ,* 4: 367.

217. Hilary McD. Beckles, "The Slave Drivers' War: Bussa and the 1816 Barbados Slave Rebellion," *Boletín de Estudios Latinoamericanos y del Caribe* 39 (December 1985): 85–109; *Niles' Weekly Register,* 1 June 1816; *Louisiana Gazette,* 3 July 1816.

218. *Annals of Congress,* Senate, 16th Cong., 1st sess., 197.

219. *Annals of Congress,* House of Representatives, 16th Cong., 1st sess., 1325.

220. *Annals of Congress,* House of Representatives, 16th Cong., 1st sess., 1343. For more on diffusionism during the Missouri debates, see McCoy, *The Last of the Fathers,* 265–276.

221. Ronald C. Woolsey, "The West Becomes a Problem: The Missouri Controversy and Slavery Expansion as the Southern Dilemma," *Missouri Historical Review* 77 (July 1983): 416.

222. Charles Tait to John Walker, 5 January 1820, Container 1, Folder 2, Walker Family Papers, ADAH.

223. Richards, *The Slave Power,* 88.

224. *Annals of Congress,* House of Representatives, 16th Cong., 1st sess., 1586–1588, and *Annals of Congress,* Senate, 16th Cong., 1st sess., 428. See also Moore, *The Missouri Controversy,* 107–112.

225. James Monroe to Thomas Jefferson, 27 May 1820, Jefferson Papers, LC.

226. For the significance of the Missouri crisis in Jacksonian politics, see John Ashworth, *Slavery, Capitalism, and Politics in the Antebellum Republic,* vol. 1: *Commerce and Compromise, 1820–1850* (New York: Cambridge University Press, 1995), 56–75.

Epilogue

1. *Louisiana Gazette,* 25 July 1818.
2. Bartlet & Cox to Henry Clay, 3 November 1815, in *The Papers of Henry Clay,* ed. James F. Hopkins (Lexington: University of Kentucky Press, 1959), 2: 92–93.
3. Robert D. Richardson to John C. Calhoun, 28 September 1819, in *The Papers of John C. Calhoun,* ed. Robert L. Meriweather (Columbia: University of South Carolina Press, 1959), 4: 351.
4. Benjamin Henry Boneval Latrobe, *Impressions respecting New Orleans: Diary & Sketches 1818–1820,* ed. Samuel Wilson, Jr. (New York: Columbia University Press, 1951), 22.
5. "The Southwest: Its History, Character and Prospects: An Oration before the Erosophic Society of the University of Alabama, December 9, 1839," in A. B. Meek, *Romantic Passages in Southwestern History* (New York: S. H. Goetzel and Co., 1857), 36.
6. Statistics from Inter-university Consortium for Political and Social Research, *Historical Demographic, Economic, and Social Data: U.S., 1790–1970* (Ann Arbor, MI: Inter-university Consortium for Political and Social Research, 197?).
7. Eleanor Myers, *A Migration Study of the Thirty-Two States and Four Organized Territories Comprising the United States in 1850 Based upon the Federal Census of 1850* (Syracuse, NY: Central New York Genealogical Society, 1977).
8. Michael Tadman, *Speculators and Slaves: Masters, Traders and Slaves in the Old South* (Madison: University of Wisconsin Press, 1989), 12; Ira Berlin, *Generations of Captivity: A History of African-American Slaves* (Cambridge, MA: Harvard University Press, 2003), chap. 4.
9. James L. Watkins, *King Cotton: A Historical and Statistical Review 1790 to 1908* (New York: James Watkins and Sons, 1908; repr., New York: Negro University Press, 1969), 147, 174, 198.
10. Lewis Cecil Gray, assisted by Esther Katherine Thompson, *History of Agriculture in the Southern United States to 1860* (New York: Peter Smith, 1941), 2: 740.
11. Stuart Bruchey, ed., *Cotton and the Growth of the American Economy: 1790–1860: Sources and Readings* (New York: Harcourt, Brace, & World, Inc. 1967), table 3M, 100; Walter Johnson, *Soul by Soul: Life inside the Antebellum Slave Market* (Cambridge, MA: Harvard University Press, 1999), 2.
12. Anthony F. C. Wallace, *The Long Bitter Trail: Andrew Jackson and the Indians* (New York: Hill and Wang, 1993).

13. Ira Berlin, *Slaves without Masters: The Free Negro in the Antebellum South* (New York: New Press, 1974), 136–137, 375.

14. Kenneth C. Martin and Gregory A. Almes, *The Historical Atlas of State Power in Congress, 1790–1990* (Washington, DC: Congressional Quarterly, 1993), 6–7.

15. David Eltis, *Economic Growth and the Ending of the Transatlantic Slave Trade* (New York: Oxford University Press, 1987); Paul Lovejoy, *Transformations in Slavery: A History of Slavery in Africa,* 2nd ed. (New York: Cambridge University Press, 2000), chaps. 8–10; J. R. McNeill and William McNeill, *The Human Web: A Bird's-Eye View of World History* (New York: W. W. Norton, 2003), 252–253; Anand A. Yang, "Indian Convict Workers in Southeast Asia in the Late Eighteenth and Early Nineteenth Centuries," *Journal of World History* 14 (June 2003): 179–208.

16. Kevin Bales, *Disposable People: New Slavery in the Global Economy* (Berkeley: University of California Press, 1999).

Acknowledgments

I am solely responsible for this book, but many people have contributed to it through their hospitality, generosity, curiosity, and expertise.

This book rests on materials that many professional librarians and archivists helped me to locate. I am especially grateful to the hardworking people at the Alabama Department of Archives and History, Columbia University's Butler Library, the Filson Historical Society, LSU's Hill Memorial Library, the Historic New Orleans Collection, Houghton Library of Harvard University, the Library of Congress, the Louisiana Division of the New Orleans Public Library, the Maryland Historical Society, the Mississippi Department of Archives and History, the National Archives, Perkins Library at Duke University, Princeton University Library, the Southern Historical Collection at the University of North Carolina, and the Supreme Court of Louisiana Collection at the University of New Orleans.

Every writer needs time and money. These were generously given to me by the Mrs. Giles Whiting Foundation, the American Council of Learned Societies, and the Georgetown University Graduate School of Arts and Sciences. Columbia University's Bancroft Dissertation Award provided Harvard University Press with funds to support the publication of *Slave Country*. Along these same general lines, I am also indebted to the Columbia University Probability Seminar.

I have presented earlier versions of parts of this book at various scholarly gatherings, including meetings of the American Historical Association, the Organization of American Historians, the Omohundro Institute of Early American History and Culture, and the Society for Historians of the Early American Republic. I would like to thank the Catholic University History Department and the Maryland Early American Seminar at the University of Maryland for inviting me to present chapters. I also benefited from participating in Bernard Bailyn's Atlantic History Seminar at Harvard University in 1998 and a conference on the domestic slave trade in the Americas sponsored by the Gilder Lehrman Center for the Study of Slavery, Resistance, and Abolition at Yale University in 1999.

I have received invaluable help from many extraordinary mentors, colleagues, and friends at Columbia, Georgetown, and elsewhere. Thanks to Tommaso Astarita, David Ball, Ed Baptist, Ira Berlin, Betsy Blackmar, Alan Brinkley, Paul Cheney, David Brion Davis, Eric Foner, Alison Games, Eugene Genovese, Gwendolyn Midlo Hall, Sam Haselby, Walter Johnson, Michael Kazin, Martin Kenner, Amy Leonard, Rebecca McLennan, John McNeill, Phil Morgan, Marcy Norton, Jim Oakes, Joe Reidy, Olutunde Rodney, Irving Rothman, Daryl Scott, Anders Stephanson, Scott Taylor, John Tutino, Steve West, and Michael Zakim. I am especially grateful to Barbara Fields, whose uncompromising intellect and dedication to the craft of history have profoundly shaped my own aspirations as a scholar and teacher.

Thanks also go to Joyce Seltzer for her guidance, to the outside readers for Harvard University Press for their suggestions, and to Julie Hagen for copy editing.

Most of all, I would like to thank my family for their humor, kindness, and love.

Index

S0-AEB-599

"*The American Statesmen Series was a pathbreaking venture in its time; and the best proof of its continuing vitality for our time lies in the testimony of the introductory essays written by eminent scholars for the volumes of the Chelsea House edition—essays that not only explain the abiding value of the texts but in many cases represent significant scholarly contributions on their own.*

"*Chelsea House is contributing vitally to the scholarly resources of the country—and, at the same time, helping us all to understand and repossess our national heritage.*"

—*Professor Arthur M. Schlesinger, jr.*

Samʳ Adams

American Statesmen Series

The State House, Boston, 1791.

Other titles in this Chelsea House series:

Forthcoming titles in this Chelsea House series:

SAMUEL ADAMS
JAMES K. HOSMER

INTRODUCTION BY
PAULINE MAIER

American Statesmen Series

GENERAL EDITOR
ARTHUR M. SCHLESINGER, JR.
ALBERT SCHWEITZER PROFESSOR OF THE HUMANITIES
THE CITY UNIVERSITY OF NEW YORK

CHELSEA HOUSE
NEW YORK, LONDON
1980

Copyright © 1980 by Chelsea House Publishers, a division of
Chelsea House Educational Communications, Inc.
Printed and bound in the United States of America

Library of Congress Cataloging in Publication Data

Hosmer, James Kendall, 1834-1927.
    Samuel Adams.

    (American statesmen)
    Reprint of the 1898 ed. published by Houghton,
Mifflin, Boston, in series: American statesmen.
    Includes bibliographical references and index.
    1. Adams, Samuel, 1722-1803.   2. United States--
History--Revolution, 1775-1783--Causes.   3. Politicians
 -United States--Biography.   I. Series: American
statesmen (New York)   II. Series: American statesmen.
E302.6.A2H6 1980   973.3'092'4 [B]   80-23753
ISBN 0-87754-195-7

Chelsea House Publishers
Harold Steinberg, Chairman & Publisher
Andrew E. Norman, President
A Division of Chelsea House Educational Communications, Inc.
70 West 40 Street, New York 10018

The old Teutonic Assembly rose again to full life in the New England town meeting. — FREEMAN.

Samuel Adams, the helmsman of the Revolution at its origin, the truest representative of the home rule of Massachusetts in its town meetings and General Court. — BANCROFT.

A man whom Plutarch, if he had only lived late enough, would have delighted to include in his gallery of worthies, — a man who in the history of the American Revolution is second only to Washington, — Samuel Adams. — JOHN FISKE.

CONTENTS

ILLUSTRATIONS
FOLLOWING PAGE 164

BLAZING THE WAY
Arthur M. Schlesinger, jr.

THE ORIGINAL AMERICAN STATESMEN SERIES consisted of thirty-four titles published between 1882 and 1916. Handsomely printed and widely read, the Series made a notable contribution to the popular appreciation of American history. Its creator was John Torrey Morse, Jr., born in Boston in 1840, graduated from Harvard in 1860 and for nearly twenty restless years thereafter a Boston lawyer. In his thirties he had begun to dabble in writing and editing; and about 1880, reading a volume in John Morley's English Men of Letters Series, he was seized by the idea of a comparable set of compact, lucid and authoritative lives of American statesmen.

It was an unfashionable thought. The celebrated New York publisher Henry Holt turned the project down, telling Morse, "Who ever wants to read American history?" Houghton, Mifflin in Boston proved more receptive, and Morse plunged ahead. His intention was that the American Statesmen Series, when complete, "should present such a picture of the development of the country that the reader who had faithfully read all the volumes would have a full and fair view of the history of the United States told through the medium of the efforts of the men who had shaped our national career. The actors were to develop the drama."

In choosing his authors, Morse relied heavily on the counsel of his cousin Henry Cabot Lodge. Between them, they enlisted an impressive array of talent. Henry Adams, William Graham Sumner, Moses Coit Tyler, Hermann von Holst, Moorfield Storey and Albert Bushnell Hart were all in their early forties when their volumes were published; Lodge, E. M. Shepard and Andrew C. McLaughlin in their thirties; Theodore Roosevelt in his twenties. Lodge took on Washington, Hamilton and Webster, and Morse himself wrote five volumes. He offered the authors a choice of $500 flat or a royalty of 12.5¢ on each volume sold. Most, luckily for themselves, chose the royalties.

Like many editors, Morse found the experience exasperating. "How I waded among the fragments of broken engagements, shattered pledges! I never really knew when I could count upon getting anything from anybody." Carl Schurz infuriated him by sending in a two-volume life of Henry Clay on a take-it-or-leave-it basis. Morse, who had confined Jefferson,

John Adams, Webster and Calhoun to single volumes, was tempted to leave it. But Schurz threatened to publish his work simultaneously if Morse commissioned another life of Clay for the Series; so Morse reluctantly surrendered.

When a former Confederate colonel, Allan B. Magruder, offered to do John Marshall, Morse, hoping for "a good Virginia atmosphere," gave him a chance. The volume turned out to have been borrowed in embarrassing measure from Henry Flanders's *Lives and Times of the Chief Justices*. For this reason, Magruder's *Marshall* is not included in the Chelsea House reissue of the Series; Albert J. Beveridge's famous biography appears in its stead. Other classic biographies will replace occasional Series volumes: John Marshall's *Life of George Washington* in place of Morse's biography; essays on John Adams by John Quincy Adams and Charles Francis Adams, also substituting for a Morse volume; and Henry Adams's *Life of Albert Gallatin* instead of the Series volume by John Austin Stevens.

"I think that only one real blunder was made," Morse recalled in 1931, "and that was in allotting [John] Randolph to Henry Adams." Half a century earlier, however, Morse had professed himself pleased with Adams's *Randolph*. Adams, responding with characteristic self-deprecation, thought the "acidity" of his account "much too decided" but blamed the "excess of acid" on the acidulous subject. The book was indeed hostile but nonetheless stylish. Adams also wrote a life of Aaron Burr, presumably for the Series. But Morse thought Burr no statesman, and on his advice, to Adams's extreme irritation, Henry Houghton of Houghton, Mifflin rejected the manuscript. "Not bad that for a damned bookseller!" said Adams. "He should live for a while at Washington and know our *real* statesmen." Adams eventually destroyed the work, and a fascinating book was lost to history.

The definition of who was or was not a "statesman" caused recurrent problems. Lodge told Morse one day that their young friend Theodore Roosevelt wanted to do Gouverneur Morris. "But, Cabot," Morse said, "you surely don't expect Morris to be in the Series! He doesn't belong there." Lodge replied, "Theodore . . . *needs the money,*" and Morse relented. No one objected to Thomas Hart Benton, Roosevelt's other contribution to the Series. Roosevelt turned out the biography in an astonishing four months while punching cows and chasing horse thieves in the Badlands. Begging Lodge to send more material from Boston, he wrote that he had been "mainly evolving [Benton] from my inner consciousness; but when he leaves the Senate in 1850 I

have nothing whatever to go by. .... I hesitate to give him a wholly fictitious date of
death and to invent all the work of his later
years." In fact, T.R. had done more research
than he pretended; and for all its defects, his
Benton has valuable qualities of vitality and
sympathy.

Morse, who would chat to Lodge about
"the aristocratic upper crust in which you & I
are imbedded," had a fastidious sense of language. Many years later, in the age of Warren
G. Harding, he recommended to Lodge that the
new President find someone "who can clothe
for him his 'ideas' in the language customarily
used by educated men." At dinner in a Boston
club, a guest commented on the dilemma of
the French ambassador who could not speak
English. "Neither can Mr. Harding," Morse
said. But if patrician prejudice improved
Morse's literary taste, it also impaired his political understanding. He was not altogether kid-
ding when he wrote Lodge as the Series was
getting under way, "Let the Jeffersonians &
the Jacksonians beware! I will poison the popular mind!!"

Still, for all its fidelity to establishment
values, the American Statesmen Series had distinct virtues. The authors were mostly from
outside the academy, and they wrote with the
confidence of men of affairs. Their books are

generally crisp, intelligent, spirited and readable. The Series has long been in demand in secondhand bookstores. Most of its volumes are eminently worth republication today, on their merits as well as for the vigorous expression they give to an influential view of the American past.

Born during the Presidency of Martin Van Buren, John Torrey Morse, Jr., died shortly after the second inauguration of Franklin D. Roosevelt in 1937. A few years before his death he could claim with considerable justice that his Series had done "a little something in blazing the way" for the revival of American historical writing in the years to come.

New York
May, 1980

INTRODUCTION
TO THE
CHELSEA HOUSE EDITION
Pauline Maier

JAMES KENDALL HOSMER'S *Samuel Adams* (1885) marks an important juncture in Americans' interpretation of their Revolution. Hosmer was one of the first to describe the Revolution as a fundamentally conservative event. And when he surveyed Americans of the 1770s, he indicated a preference for the Loyalists, another "new view" in the 1880s that would become far more common among historians in the twentieth century.

Hosmer's career also coincided with an important transition in historical studies. Before him history was the work of gentlemen scholars like George Bancroft, who produced his monumental *History of the United States* (1834-74) during a life in public service, or William V. Wells, the first biographer of Samuel Adams, who was himself a descendant of Adams. By background and social position

Hosmer resembled these men. He came from an old New England family: his ancestors left Kent County, England, for the New World in 1635 (the name appears as "Osmore" in John Winthrop's *Journal*). The first American James Hosmer was a founder of Concord, Massachusetts, where his descendants lived throughout the seventeenth and eighteenth centuries. They were, Hosmer recalled in a manuscript autobiography, "quiet, plodding people, little noted," who led "generally creditable" lives and played a prominent part in their townsmen's battle with the British on April 19, 1775.

George Washington Hosmer, the historian's father, was of the family's seventh generation in Concord, and the first to leave. He married Hannah Kendall of Plymouth and became a Unitarian minister in Northfield, Massachusetts, where James was born in 1834. Three years later he joined the westward migration of New Englanders, taking a parish in Buffalo, New York. The family's home continued to be filled with "the best of New England sweetness and light"; there visitors were "always sure of good and uplifting talk, and might encounter men and women of eminence—Henry Giles, Dorothea Dix, Horace Mann, Thomas Starr King, or indeed Ralph Waldo Emerson," whose wife was a childhood friend of Hosmer's

mother. James Kendall Hosmer returned to his
native state when he joined Harvard's class of
1855; he graduated from the Harvard Divinity
School in 1859 and became minister of the
First Unitarian Church at Deerfield, Massachusetts. There he acquired firsthand knowledge
of the New England town meeting, which
played so prominent a role in his later writings.
His first book, *The Color-Guard: Being a Cor-
poral's Notes of Military Service in the Nineteenth Army Corps* (1864), was based upon his
experiences in the Civil War as a member of the
52nd regiment of Massachusetts Volunteers.[1]

Unlike Bancroft and Wells, however, Hosmer
was also part of the new wave of professional
historians. These men, often trained in newly-
founded graduate schools and thereafter employed in colleges and universities, would dis-
place the gentlemen scholars and in time dominate the writing of history. Hosmer left the
ministry in September 1866 to become professor of rhetoric and English at Antioch College, of which his father had recently been
appointed president. Later he served as professor of English and history at the University
of Missouri (1872-74), professor of English and
German at Washington University in St. Louis
(1874-92), and librarian of the Minneapolis
Public Library, from which he retired in 1904.

He received a Ph.D. from the University of
Missouri in 1877 and an LL.D. from Washington University in 1897.

Hosmer wrote prolifically during the years
before his death in 1927 at the age of ninety-
three, leaving what he once described as a
"baker's dozen or more of volumes." They include histories of the Louisiana Purchase, the
Mississippi Valley, the American Civil War, the
Jews, German literature, and Anglo-Saxon freedom; an edition of *The Expedition of Captains Lewis and Clark,* and another of John
Winthrop's *Journal;* some fiction, a discussion
of drama in the colleges, and a volume of published reminiscences, *The Last Leaf* (1912); as
well as noteworthy biographies of Samuel
Adams, Sir Henry Vane (1888), and the Loyalist Governor of Massachusetts, Thomas
Hutchinson (1896). In the biographies above
all, Hosmer, in the style of the new professional history, emphasized his strenuous effort to
consult all available primary sources—newspapers, pamphlets, contemporary manuscript
collections. And he acknowledged his indebtedness to more recent writers, English and American, with whom he shared an obsession with
Anglo-Saxonism that united his historical work
with a wider world of scholarship.

Hosmer took up the Anglo-Saxon theme in a

sixty-page essay called "Samuel Adams, The Man of the Town-Meeting," published as part of the Johns Hopkins University Studies in Historical and Political Science in 1884, the year before his American Statesman biography of Adams appeared. He returned to it again in his biography of Vane and then explored it more fully in *A Short History of Anglo-Saxon Freedom* (1890). The "primordial cell of a free Anglo-Saxon state," he argued, was the "Folk-mote," or meeting of the people, which originated in Germany and was transplanted to England by the Saxons in a somewhat modified form. There it survived on the local level despite the Norman establishment of feudalism in England and the suppression of all traces of primitive Teutonic freedom on the Continent. Finally the tradition was fully and happily revived in America by the founders of New England. The Constitution of the United States developed further the institutions of those "white-bodied, fair-haired, blue-eyed Teutons from whom the English-speaking world descends." English Puritans, however, had failed in their effort to defend the cause of Anglo-Saxon freedom. The history of England from the Tudors through the eighteenth century was one of continued decay, with the people progressively "shut out" from participation in government. But starting with the great Reform Act of 1832 England began to recover its ancient Anglo-Saxon freedom, until in 1890 Hosmer could announce that "at the present moment, as regards popular freedom, the two countries stand nearly together."[2]

Hosmer's story had contemporary political implications. History revealed a new convergence of the English peoples, one that was strengthened, he believed, by the scholarly discovery of their common Anglo-Saxon traditions; and he heartily endorsed the reunification, moral or political, of those hundred and thirty million English-speaking people who were "in all substantial respects one ... whether settled in South Africa, in Australasia, in the primitive home, or in the United States." This was the age of unification, he noted, citing Cavour's reunification of Italy and the plaiting of "petty principalities and kingdoms" into a German nation "magnificent in size, power, and ability." An alliance of the English peoples could strengthen them against contemporary challenges, which included, for Americans of British heritage, an "undesirable foreign flood, which, pouring in yearly in volume always increasing through the unobstructed sluices of our seaports, seems likely so far to dilute our blood as to make it unequal to the task of sustaining Anglo-Saxon freedom."[3]

That great goal was obstructed, however, by a historical event. The American Revolution had divided the English-speaking peoples and left a heritage of bitterness. "We train our children," Hosmer wrote, "as we were trained ourselves, to execrate all things British, and to think only of England's tyranny."[4] Hence his intense interest in the Revolution, to which he returned continually, in his biographies of Adams and Hutchinson, in his *History of Anglo-Saxon Freedom*. Even his biography of Vane, an early Massachusetts Governor and English Puritan revolutionary who died on the scaffold in 1662, included, incongruously, a final chapter on the American Revolution. Always Hosmer wrote with a historic mission, for he sought to explain the Revolution in a way that would facilitate a reintegration of the English peoples.

In his view the Revolution was conservative in character. Those New Englanders who "drew . . . into the contest the rest of America" fought "to preserve what had been retained" by their ancestors—the ancient, democratic institutions of Teutonic origin that were the heritage of all English peoples. The Revolution did not, moreover, represent a contest between America and England, as was commonly supposed, but between political parties that spoke for minority interests in both countries. "Nine

Englishmen out of ten outside of Court influence" sided with the Americans against the
threat to Anglo-Saxon freedom posed by "the
Hanoverian George III and his Germanized
Court" who were, it seems, not fellow heirs to
Teutonic liberty but aliens whose tyranny
pointed up the common identity of the English
people. On the American side, revolution was
the work of an "energetic minority" based in
New England that prevailed over a majority
composed of the apathetic and of active
"Tories" who assumed importance by their
numbers and their strength of character.
"There were . . . no better men or women in
America, as regards intelligence, substantial
good purpose, and piety," Hosmer wrote. The
Loyalists' "stake in the country was greater
even than that of their opponents," and their
patriotism was "no doubt . . . to the full as
fervent." They were in error, of course: they
"had made the one great mistake of conceding
a supremacy over themselves to distant arbitrary masters, which a population nurtured
under the influence of the revived folk-moot
ought by no means to have made." But they
did not deserve the obloquy of later generations.[5]

The argument was hardly free of intellectual
confusion, but it allowed Hosmer to regard all

English people—all, that is, but the "German" George III—with favor. He could write an admiring biography of Hutchinson, a man of character who was, like himself, deeply committed to Anglo-American union. Henry Vane took on interest because he and his fellow seventeenth-century English Puritans had fought a losing battle for Anglo-Saxon freedom that resembled the struggle Americans won in the eighteenth century, and because his career, played out on both sides of the Atlantic, made him "so thorough an American and so thorough an Englishman" that he seemed to incarnate the common identity of both peoples. And Adams, as the title of Hosmer's 1884 essay emphasized, was "the Man of the Town-Meeting," could even be called "the creature of the town-meeting," and was certainly the "best type and representative" of that quintessential Anglo-Saxon institution.[6]

Hosmer accepted the dubious assertion that Adams was committed to independence from the 1760s, well before other colonists took up the cause. That notion had appeared in Wells's biography of 1865 and also in the writings of Hutchinson, whose authority Hosmer tended to accept uncritically. An early commitment to independence did not, however, make Adams as subversive for him as it would for some later

historians, because Hosmer considered independence essential to the conservation of
Anglo-Saxon freedom throughout the English
world.

Again from a strong dependence on Loyalist
sources, Hosmer exaggerated Adams's power
over Boston: "as a manager of men . . . Samuel
Adams was greatest. . . . He was the prince
of canvassers, the very king of the caucus. . . .
His ascendency was quite extraordinary and no
less marked over men of ability than over ordinary minds." Hosmer found this disturbing, for
it recalled the methods by which immigrants
in late-nineteenth-century cities marshaled
strength against older Americans and their
Anglo-Saxon customs. The student of revolutionary times, Hosmer commented in his biography of Hutchinson, "will see in the North
End Caucus . . . a prototype of the 'Machine,'
of such ill odor to-day in the nostrils of municipal reformers." Samuel Adams was "a man of
the strictest piety and most austere morals. . . .
But the query constantly suggests itself to him
who ponders his career, how could a man high-
minded and wise" have "stooped himself to
such questionable practices?"[7]

Adams's part in the 1773 publication of
letters written by Governor Hutchinson and
others particularly repelled Hosmer. "Nothing,"

he wrote, "can be more sly than the manoeu-
vring throughout," but he tried to explain
Adams's duplicity as part of a Yankee tradition
of "sharp practice" that claimed Adams "unconsciously." Hosmer the historian readily
exonerated Adams from charges of corruption.
What Adams did was "never for himself, but
always for what he believed the public good";
one could detect in him "no thought of personal gain or fame." Nonetheless, Hosmer
could hardly end his biography of Adams as he
ended that of Hutchinson—with a stirring
encomium to a life "thoroughly dutiful and
honorable." The limitations of his praise were
clear to readers who knew the earlier biography
by Wells, whom Hosmer considered "too indiscriminate" in admiring his ancestor and too
severe in judging the Loyalists. Occasional
commentators, however, thought that Hosmer
was not critical enough. His suggestion that
Adams rather than Washington should be remembered as the "Father of America" erred,
W. F. Poole said in a generally favorable review,
by "doubtless ranking him higher than he
deserves."[8]

Biographers after Hosmer turned against
Adams further. Ralph Volney Harlow's *Samuel
Adams: Promoter of the American Revolution*
(1923) dismissed all Adams did as the result of

a disordered psyche. No real events, it seemed, justified his hostility toward Britain; and because Adams was so influential, the entire Revolution of 1776 rested upon his derangement. The idea that Adams had "manufactured" the Revolution appeared again in Vernon L. Parrington's *The Colonial Mind, 1620-1800* (1927). Parrington described Adams as a professional agitator, "an intriguing rebel against every ambition of the regnant order," but was willing to excuse his methods because Adams sought not only independence but a democratic republic. Others proved less willing to cite ends as a justification for means. John C. Miller's *Sam Adams: Pioneer in Propaganda* (1936) described Adams as a puppeteer who "brought the people to approve his schemes and pulled the wires that set the Boston town meeting in motion against royal government," deliberately provoking crises that would "lead to the separation of mother country and colonies." Clifford Shipton reduced this interpretation of Adams to stereotype in the portrait he prepared for *Sibley's Harvard Graduates* (1958). Adams, Shipton wrote, "preached and practiced hate to a degree without rival" among New Englanders of his generation. "He taught his dog Queue to bite every Red Coat he saw, and took little children to the Common to teach them to hate

British soldiers."[9] Noel Bertram Gerson's 1973 biography of Samuel Adams was entitled *The Grand Incendiary*.

Hosmer never reduced Adams to so simple a formula. To heroicize was for him to deny weaknesses that were part of human nature; but he tried, sometimes in a mechanistic way, to balance blame with praise. More important, he sensed the complexity of Adams's character. Perhaps because he was familiar with W. E. H. Lecky's description of Adams as a latter-day Puritan covenanter, perhaps because he recognized a certain similarity between Adams and William Lloyd Garrison, Hosmer appreciated above all the ascetic qualities Adams shared with other revolutionary leaders throughout history. He stressed Adams's continual denial of self in the name of his cause and recognized in Adams's incapacity for grief after his close colleague Joseph Warren died at Bunker Hill a characteristic reticence as to his own emotions. For Hosmer Adams was in fact no one thing, but a welter of contradictions, a man "in religion the narrowest of Puritans, but in manner very genial," a person "perfectly rigid in his opinions, but in his expression of them often very compliant"; and though Adams was regarded much as the "abolitionist fanatics" had been before the emancipation proclamation, he was in fact "the most conservative of men."[10]

The elegance of such passages and the richness of Hosmer's insights redeem *Samuel Adams* from its time-bound Anglo-Saxonism and make it a book worth reading in its own right today, some one hundred years after it was first published.

Cambridge, Massachusetts
April, 1980

NOTES

1. All quoted reminiscences and much biographical information have been drawn from Hosmer's manuscript autobiography, a typescript of which is available at the Minnesota Historical Society in St. Paul. See also Solon J. Buck's brief biography in the *Dictionary of American Biography*, IX (New York, 1932), 244-45, and an obituary in *Proceedings of the American Antiquarian Society*, New Series, XXXVII (Worcester, Massachusetts; for 1927), 185-86.

2. Hosmer, "Samuel Adams, The Man of the Town Meeting," *Johns Hopkins University Studies in Historical and Political Science*, Herbert B. Adams, ed., 2nd Series, IV (Baltimore, 1884), 5; *The Life of Young Sir Henry Vane* (Boston and New York, 1889), 83; and *A Short History of Anglo-Saxon Freedom* (New York, 1890), 230.

3. Hosmer, *The Life of Thomas Hutchinson* (Boston and New York, 1896), xviii; *Life of Vane*, 550-51; and *Anglo-Saxon Freedom*, 324.

4. Hosmer, "The Work of the Revolutionary Fathers, from the Point of View of a Great-Grandson," *Address of Professor James K. Hosmer . . . at Washington University, February 23d, 1891* (St. Louis, 1891), 21.

5. *Anglo-Saxon Freedom*, 221, 219, 225-26, 228.

6. *Life of Vane*, ix-x; and Hosmer's *Samuel Adams* (Boston and New York, 1891), 352, 431.

7. *Adams*, 363; *Life of Hutchinson*, 247-48.

8. *Adams*, 368-69, and also x-xi; *Life of Hutchinson*, 349. Poole, "Samuel Adams," in *The Dial, A Monthly Journal of Current Literature*, VI (Chicago, 1885), 67.

9. Parrington, "Samuel Adams, The Mind of the American Democrat," in *The Colonial Mind, 1620-1800* (New York, 1927), 233; Miller, *Sam Adams: Pioneer in Propaganda* (Boston, 1936), 152, 276; Shipton, "Samuel Adams," in *Sibley's Harvard Graduates*, X (Boston, 1958), 463, 434. For a fuller discussion of the literature on Adams see Pauline Maier, "Coming to Terms with Samuel Adams," *American Historical Review* LXXXI (1976), 12-37.

10. *Adams*, 357-58.

AUTHOR'S PREFACE
TO THE
1898 EDITION

DURING the thirteen years since the publication of this life of Samuel Adams, which is at the same time a study of the New England town meeting at its most interesting period, the author has written three books on subjects closely relating to this, — a Short History of Anglo-Saxon Freedom;[1] a Life of Young Sir Henry Vane,[2] which is at the same time a study of the English Commonwealth; and a Life of Thomas Hutchinson,[3] royal governor of Massachusetts Bay, which is but another study of the New England Revolutionary conditions, with another personality than Samuel Adams in the foreground. While at the outset no connected series was projected, each book grew naturally out of its predecessor: the four stand, in fact, together, forming a consideration of the polity of the English-speaking race. The student whom this book may have attracted will possibly be interested to turn to its fellows. The " Anglo-Saxon Freedom " sketches the long evolution from the primitive liberty described by Tacitus to the momentous

[1] Scribners, 1890.   [2] Houghton, Mifflin & Co., 1888.
[3] Houghton, Mifflin & Co., 1896.

consummation with which Samuel Adams was so
closely bound, the coming to pass of the United
States.   The life of Vane portrays the unavailing
but heroic struggle of those close congeners of the
men of New England, the Independents, to establish in the motherland a freedom as unrestricted
as that afterwards wrought out for America.   In
the life, finally, of Thomas Hutchinson, an able
and high-minded champion who distrusted popular
government and disbelieved in the expediency of
an "Anglo-Saxon schism" in 1776, the case is
presented from a point of view in these days un-
familiar to Americans; a point of view, however,
which perhaps will not be repugnant to candid
minds, and which ought not to be overlooked in
the future as it has been in the past.

While all the books mentioned may afford help
to a reader desiring to go beyond the mere surface
of things, the "Hutchinson" bears most closely
upon the themes of the present volume.   Throughout their political lives the Tory governor and the
"man of the town meeting" were locked in the
bitterest strife; in the story of each, the great antagonist is nearly as prominent as the principal
figure; in the two presentments the operator, as
it were, but changes the position of the camera,
bringing into the foreground first one combatant,
then the other, in the same wrestle.   The cita-

tion of documents will be found to be fuller in the
" Hutchinson " than in the " Samuel Adams : " in
particular, the appendix of the " Hutchinson " will
be found useful, comprising as it does the full text
of a number of papers related in the most important ways to the story of the two men.

J. K. H.

MINNEAPOLIS PUBLIC LIBRARY,
    February 15, 1898.

AUTHOR'S PREFACE
TO THE
1885 EDITION

A LIFE of Samuel Adams from beyond the Mississippi! Of all the worthies of Boston, is there one more thoroughly Bostonian; and is it not impertinence, bordering upon profanity, for the wild West to lay hold of his name and fame? The writer of this book believes that his pages will exhibit in Samuel Adams a significance by no means circumscribed within narrow limits. The story of his career can as appropriately claim the attention of the West — yea, of the North and South — as of the East.

But if it should be thought that only New England hands can touch, without sacrilege, so sacred an ark, it may be urged that the members of that larger New England, which has forsaken the ungenerous granite of the old home for the fatter prairies and uplands of the interior, remain, nevertheless, true Yankees, and have bartered away no particle of their birthright for the more abundant pottage; they will by no means consent to resign any portion of their interest in the gods, altars, and heroes of their race.

If a personal reference may be pardoned, the

writer can claim that it has come down in his blood
to have to do with Samuel Adams.   His great-
great-grandfather, a captain of the Old French
War, was sent, in the pre-revolutionary days, by
the town of Concord to the Massachusetts Assembly, and was one of Sam Adams's faithful supporters in the long struggle when at length Bernard
and Hutchinson were foiled and driven out. In the
post-revolutionary days the writer's great-grandfather, a former officer of minute-men, sat for Concord for some years in the Massachusetts Senate,
under the sway of Samuel Adams as presiding
officer. When, on the fateful April morning, Gage
sent out the regulars, while Sam Adams and John
Hancock lay proscribed and in hiding at Lexington, the ancient captain[1] and the officer of minute-
men,[2] leaving at their homesteads the provincial
powder and cannon-balls concealed in the barns
and wells, had a main hand in organizing and
carrying through at the north bridge the Concord
Fight, during which Sam Adams was able to escape, unmolested, to the Congress at Philadelphia.
The writer's grandfather, in the next generation
again, just arrived at musket-bearing age in the
hard time of Shays's Rebellion, sustained Governor
Bowdoin and the cause of law and order among

[1] He had now become Colonel James Barrett.
[2] Adjutant Joseph Hosmer.

the rank and file, as did the aged Samuel Adams in a higher sphere.

Of all the "embattled farmers" who stood in arms at Concord bridge on the day when the arch-rebel eluded the clutch of King George, the captain of the minute-men, it is said, is the only one whose portrait has been transmitted to our time. That portrait has hung upon the wall of the writer's study while he has been busy with this book; and it has required no great stretch of imagination sometimes, among the uncertain shadows of midnight, to think that the face of the old "Revolutioner" grew genial and sympathetic, as his great-grandson tried to tell the story of the "Chief of the Revolution."

Though writing, for the most part, in St. Louis, the author has traveled far to study authorities. Whatever the Boston collections possess, — manuscripts, old newspapers, pamphlets, books, — has been freely opened to him, and examined by him. His greatest opportunity, however, was offered to him at Washington, by the kindness of Honorable George Bancroft. Mr. Bancroft held in his possession most of the manuscripts of Samuel Adams yet extant, together with a large number of autograph letters written to Mr. Adams throughout his long life by conspicuous men of the Revolutionary period. These original papers, a collection of the greatest value and interest, the writer was permitted, by the politeness of Mr. Bancroft, to use with entire freedom. This politeness the writer desires most gratefully to acknowledge.

Much help has been derived from the " Life of Samuel Adams," by William V. Wells, his great-grandson, whose three large octavos give evidence of much painstaking, and are full of interesting materials. The writer of the present biography has had no thought of superseding the important work of Mr. Wells, which must be consulted by all who desire a minute knowledge of Mr. Adams's character and career. The volumes of Mr. Wells have an especial value on account of the large number of extracts from the writings of Samuel Adams which they contain. To some extent the citations in the present work have been taken from these; in great part, however, they have been selected from old legislative reports and newspapers, and also from unprinted records, drafts, and letters. The filial piety of Mr. Wells is much too exemplary ; the career of his ancestor throughout he regards with an admiration quite too indiscriminate. Nor is his tone as regards the unfortunate men, against whom Samuel Adams fought his battle, that which candid historians of the Revolution will hereafter employ. The present book aims to give, in smaller compass, what is most important in Mr. Adams's career, and to estimate more fairly his character and that of his opponents.

JAMES K. HOSMER.

St. Louis, March 24, 1885.

SAMUEL ADAMS

CHAPTER I

THE YOUTH AND HIS SURROUNDINGS

THE Folk-mote, the fixed, frequent, accessible meeting of the individual freemen for discussing and deciding upon public matters, had great importance in the polity of the primeval Teutons, and was transmitted by them to their English descendants. All thoughtful political writers have held it to be one of the best schools for forming the faculties of men; it must underlie every representative system in order to make that system properly effective. The ancient folk-mote, the proper primordial cell of every Anglo-Saxon body-politic, which the carelessness of the people and the encroachments of princes had caused to be much overlaid in England, reappeared with great vitality in the New England town meeting.[1]

[1] Tacitus, *Germania*, xi. Waitz, *Deutsche Verfassungsgeschichte*, Band i. 4. Freeman, *Growth of English Constitution*, p. 17. May, *Constitutional History of England*, ii. 460. Phillips, *Geschichte des Angelsächsischen Rechts*, p. 12. J. Toulmin Smith, *Local Self-Government and Centralization*, p. 29, etc. Johns Hopkins Univ. Studies. E. A. Freeman, *Introd. to Am. Institut.*

At the Revolution, in Massachusetts, then including Maine, and containing 210,000 white
inhabitants, more than were found in any other
American colony, there were more than two hundred towns, whose constitution is thus described
by Gordon, a writer of the period : —

"Every town is an incorporated republic. The selectmen, by their own authority, or upon the application of a certain number of townsmen, issue a warrant
for the calling of a town meeting. The warrant mentions the business to be engaged in, and no other can be
legally executed. The inhabitants are warned to attend ;
and they that are present, though not a quarter or
tenth of the whole, have a right to proceed. They
choose a president by the name of moderator, who reg-
ulates the proceedings of the meeting. Each individual
has an equal liberty of delivering his opinion, and is not
liable to be silenced or browbeaten by a richer or greater
townsman than himself. Every freeman or freeholder
gives his vote or not, and for or against, as he pleases ;
and each vote weighs equally, whether that of the
highest or lowest inhabitant. . . . All the New England
towns are on the same plan in general."

Throughout the thirteen colonies, the folk-mote
existed in well-developed form only in the New

Hist. H. B. Adams, *Germanic Origin of N. E. Towns.* Edward
Channing, *Town and County Government in the English Colonies
of N. A.* For a sketch of the development through two thousand
years, see the author's *Short History of Anglo-Saxon Freedom*
(Scribners, 1890), in which note is made of the opinions of scholars
less certain of the derivation of that freedom than the authorities
above cited.

England town meeting; few traces of it can be found in the South; nor in the middle colonies was the case much different. At the time of the Revolution, New England stood alone in having restored a primitive liberty which had been superseded, each of her little democracies governing itself after a fashion for which there was no precedent without going back to the folk-mote of a remote day, — to a time before the kings of England began to be arbitrary, and before the people became indifferent to their birthright.

The New England town is best presented at a point when it has had time to become fully developed, and before the causes have begun to operate which in our day have largely changed it. The period of the Revolution, in fact, is the epoch that must be selected; and the town of towns, in which everything that is most distinctive appears most plainly, is Boston.

Boston was a town governed by its folk-mote almost from its foundation until 1822, more than one hundred and eighty years. In 1822, when the inhabitants numbered forty thousand, it reluctantly became a city, giving up its town meetings because they had grown so large as to be unmanageable, — the people thereafter choosing a mayor and common council to do the public business for them, instead of doing it themselves. The records of the town of Boston, carefully preserved from the earliest times, lie open to public inspection in the office of the city clerk. Whoever pores over

these records, on the yellow paper, in the faded
ink, as it came from the pens of the ancient town
clerks,[1] will find that for the first hundred years
the freemen are occupied for the most part with
their local concerns. How the famous cowpaths
pass through the phases of their evolution, — foot-
way, country-lane, high-road, — until at length they
become the streets and receive dignified names;
what ground shall be taken for burying-places,
and how it shall be fenced, as the little settlement
gradually covers the whole peninsula; how the
Neck, then a very consumptive-looking neck, not
goitred by a ward or two of brick and mortar-
covered territory, may be protected, so that it
may not be guillotined by some sharp northeaster;
what precautions shall be taken against the spread
of small-pox; who shall see to it that dirt shall
not be thrown into the town dock; that inquiry
shall be made whether Latin may not be better
taught in the public schools, — such topics as these
are considered. For the most part, the record is
tedious and unimportant detail for a modern reader,
though now and then in an address to the sovereign, or a document which implies that all is not
harmony between the town and the royal governor,
the horizon broadens a little. But soon after the
middle of the eighteenth century the record largely
changes. William Cooper at length begins his service of forty-nine years as town clerk, starting out
in 1761 with a bold, round hand, which gradually

[1] These records are now in print.

becomes faint and tremulous as the writer descends into old age. One may well turn over the musty pages here with no slight feeling of awe, for it is the record, made at the moment, of one of the most memorable struggles of human history, that between the little town of Boston on the one hand, and George III. with all the power of England at his back, on the other.

At the date of the Stamp Act, 1765, the population of Boston was not far from 18,000, in vast majority of English blood; though a few families of Huguenots, like the Faneuils, the Bowdoins, the Reveres, and the Molineux, had strengthened the stock by being crossed with it, and there was now and then a Scotchman or an Irishman. As the Bostonians were of one race, so in vast majority they were of one faith, Independents of Cromwell's type, though there were Episcopalians, and a few Quakers and Baptists. The town drew its life from the sea, to which all its industry was more or less closely related. Hundreds of men were afloat much of the time, captains or before the mast, leaving their wives and children in the town, but themselves being on shore only in the intervals between the most enterprising voyages. Of the landsmen, a large proportion were shipbuilders. The stanchest crafts that sailed slid by the dozen down the ways of the Boston yards. New England needed a great fleet, having, as she did, a good part of the carrying-trade of the thirteen colonies, with that of the West Indies also.

Another industry, less salutary, was the distilling of rum; and much of this went in the ships of Boston and Newport men to the coast of Africa, to be exchanged for slaves. It was a different world from ours, and should be judged by different standards. Besides the branches mentioned, there was little manufacturing in town or country; the policy of the mother country was to discourage colonial manufactures; everything must be made in England, the colonies being chiefly valuable from the selfish consideration that they could be made to afford a profitable market for the goods. In the interior, therefore, the people were all farmers, bringing their produce to Boston, and taking thence, when they went home, such English goods as they needed. Hence the town was a great mart. The merchants were numerous and rich; the distilleries fumed; the shipyards rattled; the busy ships went in and out; and the country people flocked in to the centre.

Though Boston lost before the Revolution the distinction of being the largest town in America, it remained the intellectual head of the country. Its common schools gave every child a good education; and Harvard College, scarcely out of sight, and practically a Boston institution, gave a training hardly inferior to that of European universities of the day. At the bottom of the social scale were the negro slaves. The newspapers have many advertisements of slaves for sale, and of runaways sought by their masters. Slavery, however, was far on the wane, and soon after the Revolution became extinguished. The negroes were for the most part servants in families, not workmen at trades, and so exercised little influence in the way of bringing labor into disrepute.

As the slaves were at the bottom, so at the top of society were the ministers, men often of fine force, ability, and education. No other such career as the ministry afforded was open in those days to ambitious men. Year by year the best men of each Cambridge class went into the ministry, and the best of them were sifted out for the Boston pulpit. Jonathan Mayhew, Andrew Eliot, Samuel Cooper, Charles Chauncey, Mather Byles, — all were characters of mark, true to the Puritan standards, generally, as regards faith, eloquent in their office, friends and advisers of the political leaders, themselves often political leaders, foremost in the public meetings, and active in private.

Together with the ministers, the merchants were a class of influence. Nothing could be bolder than the spirit in those days of Boston commerce. In ships built at the yards of the town, the Yankee crews went everywhere through the world. Timber, tobacco, tar, rice, from the southern colonies, wheat from Maryland, sugar and molasses from the West Indies, sought the markets of the world in New England craft. The laws of trade were complicated and oppressive; but every skipper was more or less a smuggler, and knew well how to brave or evade authority. Wealth flowed fast into the pockets of the Boston merchants, who built and furnished fine mansions, walked King Street in gold lace and fine ruffles, and sat at home, as John Hancock is described, in "a red velvet cap, within which was one of fine linen, the edge of this turned up over the velvet one two or three inches. He wore a blue damask gown lined with silk, a white plaited stock, a white silk embroidered waistcoat, black silk small-clothes, white silk stockings, and red morocco slippers." It is all still made real to us in the superb portraits of Copley, — the merchants sitting in their carved chairs, while a chart of distant seas unrolled on the table, or a glimpse through a richly curtained window in the background at a busy wharf or a craft under full sail, hints at the employment that has lifted the men to wealth and consequence.

Below the merchants, the class of workmen formed a body most energetic. Dealing with the tough oak that was to be shaped into storm defying hulls, twisting the cordage that must stand the strain of arctic ice and tropic hurricane, forging anchors that must hold off the lee-shores of all tempestuous seas, — this was work to bring out vigor of muscle, and also of mind and temper. The calkers were bold politicians. The ropewalk hands were energetic to turbulence, courting the brawls with the soldiers which led to the " Boston massacre." It must be said, too, that the taverns throve. New England rum was very plentiful, the cargo of many a ship that passed the

"Boston Light," of many a townsman and "high private" who came to harsh words, and perhaps fisticuffs, in Pudding Lane or Dock Square. The prevailing tone of the town, however, was decent and grave. The churches were thronged on Sundays and at Thursday lecture, as they have not been since. All classes were readers; the booksellers fill whole columns in the newspapers with their lists; the best books then in being in all departments of literature are on sale and in the circulating libraries. The five newspapers the people may be said to have edited themselves. Instead of the impersonal articles of a modern journal, the space in a sheet of the "Revolution," after the news and advertisements, was occupied by letters, in which "A Chatterer," "A. Z.," or more often some classic character, "Sagittarius," "Vindex," "Philanthrop," "Valerius Poplicola," "Nov-Anglus," or "Massachusettensis," belabors Whig or Tory, according to his own stripe of politics, — the champion sometimes appearing in a rather Chinese fashion, stilted up on high rhetorical soles, and padded out with pompous period and excessive classic allusion, but often direct, bold, and well-armed from the arsenals of the best political thinkers.

Of course the folk-mote of such a town as this would have spirit and interest. Wrote a Tory in those days: [1] "The town meeting at Boston is

[1] Sagittarius, quoted by Frothingham: "The Sam Adams's Regiments," *Atlantic Monthly*, November, 1863.

the hot-bed of sedition. It is there that all their
dangerous insurrections are engendered; it is
there that the flame of discord and rebellion was
first lighted up and disseminated over the provinces; it is therefore greatly to be wished that
Parliament may rescue the loyal inhabitants of
that town and province from the merciless hand
of an ignorant mob, led on and inflamed by self-
interested and profligate men." Have more interesting assemblies ever taken place in the history
of the world than the Boston town meetings?
Out of them grew the independence of the United
States, and what more important event has ever
occurred?

Massachusetts was unquestionably the leader
in the Revolution.[1] After the first year of war,

---

[1] On this point, which local pride might dispute, a few authorities may be cited. Englishmen at the time felt as follows:
" In all the late American disturbances and in every thought
against the authority of the British Parliament, the people of
Massachusetts Bay have taken the lead. Every new move towards independence has been theirs; and in every fresh mode of
resistance against the law they have first set the example, and
then issued out admonitory letters to the other colonies to follow
it." Mauduit's *Short View of the Hist. of the N. E. Colonies*, p. 5.
See also Anburey's *Travels*, i. 310. Hutchinson, *Hist. of Mass.
Bay*, iii. 257. Rivington, *Independence the Object of Congress in
America*, London, 1776, p. 15. Lord Camden called Massachusetts " The ring-leading Colony." Coming to writers of our own
time, Lecky declares, *Hist. of XVIIIth Century*, iii. 386: " The
Central and Southern Colonies long hesitated to follow New England. Massachusetts had thrown herself with fierce energy into
the conflict, and soon drew the other provinces in her wake."
Says J. R. Seeley, *Expansion of England*, pp. 154, 155: " The

indeed, the soil of New England, as compared with the Centre and South, suffered little from the scourge of hostile military occupation. Her sacrifices, however, did not cease. There is no way of determining how many New England militia took the field during the strife; the multitude was certainly vast. The figures, however, as regards the more regular levies, have been preserved, and are significant. With a population comprising scarcely more than one third of the inhabitants of the thirteen colonies, New England furnished 118,251 of the 231,791 Continental troops that figured in the war. Massachusetts alone furnished 67,907, more than one quarter of the entire number. As regards the giving of money and supplies, without doubt her proportion was as large. There resistance to British encroachment began; thence disaffection to Britain was spread abroad.

As Massachusetts led the thirteen colonies, the town of Boston led Massachusetts. "This province began it," wrote General Gage,[1] — " I might say this town, for here the arch-rebels formed their

spirit driving the colonies to separation from England, a principle attracting and conglobing them into a new union among themselves, — how early did this spirit show itself in the New England colonies! It was not present in all the colonies. It was not present in Virginia; but when the colonial discontents burst into a flame, then was the moment when Virginia went over to New England, and the spirit of the Pilgrim Fathers found the power to turn the offended colonists into a new nation."

[1] To Lord Dartmouth; quoted in *Diary and Letters of Thomas Hutchinson*, p. 16.

scheme long ago." The ministers of George III.
recognized this leadership and attacked Boston
first. So thoroughly did the forces of revolt centre here that the English pamphleteers, seeking
to uphold the government cause, speak sometimes
not so much of Americans, or New Englanders, or
indeed men of Massachusetts, as of "Bostoneers,"
as if it were with the people of that one little town
that the fight was to be waged. Even in the woods
and wilds the preëminence was known. When
Major George Rogers Clark was subduing the
Mississippi valley, he found that the British emissaries, rousing the Indians and simple French *hab-
itans* against him by using the terms they could
best understand, had urged them "to fight Boston." Boston led the thirteen colonies. Who led
the town of Boston? He certainly ought to be a
memorable figure. He it is whose story this book
is designed to tell.

The progenitor in America of the Adams family,
so numerous and famous, was Henry Adams, who,
with a family of eight children, settled at an early
period near Mount Wollaston in Quincy. The
inscription on his tombstone, written by President
John Adams, describes him as having come from
Devonshire, in England. English families of the
name trace their descent from a remote Welsh
ancestor; there is a possibility, therefore, of a
mixture of Celtic blood in the stock. Grandsons
of the emigrant Henry Adams were Joseph Adams,
a citizen of Braintree, and John Adams, a sea-

captain. The former was grandfather of President John Adams; the latter was grandfather of Samuel Adams, the subject of this memoir. The second son of Captain John Adams was Samuel Adams, born May 6, 1689, in Boston, where he always lived, and where he was married at the age of twenty-four to Mary Fifield. From this union proceeded a family of twelve children, three only of whom survived their father. Of these the illustrious Samuel Adams was born September 16, O. S., 1722.

The theory that great men derive their powers from their mothers rather than their fathers may, perhaps, be regarded as exploded. It will receive no support, at least, from the case of Samuel Adams. Of his mother no mention can be found except that she was rigidly pious after the Puritan standards; his father, however, was a man of most noteworthy qualities, and filled a large place in the community in which his lot was cast. He was possessed, at first, of what for those days was a large property, and in 1712 bought a handsome estate in Purchase Street, extending two hundred and fifty-eight feet along the thoroughfare and running thence to the low-water line of the harbor. The mansion, large and substantial, fronted the water, of which it commanded a fine view. Samuel Adams, senior, early made impression, passing soon from a purely private station into various public positions. He became justice of the peace, deacon of the Old South Church,

then an office of dignity, selectman, one of the
important committee of the town to instruct the
representatives to the Assembly, and at length
entered the Assembly itself. His son called him
" a wise man and a good man." He was everywhere a leader. In 1715, largely through his
influence, the " New South " religious society was
established in Summer Street. About the year
1724, with a score or so of others, generally from
the North End, where the shipyards especially lay,
he was prominent in a club designed " to lay plans
for introducing certain persons into places of trust
and power." It was known as the " Caulkers'
Club," hence, possibly, one of the best-known
terms in political nomenclature. As a representative he signalized himself by opposition to that
combative old veteran from the wars of Marl-
borough, Shute, in whose incumbency the chronic
quarrel between governor and legislature grew
very sharp. The tastes and abilities, indeed, which
made the son afterwards so famous, are also plain
in the father, only appearing in the son in a more
marked degree and in a time more favorable for
their exhibition.

" Sam " Adams (to his contemporaries it was
affectation quite superfluous to go beyond the
monosyllable in giving his Christian name) has
left but few traces of his boyhood. There is a
story that as he went back and forth between home
and the wooden schoolhouse in School Street, just
in the rear of King's Chapel, his punctuality was

so invariable that the laborers regulated their hours of work by him. One is glad to believe that this tale of virtue so portentous has no good foundation. Undoubtedly, however, he was a staid, prematurely intelligent boy, responding to the severe Puritan influences which surrounded him, and early developed through listening to the talk of the strong men of the town, for whom his father's house was a favorite meeting-place. Of his college life, too, there is almost no mention. He was a close student and always afterward fond of quoting Greek and Latin. His father's earnest wish was that he should study theology. Whitefield, as Sam Adams came forward into life, was quickening wonderfully the zeal of New England. It would have been natural for the parents and the sober-minded son to feel a warmth from so powerful a torch. A minister, however, he could not be. He received the degree of A. B. in 1740, and when three years after he became Master of Arts, the thesis which he presented showed plainly what was his true bent. " Whether it be Lawful to resist the Supreme Magistrate, if the Commonwealth cannot otherwise be preserved," was his subject, which he proceeded to discuss in the presence not only of the college dignitaries, but of the new governor, Shirley, and the crown officials, who sat in state near the young speakers at Commencement, as do their successors to-day. What he said and what effect he produced is not recorded. No one knew that as the young man spoke, then, for the first time, one of the great Revolutionary group was asserting the right of resistance by the people to arbitrary oppressors. Shirley was perhaps lost in some far-away dream of how he might get at the French; and when thirty years after, in his retirement at Dorchester, he asked who the Sam Adams could be that was such a thorn in the side to his successors Bernard and Hutchinson, he was quite unconscious of the fact that he himself had had the benefit, close at hand, of the first scratch.

In the Harvard quinquennial, where the names in the provincial period are arranged, not alphabetically, but according to the consequence of the families to which the students belong, Sam Adams stands fifth in a class of twenty-two. As he reached his majority his father became embarrassed, and, while misfortune impended, Sam Adams, whose disinclination to theology had become plain, began the study of law. This his mother is said to have disapproved; law in those days was hardly recognized as a profession, and the young man turned to mercantile life as a calling substantial and respectable. He entered the counting-house of Thomas Cushing, a prominent merchant, with whose son of the same name he was destined afterwards to be closely connected through many years of public service. For business, however, he had neither taste nor tact. The competition of trade was repulsive to him; his desire for gain was of the slightest. Leaving Mr. Cushing after a few months, he received from his father £1000 with which to begin business for himself. Half of this he lent to a friend who never repaid it, and the other half he soon lost in his own operations. Thriftless though he seemed, he began to be regarded as not unpromising, for there were certain directions in which his mind was wonderfully active. Father and son became partners in a malthouse situated on the estate in Purchase Street, and one can well understand how business must have suffered in the circumstances in which they were presently placed.

The times became wonderfully stirring. In 1745 Sir William Pepperell led his New England army to the capture of Louisburg. Boston was at first absorbed in the' great preparations; while the siege proceeded, the town was in a fever of anxiety, as it had good cause to be; for, brave though they were, whoever reads the story must feel that only the most extraordinary good luck could have brought the provincials through. When the victory was at length complete, and the iron cross from the market-place was brought home by the soldiers in token of triumph, never was joy more tumultuous. In all this time Samuel Adams, senior, was in the forefront of public affairs. He sat in the Assembly, and was proposed by that body for the Council or upper house, but was rejected by Shirley. He was a member of most of the military committees, in that day the most important of the legislature; there are facts showing that his judgment was especially deferred to in affairs of that kind.

Encouraged by the success at Cape Breton, the colonists planned still further enterprises against the French, in all which Massachusetts, stimulated by Shirley, who had the heart and the head of a soldier, took part with enthusiasm. When in 1748 the magnificent fruits of New England energy were all resigned at the peace of Aix-la-Chapelle, a deep resentment was felt.

In matters relating to peace and war the elder Adams was much concerned. The son meantime, trusting himself more and more to the element for which he was born, figured prominently in the clubs and wrote copiously for the newspapers. One can easily see how business must have been carried on with some slackness, since the two partners were marked by such characteristics.

In 1748 Samuel Adams, senior, died, bequeathing to the younger Samuel a third of his estate, — his sister and his brother (who is mentioned about this time in the town records as clerk of the market) receiving their shares. In 1749 he married Elizabeth Checkley, daughter of the minister of the " New South," established himself in Purchase Street, and gave himself, with a mind by no means undivided, to the management of the malt-house.

CHAPTER II

LEAVING "Sam the Maltster" to wait through the years that must intervene before the hour shall really strike for him, we must make a survey of the institutions into the midst of which he was born, and of the momentous dispute in which he was presently to stand forth as a figure of the first importance.

According to the original charter, which was that of a mere trading corporation, vaguely drawn, and which was converted without color of law into the foundation of an independent state, the affairs of Massachusetts were to be managed by a governor, deputy-governor, and eighteen assistants, who were to hold monthly meetings for that purpose. These officials were to be elected, and a general oversight to be exercised, by the stockholders of the company to whom the charter was granted. The colonists were " to enjoy the rights of Englishmen," but had no share in the direction of affairs. The company was transferred, however, very soon, to New England, and the settlement, instead of being subject to stockholders across the water, became then self-governed, an arrangement quite different from that at first contemplated.

For the first half century, through a provision of the General Court enacted in 1631, no man was to become a freeman unless he were a church member. Since not a fourth part of the adult population were ever church members, the democracy had many of the features of an oligarchy. Among themselves the freemen cherished a spirit strongly democratic; but towards those outside, the spiritual aristocracy preserved a haughty bearing.

At the end of fifty years, beneath Charles II. and James II., came a crisis. When at length, in 1692, Sir William Phips, a rough and enterprising son of the colony, appeared as governor, he brought with him a document which was far from pleasing to the people, who had hoped from the Protestant champion, William III., a restoration of the old institutions. High notions of his prerogative, however, were entertained by the new king, and were not opposed by even the wisest among his advisers. Massachusetts, Plymouth, and Maine were comprehended under one jurisdiction, New Hampshire being left independent. The old freedom of Massachusetts was to a large extent suspended. The theocracy, too, was abolished; toleration was secured to all religious sects except Papists; and the right of suffrage, once limited to church members, was bestowed on all inhabitants possessing a freehold of the annual value of forty shillings, or personal property to the amount of

£40. The appointment of the governor, lieutenant-governor, and colonial secretary was reserved
to the king. The governor possessed the power
of summoning, adjourning, and dissolving the General Court, and a negative upon all its acts. He
was dependent upon it, however, for his salary by
annual grant. Two boards, as before, were to constitute the legislature or General Court, a Council
and House of Representatives. The members of
the latter body were to be chosen annually by the
towns, and had the important power of the purse.
The Council was to consist of twenty-eight members, who in the first instance were to be appointed
by the king. Afterwards, a new Council for each
year was to be chosen by joint ballot of the old
Council and the Representatives, the power being
given to the governor of rejecting thirteen out of
the twenty-eight. To all official acts the concurrence of the Council was necessary, and to the king
was reserved the power of annulling any act within
three years of its passage.

To turn to judicial institutions : at the head
stood a Superior Court, presided over by a chief
justice and subordinate judges. These were appointed by the governor in Council ; so, too, were
inferior magistrates, as justices of the peace in
each county. In course of time, the regular number of judges in the Superior Court came to be
five, and to it was assigned all the jurisdiction of
the English Common Pleas, King's Bench, and
Exchequer. There were also county courts of

Common Pleas for smaller civil cases, Courts of Sessions, composed of justices of the peace in each county, for inferior criminal cases, and Courts of Probate for settling the estates of persons deceased. An attorney-general was appointed to conduct public prosecutions. From 1697 Courts of Vice-Admiralty existed, empowered to try without jury all maritime and revenue cases; but these tribunals were from the first strenuously opposed. From 1698 a Court of Chancery also existed. The governor was commander-in-chief of the militia, whose officers he was also empowered to appoint. In 1728 the charter of William and Mary was amended, after earnest disputes between Governor Shute and the Assembly (the lower house of the legislature), by a clause giving the governor power to negative the speaker chosen by the Assembly; and also by a clause making it impossible for the house to adjourn, by its own vote, for a longer term than two days.

With these representative and judicial institutions, which require from the reader careful attention, concerned as he will be in our story with a variety of constitutional disputes, Massachusetts, absorbing Plymouth and Maine, passed from her colonial into her provincial period. Though greatly restricted in her independence, the new order was really in some respects a vast improvement upon the old. Through the canceling of the condition of church membership, citizenship became practically open to all; for the pecuniary qualification was so small as to embarrass very few. Though the legislature was cramped, the town meetings were unrestrained, and through the enlargement of the franchise gained a power and interest which they had not before possessed.

The prevailing tone of American writers who, as historians or biographers, have treated the Revolutionary struggle, has been that the case against the British government was a perfectly plain one, that its conduct was aggression in no way to be justified or palliated, and as blundering as it was wicked. An illustrious Englishman, E. A. Freeman, however, has written: "In the War of Independence there is really nothing of which either side need be ashamed. Each side acted as it was natural for each side to act. We can now see that both King George and the British nation were quite wrong; but for them to have acted otherwise than they did would have needed a superhuman measure of wisdom, which few kings and few nations ever had."

Our Fourth of July orators may well assume a tone somewhat less confident, when thoughtful men in England, not at all ill-disposed toward America, and not at all blind to the blunders and crimes which strew the course of English history, pass even now, after a hundred years, such a judgment as this which has been quoted. A candid American student, admire as he may the wisdom and virtue of our Revolutionary fathers, is com-

pelled to admit, in this calmer time, that it was by
no means plain sailing for King George and his
ministers, and that they deserve something better
from us than the unsparing obloquy which for the
most part they have received.

The love of the colonists toward England had
become estranged in other ways than by " taxation
without representation."   In Massachusetts, the
destruction of the theocracy through the new charter was a severe shock to Puritan feeling.   The
enforced toleration of all sects but Papists was
a constant source of wrath; and when, as the
eighteenth century advanced, the possibility of the
introduction of bishops and a church establishment
appeared, a matter which was most persistently and
unwisely urged,[1] there was deep-seated resentment.

But another stone of offense, which, unlike the
fear of prelacy, affected all America as well as
New England, and was therefore very important,
existed in the trade regulations.   By the resolution of 1688, the royal power in England was restrained, but that of Parliament and the mercantile and manufacturing classes greatly increased.
The " Board of Trade " was then constituted, to
whom were committed the interests of commerce
and a general oversight of the colonies.   Adam

---

[1] Grahame, *Hist. of U. S.* iv. 317.   As far as New England
was concerned this fear of ecclesiasticism was as potent a source
of estrangement as any.   Some writers regard it as the principal
cause of bad feeling.   See *John Adams, the Statesman of the Revolution*, by Hon. Mellen Chamberlain.   Boston, 1884.

Smith was still in the far future, and the policy constantly pursued was neither humane nor wise. We may judge of the temper of the Board from the fact that even John Locke, its wisest and one of its most influential members, solemnly advised William to appoint a captain-general over the colonies with dictatorial power, and the whole Board recommended, in 1701, a resumption of the colonial charters and the introduction of such " an administration of government as shall make them duly subservient to England." The welfare of the colonies was systematically sacrificed to the aggrandizement of the gains of English manufacturers and merchants. Sometimes the provisions turned out to the advantage of the colonists, but more frequently there was oppression without any compensating good.

Restrictions, designed for securing to the mother country a monopoly of the colonial trade, crushed out every industry that could compete with those of England. For such products as they were permitted to raise, the colonies had no lawful market but England, nor could they buy anywhere, except in England, the most important articles which they needed. With the French West India islands a most profitable intercourse had sprung up, the colonists shipping thither lumber and provisions, and receiving in return sugar and molasses, the consumption of which latter article, in the widespread manufacture of rum, was very large. In 1733 was passed the famous " Sugar Act," the

design of which was to help the British West
Indies at the expense of the northern colonies, and
by which all the trade with the French islands
became unlawful, so that no legitimate source of
supply remained open but the far less convenient
English islands. The restrictions, indeed, were
not and could not be enforced. Every sailor was
a smuggler; every colonist knew more or less of
illicit traffic or industry. The demoralization came
to pass which always results when a community,
even with good reason, is full of law-breakers,
and the disposition became constantly more and
more unfriendly toward the mother country. Said
Arthur Young : " Nothing can be more idle than
to say that this set of men, or the other administration, or that great minister, occasioned the
American war. It was not the Stamp Act, nor
the repeal of the Stamp Act; it was neither Lord
Rockingham nor Lord North, — but it was that
baleful spirit of commerce that wished to govern
great nations on the maxims of the counter."

The Board of Trade, however, the main source
of the long series of acts by which the English dependencies were systematically repressed, should receive execration not too severe. They simply were
not in advance of their age. When, after 1688,
the commercial spirit gained an ascendency quite
new in England, the colonists, far off, little known,
and despised, were pitched upon as fair game, if
they could be made to yield advantage. In so using
them, the men in power were only showing, what

has so often passed as patriotism, that mere expansion of selfishness, inconsistent with any broad Christian sentiment, which seeks wealth and might for the state at the expense of the world outside. It was inhumanity from which the world is rising, it may be hoped, — for which it would be wrong to blame those men of the past too harshly. The injustice, however, as always, brought its penalty; and in this case the penalty was the utter estrangement of the hearts of a million of Englishmen from the land they had once loved, and the ultimate loss of a continent.

Before the Massachusetts settlement, it had been stipulated in the charter that all the colonists were to have the rights and privileges of Englishmen, and this provision they often cited. Magna Charta was but a confirmation of what had stood in and before the time of Edward the Confessor, — the primitive freedom, indeed, which had prevailed in the German woods. This had been again and again reconfirmed. Documents of Edward I. and Edward III., the Petition of Right of 1628, the Bill of Rights of 1689, had given such reconfirmations; and the descendants of the twenty thousand Puritans, who, coming over between 1620 and 1640, had been the seed from which sprung the race of New Englanders, knew these things in a general way. They were to the full as intelligent in perceiving what were the rights of Englishmen, and as tenacious in upholding them, as any class that had remained in the old home. Left to themselves for sixty years, there was little need of an assertion of rights; but when at last interference began from across the water, it was met at the outset by protest. Parliament is a thousand leagues of stormy sea away from us, said they. That body cannot judge us well; most of all, our representatives have no place in it. We owe allegiance to the king indeed, but, instead of Parliament, our General Court shall tax and make laws for us. Such claims, often asserted, though overruled, were not laid aside, and at length in 1766 we find Franklin asserting them as the opinion of America at the bar of the House of Commons.

It cannot, however, be said that New England was consistent here. In 1757, for instance, the authority of Parliament was distinctly admitted by the General Court of Massachusetts; so too in 1761; and even so late as 1768, it is admitted "that his majesty's high court of Parliament is the supreme legislative power over the whole empire."

The sum and substance is that, as to the constitutional rights of the colonists, the limits were, in particulars, quite undetermined, both in the minds of English statesmen and also among the colonists themselves. What "the privileges and rights of Englishmen" were was not always clearly outlined, and the student finds sometimes more, sometimes less, insisted on, according as the temper toward the Old World is embittered or good-natured. As events progress, through fear of prelatical contrivings and through bad trade regulations, as has been seen, the tone becomes more and more exasperated. On the one side the spirit becomes constantly more independent; on the other side, the claims take on a new shade of arrogance. When the first decided steps toward the Revolution occur in 1764, in the agitations connected with the Stamp Act, the positions in general of the parties in the dispute may be set down as follows: "Parliament asserted the right to make laws to bind the colonies in all cases whatsoever; the colonies claimed that there should be no taxation without representation, and that, since they had no representatives in Parliament, they were beyond its jurisdiction."

CHAPTER III

THE WRITS OF ASSISTANCE

Sam Adams at twenty-eight, with a wife, and his inheritance now in his hands through the death of his father, had not yet begun to play his proper part before the world. The eyes of men were beginning to turn toward him, indeed, as a man with a head to manage a political snarl, and a pen to express thoughts that could instruct and kindle. He was still, however, the somewhat shiftless manager of the Purchase Street malt-house, and the town censors no doubt said it would be vastly better for him to mind his private business rather than dabble as he did in public matters. That he was a good student and thinker was shown by his contributions to the " Public Advertiser."

He was devoted also to the discussions of the debating clubs. As yet the Revolution seemed far off. The people of Massachusetts, it has been said, were never in a more easy situation than at the close of the war with France in 1749. The whole charge for the expedition against Cape Breton was reimbursed to them by Parliament, so that the province was set free from a heavy debt, a liberality which of course made it easier to swallow the bitter pill of restoring Louisburg to the French. With his patrimony Samuel Adams had apparently inherited his father's friendships and enmities, among the latter being a feud with Thomas Hutchinson, a man fast rising to the position of leading spirit of the province, already in the Council, and destined to fill in turn, sometimes indeed to combine at once, the most distinguished positions. Governor Shirley's popularity vanished before ill success, which overtook his later enterprises. He gave way at length in 1756 to Thomas Pownall, a man of wide experience in colonial life and of much tact, so that while maintaining firmly the prerogative of the king, in the chronic dispute between ministry and Assembly, which was never long at rest, he contrived still to retain the goodwill of the people, who did him great honor at his departure. Samuel Adams, who in Shirley had opposed the union of the civil and military powers in one head, was, like his fellow citizens, better pleased with Pownall, a good opinion which the ex-governor afterward abundantly justified by bravely and intelligently defending in Parliament the cause of America.

In 1758 an incident occurred which attracted much public attention. An attempt was then made to seize and sell the property of Samuel Adams, senior, on account of his connection many years before with the "Land Bank Scheme," a device open to grave objection, which had been resorted to for avoiding great loss which threat-

ened the colony in consequence of a certain interference of the home government in the finances.[1]
At the time it had been asserted that each director
would be held individually responsible for the lia-
bilities of the concern ; but we may well believe
that for Samuel Adams it was a matter somewhat
startling to read in the " News-Letter," ten years
after his father had been in his grave, and seventeen years after the affair had taken place, a
sheriff's notice that the property he had inherited
would be sold at auction "for the more speedy
finishing the Land Bank scheme." [2]   The sale did
not take place, for when the sheriff appeared he
found himself confronted by a sturdy citizen,
whose resistance he was forced to respect.   Soon
afterward an act was passed by the legislature
liberating the directors from personal liability —
an act the significance of which was not at the
time understood, but which was often referred to
subsequently as a memorable precedent, in the
strife between the colony and Parliament.

Turning over the Boston town records, as the
venerable rolls lie in their handsome surroundings
in the great city hall that stands on the site of the
little wooden school of Samuel Adams's boyhood,
one first finds his name in 1753, on the committee
to visit schools.   Scarcely a year passes from that
date until the town meetings cease, crushed out by

---

[1] See the writer's *Life of Thomas Hutchinson*, ch. ii., for an
account of this financial crisis.

[2] *Boston News-Letter*, August 10 and 17, 1758.

the battalions of Gage, when his name does not
appear in connections becoming constantly more
honorable. The record, first in the hand of Eze-
kiel Goldthwait, town clerk, and after 1761 in that
of William Cooper, though meagre, is complete
enough to show how intimately his life is connected
with these meetings of the freemen. He serves in
offices large and small, on committees to see that
chimneys are properly inspected, as fire-ward, to
see that precautions are taken against the spread
of the small-pox, as moderator, on the committee
to instruct the representatives to the Assembly, as
representative himself. From 1756 to 1764 he
was annually elected one of the tax-collectors,
and in connection with this office came the gravest
suspicion of a serious moral dereliction which his
enemies could ever lay to his charge. Embarrassments which weighed upon the people caused
payments to be slow. The tax-collectors fell into
arrears, and it was at length entered upon the
records that they were indebted to the town in the
sum of £9878. The Tories persisted afterwards
in making this deficiency a ground of accusation,
and Hutchinson, in the third volume of his history,
deliberately calls it a " defalcation." No candid
investigator can feel otherwise than that to Samuel
Adams's contemporaries any misappropriation of
funds by him was an absurd supposition. Without stopping to inquire how it may have been with
his fellow collectors, it is quite certain that in his
case a feeling of humanity, very likely an absence

of business vigor, stood in the way of his efficiency
in the position. His townsmen wanted him for a
high office, a sure proof that they had lost no confidence in him. A successor was appointed to
collect the arrears, the province being asked to
authorize the town's action. "Neither the historian nor the contemporary records furnish any evidence to rebut the presumption that his ill success
as a collector was excusable if not unavoidable." [1]

In 1760 the prudent Pownall was succeeded by
Francis Bernard, a character of quite different
temper. Botta has described him as a man of
excellent judgment, sincerely attached to the interests of the province, and of irreproachable character. He was a defender of the prerogative of
the crown, however, ardent in disposition, and
quite without the pliancy and adroitness which had
served his predecessor so well. He had before been
governor of New Jersey, and now was promoted
to the more conspicuous post in Massachusetts.
He had received an Oxford education, was a man
of refined and scholarly tastes, and is said to have
been able to perform the astonishing feat of repeating the whole of Shakespeare from memory.
There is no reason to doubt the authorities who
speak well of Bernard, though the portrait that
has come down to us from the patriot writers is

[1] See *Province Laws*, p. 27, note, edited by Hon. Ellis Ames and
A. C. Goodell, Jr., Esq. The latter gentleman has completely
cleared the character of Samuel Adams in a paper read before
the Mass. Histor. Society in the spring of 1883.

dark. Events presently threw governor and province into positions of violent antagonism to one another. To the governor the people seemed seditious and unreasonable; to the people the governor appeared arbitrary and irritable, and the relation at length became one of thorough hatred. At first he was liberally treated, however, receiving a grant of £1300 for his salary, and the island of Mt. Desert in Maine, favors to which he would have responded no doubt graciously if, as an English country gentleman, his every nerve had not been presently rasped by the preposterous levelers with whom he was thrown into contact.

The fall of Quebec in 1759, immediately preceding the accession of Bernard, was an important crisis in the history of Massachusetts. The colonists had learned to estimate their military strength more highly than ever before. Side by side with British regulars, they had fought against Montcalm and proved their prowess. Officers qualified by the best experience to lead, and soldiers hardened by the roughest campaigning into veterans, abounded in all the towns. A more independent spirit appeared, and this was greatly strengthened by the circumstance that the destruction of the power of France suddenly put an end to the incubus which, from the foundation of things, had weighed upon New England, viz., the dread of an invasion from the north. Coincident with this great invigoration of the tone of the province came certain changes in the English policy, — changes

which came about very naturally, but which, in
the temper that had begun to prevail, aroused
fierce resentment. As the Seven Years' War drew
towards its close, it grew plain that England had
incurred an enormous debt. Her responsibilities,
moreover, had largely increased. All India had
fallen into her hands as well as French America.
At the expense of her defeated rival, her dominion
was immensely expanding; vast was the glory, but
vast also the care and the financial burden. A
faithful, sharp-eyed minister, George 'Grenville,
seeing well the needs of the hour, and searching
as no predecessor had done into the corruptions
and slacknesses of administration, at once fastened
upon the unenforced revenue laws as a field where
reform was needed. Industry on land, as we have
seen, was badly hampered in a score of ways, and
on the sea the wings of commerce were cruelly
clipped.

Grenville's imprudence was as conspicuous as
his eye was keen and his fidelity persistent. As
the first step in a series of financial measures
which should enable England to meet her enormous
debt and her great expenses, he set in operation a
vigorous exaction of neglected customs and imposts.
The vessels of the navy on the American coast
were commissioned to act in the service of the
revenue, each officer becoming a customs official.
At once all contraband trade was subjected to the
most energetic attack, no respect being shown to
places or persons. In particular, the Sugar Act,

by which an effort had been made to cut off the interchange of American lumber and provisions for the sugar and molasses of the French West Indies, was strongly enforced, and the New England sailors, with the enterprising merchants of Boston, Newport, Salem, and Portsmouth behind them, flamed out into the fiercest resentment. Whereas for many a year the collectors, from their offices on the wharves, had winked placidly at the full cargoes from St. Domingo and St. Christopher, brought into port beneath their very eyes, now all was to be changed in a moment. Each sleepy tide-waiter suddenly became an Argus, and, backed up by a whole fleet full of rough and ready helpers, proceeded to put an end to the most lucrative trade New England possessed.

To help forward this new activity in the carrying out of laws so often heretofore a dead letter, certain legal forms known as " writs of assistance " were recommended, to be granted by the Superior Court to the officers of the customs, giving them authority to search the houses of persons suspected of smuggling. The employment of such a power, though contraband goods were often, no doubt, concealed in private houses, was regarded as a great outrage. Writs of assistance in England were legal and usual. If they were ever justifiable, as English authorities said then and still say, they are justifiable under such circumstances as prevailed in America. Stephen Sewall, however, chief justice of the province, when applied to for such a writ, in November, 1760, just after the fall of Quebec, expressed doubt as to their legality, and as to the power of the court to grant them. But the application had been made on the part of the crown by Paxton, the chief officer of customs at Boston, and could not be dismissed without a hearing. While the matter was pending Sewall died, and his successor was none other than Thomas Hutchinson, who already held the offices of lieutenant-governor, member of the Council, and judge of probate. He received his new position from Governor Bernard, being preferred to Colonel James Otis, to whom the post was said to have been promised by Governor Shirley years before.

Now it is that a figure of the highest importance in the story of Samuel Adams first comes prominently upon the scene. At the sessions of the court there had lately sat among the lawyers, in the tie-wig and black gown then customary, a certain "plump, round-faced, smooth-skinned, short-necked, eagle-eyed young politician," James Otis, the younger, already a man of mark, for he held the lucrative position of advocate-general, the official legal adviser of the government. It was for him now to defend the case of the officers of the customs. He, however, refused, resigned his commission, and with Oxenbridge Thacher, a patriotic and eloquent lawyer, was retained by the merchants of Boston and Salem to undertake their cause. Hutchinson, whose invaluable history relates with a certain old-fashioned stiffness but with much calm dignity the story of Massachusetts, does not forget himself, even when he comes to the events in which he himself was an actor. His recital maintains its tone of quiet moderation even when his theme becomes that bitter strife, in which, fighting to the last, he was himself utterly borne down. It is a disfigurement of the narrative that he sometimes ascribes mean motives to the champions who faced him in the battle; but the wonder is, under the circumstances, that the men with whom he so exchanged hate for hate stand forth in his page with so little detraction. Hutchinson declares the conduct of James Otis, in the case of the writs of assistance, to have been caused by chagrin, because his father had failed to receive the position of chief justice. What weight this charge is entitled to will be considered hereafter.

Among the high services rendered by John Adams is certainly to be counted the fact that in his faithfully kept diary and familiar letters, from his youth in Shirley's day down to his patriarchal age at Quincy, when his son was president of the United States, we have the most complete and graphic picture extant of America's most memorable period. The record is in parts almost as naïve as that of Sewall, "the New England Pepys," and gains as much in value from the foibles of the writer, his self-consciousness, his honest irascibility, his narrowness, as it does from his strong qualities. Here is his picture of the case of the writs of assistance : —

"Otis was a flame of fire. With a promptitude of classical allusions, a depth of research, a rapid summary of historical events and dates, a profusion of legal authorities, a prophetic glance of his eye into futurity, and a torrent of impetuous eloquence, he hurried away everything before him. American independence was then and there born ; the seeds of patriots and heroes were then and there sown, to defend the vigorous youth, the *non sine diis animosus infans*. Every man of a crowded audience appeared to me to go away, as I did, ready to to take arms against writs of assistance. Then and there was the first scene of the first act of opposition to the arbitrary claims of Great Britain. Then and there the child Independence was born."

John Adams also took notes of the speech of Otis, which have been preserved. It lasted between four and five hours, and was indeed learned, eloquent, and bold. The most significant passage is that in which, after describing the hardships endured by the colonies through the acts of navigation and trade, with passionate invective he denounced taxation without representation. It was by no means a new claim, but the masses of the people caught the words from his lips, and henceforth it came to be a common maxim in the mouths of all that taxation without representation is tyranny. Hutchinson continued the case to the next term, " as the practice in England is not known," and James Otis went forth to be for the next ten years the idol of the people.

John Adams's assertion, that in this magnificent

outburst American independence was born, will scarcely bear examination. The speech was not to such an extent epoch-making. Both orator and audience were thoroughly loyal, and had no thought of a contest of arms with the mother country. The principle asserted was only a re-avowal of what, as has been seen, had been often maintained. The argument was simply an incident in the long-continued friction between parent-land and dependency, not differing in essential character from scores of acts showing discontent which had preceded, though possessing great interest from the ability and daring of the pleader.

CHAPTER IV

IN THE MASSACHUSETTS ASSEMBLY

In the year 1764, when the agitation concerning the impending Stamp Act was disturbing the colonies, Samuel Adams had reached the age of forty-two. Even now his hair was becoming gray, and a peculiar tremulousness of the head and hands made it seem as if he were already on the threshold of old age. His constitution, nevertheless, was remarkably sound. His frame, of about medium stature, was muscular and well-knit. His eyes were a clear steel-gray, his nose prominent, the lower part of his face capable of great sternness of look, but in ordinary intercourse wearing a genial expression. Life had brought to him much of hardship. In 1757 his wife had died, leaving to him a son, still another Samuel Adams, and a daughter. Misfortune had followed him in business. The malt-house had been an utter failure; his patrimony had vanished little by little, so that beyond the fair mansion on Purchase Street, with its pleasant harbor view, little else remained to him; the house was becoming rusty through want of means to keep it in proper repair. In his public relations, fortune had thus far treated him no more kindly. As tax-collector he had quite failed and was largely in arrears. There was a possibility of losing what little property remained to him, and of having his name stained with dishonor. His hour, however, had now come.

In May, 1764, the town of Boston appointed, as usual, the important committee to instruct the representatives just elected to the General Court. The committee were " Richard Dana, Esqr., Mr. Samuel Adams, John Ruddock, Esqr., Nathaniel Bethune, Esqr., Joseph Green, Esqr.," and to Samuel Adams was given the task of drafting the paper. He submitted it in the town meeting of the 24th, a document very memorable, because it contains the first public denial of the right of the British Parliament to put in operation Grenville's scheme of the Stamp Act, just announced; and the first suggestion of a union of the colonies for redress of grievances. Samuel Adams's original draft is still in existence, the first public document he wrote of which we have any distinct trace, though there is ample evidence that his pen had frequently before been employed in that way. One may well have a feeling of awe as he reads upon the yellowing paper, in a handwriting delicate but very firm, the protests and recommendations in which America begins to voice her aspirations after freedom. Adams says: —

" What still increases our apprehensions is, that these unexpected Proceedings may be preparatory to more extensive Taxations upon us. For if our Trade may be taxed, why not our Lands, the Produce of our lands, and in short everything we possess or make use of? This, we apprehend, annihilates our Charter Rights to govern and tax ourselves. . . . If Taxes are laid upon us in any shape without our having a legal representation where they are laid, are we not reduced from the Character of free Subjects to the miserable State of tributary Slaves?"

The instructions close with this important suggestion: —

"As his Majesty's other Northern American Colonies are embarked with us in this most important Bottom, we further desire you to use your Endeavors that their weight may be added to that of this Province; that by the united Applications of all who are Aggrieved, all may happily attain Redress." [1]

Samuel Adams drew up this document. There can be no doubt that the respectable but inconspicuous citizens associated with him on the committee looked to him to supply ideas as well as form. Patrick Henry's famous "Virginia resolutions" denying the right of Parliament to tax America did not appear until a year later. Besides the distinct denial of this right contained in Samuel Adams's instructions, and the suggestion of the union of the colonies for a redress of grievances,

[1] The first part of this extract is copied from Samuel Adams's autograph, now in the Lenox Library, New York. The concluding passage does not stand in the original draft, but is copied here from the Boston town records.

the document contained an assertion of the important position that the judges should be dependent for their salaries upon the General Assembly. Also the hint was thrown out that, if burdens should not be removed, agreements would be entered into to import no goods from Britain, as a measure of retaliation upon British manufacturers. As the story develops, it will quickly be seen how important these suggestions became. There are, in fact, few documents in the whole course of American history so pregnant with great events.

The legislature met in June, when a memorial was forthwith prepared by James Otis for transmission to the agent of the colony in England, who was expected to make the document known to the English public. The memorial followed the suggestions, almost the very words, of Samuel Adams. A committee was also appointed to address the assemblies of the sister colonies, counseling united action in behalf of their common rights. The same year, but at a later session, — for Bernard, little pleased with the tone of proceedings, made haste to prorogue the Assembly, — the house, following again the Boston instructions, petitioned the government for the repeal of the Sugar Act.

On the 6th of December of this year Samuel Adams married for his second wife Elizabeth Wells, a woman of efficiency and cheerful fortitude, who, through the forty years of hard and hazardous life that remained to him, walked sturdily at his side. It required, indeed, no common virtue to do this, for, while Samuel Adams superintended the birth of the child Independence, he was quite careless how the table at home was spread, and as to the condition of his own children's clothes and shoes. More than once his family would have become objects of charity if the hands of the wife had not been ready and skillful.

Early in 1765 Grenville brought before Parliament his scheme for the Stamp Act, notice of which had been given some time before. As discussed at home, it had excited little comment; some of the colonial agents had favored it. Even Franklin, then agent for Pennsylvania, apparently regarding its operation as a foregone conclusion, had taken steps to have a friend appointed stamp distributor in his province. In America, indeed, there had been opposition. One royal governor, no other than Bernard, was strongly opposed to it, winning from Lord Camden in a discussion with Lord Mansfield the commendation of being a " great, good, and sensible man, who had done his duty like a friend to his country." Hutchinson, too, the lieutenant-governor, opposed it. " It cannot be good policy," he said, " to tax the Americans; it will prove prejudicial to the national interests. You will lose more than you will gain. Britain reaps the profit of all their trade and of the increase of their substance." Such evidences of discontent, however, as were given, it did not seem at all worth while to regard. The bill at

length passed the house late at night, the members
yawning for bed, and listening with impatience to
the forcible protest of Barré, who in their idea had
the poor sense to magnify a mole-hill into a mountain. So little do we understand what is trifling
and what is momentous of what passes under our
eyes!

The news was brought to the colonies by a ship
which reached Boston in April, and the spirit
of resistance became universal. Patrick Henry's
resolutions, passed in May, were generally adopted
as the sentiments of America. In Boston the discontent came to a head in August, when it was
resolved to hang in effigy Andrew Oliver, who had
been appointed distributor of stamps. Decorous
though the community ordinarily was, there was a
population in the streets along the water-side quite
capable of being carried to the extreme of ruth-
lessness and folly. Hutchinson most unjustly was
made the special mark of their rage. Gordon
states that the cause in part was certain unpopular
financial enterprises, projected and carried through
by him as far back as 1748. Since then, however,
his standing with the townspeople had been as high
as possible, and it must have been well known that
he had opposed the Stamp Act as unjust and
impolitic. So far he had given but few signs of a
course obnoxious to the people. The mob, however, mad with rum, attacked with such fury the
fine mansion of Hutchinson at the North End that
he and his family escaped with difficulty. The

house was completely gutted and then destroyed. Handsome plate and furniture were shattered; worst of all, manuscripts and other documents of great importance, collected by Hutchinson for the continuation of his history, were scattered loose in the streets, and for the most part lost. The Admiralty records also were burnt and other destruction committed. The demonstration in its earlier phases had the approval of the patriots. A town meeting, however, the next day, condemned the excesses, and pledged the aid of the people to preserve order henceforth.

For the meeting of the Assembly, appointed for the end of September, Samuel Adams again, in behalf of the town, prepared instructions for the "Boston seat." John Adams, his second cousin, and some years his junior, at the same time performed a similar service for the town of Braintree. The kinsmen put their heads together in the preparation of their work, a coöperation that was to be many times repeated in the years that were coming. The "Boston Gazette" spread the documents everywhere throughout the other towns, by whom they were again and again imitated, the papers becoming the generally accepted platform of the province. Points especially insisted on were the right, secured by charter to the people of Massachusetts, of possessing all the privileges of freeborn Britons, representation as the indispensable condition of taxation, and the right of trial by jury, violated in the Admiralty Courts, whose jurisdiction of late had been much extended. The same town meeting to which the instructions were reported thanked Conway and Barré for bold speeches in their behalf, and directed that their portraits should be placed in Faneuil Hall.

Just now it was that Oxenbridge Thacher, a member of the Assembly, an ardent patriot, and the associate of James Otis in the case of the writs of assistance, died at the age of forty-five. On September 27 the town elected Samuel Adams his successor. The record in the hand of William Cooper states that the election took place on the second ballot, the candidate receiving two hundred and sixty-five votes out of four hundred and forty-eight. He appeared the same day in the Assembly-room, in the west end of the second story of the Old State House, and was immediately qualified, a moment only before the body was prorogued by the governor. It was not until October that he fairly began that life of public service which was to last almost unbroken until his death.

Samuel Adams may well be called the " Man of the Town Meeting." Though the sphere of his activity was henceforth for so much of the time the Massachusetts Assembly, he was not through that taken away from the town meeting. The connection between the Assembly and the town meetings, which stood behind it and sent the members to it, was a very close one. Each man who stood in the house, stood (if we may make use of a modern distinction) as a *deputy* and not as a *repre-*

sentative; [1] that is, he had in theory no independence, was bound as to all his acts by the instructions of the folk-mote that sent him and employed him simply as a matter of convenience. In the first days of New England there was no delegation of authority by the freemen. As the inconvenience had become plain of requiring for the transaction of all business the voices of all the freemen, the board of selectmen had at length come into existence for each town; and as the towns had multiplied, the central council was at length devised for the care of business that affected all. The town meeting, however, in the day of its strength jealously kept to itself every particle of power which it could reserve.

It was simply for convenience that the folk-motes sent each a man to the Assembly chamber in King Street. The freemen could not go in a mass; that would take them from their bread-winning. For such a crowd, too, there would be no room, nor would it be possible for all to hear and vote. A deputy must go for each town, but the liberty allowed to him was narrow. In the instructions of 1764, Samuel Adams, at the beginning, while informing the deputies that the townsmen "have delegated to you the power of acting in their publick Concerns in general as your own prudence shall direct you," takes pains immediately to qualify carefully the concession thus: "Always reserving to themselves the Constitutional Right

[1] Dr. Francis Lieber, *Political Ethics*, ii. 325.

of expressing their mind and giving you such Instruction upon particular Matters as they at any Time shall Judge proper." [1]

There is no doubt that here serious harm could come to pass; for it must be admitted that the town meeting plan can never answer for large affairs. In an ideal state, while the folk-mote is at the base, there must be found, through representation, the smaller governing and legislating body, and at length the one man, good enough and wise enough to be trusted with power to be used independently. The idea is of course quite erroneous that representative government is nothing but a substitute for the meeting of the whole people in the forum, made necessary by increased population. The representative must be held to a strict accountability indeed, — but he must be his own man, independent in judgment, with an eye to the general interests, not simply those of his constituency; he must be selected, not because he is likely to be a subservient instrument, but for his good judgment and leadership. The bond should be close between him and those who send him. Nevertheless the representative should be the superior man, selected because he is superior. " Instructions " are out of place as addressed to such a man; his judgment should be left untrammeled, and, in cases where representative and constituents are likely to differ, they should defer to him, not he to them.[2]

[1] *Boston Town Records.*
[2] See discussions of the subject by Dr. Francis Lieber, *Political*

This was not the New England theory. But, whatever may have been the New England *theory*, there is no doubt that, in *practice*, the men who sat in the Assembly, if they really had ability and force, were as free as need be. Such men as Joseph Hawley at Northampton, Elbridge Gerry at Marblehead, James Warren at Plymouth, characters about to appear in our story, shaped the opinions of the communities in which they dwelt. According to the form, they spoke simply the views of the town, and regularly after election listened respectfully to the instructions which prescribed to them a certain course of conduct, sometimes with great minuteness. They themselves, however, had led the way to the opinions that thus found voice; for, with their natural power quickened by their folk-mote training, they usually had tact and force enough to sway the town to positions near their own. How much more was this mastery held in the case of such a leader as Samuel Adams! One fancies that he must have sometimes smiled inwardly, when, after the May election, Boston, through some novice or comparatively obscure personage, charged him and his colleagues, in peremptory terms, to do this, that, and the other thing, — him whose domination in the patriot ranks became quite absolute, who at last moulded New England

Ethics, ii. 313, etc.; John Stuart Mill, *Representative Government*, p. 237; Dr. Rudolph Gneist, *Geschichte und heutige Gestalt der Aemter in England*, 112; Burke, *Speech to the Electors of Bristol*, November 3, 1774.

opinion, and could place great men and small almost as he pleased! Or was he so far self-deceived that he did not know his own strength, and believed that many a plan which came from his own powerful brain proceeded from the great heart of the people, which he so thoroughly venerated?

Practically, with all the independent thinking, the able men shaped opinion. In theory, however, all proceeded from the town meetings, and those who stood for them were deputies, who could only do the people's will. Using the term "representative" in its limited sense, it may be said that a body like the Massachusetts House was not a *representative* assembly; it was a convention of the folk-motes, the freemen of each town being concentrated for convenience into the delegate who stood in the chamber. Samuel Adams, therefore, was really scarcely less concerned with the folk-mote when he worked in the General Court than when he worked in Faneuil Hall. In the latter case he was the controlling mind of one town; in the former case, of all the Massachusetts towns, who, as it were, sat down together in the hall in King Street. For what he did in the latter sphere as well as in the former sphere he deserves to be called, above all men who have ever lived, "the Man of the Town Meeting."

No building is so associated with Samuel Adams as the Old State House. It was only now and then that a town meeting met, and seldom that it

became so large as to overflow from Faneuil Hall
into the Old South. After Samuel Adams entered the Assembly his attendance was daily at
the chamber for long periods, until he went to
Congress in 1774. From the close of the Revolution again until 1797, his public service was
almost without break. For years he was in the
Senate, was then lieutenant-governor, then governor, the functions of all which positions he discharged in one or another of the rooms of the Old
State House. No other man, probably, has dark-
ened its doorway so often. A wise reverence has
restored the building nearly to its condition of a
hundred years ago. On the eastern gable the lion
and the unicorn rear opposite one another, as in
the days of the province; belfry, roof, and windows are as of yore; the strong walls built by the
masons of 1713, though looked down upon by
great structures on all sides, stand with a kind of
unshaken independence in their place and compel
veneration. Ascending the spiral staircase, one
reaches the second story, where all stands as it
was in the former time. The Assembly chamber
occupies the western end, a well-lighted room, ample in size for the hundred and twenty-five deputies whom it was intended to accommodate. Its
decoration is simple; convenience, not beauty, was
what the Puritan architect aimed at, but it is a
well-proportioned and stately hall. On the afternoon when the writer first visited it, among other
relics there stood at the west end the old " Speak-

er's desk," as it is called, which, however, seems
ill-adapted to the use of a speaker. It has been
suggested that probably it was the clerk's desk,
for which it seems more suitable. If that is so,
here sat Samuel Adams, for he was clerk through
all those disturbed years. Here rose his voice as
he directed the stormy debate; here moved his
hands as he wrote the papers which are the first
utterances of American freedom. In the chamber
corresponding, in the eastern end of the building,
the governor met with the Council: it was also the
session-room of the Superior Court, and here took
place the scene already described, when James Otis
denounced the writs of assistance.

Of many another noteworthy event the Old
State House has also been the scene. In its halls
were held anciently the town meetings. Hither
came the deputies from the other town meetings,
in the time when the New England folk-motes
were most vigorous, most nobly active in effect-
ing great results. In the whole history of Anglo-
Saxon freedom, since the times when the Teutons
clashed their shields in token of approval in the
forests of the Elbe and Weser, what scenes are
there more memorable than these old walls have
witnessed! The Old State House is the theatre
where our actors for the most part must move.

CHAPTER V

PARLIAMENTARY REPRESENTATION AND THE MASSACHUSETTS RESOLVES

IT would be quite inexplicable how a new member at once should become to such an extent the leading man of the legislative body, deferred to upon every occasion, intrusted with the most important work, and infusing a quite new tone into all the deliberations, were it not for a fact well attested. For many previous years, while the management of the malt-house suffered, not only in Bernard's time but through the years of Pownall also, and far back into the administration of Shirley, the quick mind and ready pen of Samuel Adams had been always busy, until at length the most important documents, promulgated under quite other names, were really of his authorship. One man, and only one, there was in the Assembly, when Samuel Adams took his seat among them, who was treated by the body with equal deference, and that was James Otis, temporarily absent in New York at the Stamp Act congress, convened there at the suggestion of Massachusetts. In mind, character, and opinions, the two leaders were a strong contrast to each other in many ways. Otis's power was so magnetic that a Boston town meeting, upon his mere entering, would break out into shouts and clapping, and if he spoke he produced effects which may be compared with the sway exercised by Chatham, whom as an orator he much resembled. Long after disease had made him utterly untrustworthy, his spell remained, and we shall hereafter see the American cause brought to the brink of ruin because the people would follow him though he was shattered. Of this gift Samuel Adams possessed little. He was always in speech straightforward and sensible, and upon occasion could be impressive, but his endowment was not that of the mouth of gold. While Otis was fitful, vacillating, and morbid, Samuel Adams was persistent, undeviating, and sanity itself. While Samuel Adams never abated by a hair his opposition to the British policy, James Otis, who at the outset had given the watchword to the patriots, later, after Parliament had passed the Stamp Act, said: —

" It is the duty of all humbly and silently to acquiesce in all the decisions of the supreme legislature. Nine hundred and ninety-nine in a thousand will never entertain the thought but of submission to our sovereign, and to the authority of Parliament in all possible contingencies."

A point where the opinions of the two men were quite at variance was the idea of a representation of the colonies in Parliament. While

Samuel Adams from the first rejected it as impracticable and undesirable, James Otis advocated it with all his force. He was far from being alone in this advocacy. In England Grenville with many others was well disposed toward it, and it would probably have been considered but for the declaration made against it by the colonies themselves. Adam Smith, at this time becoming famous, espoused the view. In his ideas representation should be proportioned to revenue; and if this were conceded to the colonies, he foresaw a time when, in the growing importance of America, the seat of power would be transferred thither. A few years later than this, the British government would most willingly have granted parliamentary representation to the colonies as a solution of the difficulties. Among Americans, Franklin, as well as James Otis, earnestly favored the scheme and had anticipations similar to those of Adam Smith; and Hutchinson early had suggested the same idea. It is quite noticeable that in our own day Professor J. R. Seeley, in the " Expansion of England," treating the relations between Britain and her dependencies at the present time, advocates with eloquence an abrogation of all distinctions between mother country and dependency, and in language quite similar to that of James Otis urges the compacting and consolidating of the British empire. He would have a "great world Venice," the sea flowing everywhere, indeed, through its separated portions, but uniting instead of dividing.

Such unification now can be regarded only as advantageous, whether we look toward the general welfare, or to the internal benefits brought by such a consolidation to the powers themselves. Disintegrated Italy has in our day come together into a great and powerful kingdom under the headship of the house of Savoy. Still more memorably Germany has been redeemed from the granulation which for so many ages had made her weak, and has become a magnificent nation. The practical annihilation of space and time, as man gains dominion over the world of matter, makes it possible that states should be immense in size as never before. The ends of the earth talk together almost without shouting; the man of to-day moves from place to place more easily and speedily than the rider of the enchanted horse or the owner of the magic carpet in the Arabian Nights. Modern political unification is a step toward making real the brotherhood of the human race, the coming together of mankind into one harmonious family, to which the benevolent look forward. Who can question, moreover, that in the case of the individual citizen, whose political atmosphere is that of a mighty state, there is a largeness of view, a magnanimity of spirit, a sense of dignity, an obliteration of small prejudices, an altogether nobler set of ideas, than are possible to the citizen of a contracted land? Really, in the highest view, any limitation of the sympathies which prevents a thorough, generous going out of the heart toward the whole human race is to be regretted. The time is to be longed and labored for when patriotism shall become merged into a cosmopolitan humanity.[1] The man who can call fifty millions of men his fellow citizens is nearer that fine breadth of love than he whose country is a narrow patch. If parliamentary representation of the American colonies had come to pass, the British empire might have remained to this day undivided, and would not the welfare of the English-speaking race of the world in general have been well served thereby ?

Plausible and interesting though such considerations are, parliamentary representation in any adequate shape was for the colonies one hundred years ago probably quite impracticable; and when Samuel Adams took the lead, as he at once did, in opposing the ideas that were so powerfully advocated, he showed great practical sense and rendered a most important service. Writing to Dennys Deberdt, then colonial agent, December 21, 1765, and speaking of Parliament, he said : —

"We are far, however, from desiring any representation there, because we think the Colonies cannot be fully and equally represented; and if not equally, then in effect not at all. A representative should be, and continue to be, well acquainted with the internal circumstances of the people whom he represents. It is often necessary that the circumstances of individual towns should be brought into comparison with those of the whole; so it is particularly when taxes are in consider-

[1] Lessing, *Gespräche für Freimaürer.*

ation. The proportionate part of each to the whole can
be found only by an exact knowledge of the internal
circumstances of each. Now the Colonies are at so great
a distance from the place where the Parliament meets,
from which they are separated by a wide ocean, and
their circumstances are so often and continually vary-
ing, as is the case in countries not fully settled, that
it would not be possible for men, though ever so well
acquainted with them at the beginning of a Parliament,
to continue to have an adequate knowledge of them
during the existence of that Parliament. . . .

" The several subordinate powers of legislation in
America seem very properly to have been constituted
upon their [the colonists] being considered as free subjects of England, and the impossibility of their being
represented in Parliament, for which reason these powers ought to be held sacred. The American powers of
government are rather to be considered as matters of
justice than favor, — without them, they cannot enjoy
that freedom which, having never forfeited, no power
on earth has any right to deprive them of."

Still another consideration must have weighed
with Samuel Adams aside from those mentioned
here. He well knew how great the departure had
been in England from the primitive institutions
and standards of the old Teutonic freedom. Liberty seemed to be sinking before the encroachments of arbitrary power. Corruption was universal and scarcely noticed; the great masses of the
people, practically unrepresented in the government, apathetic or despairing, were losing the characteristics of freemen. Already he had begun to

cherish the idea of independence in his own mind. America must cut loose, not only because she was denied her rights, but because she was bound to a ship that was embarrassed almost to sinking, with few sailors in the crew that manned her likely to have strength and skill enough to keep her afloat. Precisely at this time, in the troubles connected with the election of Wilkes, the agitation was beginning that was to result, after sixty years, in the great Reform Bill of 1832. The stubborn resistance of America, of which Samuel Adams was to such an extent the heart and centre, operated most beneficently for England, by encouraging there a similar temper. Had the American disputes ended in a grant of parliamentary representation, or any result short of a complete sundering, much of the healthful pressure which afterwards brought on reform in England must have been wanting. That America insisted on independence not only saved her, but also the motherland.[1] England's other great dependencies, Canada, Australia, New Zealand, have preferred to remain in the bond; yet at the same time they are free. But in order that it should be possible for them to remain and be free, it was necessary for America to depart. Only in that way could England be brought to purify herself, and learn how to use properly the power that has been placed in her hands.

With the changed temper of the motherland,

---

[1] Buckle, *Hist. of Civilization*, i. 345.

and the changed conditions under which our lives now pass, the objections to a connection with England, so important one hundred years ago, have been to a large extent set aside. If the bond were now existing, is there really much in present circumstances to justify the severing of it? Is Freeman's anticipation to be looked upon as unreasonable and unattractive, that a time may come when, through some application of the federal principle, the great English-speaking world, occupying so rapidly north, south, east, and west the fairest portions of the planet, not only one in tongue, but substantially one in institutions and essential character, may come together into a vaster United States, the "great world Venice," the pathways to whose scattered parts shall be the subjected seas?[1]

The meeting of the legislature in September, 1765, which Bernard prorogued so summarily, scarcely giving Samuel Adams time to take his oath as a member, had yet been long enough to afford the governor opportunity to lay before them a message, in which, however he might before have shown leanings to the popular side, he now declared that the authority of Parliament was supreme, and counseled submission. The Assembly had time to arrange for an answer to the address, and a statement of their position. Samuel Adams was put at once in the forefront, the task being assigned to him of drafting the papers.

[1] See also J. R. Seeley's *Expansion of England*, and a pamphlet by Rev. F. Barham Zincke, noticed in the *Nation*, April 5, 1883.

When in October the legislature again met, two documents were soon reported, both the work of Mr. Adams, a response to Bernard, and a series of resolves destined to great fame as the "Massachusetts Resolves."

In the response, while the courtesy of the terms is consummate, the clearest assertions respecting the limitation of the powers of Parliament are made. Strong loyalty to the king is expressed, while the Assembly at the same time refuses to assist in the execution of the Stamp Act. The resolves contain the same ideas substantially, but in a different form of expression, since they were meant to be a promulgation to the world of the sentiments of Massachusetts.

Matters in Massachusetts were fast passing from the nebulous stage into clear definition. The supporters of the ministry began to withdraw from positions inconsistent with the claims now made by the government; and the Assembly, by adopting these resolves, for the first time committed itself formally to opposition. Had Otis been present there would no doubt have been less decision. In May of this year he had made the declaration, already quoted, respecting the necessity of submission to Parliament; his mind, too, was full of the thought of a parliamentary representation for the colonies. Otis, however, was absent at the Congress in New York, and the energetic new member swayed the House according to his will, with no one to cross his plans.

The New York Congress, at which delegates had appeared from nine of the colonies, had been far from harmonious in their discussions. Timothy Ruggles, the president, a delegate from Massachusetts, a brave old soldier, refused to sign the documents submitted, and cast his lot with the Tories henceforth. Ogden of New Jersey acted with him. Otis bore a prominent part, but was nevertheless forced to abandon his positions by signing the papers, which were inconsistent with the idea of submission to Parliament, and declared American representation to be impracticable. In the midst of the debates a ship loaded with stamps arrived, at which the town was thrown into the greatest turmoil. During the excitement the delegates, feeling the necessity of union, made mutual concessions, and finally, with the exceptions above mentioned, signed petitions containing substantially the ideas of the Massachusetts Resolves, by which the colonies became "a bundle of sticks, which could neither be bent nor broken."

The response to Bernard and the Massachusetts Resolves, which presently after were mocked at in England as "the ravings of a parcel of wild enthusiasts," were greeted in America with great approval. The 1st of November was the day appointed for the Stamp Act to go into operation. In Boston the morning was ushered in by the tolling of bells and the firing of minute-guns. The deep popular discontent found sullen expression, though the excesses of the August riots were avoided. The stamps had arrived and been stored at Castle William in the harbor, an additional force being appointed to guard them. Bernard, much embarrassed by the stubborn opposition, sought advice from the Council and Assembly as to what course to take, but with no good result. The Assembly, soon after convening, proceeded to consider the possibility of transacting business without the use of stamps, a matter which had been touched upon in the preceding session, and for meddling with which they had been prorogued. As was the usage, committees were appointed in which the business was to be shaped before coming under the consideration of the whole body, of all which Mr. Adams was a leading member and sometimes chairman. By his hand, too, at this time the House rebuked the governor and Council for drawing without its consent, from the provincial treasury, money to pay the additional troops at the Castle, declaring that to make expenditures unauthorized by the people's representatives was an infringement upon their rights.

Otis and his colleagues now returning from New York with a report of the proceedings of the Stamp Act Congress, the Assembly at once indorsed its action. In letters of Mr. Adams at this time sent to England, in which he writes for others as well as himself, a plan is mentioned at which he had before hinted, and which was now, under the name of the " non-importation " scheme, about to become one of the most effective means of resistance which the colonists could employ. Spreading from Massachusetts, where Adams had suggested the idea, to the thirteen colonies in general, it struck terror into the hearts of British traders, who saw ruin for themselves in the cutting off of the American demand for their products.

A general gloom now settled over Massachusetts. The courts were closed ; business, to a large extent, came to a stand. No legal or commercial papers were valid without the stamp, and the stamps lay untouched at the Castle, the province refusing to use them. The law was in many places in the colonies set at defiance and evaded. Men had recourse to arbitration in the settlement of disputes. Ships entered and cleared, and other business was done, in contempt of the statute. Newspapers were published with a death's head in the place where the law required a stamp. The strait was severe, and on the 18th of December a Boston town meeting took place to consider measures looking toward the opening of the courts. A committee was appointed, of which Samuel Adams was chairman, to petition the governor and Council, and it was agreed to employ Jeremiah Gridley, a famous lawyer of the day, James Otis, and John Adams, to support the memorial.

Samuel Adams had a quick eye for power and availability of every kind, and now that he was in the foreground he swept the field everywhere for useful allies. Of the brilliant young men who were about to come forward in Massachusetts as the contest became fierce, there is scarcely one whom Samuel Adams did not, so to speak, discover, or to whom, at any rate, he did not stand sponsor as the new-comer took his place among the strivers. He it was who suggested to the town the employment of his young Braintree kinsman, John Adams, who now for the first time steps into prominence in public affairs. The diary of John Adams gives an account of his waiting until candle-light during the winter afternoon in the representatives' chamber, in company with the town's committee and many others, until a message came across the hall from Bernard and the Council, in the east room, to Samuel Adams, directing that the memorial of the town should be presented, and that the counsel in support should attend, but no others. The memorial had no effect, and the strait remained at present unrelieved.

John Adams has interesting things to say in his diary about the clubs, at which he meets the famous characters of the day.

" This day learned that the Caucus Club meets at certain times in the garret of Tom Dawes, the adjutant of the Boston regiment. He has a large house, and he has a movable partition in his garret, which he takes down, and the whole club meets in one room. There they smoke tobacco till you cannot see from one end of the garret to the other. There they drink flip, I suppose, and there they choose a moderator who puts questions to the vote regularly; and selectmen, assessors, collectors, wardens, fire-wards, and representatives are regularly chosen before they are chosen in the town. Uncle Fairfield, Story, Ruddock, Adams, Cooper, and a *rudis indigestaque mcles* are members. They send committees to wait on the Merchant's Club, and to propose and join in the choice of men and measures."

It was the successor of this club to which Samuel Adams now introduced John Adams. The new organization was larger, and the scope of its action, too, instead of being limited to town affairs, now included a far wider range in the struggle that was beginning.

CHAPTER VI

THE STAMP ACT BEFORE ENGLAND

CAREFUL observers are remarking that the temper of the legislature, as shown by the response to Bernard and the Massachusetts Resolves, is something quite different from what it has been. This difference is to be attributed to the influence of Samuel Adams, who, although for several years well known, now for the first time finds opportunity to make himself properly felt. Meantime events are taking place across the water which require our notice.

Inasmuch as the American colonies had profited especially from the successes of the war, it had been felt, justly enough, that they should bear a portion of the burden. It might have been possible to secure from them a good subsidy, but the plan devised for obtaining it was unwise. The principle was universally admitted that Parliament had power to levy "external" taxes, those intended for the regulation of commerce. With the Stamp Act, in 1764, Grenville had taken a step· farther. This was an "internal" tax, one levied directly for the purpose of raising a revenue, not for the regulation of commerce. The unconscious

Grenville explained his scheme in an open, honest way. "I am not, however," said he to the colonial agents in London, "set upon this tax. If the Americans dislike it and prefer any other method, I shall be content. Write, therefore, to your several colonies, and if they choose any other mode, I shall be satisfied, provided the money be but raised." But Britain, pushing thus more earnestly than heretofore, found herself, much to her surprise, confronted by a stout and well-appointed combatant, not to be browbeaten or easily set aside.

No one was more astonished than Grenville that precisely now an opposition so decided should be called out. He had meant to soften his measures by certain palliatives. For the southern colonies, the raising of rice was favored; the timber trade and hemp and flax in the north received substantial encouragement; most important of all measures, all restriction was taken from the American whale fishery, even though it was quite certain, under such conditions, to ruin that of the British isles. Grenville felt that he had proceeded prudently. He had asked advice of many Americans, who had made no objection to, and in some cases had approved, the Stamp Act. Men of the best opportunities for knowing the temper of the colonies, like Shirley, fifteen years governor of Massachusetts, and for a time commander-in-chief of all the military forces in America, had decidedly favored it. Nothing better than the Stamp Act had been suggested, though Grenville had invited suggestions as to substitutes. America, however, was in a ferment, and England, too, for one reason or another, was in a temper scarcely less threatening. Something must be done at once. But the responsibility was taken out of the hands of Grenville; a new ministry had come into power, and he was once more a simple member of Parliament.

The new premier was the Marquis of Rockingham, a young statesman of liberal principles and excellent sense, though with a strange incapacity for expressing himself, which made him a cipher in debate. The secretary of state, in whose department especially came the management of the colonies, was General Conway, like Barré a brave officer and admirable man, and well-disposed toward America. On the 14th of January began that debate, so memorable both on account of the magnitude of the issues involved and the ability of the disputants who took part. A few Americans, Franklin and other colonial agents among them, listened breathlessly in the gallery, and transmitted to their country a broken, imperfect report of all the superb forensic thunder. Whoever studies candidly the accounts cannot avoid receiving a deep impression as to the power and substantial good purpose of the great speakers, and as to the grave embarrassments that clogged them in striving to point out a practicable course. The agitation out of which reform was to come was already in the air. While none of the actors in the scene appreciated the depth of the gulf into which England was sinking, all evidently felt the pressure of evil. Mansfield appears ready at one point to admit abuse, but deprecates interference with the constitution, while Pitt denounces the " rotten boroughs," and declares that they must be lopped off.

Edmund Burke made upon this occasion his maiden speech, but no one thought it worth while, in those days before systematic reporting had begun, to record the words of the unknown young man. Pitt, who followed him, hushed all into attention as he rose in his feebleness, his eloquence becoming more touching from the strange disease by which he was afflicted, and which he was accused of using purposely to increase the effect of his words; he first praised the effort of the new member, and then proceeded in that address so worthy of his fame. Pitt's advice was that the Stamp Act should be repealed absolutely and immediately, but at the same time that the sovereignty of England over the colonies should be asserted in the strongest possible terms, and be made to extend to every point of legislation, except that of taking their money without consent.

" There is an idea in some that the colonies are *virtually* represented in this house. They never have been represented at all in Parliament. I would fain know by whom an American is represented here. Is he represented by any knight of the shire in any county of this kingdom? Would to God that respectable re-

presentation were augmented by a greater number! Or
will you tell me that he is represented by any representative of a borough, a borough which perhaps no
man ever saw? This is what is called the rotten part
of the constitution: it cannot endure the century. If
it does not drop it must be amputated. The idea of a
virtual representation of America in this house is the
most contemptible that ever entered into the head of a
man. It does not deserve a serious refutation."

Later in the winter, when the debate was renewed in the House of Lords, Lord Camden, chief
justice of the Common Pleas, supported the views
of Pitt in a strain which the latter called divine.
He tried to establish by a learned citation of precedents that the parts and estates of the realm had
not been taxed until represented; but, as if he felt
that abuses had accumulated, he declared that, if
the right of the Americans to tax themselves could
not be established in this way, it would be well to
give it to them from principles of natural justice.
Among those who replied, the most noteworthy
was Lord Mansfield, chief justice of England, who
declared, in opposition to Camden, that: —

"The doctrine of representation seemed ill-founded.
There are 12,000,000 people in England and Ireland
who are not represented; the notion now taken up, that
every subject must be represented by deputy, is purely
ideal. There can be no doubt, my lord, that the inhabitants of the colonies are as much represented in Parliament as the greatest part of the people of England
are represented, among 9,000,000 of whom there are

8,000,000 who have no votes in electing members of Parliament. Every objection, therefore, to the dependency of the colonies upon Parliament, which arises to it upon the ground of representation, goes to the whole present constitution of Great Britain, and I suppose it is not meant to new-model that too ! A member of Parliament chosen by any borough represents not only the constituents and inhabitants of that particular place, but he represents the inhabitants of every other borough in Great Britain. He represents the city of London and all other the Commons of this land and the inhabitants of all the colonies and dominions of Great Britain, and is in duty and conscience bound to take care of their interests."

When, after the speech of Mansfield, the subject came to a vote in the House of Lords, the matter stood in his favor by one hundred and twenty-five to five. In the Commons the majority on the same side was as overwhelming.

Looking back upon this momentous debate after a century and a quarter has elapsed, what are we to say as to the merits of it? England has completely changed since then her colonial policy, but no sober second thought has induced her historians to believe that the position of the government was plainly a wrong one. Pitt and Camden turned the scale for us in the Stamp Act matter : their declarations put backbone into the colonial resistance, and disheartened the ministry in England; but Pitt's opinions were declared at the time to be peculiar to himself and Lord Camden, and have

ever since, in England, been treated as untenable.[1]
Mansfield's theory of " virtual representation " —
that a representative represents the whole realm,
not merely his own constituency, " all other the
Commons of this land and the inhabitants of all
the colonies and dominions of Great Britain, and
is in duty and conscience bound to take care of
their interests " — is declared by another writer
to be grandly true, though, to be sure, somewhat
overstrained as regards the colonies. Burke, a
few years afterwards, addressing the electors of
Bristol, developed the doctrine elaborately. Mansfield was right in urging that the constitution
knows no limitation of the power of Parliament,
and no distinction between the power of taxation
and other kinds of legislation. The abstract right,
continues our historian, was unquestionably on the
side of the minister and Parliament, who had imposed the tax, and that right is still acted upon.
In 1868, in the trial of Governor Eyre of Jamaica,
the English judge Blackburn decided, " although
the general rule is that the legislative assembly has
the sole right of imposing taxes in the colony, yet
when the imperial legislature chooses to impose
taxes, according to the rule of English law they
have a right to do it." [2]   Lecky says : —

"It was a first principle of the constitution, that a
member of Parliament was the representative not merely
of his own constituency, but also of the whole empire.

[1] Massey, *Hist. of Reign of George III.* i. 262.
[2] Yonge, *Const. Hist. of England*, p. 66.

Men connected with, or at least specially interested in
the colonies, always found their way into Parliament;
and the very fact that the colonial arguments were maintained with transcendent power within its walls was sufficient to show that the colonies were virtually represented."

Lecky, however, even while thus arguing, admits
that the Stamp Act did unquestionably infringe
upon a great principle ; and he acknowledges that
the doctrine, that taxation and representation are
inseparably connected, lies at the very root of the
English conception of political liberty. It was
only by straining matters that the colonies could
be said to be virtually represented, and in resisting
the Stamp Act the principle involved was the same
as that which led Hampden to refuse to pay the
ship money.[1]

It is only fair for the present generation of
Americans to weigh arguments like those of Mansfield, and to understand how involved the case was.
The statesmen of the time of George III. were neither simpletons nor utterly ruthless oppressors.
They were men of fair purposes and sometimes of
great abilities, not before their age in knowledge
of national economy and political science ; still,
however, sincerely loving English freedom, and,
with such light as they had, striving to rule in a
proper manner the great realm which was given
them to be guided. In ways which the wisest of
them did not fully appreciate, the constitution had

[1] Lecky, iii. 353, etc.

undergone deterioration through the carelessness
of the people and the arbitrary course of many of
the rulers, until the primeval Anglo-Saxon freedom was scarcely recognizable, and liberty was in
great jeopardy. Following usages and precedents,
learned lawyers could easily find justification for
an arbitrary course on the part of the ministers;
and it is a mark of greatness in Camden, that,
learned lawyer though he was, he felt disposed to
rest the cause of the colonies on the basis of " natural justice," rather than upon the technicalities
with which it was his province to deal. In the
shock of the Stamp Act and Wilkes agitations
England came to herself, and, by going back to the
primeval principles, started on a course of reform
by no means yet complete. At this very time
Richard Bland of Virginia, anticipating by a century the spirit and methods of the constitutional
writers of whom E. A. Freeman is the best-known
example, uttered sentences which might well have
been taken as their motto by the " Friends of the
People," the " Society of the Bill of Rights," and
the other organizations in England which were just
beginning to be active for the salvation of their
country. He derived the English constitution
from Anglo-Saxon principles of the most perfect
equality, which invested every freeman with a right
to vote.

" If nine tenths of the people of Britain are deprived
of the high privilege of being electors, it would be a

work worthy of the best patriotic spirits of the nation to restore the constitution to its pristine perfection."

Much as Pitt and Camden were admired, and powerful as was their brave denunciation of the Stamp Act and their demand for its repeal, their famous position that a distinction must be made between taxation and legislation, and that while Parliament could not tax it could legislate, seemed no more tenable to Americans than it did to Englishmen. As we shall see, the colonial leaders soon pass on from demanding representation as a condition of taxation to demanding representation as a condition of legislation of every kind; they deny utterly the power of Parliament to interfere in any of their affairs; they owe allegiance to the king, but of Parliament they are completely independent. So Franklin had already declared. This position was shocking to Pitt, and he would have been as willing to suppress its upholders as was Lord North himself.

It is making no arrogant claim to say that in all this preliminary controversy the American leaders show a much better appreciation of the principles of Anglo-Saxon liberty, and a management much more statesmanlike, than even the best men across the water. It was to be expected. As far as New England is concerned, there is no denying the oft-quoted assertion of Stoughton, that God sifted a whole nation to procure the seed out of which the people was to be developed. The colonists were picked men and women, and the circumstances

under which they were placed on their arrival on
these shores forced upon them a revival of institutions which in England had long been overlaid.
The folk-mote had reappeared in all its old vigor,
and wrought in the society its natural beneficent
effect. Together with intelligence and self-reliance
in every direction, it had especially trained in
the people the political sense. In utter blindness
the Englishman of our Revolutionary period looked
down upon the colonist as wanting in reason and
courage. Really the colonist was a superior being,
both as compared with the ordinary British citizen and with the noble. Originally of the best
English strain, a century and a half of training
under the institution best adapted of all human
institutions to quicken manhood had had its effect.
What influences had surrounded lord or commoner
across the water to develop in them a capacity
to cope with the child of the Puritan, schooled
thoroughly in the town meeting?

CHAPTER VII

THE TRUE SENTIMENTS OF AMERICA

FROM the imposing British Parliament, sitting in the shadow of Westminster Abbey, with Westminster Hall close at hand, and just beyond these the City, fast becoming the heart of the civilized world, to come to the little provincial town and the Old State House with its modest company of town meeting deputies is a change marked indeed. But the deputies are as worthy of regard as their high placed contemners at St. Stephen's.

Though Otis was still the popular idol, Samuel Adams became every day more and more the power behind all, preparing the documents, laying trains for effects far in the future, watchful as regards the slightest encroachments. In Faneuil Hall as plain townsman, and also in his place as deputy, he is found busy with plans for helping on the work of the courts without yielding to the requirements of the Stamp Act, while the crown officials on their side uphold the authority of Parliament. On the 16th of May, 1766, however, the Harrison, a brigantine, six weeks out from England, cast anchor in the inner harbor with news of the repeal of the Stamp Act. The powerful voices raised in opposition to it in Parliament, the pressure from the trading and manufacturing centres, the clamor of the people, had brought about the change. The measure, however, was accompanied by the Declaratory Act, in which the ground of Pitt was by no means taken, but the assertion was made that Parliament was supreme over the colonies in all cases whatsoever. For expediency's sake the obnoxious tax was repealed, but the right to tax and to legislate in every other way for the colonies was plainly stated. The people in general, nevertheless, noticed only the repeal, and were transported with joy. Salutes were fired from the different batteries, the shipping was dressed with flags, the streets were full of music. At night Liberty Tree was hung full of lanterns, transparencies were shown, fireworks were displayed on the Common, and high and low feasted and reveled. John Hancock, a rich young merchant twenty-nine years old, lately come into a great fortune through the death of his uncle, Thomas Hancock, particularly signalized himself by his liberality. Before his handsome mansion opposite the Common, a pipe of Madeira wine was distributed to the people. His house and those of other grandees near were full of the finer world, while the multitude were out under the trees, just leafing out for the spring. One is glad to record that for once poor Bernard cordially sympathized with the popular feeling. He and his Council had a congratulatory meeting in the afternoon, and in the evening walked graciously

about among the people, a brief harmonious inter-
lude with discord before and triple discord to come
in the near future.

In May, as usual, the elections for representatives were held. Boston returned, as the four to
whom it was entitled, Samuel Adams, Thomas
Cushing, James Otis, and a new member, destined in the time coming to great celebrity, John
Hancock. True to his self-imposed function of
enlisting for the public service young men likely
for any reason to be helpful, it was Mr. Adams
who brought forward the new member. The handsome, free-handed young merchant, perhaps the
richest man of the province, began now a public
career, in the main though not always useful,
almost as continuous and protracted as that of
Mr. Adams himself.

Still another noteworthy addition was made
this year to the Assembly in Joseph Hawley, sent
as member for Northampton on the Connecticut
River, a man of the purest character, of bright
intellect, devoted to the cause of the patriots, and
especially helpful through his profound legal knowledge. His influence was powerful with the country members, who sometimes showed a jealousy,
not unusual in the present day, of the representatives of the metropolis. Samuel Adams and
Hawley thoroughly appreciated one another, and
worked hand in hand through many a difficult
crisis in the years that were approaching.

During the troubled sessions to come, Thomas

Cushing was chosen each year the speaker, — an honorable but not especially significant man among the patriots, who, through the fact that he was figurehead of the House, was sometimes credited in England and among the other colonies with an importance which he never really possessed. Samuel Adams at the same time was made clerk, a position which gave him some control of the business of the House, and was worth about a hundred pounds a year. His ability in drafting documents was now particularly in place; at the same time he was not at all debarred from appearing in debate. From this time forward, until he went to Congress at Philadelphia, he was annually made clerk, the little stipend forming often his sole means of support.

At the instance of James Otis, on the 3d of June, the debates of the Assembly were thrown open to the public, and arrangements were made for a gallery where the sessions could be witnessed by all. For the first time in the history of legislative associations it was made the right of the plain citizen to hear and see, — a usage which has modified in important ways the proceedings and very character of deliberative bodies.

No long-headed statesman in the colonies, in face of the Declaratory Act, could feel that the contest with the home government was anything more than adjourned, and the wary Massachusetts managers were careful not to be caught napping. The constitution of the Council or upper house will be remembered. It consisted of twenty-eight members, elected each year by the Assembly and the preceding Council, voting together; the governor possessed the power of rejecting thirteen of the twenty-eight elected. Immediately after the organization of the Assembly at the end of May, Bernard and the leaders came to strife as to the composition of the new Council. There were five persons upon the election of whom the governor's heart was especially fixed, — Hutchinson, Andrew and Peter Oliver, Trowbridge, and Lynde. They were "prerogative men" and very important in the way of keeping in check in the upper house any feeling of sympathy with the spirit of opposition, which was sure to be rife in the Assembly. As Bernard was anxious to retain them, the popular leaders were just as anxious to exclude them; Hutchinson, in particular, from his great ability and influence, was especially desired on the one hand and dreaded on the other. These five the Assembly refused to reëlect, taking the ground that, as crown officials, it was inappropriate that they should sit in the legislature. Hutchinson was lieutenant-governor, chief justice, and judge of probate; the Olivers were respectively secretary and judge in the Superior Court, Lynde was a judge also, and Trowbridge was attorney-general. In a paper justifying the course of the Assembly, drafted by Adams, but in the composition of which Otis no doubt had a share, the desire was expressed to release " the judges from the cares and perplex-

ities of politics, and give them an opportunity to
make still further advances in the knowledge of
the law." Bernard possessed no means of con-
straining the election of his friends. He rejected
six of the councilors elected by the Assembly, by
way of retaliation, and scolded the body sharply.
The vacancies remained unfilled, although Hutchinson tried to retain his place on the strength of
his office as lieutenant-governor. The Assembly
was inflexible. Into the place of leader of the
Council stepped the excellent James Bowdoin, a
well-to-do merchant of Huguenot descent, of the
best sense and character, who henceforth for many
years played a most useful part; at present he rendered great service by keeping the Council and the
Assembly in accord.

Hawley at once made himself felt as a bold
and clear-headed statesman. " The Parliament of
Great Britain," said he, during this session, " has
no right to legislate for us." Hereupon James
Otis, rising in his seat, and bowing toward Hawley, exclaimed : " He has gone farther than I have
yet done in this house." With his lawyer's acumen the Northampton member seemed to appreciate the untenability of Pitt's opinion and to reject
it at once. In 1766, to deny to Parliament the
right of legislating for the colonies was advanced
ground, but it came soon to be generally occupied.

In December, 1766, soon after the adjournment
of the legislature, a vessel, having on board two
companies of royal artillery, was driven by stress

of weather into Boston harbor.   The governor, by advice of the Council, directed that provision should be made for them at the expense of the province, following the precedent established shortly before, when a company had been organized to be paid by the province, but without the consent of the representatives, for the protection of the stamps at the Castle.   In the case in hand humanity demanded that the soldiers should be received and provided for; a principle, however, was again violated in a way which sharp-eyed patriots could not overlook. Here resistance was made, as in the previous case, and we find now the beginnings of a matter which developed into great importance.

According to the account of Hutchinson, the jealousy which the country towns had felt of the influence of Boston was disappearing at the time of the Stamp Act.   Thenceforward the leaders are for the most part the Boston men, who project and conduct all the measures of importance.   In the intervals between the sessions of the Assembly, town meetings are frequent, in which general interests, as well as things purely local, are considered.   In town meeting and Assembly the leaders are the same, a select body of whom meet at stated times and places in the evening, at least once a week, to concert plans, inspire the newspapers, arrange for news.

With calmness and accuracy Hutchinson states the gradual changes of position which the colonies assume as the contest proceeds.   The view which

advanced minds had some time before adopted
became general. The authority of Parliament to
pass any acts whatever affecting the interior polity
of the colonies was called in question, as destroying the effect of the charters. King, lords, and
commons, it is said, form the legislature of Great
Britain; so the king by his governors, the coun-
cils and assemblies, form the legislatures of the
colonies. But as colonies cannot make laws to
extend farther than their respective limits, Parliament must interpose in all cases where the legislative power of the colonies is ineffectual. Here
the line of the authority of Parliament ought to
be drawn; all beyond is encroachment upon the
constitutional powers of the colonial legislatures.
This doctrine, says Hutchinson, was taught in
every colony from Virginia to Massachusetts, as
early as 1767.

The liberal Rockingham administration, after a
few months of power, disappeared, having signalized itself as regarded America by the repeal of
the Stamp Act, and by the Declaratory Act. Of
the new ministry the leading spirit was Charles
Townshend, a brilliant statesman, but unscrupulous and unwise. His inclinations were arbitrary;
he regretted the repeal of the Stamp Act, as did
also the king and Parliament in general, who felt
themselves to have been humiliated. Pitt, indeed, now Earl of Chatham, was a member of the
government; but, oppressed by illness, he could
exercise no restraint upon his colleague, and the

other members were either in sympathy with Townshend's views, or unable to oppose him. Townshend's three measures affecting America, introduced on the 13th of May, 1767, were: a suspension of the functions of the legislature of New York for contumacy in the treatment of the royal troops; the establishment of commissioners of the customs, appointed with large powers to superintend laws relating to trade; and lastly an impost duty upon glass, red and white lead, painters' colors, paper, and tea. This was an "external" duty to which the colonists had heretofore expressed a willingness to submit; but the grounds of the dispute were shifting. Townshend had declared that he held in contempt the distinctions sought to be drawn between external and internal taxes, but that he would so far humor the colonists in their quibble as to make his tax of that kind of which the right was admitted. A revenue of £40,000 a year was expected from the tax, which was to be applied to the support of a "civil list," namely, the paying the salaries of the new commissioners of customs, and of the judges and governors, who were to be relieved wholly or in part from their dependence upon the annual grants of the Assemblies; then, if a surplus remained, it was to go to the payment of troops for protecting the colonies. To make more efficient, moreover, the enforcement of the revenue laws, the writs of assistance, the denunciation of which by James Otis had formed so memorable a crisis, were formally legalized.

The popular discontent, appeased by the repeal of the Stamp Act, was at once awake again, and henceforth, in the denial of the right of Parliament to tax, we hear no more of acquiescence in commercial restrictions and in the general legislative authority of Parliament. A knowledge of the scandalous pension list in England, the monstrous abuses of patronage in Ireland, the corruptions which already existed in America, made the people indignant at the thought of an increase in the numbers and pay of placemen.

Now it is that still another of the foster children of Samuel Adams emerges into prominence, the bright and enthusiastic Josiah Quincy, already at the age of twenty-three becoming known as a writer, who urges an armed resistance at once to the plans of the ministry. It was the over-hasty counsel of youth, and the plan for resistance adopted by the cooler heads was that of Samuel Adams, namely, the non-importation and the non-consumption of British products. From Boston out, through an impulse proceeding from him, town meetings were everywhere held to encourage the manufactures of the province and reduce the use of superfluities, long lists of which were enumerated. Committees were appointed everywhere to procure subscriptions to agreements looking to the furtherance of home industries and the disuse of foreign products.

But while some were watchful, others were supine or indeed reactionary. Pending the operation of the non-consumption arrangements, which were not to go into effect until the end of the year, a general quiet prevailed, at which the friends of the home government felt great satisfaction. They declared that the "faction dared not show its face," and that "our incendiaries seem discouraged," and in particular they took much hope from the course pursued by James Otis. He, on the 20th of November, in town meeting, made a long speech on the side of the government, asserted the right of the king to appoint officers of customs in what number and by what name he pleased, and declared it imprudent to oppose the new duties. Of the five commissioners of customs three had just arrived from England, the most important among them being Paxton, whose influence had been felt in the establishment of the board. Robinson and Temple, the other members, were already on the ground. In their early meetings, while the province in general seemed quiet, and the voice of Otis in Faneuil Hall advocated a respectful treatment of the board and a compliance with the regulations they were to enforce, they had some reason to feel that, in spite of the hot-headed boy Quincy, and Samuel Adams, with his impracticable non-consumption schemes, the task of the commissioners was likely to be an easy one.

Before the full effects of the new legislation could be seen, Townshend suddenly died; but in the new ministry that was presently formed Lord North came to the front, and adopted the policy of

his predecessor, receiving in this course the firm
support of the king, whose activity and interest
were so great in public affairs that he "became his
own minister." As the business of the colonies
grew every day more important, it was thought
necessary at the end of the year to appoint a secretary of state for the American department. For
this office Lord Hillsborough was named, who had
been before at the head of the Board of Trade.
The new official did not hesitate to adopt aggressive measures, granting, for his first act, to the
many functioned Hutchinson a pension of two hundred pounds, to be paid by the commissioners of
customs, through which he became in a measure
independent of the people.

Of the three men now leaders of the Assembly,
Hawley lived at a distance and was only occasionally in Boston, which became more and more the
centre of influence. A certain excitability, moreover, which made him sometimes over-sanguine
and sometimes despondent, hurt his usefulness.
Otis, sinking more and more into the power of
the disease which in the end was to destroy him,
grew each year more eccentric. Samuel Adams,
always on the ground, always alert, steady, indefatigable, possessing daily more and more the confidence of the province, as he had before gained
that of the town, became constantly more marked
as, in loyalist parlance, the "chief incendiary."
Just at this time, in the winter session of the
legislature of 1767–68, he produced a series of

remarkable papers, in which the advanced ground now occupied by the leaders was elaborately, firmly, and courteously stated.

The first letter, adopted by the Assembly January 13, 1768, is to Dennys Deberdt, the agent of the Assembly in London, and intended of course to be made public. The different members of the ministry and the lords of the treasury were also addressed, and at last the king. There is no whisper in the documents of a desire for independence.

"There is an English affection in the colonists towards the mother country, which will forever keep them connected with her to every valuable purpose, unless it shall be erased by repeated unkind usage on her part."

The injustice of taxation without representation is stated at length, the impossibility of a representation of the colonies in Parliament is dwelt upon, and a voluntary subsidy is mentioned as the only proper and legal way in which the colonies should contribute to the imperial funds. The impropriety of giving stipends to governors and judges independent of the legislative grants is urged, and the grievance of the establishment of commissioners of customs with power to appoint placemen is assailed. No passage is more energetic than that in which the Puritan forefends the encroachments of prelacy.

"The establishment of a Protestant episcopate in America is also very zealously contended for; and it is very alarming to a people whose fathers, from the hardships they suffered under such an establishment, were obliged to fly their native country into a wilderness, in order peaceably to enjoy their privileges, civil and religious. Their being threatened with the loss of both at once must throw them into a disagreeable situation. We hope in God such an establishment will never take place in America, and we desire you would strenuously oppose it. The revenue raised in America, for aught we can tell, may be as constitutionally applied towards the support of prelacy as of soldiers and pensioners."

As a final measure a "Circular Letter" was sent to "each House of Representatives or Burgesses on the Continent."

The authorship of these documents has been claimed for Otis, the assertion being made that Adams was concerned with them only as his assistant. The claim is, however, quite untenable. In style and contents they reflect Adams, while they are in many points inconsistent with the manner and opinions of Otis. Aside from the strong internal evidence, the most satisfactory external proofs have been produced. Mrs. Hannah Wells, the daughter of Samuel Adams, used to say that, when her father was busy with the composition of the petition to the king, she one day said to him, in girlish awe before the far-off mighty potentate, that the paper would doubtless be soon touched by the royal hand. "It will, my dear," he replied, "more likely be spurned by the royal foot." It

is a significant anecdote as showing that he himself had little confidence that the effort of the province would meet with favor. Though eminent
statesmen had been personally appealed to, and
finally the king, the Assembly were careful to send
no memorial to Parliament, not recognizing its
right to interfere.

Even more important than the documents sent
abroad was the " Circular Letter " dispatched by
the Assembly to its sister bodies throughout
America during the same session. When the
measure was first proposed by Mr. Adams, there
was a large majority against it, for the feeling in
England against concerted action in the colonies
was well known, and there was a disinclination to
cause any unnecessary friction. In a fortnight,
however, a complete change had been wrought,
for the measure was carried triumphantly, the
preceding action of the House being erased from
the record. A few days after, on February 11,
the form of the letter was reported, again from the
hand of Mr. Adams. In it a statement was made
of the expediency of providing for a uniform plan
in the action of the different legislatures for remonstrances against the government policy, information was given as to the action of Massachusetts, and communication was invited as to the
measures of the rest. Great pains were taken to
·disclaim all thought of influencing others.

" The House is fully satisfied that your Assembly is

too generous and enlarged in sentiment to believe that this letter proceeds from an ambition of taking the lead or dictating to the other Assemblies. They freely submit their opinion to the judgment of others, and shall take it kind in your House to point out to them anything further that may be thought necessary."

The utmost care and tact were evidently believed to be in place, to avoid exciting jealousy. The "Circular Letter" had a good reception from the various bodies to which it was addressed, and exasperated correspondingly the loyalists. The crown officers of Massachusetts sent energetic memorials to England; Bernard in particular, besides detailing the new outrage, enlarged upon the older grievance, the determination of the Assembly to exclude the crown officers from the Council.

The same month of February was still further signalized by the coming forward into prominence of yet another of the *protégés* of Samuel Adams, perhaps the ablest and most interesting of all, Joseph Warren, who, although for some years a writer for the newspapers, now, at the age of twenty-seven, made for the first time a real sensation by a vehement arraignment of Bernard in the "Boston Gazette." The sensitive governor, touched to the quick by the diatribe, for such it was, and unable to induce the legislature to act in the matter, prorogued it in a mood of exasperation not at all surprising; not, however, until a series of resolutions had been reported, by a committee of which Otis and Adams were members, discouraging foreign importations and stimulating home industries. These were passed with no dissenting voice but that of stalwart Timothy Ruggles, who, having honestly espoused the cause of king and Parliament, opposed himself now to the strong set of the popular current, careless of results to himself, with the same soldierly resolution he had brought to the aid of Abercrombie and Sir Jeffrey Amherst in the hard fighting of the Old French War.

CHAPTER VIII

THE ARRIVAL OF THE TROOPS

IF we look back through the controversy that preceded the independence of America, the year 1768 stands out as an important one. The adoption by the Assembly of Massachusetts of the state papers described in the preceding chapter signalized the opening of the year. These were presently after published together in England by that liberal-handed friend of America, Thomas Hollis, under the title, "The True Sentiments of America." They impressed profoundly public sentiment on both sides of the Atlantic. Events of commensurate importance presently followed, and the year was not to close without a marked increase in the estrangement between motherland and colonists.

In Pennsylvania the "Farmer's Letters" of John Dickinson were meeting with wide approval, and quickly obtained circulation in the colonies in general. They were entirely in accord with the Massachusetts utterances, and proved that, while Franklin was in England, he had left men behind in his province well able to take care of the public welfare. Boston town meeting, in the spring, appointed Samuel Adams, John Hancock, and Joseph

Warren to express to Dickinson its thanks. Meantime though, as has been seen, the author of the papers of January had little hope that they would meet with a kind reception, the people were more sanguine, and looked for a good result. Hillsborough, however, never presented the letter to the king. The government found nothing but unreasonable contumacy in the "True Sentiments of America." The "Circular Letter" was regarded as distinctly seditious, and Bernard was required to demand of the legislature that it should be rescinded, under threat of constant prorogation until it should be done. To give emphasis to the government threat, General Gage, commander of the forces in America, with headquarters in New York, was ominously directed "to maintain the public tranquillity."

A naval force also was dispatched to Boston, of which the first vessel to arrive was the fifty-gun ship Romney, which signalized its approach from Halifax in May by impressing New England seamen from vessels met off the coast. Great ill-will existed between the people and the ship's crew, which burst into flame a few weeks after in the affair of the Liberty, a sloop owned by Hancock, which had broken the revenue laws. A serious riot came near resulting. The commissioners of customs, having in mind the Stamp Act riots four years before, took refuge at the Castle; Bernard withdrew to his house in Roxbury; while the people thronged to town meeting, which, as usual, when the numbers overflowed, flocked from Faneuil Hall to the Old South. As James Otis entered he was received with cheers and clapping of hands; he was made moderator by acclamation, and presently was storming magnificently before the enthusiastic thousands. No alarming result, however, followed. Bernard, reasonably somewhat anxious at Roxbury, with scarcely a man to rely on if force should be used, heard at last that the emissaries of the people were coming. It must have been with much relief that he saw presently a quiet procession of eleven chaises draw up before his door, from which alighted two-and-twenty citizens, with a member of his Council at their head, and Otis and Samuel Adams among the number. A representation of grievances was made in decided but temperate terms; chief of all, the demand was urged that the Romney should be removed from the harbor.

"I received them," wrote Bernard, " with all possible civility, and having heard their petition I talked with them very freely upon the subject, but postponed giving them a final answer until the next day, as it should be in writing. I then had wine handed around, and they left me highly pleased with their reception."

Bernard declared that he had no authority to remove the Romney, and the matter rested there, the crown officials, not unreasonably, pressing more urgently than ever for a body of troops for their protection. The disturbance had, to be sure, proved slight, but it might easily have become a grave affair. In the instructions of the town to the representatives, adopted in May, written by John Adams, now resident in Boston, Hutchinson calls attention to a significant attenuation of the usual loyal expression.

" They declare a reverence and due subordination to the British Parliament, as the supreme legislative, *in all cases of necessity for the preservation of the whole empire.* This is a singular manner of expressing the authority of Parliament."

The whole continent had approved the " Circular Letter." Connecticut, New Jersey, Georgia, and Virginia had responded, which caused Samuel Adams to exclaim in terms which he afterwards used on a still more memorable occasion, " This is a glorious day ! " When the demand that the " Circular Letter " should be rescinded became known to the Assembly, through a message from Bernard in which a letter from Hillsborough was quoted, a letter written by Samuel Adams was twice read and twice accepted, by a vote of ninety-two to thirteen, and ordered to be sent to Hills-borough by the first opportunity, without imparting its contents to the governor or the public. The letter closes with the hope that " to acquaint their fellow subjects involved in the same distress of their having invited the union of all America in one joint supplication, would not be discountenanced by our gracious sovereign as a measure of an inflammatory nature."

The letter was sent by the first conveyance. Mr. Adams withheld it from publication as long as he considered that the public interests were subserved by so doing; then he resolved to have it printed in the "Boston Gazette." Bernard thus relates a scene reported to him: —

"This morning the two consuls of the faction — Otis and Adams — had a dispute upon it in the representatives' room, where the papers of the house are kept, which I shall write as a dialogue to save paper: —

"*Otis.* — What are you going to do with the letter to Lord Hillsborough?

"*Adams.* — To give it to the printer to publish next Monday.

"*Otis.* — Do you think it proper to publish it so soon, that he may receive a printed copy before the original comes to his hand?

"*Adams.* — What signifies that? You know it was designed for the people, and not for the minister.

"*Otis.* — You are so fond of your own drafts that you can't wait for the publication of them to a proper time.

"*Adams.* — I am clerk of this house, and I will make that use of the papers which I please.

"I had this," continues the governor, "from a gentleman of the first rank, who I understood was present."

On the day of the adoption of the letter to Hillsborough, the House considered also the question of rescinding, which was promptly decided in the negative by a vote of ninety-two to seventeen. Addressing the governor, still by the hand of Samuel Adams, they declared: —

"The Circular Letters have been sent and many of them have been answered ; those answers are now in the public papers ; the public, the world, must and will judge of the proposals, purposes, and answers. We could as well rescind those letters as the resolves; and both would be equally fruitless if by rescinding, as the word properly imports, is meant a repeal and nullifying the resolution referred to."

Immediately upon this action, Bernard, as required, prorogued the Assembly, but not until a committee had been appointed to prepare a petition praying "that his majesty would be graciously pleased to remove his excellency, Francis Bernard, from the government of the province." Adams justly looked upon the persistence of the Assembly in this matter as an important triumph, and often referred to it in times when the people's cause was depressed, during the years that were coming, to invigorate the spirit of his party. Since the governor had been directed to prorogue the Assembly as often as it should come together, until the "Circular Letter" should be rescinded, Massachusetts in July, 1768, had practically no legislature. The colonies in general approved the stand of that province, and the necessity of union began to be felt.

In the democracy of Boston, Samuel Adams, among the leaders, was especially the favorite of the mechanics and laborers. His popularity was particularly marked in the shipyards, the craftsmen in which exercised a great influence. His

own poverty, plain clothes, and carelessness as to
ceremony and display, caused them to feel that he
was more nearly on a level with themselves than
Bowdoin, Cushing, Otis, or Hancock, who through
wealth or distinguished connections were led to
affiliate with the rich and high-placed. Though
the legislature could not convene, the restless patriot could find his opportunity in the town meetings; and if they were infrequent, he poured himself into the newspapers. Constant, too, were the
harangues which he delivered in his intercourse
with the townsmen, sitting side by side with some
ship-carpenter on a block of oak, just above the
tide, or with some shopkeeper in a fence corner
sheltered from the wind. Most of his writing was
done in a study adjoining his bedroom in the Purchase Street house. His wife used to tell how she
was accustomed to listen to the incessant motion
of his pen, the light of his solitary lamp being
dimly visible. Passers in the street would often
see, long after midnight, the light from his well-
known window, and " knew that Sam Adams was
hard at work writing against the Tories." Of his
ways, as he moved about in his daily walks, some
graphic hints are given in an affidavit which was
taken at a time when an effort was made to collect
evidence against him. Under a statute of the
reign of Henry VIII., which had been produced
from under the dust of centuries, subjects could be
taken from foreign parts to England, to be tried
for treason. A great desire was felt by the gov-

ernment party to make out a case against Samuel Adams sufficiently strong to justify such deportation. The project was abandoned, but the following curious memorial of the attempt is still preserved in the London State Paper Office : —

"The information of Richard Sylvester of Boston, inn-holder, taken before me, Thomas Hutchinson, Esq., chief justice of said province, this twenty-third of January, in the ninth year of his Majesty's reign:

"This informant sayeth that the day after the boat belonging to Mr. Harrison was burnt, the last summer, the informant observed several parties of men gathered in the street at the south end of the town of Boston, in the forenoon of the day. The informant went up to one of the parties, and Mr. Samuel Adams, then one of the representatives of Boston, happened to join. the same party near about the same time, trembling and in great agitation.[1] The party consisted of about seven in number, who were unknown to the informant, he having but little acquaintance with the inhabitants, or, if any of them were known, he cannot now recollect them. The informant heard the said Samuel Adams then say to the said party, ' If you are men, behave like men. Let us take up arms immediately, and be free, and seize all the king's officers. We shall have thirty thousand men to join us from the country.' The informant then walked off, believing his company was disagreeable. The informant further sayeth, that after the burning of the boat aforesaid, and before the arrival of the troops, the said Samuel Adams has been divers times at the

[1] The constitutional tremulousness of hand and voice common to Mr. Adams is elsewhere described.

house of the informant, and at one of those times particularly the informant began a discourse concerning the times ; and the said Samuel Adams said : ' We will not submit to any tax, nor become slaves. We will take up arms, and spend our last drop of blood before the king and Parliament shall impose on us, and settle crown officers in this country to dragoon us. The country was first settled by our ancestors, therefore we are free and want no king. The times were never better in Rome than when they had no king and were a free state ; and as this is a great empire, we shall have it in our power to give laws to England.' The informant further sayeth, that, at divers times between the burning of the boat aforesaid and the arrival of the troops aforesaid, he has heard the said Adams express himself in words to very much the same purpose, and that the informant's wife has sometimes been present, and at one or more of such times George Mason of Boston, painter, was present. The informant further sayeth, that about a fortnight before the troops arrived, the aforesaid Samuel Adams being at the house of the informant, the informant asked him what he thought of the times. The said Adams answered, with great alertness, that, on lighting the beacon, we should be joined with thirty thousand men from the country with their knapsacks and bayonets fixed, and added, ' We will destroy every soldier that dare put his foot on shore. His majesty has no right to send troops here to invade the country, and I look upon them as foreign enemies ! ' This informant further sayeth, that two or three days before the troops arrived, the said Samuel Adams said to the informant, that Governor Bernard and Mr. Hutchinson and the commissioners of the customs had

sent for troops, and the said Adams made bitter excla-
mations against them for so doing, and also repeated
most of the language about opposing the king's troops,
which he had used as above mentioned about a fortnight before.   The informant contradicted the said
Samuel Adams, and attributed the sending troops to the
resolve of the General Court and the proceedings of the
town meeting.

" Sworn to: T. Hutchinson."

The steps taken in America had only strengthened the determination of the government to break
the spirit of the colonists.   Not only was the project entertained of sending Samuel Adams and
other leaders to England for trial, but town meetings were to be forbidden, and an armed force,
consisting of two regiments and a frigate, was to
be sent at once to Boston.   Samuel Adams afterward said that from this time he dismissed all
thought of reconciliation, and looked forward to,
and labored for, independence.   Hutchinson declares that Adams's efforts for independence began
as early as 1765.   It is well established, at any
rate, that though the vague dream of a great independent American state, some time to exist, had
now and then found expression, Samuel Adams,
first of men, saw clearly that the time for it had
come in the critical period of the reign of George
III., and secretly began his labors for it.   Up to
the year we have reached, indeed, and possibly
afterwards, documents which he prepared contain
loyal expressions, and sometimes seem to disclaim

the wish or thought of ever severing the connection with the mother country. His Tory contemporaries found great duplicity in Mr. Adams's conduct. He himself would, no doubt, have said that when he disclaimed the thought of independence he spoke for others, — the bodies, namely, which employed his hand to express their conclusions; that he could not be and was not bound in such cases to speak his own private views. It must be confessed that some casuistry is necessary now and then to make the conduct of Samuel Adams here square with the absolute right. An advocate, whose sense of honor is nice, hesitates to screen a criminal of whose guilt he is convinced, by any reticence as to his own views. A newspaper writer of the highest character will refuse to postpone his own sentiments, while he expresses the differing sentiments adopted by the journal which employs him. One wonders if the Puritan conscience of Samuel Adams did not now and then feel a twinge, when at the very time in which he had devoted himself, body and soul, to breaking the link that bound America to England, he was coining for this or that body phrases full of reverence for the king and rejecting the thought of independence. The fact was, he could employ upon occasion a certain fox-like shrewdness, which did not always scrutinize the means over narrowly, while he pushed on for the great end. Before our story is finished other instances of wily and devious management will come under our notice, which a proper plumb-line will prove to be not quite in the perpendicular. Bold, unselfish, unmistakably pious as he was, the Achilles of independence was still held by the heel when he was dipped.

In September, the Senegal and Duke of Cumberland, ships of the fleet, set sail from the harbor, and Bernard caused the rumor to be spread abroad that they were going for troops. A town meeting was summoned, and Bernard, apprehending insurrection, caused the beacon on Beacon Hill to be so far dismantled that signals could not be sent to the surrounding country. At the meeting, over which Otis presided, four hundred muskets lay on the floor of Faneuil Hall. A committee, of which Samuel Adams was a member, was appointed to inquire of the governor as to his reasons for expecting the troops, and to request him to convoke a general assembly. Bernard refused, which conduct the committee reported to an adjourned meeting on the day following, when a spirited declaration was made by the town of its purpose to defend its rights. The governor described the meeting to Hillsborough in these terms: —

"An old man protested against everything but rising immediately, and taking all power into their own hands. One man, very profligate and abandoned, argued for massacring their enemies. His argument was, in short, liberty is as precious as life; if a man attempts to take my life, I have a right to take his; *ergo*, if a man attempts to take away my liberty, I have a right to take his life. He also argued, that when a people's liberties were threatened, they were in a state of war, and had a right to defend themselves; and he carried these arguments so far, that his own party were obliged to silence him."

For the leaders there was plainly work to be done in the way of restraining as well as stimulating. The policy decided upon was bold, but not without precedent. Since the governor refused to convene the legislature, the town meeting of Boston resolved to call a convention of the towns of the province, by their representatives, as had been done in 1688, choosing at the same time Cushing, Otis, Samuel Adams, and Hancock as their own delegates. Every inhabitant also was exhorted to provide himself with arms and ammunition, on the pretext that a war with France was impending. At once, on September 22, the convention assembled; ninety-six towns and four districts sent deputies. It was much embarrassed during the first three days of its sitting by the unaccountable absence of Otis, whose importance was so great that, however strange his freaks might be, his presence could not be dispensed with. The government party regarded this convention as the most revolutionary measure yet undertaken; Bernard declared it to be illegal, and solemnly warned it to disperse. The temper of the body, however, was somewhat reactionary, the country members in particular holding back from the course to which the " Bostoneers " would have committed them. Adams, who was always in advance, was little pleased.

His daughter remembered afterwards that he exclaimed: "I am *in* fashion and *out* of fashion, as the whim goes. I will stand alone. I will oppose this tyranny at the threshold, though the fabric of liberty fall and I perish in its ruins." The petition of the preceding legislature to the king, however, and a letter to Deberdt, also written by Adams, both which papers were manly and strong, were adopted. The great end gained was in the way of habituating the people to coming together in other than the established ways; and the precedent was found useful in the times that were approaching.

On the very day that the convention adjourned, after a session of a week, there arrived from Halifax the 14th and 29th regiments, which have come down in history, following the designation of Lord North, as the "Sam Adams regiments," for reasons which will abundantly appear. While the ships which brought them lay close at hand in the harbor in a position to command the town, the regiments after landing marched with all possible pomp from Long Wharf to the Common, where they paraded, each soldier having in his cartridge-box sixteen rounds, as if entering an enemy's country. The 29th regiment encamped on the Common, but the 14th was quartered in Faneuil Hall, Bernard insisting that both should be in the body of the town. Samuel Adams wrote the next week to Deberdt: —

"The inhabitants preserve their peace and quietness.

However, they are resolved not to pay their money without their own consent, and are more than ever determined to relinquish every article, however dear, that comes from Britain. May God preserve the nation from being greatly injured, if not finally ruined, by the vile ministrations of wicked men in America!"

CHAPTER IX

THE RECALL OF BERNARD

THE troops had arrived, and it is absurd to think that Bernard and the crown officers had no reason on their side in demanding them. With three quarters of the people of the province, as shown by the composition of the Assembly, directly hostile to the government policy, and in Boston a still larger proportion in opposition, with the upper house of the legislature through its constitution scarcely less in sympathy with the people than the lower, the governor had no support in his honest efforts to maintain the parliamentary supremacy, unless he could have the regiments. That the commissioners of the customs had been foolish and cowardly in fleeing with their families to the Castle after the affair of the Liberty, it is quite wrong to assert. They were unquestionably in danger, and had no means of defending themselves. The unpopular laws which they were expected to administer could only be carried out under protection of a military force.

When General Gage came on from New York to demand quarters for the regiments, the Council refused to grant them until the barracks at the

Castle were filled, which was required by the letter
of the law. The main guard was finally established
opposite the State House in King Street, with the
cannon pointed toward the door, while the troops
were housed in buildings hired by their commander, the attempt to obtain possession of a ruinous building belonging to the province being foiled
by its occupants, who were backed by town and
country in refusing to vacate.

The troops presented a formidable appearance
as they marched through the streets and paraded
on the Common. However objectionable in actual
service, for imposing display all who are familiar
with armies must admit that nothing is equal to
the British scarlet, when spread out over ranks
well filled and drilled, with the glitter of bayonets
above the mass of superb color. The Tories took
great heart. Good-natured Dr. Byles congratulated the patriots because their grievances were at
length *redressed* [red-dressed], and Hutchinson
wrote cheerful letters. The people were at first
quiet and orderly, but by no means cowed ; and
when familiarity at length had bred its usual consequence, a threatening turbulence appeared. A
crowd of abandoned women followed the troops
from Halifax, many of whom before long became
inmates of the almshouses. Before a month had
passed, forty men had deserted, and one who was
recovered was summarily shot. The town, moreover, was shocked by the flogging of troops, which
was administered by negro drummers in public on

the Common. Strangely enough, Samuel Adams was once appealed to by the wife of a soldier sentenced to receive a number of lashes almost sufficient to kill him. How the poor creature could have formed the idea that the arch rebel would have influence with the commanders it is hard to say. He made the effort, however, and the intervention was successful, in the hope, his daughter surmises, who tells the story, that the concession would pave the way for conciliatory overtures, with which he was afterwards approached. Through policy, and no doubt also through humane inclination, occasions of friction between soldiers and townsmen were avoided as far as possible by the commanders; the legal restriction was fully recognized, that the troops could not be employed except upon the requisition of a civil magistrate.

Some amusing traditions have come down as to the extent to which non-interference was pursued. At a legal inquiry, a soldier, who had been on duty, was said to have been thus interrogated : —

" The sentinel being asked whether he was on guard at the time, he answered — Yes. Whether he saw any person break into Mr. Grey's house ? — Yes. Whether he said anything to them ? — No. Why he did not ? — Because he had orders to challenge nobody. Whether he looked upon them to be thieves ? — Yes. Why he did not make an alarm and cause them to be secured ? — Because he had orders to do nothing which might deprive any man of his liberty ! "

This story is perhaps an invention, but the

policy which it parodies was real. Occasions of
offense were avoided; a good discipline was maintained, and the collisions which at length came to
pass grew rather out of the aggressions of the
townsmen than from the conduct of the troops.

As the fall and winter proceeded, we find Samuel
Adams busy in the newspapers, among which his
principal organ was the "Boston Gazette," whose
bold proprietors, Edes & Gill, made their sheet
the voice of the patriot sentiment, and gave their
office also to be a rallying-point for the popular
leaders. Adams's signatures at this time are significant: "Obsta principiis," "Arma cedant togæ,"
and "Vindex." Through him the popular ideas
find expression. He shows the illegality and use-
lessness of billeting troops. He assails the commissioners of customs, who, having returned from
the Castle, and been censured by the Council because "they had no just reason for absconding
from their duty," had taken up their quarters in
Queen Street. He considers the arguments of the
opponents of America in Parliament, and upon this
latter theme is particularly wise and forcible. The
following letter he contributed, as "Vindex," to
the "Boston Gazette" of December 19, 1768, and
it would perhaps be impossible to find a better
illustration of the superior political sense of the
New Englanders, trained in town meeting, as compared with their contemporaries in England.
Speaking of a certain just claim of the colonies,
he says : —

"I know very well that some of the late contenders
for a right in the British Parliament to tax Americans
who are not, and cannot be, represented there, have denied this.   When pressed with that fundamental principle of nature and the Constitution, that what is a
man's own is *absolutely* his own, and that no man *can*
have a right to take it from him without his consent,
they have alleged, and would fain have us believe, that
by far the greater part of the people in Britain are
excluded the right of chusing their representatives,
and yet are taxed ; and therefore that they are taxed
without their consent.   Had not this doctrine been repeatedly urged, I should have thought the bare mention-
ing it would have opened the eyes of the people there to
have seen where their pretended advocates were leading
them : that in order to establish a right in the people in
England to enslave the Colonists under a plausible shew
of great zeal for the honor of the nation, they are driven
to a bold assertion, at all adventures, that truly the
greater part of the nation are themselves subject to the
same yoke of bondage.   What else is it but saying that
the greater part of the people in Britain are slaves ?
For if the fruit of all their toil and industry depends
upon so precarious a tenure as the will of a few, what
security have they for the utmost farthing ?   What are
they but *slaves*, delving with the sweat of their brows,
not for the benefit of themselves, but their *masters ?*
After all the fine things that have been said of the British Constitution, and the boasted freedom and happiness
of the subjects who live under it, will they thank these
modern writers, these zealous assertors of the honor of
the nation, for reducing them to a state inferior to that

of indented servants, who generally contract for a maintenance, at least, for their labor ? " [1]

In Parliament, the American cause was by no
means without friends and advocates, among whom
the conspicuous figure was now Edmund Burke.
Even Grenville declared that the order requiring the
rescinding of the Circular Letter was illegal. Lord
North, however, in November was " determined
to see America at the king's feet;" he led the ministry, and through both houses England pledged
itself to maintain entire and inviolate the supreme
authority of the legislature of Great Britain over
every part of the empire. Hillsborough introduced
resolutions in the House of Lords condemning the
legislature of Massachusetts and the September
convention, approving the sending of the military
force, and preparing changes in the charter of the
province which would lessen the popular power.
Through the Duke of Bedford steps were taken
toward bringing " the chief authors and instiga-
tors " to trial for treason, and yet the riots at this
time in England were beyond comparison greater
and more threatening than any disturbances in
the colonies. Obstacles, however, were found to
bringing these men to trial. It was declared by
the attorney and solicitor-general to be impossible,
from the evidence furnished, to make out a case of
treason against Samuel Adams or any other person

[1] In most of the extracts given, punctuation, spelling, capitals,
and italics follow those of the originals, as they stand in the old
newspapers or the manuscripts.

named. The straits to which the trade of England
had been brought, through the course pursued by
the colonies, produced at length an effect greater
than any remonstrances. The tax upon glass,
paper, and painters' colors was taken off; it was,
however, allowed to remain on the one article,
tea.

In the mean time, in Boston, the controversy
was fast and furious. Of the half dozen newspapers, the " Massachusetts Gazette," also known
as " Draper's " and the " Court Gazette," was the
usual organ of the administration, as the " Boston Gazette " was of the popular leaders, though
other sheets as well teemed with combative periods.
The government writers, among whom were some
of the commissioners of customs, received liberal
pay. On the popular side Samuel Adams was the
writer most forcible and prolific, and his contributions went also to newspapers at a distance. The
following extract is taken from an appeal to the
Sons of Liberty, prepared on the anniversary of
the repeal of the Stamp Act, and found posted
on the Liberty Tree in Providence, R. I., on the
morning of the 18th of March, 1769. It appeared
the same morning in the " Providence Gazette,"
and afterward in the " Boston Gazette." It is the
closing paragraph .of the appeal, and remarkable
from the significant words at the end. It is the
first instance, perhaps, where Samuel Adams in
any public way hints at independence as the probable issue of the difficulties.

" When I consider the corruption of Great Britain, — their load of debt, — their intestine divisions, tumults, and riots, — their scarcity of provisions, — and the Contempt in which they are held by the nations about them; and when I consider, on the other Hand, the State of the American Colonies with Regard to the various Climates, Soils, Produce, rapid Population, joined to the virtue of the inhabitants, — I cannot but think that the Conduct of Old England towards us may be permitted by Divine Wisdom, and ordained by the unsearchable providence of the Almighty, for hastening a period dreadful to Great Britain.

" A Son of Liberty.

"Providence, March 18th, 1769."

Great efforts were made to obtain circulation for the Tory papers (for now the terms Tory and Whig, borrowed from England, had come into vogue) ; but they had no popular favor as compared with the "Boston Gazette." Hutchinson declared that seven eighths of the people read none but this, and so were never undeceived. The site of the office of Edes & Gill, in Court Street, is really one of the memorable spots of Boston. Here very frequently met Warren, Otis, Quincy, John Adams, Church, and patriots scarcely less conspicuous. In those groups Samuel Adams becomes constantly more and more the eminent figure. Here they read the exchanges, corrected the proof of their contributions, strengthened one another by the interchange of ideas, and planned some of the most remarkable measures in the course to independence. At this time, also, Samuel Adams's controversial pen found other subjects than British machinations. His friend, Dr. Chauncy, becoming concerned in a sharp dispute with Seabury, afterwards the first bishop of the American Episcopal Church, Adams smote the prelatical adversary with a true Roundhead cudgel. To such as Seabury he was uncompromisingly hostile till the day of his death, though on one remarkable occasion hereafter to be mentioned he postponed his prejudice to secure a certain ulterior end. For Mr. Seabury's cloth at this time he shows little respect, declaring that " he had managed his cause with the heart, though he had evidently discovered that he wanted the head, of a Jesuit."

Massachusetts had been nearly a year without a legislature, when in May, 1769, the governor issued a summons for a meeting. Otis, Cushing, Samuel Adams, and Hancock were elected almost unanimously in town meeting, and forthwith " instructed," by the hand of John Adams, in the most determined manner. The Assembly, as soon as the members were sworn, neglecting the usual preliminary, the election of the clerk, who then superintended the election of the speaker, adopted a remonstrance, prepared by Samuel Adams, demanding the removal of the troops. When Bernard alleged that the power did not lie with him, a committee, of which Samuel Adams was a member, declared in answer to the assertion : —

"That the king was the supreme executive power through all parts of the British empire, and that the governor of the Province being the king's lieutenant and captain-general and commander-in-chief, it indubitably follows that all officers, civil and military, within the colony are subject to his Excellency."

In adopting the report the Assembly declined to proceed to business under military duress, upon which Bernard adjourned them to Cambridge, urging that in that place the objection would be removed. The Assembly went to Cambridge, although, in 1728, the power of the governor to convene the legislature elsewhere than in Boston had been denied. They went, however, under protest, and when in the succeeding administration they were again and again convened at Cambridge, a sharp controversy resulted, with which we shall presently be concerned. When the governor urged them to hasten their proceedings in order to save time and money, the house replied by Samuel Adams: —

"No time can be better employed than in the preservation of the rights derived from the British Constitution, and insisting upon points which, though your Excellency may consider them as non-essential, we esteem its best bulwarks. No treasure can be better expended than in securing that true old English liberty which gives a relish to every other enjoyment."

News reached Massachusetts of the bold resolves of the Virginia House of Burgesses of this year.

" The committee on the state of the province," of which Mr. Adams was a member, at once reported resolutions embodying those of Virginia in so far as they related to taxation, intercolonial correspondence, and trial by jury of the vicinage. They went back to the "Massachusetts Resolves" of 1765, and made so definite an expression of the claims of the patriots that Hutchinson declared "no such full declaration had ever before been made, that no laws made by any authority in which the people had not their representatives could be obligatory on them." Two additional regiments had come in the spring to Boston, which, being judged quite unnecessary, had been ordered to Halifax. One had already sailed, and the other was about to embark, when the new resolutions appeared in the "Boston Gazette." Then the regiment was detained; for the government felt that the declarations were more pronounced in their rebellious tone than any that had yet been made. At this the Assembly took alarm, and although the resolves had passed in a full house unanimously, one hundred and nine being present, it was voted to modify them. This was done in spite of the more zealous spirits. The regiment then departed, leaving behind the original force, the 14th and 29th, which were now fast nearing an hour destined to bestow upon them a somewhat unenviable immortality in the history of America.

Another noteworthy incident in this animated session was the demand by Bernard, in accordance with the terms of the Billeting Act by which the troops had been quartered on the town, of a sum to defray the expenses of the troops. Samuel Adams, speaking for his committee, showed at length the conflict of the demand with the chartered rights of the province, ending with the declaration: —

"Your Excellency must therefore excuse us in this express declaration, that as we cannot consistently with our honor or interest, and much less with the duty we owe our constituents, so we shall *never* make provision for the purposes in your several messages above mentioned."

But the career of Francis Bernard in America had now reached its close. The petitions for his removal that had been sent from the province had probably little effect in producing this result; but the merchants of England, alarmed at the non-importation agreements in the colonies, and selfishly anxious to stem, if possible, the disaffection that was beginning to tell with such effect on their pockets, made representations that were heeded. While retaining his office, he was summoned to England, ostensibly to help the government with information and advice; and, as a mark of the approval with which the king and ministry regarded his course, he was made a baronet under the title of Sir Francis Bernard of Nettleham. His demand from the legislature of a grant for the salary during the year to come, made under instruction from the king, was sufficiently legal, inasmuch as he remained governor and was to serve, according to his own ideas, the interests of the province. Half the salary, moreover, was to be paid to the lieutenant-governor. But the General Court scornfully refused the demand. It was prorogued early in July " to the usual time for its meeting for the winter session," and on the last day of the month Sir Francis sailed for England. The day of his departure was made a public gala-day. Flags were hoisted, the bells sounded from the steeples, cannon roared from the wharves, and on Fort Hill blazed a great bonfire. For more than a year he retained in England the title of governor of Massachusetts Bay. Samuel Adams, in the "Boston Gazette," May 1, thus mocked the outgoing magistrate : —

"Your promotion, sir, reflects an honor on the Province itself ; an honor which has never been conferr'd upon it since the thrice-happy administration of Sir Edmond Andross of precious memory, who was also a baronet ; nor have the unremitted Endeavors of that very amiable and truly patriotick Gentleman to render the most substantial and lasting services to this people, upon the plan of a wise and uncorrupt set of m——rs, been ever *parallelled* till since you adorned the ch—r. . . . Pity it is that you have not a pension to support your title. But an Assembly *well chosen* may supply that want even to *your* wish. Should this fail, a late letter, said to have strongly recommended a tax upon the improved LANDS of the Colonies, may be equally successful with the other letters of *the like nature*, and funds sufficient may be rais'd for the Use and Emolument of yourself and friends, without a Dependence upon a '*military establishment supported* by the Province at Castle William.'

"I am, sir, with the most profound respect, and with the sincerest Wishes for your further Exaltation, the most *servile* of all *your* tools.   A TORY."

Francis Bernard was an honorable and well-meaning man, and by no means wanting in ability. As with the English country gentlemen in the eighteenth century, in general, the traditions of English freedom had become much obscured in his mind. He leaned toward prerogative, not popular liberty, and honestly felt that the New Englanders were disposed to run to extremes that would ruin America and injure the whole empire. Where among the rural squires or the Oxford scholars of the time can be found any who took a different view? This being his position, no one can deny that during the nine years of his incumbency he fought his difficult fight with courage, persistency, and honesty. He leaned as far as such a man could be expected to lean toward the popular side, showing wisdom in 1763 and 1764, as we have seen, in trying to procure a lowering or abolition of the duties in the Sugar Act, and regarding the Stamp Act as most inexpedient. The best friends of America in Parliament, like Lord Camden, extolled in strong terms his character and good judgment. His refined tastes and good dispositions were shown in his interest in Harvard College. After the fire of 1764, he did what he could from his own library to make good the loss of the books which had been burned; certainly the alumnus in whose youthful associations the plain but not ungraceful proportions of Harvard Hall have become intimately bound may have a kind thought for its well-meaning and much-maligned architect. The accusations of underhand dealing that were brought against him will not bear examination.

Bollan, agent in England of the Massachusetts Council, obtained from Beckford, a liberal member of Parliament, copies of six letters, written by Bernard to influence parliamentary action in November and December, 1768. The letters contain estimates of public characters, an account of events in Massachusetts, and proposals of certain changes in the charter. When sent to America these papers aroused great indignation. They were felt to be so important that, despite sabbatarian scruples, they were considered by the Council on Sunday. The utmost wrath was poured out upon their author. Yet really the letters contain nothing more than views which Bernard had made no secret of. That he was profoundly dissatisfied with the constitution of the colonies and desired changes, every one knew. What opinion he had of his active opponents and their measures was no secret. He did them no more justice than they did him. The changes he advocated were that the provincial governments should be brought to a uniform type ; the Assemblies he would have remain popular, as before ; but for the Council, or

upper house, he recommended a body made up
of a kind of life peers, appointed directly by the
king. He recommended, also, that there should
be a fixed civil list from which the king's officers
should derive a certain provision, declaring that in
the existing state of things it was impossible to
enforce in the colonies any unpopular law or punish any outrage favored by the people, since civil
officers were mainly dependent on annual grants
from the Assembly. For a prerogative man, such
views were not unreasonable; certainly Bernard
had made no pretense of holding others. He was,
however, bitterly denounced and insulted.

As the Baronet of Nettleham was borne out to
sea that quiet summer evening, amid the pealing
of bells, the salvos of cannon, and the glare of the
great bonfire on Fort Hill, the populace of Boston,
as it were, shouted after him their contumely.
Fine Shakespearean scholar that he was, one may
well believe that the bitter outbursts of Coriolanus
against the common cry of curs, whose breath was
hateful as the reek of rotten fens, rose to the lips
of the aristocrat. Neither side could do justice to
the other. The student of history knows well that
mutual justice and forbearance are in such cases
not to be expected. They were the fighters in
a fierce conflict, and of necessity bad blood was
engendered. A different tone, however, may be
demanded at the present time. When a writer,
after the lapse of a hundred years, declares, "He
displayed his malignity to the last, and having

done his best to ruin the province, and to reap all possible benefit from its destruction, took his departure,"[1] one feels that a well-meaning man is pursued quite too far, and the desire for fair play suggests the propriety of a word or two in his favor.

[1] Wells, *S. Adams*, i. 206.

CHAPTER X

THE NON-IMPORTATION AGREEMENTS

BERNARD had gone, and in his place stood Thomas Hutchinson. For the next two years he remained lieutenant-governor, but to all intents and purposes he was chief magistrate, in which position he remained until the king found no way of disentangling the ever-increasing perplexities except through the sword of a soldier. Since for five most important years the figure of Hutchinson is to be scarcely less prominent in our story than that of Samuel Adams himself, the main facts in his career hitherto may be recapitulated, that the character may be fully understood with which now, in the summer of 1769, and in his fifty-eighth year, he comes into the foreground.

Born in 1711, he left Harvard in 1727, and soon made some trial of mercantile life. From a line of famous ancestors, among them Mrs. Anne Hutchinson, that strong and devout spirit of the earliest days of Boston, he had inherited a most honorable name and great abilities. He was a Puritan to the core; his wealth was large; his manners conciliated for him the good-will of the people, which for a long time he never forfeited.

He became a church member at twenty-four, select-man of Boston at twenty-six, and at thirty was sent as agent of the province to London on important business, which he managed with ability. For ten years after his return he was representative, dur-ing three of which he served as speaker. In par-ticular, he did good service in the settlement of the province debt in 1749. For sixteen years he was a member of the Council, and while in the Council he became judge of probate, lieutenant-governor, and chief justice, holding all these posi-tions at once. It is shooting quite wide of the mark to base any accusation of self-seeking on the number of Hutchinson's offices. The emoluments accruing from them all were very small ; in some, in fact, his service was practically gratuitous. Nor was any credit or fame he was likely to gain from holding them at all to be weighed against the labor and vexation to be undergone in discharging their functions. A more reasonable explanation of his readiness to uphold such burdens is that the rich, high-placed citizen was full of public spirit. That he performed honorably and ably the work of these various offices there is no contradicting tes-timony. As a legislator no one had been wiser. As judge of probate he had always befriended widows and orphans. As chief justice, though not bred to the law, he had been an excellent magis-trate. Besides all this, he had found time to write a history of New England, which must be regarded as one of the most interesting and important literary monuments of the colonial period, — a work digested from the most copious materials with excellent judgment, and presented in a style admirable for dignity, clearness, and scholarly finish.

Now that battle was joined between the people and the prerogative men, he had taken sides with the latter, following his honest opinions, and keeping his head cool even after the exasperations of years of controversy. On the 14th of February, 1772, he writes: —

"It is not likely that the American colonies will remain part of the dominion of Britain another century, but while they do remain, the supreme, absolute legislative power must remain entire, to be exercised upon the colonies so far as is necessary for the maintenance of its own authority and the general weal of the whole empire, and no farther." [1]

With these views Hutchinson comes into the leading place among the Tory champions, a place which he had not sought, but which, when urged upon him, he did not refuse.

As Hutchinson becomes now the conspicuous figure among the royalists, Samuel Adams stands out in a prominence which he has not before possessed in the camp of the patriots. To Bernard "he was one of the principal and most desperate chiefs of the faction." To Hutchinson, however, he becomes "the chief incendiary," the "all in all," the "*instar omnium*," "the master of the

[1] From Hutchinson's autograph letter to John H. Hutchinson, Dublin, in Mass. Archives.

puppets." Whereas to Bernard Samuel Adams
has been only one among several of evil fame, to
Hutchinson he stands like Milton's Satan among
the subordinate leaders of the hellish cohorts, isolated in a baleful supremacy. This new eminence
of Samuel Adams is mainly due to an event which
took place in the beginning of September. James
Otis, who was far enough from looking forward to
independence, whose favorite scheme, as we have
seen, was an American representation in Parliament, and who with all his opposition was very
desirous to be thought loyal, felt outraged beyond
measure at the reports of seditious conduct on his
part, that had been made in letters written by
the crown officers to the government in England.
While in this frame of mind he met, at the British
coffee-house in King Street, Robinson, one of the
commissioners of customs, who was there in company with officers of the army and navy and various civil dignitaries. A violent altercation took
place which ended in a fight, in the course of which
Otis was severely cut and bruised, his head in particular receiving ugly wounds. The proceeding was
regarded in the town as most cowardly and brutal,
since Otis, while alone, was set upon by several
assailants. The hostile temper of the people was
greatly incensed by the occurrence, the resentment
becoming mixed with passionate grief when it presently appeared that the mind of the popular idol
had become practically wrecked by reason, as was
generally believed, of the injuries received.

For years already the eccentricities of Otis, which plainly enough indicate a certain morbidness of mind, had aroused anxiety, and made him sometimes almost unendurable to those who were forced to work with him. When Oxenbridge Thacher, the admirable man whose untimely death opened the way for Samuel Adams to enter the Assembly, had happened to think differently from Otis, the latter had treated him in so overbearing and insolent a way that he was obliged to call on the speaker of the house for protection. The bar were sometimes all up in arms against him on account of his arrogant affronts. Adams usually got on with him better than others did. Gordon says that "Sam Adams was well qualified to succeed Thacher, and learned to serve his own views by using Otis's influence." The old historian regards it as part of Samuel Adams's tact, who, he says, acquired great ascendency by being ready to "acquiesce in the proposals and amendments of others, while the end aimed at by them did not eventually frustrate his leading designs. He showed in smaller matters a pliableness and complaisance which enabled him at last to carry those of much greater consequence."

But, deft though he was, Adams could not always manage Otis, as is indicated by the scene between "the two consuls of the faction," of which we know through Bernard's description, already quoted. At the time of the violence, as is learned from John Adams's report, Otis was in a strange

frame of mind, and no doubt comported himself
in such a way as to bring the assault upon himself. Although the abilities and services of James
Otis were so magnificent, contemporary testimony
makes it plain that he must often have been a
source of great embarrassment through his vacillations and infirmities. That his motives were
sometimes far enough from being the highest
seems probable. The assertion of Hutchinson that
his opposition to the government cause was due to
wrath, into which he fell because his father had
not been made chief justice in 1760, would not,
unsupported, be sufficient to establish the fact.
Gordon, however, who stood with the patriots,
makes the same statement. The story is that
Shirley had promised the place to the elder Otis,
and that the son had exclaimed, " If Governor
Bernard does not appoint my father judge of the
Superior Court, I will kindle such a fire in the
province as shall singe the governor, though I myself perish in the flames; " and that his resistance
to the government began at the appointment of
Hutchinson instead of his father. John Adams,
too, touched by a slighting remark of Otis, and
dashing down an odd outburst of testiness in his
diary, hints at much self-seeking.

From 1769 Otis, who had always been an un-
comfortable ally, however useful at times, became
simply a source of anxiety and embarrassment.
His influence with the people yet remained; by
fits and starts his old eloquence still flashed forth,

and town meeting and Assembly, which he had
so often made to thrill, were slow to give him up.
It required all Samuel Adams's adroitness, however, to hold his crazy associate within some kind
of limits, who frequently, as we shall see, put
things in the gravest peril in spite of all that could
be done. With Bernard gone, therefore, and Otis
incapacitated, Hutchinson and Samuel Adams, in
the deepening strife, confront one another, each
assisted by, but quite above, his fellow combatants, fighters well worthy of one another in point
of ability, honesty, and courage.

For years now Samuel Adams had laid aside all
pretense of private business, and was devoted simply and solely to public affairs. The house in Purchase Street still afforded his family a home. His
sole source of income was the small salary he received as clerk of the Assembly. His wife, like
himself, was contented with poverty; through good
management, in spite of their narrow means, a
comfortable home life was maintained in which
the children grew up happy, and in every way
well trained and cared for. John Adams tells of
a drive taken by these two kinsmen, on a beautiful
June day not far from this time, in the neighborhood of Boston. Then, as from the first and ever
after, there was an affectionate intimacy between
them. They often called one another brother,
though the relationship was only that of second
cousin. "My brother, Samuel Adams, says he
never looked forward in his life; never planned,

laid a scheme, or formed a design of laying up anything for himself or others after him." The case of Samuel Adams is almost without parallel as an instance of enthusiastic, unswerving devotion to the public service throughout a long life. His pittance scarcely supplied food, and when clothing was required, as we shall see, it came by special gift from his friends. Yet with all this, according to the confession of his enemies, he was absolutely incorruptible.

Bernard before his departure had written that the most respectable of the merchants would not hold to the non-importation agreements, and British merchants accordingly felt encouraged to send cargoes to America. On September 4 a factor arrived in charge of a large consignment of goods. The town was expecting him; Samuel Adams, in the "Boston Gazette," had prepared the public mind. At once a meeting of merchants was held at which the factor was "required to send his goods back again." At a town meeting held on the same day Samuel Adams with others was appointed to vindicate the town from the false representations of Bernard and other officials, and the case of those who had broken the non-importation agreements was considered. The names of four merchants were placed on the records as infamous; among those thus gibbeted were a son of Bernard and the two sons of Hutchinson, with whom the father was believed by the people to be in collusion. Such goods as had been landed were housed, and the key was kept by a committee of patriots. The troops meanwhile stood idle spectators, for no act could be alleged of which any justice of the peace would take notice, although the temper of the people was so plainly hostile. An invitation from New York, to continue the non-importation agreement until *all* the revenue acts should be repealed, was at once accepted by the merchants. Hutchinson, in letters to Bernard, hopes, consistently enough, "that Parliament will show their indignation. . . . A rigorous spirit in Parliament will yet set us right; without it the government of this province will be split into innumerable divisions."

The committee chosen to defend the town from the aspersions of the crown officials reported at an adjourned meeting, held a fortnight later, an address written by Samuel Adams, which obtained great fame under the title, "An Appeal to the World." It occupies twenty-nine pages of the town records, and was circulated widely in America and also in England, where it was republished. In the case of Wilkes the principle of representation was at this time undergoing attack in England as well as in America, and there were many who read with eagerness the Boston statement. Speaking of Bernard, the appeal declares : —

"He always discovered an aversion to free assemblies; no wonder then that he should be so particularly disgusted at a legal meeting of the town of Boston, where a noble freedom of speech is ever expected and maintained; an assembly of which it may be justly said, 'Sentire quæ volunt et quæ sentiunt dicere licet,' — they think as they please and speak as they think. Such an assembly has ever been the dread, often the scourge of tyrants."

A remarkable forbearance, one is forced to admit, characterizes the conduct of the soldiers during the fall and winter of 1769. In October a man who had given information regarding certain smuggled wine, which had arrived from Rhode Island, was tarred and feathered, carted for three hours through the streets, and finally made to swear under the Liberty Tree never again to do the like. John Mein, publisher of the "Chronicle," a paper which, from having been neutral, at length took the government side, was a recent Scotch immigrant of intelligence and enterprise. His advertisements as a bookseller are still interesting reading, filling as they do whole columns of the newspapers with lists of his importations, comprising the best books in that day published. He deserves to be gratefully remembered also as the founder in Boston of circulating libraries. For ridiculing certain of the patriots he was attacked, and goaded into firing a pistol among the crowd; he was forced to fly to the main guard for protection, whence he escaped in disguise, to return soon after to England. Difficulty was experienced in maintaining the non-importation agreements. Certain merchants who had signed them reluctantly, interpreting them now according to the letter,

which made them expire on January 1, 1770, at
once threw off restrictions on that date and began
to sell tea. Among these were the sons of Hutchinson, who were upheld by their father. The people, however, had a different understanding of the
agreement. The restriction, they thought, must
remain in force until other merchants could import. A crowd of citizens, merchants, justices of
the peace, selectmen, representatives, and magistrates, as well as men of a lower degree, waited
upon Hutchinson, demanding redress. Hutchinson from the window warned them of the danger
of their illegal and riotous proceedings, but finally
succumbed to the demands of the crowd, a course
which he later regretted. "Some of your friends
and mine," he afterward wrote to a royalist, "wish
matters had gone to extremities, this being as good
a time as any to have called out the troops." He
felt great doubt whether he was competent, as
governor, to order the soldiers to fire, as appears
from his diary, a doubt shared by the legal lights
in England ; he was chief magistrate, but did that
imply the powers of a justice of the peace ?

The same method seems to have been employed
or at least threatened by the people, in other
cases, and to have been much dreaded. A certain
Scotchman, a large importer, having been remonstrated with and proving utterly contumacious,
Samuel Adams arose in the meeting and moved
grimly that the crowd, consisting of two thousand people, should resolve itself into a committee

of the whole and wait upon him to urge his compliance with the general wish. Thereupon the Scotchman, a little fellow in a reddish, smokedried wig, with a squeaking voice and a roll of the *r*'s like a well-played drum, rushed before the crowd exclaiming: "Mr. Mode-r-r-rator, I agr-r-ree, I agr-r-ree!" greatly to the people's amusement. Samuel Adams pointed to a seat near himself with a polite, condescending bow of protection, and the frightened man was quieted.

It had been intimated from England that, since the government had become convinced that duties like those of the Townshend act were not consistent with the laws of commerce, the imposts would be removed from glass, paper, and painters' colors, but not, as we have seen, from the one article, tea. The people were not conciliated, for it was easy to see that, in retaining the duty upon tea, the government proposed to cling to the right of taxing the colonies. This principle the colonists were just as determined to repudiate, and therefore, although as a matter of dollars and cents it was a thing of trifling moment, a resistance to the use of tea from the present time is a main feature of the disturbance. Tea it was which the sons of Hutchinson were anxious to bring into the market at the expiration of the non-importation agreements, when the resistance of the people was so determined. It was voted by the citizens soon after at Faneuil Hall to abstain totally from the use of tea. Since the men were less concerned in the

matter than the women, the mistresses of four
hundred and ten families pledged themselves to
drink no more tea until the revenue act was repealed, and a few days later one hundred and
twenty young ladies formed a similar league.

"We, the daughters of those patriots," said they,
"who have and do now appear for the public interest,
and in that principally regard their posterity, — as such
do with pleasure engage with them in denying ourselves
the drinking of foreign tea, in hope to frustrate a plan
which tends to deprive a whole community of all that is
valuable in life."

At the social gatherings the void created by the
absence of the popular beverage was quite unfilled,
save by the rather melancholy notes of the spin-
net.

The importers had no peace. They were pointed
out as proscribed men, and were hooted at by boys
in the street. It was during such a disturbance
that, on the 22d of February, the first bloodshed
took place in Boston, in a contest which had for
so long been a mere war of words. A crowd of
boys, engaged in tormenting a trader who had made
himself obnoxious by selling tea, was fired into
by a partisan of the government. One boy was
wounded, and another, Christopher Snyder, son of
a poor German, was killed. An immense sensation was created. The boy who was slain was
eleven years old. At his funeral five hundred of
his schoolmates walked before the coffin, and a

crowd of more than a thousand people followed. The procession marched from the Liberty Tree to the town-house, and thence to the burying-ground on the Common. The man who had fired the shot narrowly escaped being torn in pieces. So step by step the estrangement increased, and at length came a formidable explosion.

CHAPTER XI

THE SAM ADAMS REGIMENTS

As the spring of the year 1770 appeared, the 14th and 29th regiments had been in Boston about seventeen months. The 14th was in barracks near the Brattle Street Church; the 29th was quartered just south of King Street; about midway between them, in King Street, and close at hand to the town-house, was the main guard, whose nearness to the public building had been a subject of great annoyance to the people. During a period when the legislature was not in session a body of troops had occupied the unused representatives' chamber. James Otis had characteristically given voice to the general aversion at this time. At a meeting of the Superior Court in the council chamber he moved an adjournment to Faneuil Hall, saying, with a gesture of contempt and loathing, " that the stench occasioned by the troops in the representatives' chamber might prove infectious, and that it was utterly derogatory to the court to administer justice at the points of bayonets and the mouths of cannon." During their Boston sojourn the troops were carefully drilled. John Adams, whose house was near the barracks of the 14th, has left a description of the music and exercises to which he and his family were constantly treated. One is forced to admit, also, that a good degree of discipline was maintained; no blood had as yet been shed by the soldiers, although provocations were constant, the rude element in the town growing gradually more aggressive, as the soldiers were never allowed to use their arms. Insults and blows with fists were frequently taken and given, and cudgels also came into fashion in the brawls. Whatever awe the regiments had inspired at their first coming had long worn off. In particular the workmen of the ropewalks and shipyards allowed their tongues the largest license, and were foremost in the encounters.

About the 1st of March fights of unusual bitterness had occurred near Grey's ropewalk, not far from the quarters of the 29th, between the hands of the ropewalk and soldiers of that regiment, which had a particularly bad reputation. The soldiers had got the worst of it, and were much irritated. Threats of revenge had been made, which had called out arrogant replies, and signs abounded that serious trouble was not far off. From an early hour on the evening of the 5th of March the symptoms were very ominous. There was trouble in the neighborhood of the 14th regiment, which was stopped by a sudden order to the soldiers to go into their barracks. A crowd of townspeople remained in Dock Square, where they listened to an harangue from a certain mysterious stranger in a long cloak, who has never been identified. An alarm was rung from one of the steeples, which called out many from their houses under the impression that there was a fire. At length an altercation began in King Street between a company of lawless boys and a few older brawlers on the one side, and the sentinel, who paced his beat before the custom-house, on the other. Somewhat earlier in the evening the sentry had pushed or struck lightly with his musket a barber's apprentice, who had spoken insolently to a captain of the 14th as he passed along the street. The boy was now in the crowd, and, pointing out the sentry as his assailant, began with his companions to press upon him, upon which the soldier retreated up the steps of the custom-house, and called out for help. A file of soldiers was at once dispatched from the main guard, across the street, by Captain Preston, officer of the guard, who himself soon followed to the scene of trouble. A coating of ice covered the ground, upon which shortly before had fallen a light snow. A young moon was shining; the whole transaction, therefore, was plainly visible. The soldiers, with the sentinel, nine in number, drew up in line before the people, who greatly outnumbered them. The pieces were loaded and held ready, but the mob, believing that the troops would not use their arms except upon requisition of a civil magistrate, shouted coarse insults, pressed upon the very muzzles of the pieces, struck them with sticks, and assaulted the soldiers with balls of ice.

In the tumult precisely what was said and done cannot be known. Many affidavits were taken in the investigation that followed, and, as always at such times, the testimony was most contradictory. Henry Knox, afterwards the artillery general, at this time a bookseller, was on the spot and used his influence with Preston to prevent a command to fire. Preston declared that he never gave the command. The air, however, was full of shouts, daring the soldiers to fire, some of which may have been easily understood as commands, and at last the discharge came. If it had failed to come, indeed, the forbearance would have been quite miraculous. Three were killed outright, and eight wounded, only one of whom, Crispus Attucks, a tall mulatto who faced the soldiers, leaning on a stick of cordwood, had really taken any part in the disturbance. The rest were bystanders or were hurrying into the street, not knowing the cause of the tumult. A placid citizen, standing in his doorway on the corner of King and Congress streets, was struck by two balls in the arm, upon which, says tradition, he turned about and quietly remarked, " I declare, I do think these soldiers ought to be talked to." A wild confusion, with which this curious little spill of milk and water was in strong enough contrast, took possession of the town. The alarm-bells rang frantically; on the other hand, the drums of the regiments thundered to arms. The people flocked to King Street, where the victims lay weltering, the whiteness of the ground under the moon giving more ghastly emphasis to the crimson horror. The companies of the 29th regiment, forming rapidly, marched to the same spot, upon which, with steady discipline, they kneeled in obedience to command, prepared for street-firing. The 14th meanwhile stood ready in their barracks. " The soldiers are rising. To arms! to arms! Town-born, turn out!" were the wild cries with which the air was filled.

What averted a fearful battle in the streets was the excellent conduct of Hutchinson. He had supposed at first that the confusion was due to an alarm of fire, but was presently called out by people running from King Street, with the tidings that he must appear, or the town would soon be all in blood. Making his way to Dock Square, he could produce no impression upon the confusion. He avoided the crowd by entering a house, and by a private way at length reached the custom-house. His first act was to take Preston sharply to task.

" Are you the commanding officer ? "

" Yes, sir."

" Do you know, sir, you have no power to fire on any body of people collected together, except you have a civil magistrate with you to give orders ? "

" I was obliged to, to save the sentry."

As a catastrophe seemed imminent, the lieutenant-governor made his way as quickly as possible to the council chamber, from the balcony of which facing eastward down King Street, with the soldiers in their ranks, the angry people and the bloody snow directly beneath him, he made a cool and wise address. He expressed heartfelt regret at the occurrence, promised solemnly that justice should be done, besought the people to return to their homes, and desired the lieutenant-colonels who stood at his side to send the troops to their quarters. " The law," he declared, " should have its course. He would live and die by the law."

The officers, descending to their commands, gave orders to the troops to shoulder arms and return to their barracks. No opposition was made to the arrest of Captain Preston and the nine soldiers who had been concerned in the firing, which was presently effected. The crowd gradually fell away, leaving about a hundred to attend the investigation, which at once began under Hutchinson's eye, and continued until three o'clock in the morning. In good season the next forenoon, Hutchinson, sitting in the council chamber, with such members of the Council as could be assembled, was waited upon by the selectmen of Boston and most of the justices of the county, who told him that townspeople and troops could no longer live together, and that the latter must depart. Hutchinson alleged, as he had done before, that the troops were not under his command, and while the interview went forward the selectmen were peremptorily summoned elsewhere. To Faneuil Hall the people had flocked betimes, the number of the townsmen swelled by crowds who poured in from the country.

William Cooper, the town clerk, acted as chairman at first. When presently the selectmen appeared, and things took on a more formal shape, Thomas Cushing became moderator, and Dr. Cooper, of the church in Brattle Street, by invitation of the multitude, offered an earnest prayer. Depositions were then taken, graphic statements of facts connected with the Massacre, by various eye-witnesses, and then at length Samuel Adams addressed the meeting. What he said must be inferred from the action which the meeting immediately took. A committee of fifteen was appointed, among them Samuel Adams, although he was not at the head of it, who were instructed to wait upon Hutchinson to demand the instant removal of the troops. Measures were then taken for a town meeting in regular form at three o'clock in the afternoon, the selectmen preparing, and the constables posting the warrants. While the people dispersed, the committee proceeded to discharge their duty that they might be ready to report in the afternoon. Their spokesman announced to Hutchinson that it was the determination of Boston and all the country round that the troops should be removed. According to Hutchinson's own account, when he, with his Council and the officers of the army and navy stood face to face with the committee of fifteen, he reiterated his declaration that he had no authority to remove the troops. The committee, dissatisfied, waited after the interview in a room adjoining the council chamber.

At three o'clock the town meeting assembled in regular form at Faneuil Hall, but the multitude, swollen by the people of the surrounding towns, became so vast that they adjourned to the Old South. As Hutchinson sat deliberating with the Council and crown officers, the crowd swept past the town-house, over the snow still crimson with the Massacre. How they looked as they moved past, now in groups, now singly, now in a numerous throng, we may get through side-lights. It was a disorderly mob which the evening before had pressed upon the soldiers. But now said a member of the Council to Hutchinson, as they looked from the windows down upon the street: "This multitude are not such as pulled down your house; but they are men of the best characters, men of estates, and men of religion; men who pray over what they do." And Hutchinson himself declares, that they were "warmed with a persuasion that what they were doing was right, that they were struggling for the liberties of America," and he judged "their spirit to be as high as was the spirit of their ancestors when they imprisoned Andros, while they were four times as numerous." It must be owned that there is a tone of candor in these expressions; nevertheless, it was the view of Hutchinson that the demand of the people for the removal of the regiments ought to be resisted, and he has recorded that it was not he who yielded. Colonel Dalrymple, of the 14th regiment, the ranking officer, had indicated that as the first intention

had been to station the 29th at the Castle, though
he could receive an order from no one but Gage,
he would respect the expression of a *desire* from
the magistrates, and would, if it were thought
best, send the 29th to the Castle. The town's
committee were informed of this, Hutchinson declaring that he would receive no further communication on the subject. The Council, however, with
Dalrymple, induced him to meet them again for
further deliberation.

Issuing, as we may suppose, from the southern
door, the committee of fifteen appeared upon the
steps of the Old State House, on their way to the
Old South to make their report, Samuel Adams at
their head. The crowd had overflowed from the
church into the street, and the cry went before,
"Make way for the committee." Samuel Adams
bared his head: he was but forty-eight, but his
hair was already so gray as to give him a venerable look. He inclined to the right and left, as they
went through the lines of men, saying as he did
so: "Both regiments or none!" "Both regiments
or none!" Densely as they could be packed, the
floor and the double range of galleries in the Old
South were filled with the town meeting, the crowd
in the street pushing in on the backs of those
already in place, till stairs, aisles, and windows
were one mass of eager faces. The reply of the
lieutenant-governor was rendered in this presence,
— namely, that the commander of the two regiments received orders only from the general in

New York, but that at the desire of the civil magistrates the 29th, because of the part it had played in the disturbance, should be sent to the Castle, and also that the position of the main guard should be changed; the 14th, however, must remain in the town, but should be so far restrained as to remove all danger of further differences. But now resounded through the building the cry, "Both regiments or none!" from the floor, from the galleries, from the street outside, where men on tiptoe strove to get a view of proceedings within. "Both regiments or none!" and it became plain what the leader had meant, as he spoke to the right and to the left a moment before, while the committee had proceeded from the council chamber to the town meeting. The watchword had been caught up as it was suggested; and now with small delay a new committee, this time consisting of seven, upon which the town took more care than ever to put the best men, was sent back to the governor.

Of the committee, Hancock, Henshaw, and Pemberton had wealth, ability, and worth, and were moreover selectmen; Phillips was a merchant, generous and respected; Molineux, too, was a merchant, a man of much executive force, but more valued perhaps in action than in counsel; while Joseph Warren, the physician, impetuously eloquent, had for some years been pushing always higher. On the list of the committee, while Hancock is first, Samuel Adams comes second. Probably the rich, luxurious chairman did not forget, even on an occasion like this, to set off his fine figure with gay velvet and lace, and a gold-headed cane. About four o'clock that afternoon, the 6th of March, the new committee entered the council chamber ; and now as the power of the people and the power of the government, like two great hulls in a sea-fight, are about to crash together, in the moment of collision, on the side of the province the gilded figurehead is taken in and " a wedge of steel " [1] is thrust forth in front to bear the brunt of the impact. Hancock disappears from the fore, and Samuel Adams stands out to take the shock! Day was already waning, and we may fancy the council chamber lighting up with a ruddy glow from the open fireplaces.   John Adams long after suggested the scene that took place as a fit subject for a historical painting.

"Now for the picture. The theatre and the scenery are the same with those at the discussion of the writs of assistance. The same glorious portraits of King Charles the Second, and King James the Second, to which might be added, and should be added, little miserable likenesses of Governor Winthrop, Governor Bradstreet, Governor Endicott, and Governor Belcher, hung up in obscure corners of the room. Lieutenant-Governor Hutchinson, commander-in-chief in the absence of the

[1] John Adams, who found the legitimate resources of rhetoric quite inadequate for the expression of his admiration for his kinsman, says Sam Adams was " born and tempered a wedge of steel to split the knot of *lignum vitæ* that tied America to England."

governor, must be placed at the head of the council-
table.   Lieutenant-Colonel Dalrymple, commander-in-
chief of his majesty's military forces, taking rank of
all his majesty's councillors, must be seated by the side
of the lieutenant-governor and commander-in-chief of
the Province.   Eight-and-twenty councillors must be
painted, all seated at the council-board.   Let me see, —
what costume?   What was the fashion of that day in
the month of March ?   Large white wigs, English scar-
let-cloth coats, some of them with gold-laced hats ; not
on their heads indeed in so august a presence, but on
the table before them or under the table beneath them.
Before these illustrious personages appeared SAMUEL
ADAMS, a member of the House of Representatives and
their clerk, now at the head of the committee of the
great assembly at the Old South Church."

Adams spoke in his straightforward, earnest
way, asserting the illegality of quartering troops
on the town in time of peace without the consent
of the legislature; he described the trouble that
must come if the troops remained, and urged the
necessity of compliance with the demand of the
town.   Gordon says that the peculiar nervous
trembling, of which he was the subject, communicated itself as he spoke to Colonel Dalrymple.
Hutchinson showed no irresolution.   He briefly
defended both the legality and the necessity of the
presence of the troops, and declared once more
that they were not subject to his authority.   Samuel Adams once more stood forth: —

"It is well known," he said, "that acting as governor of the province, you are by its charter the commander-in-chief of the military forces within it; and as such, the troops now in the capital are subject to your orders. If you, or Colonel Dalrymple under you, have the power to remove one regiment, you have the power to remove both; and nothing short of their total removal will satisfy the people or preserve the peace of the province. A multitude highly incensed now wait the result of this application. The voice of ten thousand freemen demands that both regiments be forthwith removed. Their voice must be respected, their demand obeyed. Fail not then at your peril to comply with this requisition! On you alone rests the responsibility of this decision; and if the just expectations of the people are disappointed, you must be answerable to God and your country for the fatal consequences that must ensue. The committee have discharged their duty, and it is for you to discharge yours. They wait your final determination."

A long discussion now took place, in which Hutchinson appears to have stood alone in his wish to continue to oppose the town. His belief, he says, was that, if officers and Council had supported him in the beginning in the firm assertion that the troops could not be removed without the orders of Gage, the people could have been put off. The Council, however, yielded; the colonels, too, gave way, Dalrymple at last signifying his readiness to remove the 14th as well as the 29th.

The position of affairs remained no secret. The people were promptly informed that the governor stood alone. At length Andrew Oliver, the secretary, upon whom Hutchinson much relied, who had at first advised resistance, declared that it could go no farther, that the governor must give way or instantly leave the province. At last, therefore, the formal recommendation came from him to Dalrymple to remove the troops. The soldier's word of honor was given that it should be done at once, and at dark the committee carried back to the meeting the news of success, upon which, so say the records, "the inhabitants could not but express the high satisfaction which it afforded them."

A week was required for the transportation of the troops and their baggage, during which the town, dissatisfied with what appeared like unnecessary delay, remonstrated through the same committee of seven. A night-watch during this time continued in organization, under the same committee. Says John Adams:—

"Military watches and guards were everywhere placed. We were all upon a level; no man was exempted; our military officers were our superiors. I had the honor to be summoned in my turn, and attended at the State House with my musket and bayonet, my broadsword and cartridge-box, under the command of the famous Paddock."

During this week occurred the funeral of the victims of the Massacre, which took place under circumstances of the greatest solemnity. Four hearses, for one of the wounded had meantime died, containing the bodies, and coming from different directions, met upon the spot in King Street in which the victims had fallen. The assemblage was such as had never before been known; the bells of Boston and the whole neighborhood tolled, and a great procession, marching in ranks of six abreast, followed to the Granary Burying Ground, where the bodies were laid in a common grave near the northeast corner. There they rest to this day. In England the affair was regarded as a "successful bully" of the whole power of the government by the little town, and when Lord North received details of these events he always afterward referred to the 14th and 29th as the "Sam Adams regiments."

From that day to this, both in England and America, it has been held that there was a great exhibition of weakness, if not actual poltroonery, on the part of the civil and military officers of the government in this conflict with the town of Boston. The idea is quite wrong. Hutchinson, so far from showing any weakness, was resolute even to rashness. Loving his country truly, honestly believing that Parliament must be supreme over the provincial legislature, and that the people would acquiesce in supremacy if only a few headstrong leaders could be set aside, he was in a position as chief magistrate which he had not sought. Now that he was in it, however, he pursued the course which seemed to him proper, saddened

though he must have been by the unpopularity,
fast deepening into hatred, of which he had become the subject.   To uphold the government
cause, the presence of the troops was, in his view,
indispensable. The taxes imposed by Parliament
there could be no hope of collecting in the misled
province except with the support of bayonets.
Upon what could his own authority rest, with
Council and Assembly in vast proportion hostile,
if the troops were removed? He had avoided occasions of conflict, as he had reason to feel, with
much forbearance. The Massacre of the 5th of
March he deeply regretted; he was determined to
have justice done. But when the peremptory demand came from the town for the removal of the
regiments, then he felt it right to remain passive;
he thought he had no power in the matter. There
is no reason to doubt his own representation, made
in private letters,[1] in his history,[2] in his private
diary [3] now just come to light, that he would not
have yielded but for the course pursued by those
about him, whose support he could not do without. Possibly he was right in thinking that a
firm front shown from the first by the crown officers would have won over the people in spite of
the machinations of the "faction."   All men about
the governor, however, were at last for yielding,
and the people knew it, and were encouraged by
it in their own course.   In the "Diary," where he

[1] To Bernard, March 18, 1770.   [2] *Hist.* iii. 275.
[3] *Diary*, 79, 80.

expresses himself with more freedom than elsewhere, Hutchinson charges Dalrymple with being
especially responsible for the result: —

"Colonel Dalrymple offered to remove one regiment,
to which the soldiers on guard belonged. This was
giving up the point. . . . The regiments were removed.
He was much distressed, but he brought it all upon himself by his offer to remove one of the regiments."

Nor is it necessary to regard Dalrymple as a
coward. His character as a brave and prudent
soldier is certified to in the strongest terms by the
famous Admiral Hood, shortly before the commodore on the Boston station. The regiments together numbered scarcely six hundred effective
men. Boston was evidently sustained by the country. What could six hundred men do against a
populous province? It was, no doubt, a stretch
of authority to order the troops away, but a prudent soldier may well have felt that the circumstances justified it. He took the responsibility,
and although the mortification which the act caused
in England was so great, it is to be noticed that he
never received any censure for it.

But while we try to do justice to men who have
received contemptuous treatment for a hundred
years, we must not lose sight of their mistake.
Hutchinson's conduct was manful and consistent
with his views. He ought, however, to have had
better views. Out of the best strain of New England as he was, sprung from liberty-loving sires

and trained in the folk-mote, what business had he
to stand there for arbitrary power against government of the people, by and for the people? It
was a position in which such a man should never
have been found. And now let us look at the great
contrasting figure. In the scenes we have been
contemplating, the two men stand over against
each other in a definite opposition and prominence which we have not before seen. It has been
regarded as the most dramatic point of Samuel
Adams's career. One may well dwell with admiration on the incidents of his conduct. Where
his adversary failed, he was strong. Of like origin and training with him, in Samuel Adams's case
the fruit had been legitimate. He believed with
all his heart in the people, that they should be
governed only by themselves or their representatives, and was perfectly fearless and uncompromising against all power, whether king, Parliament, or soldiery, which contravened the great
right. While he moves in obedience to the principle he recognizes, how effective at this time is his
work! As is so often the case, he is, for the most
part, somewhat withdrawn, — not the moderator
of the town meeting, nor indeed chairman of the
famous committees, — but nevertheless the controlling mind. His speech at Faneuil Hall in
the forenoon of the 6th of March without doubt
outlined the whole policy that must be pursued.
When, as the first committee passed from the
south door of the State House to the Old South,

he kept repeating to right and left, "Both regiments or none," he guided the whole action of the people as the crisis approached. When, an hour or two later, Hancock stepped aside and Samuel Adams walked forward in the council chamber into the spokesman's place, probably he was the one man of the province who could then have brought the British lion to confusion. He himself seems to have felt that it was the great moment in his life. For almost the only time in his whole career, we find something like a strain of personal exultation in his reference to this scene. Writing of Hutchinson's bearing in it to James Warren of Plymouth, in the following year, he says : —

"It was then, if fancy deceived me not, I observed his knees to tremble. I thought I saw his face grow pale (and I enjoyed the sight) at the appearance of the determined citizens peremptorily demanding the redress of grievances."

The contemporary historian, as we have seen, says that Dalrymple, too, trembled. We need not feel, however, that either soldier or civilian played then the part of the craven. The circumstances were for them full of danger and difficulty. The determination of ten thousand freemen was focused in the steel-blue eyes of Samuel Adams as he stood in the council chamber; the tramp of their feet and the tumult of their voices made a heavy groundtone behind his earnest, decisive words. It was a time when even a brave man might for a moment blench.

By rare good-fortune, the world possesses what is probably the best representation that could at that time have been made of Samuel Adams as, on that March day, he drove the British uniform out of the streets of Boston. John Hancock, two years later, employed the famous John Singleton Copley to paint portraits of himself and Samuel Adams, which hung for fifty years on the walls of the Hancock House in Beacon Street, which were then removed to Faneuil Hall, and are now in the Art Museum. Copley was at first well disposed to the popular cause. At the time of the Massacre he testified against the soldiers, and seems to have admired the bearing of Samuel Adams throughout the disturbances. At any rate, for this portrait, he has chosen to give Samuel Adams as he stood in the scene with Hutchinson in the council chamber. Against a background suggestive of gloom and disturbance, the figure looks forth. The face and form are marked by great strength. The brow is high and broad, and from it sweeps back the abundant hair, streaked with gray. The blue eyes are full of light and force, the nose is prominent, the lips and chin, brought strongly out as the head is thrown somewhat back, are full of determination. In the right hand a scroll is held firmly grasped, the energy of the moment appearing in the cording of the sinews as the sheets bend in the pressure. The left hand is thrown forth in impassioned gesture, the forefinger pointing to the provincial charter, which, with the great seal

affixed, lies half unrolled in the foreground. The
plain dark red attire announces a decent and simple respectability. The well-knit figure looks as
fixed as if its strength came from the granite on
which the Adamses planted themselves when they
came to America; the countenance speaks in every
line the man.

The BLOODY MASSACRE perpetrated in King — Street BOSTON on March 5th 1770 by a party of the 29th REGt.

Unhappy BOSTON! see thy Sons deplore,
Thy hallow'd Walks besmear'd with guiltless Gore:
While faithless P—n and his savage Bands,
With murd'rous Rancour stretch their bloody Hands;
Like fierce Barbarians grinning o'er their Prey,
Approve the Carnage and enjoy the Day.

If scalding drops from Rage from Anguish Wrung
If speechless Sorrows lab'ring for a Tongue,
Or if a weeping World can ought appease
The plaintive Ghosts of Victims such as these;
The Patriot's copious Tears for each are shed,
A glorious Tribute which embalms the Dead

But know, FATE summons to that awful Goal,
Where JUSTICE strips the Murd'rer of his Soul:
Should venal C—ts the scandal of the Land,
Snatch the relentless Villain from her Hand,
Keen Execrations on this Plate inscrib'd,
Shall reach a JUDGE who never can be brib'd.

Engrav'd Printed & Sold by PAUL REVERE BOSTON.

The unhappy Sufferers were Messrs. Saml. Gray, Saml. Maverick, Jams. Caldwell, Crispus Attucks & Patk. Carr
Killed. Six wounded; two of them (Christr. Monk & John Clark) Mortally

James Bowdoin

CHAPTER XII

In the fall of the year Captain Preston and the soldiers were brought to trial. However the rude part of the people may have thirsted for their blood, it was not the temper of the better-minded. By an arrangement in which Samuel Adams had a share, John Adams and Josiah Quincy, eminent patriots and lawyers, appeared as counsel for the prisoners, while Robert Treat Paine, also eminent, undertook the prosecution. Everything was done to secure for the prisoners a fair trial. The town attempted to suppress the publication of the official account of the Massacre until proceedings were over, that the minds of the jurors might be quite unprejudiced. Preston was entirely acquitted; most of the soldiers, too, were brought in "Not guilty." Two were found guilty of manslaughter, but let off with no more severe punishment than being branded in the hand in open court. John Adams, fully persuaded of the innocence of the accused, and Quincy, exerted themselves to the utmost for their clients, and every extenuating circumstance was allowed its full weight. Samuel Adams, it must be confessed, appears not always

to advantage at this time. He was little satisfied
with the postponement of the trial, and quite displeased with the issue. With William Cooper,
Warren, and a concourse of people, if we may
trust Hutchinson, he appeared before the Superior
Court after the judges had decided not to proceed
at once, and sought to induce them to alter their
decision. The trial he followed carefully, constantly taking notes. At its conclusion, over the
signature "Vindex," he examined the evidence at
length, pronounced much of that given for the soldiers false, and battled fiercely with the royalist
writers who ventured into the lists against him.

The conduct of the town of Boston was really
very fine. The moderation which put off the arraignment of the accused men until the passions
of the hour had subsided, the appearance of John
Adams and Josiah Quincy, warm patriots, in the
defense, the acquittal at last of all but two, and
the light sentence inflicted upon these, — all together constituted a grand triumph of the spirit of
law and order, at a time when heated feeling might
have been expected to carry the day. If Samuel
Adams's counsels had prevailed, it cannot be denied that the outcome would have been less creditable. The course of things would have been
hurried, the punishment have been more severe.
Yet with all their undue vehemence, his utterances
possess sometimes a noble grandeur. As "Vindex " he declares : [1] —

[1] January 21, 1771.

"Philanthrop may tell us of the hazard of 'disturbing and inflaming the minds of the multitude whose passions know no bounds.' The multitude I am speaking of is the body of the people, no contemptible multitude, for whose sake government is instituted, or rather who have themselves erected it, solely for their own good, — to whom even kings and all in subordination to them, are, strictly speaking, servants, not masters."

On the very day of the Boston Massacre, Parliament debated the repeal of the taxes imposed by Townshend upon glass, paper, and paints, voting at last, as has been said, to retain only the duty upon tea. Since the right of taxation without representation was thus adhered to, the concession amounted to nothing, and the breach between motherland and colonies remained as wide as ever.

When at length the General Court convened, in March, a most tedious dispute arose at once. Says Hutchinson : —

"There came a signification of the king's pleasure that the General Court should be held in Cambridge, unless the lieutenant-governor should have more weighty reasons for holding it at Boston than those which were mentioned by the secretary of state against it."

Bernard, as we know, had already convened the court at Cambridge, in violation, as was claimed, of the charter, causing no small inconvenience to the members and also to Harvard College, the "Philosophy Room" in which was given up to the sessions. The main point, however, upon which

the Whigs stood was the insufficiency of the plea
of royal " instructions " for violating a provision
of the charter. The quarrel continued until 1772,
when Hutchinson felt forced to yield the point,
although shortly before he had been on the brink
of success. Both Otis and Hancock came out at
one time on the government side, and Cushing,
too, was weak-kneed. Hutchinson might well have
felt that he was made even with his adversary for
his discomfiture at the time of the Massacre, when
one day he was waited upon by a legislative committee with Sam Adams among them, bearing a
message to the effect that they recognized his
power under royal instruction to remove the legislature " to Housatonic, in the extreme west of the
province, if he chose." For the patriot cause all
seemed imperiled, and Hutchinson wrote cheer-
fully, looking forward to the most substantial cleav-
ing of difficulties from the success of this entering
wedge. He was foiled, however; Bowdoin and
Hawley stood steadfastly by Samuel Adams, while
Otis, speedily falling once more under the power
of his disease, was carried off bound hand and foot.
Hancock came round again to his old friends. The
tail of the British lion remained in the grasp of
these remorseless twisters.

While the debate was in progress Hutchinson
received his commission as governor, not without
many tokens of favor in spite of the lowering
brows of the patriots. His brother-in-law, Andrew
Oliver, became at the same time lieutenant-gov-

ernor, and Thomas Flucker secretary. Among the felicitations Harvard College paid a tribute, while the students made the walls of Holden Chapel ring with the anthem : —

"Thus saith the Lord : from henceforth, behold, all nations shall call thee blessed ; for thy rulers shall be of thy own kindred, your nobles shall be of yourselves, and thy governor shall proceed from the midst of thee."

Shortly before, in 1770, died Dennys Deberdt, who had served the Assembly long and faithfully in England as agent; and in his place, not without considerable resistance, Franklin was elected. This famous Boston boy, who as a youth had gone to Pennsylvania, and after a remarkable career had at length proceeded to England, was already the agent of Pennsylvania. No American as yet had gained so wide a fame on both sides of the Atlantic. His discoveries in natural philosophy gave him high rank among men of science, and his abilities in politics had also become generally recognized. In Massachusetts, nevertheless, a considerable party distrusted him, among whom stood Samuel Adams; and it is easy to understand why. Franklin's wide acquaintance with the world, joined to a disposition naturally free, had lifted him to a degree that might well seem alarming above the limitations recognized as proper by all true New Englanders. The boy who, according to the well-known story, had advised his father to say grace once for all over the whole barrel of beef in the cellar, and so avoid the necessity of a blessing at table over each separate piece, was indeed the father of the man. Plenty of stories were rife respecting Franklin, that touched the Puritan corns as much as would this. At the present time, indeed, it is not merely the over-fastidious who take exception to certain passages in Franklin's life. To stern Samuel Adams and his sympathizers, no man upon whom rested a suspicion of free thinking or free living could be congenial.

There were still other reasons which had probably more weight than that just mentioned in bringing it about that just at this time Franklin should be opposed in Massachusetts. In some respects, to be sure, his political declarations were exceedingly bold; witness his famous "examination" in 1765. With all this, however, Franklin was strenuously opposed to any revolution. The British empire he compared to a magnificent china bowl, ruined if a piece were broken out of it, and he earnestly recommended that it should be kept together. With grand foresight he anticipated the speedy peopling of the Mississippi valley, though at that time few Europeans had crossed the Alleghanies; and he thought the time was not far off when this portion of the English dominions would preponderate, when even the seat of government might be transferred hither, and America become principal, while England should become subordinate. For the views of Samuel Adams,

Franklin, probably, had as little liking as Adams had for those of Franklin. As late as the summer of 1773 Franklin wrote to Boston, deprecating the influence of the violent spirits who were for a rupture with the mother country. " This Protestant country (our mother, though of late an unkind one) is worth preserving; her weight in the scale of Europe, and her safety in a great degree, may depend on our union with her." To his well-known desire to remain united to England was added the fact that Franklin, as deputy postmaster-general, held an important crown office, while his natural son, William Franklin, was royal governor of New Jersey, and a pronounced Tory.

Samuel Adams acquiesced in the appointment of Franklin, though his party succeeded in associating with him the Virginian, Arthur Lee; and at the fall session of 1770, by the bidding of the House, Samuel Adams had sent the new agent a long letter of instructions, in which the grievances were recapitulated for which Franklin was to seek redress. These include the quartering of troops on the people in time of peace; the policy of arbitrary instructions from his majesty's secretaries of state in violation of the charter; the removal of the legislature from Boston; the secrecy as to intended measures of government, with the concealment from the colonies of the names of their accusers and of the allegations against them; the sending to England of false reports of speeches and legislative proceedings under the province seal; the enormous extension of the jurisdiction of the Admiralty Courts, in violation of the clause of Magna Charta by which every freeman on trial was entitled to the "judgment of his peers on the law of the land;" and finally the threatened bestowal by the king of salaries upon the attorney-general, judges, and governor of the province, thus removing their dependence upon the people. All these subjects are treated in detail. The letter was not only sent to Franklin, but was published in full in the "Boston Gazette." Hutchinson sent a copy to England, denouncing Samuel Adams by name as the author, and calling him the "all in all," the "great incendiary leader."

In August, 1771, a strong fleet of twelve sail, under Admiral Montague, brother of the Earl of Sandwich, a commander who among the old sea-dogs of England seems to have been marked by characteristics especially canine, cast anchor before the town. The pretext was the impending war with Spain, but all knew it was intended to check the spread of sedition. It is hard to see in these years how the Whig cause could have been prevented from going by the board but for Samuel Adams. Now in the newspapers, now in the Boston town meeting, now at the head of his party in the House, at the first symptom of danger he was on the alert with resolute remonstrance, the more vigorous as those about him grew weary and reactionary. Fighting steadily the removal of the legislature, he was once more up in arms when

Hutchinson, in obedience again to "instructions," was about to surrender the command of the Castle to Dalrymple, though the charter required that the commander should be an officer of the province. Again, at the hint that the governors and the law officers were to receive salaries from the king and be no longer dependent on the province, there was the fiercest "oppugnation." This point, indeed, became at once the subject of a quarrel of the sharpest, just as the long dispute was closing respecting the removal of the legislature.

Almost the first business to which the House turned in May, 1772, was the question of the governor receiving a salary from the king. Hutchinson now avowed that his support in future was to proceed from the king, and declined to accept compensation from the province. Vigorous resolutions were passed declaring this to be a violation of the charter, "exposing the province to a despotic administration of government." Hawley was chairman of the committee reporting the resolutions, but Samuel Adams was concerned in their composition. When they passed by a vote of eighty-five to nineteen, several of the loyalists withdrew discouraged. The legislature, made sullen, refused to repair the Province House, and Hutchinson, after an energetic reply to Hawley's resolutions, prorogued the court until September. During the summer Lord Hillsborough retired from his secretaryship, making it known to the lords of trade on the eve of that event that the king, "with the entire concurrence of Lord North, had made provision for the support of his law servants in the Province of Massachusetts Bay." In September this news became known in Boston, and that warrants had been ordered on the commissioners of customs for the payments. The rising tone in the writings of Samuel Adams is very apparent. As "Vindex" he had declared in the "Boston Gazette," when only rumors were rife, —

"I think the alteration of our free and mutually dependent constitution into a dependent ministerial despotism, a grievance so great, so ignominious and intolerable, that in case I did not hope things would in some measure regain their ancient situation without more bloodshed and murder than has been already committed, I could freely wish at the risk of my all, to have a fair chance of offering to the manes of my slaughtered countrymen a libation of the blood of the ruthless traitors who conspired their destruction."

As "Valerius Poplicola," October 5, 1772, he is even more earnest.

"Is it not enough," he cried, " to have a Governor an avowed advocate for ministerial measures, and a most assiduous instrument in carrying them on, model'd, shaped, controul'd, and directed, totally independent of the people over whom he is commissioned to govern, and yet absolutely dependent upon the Crown, pension'd by those on whom his existence depends, and paid out of a revenue establish'd by those who have no authority to establish it, and extorted from the people in a Manner most odious, insulting, and oppressive? Is not this indignity enough to be felt by those who have any feeling? Are we still threatened with more? Is Life, Property, and everything dear and sacred to be now submitted to the Decisions of PENSIONED judges, holding their places during the pleasure of *such* a Governor, and a Council *perhaps* overawed? To what a state of Infamy, Wretchedness, and Misery shall we be reduced, if our Judges shall be prevail'd upon to be thus degraded to HIRELINGS, and the BODY of the people shall suffer their free Constitution to be overturned and ruin'd. *Merciful God! inspire thy people with wisdom and fortitude, and direct them to gracious ends. In this extreme distress, when the plan of slavery seems nearly compleated, O save our country from impending ruin. Let not the iron hand of tyranny ravish our laws and seize the badge of freedom, nor avow'd Corruption and the murderous Rage of lawless Power be ever seen on the sacred Seat of Justice!*

" Let us converse together upon this most interesting Subject, and open our minds freely to each other. Let it be the topic of conversation in every social club. Let every Town assemble. Let Associations and Combinations be everywhere set up to consult and recover our just Rights.

> ' The country claims *our* active *aid*.
> That let us roam ; & where we find a spark
> Of public Virtue, blow it into Flame.' "

CHAPTER XIII

"LET associations and combinations be every-where set up to consult and recover our just rights." This suggestion, contained at the end of the paper quoted at the close of the last chapter, Samuel Adams proceeded to put at once in prac-tice, setting on foot one of the most memorable schemes with which his name is associated. As his career has been traced, we have seen that, in the instructions of 1764 and frequently since, his recognition of the importance of a thorough under-standing between the widely separated patriots has appeared. A letter of the previous year to Arthur Lee contains the definite suggestion of a Commit-tee of Correspondence, "a sudden thought which drops undigested from my pen," which should not only promote union among the Americans, but also with men similarly minded in England, like the society of the Bill of Rights. The task before Samuel Adams was a hard one. Not only must he thwart the Tories, but he found the patriots for the most part quite indifferent; he may be said, indeed, to have worked out the scheme alone. Cushing, Hancock, and Phillips, his associates of the Boston seat, were against his idea, as were also the more influential among the selectmen. Warren indeed was a strenuous helper, but had not yet risen into great significance. Church appeared zealous, but he was secretly a traitor. Three petitions were presented to the selectmen, and three weeks passed before the meeting could be brought about. In the last petition the number of names was much diminished, indicating the difficulty which Samuel Adams found in holding the people to the work. He used what influence he could outside of Boston to prepare the way for his idea in other towns. Writing to Elbridge Gerry, a young man of twenty-eight, with whom he was just coming into a connection that grew into a close and unbroken lifelong friendship, who had encouraged him with an account of interest felt at Marblehead, he says : —

"Our enemies would intimidate us by saying our brethren in the other towns are indifferent about this matter, for which reason I am particularly glad to receive your letter at this time. Roxbury I am told is fully awake. I wish we could arouse the continent."

A town meeting took place, which was adjourned and again adjourned, in the general lethargy ; so slight was the interest with which the successive steps in a movement of the first importance were regarded! Hutchinson, in answer to a resolution of inquiry and a request that the legislature, which was to meet December 2, might not be prorogued, replied, —

" That the charter reserved to the governor the full
power, from time to time, to adjourn, prorogue, or dis-
solve the Assembly. A compliance with the petition
would be to yield to them the exercise of that part of
the prerogative.   There would be danger of encouraging the inhabitants of other towns in the province to
similar procedures, which the law had not made the
business of town meetings."

The town meeting caused the governor's words
to be read again and again before it, and voted
them to be " not satisfactory." The proceeding
illustrates well the astuteness and knowledge of
men of Samuel Adams, who was certainly as consummate a political manager as the country has
ever seen. He drafted for the town the resolution
and request to the governor, which have just been
referred to, and which apparently relate to something very different from his real purposes ; he was
chairman of the committee which presented these
documents. The whole thing was a trap. He wrote
afterwards to Gerry that he knew such requests,
couched in such terms, must provoke from Hutchinson an arrogant answer, the effect of which
would be to touch the people in a point where
they were sensitive, and produce unanimity for
the course which he desired to pursue. As he had
expected and planned, the town meeting resolved
unanimously that " they have ever had, and ought
to have, a right to petition the king or his representative for a redress of such grievances as they
feel, or for preventing such as they have reason to

apprehend, and to communicate their sentiments to other towns."

The town meeting having been brought into an appropriate mood, there followed the motion which in its consequences was perhaps the most important step which had so far been taken in bringing into existence the new nation. The town records of Boston say : —

"It was then moved by Mr. Samuel Adams that a Committee of Correspondence be appointed, to consist of twenty-one persons, to state the rights of the colonists and of this province in particular as men and Christians and as subjects ; and to communicate and publish the same to the several towns and to the world as the sense of this town, with the infringements and violations thereof that have been or from time to time may be made."

The motion occasioned some debate, and seems to have been carried late at night ; the vote in its favor, at last, was nearly unanimous. The colleagues of Adams, who had left him almost alone thus far, now declined to become members of the committee, regarding the scheme as useless or trifling. The committee was at last constituted without them ; it was made up of men of little prominence but of thorough respectability. James Otis, in another interval of sanity, was made chairman, a position purely honorary, the town in this way showing its respect for the leader whose misfortunes they so sincerely mourned.

The Committee of Correspondence held its first meeting in the representatives' chamber at the

town-house, November 3, 1772, where at the outset
each member pledged himself to observe secrecy
as to their transactions, except those which, as a
committee, they should think it proper to divulge.
According to the motion by which the committee
was constituted, three duties were to be performed:
1st, the preparation of a statement of the rights
of the colonists, as men, as Christians, and as subjects; 2d, a declaration of the infringement and
violation of those rights; 3d, a letter, to be sent to
the several towns of the province and to the world,
giving the sense of the town. The drafting of
the first was assigned to Samuel Adams, of the
second to Joseph Warren, of the third to Benjamin Church. In a few days tidings came from
the important towns of Marblehead, Roxbury, Cambridge, and Plymouth, indicating that the example
of Boston was making impression and was likely
to be followed. On November 20, at a town meeting in Faneuil Hall, the different papers were presented: Otis sat as moderator, appearing for the
last time in a sphere where his career had been
so magnificent. The report was in three divisions,
according to the motion. The part by Samuel
Adams, which has absurdly been attributed to
Otis by later writers, is still extant in his autograph. The paper of Warren recapitulated the
long list of grievances under which the province
had suffered; while Church, in a letter to the
selectmen of the various towns, solicited a free
communication of the sentiments of all, expressing

the belief that the wisdom of the people would not "suffer them to doze or sit supinely indifferent on the brink of destruction."

In the last days of 1772, the document, having been printed, was transmitted to those for whom it had been intended, producing at once an immense effect. The towns almost unanimously appointed similar committees; from every quarter came replies in which the sentiments of Samuel Adams were echoed. In the library of Bancroft is a volume of manuscripts,[1] worn and stained by time, which have an interest scarcely inferior to that possessed by the Declaration of Independence itself, as the fading page hangs against its pillar in the library of the State Department at Washington. They are the original replies sent by the Massachusetts towns to Samuel Adams's committee, sitting in Faneuil Hall, during those first months of 1773. One may well read them with bated breath, for it is the touch of the elbow as the stout little democracies dress up into line, just before they plunge into actual fight at Concord and Bunker Hill. There is sometimes a noble scorn of the restraints of orthography, as of the despotism of Great Britain, in the work of the old town clerks, for they generally were secretaries of the committees; and once in a while a touch of Dogberry's quaintness, as the punctilious officials, though not always "putting God first," yet take pains that there shall be no mistake as to their

[1] Now in the Lenox Library, New York.

piety by making every letter in the name of the
Deity a rounded capital. Yet the documents
ought to inspire the deepest reverence. They constitute the highest mark the town meeting has
ever touched. Never before and never since have
Anglo-Saxon men, in lawful folk-mote assembled,
given utterance to thoughts and feelings so fine in
themselves and so pregnant with great events. To
each letter stand affixed the names of the committee in autograph. This awkward scrawl was made
by the rough fist of a Cape Ann fisherman, on
shore for the day to do at town meeting the duty
his fellows had laid upon him; the hand that
wrote this other was cramped from the scythe-
handle, as its possessor mowed an intervale on the
Connecticut; this blotted signature, where smutted
fingers have left a black stain, was written by a
blacksmith of Middlesex, turning aside a moment
from forging a barrel that was to do duty at Lexington. They were men of the plainest; but as
the documents, containing statements of the most
generous principles and the most courageous determination, were read in the town-houses, the
committees who produced them, and the constituents for whom the committees stood, were lifted
above the ordinary level. Their horizon expanded
to the broadest; they had in view not simply themselves, but the welfare of the continent; not solely
their own generation, but remote posterity. It
was Samuel Adams's own plan, the consequences
of which no one foresaw, neither friend nor foe.

Even Hutchinson, who was scarcely less keen than Samuel Adams himself, was completely at fault. " Such a foolish scheme," he called it, " that the faction must necessarily make themselves ridiculous." But in January the eyes of men were opening. One of the ablest of the Tories, Daniel Leonard, wrote : —

" This is the foulest, subtlest, and most venomous serpent ever issued from the egg of sedition. I saw the small seed when it was implanted ; it was a grain of mustard. I have watched the plant until it has become a great tree."

It was the transformation into a strong cord of what had been a rope of sand.

Though Samuel Adams could be terribly in earnest, as sufficiently appears from the extracts which have been made, there is never an excess of zeal and rage, such as shows itself sometimes in his more youthful and hot-headed disciples, Warren and Quincy. During the occupation of Boston by the troops, Warren was known to be ready with knock-down arguments, upon occasion, for red-coats that were too forthputting, and once exclaimed to William Eustis, afterwards governor of Massachusetts : " These fellows say we won't fight ; by heavens, I hope I shall die up to my knees in blood !" During the agitation before the formation of the Committee of Correspondence, Josiah Quincy wrote : —

" The word of God has pointed the mode of relief

from Moabitish oppression: prayers and tears with the help of a dagger. The Lord of light has given us the fit message to send to a tyrant: a dagger of a cubit in his belly; and every worthy man who desires to be an Ehud, the deliverer of his country, will strive to be the messenger."

Such outbreaks of vindictive frenzy never appeared in the speech or conduct of Samuel Adams, though as a dire necessity from which there could be no shrinking without sacrifice of principle, an appeal to the sword at some time not far distant began to seem to him inevitable.

How high the name of Samuel Adams stood elsewhere than in Massachusetts was shown early in 1773 in the matter of the burning of the British man-of-war Gaspee, in Narragansett Bay. The zealous officer who commanded her had brought upon himself the ill-will of the people by the faithfulness with which he carried out his instructions in executing the obnoxious revenue laws. His vessel running ashore, a party from Providence attacked her in boats, and after a fight, in which the commander was wounded, the Gaspee was burned. The wrath of the Tories and of the officers of the British army and navy was great. A board of commissioners appointed by the crown convened at Providence, who, it was believed, would send the culprits to England for punishment, and perhaps take away the charter of Rhode Island. Through the general connivance of the people, the British admiral and the governor could not find the actors in the affair, although they were well known. Matters wore a dark look. In their distress, the leading men of the colony, looking about for an adviser, made respectful application to Samuel Adams: "Give us your opinion in what manner this colony had best behave in this critical situation, and how the shock that is coming upon us may be best evaded or sustained." Samuel Adams, while giving advice in detail, makes a suggestion which plainly shows what thought now especially occupies him: —

"I beg to propose for your consideration whether a circular letter from your Assembly on the occasion, to those of the other colonies, might not tend to the advantage of the general cause and of Rhode Island in particular."

CHAPTER XIV

THE CONTROVERSY AS TO PARLIAMENTARY AUTHORITY

In the long struggle between the patriots and the government the student becomes bewildered, so numerous are the special discussions, and so involved with one another. Hutchinson and Samuel Adams stand respectively at the heads of the opposed powers, each dexterous, untiring, fearless; and, as the spectator of a mortal combat with swords between a pair of nimble, energetic strivers might easily become confused in the breathless interchange of thrust and parry, so in trying to follow this unremitting ten years' fight there is absolutely no place where one can rest. The attention must be fixed throughout, or some essential phase of the battle is lost.

However deceived Hutchinson may have been for an instant as to the effect of his great rival's stroke in the establishment of the Committee of Correspondence, his eyes were in a moment opened, and with his usual quickness he was ready at once with his guard. He convened the legislature January 6, 1773, and whereas he had always heretofore avoided a formal discussion of the great question at issue, preferring to assume the authority of Parliament over the colonies as a matter of course, he now sent to the legislature a powerful message in which the doctrine of parliamentary supremacy was elaborately vindicated. The reception of such a paper was to the legislature a matter of the gravest moment. Hutchinson was unsurpassed in acuteness ; no one knew so thoroughly as he the history of the colonies from the beginning; his legal reading had been so wide that few could match him in the citation of precedents. At his command, too, were all the skill and learning of the Tory party, which included strong men, like Daniel Leonard, the newspaper writer, and Jonathan Sewall, the attorney-general. Reviewing the past usages of Massachusetts, the governor undertook to show that the course of things favored the idea of the supremacy of Parliament, which had never been denied until the time of the Stamp Act. The grant of liberties and immunities in the charter could not be understood as relieving the province from obligations toward the supreme legislature, but was only an assurance on the part of the crown to the Americans that they had not become aliens, but remained free-born subjects everywhere in the dominions of Britain. By their voluntary removal from England to America, they relinquished a right which they could assume whenever they chose to return to England, — the right, namely, of voting for the persons who made the laws. The fact that they had voluntarily relinquished this right by removing could by no means be understood as destroying the authority of the law-makers over them. No line, he alleged, could be drawn between an acknowledgment of the supremacy of Parliament and independence; and the governor asked if there was anything they had greater reason to dread than independence, exposed as they would then be in their weakness to the attacks of any power which might choose to destroy them. Hutchinson supported and illustrated his positions by references to history and constitutional authorities far and near. The tone of the document was moderate and candid : " If I am wrong I wish to be convinced of my error. . . . I have laid before you what I think are the principles of your constitution; if you do not agree with me, I wish to know your objections." Nothing could be better adapted to weaken the spirit of opposition, to which the Committees of Correspondence were giving new strength.

The governor's message produced a wide and profound effect. The newspapers spread it to the world. It was read not only throughout Massachusetts, but throughout America; in England, too, it was widely circulated. Many a patriot knit his brows over it as a paper most formidable to his cause; the Tories called it unanswerable, and extolled its author as a reasoner whom none could overthrow. But over against him stood his adversary, wary, watchful, undismayed, and the counter-stroke was at once delivered. As Hutchinson had summoned to his help all the acumen and learning of the loyalists, so his opponent laid under contribution whatever shrewdness or knowledge could be found in the opposite camp. Hawley and John Adams, in particular, lent their help. The master agitator, however, himself arranged and combined all, presenting at last an instrument in his own clear, unequivocal English, which the simplest could grasp, which the ablest found it difficult to gainsay. On January 8 the speech of the governor had had a second reading; then a committee, with Samuel Adams for its chairman, was appointed to reply, which reported its answer on the 22d. The Assembly entered into long and careful deliberation concerning it. They had been accustomed to follow with little question their strongest minds, particularly of late the members of the Boston seat; but in the present crisis they seem to have resolved to take no leap in the dark. The answer of the committee was taken up paragraph by paragraph, and thorough proof was demanded for the soundness of all the arguments and the correctness of the citations from authorities. All this the committee furnished.

The reply, as it came out from this inquisition, traversed the governor's speech, position by position. The disturbed condition of the province, to which he had made allusion, was attributed to the unprecedented course of Parliament. The charters granted by Elizabeth and James were cited, and much space was taken in showing that the laws

of the colonies were intended to conform to the
fundamental principles of the English Constitution, and that they did not imply the supremacy
of Parliament. The territory of America was at
the absolute disposal of the " crown," and not an-
nexed to the " realm." The sovereignty of Parliament was not implied in the granting of the charters ; Parliament had never had the inspection of
colonial acts, for the king alone gave his consent
or allowance. The reply denied that the settlers,
when removing to America, relinquished any of
the rights of British subjects, one of which was
to be governed by laws made by persons in whose
election they had a voice. " His excellency's manner of reasoning on this point seemed to them to
render the most valuable clauses of their charter
unintelligible."

The paper passed on to a consideration of the
views of the founders of New England. From
Hutchinson's own declarations in his history, they
sought here to make good their case in opposition
to his plea. As regarded the dilemma proposed
by the governor, that if Parliament were not supreme the colonies were independent, the alternative was accepted, and the claim made that, since
the vassalage of the colonies could not have been
intended, therefore they must be independent.
There cannot be two independent legislatures in
one and the same state, Hutchinson had urged.
Were not the colonies, then, by their charters
made different states by the mother country?

queried the reply. Although, said Hutchinson, there may be but one head, the king, yet the two legislative bodies will make two governments as distinct as the kingdoms of England and Scotland before the union. Very true, may it please your excellency, was the answer; and if they interfere not with each other, what hinders their living happily in such a connection, mutually supporting and protecting each other, united under one common sovereign? As to the dangers of independence, the answer states that the colonists stand in far more fear of despotism than of any perils which could come to them if they were cut loose. The Assembly discussed the paper with the greatest care, point by point. At length it passed, and Samuel Adams himself, at the head of the committee, put the document into the hand of Hutchinson.

A controversy has arisen, which need not be entered into here, as to how far the credit of this memorable reply belongs to any one man. That Samuel Adams consulted whoever might be able to give him help is certain, and he gained much from the suggestions of others. In the main, however, the work is undoubtedly his. Wide as is the range of reading implied, it was not beyond him. Devoted heart and soul as he was to the public service, there were few great writers upon the subject of politics, ancient or modern, with whom he was unacquainted. Though not a lawyer, wherever law touched questions of state he was at home.

Hutchinson had felt that his message was irrefutable. The reply made him think that he had perhaps made a mistake in submitting the matter to argument. Heretofore the policy had been to regard the matter of parliamentary supremacy as something so clear that it did not admit of discussion; doubts now began to arise whether it had been wise to abandon this policy. But it was too late to withdraw. To the reply of the House he opposed a rejoinder longer than his original message, adding little, however, to its strength. When the Assembly, through Samuel Adams, met this also, the indefatigable governor once more appeared. The Council, too, by the hand of Bowdoin, took part in the controversy.

The patriots published the debate, *pro* and *con*,[1] far and wide, confident that their side had been well sustained. On the other hand, the friends of government in England and America extolled the effort of Hutchinson, and found only sophistry in the argument of his opponents. Thurlow, then attorney-general, found the governor's course admirable; and Lord Mansfield, whom Hutchinson met in England the following year, passed the highest encomiums upon his work.

In spite of commendation from such high sources, many friends of the government disapproved Hutchinson's course. They felt, says Grahame, that " the principles solemnly established by

[1] For the text of these important documents see the author's *Life of Thomas Hutchinson*, appendix B.

the crown and Parliament were unhinged and degraded by the presumptuous, argumentative patronage of a provincial governor." Hutchinson himself was ill at ease. He wrote Lord Dartmouth that he did not "intend ever to meet the Assembly again. . . . Your lordship very justly observes that a nice distinction upon civil rights is far above the reach of the bulk of mankind to comprehend. I experience the truth of it both in the Council and House of Representatives. The major part of them are incapable of those nice distinctions, and are in each house too ready to give an implicit faith to the assertion of a single leader."

As one reviews the strife at this distance, it may be said that both sides argued well. As far as precedents went, Hutchinson certainly could brace himself thoroughly. For centuries the principles of the primeval liberty had undergone wide perversion. Kings had persisted, and people had acquiesced in all sorts of arbitrary procedure. The first charter, intended only for a trading company, had been put to a use for which it was never designed in being made the basis of a great body-politic. In the second charter, many provisions were indefinite. The relation of government and governed throughout the colonial history had been full of quarreling. It was often hard enough to say what could be claimed, what rulers and people really thought or intended. A good basis for Hutchinson's argument existed in the British Constitution as it was. Samuel Adams presented that constitution rather as it had been before the ancient freedom had been overlaid ; as it should be, moreover, and as it tends to become in these later days, when the progress of reform gives back constantly more and more of the old Anglo-Saxon liberty.[1] Hutchinson honestly felt that he was right ; he was sustained by many of the best Englishmen of his day ; in fact, at the present time Britons of the highest position and intelligence hold the same conclusions. The ideas of his opponent, however, are those higher and broader ones which are to rule the world of the future.

Before the session ended, the House through Samuel Adams contended with Hutchinson as to the salaries of the judges of the Superior Court, which, like that of the governor, it had been resolved in England should be independent of the province. The prorogation took place on the 6th of March.

When on the 5th of March the anniversary of the Massacre was celebrated, the oration before the crowded auditory in the Old South was delivered by the brilliant but double-faced Benjamin Church. He was eloquent and seemingly patriotic ; the following prophetic passage is found in the address : " Some future Congress will be the glorious source of the salvation of America. The Amphictyons of Greece, who formed the diet or great council of the states, exhibit an excellent model for the rising Americans."

[1] Freeman, *Growth of the Eng. Const.*

Hutchinson having alleged the illegality of the proceedings of the Boston town meeting, which established the Committee of Correspondence, and considered the matter of the salaries of the judges, Samuel Adams was chairman of the committee to reply. "By an unfortunate mistake," wrote the governor, "soon after the charter a law passed which made every town in the province a corporation perfectly democratic, every matter being determined by the major vote of the inhabitants; and although the intent of the law was to confine their proceedings to the immediate proceedings of the town, yet for many years past the town of Boston has been used to interest itself in every affair of moment which concerned the province in general."

The legislature during the late session had been so thoroughly occupied by the controversy concerning the parliamentary authority that Samuel Adams had found no opportunity to develop his plan of Committees of Correspondence in ways that he had projected. He was of course not sorry to have circumstances bring it about that the initiative in the greater work, the binding together of the separate colonies as the Massachusetts towns were bound together, was taken by Virginia. Early in March, the House of Burgesses debated the matter of an intercolonial system of correspondence; before the middle of the month the measure had passed, and as soon after as the slow-moving posts of those days could bring the news, the intelligence reached Massachusetts. The controversy as to whether the idea of intercolonial Committees of Correspondence really originated with Samuel Adams is hardly worth dwelling upon. Indeed, the scheme was so obvious that doubtless it occurred originally to many persons. None, however, are known to have been before Samuel Adams in the matter.

That the special action of the House of Burgesses in March, 1773, came to pass through Boston incitement is a matter which Virginia local pride would no doubt strenuously deny. Boston claimed it, however.

"Our patriots say that the votes of the town of Boston, which they sent to Virginia, have produced the resolves of the Assembly there, appointing a Committee of Correspondence, and I have no doubt it is their expectation that a committee for the same purpose will be appointed by most of the other Assemblies upon the continent." [1]

Whatever may have been the secret springs, the news of the Virginia action was most warmly welcomed. The General Court had adjourned, but the Boston Committee of Correspondence distributed the Southern resolutions far and wide. Samuel Adams at once testified his joy, in a letter to R. H. Lee; and immediately upon the convening of the new legislature, to which he, with Hancock, Cushing, and Phillips, had been elected by an almost

[1] Hutchinson, manuscript letter in Mass. Archives, April 19, 1773.

unanimous vote, resolves were introduced responding warmly to the Southern overtures and establishing a legislative Committee of Correspondence. Fifteen members were to constitute it, eight of them forming a quorum. Though Cushing was nominally chairman, Samuel Adams was of course the inspirer and chief mover, as he also was of the Boston committee. In both he was by far the foremost man, fanning, as it were, with one hand the fires of freedom already alight in the Massachusetts towns, and with the other holding the torch to the tinder piled up and ready, though not yet kindled, in the slower colonies, until at last the whole land was brought into a conflagration of discontent.

CHAPTER XV

THE HUTCHINSON LETTERS

In the session of the General Court which came after the May elections of 1773, the governor, following instructions, signified the king's disapprobation of the appointment of Committees of Correspondence, which sit and act during the recesses. The House replied, and Hutchinson gives in his history a summary of their argument. It is strange, when he was able to state so fairly the positions of his opponents, that he did not feel more strongly the justice of those positions. The House said : —

"When American rights are attacked at times when the several Assemblies are not sitting, it is highly necessary that they should correspond, in order to unite in the most effectual means to obtain redress of grievances ; and as in most colonies the Assemblies sit at such times as governors who hold themselves under the direction of administration think fit, it must be expected that the intention of such correspondence will be made impracticable, unless committees sit in the recess. The crown officers had corresponded with ministers of state and persons of influence, in order to make plans for a policy deemed grievous by the colonists ; it ought not to be thought unreasonable or improper for the colonists to correspond with their agents as well as each other, that

their grievances might be explained to his majesty, that
in his justice he might afford them relief; and as heretofore the province had felt the displeasure of their sovereign from misrepresentations, there was room to apprehend that in this instance he had been misinformed
by such persons as had in meditation further measures
destructive to the colonies, and which they were apprehensive would be defeated by means of Committees of
Correspondence, sitting and acting in the recess of the
respective Assemblies."

The "misinformation" conveyed to the king by
persons who favored "measures destructive to the
colonies" was a matter which troubled the patriots
not a little, leading in the summer of 1773 to a
series of proceedings on their part full of adroitness, but quite irreconcilable, one is forced to admit, with fair dealing. The conviction had long
prevailed that the policy of the ministry toward
America was suggested by persons residing in the
colonies, who studied on the spot the course of
events and the temper of the people, and by secret
correspondence gave advice which led to obnoxious
acts. Franklin at length obtained possession in
England of certain private letters from Hutchinson, Andrew Oliver the lieutenant-governor, Paxton the head of the commissioners of customs, and
one or two other loyalists, which were put to an
extraordinary use. Precisely how Franklin obtained the letters was a secret for more than a
hundred years. Whether his course was altogether
honorable in the matter need not be considered

here. In the recriminations that followed, an innocent man nearly lost his life in a duel, and
Franklin himself, after having been exposed to a
bitter denunciation by Wedderburn, the solicitor-
general, in the presence of the Privy Council, was
ostracized by English society.

However it may have been with the obtaining
of the letters, the manner in which they were employed to bring obloquy upon Hutchinson really
admits of no defense. Less than half of the letters
were from Hutchinson, and in these not a sentence
can be found inconsistent with his public declarations, or expressing more than a mild disapproval
of the course of the Whigs. His conviction that
Parliament should be supreme in the colonies is
apparent, but this he had a thousand times asserted
before the world. He writes in no unfriendly
spirit, and makes suggestions remarkable only for
their great moderation. In the only one of the six
letters in which Hutchinson trenches closely upon
controverted points, his expressions, copied here
from the pamphlet published by the Massachusetts
Assembly, are as follows: —

"I never think of the measures necessary for the
peace and good order of the colonies without pain;
there must be an abridgment of what are called English
liberties. I relieve myself by considering that in a remove from the state of nature to the most perfect state
of government, there must be a great restraint of natural liberty. I doubt whether it is possible to project a
system of government in which a colony, three thousand

miles distant from the parent state, shall enjoy all the liberty of the parent state. I am certain I have never yet seen the projection."

In Hutchinson's own defense, he says of these words, in his history: —

"To a candid mind, the substance of the whole paragraph was really no more than this: 'I am sorry the people cannot be gratified with the enjoyment of all they call English liberties, but in their sense of them it is not possible for a colony at three thousand miles' distance from the parent state to enjoy them, as they might do if they had not removed.'"

In no way does the governor say more here than he had repeatedly said in public. He makes no recommendation that the charter should be changed or troops be sent. Such liberties as the establishment of Committees of Correspondence, the discussion of great affairs of state by the town meetings, the resistance to the ministerial policy in the matter of the payment of the judges and the crown officials, Hutchinson felt, and in the most open manner had said, ought to be abridged. These, in his idea, were excesses, but they could be remedied without touching the charter. He was undoubtedly wrong, of course, but there was nothing underhanded in his fight. He declares further that he wishes well to the colony, and *therefore* desires an abridgment of its liberty, and that he hopes no more severity will be shown than is necessary to secure its dependence.

As to the other letters sent by Franklin at the same time with those of Hutchinson, there is no reason at all for supposing that the latter had known anything about them. Oliver goes farther than the governor: he recommends changes in the constitution, hints at taking off the "principal incendiaries," and proposes the formation of a colonial aristocracy from whom the Council shall be drawn. Paxton demands plainly "two or three regiments." Oliver and Paxton did say enough to compromise themselves, but they were comparatively small game, about whom the patriots cared little. We have now to see what was made out of these letters.

For some months they remained in the hands of the patriots unused. In June, however, soon after the governor's return from Hartford, where he had been concerned with the settlement of the boundary line between New York and Massachusetts, a public service which he skillfully turned much to the advantage of the province, Hancock informed the Assembly darkly that within eight-and-forty hours a discovery would be made which would have great results. This the spectators in James Otis's gallery caught up, and it was spread throughout the town and the province. At the time named, Samuel Adams desired that the galleries might be cleared, as he had matters of profound moment to communicate. After the clearing, he spoke of a prevailing rumor that letters of an extraordinary nature had been written and

sent to England, greatly to the prejudice of the
province. He added that he had obtained the letters, and the consent of the person who had received
them to their being read to the House, under the
restriction, however, that they were neither to be
printed nor copied, in whole or part. The letters
were then read. After the reading, amid these
mysterious surroundings, a committee reported, the
letters being lumped together, that they tended and
were designed to overthrow the constitution of government, and to introduce arbitrary power into the
province. The report was accepted almost unanimously. These proceedings were spread abroad,
and the curiosity of the people became wonderfully
roused as to what the dreadful letters contained.
This temper of mind was stimulated by rollings of
the eyes and raisings of the hands on the part of
the Whig leaders over the enormities which could
not be spoken.

Hutchinson did not prorogue the court, which
would have looked like an attempt on his part to
smother the subject, indicative of consciousness of
guilt; but he sent a message asking for copies
of the letters, declaring that he had never written
letters, public or private, of any such character as
was reported. The House replied by sending him
the dates, and asking him for copies of his letters
written on those dates. Hutchinson declined to
send the copies, on the ground that there would be
an impropriety in laying before them his private
correspondence, and that he was restrained by the

king from showing that of a public nature. But he said that he could assure them that neither private nor public letters of his " tended, or were designed to subvert, but rather to preserve entire the constitution of the government." He declared that his letters, of the dates mentioned by the House, contained nothing different from what had been published in his speeches to the Assembly, as well as to the world in his history, and that none of them related to the charter.

The popular pressure to know more of the direful discoveries became very earnest. Hancock at length told the House that copies of the letters had been put into his hands in the street. These were found upon comparison to correspond with the letters in possession of the House, and a committee was appointed to consider how the House might become " honorably " possessed of the letters, so that they could be published. Hawley soon reported from this committee that Samuel Adams had said that, since copies of the letters were already abroad, the gentleman from whom the letters themselves were received gave his consent that they should be copied and printed. The legislature then ordered that the letters should be printed; but beforehand, with very Yankee cunning, they took pains to circulate everywhere their resolves. These resolves, putting as they did the worst construction upon the letters, declaring that they tended to alienate the affections of the king, to produce severe and destructive measures, and that they contained proofs of a conspiracy against the country, went to all the towns. As if Hutchinson had been privy to, if not the author of, all the letters, the implication was that it was right to hold him responsible for everything they contained. The towns became prepossessed with the darkest anticipations.

The printed letters were at length allowed to go forth.[1] In the popular excitement, and influenced by the interpretation which had been given to them, the people universally saw abominable treachery in what was really harmless. In the midst of the rage against the governor, a petition for his removal and that of Oliver was dispatched by the legislature to Franklin, to be presented to the ministry. The rough draft of this petition, in the hand of Samuel Adams, runs as follows:—

PETITION TO THE KING.

June 23, 1773.

Nothing but a Sense of the Duty we owe to our Sovereign and the obligation we are under to consult the Peace and Safety of the Province could induce us to remonstrate to your Majesty the Malconduct of those who, having been born and educated and constantly resident in the Province and who formerly have had ye confidence and were loaded with ye honours of this People, your Majesty, we conceive from the purest Motives of rendering the People most happy, was graciously pleased

---

[1] The letters and also the resolves, taken from the pamphlet published by order of the legislature, are given in the author's *Life of Thomas Hutchinson*, appendix C.

to advance to the highest places of Trust and Authority in the Province. . . . We do therefore most humbly beseech your Majesty to give order that Time may be allowed to us to support these our Complaints by our Agents and Council. And as the said Thomas Hutchinson, Esq., and Andrew Oliver, Esq., have by their above mentioned Conduct and otherwise rendered themselves justly obnoxious to your Majesty's loving Subjects, we pray that your Majesty will be graciously pleased to remove them from their posts in this government, and place such good and faithfull men in their stead as your Majesty in your great Wisdom shall think fit.

This transaction, which has been dwelt on at considerable length, deserves attention because it is probably the least defensible proceeding in which the patriots of New England were concerned during the Revolutionary struggle. Nothing can be more sly than the manœuvring throughout. The end aimed at, to excite against Hutchinson the strongest animosity at a time when his management of the controversy as to parliamentary authority had made an impression of ability, and his service in settling the boundary line so satisfactorily might have conciliated some good-will, was completely successful. His position was henceforth intolerable. When one reads at this distance of time the little pamphlet containing the letters which the General Court caused to be published, one sees plainly the justice of the remark of Dr. George E. Ellis: "The whole affair is a marvelously strong illustration of the most vehement possible cry, with the slightest possible amount of wool."

Without this means of forming a judgment for ourselves, Hutchinson's statements as to the matter would require to be taken with much allowance. View them in connection with this plain evidence, however, and they have great weight, and it is hard to resist the conviction that the man was deeply injured. He said: "They [the letters] have been represented as highly criminal, though there is nothing more than what might naturally be expected from a confidential correspondence."[1] Again he declared them to be "the most innocent things in the world; but if it had been Chevy Chace, the leaders are so adroit they would have made the people *believe* it was full of evil and treason."[2] The following letter, written a little later in the year, copied here from Hutchinson's letter book, contains a clear and manly statement: —

"I differ in my principles from the present leaders of the people. . . . I think that by the constitution of the colonies the Parliament has a supreme authority over them. I have nevertheless always been an advocate for as large a power of legislation within each colony as can consist with a supreme controul. I have declared against a forcible opposition to the execution of acts of Parliament which have laid taxes on the people of America; I have notwithstanding ever wished that such

[1] From Hutchinson's manuscript, Mass. Archiv.
[2] From manuscript in Mass. Archiv.

acts might not be made as the Stamp Act in particular.
I have done everything in my power that they might be
repealed. I do not see how the people in the colonies
can enjoy every liberty which the people in England enjoy, because in England every man may be represented
in Parliament, the supreme authority over the whole;
but in the colonies, the people, I conceive, cannot have
representatives in Parliament to any advantage. It
gives me pain when I think it must be so. I wish also
that we may enjoy every priviledge of an Englishman
which our remote situation will admit of. These are
sentiments which I have without reserve declared among
my private friends, in my speeches and messages to the
General Court, in my correspondence with the ministers
of state, and I have published them to the world in my
history; and yet I have been declared an enemy and a
traitor to my country because in my private letters I
have discovered the same sentiments, for everything else
asserted to be contained in those letters, I mean of mine,
unfriendly to the country, I must deny as altogether
groundless and false."

On a fly-leaf of his diary two years later, after
quoting a sentence from Erasmus as to the injustice of garbled quotations from a man's words, he
continues : " How applicable is this to the case of
my letters to Whately, and the expression, 'there
must be an abridgment of what are called English
liberties'! Everything which preceded and followed, which would have given the real sentiment
and taken away all the odium, was left out."

It is hard to palliate the conduct of the patriots.
Had the leaders lost in the excitement of the con-

troversies the power of weighing words properly, and did they honestly think Hutchinson's expressions deserved such an interpretation? Did they honestly believe that it was right to hold him responsible for what Oliver and Paxton had said? Unfortunately there is some testimony to show that their conduct was due to deliberate artifice. Says their victim: —

" When some of the governor's friends urged to the persons principally concerned . . . the unwarrantableness of asserting or insinuating what they knew to be false and injurious, they justified themselves from the necessity of the thing; the public interest, the safety of the people, making it absolutely necessary that his weight and influence among them should by any means whatever be destroyed."

Further, if Hutchinson's testimony in his own case is not to be received, what are we to say of Franklin's suspicious hint, who, in transmitting the letters, counsels the use of mystery and manœuvring, that, "as distant objects seen only through a mist appear larger, the same may happen from the mystery in this case."[1] There never were cooler heads than stood on the shoulders of some of those leaders; it is impossible to think that they were blinded.

The complicity of Samuel Adams with the whole affair is unmistakable. His name occurs

---

[1] G. E. Ellis, *Atlantic Monthly*, May, 1884, p. 672 ; also Curwen's *Jour.*, App., art. " Hutchinson." I cannot, however, find the letter to Cooper in which this passage is said to occur.

constantly in the course of the proceedings; his
ascendency among the Whigs at the moment was
at its highest. "Master of the puppets," his
writhing adversary calls him, while also declaring
that through some kind of evil sorcery many of
the representatives, in spite of themselves, were
made by him to vote against their will and judgment. The whole transaction has a more than
questionable color; and though patriotic historians
and biographers have been able to see nothing in
it except, so to speak, a dove-like iridescence, an
unprejudiced judge will detect the scaly gleam
of a creature in better repute for his wisdom than
his harmlessness. Dr. Johnson might have folded
Hutchinson and Samuel Adams to his burly breast
in an ecstacy, such thoroughly good haters of one
another were they. It is hard to say what the
casuistry was which enabled the Puritan politician,
upright though he was, to make crooked treatment
of his Tory *bête noire* square with his sense of
right. Apparently he felt that Hutchinson was
the devil, who might rightly be fought with his
own fire.

Besides the controversy over the letters sent by
Franklin, the House, in the summer session of
1773, discussed the independency of the judges
of the Supreme Court. A series of resolves was
passed demanding of those officers whether they
would receive the grants of the Assembly or accept
their support from the crown, and making it the
indispensable duty of "the Commons" of the pro-

vince to impeach them before the governor and
Council if their reply should be delayed. Hutchinson upon this at once prorogued the House. The
term "the Commons" had only lately been applied
to the Assembly. Says Hutchinson : —

"Mr. Adams would not neglect even small circumstances. In four or five years a great change had been
made in the language of the general Assembly. That
which used to be called the 'court-house,' or 'town-
house,' had acquired the name of the 'state-house ; ' the
'House of Representatives of Massachusetts Bay' had
assumed the name of 'his majesty's Commons ; ' the
debates of the Assembly are styled 'parliamentary debates ; ' acts of Parliament, 'acts of the British Parliament ; ' the Province laws, 'the laws of the land ; ' the
charter, a grant from royal grace or favor, is styled the
'compact ; ' and now 'impeach' is used for 'complain,'
and the 'House of Representatives' are made analogous
to the 'commons,' and the 'Council' to the 'Lords,' to
decide in case of high crimes and misdemeanors."

Townshend's revenue act of 1767, by which a
tax was laid upon painters' colors, glass, paper,
and tea, was passed less for the sake of gaining
a revenue than for maintaining the abstract right
of taxation. The yield had been from the first
quite insignificant, and, as has been seen, the tax
was now entirely repealed, except upon the single
article of tea. In the hampered commerce of that
time, duties were levied upon articles both when
exported and when imported. In the present case
the duty upon tea exported from England was

taken off, and threepence a pound was assigned as
the impost to be paid on the importation into
America.   As the export duties to be removed
were far larger than this import duty, the tea could
be sold for a price considerably lower than heretofore.   A double benefit was hoped for, — that the
Americans, won by cheap tea, might be brought
to acquiesce in a tax levied by Parliament, and
also that the prosperity of the important East
India Company would be furthered, which for
some time past, owing to the colonial non-importation agreements, had been obliged to see its tea
accumulate in its warehouses, until the amount
reached 17,000,000 pounds.   The project was Lord
North's, and passed Parliament in May, by a large
majority.

Samuel Adams, forever alert, saw the danger
in a moment, and was ready with his expedient.
Steps must be forthwith taken for a closer bond
among the colonies, " after the plan first proposed
by Virginia."   A congress of delegates, to meet at
some central point, must be arranged for ; it was
time for the representatives of the colonies to come
together face to face.   The credit of originating
the idea of a continental congress belongs to Franklin, who in 1754 brought about the congress at Al-
bany.   Its main object then, however, had been to
take measures for a united resistance against the
French.   The Stamp Act congress, ten years later,
suggested in Samuel Adams's often referred to
"instructions " of that year, was the first meeting

of colonial delegates to resist England. In 1766,
'68, '70, and '71, we find him pushing measures
looking toward union; now in 1773 he is out-
spoken and urgent. His position in the leading
colony gave him an opportunity to work effectively,
such as others elsewhere did not possess. When
in July of this year Franklin wrote to Cushing
from London suggesting a congress, Samuel Adams
had already hinted at it strongly in the preceding
January, and Church in his oration on the 5th of
March had uttered the prophetic passage that has
been quoted.

Samuel Adams urged during the present summer, in a series of essays in the "Boston Gazette,"
the project of a congress as the only salvation
of the country. Though Hutchinson was under
obloquy, the cause of the Whigs was far from being in a satisfactory condition. Many were tired
of controversy. Cushing, for instance, who had
been addressed directly by Dartmouth, the colonial
secretary, favored a submissive policy, believing
that grievances would be redressed, "if these high
points about the supreme authority of Parliament
were to fall asleep." Such laxness Samuel Adams
tried hard to counteract. Lord Dartmouth to be
sure was thoroughly well-meaning. His marked
religious character, unusual among men of his station, made him acceptable to the New Englanders.
He proposed that there should be mutual concessions. Only submit and you shall be treated most
graciously, was his tone. But Samuel Adams opposed with all his might.

At length, as "Observation" in the "Boston Gazette," September 27, 1773, Samuel Adams wrote : —

"The very important dispute between Britain and America has, for a long time, employed the pens of statesmen in both countries, but no plan of union is yet agreed on between them ; the dispute still continues, and everything floats in uncertainty. As I have long contemplated the subject with fixed attention, I beg leave to offer a proposal to my countrymen, namely, that a CONGRESS OF AMERICAN STATES be assembled as soon as possible; draw up a Bill of Rights, and publish it to the world; choose an ambassador to reside at the British Court to act for the united Colonies; appoint where the Congress shall annually meet, and how it may be summoned upon any extraordinary occasion, what farther steps are necessary to be taken, &c."

Three weeks later, October 11, in the "Gazette" appeared the following : —

"But the Question will be asked, — How shall the Colonies force their Oppressors to proper Terms ? This question has been often answered already by our Politicians, viz: ' Form an Independent State,' ' AN AMERICAN COMMONWEALTH.' This Plan has been proposed, and I can't find that any other is likely to answer the great Purpose of preserving our Liberties. I hope, therefore, it will be well digested and forwarded, to be in due Time put into Execution, unless our Political Fathers can secure American Liberties in some other Way. As the Population, Wealth, and Power of this Continent are swiftly increasing, we certainly have no Cause to doubt of our Success in maintaining Liberty by forming a Commonwealth, or whatever Measure Wisdom may point out for the Preservation of the Rights of America."

The legislative Committee of Correspondence had heretofore done little. Samuel Adams, who by means of the Boston committee had largely reinvigorated the spirit of liberty in the province, now set the other agency at work, that a similar spirit might be sent throughout the thirteen colonies. It was necessary that Cushing, who, as speaker, was *ex-officio* chairman of the committee, should sign the manifesto. Hutchinson's term " the puppets," of whom Samuel Adams was said to be the master, was perhaps more applicable to Cushing than to some of his fellows. By a skillful touch of the master's fingers, the respectable wooden personality that did duty as the legislative figurehead, responded to his wire and danced to the patriot measure. The document is wise, moderate, thoroughly appreciative of the circumstances of the hour.

"We are far from desiring," thus the paper concluded, "that the Connection between Britain and America should be broken. *Esto perpetua* is our ardent wish, but upon the Terms only of Equal Liberty. If we cannot establish an Agreement upon these terms, let us leave it to another and a wiser Generation. But it may be worth Consideration, that the work is more likely to be well done at a time when the Ideas of Liberty and its Importance are strong in men's minds.

There is Danger that these Ideas may grow faint and languid. Our Posterity may be accustomed to bear the Yoke, and being inured to Servility, they may even bow the Shoulder to the Burden. It can never be expected that a people, however *numerous*, will form and execute as wise plans to perpetuate their Liberty, when they have lost the Spirit and feeling of it."

The document was of course written by Mr. Adams, and the selection given is copied from his autograph.

Hutchinson now wrote to Dartmouth a letter containing the following passage. Speaking of the Whigs he said : —

" They have for their head one of the members from Boston, who was the first person that openly, in any public assembly, declared for absolute independence, and who, from a natural obstinacy of temper, and from many years' practice in politics, is, perhaps, as well qualified to excite the people to any extravagance in theory and practice as any person in America. From large defalcations, as collector of taxes for the town of Boston, and other acts in pecuniary matters, his influence was small until within these seven years ; but since that, it has been gradually increasing, until he has obtained such an ascendency as to direct the town of Boston and the House of Representatives, and consequently the Council, just as he pleases. A principle has been avowed by some who are attached to him, the most inimical that can be devised, that in political matters the public good is above all other considerations ; and every rule of morality, when in competition with it, may very well be dispensed with. Upon this principle, the whole proceeding, with respect to the letters of the governor and lieutenant-governor, of which he was the chief conductor, has been vindicated. In ordinary affairs, the counsels of the whole opposition unite. Whenever there appears a disposition to any conciliatory measures, this person, by his art and skill, prevents any effect; sometimes by exercising his talents in the newspapers, an instance of which is supposed to have been given in the paper enclosed to your lordship in my letter, number twenty-seven, at other times by an open opposition, and this sometimes in the House, where he has defeated every attempt as often as any has been made. But his chief dependence is upon a Boston town meeting, where he originates his measures, which are followed by the rest of the towns, and of course are adopted or justified by the Assembly.

"I could mention to your lordship many instances of the like kind. To his influence it has been chiefly owing, that when there has been a repeal of acts of Parliament complained of as grievous, and when any concessions have been made to the Assembly, as the removal of it to Boston and the like, (notwithstanding the professions made beforehand by the moderate part of the opposition, that such measures would quiet the minds of the people,) he has had art enough to improve them to raise the people higher by assuring them, if they will but persevere, they may bring the nation to their own terms; and the people are more easily induced to a compliance from the declaration made, that they are assured by one or two gentlemen in England, on whose judgment they can depend, that nothing more than a firm adhesion to their demands is necessary to obtain a compliance with every one of them. Could he have been made dependent, I am not sure that he might

not have been taken off by an appointment to some public civil office. But, as the constitution of the Province
is framed, such an appointment would increase his abilities, if not his disposition to do mischief, for he well
knows that I have not a Council which in any case
would consent to his removal, and nobody can do more
than he to prevent my ever having such a Council."

CHAPTER XVI

THE TEA-PARTY

THE colonies generally were resolved not to receive the tea. Resolutions were adopted in Philadelphia, October 18, requesting the agents of the East India Company, who were to sell the tea, to resign, which they did. Boston at once followed the example. Acting upon the precedent of the time of the Stamp Act, when Oliver, the stamp commissioner, had resigned his commission under the Liberty Tree, a placard was posted everywhere on the 3d of November, inviting the people of Boston and the neighboring towns to be present at Liberty Tree that day at noon, to witness the resignation of the consignees of the tea, and hear them swear to re-ship to London what teas should arrive. The placard closed, —

" ☞ Show me the man that dares take this down."

At the time appointed, representatives Adams, Hancock, and Phillips, the selectmen and town clerk, with about five hundred more, were present at the Liberty Tree. But no consignees arrived, whereupon Molineux and Warren headed a party who waited upon them. The consignees, Clarke, a rich merchant, and his sons, Benjamin Faneuil, Winslow, and the two sons of Hutchinson, Thomas and Elisha, sat together in the counting-house of Clarke in King Street. Admittance was refused the committee, and a conversation took place through a window, during which the tone of the consignees was defiant. There was some talk of violence, and when an attempt was made to exclude the committee and the crowd attending them from the building, into the first story of which they had penetrated, the doors were taken off their hinges and threats uttered. Molineux, generally impetuous enough, but now influenced probably by cooler heads, dissuaded the others from violence. A few days later, a serious riot came near taking place before the house of Clarke in School Street; the people outside broke some windows, while from the inside a pistol was fired from the second story. Judicious men among the patriots, however, exerted themselves successfully to prevent a repetition of the excesses at the time of the Stamp Act.

A town meeting on November 5, in which an effort of the Tories to make head against the popular feeling came to naught, showed how overwhelming was the determination to oppose the introduction of the tea. Precisely how the plans were organized — precisely who many of the actors were in the few eventful weeks that remained of 1773 — can now never be known. A frequent meeting-place was the room over the printing-office

of Edes & Gill, now the corner of Court Street
and Franklin Avenue. Samuel Adams, never more
fully the master than during these lowering autumn and winter days when such a crisis was encountered, was often at the printing-office; and
there and at meetings of the North End Club
much was arranged. No voice needs to speak out
of the silence of those undercurrents to let us
know that he was at the head. When news arrived on the 17th that three tea-ships were on the
way to Boston, for a second time a town meeting
demanded through a committee, of which Samuel
Adams was a member, the resignation of the consignees. They evaded the demand; the town meeting voted their answer not satisfactory, and at once
adjourned without debate or comment. The silence
was mysterious; what was impending none could
tell.

The consignees, appreciating their danger, tried
to shift their responsibility upon the governor and
Council, but without effect. The Committee of
Correspondence of the town, combining with itself
the committees of Roxbury, Dorchester, Brookline,
Cambridge, and Charlestown, and so forming what
Hutchinson called "a little senate," met frequently
and maintained a general oversight. They pledged
themselves to resist the landing and sale of the tea,
and sent out through the province a joint letter,
the composition of Samuel Adams: "We think,
gentlemen," this document said, "that we are in
duty bound to use our most strenuous endeavors to

ward off the impending evil, and we are sure that upon a fair and cool inquiry into the nature and tendency of the ministerial plan, you will think this tea now coming to us more to be dreaded than plague and pestilence." The necessity of resistance was strongly declared, and the advice of the committees urgently asked.

The incipient union is becoming very plain at the time of the Boston tea-party. In the crises of an earlier date, each town or province had met the occasion in a condition of more or less isolation. Now, however, as never before, there appears a formal bond; the newspapers teem with missives, not only from Massachusetts towns, but from the colonies in general, expressing sympathy, fear that the peril will not be adequately met, encouragement to boldness, praise for decision, — missives proceeding from the regularly organized committees, showing how the ligaments are knitting that are to bind so great a body.

On the 28th, the first of the tea-ships, the Dartmouth, Captain Hall, sailed into the harbor. Sunday though it was, the Committee of Correspondence met, obtained from Benjamin Rotch, the Quaker owner of the Dartmouth, a promise not to enter the vessel until Tuesday, and made preparations for a mass meeting at Faneuil Hall for Monday forenoon, to which Samuel Adams was authorized to invite the surrounding towns. A stirring placard the next morning brought the townsmen and their neighbors to the place. After the organization, Samuel Adams, arising among the thousands, moved that: "As the town have determined at a late meeting legally assembled that they will to the utmost of their power prevent the landing of the tea, the question be now put, — whether this body are absolutely determined that the tea now arrived in Captain Hall shall be returned to the place from whence it came." There was not a dissenting voice. The meeting had now become larger even than the famous one of the Massacre. As usual they surged across King Street to the Old South, once more under the eyes of Hutchinson, who, as at the time of the Massacre, could look down upon them from the chamber in the State House where he was sitting with the Council. Samuel Adams's motion was repeated, with the addition: "Is it the firm resolution of this body that the tea shall not only be sent back, but that no duty shall be paid thereon?" Again there was no dissenting voice. In the afternoon, the meeting having resolved that the tea should go back in the same ship in which it had come, Rotch, the owner of the Dartmouth, protested, but was sternly forbidden, at his peril, to enter the tea. Captain Hall also was forbidden to land any portion of it. "Adams was never in greater glory," says Hutchinson.

The next morning, November 30, the people again assembling, the consignees made it known that it was out of their power to send the tea back; but they promised that they would store it until

word should come from their "constituents" as
to its disposal. While the meeting deliberated,
Greenleaf, the sheriff of Suffolk, appeared with a
message from the governor. Samuel Adams gave
it as his judgment that the sheriff might be
heard; upon which the paper was read. Hutchinson blamed the meeting sharply, and concluded
by "warning, exhorting, and requiring" the assemblage to disperse, and to "surcease all further unlawful proceedings at their utmost peril." The
crowd hissed the official heartily, who at once beat
a retreat. Copley, the artist, who has already appeared in our story as painting the portrait of the
"man of the town meeting," at the time when the
regiments were driven to the Castle, was much
liked for his honesty and good-nature. As the
son-in-law of the consignee, Richard Clarke, and at
the same time popular in the town, he was well-
fitted to be a mediator. He now asked of the meeting whether the consignees would be civilly treated
if they should appear before it. Upon assurance
that they would be, he went at once to the Castle,
whither the Clarkes had betaken themselves, one
must allow with perfect good reason, if they valued
their safety. He could not prevail upon them,
however, to face the assembly, and not long after
we find him on the Tory side, until at length he
leaves America.

The Dartmouth each night was watched by a
strong guard; armed patrols, too, were established,
and six couriers held themselves ready, if there

should be need, to alarm the country. The most vigorous resolutions were passed, and a committee was appointed, with Samuel Adams at the head, to send intelligence far and wide. During the first week in December arrived the Eleanor and the Beaver, also tea-ships, which were moored near the Dartmouth, and subjected to the same oversight. The "True Sons of Liberty" posted about the town the most spirited placards. From the sister towns the post-riders came spurring in haste with responses to the manifesto of the Committee of Correspondence, all which Samuel Adams took care to have at once published, with whatever rumors there might be as to the conduct of the other provinces respecting tea, which, as all knew, might be expected to arrive in other ports besides Boston.

Hutchinson, in spite of himself, had become, one is forced to say through the machinations of the Whigs, little more than a cipher in his own jurisdiction. His influence was for the time being completely broken down, and though the fleet lay in the harbor, and the weak regiments were at the Castle, yet the popular manifestation was so general and threatening that he could make no head against it. It is absurd to accuse him or the consignees of cowardice because they felt they were in danger in the town. The latter had good reason to seek the protection of the Castle, and the governor might well prefer to occupy his country house. For several times the air was full of riot, and

Hutchinson and his friends had cause to know that a Boston riot might be a terrible thing. The governor could not depend upon any justice of the peace to make a requisition for the use of the military. Whether he himself had power to make such a requisition lawfully was a matter open to doubt. He could expect no support from his Council, — his own party were completely overawed. He showed no want of spirit at this time. Says Richard Frothingham: "His course does not show one sign of vacillation from first to last, but throughout bears the marks of clear, cold, passionless inflexibility." It is rather amusing to read his summons to Hancock, commander of the Boston cadets, to hold his force in readiness for the preservation of order; for Hancock, however he may have coquetted with the Tories shortly before, was now a red-hot Whig, as were most of the cadets, who were in great part themselves in the "rabble." The governor denounced, threatened, pleaded, without yielding a hair from his position that the authority of Parliament must be maintained, although, as we know now, it went sorely against his wish that the tax on tea was retained, and he would gladly have had things as they were before the Stamp Act.

The days flew by. At length came the end of the time of probation. If the cargo of the Dartmouth had not been "entered" within that period, the ship, according to the revenue laws, must be confiscated. Rotch, the Quaker owner, had signified his willingness to send the ship back to England with the cargo on board, if he could procure a clearance. The customs officials stood on technicalities; under the circumstances a clearance could not be granted. The grim British admiral ordered the Active and the Kingfisher from his fleet to train their broadsides on the channels, and sink whatever craft should try to go to sea without the proper papers. The governor alone had power to override these obstacles. It was competent for him to grant a permit which the revenue men and the admiral must respect. If he refused to do this, then on the next day the legal course was for the revenue officers to seize the Dartmouth and land the tea under the guns of the fleet.

It was the 16th of December. A crowd of seven thousand filled the Old South and the streets adjoining. Nothing like it had ever been known. Town meeting had followed town meeting until the excitement was at fever heat. The indefatigable Committee of Correspondence had, as it were, scattered fire throughout the whole country. The people from deep in the interior had poured over the "Neck" into the little peninsula to see what was coming; the beacons were ready for lighting, and everywhere eyes were watching, expecting to see them blaze. Poor Quaker Rotch, like his sect in general, quite indifferent to great political principles at stake, ready to submit to "the powers that be," and anxious about his pelf, felt himself, probably, the most persecuted of men, when the monster meeting forced him in the December weather to make his way out to Milton Hill to seek the permit from Hutchinson. While the merchant journeyed thither and back, the great meeting deliberated. Even as ardent a spirit as Josiah Quincy counseled moderation; but when the question was put whether the meeting would suffer the tea to be landed, the people declared against it unanimously.

Meantime darkness had fallen upon the short winter day. The crowd still waited in the gloom of the church, dimly lighted here and there by candles. Rotch reappeared just after six, and informed the meeting that the governor refused to grant the permit until the vessels were properly qualified. As soon as the report had been made, Samuel Adams arose, for it was he who had been moderator, and exclaimed: "This meeting can do nothing more to save the country." It was evidently a concerted signal, for instantly the famous war-whoop was heard, and the two or three score of "Mohawks" rushed by the doors, and with the crowd behind them hurried in the brightening moonlight to Griffin's wharf, where lay the ships. The tea could not go back to England; it must not be landed. The cold waters of the harbor were all that remained for it. Three hundred and forty-two chests were cast overboard. Nothing else was harmed, neither person nor property. All was so quiet that those at a distance even could hear in the calm air the ripping open of the thin chests as the tea was emptied. The "Mohawks" found helpers, so that in all perhaps one hundred and fifty were actively concerned. Not far off in the harbor lay the ships of the fleet, and the Castle with the "Sam Adams regiments." But no one interfered. The work done, the "Mohawks" marched to the fife and drum through the streets, chaffing on the way Admiral Montague, who was lodging in the town. He gave a surly growl in return, which tradition has preserved. "Well, boys, you've had a fine pleasant evening for your Indian caper, haven't you? But mind, you have got to pay the fiddler yet!" "Oh, never mind!" shouted Pitts, the leader, "never mind, squire; just come out here, if you please, and we'll settle the bill in two minutes."[1]

Next morning, while the good Bohea, soaked by the tide, was heaped in windrows on the Dorchester shore, the rueful Boston mothers steeped from catnip and pennyroyal a cup which certainly could not inebriate, and which even Sam Adams's robust patriotism could hardly have regarded as cheering.

Through this whole crisis Hancock was in the front, like a brave man, risking his life and his means. Warren, too, and another public-spirited physician, Dr. Thomas Young, who soon after, by

[1] Lossing's *Field Book*, i. 499.

removal from the country, brought to an end a career which had promised to become illustrious, were earnestly engaged. To these must be added Josiah Quincy, John Pitts, John Scollay, and the other selectmen, with William Cooper, the intrepid town clerk. But in the whole affair Samuel Adams was more than ever the supreme mind. To his discretion was left the giving of the signal; as the controller of the Committee of Correspondence, he was practically the ruler of the town; his spirit pervaded every measure. In regard to the whole secret development, which can now never be known, it is probable that his influence was no less dominant than in what was done before the world.

The couriers galloped with all the four winds to spread the news, Paul Revere reaching Philadelphia shortly before Christmas. Here is a specimen of the hastily prepared notes they carried from the Committee of Correspondence. It is copied from the autograph in Samuel Adams's papers, the *t*'s for the most part uncrossed, and punctuation neglected in the breathless haste in which it was written.

BOSTON, Dec. 17th, 1773.

GENTLEMEN, — We inform you in great Haste that every chest of Tea on board the three Ships in this Town was destroyed the last evening without the least Injury to the Vessels or any other property. Our Enemies must acknowledge that these people have acted upon pure and upright Principle. the people at the

Cape will we hope behave with propriety and as becomes men resolved to save their Country.

    To Plym°

        & to Sandwich with this addition

  We trust you will afford them

Your immediate Assistance and Advice.

The reference at the close of the note is to still a fourth tea-ship which had been cast away on the back of Cape Cod.

CHAPTER XVII

HUTCHINSON AND THE TORIES

THE Boston leaders were now in great danger of arrest and deportation to England for trial, the members of the Committee of Correspondence in particular being shadowed by spies who tried to obtain all information that could be made to count against them. For mutual protection fifteen members of the committee bound themselves to support and vindicate one another, by an agreement which it is interesting to read. In this document a circumstance slight in itself, but important as revealing the recognized leadership of Samuel Adams, is to be noticed. The first signer is a worthy citizen, Robert Pierpont, but the name has been erased, and that of Samuel Adams put in its place, Pierpont and the other associates coming afterward. Plainly the committee regarded it as presumptuous that any name should be written before his. The energy of the body was untiring. South Carolina was encouraged, and the tea received there was left to rot in cellars in Charleston. Philadelphia and New York responded with equal spirit. Through the committees the thirteen colonies were now linked, and the desire for a congress was becoming general and imperative.

When the legislature met in January, 1774, to which time it had been prorogued, Samuel Adams vindicated the Committees of Correspondence, and their activity in the intervals between the sessions, in reply to a message of Hutchinson, who declared the king's disapprobation of such institutions. Comparing the state papers of the veteran disputant at this time with those of ten years previous, one notes a change in the grounds upon which he chooses to base his striving. There is less reference to precedents and documentary authorities, and more frequent appeal to natural right. "The welfare and safety of the people," "the good of the people," are phrases which appear more often. Whether it was that he felt that he could express himself more freely since public sentiment had become so far educated, or whether his own conceptions ripened and altered, his arguments and his watchwords became different. Hutchinson wrote:

"The leaders here seem to acknowledge that their cause is not to be defended on constitutional principles, and Adams now gives out that there is no need of it; they are upon better ground; all men have a natural right to change a bad constitution for a better, whenever they have it in their power." [1]

Elsewhere, too, Hutchinson declares to Lord Dartmouth that a principle had been avowed by the patriots that "the public good was above all considerations."

[1] Copied from autograph in Mass. Arch., April 7, 1773.

An important topic during the present session
was the one which had now for some time been
agitated, and which had been pointedly dwelt upon
at the session of the preceding summer, whether
the judges of the Superior Court should be suffered to receive salaries from the king, and thus
be made quite independent of the province. The
legislature had passed resolves requiring the judges
to decline the royal grant; and one of the five,
Trowbridge, whose feeble bodily condition was believed, at any rate by the Tories, to have unnerved
him, had obeyed. His associates followed his example. "One of them assured me," says Hutchinson, "that he was constrained to a compliance,
merely because his person, his wife and children,
and his property, were at the mercy of the populace, from whom there was nothing which he had
not to fear." Peter Oliver alone, the chief justice,
refused to yield to the legislative pressure, and
was at once taken in hand. The judges, in truth,
seem to have been miserably starved. Even their
doorkeeper is said to have had a larger stipend
than theirs. On circuits they traveled eleven hundred, sometimes thirteen hundred miles a year.
The highest grant made to any one of them was
£120 a year, and it had been much less. The chief
justice received only £150. Small as the salary
was, the grant was sometimes postponed. Respected members of the bench, not long before, had
lived in penury and died insolvent. Peter Oliver
set forth that he had been a justice of the Superior

Court seventeen years; that his salary had been insufficient for his support; that his estate had suffered; and that he had repeatedly had it in mind to resign, but had been encouraged to hope for something better. It had always been a hope deferred, and he announced that he proposed now to accept the offer of the king.

When Oliver's purpose became plain, steps were promptly taken in the legislature for his impeachment. Hereupon sprang up a new controversy with the governor. The Assembly assumed that, since the chief justice was appointed by the governor by the advice and consent of the Council, the governor and Council by implication, though it might not be plainly expressed, possessed also a power of removal. Hutchinson declared that the governor and Council had no power to sit as a court in such a case; and when the committee of the Assembly, with Samuel Adams at its head, presented themselves before the Council to institute proceedings, the governor held aloof. A neat piece of management here occurred, in which Adams and Bowdoin played into one another's hands as they had long been accustomed to do, dexterously circumventing an obstacle, and making a precedent sure to be afterwards useful. Poor Hutchinson, not less shrewd than they, saw it all, but he had become the merest shadow of power.

"Mr. Adams addressed the Council in this form: 'May it please your Excellency and the honorable Council.' Mr. Bowdoin, no doubt by concert, observed to him that the governor was not in Council. This gave opportunity for an answer : 'The governor is "presumed" to be present.' This was certainly a very idle presumption. It gave pretense, however, for Mr. Adams to report to the House, and, being clerk of the House, afterwards to enter upon the journals, that the committee had impeached the chief justice before the governor and Council, and prayed that they would assign a time for hearing and determining thereon."

The cunning coryphœi of the two houses in this way were preparing to dispense with the governor entirely. He prorogued the court before proceedings could go farther, sending his secretary for that purpose. The Council received the message, but the House barred its door against him until they had completed certain important measures. The last act of the session, while the door was still kept fast, was to direct the Committee of Correspondence to write to Franklin with respect to the public grievances, — the final appeal, direct or indirect, which Massachusetts made for redress.

Hutchinson, broken in health by the treatment he had received from a people whom he sincerely loved and honestly desired to serve, begged the king for leave of absence. It was promptly granted, and the governor would have early availed himself of it, but for the death of Andrew Oliver, the lieutenant-governor. If Hutchinson should now absent himself, authority must fall into the hands of the Council, which would be a complete surrender to the Whigs. He therefore postponed his departure until a new appointment could be made.

On the 5th of March the oration in commemoration of the Massacre was given by John Hancock. He is described as making a fine appearance, and produced upon the vast assembly a great impression. Wells, whose admiration for his great-grandfather is perfectly unqualified, insists, with rather naïve unconsciousness that there can be anything crooked in such a proceeding, that Samuel Adams wrote the oration for Hancock, and then sat blandly by as moderator while the people were deceived into the belief that the man who surpassed all in social graces and length of purse could thunder also from the rostrum with the best. At the end, moreover, the moderator, at the head of the committee appointed by the meeting, thanked the orator in the name of the town for his " elegant and spirited oration." Really there is nothing in the character of either man, it must be admitted with some sadness, to make the assertion seem unreasonable. Hancock was quite capable, as in his love for popularity he wooed the turbulent crowd, of appropriating without acknowledgment the strength of some convenient Siegfried, standing invisible at his side. As to Adams, since we have been forced to believe that he had a principal hand in the manœuvring as regards Hutchinson's letters, it will require no strain to believe him capable of a peccadillo so trifling in comparison, as lending Hancock a little brains, that he might gain a credit he did not deserve. The transaction has unquestionably a good side. The cause would be helped by a spirited, patriotic speech from the handsome, well-born man whose wealth and prodigality gave him prestige. Hancock, too, would be pleased, and so more firmly bound. No American public man ever postponed more utterly the thought of self than Samuel Adams. Only let the cause be helped! No man's end was ever better, but now and then in the means there was a touch of trickery.

When the news of the Boston tea-party reached England, Parliament, naturally much incensed, prepared promptly to retaliate. Says the authority from whom so much has been taken, whose help, however, we are about to lose : —

" This was the boldest stroke which had yet been struck in America. . . . The leaders feared no consequences. And it is certain that ever after this time an opinion was easily instilled and was constantly increasing, that the body of the people had also gone too far to recede, and that an open and general revolt must be the consequence ; and it was not long before actual preparations were visibly making for it in most parts of the province."

While one party thus girded itself for a war that was no longer to consist in words, the other party pressed on with equal spirit. The first retaliatory measure was the Boston Port Bill, which passed about the end of March in spite of the strenuous opposition of the friends of America, and against the best judgment also of Hutchinson and some of the wiser Tories. The faithful Colonel Barré showed at this time a curious inconsistency and confusion of ideas. In a speech which causes one almost to believe that the good veteran at the time had fortified himself for his forensic bout with a nip of Dutch courage, he declared " that he liked the measure, harsh as it was; he liked it for its moderation. . . . He said, I think Boston ought to be punished. *She* is your oldest *son*. (Here the House laughed)." [1] A fortnight later, however, he stood sturdily with Burke and Pownall in strong opposition. By the Port Bill all ships were forbidden to enter or depart from the port of Boston until the contumacious town should agree to pay for the destroyed tea, and in other respects make the king sure of its willingness to submit. Many who had hitherto been brave showed now a disposition to quail. Franklin wrote from England to the four Boston representatives, advising that compensation for the destroyed tea should be made to the East India Company, as a conciliatory step. Samuel Adams dismissed the advice with the contemptuous remark that " Franklin might be a great philosopher, but that he was a bungling politician."

A second act was also passed by Parliament to change the constitution of Massachusetts, according to which act the Council was to be appointed by the crown, the judges were to be appointed and

[1] Tudor's *Otis*, p. 438.

removed by the governor, the juries were to be nominated and summoned by the sheriffs, instead of chosen among the people, and, most serious of all, an end was to be put to the free town meetings, which henceforth were to assemble only as convened by the governor, and to discuss only such topics as he prescribed.

A third act was designed to protect soldiers who might use violence in opposing popular disturbances. Such trials as those of Captain Preston and the men who fired at the Massacre were not to be repeated, but any persons similarly accused were to be sent to Great Britain, or to some other colony, to be judged.

A fourth act, affecting Massachusetts less directly than the three which have been described, was, however, scarcely less exasperating. It was known as the Quebec Act, and had as its ostensible object the settling of the constitution of Canada. But the measure did far more than this. In disregard of the charters and rights of Massachusetts, Connecticut, New York, and Virginia, the boundaries of "Quebec" were extended to the region now occupied by Ohio, Michigan, Indiana, Illinois, and Wisconsin, — the whole Northwest; for all this vast territory an arbitrary rule was decreed. There was to be no habeas corpus; the people were to have no power; the religion of the pope was not only tolerated, but favored. Said Thurlow, in the House of Commons: "It is the only proper constitution for the colonies; it ought

to have been given to them all when first planted;
and it is what all now ought to be reduced to."
Measures were also taken to meet the case of riots,
and special instructions were sent for the arrest, at
a proper and convenient time, of Samuel Adams,
as the "chief of the revolution" above all others.
General Gage, commander-in-chief in America, was
appointed to supersede Hutchinson temporarily,
the quartering of soldiers upon the people was
made legal, and arrangements were entered upon
for increasing the military force.

Meantime in the province, the legislature being
prorogued, and Hutchinson's power practically at
an end, authority lay in the hands of the Committee of Correspondence.

"The governor," says Hutchinson, "retained the title
of captain-general, but he had the title only. The inhabitants in many parts of the province were learning
the use of firearms, but not under the officers of the
regiments to which they belonged. They were forming
themselves into companies for military exercise under
officers of their own choosing, hinting the occasion there
might soon be for employing their arms in defense of
their liberties."

Letters were addressed to the sister colonies,
deploring their silence as to the question of parliamentary authority. Adams, writing to Franklin
for the committee, recapitulates the old positions:

"It will be vain for any to expect that the people of
this country will now be contented with a partial and

temporary relief, or that they will be amused by court promises, while they see not the least relaxation of grievances. By the vigilance and activity of Committees of Correspondence among the several towns in this province, they have been wonderfully enlightened and animated. They are united in sentiment, and their opposition to unconstitutional measures of government is become systematical. Colony communicates freely with colony. There is a common affection among them, — the *communis sensus;* and the whole continent is now become united in sentiment and in opposition to tyranny. Their old good-will and affection for the parent country is not, however, lost. If she returns to her former moderation and good humor, their affection will revive. They wish for nothing more than permanent union with her, upon the condition of equal liberty. This is all they have been contending for, and nothing short of this will, or ought to, satisfy them. When formerly the kings of England have encroached upon the liberties of their subjects, the subjects have thought it their duty to themselves and their posterity to contend with them till they were restored to the footing of the Constitution. The events of such struggles have sometimes proved fatal to crowned heads, — perhaps they have never issued but in establishments of the people's liberties."

Already Hutchinson had written to Dartmouth: " There are some who are ready to go all the lengths of the chief incendiary, who is determined, he says, to get rid of every governor who obstructs them in their course to independency." [1] Samuel Adams himself now wrote to Arthur Lee : —

[1] From letter book in Mass. Archiv., July 10, 1773.

"The body of the people are now in council. Their opposition grows into a system. They are united and resolute. And if the British administration and government do not return to the principles of moderation and equity, the evil, which they profess to aim at preventing by their rigorous measures, will the sooner be brought to pass, viz., *the entire separation and independence of the colonies.*"

News of the Port Bill and of the removal of the seat of government to Salem were received in Boston on the 10th of May, which was at the same time election day. The spirit of the town may be inferred from the voting. Of the five hundred and thirty-six votes cast, Hancock received all, Samuel Adams all but one, and Cushing and Phillips were returned with nearly the same emphasis. The Committee of Correspondence on the same day issued an invitation to the committees of the eight neighboring towns to meet them in convention on the 12th. The towns, Charlestown, Cambridge, Newton, Brookline, Roxbury, Dorchester, Lynn, and Lexington, were promptly on hand by their committees. The proceedings were open to the public. Samuel Adams was moderator, while Joseph Warren, who every day now becomes more conspicuous, managed proceedings on the floor. The injustice and cruelty of the act closing the port were denounced, and the idea indignantly spurned of purchasing exemption from the penalty by paying for the tea. A circular letter prepared by Samuel Adams was sent from the convention to

New England and the middle colonies. The paper, having pointed out the injustice and cruelty of the act by which the inhabitants had been condemned unheard, proceeds : —

"This attack, though made immediately upon us, is doubtless designed for every other colony who shall not surrender their sacred rights and liberties into the hands of an infamous ministry. Now, therefore, is the time when *all* should be united in opposition to this violation of the liberties of all. . . .

"The single question then is, whether you consider Boston as now suffering in the common cause, and sensibly feel and resent the injury and affront offered to her. If you do, and we cannot believe otherwise, may we not, from your approbation of our former conduct in defense of American liberty, rely on your suspending your trade with Great Britain at least, which it is acknowledged will be a great but necessary sacrifice to the cause of liberty, and will effectually defeat the design of this act of revenge? If this should be done, you will please consider it will be through a voluntary suffering, greatly short of what we are called to endure from the immediate hand of tyranny."

The town, too, took action in the matter. May 13 a town meeting was held, at which, after prayer by Dr. Samuel Cooper, William Cooper read the text of the Port Bill, which the meeting straightway pronounced repugnant to law, religion, and common sense. Samuel Adams was moderator. The Tories were out in force, and strove hard to bring the meeting to an agreement to pay for the tea, which course would buy off the ministry from the enforcement of the act. As has been mentioned, even Franklin counseled this ; but a truer instinct caused the Boston Whigs to regard such a course as a virtual admission that in destroying the tea they had done wrong, and a concession therefore of the principle for which they had been contending. They carried the day. Samuel Adams, as moderator, transmitted the action of Boston to all the colonies, accompanying his report with these words : —

"The people receive the edict with indignation. It is expected by their enemies, and feared by some of their friends, that this town singly will not be able to support the cause under so severe a trial. As the very being of every colony, considered as a free people, depends upon the event, a thought so dishonorable to our brethren cannot be entertained as that this town will be left to struggle alone."

Paul Revere, the patriot Mercury, carried the document and also the manifesto of the convention of Committees of Correspondence to New York and Philadelphia, consuming in his ride to the latter town six days. The effect of the papers was marvelous. Philadelphia recommended a congress, and from every quarter came expressions of sympathy and promises of help. During the summer the people in all the New England and middle colonies came together, and for the most part adopted the phrase that "Boston must be regarded as suffering in the common cause." Everywhere there was manful resolution that Boston must be sustained.

Thomas Gage, the new military governor, on the 13th of May, while the town meeting just described was in session, sailed up the harbor in the frigate Lively, the cannon of which, a year later, were to open the battle of Bunker Hill. Landing first at the Castle, he entered the town on the 17th with great circumstance. Crowds filled the streets, and outwardly all was decorous and respectful. Hancock, at the head of the cadets, received him at the wharf; there were proper ceremonies in the council chamber, and a great banquet at Faneuil Hall, where many loyal toasts were drunk. The day was raw and rainy, and the public temper, in spite of the outward show, no better. The instructions of Gage were to proceed promptly against the ringleaders, who, as Dartmouth wrote, were regarded as having sufficiently compromised themselves by the tea-party to receive the heaviest punishment. Gage, however, was reluctant to act, through a well-grounded prudence. Though his force was increased to four regiments, no leader could be arrested without certainty of a popular uprising not to be lightly encountered.

We have now to bid farewell to a figure who has for more than ten years been scarcely less conspicuous in these pages than Samuel Adams himself. So far as the unfortunate Thomas Hutchinson is concerned, the battle is over. As he disappears from the scene, the reader will not feel that it is an undue use of time if a page or two is devoted to a final consideration of him and the class he represented.

History, at this late date, can certainly afford a compassionate word for the Tories, who, besides having been forced to atone in life for the mistake of taking the wrong side by undergoing exile and confiscation, have received while in their graves little but detestation. At the evacuation of Boston, says Mr. Sabine in the "American Loyalists," eleven hundred loyalists retired to Nova Scotia with the army of Gage, of whom one hundred and two were men in official station, eighteen were clergymen, two hundred and thirteen were merchants and traders of Boston, three hundred and eighty-two were farmers and mechanics, in great part from the country. The mere mention of calling and station in the case of the forlorn, expatriated company conveys a suggestion of respectability. There were, in fact, no better men or women in Massachusetts, as regards intelligence, substantial good purpose, and piety. They had made the one great mistake of conceding a supremacy over themselves to distant arbitrary masters, which a population nurtured under the influence of the revived folk-mote ought by no means to have made; but with this exception, the exiles were not at all inferior in worth of every kind to those who drove them forth. The Tories were generally people of substance, their stake in the country was greater even than that of their opponents, their patriotism, no doubt, was to the full as fervent. There is much that is melancholy, of which the world knows but little, connected with their expulsion from the land they sincerely loved. The estates of the Tories were among the fairest; their stately mansions stood on the sightliest hill-brows; the richest and best tilled meadows were their farms; the long avenue, the broad lawn, the trim hedge about the garden, servants, plate, pictures, — the varied circumstance, external and internal, of dignified and generous housekeeping, — for the most part, these things were at the homes of Tories. They loved beauty, dignity, and refinement. It seemed to belong to such forms of life to be generously loyal to king and Parliament, without questioning too narrowly as to rights and taxes. The rude contacts of the town meeting were full of things to offend the taste of a gentleman. The crown officials were courteous, well-born, congenial, having behind them the far-away nobles and the sovereign, who rose in the imagination, unknown and at a distance as they were, surrounded by a brilliant glamour. Was there not a certain meanness in haggling as to the tax which these polite placemen and their superiors might choose to exact, or inquiring narrowly as to their credentials when they chose to exercise authority? The graceful, the chivalrous, the poetic, the spirits over whom these feelings had power, were sure to be Tories. Democracy was something rough and coarse; inde-

pendence, — what was it but a severing of those
connections of which a colonist ought to be proud-
est! It was an easy thing to be led into taking
sides against notions like these. Hence, when the
country rose, many a high-bred, honorable gentleman turned the key in his door, drove down his
line of trees with his refined dame and carefully
guarded children at his side, turned his back on
his handsome estate, and put himself under the
shelter of the proud banner of St. George. It was
a mere temporary refuge, he thought, and, as he
pronounced upon "Sam Adams" and the rabble
a gentlemanly execration, he promised himself a
speedy return, when discipline and loyalty should
have put down the shipyard men and the misled
rustics.

But the return was never to be. The day went
against them; they crowded into ships with the
gates of their country barred forever behind them.
They found themselves penniless upon shores often
bleak and barren, always showing scant hospitality
to outcasts who came empty-handed, and there they
were forced to begin life anew. Having chosen
their side, their lot was inevitable. Nor are the
victors to be harshly judged. There was no unnecessary cruelty shown to the loyalists. The land
they had left belonged to the new order of things,
and, good men and women though they were, there
was nothing for them, and justly so, but to bear
their expatriation and poverty with such fortitude
as they could find. Gray, Clarke, Erving, and

Faneuil, — Royall and Vassall, Fayerweather and Leonard and Sewall, — families of honorable note, bound in with all that was best in the life of the province, — who now can think of their destiny unpitying? Let us glance at the stories of two or three whose names have become familiar to the reader in these pages.

Andrew Oliver, the lieutenant-governor, thought Parliament ought to be supreme. With perfect honesty he upheld his view, believing not only that it was England's right, but that in this sovereignty lay his country's only chance for peace and order. The old Tory atoned heavily for his mistake in life and even in death. It broke his heart when his private letters, sent by Franklin, were used to rouse against him the people's ill-will. In the streets he was exposed to execration. At his funeral the Assembly, taking umbrage because precedence was given to the officers of the army and navy, withdrew, insisting even in presence of the corpse upon an unseemly punctilio. When the body was lowered into the grave the people cheered, and Peter Oliver, the chief justice, was prevented by fear for his life from doing a brother's office at the burial.

Stout Timothy Ruggles was the son of the minister of Rochester. He was six feet six inches tall, and as stalwart in spirit as in frame. He became a soldier, and as the French wars proceeded was greatly distinguished for his address and audacity. At the battle of Lake George he was in important

command, having charge especially of the New
England marksmen, whose sharp fire it was that
caused the defeat of the Baron Dieskau. As a
lawyer, after his return from his campaigns, his
reputation equaled that which he had gained in the
field. His bold, incisive character, and a caustic
wit which he possessed, caused men to give way
before him. John Adams, in 1759, mentions Ruggles first and most prominently in making a comparison of the leading lawyers of the province, and
tells us in what his " grandeur " consisted. Ruggles then lived in Sandwich, but removing soon
after to Hardwick, in Worcester County, he laid
out for himself a noble domain, greatly benefiting
the agriculture of the neighborhood by the introduction of improved methods, by choice stock, and
an application of energy and intelligence in general. In public and professional life he was a rival
of the Otises, father and son. He was at one time
speaker of the Assembly. He was president of the
Stamp Act congress in New York, where his opposition to the patriot positions caused him to be
censured. As the conflict between crown and Assembly proceeded, he was one of Samuel Adams's
most dreaded opponents. Through force of character he did much to infuse a loyalist tone into the
western part of the province, which might have
been fatal to the Whigs, had there not been on the
spot a man of Hawley's strength to counteract it.
In the Assembly he was Hutchinson's main reliance, able to accomplish little on account of the

overwhelming Whig majority, but always consistently working for the ideas in which he believed. When war became certain, " Brigadier " Ruggles was counted as the best of the veterans who still survived from the struggles with the French ; he was much more distinguished than Washington. On the day of the battle of Lexington he organized a force of loyalists two hundred strong. Later he was in arms on Long Island. But fortune no more favored him. As an exile in Nova Scotia he fared as best he could, dying at last in 1798, a man without a country.

But of all the Americans who took the loyal side at the Revolution, Thomas Hutchinson is the most distinguished figure. His early career has been already sketched. His work as a financier had been particularly important, his ability in this direction being conceded by his enemies. John Adams wrote in 1809 : —

"If I was the witch of Endor, I would wake the ghost of Hutchinson and give him absolute power over the currency of the United States and every part of it, provided always that he should meddle with nothing but the currency. As little as I revere his memory, I will acknowledge that he understood the subject of coin and commerce better than any man I ever knew in this country."

Judging him at this distance of time, we certainly can see that Hutchinson was a good and able man in many other directions than as a financier.

His one mistake in fact, for which he was made
to atone so bitterly in life and death, was disloyalty to the folk-mote, that sovereign People so long
discrowned, which on the soil of New England resumed its rights, and fought its hot battle with the
usurper, Prerogative. He should have chosen his
master better; he ought to have known how to
choose better, sprung as he was from the best New
England strain, and nurtured from his cradle in
the atmosphere of freedom. But his choice was
honest, and no one, who examines the evidence,
can say that in his losing cause he did not fight
his guns like a man, — a sleepless, able captain
who went down at last with his ship. He hoped,
no doubt, for advancement for himself and his
sons, stood in some undue awe, natural enough in
a colonist, before the king and English nobles, and
came to feel a personal hatred for the men who
opposed him, so that he could no more do them
justice than they could do it to him. It has been
charged that, for the sake of winning favor with
the people, he wrote letters of a character likely to
give them pleasure, which he exhibited in public
as letters which he intended to send to persons in
power; that, however, they were never sent; that,
the impression on the minds of the people having
been produced, the letters were destroyed. The
charge has been confidently made, but it has no
grounds. He was above a trick so discreditable;
it is as inconsistent with his general character as
were some of the alleged shortcomings of Samuel

Adams with his. We may admit the faults of
Hutchinson, that he was sometimes subservient,
that he sometimes bore malice, sometimes, possibly, for a moment under temptation stooped to
duplicity, though proof of this is rare indeed.
Nevertheless, the obloquy of which he has been
the victim is for the most part quite undeserved,
and any lover of fair play will feel that it ought to
be refuted. He held, to be sure, many offices; it
is rather the case, however, that they were thrust
upon him than that he sought them; they were
miserably paid, excepting the governorship, to
which he attained only at a late period; they were
positions of burden rather than honor; his administration of his trusts in every point, excepting as
he favored parliamentary supremacy, was wise and
faithful, according to the testimony of all. He has
been called covetous; rather he sacrificed his means
for what he thought the public good, and when, as
the cause of the king went down, his beautiful
home and fine fortune underwent confiscation, he
speaks of the loss in his diary and private letters
with the dignified equanimity of a high-minded
philosopher.

Pleasant traditions of the most royal governor
yet linger about Milton Hill, the spot which he
loved above all others. Old people are still there
who have heard from their grandparents the story
of Hutchinson's leave-taking, on the June day
when at length the soldiers had come with Gage,
and he was about setting out for England to give

the king the account of his stewardship. As he stepped forth from his door the beautiful prospect was before him, the Neponset winding through the meadows waving for the scythe, the villages on the higher ground, the broad blue harbor, unfolded from the wharves to the Boston Light, with the ships on its breast, and the flag above the Castle. He looked up, no doubt, into the branches of the thrifty buttonwoods he had planted, with a good-by glance, then turned his back upon it all, with no thought that it was for the last time. He went down the road on foot, affably greeting his neighbors, Whig and Tory, for the genial magnate was on the best terms with all. At the foot of the hill, his coach, which the next year was taken to Cambridge and appropriated to the use of Washington, received him and carried him to Dorchester Neck, whence in his barge he proceeded to the man-of-war Minerva, and so passed away forever.

All that he possessed was confiscated, even the dust of his forefathers, and those still nearer ; and here may be mentioned a circumstance in which the grotesque and the melancholy are strangely commingled. In his tomb on Copp's Hill lay his father and grandfather, and also his wife, whose memory he tenderly cherished. He wrote from England a moving letter to his son, asking that the coffin might be removed to Milton, to a new tomb to be there built, near the home to which he expected to return, prescribing carefully the steps to be taken, that all might be done reverently.

But the son, leaving with the other Tories at the time of the evacuation of Boston, never found the opportunity. The tomb with its dead, like everything else belonging to the old governor, was sold. The canny patriot who bought it had a thrift as close as that of the character in the "Pirates of Penzance," who appropriates in the old burying-ground on his freshly purchased estate the ancestors of the former possessor. "I do not know whose ancestors they may formerly have been, but they are now mine," and so he weeps among their graves upon proper occasion. The governor's tomb had before it a stone bearing the name "Hutchinson," and, underneath, the finely-carved escutcheon of the family. A great-grandson of the governor, on a pious pilgrimage to the spot, found the old lettering erased. The armorial bearings, however, remained distinct and handsome, and over them, as if they were his own, the new proprietor had caused his own name to be carved. The coat of arms he felt apparently to be part of his bargain; so, too, the buried Hutchinsons beneath. The stone is still to be seen in its place above the tomb on Copp's Hill, and under it no doubt lies, with his appropriated ancestors, the clever Whig, whose name it now bears, snugly tucked in, like a hermit-crab in his stolen shell, awaiting Gabriel's trump.

When Hutchinson reached England his reception was of the best. Lord Dartmouth carried him to the king without giving him time to change his clothes after the journey. A conversation of an hour or two took place, of which he has left a careful report, in which both king and governor appear to good advantage. He was offered a baronetcy, and was as well received as possible by the people in power. His diary, just given to the world, offers an unaffected account of his experiences, from which the conclusion is irresistible that he bore himself well in his new surroundings, was felt by good men to have played a creditable part, and made all whom he met regard him as a man of good sense. Not Samuel Adams himself could have moved with a stricter conformity to Puritan standards in the midst of a life often frivolous and corrupt. In fact, the two men, much as they hated one another, were in some respects alike. In point of adroitness they were not ill-matched; each sought what he believed to be his country's good, with sincere patriotism, in his separate way; there was in each the same indefatigability, the same deep gravity of character, combined with a genial manner. From the fashionable amusements of London Hutchinson turned with disgust. Garrick utterly displeased him; he could see nothing attractive in the sports which he was taken to witness. After John Adams's fashion, he notes carefully each Sunday the preacher and the sermon. Like the " chief incendiary," his ideal community would have been his dear Boston straitened into a " Christian Sparta." " I assure you," he writes, " I had rather die in a little country farm-

house in New England, than in the best nobleman's seat in Old England, and have therefore
given no ear to any proposal of settling here." So
frequently in these pages we have the utterances
of a homesick spirit, that would gladly have left
the splendors and attentions of the court of George
III. to return to the land he sincerely loved. The
exile was keenly sensitive to opprobrium, and de-
fends himself in his letters and sometimes in more
formal ways. Speaking of his letter books left behind in his house at Milton, now in the Massachusetts archives, and from which much has been
quoted in this volume, he says : —

"When I was threatened by the tea-mobs, I carried
them to Milton, and when I was obliged to return to the
Castle upon Gen. Gage's arrival, it did not come into
my mind where I had put them. I am sure there is
nothing in them but what will evidence an upright aim,
and an endeavor to keep off the miseries which in spite
of my endeavors a few men have brought upon the
country ; and if they will take the whole of them, they
will find a uniform plan for preserving the authority of
Parliament, and at the same time indulging the colonies
in every point in which the people imagined they were
aggrieved."

To attacks which were made upon him by the
Whigs in Parliament he replied by a formal " Vin-
dication," in which he speaks of himself in the
third person. The paper was not printed then,
and appears now for the first time in the diary.
It is a document full of clearness and dignity, and

has much interest to the student of our Revolutionary history. A passage from this follows : —

"It is asserted that no one fact has ever appeared to have been materially misrepresented by him, nor any one proposal made unfriendly to the rights and liberties of mankind in general, or tending to take from the province of which he was governor, the privileges enjoyed by its charter, or any powers or privileges from the inhabitants of the colonies, which can be made to consist with their relation to Parliament as the supreme authority of the British dominions. . . .

"It is a remark more ancient than any British colony that ' Gubernatorum vituperatio populo placet,' and every governor of Massachusetts Bay, for near a century past, has by experience found the truth of it."

With this outburst we dismiss the ruined exile from our attention.

CHAPTER XVIII

PREPARATIONS FOR THE FIRST CONGRESS

As Hutchinson looked his last upon Boston harbor, having his mind cheered by a warm address, expressing for him deep respect, which had been sent in to him by a hundred and twenty respectable merchants, and by a second similar address coming from the lawyers, he must have heard the tolling of the bells that announced the closing of the port of Boston in retaliation for the destruction of the tea.

The steps which the government had taken were decided enough, but the instrument through whom they were to be carried into execution was a man far different from the astute, energetic Hutchinson. Gage was mild in temper, and of very moderate ability. His disposition was to treat Boston good-naturedly, and it was only when fortified by others that he made up his mind to put the Port Bill in force. The Whig leaders, relieved from the opposition of their great antagonist, manoeuvred and drove forward relentlessly, outwitting or overriding the general at every step, until his weak amiability gave way to outbreaks of testy ill-nature.

The General Court which had convened on the

26th of May was memorable as the last under the colonial charter. The other colonies, as well as Massachusetts, were now ripe for the Congress, and Samuel Adams, who in the gathering Revolution had attained in his own province an almost autocratic ascendency, prepared to secure the nomination of delegates. For a few days nothing could be done, for Gage prorogued the court, to meet early in June at Salem. The session presently took place in that town, and never had the hand of the great master been so deft and at the same time so daring; one moment pulling strings with the nicest caution, the next it was, as it were, clenched and delivered in a telling blow. But, whether in the form of flattering palm or doubled fist, it ruled the hour omnipotently, and brought to pass a triumphant success.

Samuel Adams, working with the Committee of Correspondence to the last moment, then hurrying over the country roads to Salem, was late in reaching the place of meeting, giving much anxiety to the patriots, who followed him now like children, and much joy to the Tories, for the report spread that at last the soldiers had seized him. While the Assembly waited, he entered the hall. The Tories, made bold by the presence in town of a general as chief magistrate, with soldiers at his back, bore themselves with much arrogance. The pressure of the crowd of spectators in the hall in which the court was to assemble was considerable, and a group of Tories had taken possession of the space about the chair appropriated to the clerk. When Samuel Adams entered, one of their number, in a gold-laced coat and otherwise richly dressed, had seated himself in the chair, which he seemed disposed to retain. "Mr. Speaker, where is the place for your clerk?" said Samuel Adams, with his eyes fixed upon the intruder and the group that surrounded him. The speaker pointed to the chair and desk. "Sir," said Mr. Adams, "my company will not be pleasant to the gentlemen who occupy it. I trust they will remove to another part of the house." The Tories gave way before him, and his bearing soon dispelled the idea, with which some of the Tories had flattered themselves, that Samuel Adams had been delayed by his fears.

The House at once after organization protested against the removal from Boston. The Council presented to the governor a respectful address; but when at last a wish was expressed that his administration might be a happy contrast to that of his two immediate predecessors, Gage angrily interrupted the chairman, refused to listen farther, and denounced the address as insulting to the king and Privy Council, and to himself. Affairs were indeed critical. Boston, with many of its Whigs weak-kneed and its latent Toryism all brought to the surface and made demonstrative by the display of power by the ministry, was in danger of adopting a measure for giving compensation for the tea, and perhaps going still farther in the path of concession, to win relief from the calamity that had come. A town meeting was called. Samuel Adams could not be in two places at once, and to Joseph Warren was left the responsibility of bringing things to a good issue. Warren, gallant as he was, felt his heart sink. He was like a general of division, who, having fought long with great effect under the eye of an old field-marshal, suddenly in a day of the utmost danger finds himself intrusted with an independent command. He begged the generalissimo to come back. " I think your attendance can by no means be dispensed with over Friday, as I believe we shall have a warm engagement." But on that very day — it was the 17th of June, one year before Bunker Hill — there was work to be done at Salem too, and Warren had to fight it out by himself. With John Adams in the chair as moderator, the lieutenant on the floor brought all to a victorious issue. At that time he first realized his own great power and became self-reliant. Meanwhile Samuel Adams, in his field, having burrowed for days like a skillful engineer, at length sprung his mine, and in the most audacious of assaults carried the position.

A larger number of representatives had appeared than ever before, drawn together by the greatness of the crisis, many of whom were disposed to be reactionary, if not actually Tories. A committee of nine on the state of the province, consisting of the principal members of the Assembly, and of which Samuel Adams was chairman, had been appointed in May before the prorogation. By this committee all action must be initiated. If a hint should reach Gage that the Assembly were engaged in the election of delegates to a Congress, it was known that he would at once prorogue the court to prevent such action. Samuel Adams studied his problem warily. Sounding the members of his committee, he found some of them doubtful in the cause. In particular Daniel Leonard of Taunton, a man of ability, who is now known to have been one of Hutchinson's sharpest writers, was to be dreaded. The plan pursued was to entertain in meetings of the committee vague propositions for conciliation, until the lukewarm or Tory members should form the idea that some compromise was likely to be proposed. Meantime Samuel Adams secretly made sure of those in the committee upon whom he could rely, and gradually ascertained precisely what other members of the House could be counted upon. All must be done with the most velvet-footed caution, and days must pass. A sufficient majority must be secured and instructed, so that the measure might be carried with little debate, as soon as proposed, and no hint of it reach Gage.

The days passed. At meetings of the committee the old cat purred of conciliation with half-closed, sleepy eyes, until the doubtful men were completely deceived. Leonard himself, at length, went home to Taunton on legal business, feeling that, if Sam Adams was ready to yield, there was no need of being watchful. At once Adams set one of his best lieutenants, James Warren of Plymouth, an apt and faithful pupil, to keep the committee in play, while he worked as secretly but more actively outside. At first he was sure of but five; in two days he could count on thirty; at length he had under his hand a majority, and all was ready. One feels that, if sharp-eyed Hutchinson had been on the spot, there would have been trouble. Gage, however, satisfied with his show of energy in rebuking the Council, and abundantly assured that the temper of the Assembly was peaceful, looked amiably on with his hands folded.

The spring at last was like lightning. On Friday, the 17th of June, one hundred and twenty-nine members were present. Sam Adams, at the head of the committee on the state of the province, suddenly caused the door to be locked, and charged the doorkeeper to let no one in or out. The next instant a series of resolves was produced providing for the appointment of James Bowdoin, Thomas Cushing, Samuel Adams, John Adams, and Robert Treat Paine, to meet the delegates of other colonial Assemblies, on the 1st of September, at Philadelphia, or any other place that should be decided upon. The House was at once in an uproar, and an earnest effort was made to choke off the measure. But the majority rose in its power; the lieutenants, secretly drilled, were each in place, and the arch conspirator, cool and genial, but adroit and forceful as any man who ever ruled a senate, held every string in his hand. Attempts were made by Tory members to leave the hall, when it became plain how things must go. The doorkeeper, beset and browbeaten by heated men, grew uneasy under the responsibility which was placed upon him; whereupon Sam Adams, with a curious inversion of the great Cromwellian precedent, but with a spirit as self-reliant and straightforward as that of the other great Puritan brewer himself, did not turn his Parliament out, but bolted them in. Making sure that the door was still fast, he put the key into his own pocket.

Some debate there must be, and while it went forward a Tory member, pleading sickness, in some way did manage to make his escape, and hurried at once to Gage with the news. Forthwith the general prepared the shortest possible message of prorogation, and his secretary hurried with it to the hall. The door was still locked, with the key in Samuel Adams's pocket, and even Thomas Flucker, Esquire, no inconsiderable personage himself, and now the messenger of the governor and commander-in-chief, demanded admission in vain. The fact that he was without was imparted to the speaker, who communicated it formally to the House, but the majority ordered the door to be kept fast. By this time rumors of a great legislative *coup d'état* were flying through the town, and a crowd began to collect in the approaches to

the hall.   To these, for want of a better audience,
and also to several members of the House who had
come late to the session, Flucker read his message.
No tactics, meantime, could long stave off the end
at which Sam Adams aimed.   The Tories succumbed, the doubtful went over in a troop to the
Whig side, the delegates were elected with only
twelve dissenting voices, and five hundred pounds
were voted to pay their expenses.   Since no money
could be drawn from the public treasury without
the governor's consent, every town in the province
was assessed in proportion to its last tax-list, to
provide the sum.   Resolves were then passed for
the relief of Boston and Charlestown, as the special sufferers by the Port Bill, renouncing the use
of tea and all goods and manufactures coming from
Great Britain, and encouraging home productions
to the utmost.   All that was necessary having been
fully and satisfactorily performed, Mr. Flucker was
admitted, the Assembly with all grace submitted
to the mandate of prorogation, and the members
scattered.   The horse was stolen, and General Gage
locked the barn-door with great vigor.

Samuel Adams dispatched the news by printed
circular to the selectmen of the towns, with the
apportionment made in each case for the fund to
defray the expenses of the delegates, and himself
received the sums that were sent.   Notice was sent,
too, by Cushing, as speaker, to all the colonies, informing them of the action of Massachusetts.   This
it was which had been generally awaited, and now,

following in her wake, the thirteen colonies, from
New Hampshire to Georgia, prepared for the great
Congress at Philadelphia on September 1.

The interval between the prorogation of the
legislature and the departure of the delegates to
Philadelphia was by no means an idle one for the
patriots. As chairman of the committees for devising plans for the relief of the poor, and distributing the donations which began to arrive from all
quarters, Samuel Adams was kept busy. On the
27th of June occurred a town meeting, memorable
as being the last occasion upon which the Tories
made an effort to stem in that community the
course of the Revolution; after this they threw
themselves back upon the military power. Taking
advantage of the public distress, which became
every day greater, a meeting was called by them
at Faneuil Hall. In the enforced idleness of all
classes, a multitude attended, and, as usual, the
meeting adjourned to the Old South. A few weeks
previous, a "solemn league and covenant" against
using British productions of every kind had been
drawn up by Warren, and had received many signatures. This document having been read, a Tory
denounced it, and presently after a vote of censure
was moved upon the Committee of Correspondence,
providing also for its annihilation. Samuel Adams, the moderator, quickly left the chair to Cushing, taking his place on the floor as champion of
the committee of which he had been the creator
and the ruling spirit. The debate was long and

vehement, lasting until dark of the long June day, and was resumed the following forenoon. It was conducted in the presence of an audience of ruined men; merchants whose idle ships had nothing before them but to rot at the wharves, mechanics whose labor had suddenly become a drug in the market, sailors to whom the sea was barred. A slight yielding from the course into which the Whigs had struck would remove at once the incubus. It was not at all necessary to become Tories; certain small concessions, like the payment for the tea and an admission that its destruction had been a mistake, would be enough. Even Josiah Quincy had advised moderation at the time, and now great patriots like Franklin declared this to be a proper step.

To Samuel Adams, who saw no safety in such a course, the time was indeed critical. But when the question was put as to the annihilation of the committee, the meeting "*by a great majority*" [1] voted in the negative, and then almost unanimously the resolve passed: "That the town bear open testimony that they are abundantly satisfied of the upright intentions and much approve of the honest zeal of the Committee of Correspondence, and desire that they will persevere with their usual activity and firmness, continuing steadfast in the way of well-doing." This was an indorsement of an unyielding course. The Tories, so utterly defeated

[1] These words in the town records are underscored by William Cooper, showing his strong feeling.

in town meeting, signed a protest, which was widely
distributed, against the "solemn league and covenant;" but their sleepless and implacable opponent stormed at them as "Candidus" from the
columns of the "Boston Gazette." The "solemn
league and covenant" spread throughout the Massachusetts towns, through all New England, and
into the colonies in general, becoming a most formidable non-importation agreement, which the
royal governors denounced in vain.

The patriots now lived in daily fear of the arrest
of Samuel Adams and his prominent supporters.
Urgent letters are extant, entreating him to be on
his guard; steps were taken to make his house
more secure. But Gage delayed; the matter was
left largely to his discretion, and he was quite justified in thinking it would be imprudent. A public
seizure would have been the height of rashness,
and a private arrest would have brought upon the
British force, still far from large, though it was
gradually increasing, such an avalanche of patriots
as would infallibly have crushed it. It came very
near being the case that positive orders were sent
to Gage for the seizure. Says Hutchinson: "The
lords of the Privy Council had their pens in their
hands in order to sign the warrant to apprehend
Adams, Molineux, and other principal incendiaries,
try them, and, if found guilty, put them to death."
Lord Mansfield told Hutchinson that the warrant
was not sent, "because the attorney and solicitor
general were in doubt whether the evidence was

sufficient to convict them; but he said things would never be right until some of them were brought over."

More insidious assaults were made, however, without success. Hutchinson in his day had known Adams too well to try such means. "Why hath not Mr. Adams been taken off from his opposition by an office?" inquired members of the ministry. "Such is the obstinacy and inflexible disposition of the man," was the reply, "that he never would be conciliated by any office of gift whatever." Gage was less wise, and made a trial which had an ignominious failure. In 1818 Mr. Adams's daughter related: The governor sent, by Colonel Fenton, who commanded one of the newly arrived regiments, a confidential and verbal message, promising Adams great gifts and advancement if he would recede, and saying it was the advice of Governor Gage to him not to incur the further displeasure of his majesty. Adams listened with apparent interest to this recital, until the messenger had concluded. Then rising, he replied, glowing with indignation: "Sir, I trust I have long since made my peace with the King of kings. No personal consideration shall induce me to abandon the righteous cause of my country. Tell Governor Gage it is the advice of Samuel Adams to him no longer to insult the feelings of an exasperated people." There is some reason also for supposing that he was offered afterward a pension of two thousand guineas, and a patent of nobility in the American peerage which was projected.

Early in August Gage received official news of the act of Parliament changing the charter, which had been for some time unofficially known, and instructions to put it at once in force. Thirty-six councilors were nominated by the crown, according to the new method, called the "mandamus" councilors; of these twenty-four accepted. They at once met, and other arbitrary measures were taken. The Committee of Correspondence retaliated by recommending that all men should practice military drill, and that a Provincial Congress should be summoned. Preliminary to this the counties met in convention, one hundred and fifty delegates from the towns of Middlesex assembling at Concord, and the towns of Essex convening at Ipswich. Gage, meantime, took cannon from Cambridge, and in defiance of the protests of the selectmen began to fortify Boston Neck.

During the summer of 1774, Samuel Adams while preparing for his departure to Philadelphia, continued to direct affairs in straitened Boston. The committees of which he was the chairman made gifts and afforded employment to the poor in the repairing of streets and building of wharves on the town's land. His correspondence continues. To R. H. Lee he writes: "It is the virtue of the yeomanry we are chiefly to depend upon." The sentence lets us know the kind of democracy in which Adams believed. His disposition was to

put the fullest reliance upon the people, yet sometimes he is careful to specify that it is the "yeomanry" or "the *bulk* of the people" who are to be
built upon. As he distrusted the fine world which
was ready to cringe before power, he recognized,
too, the possibility of danger at the other end of
the scale, from the "mob." In March of the present year there had been a riot at Marblehead,
the people burning lawlessly a small-pox hospital.
Through Elbridge Gerry the facts came to Samuel
Adams, and the Assembly were petitioned for
armed assistance. It would have been mortifying
to the patriots and a triumph to the Tories if the
Assembly had been brought to use arms against
the people. The House delayed, probably through
Adams's influence, and the matter meanwhile fortunately quieted itself. At a later time, however,
in the Shays rebellion, we shall find the man of
the town meeting standing as sternly against the
misguided people as he ever did against Tory or
crown official. "Vox populi vox Dei" was a sentiment to which he fully subscribed, but it must be
the voice of the *substantial* people.

Donations came from near and far to the support of suffering Boston. Salem and the ports
adjacent commonly received what was sent, and
thence the carriage was made by land to the centre.
As the time drew near for the departure to Philadelphia, Samuel Adams gave his parting charge to
the Committee of Correspondence, a charge which
they spoke of as "instructions," from which they

must on no account deviate, so authoritative had his word become. The very last business performed was to arrange for a convention of deputies from Boston and the adjoining towns at some inland point, out of the way of interruptions. This, it was felt, might pave the way for a general congress of the province, which was likely before long to be wanted. The execution of this project, and the general direction of affairs, was to lie with Joseph Warren, who, since the " Port Bill meeting" of June 17, had fully found his powers, and during the short remnant of his life was to show himself a man of great executive force.

And now let us pause for a moment, as Samuel Adams is on the point of leaving Massachusetts for the first time, to look at his home life.

He still occupied the house in Purchase Street, the estate connected with which had, as time went forward, through the carelessness of its preoccupied owner, become narrowed to a scanty tract. It was nevertheless a sightly place, from which stretched seaward before the eye the island-studded harbor, with the many ships, the bastions of the Castle, low lying to the right, and landward the town, rising fair upon its hills. Samuel Adams, shortly before this time, had been able, probably with the help of friends, to put his home in good order, and managed to be hospitable. For apparently life went forward in his home, if frugally, not parsimoniously, his admirable wife making it possible for him, from his small income as clerk of the House, to maintain a decent housekeeping. His son, now twenty-two years old, was studying medicine with Dr. Warren, after a course at Harvard, a young man for whom much could be hoped. His daughter was a promising girl of seventeen. With the young people and their intimates the father was cordial and genial. He had an ear for music and a pleasant voice in singing, a practice which he much enjoyed. The house was strictly religious; grace was said at each meal, and the Bible is still preserved from which some member of the household read aloud each night. Old Surry, a slave woman given to Mrs. Adams in 1765, and who was freed upon coming into her possession, lived in the family nearly fifty years, showing devoted attachment. When slavery was abolished in Massachusetts, papers of manumission were made out for her in due form; but these she threw into the fire in anger, saying she had lived too long to be trifled with. The servant boy, whom Samuel Adams carefully and kindly reared, became afterwards a mechanic of character, and worked efficiently in his former master's behalf when at length in old age Adams was proposed for governor. Nor must Queue be forgotten, the big, intelligent Newfoundland dog, who appreciated perfectly what was due to his position as the dog of Sam Adams. He had a vast antipathy to the British uniform. He was cut and shot in several places by soldiers, in retaliation for his own sharp attacks; for the patriotic Queue anticipated even the " embattled farmers" of Concord bridge in inaugurating hostilities, and bore to his grave honorable scars from his fierce encounters. The upholders of the house of Hanover had received no heartier bites than those of Queue since the days of the Jacobites.

Until now, in his fifty-third year, Samuel Adams had never left his native town except for places a few miles distant. The expenses of the journey and the sojourn in Philadelphia were arranged for by the legislative appropriation. But the critical society of a populous town, and the picked men of the thirteen colonies were to be encountered. A certain sumptuousness in living and apparel would be not only fitting but necessary in the deputies, that the great province which they represented might suffer no dishonor. Samuel Adams himself probably would have been quite satisfied to appear in the old red coat of 1770 in which Copley had painted him, and which no doubt his wife's careful darning still held together; but his townsmen arranged it differently. The story will be best told in the words of a writer of the time : —

"The ultimate wish and desire of the *high* government party is to get Samuel Adams out of the way, when they think they may accomplish every of their plans; but, however some may despise him, he has certainly very many friends. For, not long since, some persons (their names unknown) sent and asked his permission to build him a new barn, the old one being decayed, which was executed in a few days. A second sent to ask leave to repair his house, which was thoroughly effected soon. A third sent to beg the favor of him to call at a tailor's shop, and be measured for a suit of clothes, and choose his cloth, which were finished and sent home for his acceptance. A fourth presented him with a new wig, a fifth with a new hat, a sixth with six pair of the best silk hose, a seventh with six pair of fine thread ditto, an eighth with six pair of shoes, and a ninth modestly inquired of him whether his finances were not rather low than otherwise. He replied it was true that was the case, but he was very indifferent about these matters, so that his *poor* abilities were of any service to the public; upon which the gentleman obliged him to accept of a purse containing about fifteen or twenty Johannes." [1]

On the 10th of August the four delegates set forth: Thomas Cushing, Samuel and John Adams, and Robert Treat Paine. Bowdoin was unfortunately kept at home by the sickness of his wife. They left the house of Cushing in considerable state. "Am told," says John Andrews, "they made a very respectable parade in sight of five of the regiments encamped on the Common, being in a coach and four, preceded by two white servants well mounted and armed, with four blacks behind in livery, two on horseback and two footmen." At Watertown they dined with a large number of their

[1] John Andrews to William Barrell, Boston, August 11, 1774. *Mass. Hist. Soc. Coll.* 1865. The new suit was given just before the departure for Philadelphia.

friends, who drove out thither for the final parting.
Hence they proceeded in a coach arranged for their
special convenience. The journey, with the great
attentions they received, is graphically related in
the diary of John Adams, who was, as the reader
of these pages by this time well knows, a most
admirable observer and reporter, in part for the
same reason Lowell gives for Margaret Fuller's
sharpness : —

> "A person must surely see well, if he try,
> The whole of whose being 's a capital I."

In Connecticut they were received with great
circumstance. Cavalcades accompanied them from
town to town.

"At four we made New Haven. Seven miles out of
town, at a tavern, we met a great number of carriages
and horsemen who had come out to meet us. The
sheriff of the county, and constable of the town, and
the justices of the peace were in the train. As we were
coming, we met others to the amount of I know not
what number. As we came into the town, all the bells
in town were set to ringing, and the people, men, women,
and children, were crowding at the doors and windows
as if it was to see a coronation. At nine o'clock the
cannon were fired, about a dozen guns, I think."

Bears, the landlord of the tavern, afterwards
tells them : "The parade which was made to introduce us into town was a sudden proposal in order
to divert the populace from erecting a liberty pole,"
engineered by the Tories.

Rarely enough in his life did Sam Adams take a holiday, and now one thinks that, with so much that was tremendous impending, a man could hardly be in a mood for the enjoyment of new scenes and people, and the reception of honors, however flattering. He had long lived, however, with his head in the lion's mouth, and, though the beast roared as never before, he had good reason to feel that in the general rising of America, of which he everywhere found tokens, the bite might at last be risked. As they passed onward in the pleasant summer weather, there was no doubt much to enjoy; but whether his experiences were agreeable or otherwise, of matters purely personal he makes no more mention now than at other times. The two kinsmen, so long already companions, and now in closer relations than ever, good friends though they were, were in some points strangely unlike. Honest John parades himself artlessly in every page he writes, now in self-chastening, now in comfortable self-complacency. Reticent Sam, on the other hand, though he lived with the pen in his hand, and wrote reams every year which went into print, is as silent as to himself as if he had been dumb. Whether he was elated or discouraged, happy or wretched, his mood rarely leaves on his page any trace of itself.

The biographer of Samuel Adams, therefore, is thankful enough for the help rendered him by the unreserved Hutchinson and the naïve chat of the Braintree statesman. So in the agreeable record of the latter we follow the deputies onward. Each Sunday we know the country parson whose preaching they experience, his text, his subject, perhaps the heads of his discourse. At each stage we know not so well the name of the town as that of the cheerful landlord with whom they lodge. Starting from Coolidge's in Watertown, we have seen them bring up at Isaac Bears's in New Haven, — the curt host who dampens any self-complacency they may incline to feel by declaring the demonstration in their honor to be nothing but a Tory device to head off the raising of a liberty pole. Thence on to Curtiss's, to Quintard's, to Fitch's, Haviland's, Cock's, and Day's, until at length they drive up before Hull's, "The Bunch of Grapes," in New York. Here they rest for several days, seeing the town under the guidance of McDougall, afterwards major-general, and meeting John Morin Scott, John Jay, Duane, and members of the great Livingston family, as they had met in Connecticut Silas Deane and Roger Sherman.

On the 27th they reached Princeton, where, attending the college prayers, they find the Scotch president, Dr. Witherspoon, "as high a son of liberty as any man in America." They cross the Delaware at Trenton, a pleasant summer transit. The men of Glover's amphibious regiment who are to struggle with ice cakes here in a year or two are still quietly fishing off Marblehead, and the Hessians of Colonel Rahl are still free and happy farmers in the petty villages about Marburg and

Cassel. In Philadelphia presently after, "dirty and fatigued," they take lodgings, the four Massachusetts delegates together, "with Miss Jane Port in Arch Street."

CHAPTER XIX

On September 5 the delegates, fifty-three in number, met at the city tavern, then viewed the famous hall built for the Society of House Carpenters, and concluded it was sufficient for their purpose. Peyton Randolph of Virginia was made chairman, and Charles Thomson secretary. The Massachusetts delegates had adopted the policy of keeping in the background, influenced greatly, no doubt, by an incident that happened as they were on the point of entering Philadelphia, and which John Adams thus detailed in his old age: —

"We were met at Frankfort by Dr. Rush, Mr. Mifflin, Mr. Bayard, and several other of the most active sons of liberty in Philadelphia, who desired a conference with us. We invited them to take tea with us in a private apartment. They asked leave to give us some information and advice, which we thankfully granted. They represented to us that the friends of government in Boston and in the Eastern states had represented us to the Middle and South as four desperate adventurers. 'Mr. Cushing was a harmless kind of man, but poor, and wholly dependent upon his popularity for his subsistence. Mr. Samuel Adams was a very artful, designing man, but desperately poor, and wholly dependent on his popularity with the lowest vulgar for his living. John Adams and Mr. Paine were two young lawyers, of no great talents, reputation, or weight, who had no other means of raising themselves into consequence than by courting popularity.' We were all suspected of wishing independence. Now, said they, you must not utter the word independence, nor give the least hint or insinuation of the idea, either in Congress, or any private conversation; if you do, you are undone; for independence is as unpopular in all the Middle and South as the Stamp Act itself. No man dares to speak of it. . . . You are thought to be too warm. You must not come forward with any bold measure; you must not pretend to take the lead. You know Virginia is the most popular state in the Union — very proud — they think they have a right to lead. The South and Middle are too much disposed to yield it. . . . This was plain dealing, but it made a deep impression. That conversation has given a coloring to the whole policy of the United States from that day to this (1822)."

As the presidency of Congress was given to Virginia, so the first memorable event of the session was an impassioned speech by Patrick Henry, reciting the colonial wrongs, the necessity of union, and of the preservation of the democratic part of the constitution. Applause was general, and a debate followed, in which for the most part only the Southern members appeared, though John Jay took part. Samuel Adams was without doubt the most conspicuous and also the most dreaded member of the body. All knew that he had been especially singled out as the mark of royal vengeance;

with the leading men he had long been in correspondence; his leadership in the most populous
colony, which had so far borne the brunt of the
struggle, was a familiar fact, as was also his authorship of the documents and measures which had
done most to bring about a crisis. His views were
generally felt to be quite too extreme.

His first move was one of the most long-headed
proceedings of his whole career, — a wily master-
stroke even for him. In the differences of religious belief, so many of the members holding to
their views with ardent intolerance, it was felt by
many to be quite inexpedient to open the Congress
formally, after the preliminaries were arranged,
with prayer. Samuel Adams, however, sternest
of the Puritans, and well known to hate everything
that had to do with prelacy ten times more because
a large proportion of the Episcopalians in the colonies held the popular cause in contempt, electri-
fied friend and foe by moving that the Rev. Mr.
Duché, an Episcopal clergyman, should be asked
to open their deliberations with a religious service.
Few acts in his career, probably, cost him a greater
sacrifice, and few acts were really more effective.
A rumor came at the moment that Boston had
been bombarded. In the excitement that prevailed Mr. Duché performed the service impres-
sively, although his conduct afterward proved him
to be a wretched character.[1] "Joseph Reed, the
leading lawyer of Philadelphia," says John Adams,

[1] Graydon's *Memoirs*, p. 98, note.

"returned with us to our lodgings. He says we never were guilty of a more masterly stroke of policy than in moving that Mr. Duché might read prayers. It has had a very good effect." If Prynne in the Long Parliament had asked for the prayers of Laud, the sensation could not have been greater. Before such a stretch of catholicity, the members became ashamed of their divisions, and a spirit of harmony, quite new and beyond measure salutary, came to prevail.

Immediately afterward a committee was formed, the description of whose duties recalls the language used by the Boston town meeting in 1772, when the Committee of Correspondence was formed. The committee was " to state the rights of the colonies in general, the several instances in which those rights are violated and infringed, and the means most proper to be pursued for obtaining a restoration of them." The committee was to consist of two delegates from each province, Samuel and John Adams acting for Massachusetts. Another committee was also appointed to examine and report the several statutes which affected trade and manufactures.

Meantime the plans concerted between Samuel Adams on the one hand, and Warren with the home-keeping patriots on the other, were carried to fulfillment. Warren engineered the famous " Suffolk Resolves," that " no obedience was due to either or any part of the recent acts of Parliament, which are rejected as the attempts of a wicked administration to enslave America." The determination was expressed to remain on the defensive so long as such conduct might be vindicated by the principles of reason and self-preservation, but no longer, and to seize as hostages the servants of the crown as an offset to the apprehension of any persons in Suffolk County who had rendered themselves conspicuous in the defense of violated liberty. A provincial congress was recommended, and all tax-collectors were exhorted to retain moneys in their hands until government should be constitutionally organized. So far there had been no utterance quite so bold as this, and Warren at once committed his resolves to the faithful saddlebags of prompt Paul Revere, who conveyed them in six days to the banks of the Schuylkill. The hosts now faced each other with weapons drawn, and any day might see an encounter.

Samuel Adams was believed by the moderate men and the Tories to manage things both in and out of Congress.

"While the two parties in Congress remained thus during three weeks on an equal balance, the republicans were calling to their assistance the aid of their factions without. Continued expresses were employed between Philadelphia and Boston. These were under the management of Samuel Adams, — a man who, though by no means remarkable for brilliant abilities, yet is equal to most men in popular intrigue and the management of a faction. He eats little, drinks little, sleeps little, thinks much, and is most decisive and indefatigable in the pursuit of his objects. It was this man, who, by his superior application, managed at once the faction in Congress at Philadelphia and the factions in New England. Whatever these patriots in Congress wished to have done by their colleagues without, to induce General Gage, then at the head of his majesty's army at Boston, to give them a pretext for violent opposition, or to promote their measures in Congress, Mr. Adams advised and directed to be done; and when done, it was dispatched by express to Congress. By one of these expresses came the inflammatory resolves of the county of Suffolk, which contained a complete declaration of war against Great Britain." [1]

Galloway, the writer quoted, an able lawyer, who had just before been speaker of the Pennsylvania Assembly, was a leader in Congress of the strong party who desired conciliation. The plan proposed by him, and which came within one vote of being accepted, was a union of the colonies under a general council, which, in conjunction with the British Parliament, was to care for America. Galloway confesses to have been fairly frightened out of his purpose by what he supposed to be the power of Samuel Adams.

The Declaration of Rights, embodying a non-consumption and non-importation of British goods; the addresses to the king, to the people of England,

[1] *Historical and Political Reflections on the Rise and Progress of the American Revolution,* by Joseph Galloway. London, 1780. Page 67.

of Canada, and of the British American colonies, and a letter to the agent of the colonies in England, comprise the published papers of the first Congress, seven weeks passing while they were in preparation. Of these the first and most important is substantially the same as that adopted by the people of Boston in 1772. What part precisely Samuel Adams took, we cannot tell. He himself says nothing, and there was no formal report. John Adams's pictures are as vivid as possible, but the value of his evidence is impaired by his evident prejudice and sense of self-importance. Bits of testimony, such as that just quoted from Galloway, throw some further light. Gordon states : —

"In some stage of their proceedings the danger of a rupture with Britain was urged as a plea for certain concessions. Upon this Mr. S. Adams rose up, and, among other things, said in substance: ' I should advise persisting in our struggle for liberty, though it was revealed from heaven that nine hundred and ninety-nine were to perish, and only one of a thousand to survive and retain his liberty. One such freeman must possess more virtue and enjoy more happiness than a thousand slaves; and let him propagate his like, and transmit to them what he hath so nobly preserved.' "

All his tact and all his force were brought into the fullest play, and we can be certain that his influence was great. He writes to Warren, September 25, indicating that the disposition to regard Massachusetts as over-rash is somewhat overcome, but that great caution must be used on account of a pervading fear that independence is aimed at, and a subsequent subjugation of America by the power of New England. If the first Congress was not won to thoughts of independence, it was kept, at any rate, from measures disastrously reactionary. When Congress adjourned, October 26, appointing a second convention for May 20, 1775, Samuel Adams had reason to feel that the course of things had been not unsatisfactory.

The two Adamses and Cushing were received, upon their arrival in Boston, November 9, with public demonstrations. Letters are extant from the patriots who had remained behind in Boston, addressed to Samuel Adams while at Philadelphia, full of regard and a reverence almost filial, showing in every line how his wisdom was deferred to. The uneducated people, indeed, are said to have become superstitious with regard to him, believing that he had a prophetic power, and had in his keeping war and peace. As usual, there was no respite for him. Gordon is authority for the statement that the presence of Samuel Adams in the Provincial Congress, which had come into being, caused it to push preparations for war, and that, since many members were timid, and excused themselves from attendance under plea of sickness, at his instance measures were taken to keep them at their work. He was like a stout sergeant, who makes it his duty not only to face the foe, but sometimes to pass along the rear of the line of battle, with an admonitory prick of the bayonet for the timid ones who may be disposed to run before the enemy's fire. As a body, however, the Provincial Congress was brave and united, and included the best men in Massachusetts.

To the second Continental Congress the interval is short, but the factotum crowds it with work. He leads the Provincial Congress in measures for making the people aware of the imminence of their danger; he is at the head of the town's committee to distribute donations from abroad; he reaches out on the one hand to Canada, on the other to the Mohawk and Stockbridge Indians, in efforts to induce them to march to the patriotic music; but his most remarkable manifestation is in connection with the fifth celebration of the Boston Massacre, on the 6th of March, the 5th being Sunday. The truth was, that since the change in the charter in the preceding year no town meeting could be legally held save such as the governor expressly called. The well-trained " Bostoneers," however, had a ruse ready, over which the dazed Gage stroked his chin, without being able to make up his mind to interfere. The clause of the Government Act was clear as to the prohibition of town meetings. The preceding August, Gage, disposed as usual to be good-natured, had summoned the selectmen to the Province House. " If a meeting were wanted he would allow one to be called, if he should judge it expedient." The fathers of the town told him they had no occasion for calling a meeting; they had one alive. Gage looked serious: "I must think of that; by thus doing you can keep the meeting alive for ten years." Foreseeing the storm, indeed, the May meeting of 1774 had not "dissolved," but "adjourned." So, too, had the Port Bill meeting of June 17. During the remainder of the year, therefore, and into the year following, as one turns over the pages of the town records, the "adjourned" May meeting, or the "adjourned" Port Bill meeting, are reported, which serve perfectly every purpose, the town comfortably riding out the storm by the parliamentary technicality. The meeting of the 6th of March was an adjournment of the Port Bill meeting. Warren, knowing that the orator would be in danger, with characteristic bravery solicited the post for himself.

Generally it is as the manager, somewhat withdrawn behind the figures in the foreground, that Samuel Adams makes himself felt. In 1770, at the driving out of the regiments, he is not chairman of the town's committee that waits upon Hutchinson, but stands behind Hancock, only coming forward at the moment of danger. At the destruction of the tea, he is not in the company, but his sentence from the chair was evidently the concerted signal for which all were waiting. Again, at the last great town meeting before Lexington and Concord, March 6, 1775, the fifth celebration of the Boston Massacre, while Warren is the heroic central figure, Samuel Adams is behind all as

chief director. On that day Gage had in the town
eleven regiments. Of trained soldiers there were
scarcely fewer than the number of men on the
patriot side; and when we remember that many
Tories throughout the province, in the disturbed
times, had sought refuge in Boston, under the protection of the troops, we can feel what a host there
was that day on the side of the king. Nevertheless, all went forward as usual. The warrant appeared in due form for the meeting, at which an
oration was to be delivered to commemorate the
" horrid Massacre," and to denounce the " ruinous
tendency of standing armies being placed in free
and populous cities in time of peace." The Old
South was densely thronged, and in the pulpit as
moderator once more, by the side of the town
clerk, William Cooper, quietly sat Samuel Adams.
Among the citizens a large party of officers were
present, apparently intent upon making a disturbance with the design of precipitating a conflict.
The war, it was thought, might as well begin then
as at any time. Warren was late in appearing;
Samuel Adams sat meantime as if upon a powder-
barrel that might at any minute roar into the air
in a sudden explosion. The tradition has come
down that he was serene and unmoved. He
quietly requested the townsmen to vacate the front
seats, into which, in order that they might be well
placed to hear, he politely invited the soldiers,
whose numbers were so large that they overflowed
the pews and sat upon the pulpit stairs. Warren

came at last, entering through the window behind
the pulpit to avoid the press. Wells gives, from
a contemporary, the following report : —

"The Selectmen, with Adams, Church, and Hancock,
Cooper, and others, assembled in the pulpit, which was
covered with black, and we all sat gaping at one another above an hour, expecting! At last a single horse
chair stopped at the apothecary's opposite the meeting,
from which descended the orator (Warren) of the day ;
and entering the shop, was followed by a servant with a
bundle, in which were the Ciceronian toga, etc.

" Having robed himself, he proceeded across the street
to the meeting, and being received into the pulpit, he
was announced by one of his fraternity to be the person
appointed to declaim on the occasion. He then put himself into a Demosthenian posture, with a white handkerchief in his right hand, and his left in his breeches, —
began and ended without action. He was applauded by
the mob, but groaned at by people of understanding.
One of the pulpiteers (Adams) then got up and proposed
the nomination of another to speak next year on the
bloody Massacre, — the first time that expression was
made to the audience, — when some officers cried, 'O
fie, fie!' The gallerians, apprehending fire, bounded
out of the windows, and swarmed down the gutters, like
rats, into the street. The Forty-third Regiment returning accidentally from exercise, with drums beating, threw
the whole body into the greatest consternation. There
were neither pageantry, exhibitions, processions, or bells
tolling as usual, but the night was remarked for being
the quietest these many months past."

A picturesque incident in the delivery of the

oration was that, as Warren proceeded, a British captain, sitting on the pulpit stairs, held up in his open palm before Warren's face a number of pistol bullets. Warren quietly dropped his handkerchief upon them and went on. It was strange enough that that oration was given without an outbreak.

"We wildly stare about," he says, "and with amazement ask, 'Who spread this ruin around us?' What wretch has dared deface the image of his God? Has haughty France or cruel Spain sent forth her myrmidons? Has the grim savage rushed again from the far-distant wilderness? Or does some fiend, fierce from the depth of Hell, with all the rancorous malice which the apostate damned can feel, twang her destructive bow and hurl her deadly arrows at our breast? No, none of these; but how astonishing! It is the hand of Britain that inflicts the wound. The arms of George, our rightful king, have been employed to shed that blood which freely should have flowed at his command, when justice, or the honor of his crown, had called his subjects to the field." [1]

The oration was given without disturbance, though the tension was tremendous. In the proceedings that followed the quiet was not perfect, but the collision was averted for a time. The troops were not quite ready, and on the patriot side the presiding genius was as prudent as he was bold.[2] Shortly afterward Samuel Adams sent

[1] Frothingham's *Warren*, p. 433.

[2] Hutchinson gives an interesting fact respecting this memo-

the following quiet account to Richard Henry Lee in Virginia, which is taken here from the autograph: —

BOSTON, March, 1775.

On the sixth Instant, there was an Adjournment of our Town-meeting, when an Oration was delivered in Commemoration of the Massacre on the 5th of March, 1770. I had long expected they would take that occasion to beat up a Breeze, and therefore (having the Honor of being the Moderator of the Meeting, and seeing Many of the Officers present before the orator came in) I took care to have them treated with Civility, inviting them into convenient Seats, &c., that they might have no pretence to behave ill, for it is a good maxim in Politicks as well as War, to put and keep the enemy in the wrong. They behaved tolerably well till the oration was finished, when upon a motion made for the appointment of another orator, they began to hiss, which irritated the

rable town meeting, in his Diary. "September 6, 1775. Col. James tells an odd story of the intention of the officers the 5 March; that 300 were in the meeting to hear Dr. Warren's oration; that if he had said anything against the King, &c., an officer was prepared, who stood near, with an egg to have thrown in his face, and that was to have been a signal to draw swords, and they would have massacred Hancock, Adams, and hundreds more; and he added he wished they had. I am glad they did not: for I think it would have been an everlasting disgrace to attack a body of people without arms to defend themselves.

"He says one officer cried 'Fy! Fy!' and Adams immediately asked who dared say so? And then said to the officer he should mark him. The officer answered, 'And I will mark you. I live at such a place, and shall be ready to meet you.' Adams said he would go to his General. The officer said his General had nothing to do with it; the affair was between them two." *Diary and Letters*, pp. 528, 529.

assembly to the greatest Degree, and Confusion ensued. They, however, did not gain their End, which was apparently to break up the Meeting, for order was soon restored, and we proceeded regularly and finished. I am persuaded that were it not for the Danger of precipitating a Crisis, not a Man of them would have been spared. It was provoking enough to them, that while there were so many Troops stationed here for the design of suppressing Town-Meetings, there should yet be a Meeting for the purpose of delivering an oration to commemorate a massacre perpetrated by soldiers, and to show the danger of standing armies.

And now Gage was preparing for the expedition to secure the stores at Concord, and make the oft-threatened seizure of Hancock and Adams. However the general may have vapored shortly before in England, he had shown since his arrival in Boston a judicious - hesitation as to precipitating hostilities, which he saw well must at once follow the arrest of the important men. Reinforcements, however, were now on the way; he had been urged forward by letters from England, and he made ready for the attempt. Several months before this time, in the Provincial Congress, Samuel Adams had called attention to the danger of allowing expeditions of regulars into the interior, and had recommended opposition if they should proceed more than ten miles from Boston. From this suggestion it may have come about that the militia everywhere were so on the alert, and that on the evening of the 18th, when the news spread that the regulars

were coming out, Jonas Parker's company paraded
so promptly on Lexington Green. That night,
in the house of the Rev. Jonas Clark, which still
stands a few rods from the Common, lodged Samuel Adams and John Hancock, about to start upon
their journey southward. Rumors of the coming
of the troops had reached the village through several channels, and when an hour after midnight
Parker's men loaded with powder and ball, Hancock and Adams, stepping over from the minister's, looked on. Shortly before, the centaur, Paul
Revere, having escaped from the clutches of the
British, had galloped up, and found all asleep.
The sergeant, who with eight men was stationed at
the house, roused by the courier's urgency, stated
that the family did not wish to be disturbed by
any noise. "Noise," cried Paul Revere, "you'll
have noise enough before long. The regulars are
coming out." On came the light infantry, moving
swiftly in the fresh night air. In a moment more
occurred the incident of Major Pitcairn's order
and pistol shot; then while the smoke cleared after
the memorable volley, Adams and Hancock were
making their way across the fields to Woburn.
For Adams it was an hour of triumph. The
British had fired first; the Americans had "put
the enemy in the wrong;" the two sides were
committed; conciliation was no longer possible.
As the sun rose there came from him one of the
few exultant outbursts of his life: "What a glorious morning is this!" They waited in the second

precinct of Woburn, now Burlington, while the
minute-men, through the forenoon, hurried by with
their arms. At noon a man broke in upon them,
at the house of the minister, with a shriek, and
for a moment they thought themselves lost. They
were then piloted along a cart-way to a corner of
Billerica, where they were glad to dine off cold salt
pork and potatoes served in a wooden tray. A day
or two later they set out for Philadelphia.

A spirited, manly letter is extant, written by
John Hancock, at Worcester, to the Committee of
Safety. We have already had occasion to notice
his weakness; his conduct hereafter will show
greater shortcomings. One is glad to view him
at his best; for at his best he was a generous and
able man.

CHAPTER XX

THE DECLARATION OF INDEPENDENCE

HARTFORD was reached on the 29th by the two delegates, where, in a secret meeting with Governor Trumbull and others, they heard the plan arranged for the surprise of Ticonderoga. Cushing, John Adams, and Paine joined them, and soon afterward, in company with the Connecticut delegation, the Massachusetts deputies entered New York with great ceremony. With their number increased to fourteen by the addition of the New York delegates, they crossed the Hudson, escorted by five hundred gentlemen and two hundred militia. Through New Jersey the honors continued, and at Philadelphia the climax was reached. Says Curwen's "Journal: " —

"Early in the morning a great number of persons rode out several miles, hearing that the Eastern delegates were approaching, when, about eleven o'clock, the cavalcade apeared (I being near the upper end of Fore Street) ; first, two or three hundred gentlemen on horseback, preceded, however, by the newly chosen city military officers, two and two, with drawn swords, followed by John Hancock and Samuel Adams in a phaeton and pair, the former looking as if his journey and high living, or solicitude to support the dignity of the first man in Massachusetts, had impaired his health. Next came John Adams and Thomas Cushing in a single-horse chaise: behind followed Robert Treat Paine, and after him the New York delegation and some from the Province of Connecticut, etc., etc. The rear was brought up by a hundred carriages, the streets crowded with people of all ages, sexes, and ranks. The procession marched with a slow solemn pace. On its entrance into the city, all the bells were set to ringing and chiming, and every mark of respect that could be was expressed; not much, I presume, to the secret liking of their fellow delegates from the other colonies, who doubtless had to digest the distinction as easily as they could."

The events of the 19th of April had widened the breach greatly; nevertheless, when Samuel Adams, now more than ever looking forward to nothing less than independence, stood among his fellow members in the second Continental Congress, he found himself still alone. Even John Adams and Jefferson were as yet far from being ready for such a step, and in the debates the only questions raised were between a party which was in favor of resisting British encroachments by force of arms and a party which desired to make still further appeal to king and Parliament, both parties looking forward only to a restoration of the state of things existing before the disputes began. Among the leading statesmen of America, independence was the desire of Samuel Adams alone. He lost a stanch supporter just now in the untimely death of Josiah Quincy, Jr., by consumption, which occurred on shipboard in April, on his return from England, whither he had gone hoping for an improvement in health. Quincy's relations with Samuel Adams, who was twenty-two years older than he, were almost those of a son. Except Warren, no one stood higher in Adams's esteem, who always referred to him with respect and tenderness. Quincy, in turn, was devoted. "Let our friend, Samuel Adams, be one of the first to whom you show my letters," he wrote to his wife, — and again, speaking of England: "The character of your Mr. Samuel Adams stands very high here. I find many who consider him the first politician in the world. I have found more reason every day to convince me he has been right when others supposed him wrong."

His reputation as a desperate and fanatical adventurer, with nothing to lose, still followed him, and his advocacy of a scheme was often an injury to it. Massachusetts, through Warren, now beyond all men the leader at home, sought to secure an authorization of the Provincial Congress, which many in the Continental Congress hesitated to grant, since it would be practically a recognition of the independence of Massachusetts. When Peyton Randolph, however, retired from the chair to attend the session of the Virginia legislature, the presidency was given to Massachusetts, in the person of John Hancock, — a measure for which the two Adamses worked hard, having in view a double advantage; by putting the richest man in New England into conspicuous position, the idea was dispelled that only needy adventurers were concerned; and, on the other hand, Hancock himself was likely to be clamped firmly to the popular cause by the honor which was shown him.

By far the most important business transacted by the second Continental Congress was the appointment of Washington as commander-in-chief, — a service principally due to John Adams, though the nomination was seconded by Samuel Adams.

"Full of anxieties," says John Adams, " concerning these confusions, and apprehending daily that we should hear very distressing news from Boston, I walked with Mr. Samuel Adams in the State House yard, for a little exercise and fresh air, before the hour of Congress, and there represented to him the various dangers that surrounded us. He agreed to them all, but said, ' What shall we do?' I answered him . . . I was determined to take a step which should compel all the members of Congress to declare themselves for or against something. I am determined this morning to make a direct motion that Congress should adopt the army before Boston, and appoint Colonel Washington commander of it. Mr. Adams seemed to think very seriously of it, but said nothing.

"Accordingly, when Congress had assembled, I rose in my place . . . Mr. Washington, who happened to sit near the door, as soon as he heard me allude to him, from his usual modesty, darted into the library-room. Mr. Hancock heard me with visible pleasure, but when I came to describe Washington for the commander, I never remarked a more sudden and striking change of countenance. Mortification and resentment were expressed as forcibly as his face could exhibit them. Mr. Samuel Adams seconded the motion, and that did not soften the president's physiognomy at all."

On the 12th of June Gage made his proclamation, offering pardon "to all persons who shall forthwith lay down their Arms and return to the Duties of peaceable Subjects, excepting only from the Benefit of such Pardon Samuel Adams and John Hancock, whose Offences are of too flagitious a Nature to admit of any other Consideration than that of condign Punishment." News of his proscription probably reached Samuel Adams at the same time with that of the battle of Bunker Hill, and of the death of the man whom he is believed to have loved beyond all others, Dr. Warren. The following letter to his wife is contained among his manuscripts : —

PHIL., June 28th, 1775.

MY DEAREST BETSY, yesterday I received Letters from some of our Friends at the Camp informing me of the Engagement between the American Troops and the Rebel Army in Charlestown. I cannot but be greatly rejoyced at the tryed Valor of our Countrymen, who by all Accounts behaved with an intrepidity becoming those who fought for their Liberties against the mercenary Soldiers of a Tyrant. It is painful to me to reflect on the Terror I must suppose you were under on hearing the Noise of War so near. Favor me my dear with an Account of your Apprehensions at that time, under your own hand. I pray God to cover the heads of our Countrymen in every day of Battle and ever to protect you from Injury in these distracted times. The Death of our truly amiable and worthy Friend Dr. Warren is greatly afflicting; the Language of Friendship is, how shall we resign him; but it is our Duty to submit to the Dispensations of Heaven " whose ways are ever gracious, ever just." He fell in the glorious Struggle for publick Liberty. Mr. Pitts and Dr. Church inform me that my dear Son has at length escaped from the Prison at Boston. . . . Remember me to my dear Hannah and sister Polly and to all Friends. Let me know where good old Surry is. Gage has made me respectable by naming me first among those who are to receive no favor from him. I thoroughly despise him and his Proclamation. . . . The Clock is now striking twelve. I therefore wish you a good Night.

Yours most affectionately,

S. ADAMS.

Wells has stated that no letter of Samuel Adams can be found in which any reference is made to the death of Warren, overlooking that which has just been given. It is, perhaps, singular that Adams expressed no more. " Their kindred souls were so closely twined that both felt one joy, both one affliction," said the orator at Warren's re-interment after the British evacuation. That Samuel Adams wore him in his heart of hearts all men knew, and his silence is part of that reticence as to his own emotions which has been referred to as so constantly marking him. His relation to Warren, who died at thirty-five, was similar to that in which he stood to Quincy, though somewhat more intimate. "The future seemed burdened with his honors," says Bancroft of Warren, and it is hard to see how promise could be finer. His powers were becoming calmed and trained, while losing no particle of their youthful force. He was at once prudent and yet most impetuous, — able in debate in town meeting or Assembly, — prompt and intrepid in the field. Either as statesman or as soldier he might have been his country's pride.

Samuel Adams swept aside personal griefs and perils. He adopted Washington cordially, and poured out for him whatever information could be of value to a man of the South about to take command of an army of New England troops. He strove to prepare for him a good reception by sending beforehand to the important men the most favorable commendations. Less fortunate was the work of the Adamses in behalf of Charles Lee, who, largely through them, was appointed second in command, the eccentric, selfish marplot, who so nearly wrecked the cause he assumed to uphold. On the 1st of August the second Continental Congress adjourned until the 5th of September, the Massachusetts delegation, on their return, having in care five hundred thousand dollars for the use of the army of Washington.

When Samuel Adams, with his fellow delegates, arrived from Philadelphia, he found in session "The General Assembly of the territory of Massachusetts Bay," in which he was to sit as one of the eighteen councilors. He was at once made secretary of state. His son became a surgeon in the army of Washington, while his wife and daughter were inmates of the family of Mrs. Adams's father at Cambridge. Leaving his public functions in the hands of a deputy secretary, Samuel Adams is in the saddle again on the 12th of September, and, after riding three hundred miles on a horse lent him by John Adams, with great benefit to his health, he is soon once more at Philadelphia, for the opening of the third Continental Congress.

The jealousy toward New England was now even greater than ever before in the proprietary and some of the southern colonies. Gadsden, R. H. Lee, Patrick Henry, and a few others were ready for independence. As yet, however, there was no discussion of this matter. Samuel Adams, impatient, began to entertain the idea of establishing independence for the New England colonies by themselves, cherishing the hope that the rest would follow in time.

The defection of Dr. Benjamin Church, which was discovered in the fall of 1775, must have caused him pain scarcely less than the deaths of Quincy and Warren. Next to these, no one of the younger men had promised more fairly than Church. His abilities were brilliant, his interest in all the Whig projects apparently most sincere. He had been implicitly trusted. Years before, while secretly a writer for the government, he had escaped discovery. Now he was detected, while betraying to the enemy, by letters written in cipher, the plans of the Massachusetts patriots. He narrowly escaped execution. He was allowed to take passage for the West Indies in a ship which was never heard of more.

To relate particularly the doings of the Continental Congress must be left to the general historian. The reports are meagre; a thousand details came up for consideration, and Samuel Adams was busy in many different ways which it would be wearisome to try to trace. Independence was more than ever at his heart, but seemed as far off as ever. John Adams, who had reached his ground at last, went home in the winter and remained two months; Hancock, becoming estranged from his plain companions, affiliated with the aristocratic members from the middle and southern colonies; both Cushing and Paine favored conciliation. Jefferson remembered Samuel Adams as the chief promoter of the invasion of Canada. He became warmly friendly to the brave Montgomery, followed with ardent hope the reduction of St. Johns, Chambly, and Montreal, and was much afflicted when the young conqueror was struck down in the winter storm at Quebec. Disaster, as always, nerved him to new efforts.

The reader will be interested in the following letter from his wife, copied from the autograph, which the "bad paper" and the "pen made with scissars" make not easily decipherable: —

CAMBRIDGE Feb. 12th, 1776.

MY DEAR, I Received your affectinate Letter by Fes-
enton and I thank you for your kind Concern for My
health and Safty. I beg you Would not give yourself
any pain on our being so Near the Camp ; the place I
am in is so Situated, that if the Regulars should ever
take Prospect Hill, which god forbid, I should be able
to Make an Escape, as I am Within a few stone casts of
a Back Road, Which Leads to the Most Retired part of
Newtown. . . . I beg you to Excuse the very poor
Writing as My paper is Bad and my pen made with
Scissars. I should be glad (My dear), if you should 'nt
come down soon, you would Write me Word Who to
apply to for some Monney, for I am low in Cash and
Every thing is very dear.

        May I subscribe myself yours

                ELIZA'ᴴ ADAMS.

The chafing fanatic of independence, whose fire
was rising more and more, sent out in February an
" Earnest Appeal to the People." The opponents
of independence, led now by the able Wilson of
Pennsylvania, conspicuous afterwards in the debates on the Constitution, and as a justice of the
Supreme Court of the United States, pursued a
vigorous course. Helped especially by Wythe of
Virginia, Samuel Adams stood against them. His
abilities were greater in other fields than on the
floor of debate, ready and impressive though he
was, and he at this time sadly missed the help of
John Adams, whose power here was of the highest.
The baffled striver, borne down for the time by the

odds against him, gnashed his teeth against his colleagues, Hancock, Paine, and Cushing, who rendered him no help. " Had I suggested an idea of the vanity of the ape, the tameness of the ox, or the stupid servility of the ass, I might have been liable to censure," — thus he wrote. Massachusetts stood nobly by him, for at the reëlection of delegates, though Hancock was returned, like the two Adamses, by a good majority, Paine was barely chosen, and Cushing was entirely dropped, Elbridge Gerry of Marblehead taking his place, and showing himself at once a capable combatant side by side with the veteran.

But a change was preparing. Speaking of the work of Thomas Paine, Samuel Adams bore this testimony to its value : " 'Common Sense' and 'The Crisis' undoubtedly awakened the public mind, and led the people loudly to call for a declaration of independence." But months were to pass before the new mood of the people was to make itself felt in Congress. Adams, with the small phalanx of advanced men, among whom, besides Wyeth, were Ward of Rhode Island, Chase of Maryland, and Oliver Wolcott and Roger Sherman of Connecticut, faced the moderate men. He fought also outside, trying especially to counteract the influence of the Quakers, a sect whose conduct in general tried his patience greatly, and which in convention just before had issued an address strongly urging unqualified submission. Samuel Adams handled without gloves the respectable broad-brims : —

" ' But,' say the puling, pusillanimous cowards, ' we shall be subject to a long and bloody war, if we declare independence.' On the contrary, I affirm it the only step that can bring the contest to a speedy and happy issue. By declaring independence we put ourselves on a footing for an equal negotiation. Now we are called a pack of villainous rebels, who, like the St. Vincent's Indians, can expect nothing more than a pardon for our lives, and the sovereign favor, respecting freedom and property, to be at the king's will. Grant, Almighty God, that I may be numbered with the dead before that sable day dawns on North America."

Samuel Adams undoubtedly prepared the resolutions respecting the disarming of the Tories, being chairman of the committee on that matter. It was more and more the case that his state papers before the war became the models for important documents, and were used directly to explain to the public the justice of the American cause. John Adams, until within a few months, and Jefferson, to the present moment, had regarded independence with disfavor, only to be accepted as a last resort. Franklin looked upon it as an event which, if it must come, was lamentable. Washington, in the first Congress, denied that the colonies desired, or that it was for their interest, " separately or collectively, to set up for independence." Up to the time when he became commander-in-chief, he desired peace and reconciliation on an honorable basis. Joseph Warren died without desiring American freedom. Even after

Lexington he favored reconciliation, founded on the maintenance of colonial rights. "This," said he, "I most heartily wish, as I feel a warm affection for the parent state." Samuel Adams had a few correspondents of views similar to his own. Such were Joseph Hawley, who, because he was ill, or through some unaccountable neglect, was suffered to hide his fine powers and accomplishments during all these mighty years in the seclusion of Northampton; also Dr. Samuel Cooper, and James Warren of Plymouth, fast rising in Massachusetts to take his namesake's place in council, though he never appeared in the field. To the latter Adams writes in April: "The child Independence is now struggling for birth. I trust that in a short time it will be brought forth, and, in spite of Pharaoh, all America will hail the dignified stranger." The plain people, too, whom he loved and trusted, rallied to him. At last, on the 6th of April, while the Pennsylvania Assembly, under the lead of the incorrigible Dickinson, who was now as energetic at the brake as he had once been on the engine, was instructing its delegates to discourage separation, a measure was passed abolishing British custom-houses in the thirteen colonies, and opening their ports to the commerce of the world. Samuel Adams was on the committee that reported it, and wrote to Hawley that the " united colonies had torn into shivers the British acts of trade." By May 10, under the lead of John Adams, Congress had recommended to the colonies to set up governments of their own, suppressing all crown authority. In May, also, the Virginia delegates were instructed from home to declare for independence; Maryland was won through the influence of Thomas Chase; in Pennsylvania the power of Dickinson visibly waned; everywhere there was movement, until on the 5th of June Richard Henry Lee of Virginia offered his resolution declaring the colonies free and independent states, recommending the formation of foreign alliances, and a plan of confederation.

As in some elaborate piece of music, a mighty march, with distinct, slowly succeeding tones goes forward, while the intervals are filled in with innumerable subordinated notes, so in this advance toward independence, while the solemn steps are measured, a thousand minor details are everywhere interspersed. The hour at hand constantly pressed. Powder in this direction, provisions and clothes in that; troops to be recruited; roads to be built; inert Whigs to be stimulated; active Tories to be suppressed; officers to be commissioned; plans of campaign to be devised; hostile projects to be counteracted, — all this must go forward. Samuel Adams bore his part in all the intricacies, but saw to it that the main theme should be forever thundered with a volume more and more prevailing.

On the 8th of June began the debate on Lee's resolution. We do not know the special arguments used, nor with certainty the names of the speakers on the side of independence, excepting John

Adams. Elbridge Gerry, many years after, told the daughter of Samuel Adams that the success of Lee's measure was largely due to the "timely remarks" of her father; that in one speech he occupied an unusually long time, and that two or three wavering members were finally convinced by him. He remembered it as Samuel Adams's ablest effort. Edward Rutledge, at length, brought about a postponement of the question for three weeks, that the hesitating delegates of the central colonies might have time to consult their constituents; but not before Jefferson, John Adams, Franklin, Roger Sherman, and Robert R. Livingston had been made a committee to prepare the Declaration. One who follows this story must feel regret that Samuel Adams was not of this number. It happened not through neglect, for at the same time he was appointed to stand for Massachusetts on a committee regarded, probably, as certainly not less important, — a committee, namely, consisting of one from each colony, to prepare a plan of confederation.

The three weeks passed, during which the ripening sentiment of the country made itself strongly felt by Congress. For Samuel Adams it was a time of labor, for now it was, in personal conferences with hesitating members, that he brought to bear his peculiar powers. When the measure was again taken up, on the first days of July, all was secured. There was no longer a dissenting voice, and the delegates, after the memorable form, pledged their lives, their fortunes, and their sacred honor.

It seems to have been not at all a solemn hour.
The weather was very hot, and through the open
windows there came in from a stable close by a
swarm of mosquitoes and horse-flies, who bit vi-
ciously at the legs of the members through their
silk stockings. American patriotism owes to these
energetic insects an obligation very great and by
no means adequately recognized ; for the Fathers,
wrought upon by the sedulously applied torment,
hastened to sign the famous document of Jefferson, submitted at last by the committee. Now that
the struggle was over, the members became posi-
tively hilarious in their good-nature. John Hancock dashed down his great signature in such shape
"that George the Third might read it without
his spectacles." "Now we must all hang together,"
it was remarked. "Yes," said Franklin, "or we
shall all hang separately." "When it comes to
the hanging," said fat Mr. Harrison of Virginia
to lean little Elbridge Gerry of Massachusetts, "I
shall have the advantage of you, for my neck, probably, will be broken at the first drop, whereas you
may have to dangle for half an hour."

For Samuel Adams it was the most triumphant
moment of his life ; but he writes thus calmly to
his friend, John Pitts, at Boston : —

PHIL. July, 1776.

MY DEAR SIR, you were informed by the last Post
that Congress had declared the thirteen United Colonies
free and independent States. It must be allowed by
the impartial World that this Declaration has not been

made rashly. . . . Too Much I fear has been lost by
Delay, but an accession of several colonies has been
gained by it. Delegates of every Colony were present
and concurred in this important Act except those of
New York, who were not authorized to give their voice
on the Question, but they have since publickly said that
a new Convention was soon to meet in that Colony, and
they had not the least doubt of their acceding to it. Our
Path is now open to form a plan of Confederation and
propose Alliances with foreign States. I hope our Affairs will now wear a more agreeable aspect than they
have of late.

S. A.[1]

[1] Copied from the autograph.

CHAPTER XXI

WE have reached a point in the career of Samuel Adams from which it will be convenient to take a retrospect. He was now fifty - four years old. Although his life was destined to continue more than a quarter of a century longer, and although the work that he accomplished in the years that were coming was important, his great and peculiar desert is for the work done during these twelve years from 1764 to 1776, with the description of which this book has been thus far occupied. That Massachusetts led the thirteen colonies during the years preliminary to the Revolution has been sufficiently set forth ; that Boston led Massachusetts is plain ; the reader of the foregoing pages will clearly understand that it was Samuel Adams who led Boston. If the remark that Bancroft somewhere makes is just, that " American freedom was more prepared by courageous counsel than successful war," it would be hard to exaggerate the value of the work of Samuel Adams in securing it.

Bancroft has spoken of Samuel Adams as, more than any other man, " the type and representative of the New England town meeting." [1]   Boston, as we have seen, is the largest community that ever maintained the town organization, probably also the most generally able and intelligent.   No other town ever played a more conspicuous part in connection with important events.   Probably in the whole history of the Anglo-Saxon race there has been no other so interesting manifestation of the activity of the folk-mote.   Of this town of towns Samuel Adams was the son of sons.   He was strangely identified with it always.   He was trained in Boston schools and Harvard College. He never left the town except on the town's errands, or those of the province of which it was the head.   He had no private business after the first years of his manhood ; he was the public servant simply and solely in places large and small, — fire-ward, committee to see that chimneys were safe, tax-collector, moderator of town meeting, representative.   One may almost call him the creature of the town meeting.   His development has taken place among the talk of the town politicians at his father's house, on the floors of Faneuil Hall and the Old South, from the time when he looked on as a wondering boy to the time when he stood there as the master-figure.   " His chief dependence," wrote Hutchinson, in a passage already quoted, " is upon Boston town meeting, where he originates the measures which are followed by the

[1] In a private conversation with the writer; also, *Hist. of Constitution*, ii. 260.

rest of the towns, and, of course, are adopted or justified by the Assembly." Edward Everett declared too, in the Lexington oration, that —

"The throne of his ascendency was in Faneuil Hall. As each new measure of arbitrary power was announced from across the Atlantic, or each new act of menace and violence on the part of the officers of the government or of the army occurred in Boston, its citizens, oftentimes in astonishment and perplexity, rallied to the sound of his voice in Faneuil Hall; and there, as from the crowded gallery or the moderator's chair he animated, enlightened, fortified, and roused the admiring throng, he seemed to gather them together beneath the ægis of his indomitable spirit, as a hen gathereth her chickens under her wings."

Though the sphere of his activity was to so large an extent the Massachusetts Assembly, he was not the less for that, as has appeared, the "man of the town meeting." The Assembly was a collection of *deputies*, of whom each was the mouthpiece of his constituency, having the folk-mote behind him, which limited his action by careful instructions, kept sharp watch of his behavior, and suffered him to hold office for so short a term that he was in no danger of getting beyond control. The Assembly was, therefore, rather a convention of town meetings than a *representative* body, bearing in mind Dr. Lieber's distinction; and when Samuel Adams arrayed and manœuvred them in the west chamber of the Old State House against Bernard or Hutchinson in the east chamber, — the regiments lying threateningly just behind, either in the town or at the Castle, — it was the Massachusetts towns that he marshaled almost as much as if the population had actually come from the hills and the plains, gathering as do the hamlets of Uri and Appenzell in Switzerland, to legislate for themselves without any delegation of authority.[1]

We have seen that New England had been prolific of children fitted for the time. Men like John Scollay, William Cooper, William Molineux, William Phillips, Robert Pierpont, John Pitts, Paul Revere, — plain citizens, merchants, mechanics, selectmen of the town, deacons in the churches, cool-headed, well-to-do, persistent, courageous, — were sturdy wheel-horses for the occasion. Of a higher order, and great figures in our story, have been James Otis, James Bowdoin, Joseph Hawley, Thomas Cushing ; and of the younger generation, John Hancock, Josiah Quincy, Joseph Warren, John Adams, Benjamin Church, — men who had some of them a gift of eloquence to set hearts on fire, some of them executive power, some of them cunning to lay trains and supply the flash at the proper time, some wealth, and birth, and high social position. It was a wonderful group, but in every one there was some inadequacy. The splendid Otis, whose leadership was at first unquestioned, who had only to enter Boston town meeting to call forth shouts and clapping of hands, and who had equal authority in the Assembly, was, as early

[1] Freeman, *Growth of the English Const.*

as 1770, fast sinking into insanity. In spite of fits of unreasonable violence and absurd folly, vacillations between extremes of subserviency and audacious resistance, his influence with the people long remained. He was like the huge cannon on the man-of-war, in Victor Hugo's story, that had broken from its moorings in the storm, and become a terror to those whom it formerly defended. He was indeed a great gun, from whom in the time of the Stamp Act had been sent the most powerful bolts against unconstitutional oppression. With lashings parted, however, as the storm grew violent he plunged dangerously from side to side, almost sinking the ship, all the more an object of dread from the calibre that had once made him so serviceable. It was a melancholy sight, and yet a great relief, when his friends saw him at last bound hand and foot, and carried into retirement.

Bowdoin, also, was not firm in health, and, though most active and useful in the Council, has thus far done little elsewhere. Hawley, far in the interior, was often absent from the centre in critical times, and somewhat unreliable through a strange moodiness; Cushing was weak; Hancock was hampered by foibles that sometimes quite cancelled his merits; Quincy was a brilliant youth, and, like a youth, sometimes fickle. We have seen him ready to temporize when to falter was destruction, as at the time of the casting over of the tea; again, in unwise fervor, he could counsel assassination as a proper expedient. Warren, too, could rush into extremes of rashness and ferocity, wishing that he might wade to the knees in blood, and had just reached sober, self-reliant manhood when he was taken off. John Adams showed only an intermittent zeal in the public cause until the preliminary work was done; and Benjamin Church, half-hearted and venal, early began the double-dealing which was to bring him to a traitor's end.

There was need in this group of a man of sufficient ascendency, through intellect and character, to win deference from all, — wise enough to see always the supreme end, to know what each instrument was fit for, and to bring all forces to bear in the right way, — a man of consummate adroitness, to sail in torpedo-sown waters without exciting an explosion, though conducting wires of local prejudice, class-sensitiveness, and personal foible on every hand led straight down to magazines of wrath which might shatter the cause in a moment, — a man having resources of his own to such an extent that he could supplement from himself what was wanting in others, — always awake though others might want to sleep, always at work though others might be tired, — a man devoted, without thought of personal gain or fame, simply and solely to the public cause. Such a man there was, and his name was Samuel Adams.

In character and career he was a singular combination of things incongruous. He was in religion the narrowest of Puritans, but in manner very genial. He was perfectly rigid in his opinions, but in his expression of them often very compliant. He was the most conservative of men, but was regarded as were the "abolition fanatics" in our time, before the emancipation proclamation. Who will say that his uprightness was not inflexible? Yet a wilier fox than he in all matters of political manœuvring our history does not show. In business he had no push or foresight, but in politics was a wonder of force and shrewdness. In a voice full of trembling he expressed opinions, of which the audacity would have brought him at once to the halter if he could have been seized. Even in his young manhood his hair had become gray and his hand shook as if with paralysis; but he lived, as we shall see, to his eighty-second year, his work rarely interrupted by sickness, serving as governor of Massachusetts for several successive terms after he had lived his threescore and ten years, almost the last survivor among the great pre-Revolutionary figures.

Among his endowments eloquence was not his most conspicuous power. As an orator Samuel Adams was surpassed by several of his contemporaries. His ordinary style of speech was plain and straightforward, rarely, it is probable, burning out into anything like splendor. For swelling rhetoric he was quite too sincere and earnest. John Adams, in his old age, said : —

"In his common appearance, he was a plain, simple, decent citizen, of middling stature, dress, and manners

He had an exquisite ear for music, and a charming voice when he pleased to exert it. Yet his ordinary speeches in town meetings, in the House of Representatives, and in Congress, exhibited nothing extraordinary; but upon great occasions, when his deeper feelings were excited, he erected himself, or rather nature seemed to erect him, without the smallest sympton of affectation, into an upright dignity of figure and gesture, and gave a harmony to his voice which made a strong impression on spectators and auditors, — the more lasting for the purity, correctness, and nervous elegance of his style."

In Philadelphia, in 1774, 1775, and 1776, John Adams probably was by far the best debater in Congress. Jefferson wrote: —

" As a speaker Samuel Adams could not be compared with his living colleague and namesake, whose deep conceptions, nervous style, and undaunted firmness made him truly our bulwark in debate. But Mr. Samuel Adams, although not of fluent elocution, was so rigorously logical, so clear in his views, abundant in good sense, and master always of his subject, that he commanded the most profound attention whenever he rose in an assembly by which the froth of declamation was heard with the most sovereign contempt."

Samuel Adams had his say and ceased. One may be quite certain that he was seldom tedious. He was never the " dinner-bell " of town meeting or Assembly; but James Otis and John Adams certainly surpassed him as orators, the former of whom might with good reason contest with Patrick Henry the title of " the American Chatham," while the latter was well called " the Colossus of debate."

Nor is it as a writer that Samuel Adams is at his best. It is probable that he was one of the most voluminous writers whom America has as yet produced. Some twenty-five signatures have been identified as used by him in the newspapers at different times. At the same moment that he filled the papers, he went on with his preparation of documents for the town and the Assembly till one wonders how a single brain could have achieved it all. If those writings only which can be identified were published, the collection would present a formidable array of polemical documents, embracing all the great issues out of whose discussion grew our independence. They were meant for a particular purpose, to shatter British oppression, and when that purpose was secured, their author was perfectly careless as to what became of them. Like cannon-balls which sink the ship, and then are lost in the sea, so the bolts of Samuel Adams, after riddling British authority in America, must be sought by diving beneath the oblivion that has rolled over them. Of the portion that has been recovered, these pages have given specimens enough to justify a high estimate of the genius and accomplishments of their author. It was an age of great political writers. Contemporary in England were Burke and " Junius," — in France, Montesquieu, Rousseau, and Voltaire, — in America, Dickinson, Franklin, and Paine

Samuel Adams will bear a good comparison with them, generally offering for any shortcoming some compensating merit. If there is never the magnificence of Burke, there is an absence, too, of all turgid and labored rhetoric. If there is a lack of Franklin's pith and wit, there is a lack, too, of Poor Richard's penny wisdom. If we miss the tremendous invective of " Junius," we find instead of acrid cruelty the spirit of humanity. If there is no over-bitter denunciation, there is on the other hand no milk and water. While he is never pedantic, the reader has had occasion to see his familiarity with ancient and modern literature, and in particular his acquaintance with writers upon constitutional history. The clearness of his style is admirable, his logic unvaryingly good. His intensity of conviction, both religious and political, sometimes makes him narrow. He can speak only in stern terms of a Tory ; scarcely otherwise of a Catholic or Episcopalian ; to free-thinkers like Franklin and Paine he did not at first find it easy to be cordial. But had he been more tolerant he must have been less intense and forceful.

That the power of Samuel Adams as a writer was better appreciated by his contemporaries than it has been by his successors is abundantly apparent. The man who more than any other felt his blows has left it on record that Samuel Adams had been " for near twenty years a writer against government in the public newspapers, at first but an indifferent one ; long practice caused him to arrive at great perfection, and to acquire a talent of artfully and fallaciously insinuating into the minds of his readers a prejudice against the character of all whom he attacked, beyond any other man I ever knew." " Bernard," says a contemporary, " used to ' damn that Adams. Every dip of his pen stings like a horned snake.' " These are the bitter, chagrin-charged comments of his opponents. His friends found no words strong enough to make known their appreciation. That the patriots were in the majority they directly attributed to him. Says James Sullivan : " By his speeches and ' Gazette ' productions a large majority was produced and maintained in Massachusetts in opposition to the claims of the ministry." Says John Adams: " A collection of his writings would be as curious as voluminous. It would throw light upon American history for fifty years. In it would be found specimens of a nervous simplicity of reasoning and eloquence that have never been rivaled in America."

It was, however, as a manager of men that Samuel Adams was greatest. Such another master of the ways by which a town meeting may be swayed the world has not seen. On the best of terms with the people, the shipyard men, the distillers, the sailors, as well as the merchants and ministers, he knew precisely what springs to touch. He was the prince of canvassers, the very king of the caucus, of which his father was the inventor. His ascendency was quite extraordinary, and no less marked over men of ability than over ordinary minds.   Always clear-headed and cool in the most confusing turmoil, he had ever at command, whether he was button-holing a refractory individual or haranguing a Faneuil Hall meeting, a simple but most effective style of speech.   As to his tact, was it ever surpassed?   We have seen Samuel Adams introduce Hancock into the public service, as he did a dozen others.   It is curious to notice how he knew afterwards in what ways, while he stroked to sleep Hancock's vanity and peevishness, to bring him, all unconscious, to bear, — now against the Boston Tories, now against the English ministry, now against prejudice in the other colonies.   Penniless as he was himself, it was a great point, when the charge was made that the Massachusetts leaders were desperate adventurers who had nothing to risk, to be able to parade Hancock in his silk and velvet, with his handsome vehicle and aristocratic mansion.   One hardly knows which to wonder at most, the astuteness or the self-sacrifice with which, in order to present a measure effectively or to humor a touchy co-worker, he continually postpones himself while he gives the foreground to others.   Perhaps the most useful act of his life was the bringing into being of the Boston Committee of Correspondence; yet when all was arranged, while he himself kept the laboring oar, he put at the head the faltering Otis.   Again and again, when a fire burned for which he could not trust himself, he would turn on the magnificent speech of Otis, or Warren, or Quincy, or Church, who poured their copious jets, often quite unconscious that cunning Sam Adams really managed the valves and was directing the stream.

The same ability at management has showed itself in his career in the Continental Congress. "I always considered him," said Jefferson, "more than any other member, the *fountain* of our more important measures;" and again, writing in 1825:

"If there was any Palinurus to the Revolution, Samuel Adams was the man. Indeed, in the Eastern States, for a year or two after it began, he was truly the Man of the Revolution. He was constantly holding caucuses of distinguished men (among whom was R. H. Lee), at which the generality of the measures pursued were previously determined on, and at which the parts were assigned to the different actors who afterwards appeared in them. John Adams had very little part in these caucuses; but as one of the actors in the measures decided on in them, he was a Colossus."

How profound was the belief which the Tories held in his cunning has been illustrated in the case of Hutchinson. Here are still other testimonies. The charge of duplicity becomes intelligible, from that Machiavellian streak in his character, the existence of which it is useless to attempt to deny: —

"John Adams is the creature and kinsman of Samuel Adams, the Cromwell of New England, to whose intriguing arts the Declaration of Independence is in a great measure to be attributed, the history of which will not be uninteresting.

"When the Northern delegates broached their political tenets in Congress, they were interrogated by some of the Southern ones, whether they did or did not aim at independence, to which mark their violent principles seemed to tend. Samuel Adams, with as grave a face as hypocrisy ever wore, affirmed that they did not, but in the evening of the same day, in a circle of confidential friends (as he took them to be), confessed that the independence of the colonies had been the great object of his life; that whenever he had met with a youth of parts, he had endeavored to instil such notions into his mind, and had neglected no opportunity, either in public or in private, of preparing the way for that event which now, thank God, was at hand.

"He watched the favorable moment when, by pleading the necessity of a foreign alliance, and urging the impracticability of obtaining it without a declaration of independence, he finally succeeded in the accomplishment of his wishes." [1]

Another Tory, writing from Boston early in this year, assails Adams and Hancock in this wise: —

"This man, whom but a day before hardly any man would have trusted with a shilling, and whose honesty they were jealous of, now became the confidant of the people. With his oily tongue he duped a man whose brains were shallow and pockets deep, and ushered him to the public as a patriot too. He filled his head with importance, and emptied his pockets, and as a reward kicked him up the ladder where he now presides over the 'Twelve United Provinces,' and where they both are

[1] "Decius," *Lond. Morn. Post*, 1779 (Moore's *Diary of the Revolution*, ii. 144).

at present plunging you, my countrymen, into the depths of distress."

After the destruction of Rivington's press in New York, the loyalist printer returned to England, and published a pamphlet to show that the intention of Congress was to assert American independence and maintain it with the sword.

"That I may thoroughly explain this matter," he continues, "it is necessary the public should be made acquainted with a very conspicuous character, no less a man than Mr. SAMUEL ADAMS, the would-be Cromwell of America. As to his colleague, JOHN HANCOCK, that gentleman is, in the language of Hudibras, —

> 'A very good and useful tool
> Which knaves do work with, called a fool.'

But he is too contemptible for animadversion. He may move our pity, not our indignation. Mr. Adams, on the other hand, is one of those demagogues who well know how to quarter themselves on a man of fortune, and, having no property of his own, has for some time found it mighty convenient to appropriate the fortune of Mr. Hancock to public uses, — I mean the very laudable purpose of carrying on a trade in politics.

"Mr. Adams finding, therefore, how very profitable a business of this kind might be made without the necessity of a capital of his own, it is no wonder he should eagerly embrace the opportunity of dealing in political wares with the demagogues of Britain.

"In justice to that gentleman's talents and virtues, it must be confessed that he is an adept in the business, and is as equal to the task of forwarding a rebellion as most men. He is therefore far from being unworthy the notice of British patriots. His politics are of a nature admirably adapted to impose on a credulous multitude.

"Mr. Adams's character may be defined in a few words. He is a hypocrite in religion, a republican in politics, of sufficient cunning to form a consummate knave, possessed of as much learning as is necessary to disguise the truth with sophistry, and so complete a moralist that it is one of his favorite axioms, 'The end will justify the means.' When to such accomplished talents and principles we add an empty pocket, an unbounded ambition, and a violent disaffection to Great Britain, we shall be able to form some idea of Mr. Samuel Adams."

"That Machiavellian streak in his character!" But do we need to go out of our way and call it Machiavellian? He would have been, alas! a less typical New Englander had he not stooped now and then to a piece of sharp practice. No Sam Slick, peddling out his cargo of clocks, or whittling away at a horse-swap, or (we must regretfully say it) inventing and distributing his wooden nutmegs, was ever "cuter" than Samuel Adams. The unconscionable outside world, while it ascribes to the Yankee character a thousand traits of worth, persists in detecting in the pot of ointment a most egregious fly. Who will deny that the defect is there? Sam Adams was too thorough a Yankee to be quite without it. We believe that he fell into it unconsciously. In the cases of sharp practice that can be brought home against him, it was, at any rate, never for himself, but always for what he believed the public good ; for from first to last one can detect in him no thought of personal gain or fame.

As Samuel Adams's followers often did not know that they were being led, so, possibly, he himself failed to see sometimes that he was leading, believing himself to be the mere agent of the will of the great people, which decided this way or that. Quite careless was he as regards wealth, as regards his position before his contemporaries and in history. Time and again the credit for great measures which he originated was given to men who were simply his agents, and there was never a remonstrance from him ; time and again the men whom he brought forward from obscurity, and whom he set here and there with scarcely more volition of their own than so many chessmen, stood in an eminence before the world which is not yet lost, obscuring the real master. Papers which would have established his title to a position among the greatest, he destroyed by his own hand, or left at haphazard.

If we briefly sum up the services rendered during these twelve years, the particulars of which, as they have been detailed, have seemed involved and confusing, it is easy to see how the men of his own day came to set him by the side of Washington, and how writers of our time can declare him "second only to Washington."[1] Those instruc-

[1] "A man whom Plutarch, if he had only lived late enough,

tions to the Boston representatives in 1764, in which Samuel Adams spoke for the town, emerging then, at the age of forty-two, into the public life where he remained to the end, contain the first suggestion ever made in America for a meeting of the colonies looking toward a resistance to British encroachments. From that paper came the "Stamp Act Congress." While the contemporaries of Samuel Adams rejoiced over the repeal of the Stamp Act, he saw in the declaration of Parliament by which it was accompanied, — " that it was competent to legislate for the colonies in all cases whatsoever," — plain evidence that more trouble was in store ; and he was the most influential among the few who strove to prevent a disastrous supineness among the people. From this time forward, in Massachusetts, the substantial authorship of almost every state paper of importance can be traced to him ; so, too, the initiation of almost every great measure.

Nor was he the less a man of national importance from the circumstance that his activity for the most part, up to this time, has been circumscribed by the limits of Massachusetts. As in Massachusetts the stirrings of freedom were most early and most earnestly felt, so for many years Massachusetts was a battle-ground in which arbi-

would have delighted to include in his gallery of worthies, a man who in the history of the American Revolution is second only to Washington, Samuel Adams." JOHN FISKE, a statement to the writer.

trary power and popular liberty were hotly contending, while the remaining provinces had little
to disturb their peace. "Boston is suffering in the
common cause," became the cry of America, at the
time of the Port Bill, in 1774. Massachusetts had
been no less suffering in the common cause for a
full decade before, the long parliamentary wrestle
between her General Court and the royal governors having been waged for the benefit of the whole
thirteen colonies no less than for herself. Elsewhere, no doubt, there was disturbance : in Virginia, in particular, the discord was grave between
the burgesses and the royal representatives. Massachusetts, however, was far more than any other
province the field of strife, the critical point beyond
all others being the Old State House in Boston,
with Hutchinson or Bernard in one end, and the
Assembly in the other. The great leader of the
Massachusetts folk-motes manœuvred and fought
in a small space ; but what was done was done for
an entire continent. It was no combat of mere
local significance. Who can estimate the greatness of the interests involved ?

From 1768, perhaps from an earlier period, he
saw no satisfactory issue from the dispute but in
the independence of America, and began to labor
for it with all his energy. It had been a dream
with many, indeed, that some time there was to be
a great independent empire in this western world ;
but no public man saw so soon as Samuel Adams
that in the latter half of the eighteenth century

the time for it had come, and that to work for it
was the duty of all patriots.[1] We have passed
in review the great figures of our Revolutionary
epoch one by one, and seen that neither then, seven
years before the Declaration of Independence, nor
long after, was there a man except Samuel Adams
who looked forward to it and worked for it. The
people generally had not conceived of the attain-
ment of independence as a present possibility.
Those who came to think it possible, like Franklin, Dickinson of Pennsylvania, and James Otis,
shrank from the idea as involving calamity, and
only tried to secure a better regulated dependence.
As late as 1775 the idea of separation, according
to Jefferson, had " never yet entered into any person's mind." [2] It was well known, however, what
were the opinions of Samuel Adams. He was isolated even in the group that most closely sur-

[1] July 1, 1774, Hutchinson, having just reached London, was
hurried by Lord Dartmouth into the presence of the king, without being allowed time to change his clothes after the voyage.
A conversation of two hours took place, the king showing the
utmost eagerness to find out the truth as to America. While
answering the king's inquiries concerning the popular leaders,
Hutchinson remarked that Samuel Adams was regarded " as the
opposer of government and a sort of Wilkes in New England.

" *King:* What gives him his importance ?

" *Hutchinson:* A great pretended zeal for liberty and a most
inflexible natural temper. He was the first that publicly asserted
the independency of the colonies upon the kingdom." *Diary and
Letters of Hutchinson*, p. 167.

Hutchinson had before declared the same thing in a letter to
Dartmouth, already quoted.

[2] Cooke's *Virginia*, p. 375.

rounded him. Even so trusty a follower and attached a friend as Joseph Warren could not stand
with him here. What Garrison was to the abolition of slavery, Samuel Adams was to independence, — a man looked on with the greatest dread
as an extremist and fanatic by many of those who
afterwards fought for freedom, down almost to
that very day, July 4, 1776, when, largely through
his skillful and tireless management, independence
was brought to pass.

We are accustomed to call Washington the
"Father of his country." It would be useless, if
one desired to do so, to dispute his right to the
title. He and no other will bear it through the
ages. He established our country's freedom with
the sword, then guided its course during the first
critical years of its independent existence. No one
can know the figure without feeling how real is its
greatness. It is impossible to see how, without
Washington, the nation could have ever been. His
name is and should be greatest. But after all is
"Father of America" the best title for Washington? Where and what was Washington during
those long preliminary years while the nation was
taking form as the bones do grow in the womb of
her that is with child? A quiet planter, who in
youth as a surveyor had come to know the woods ;
who in his young manhood had led bodies of provincials with some efficiency in certain unsuccessful
military expeditions ; who in maturity had sat, for
the most part in silence, among his talking col-

leagues in the House of Burgesses, with scarcely a suggestion to make in all the sharp debate, while the new nation was shaping. There is another character in our history to whom was once given the title, "Father of America," — a man to a large extent forgotten, his reputation overlaid by that of those who followed him, — no other than this man of the town meeting, Samuel Adams. As far as the *genesis* of America is concerned, Samuel Adams can more properly be called the "Father of America" than Washington.

CHAPTER XXII

CLOSING YEARS

BRITISH authority in America, so far at any rate as this could be done in the forum, was shattered by the Declaration of Independence. The work was then transferred to the field. Samuel Adams's heroic time has come to an end; his distinctive work is done; if he had died at the Declaration, his fame would be as great as it is now; what further he accomplished, though often of value, an ordinary man might have performed. The events of his life may be given henceforth with little detail.

So long as the war continued he remained in Congress, with the exception of one year, when infirmity, and the fact also that Massachusetts was in the act of adopting her state Constitution, in connection with which he rendered important service, kept him at home. Congress fell woefully in popular esteem, but the work and the responsibility remained vast for the few who were faithful. Samuel Adams has been accused of unfriendliness to Washington, and of having been concerned in the Conway cabal. The papers are in perfect preservation which put at rest this calumny, and

enable us to understand precisely what feeling
Samuel Adams did at this time entertain for
Washington. It was neither strange nor at all
discreditable at that period in the war to doubt
whether Washington was the best man in the
country for the head of the army. The supreme
position in the hearts of Americans, which he came
afterwards to hold, was at that time far enough
from being achieved. In the flood of disaster which
had so often overwhelmed the American efforts,
could any human eye then see clearly what portion
of responsibility for it rested on the commander,
what portion on his subordinates, and what was
due to things in general? So far, the only brilliant achievements of Washington had been the
victories at Trenton and Princeton, and that the
credit for those successes belonged to him was less
clear than it is now. The " Fabian policy," which
he had to so large an extent pursued, and which
the world now believes to have been masterly, did
not vindicate itself at once to the contemporaries
of Washington. To Samuel Adams, so straight
and impetuous, who from the beginning of his
course had sought his object with the directness
and force of a cannon-ball, and who felt that a fair
exertion of the military strength of America ought
to burst to pieces the British opposition, Washington, not unnaturally, seemed unenergetic.

But though Samuel Adams might be secretly
impatient, and might give his impatience expression in directions where he thought good might

result, he had no desire but to sustain the leader
in all efficient work. He had even been willing to
make him dictator. His own declarations, repeatedly uttered under circumstances which must cause
them to seem true to the most suspicious, make it
clear that he was never Washington's enemy, and
never plotted for his removal. A word must be said
about the origin of this calumny, which troubled
Adams in his lifetime, and followed him after
his death. We have already seen Samuel Adams
the object of the enmity of John Hancock, in the
old days of the struggle with Hutchinson. Now,
again, Hancock's worse nature has the upper
hand, and gives disgraceful evidence of itself.
His disposition to associate with the aristocratic,
temporizing element, his obstructive course when
the Declaration of Independence was pending, the
absurd pomp which he persisted in maintaining
as president of Congress, even when the nation
seemed at the last gasp, offended much his austere
and simple-minded colleague. Undoubtedly these
things had provoked from Adams severe remark.
This sharp criticism, combined with the fact that
the Tories, and indeed others, habitually spoke of
Hancock in a way quite exasperating to one so
vain, as the "ape" or "dupe" of Samuel Adams,
gives abundant explanation why an estrangement
should have come about. Hancock pursued his
former friend with great malignity. He circulated, if he did not originate, the slander that Samuel Adams was the enemy of Washington; and in

other ways used his high prestige to spread false
ideas as to his colleague's opinions and aims.

Said Mr. Adams: —

"The Arts they make use of are contemptible. Last
year, as you observe, I was an Enemy to General Washington. This was said to render me odious to the people. The man who fabricated that Charge did not believe it himself." [1]

In July, 1778, the British fleet left the Delaware
in haste, fearing to be blocked up by the superior
force of d'Estaing, about to arrive, and immediately Clinton, abandoning Philadelphia, retreated
through New Jersey, fighting on the way the battle
of Monmouth, where victory was so balked for
the Americans by the misconduct of Charles Lee.
Immediately afterward the French admiral, with
twelve sail of the line, four frigates, and four thousand troops, sailed into the Delaware, bringing M.
Gérard, the ambassador, for whom Congress, at
once returning to Philadelphia, prepared a great
reception. The ceremonies took place on August
5, and were more elaborate than had ever before
been witnessed in America. Somewhat ludicrously,
in this pompous pageant, Samuel Adams, associated with his old friend, Richard Henry Lee, appears as master of ceremonies, leading off in the
bowings and parade by which the man of Versailles

[1] In the Adams papers are several letters of interest as bearing
upon this point. One written to General Greene has an especial
value.

was to be made to feel that he had not fallen
among the Goths. But more than once before
this we have seen that Samuel Adams could pocket
his preferences to serve an occasion.

The French alliance came near going to ship-
wreck at the outset. Great was the mortification,
great the wrath at the French, to whose desertion,
as it was called, the failure in Rhode Island was
attributed. A serious riot between American and
French sailors occurred in Boston, in which all the
old animosity of the French war, which for the
time had slumbered, seemed on the point of reap-
pearing. Washington and Congress took all means
possible to restore a cordial understanding, in which
efforts Samuel Adams bore a great part. Here it
was, too, that Hancock rendered one of his greatest
services, his very vanity and profuseness, for once,
helping to an excellent result. He threw his house
open to d'Estaing and his officers, entertaining
them magnificently. Thirty or forty dined with
him each day, whom he dazzled with his liveries
and plate. At Concert Hall, too, he gave them a
great ball, and stimulated other Whigs to similar
hospitalities. The *entente cordiale*, which the Newport storm had disturbed, grew firm again amid
the steam of punch and the airs of the Boston fid-
dlers.

Adams opposed, in 1780, Washington's plan for
giving to officers serving through the war half pay
for life. To this period, too, belongs one of the
greatest mistakes of his career, which must be

referred to what may be called his town meeting ideas. He showed his dislike to the delegation of power to such an extent as to oppose the establishment of departments presided over by secretaries, preferring as the executive machinery of Congress the form of committees, which had prevailed from the first, and had often proved inconvenient. There was probably a degree of justice in the criticism of Luzerne, the French minister: —

" Divisions prevail in Congress about the new mode of transacting business by secretaries of different departments. Samuel Adams, whose obstinate, resolute character was so useful to the Revolution at its origin, but who shows himself so ill suited to the conduct of affairs in an organized government, has placed himself at the head of the advocates of the old system of committees of Congress, instead of relying on ministers or secretaries under the new arrangement."

He opposed the establishment of a Foreign Office; so, too, of a War Department, for the secretaryship of which the name of General Sullivan had been mentioned. He opposed, with equal decision, the appointment of a secretary of finance, which position, however, was created and bestowed upon Robert Morris, with results most important and beneficent. For the moment he consented to the dictatorship of Washington, but generally he looked askance at all approaches to the " one-man power," standing ready to sacrifice efficiency even in desperate circumstances, rather than contravene the principle that authority should rest, as immediately as possible, in the hands of the plain people.

On February 24, 1781, at length, four years and a half after the scheme had been initiated, the Articles of Confederation were ratified, and the affixing of his signature to these was the last act of Samuel Adams in Congress. The committee appointed to draw up the Articles of Confederation, created at the same time with the committee to draw up the Declaration of Independence, had found their work one of the greatest difficulty. Samuel Adams, it will be remembered, represented Massachusetts on the former committee, while John Adams served upon the latter. The embarrassing labor had gone forward whenever, from time to time, a moment could be snatched from the ever-pressing conduct of the war. It seemed scarcely possible to frame a practicable scheme. The several States, having declared themselves free from the authority of England, exulted in their independence, and regarded with great jealousy any scheme by which their liberty might be curtailed. Some bond must of necessity be devised, which would enable them to present front to the danger which threatened all alike. But the smaller States feared to be swallowed up by the larger, and the larger sometimes felt it to be beneath their dignity to stand on an equal footing with the smaller. There was as yet no common sentiment of nationality. Constitution framers never had a harder task. There was little enough precedent for a great federal league. The architects were inexperienced, those for whom they worked were most suspicious, the dangers and distractions, in the midst of which they must deliberate, were quite overwhelming. The Constitution of 1787 we feel to be vastly better, but the Confederation that preceded it is, of course, not to be despised. The Constitution was the child of the Confederation, its existence not possible without its parent. The Confederation was tentative, temporary, and no doubt as close and effective as it was possible, under the circumstances, to make it. The intermittent debates had tediously proceeded while often cannon thundered north and south, and the Congress, scarcely less than the commanders, were forced to live in the saddle. One by one the greater leaders of 1774, 1775, and 1776 had retired, yielding place often to inferior men, while they themselves served sometimes in the field, sometimes in their home legislatures, sometimes remained idle on their farms. At length, of all those who took part in sketching the original plan, Samuel Adams was left alone.

The adoption of the Articles of Confederation, so far from increasing, rather limited the powers of Congress. Sessions were to be annual, to commence on the first Monday in November; the delegates were to be appointed for a year, but were liable at any time to be recalled by the States that had sent them. To all important points nine States must consent, whereas before a mere major-

ity had been decisive. No State could vote unless
represented by at least two delegates. As regards
peace, war, and foreign intercourse, Congress possessed most of the powers now exercised by the
federal government; but it had no means of raising a revenue independent of state action, except
the resources, already exhausted and fallen into
disrepute, of paper issues and loans. Congress
could make requisitions on the States, but had no
power to enforce them; the oftener they were
made the less they were heeded.

It is worth while to look somewhat particularly
at the Articles of Confederation, because in the
framing of them Samuel Adams was so largely
concerned, and because, too, as will be seen, they
appeared to him, for the most part, quite satisfactory as a bond of union between the States. He
reluctantly gave them up afterwards for the Constitution, even after their weakness had become
very plain, dreading of all things a disposition to
centralize. In the States the legislatures should
be held in strict subordination to the town meetings; and, again, in the federation, there should be
no compromise of the independence of the States.
In April Samuel Adams took leave of Congress
for Massachusetts, from whose soil he never afterwards departed.

The following correspondence can be appropriately introduced here, as showing what men
in these times were after Samuel Adams's own
heart: —

WEST POINT, Dec. 10th, 1781.

Maj. Gibbs of your line is the bearer of this, by whom I have sent you a plate, a specimen of the material which covers my board. It is made, as the set is, of old unserviceable camp-kettles.

TO MAJ. GEN. ALEX. MACDOUGAL.

May 13th, 1782.

The present you sent me by Maj. Gibbs gratified me exceedingly. I intend to transmit it to my posterity as a specimen of Spartan frugality in an American general officer. The citizen and the soldier are called to the exercise of self-denial and patience, and to make the utmost exertions in support of the great cause we are engaged in.

S. A.

Always, when at home from Congress, as the town records of Boston show, he had been at the town meetings, serving as moderator, on committees of correspondence, safety, and inspection, committees for obtaining orators for the celebration of the anniversary of the Massacre, for the reformation of the manners of the town, for the instruction of representatives to address Lafayette, to take care of schools, etc., etc.[1] So it is that this Antæus of democracy touches, as he can, his mother earth, to draw in strength for the battle he is waging. Now that he is at home again permanently, he seems to be constantly present at the

[1] Town records of Boston from 1775 to 1781.

town meetings, acting as moderator whenever he is willing to serve as such, and intrusted with business great and small. Once more, too, the old man found himself under the roof of the Old State House, which had seen so many of his early battles and triumphs, for he was straightway elected to the Senate of the State, and became at once its presiding officer. As such he sat in that famous chamber to the east, where James Otis had denounced the writs of assistance, and where he himself had confronted Hutchinson in the stormy day of the Massacre.

One last scene of military pomp signalized the close of the war. In the late fall of 1782 the French army, which had fought well in the field and gained honor among the people, holding aloof from marauding and deeds of license, — a fact which put it often in favorable contrast even with the American levies, — marched from the Hudson to Boston, to embark for the West Indies. In uniforms of white and violet, with the fleur-de-lis waving over their ranks, in gaiters, queues, and great cocked hats, such as had figured at Fontenoy and in the wars of Frederick, the long column worked its way through the interior villages to the seaboard. The Baron Vioménil, who had done brilliantly at Yorktown, was their commander. Boston town meeting did all honor to their guests, for the Frenchmen remained some days while the transports were preparing. Samuel Adams was the prominent figure in the demonstrations.

Efforts having been made to restore the refugee Tories to their original rights, Adams, appointed by the town of Boston, instructed the Committee of Correspondence, Inspection, and Safety in terms which show that his implacability was undiminished. The committee are directed to oppose " to the utmost of their power every enemy to the just rights and liberties of mankind; after so wicked a conspiracy against these rights and liberties by certain ingrates, most of them natives of these States, and who have been refugees and declared traitors to their country, it is the opinion of this town that they ought never to be suffered to return, but excluded from having lot or place among us." However harsh this expression may appear, no fair student of the history of those days will deny the reasonableness of the judgment. There was every motive for prudence as to the admission of British emissaries and men of Tory sentiments. Whatever their professions, they could scarcely fail to treat with contempt the new order of things, and try secretly to undermine it. Efforts were made in 1784 and 1785 to exchange the Boston town meeting for a city organization, which, it was felt, would be much more convenient for managing the affairs of so large a population. The people, however, could not bring themselves to give up the venerable system which had accomplished such memorable results. Samuel Adams took a leading part in the discussions, and was chairman of the important committee to whom was left the duty of stating the " defects of the town constitution." In this capacity he reported to the town that " there were no defects," [1] and in his time there was no change.

In 1786 came the formidable popular outbreak known as Shays's Rebellion. The weight of federal and state taxes, combined with the pressure of a vast private indebtedness, well-nigh crushed the people. Circumstances made proper the most rigid economy, but the vicious spirit of extravagance prevailed. The courts, whose agency had been invoked for the collection of the debts, were declared in the western counties to be engines of destruction. Other grievances, sometimes partly reasonable, sometimes absurd, were the cost of litigation, the inordinate salaries of many public officers, and the existence of the Senate in the state Constitution, which was condemned as needless and aristocratic. At conventions of the people, sometimes imposing through numbers, demagogues dwelt in exaggerated terms upon these topics, and, in no secret way, violence was counseled against the laws of the land. The means employed, indeed, were the same used against British authority, which had resulted in the Revolution. Those precedents, in that time recent, were in the minds of the agitators; and it could be plausibly urged that the men now in authority under the new order could not consistently find fault with this application of their own machinery, which the people were setting at work once more to right great wrongs by which they felt

[1] Town records, November 9, 1785.

themselves oppressed. Samuel Adams and those who believed with him certainly had reason to be much embarrassed by the situation. There is nevertheless no evidence that the old democrat hesitated for a moment as to his course. While the public suffering could not be doubted, it was the result of a terrible war and could not be helped. Whatever injustice existed could be reached and remedied by constitutional means, without an overturn, — a thing which could not at all be said of the old oppressions. He wrote to John Adams : —

"Now that we have regular and constitutional governments, popular committees and county conventions are not only useless but dangerous. They served an excellent purpose, and were highly necessary when they were set up, and I shall not repent the small share I then took in them."

As the danger thickened, Samuel Adams was one of those who declared for the sternest measures to maintain the Constitution and the laws. Once more at the head of Boston town meeting, which he guided as moderator, and whose spokesman he as usual became, as first on the committee appointed to draft an address, he strengthened the hands of his old fellow fighter, the fearless, energetic Bowdoin, then governor, who was ready to do his full duty. The entire state militia was called out, and was well commanded, for fortunately the veteran officers of the Revolution stood stoutly on the side of law and order.

The gossiping William Sullivan gives a good picture of the noble Bowdoin, standing on the steps of the court-house at Cambridge while the troops of General John Brooks pass by in review. He was fifty-eight years old, tall and dignified, dressed in a gray wig, cocked hat, white broadcloth coat and waistcoat, red smallclothes, and black silk stockings. His air and manner were quietly grave, his features rather small for a man of his size, his colorless face giving evidence of the delicate health which no doubt had prevented him from taking a stand among the first of the patriots. Blood was shed at Springfield, and at length in midwinter came the famous march of General Lincoln to Petersham, thirty miles in one night through a driving snowstorm, which scattered the main power of the insurgents, and ended the danger.

The attitude in which Samuel Adams stood to the federal Constitution was much misrepresented during his lifetime, and a misunderstanding as regards it has clouded his fame to the present day. He disliked to confer great powers, as we have repeatedly seen, on a body far removed from its constituents. According to his town meeting ideas there should always be as few removes as possible of the power from the people. In 1785 Samuel Adams writes to Elbridge Gerry, advising against " a general revision of the Confederation," which seems to him dangerous and unnecessary, and he

appears to strike hands with Gerry and his colleague King, the representatives from Massachusetts, to embarrass those who favor a stronger central government.[1] At the same time, however, he
declares : " It would have been better to have fallen
in the struggle than now to become a contemptible
nation," and he seems to be persuaded that there
must be in some way a strong, effective union.
His declarations are perhaps not altogether consistent, and imply some uncertainty.

At the beginning of the convention assembled
in Massachusetts for the ratification or rejection
of the Constitution, Samuel Adams underwent a
severe affliction in the death of his son, who, with
his constitution broken by the hardships of a surgeon's life during the war, died at thirty-seven.
For two weeks debates went forward without result, Mr. Adams sitting silent, though it should be
mentioned that at the beginning, no doubt with the
idea of securing harmony, he made a motion quite
similar to that which preceded the deliberations at
Philadelphia in 1774, and which was regarded as
such a master-stroke. It was that the ministers of
the town in turn, without regard to sect, should be
invited to open the meetings with prayer.

An effort was made to bring the convention to
an abandonment of the consideration of the instrument by paragraphs, and induce it to vote upon
the document as a whole, which without doubt
would have resulted in its rejection. This Samuel

[1] Bancroft, *Hist. of Constit.* i. 199.

Adams opposed in a speech still extant. He declared that he had difficulties and doubts as regards the proposed Constitution, as had others, and he desired to have a full investigation instead of deciding the matter in a hurry. This prevailed, and in the course of the following week the shrewd managers who favored the acceptance of the form submitted devised a way to secure victory. Nine amendments were prepared, famous as the " conciliatory propositions," the story of which is told as follows by Colonel Joseph May : [1] —

" Adams and Hancock [then governor] were both members of the convention in Massachusetts, and the two most powerful men in the State. Adams questioned the policy of the adoption without amendments, and let men know his reasons; but Hancock was in great trouble, and, as usual on such occasions, he had, or affected to have, the gout, and remained at home, wrapped up in flannel. The friends of the Constitution gathered about him, flattered his vanity, told him the salvation of the nation rested with him: if the Constitution was not accepted, we should be a ruined nation; if he said accept it, Massachusetts and the nation would obey. They persuaded him to that opinion. It was reported abroad that he had made up his mind, and had recovered from his illness so far that, on a certain day, he would appear again in the convention, and would make a speech which would probably be in favor of adopting the Constitution. Theophilus Parsons, afterwards the famous judge, was the most active in procuring this result. He wrote a speech for Hancock to read in the convention.

[1] Wells, iii. 258.

"So when the day arrived, Mr. Hancock was helped out of his house into his coach, and driven down to the place where the convention was held, — Federal Street, — and thence carried into the convention by several young gentlemen, who were friends of the family and in the secret. He rose in his place and apologized for his absence, for his feebleness, and declared that nothing but the greatness of the emergency would have brought him from his bed of sickness; but duty to his country prevailed over considerations of health. He hoped they would pardon him for *reading* a speech which he had carefully prepared, not being well enough to make it in any other manner. Then he read the speech which Parsons had written for him, and from Parsons's manuscript, and sat down. One of his friends took the manuscript hastily from him, afraid that the looker-on might see that it was not in Hancock's hand, but Parsons's."

Colonel May next relates the course adopted to secure the coöperation of Adams: —

"The same means were undertaken to influence Mr. Adams. It was not, however, so easy. They had done what they could with experiment; flattery would have no effect upon him; but they knew two things, — first, that he had great confidence in the democratic instincts of the people; and second, that he was a modest man, and sometimes doubted his own judgment when it differed from the democratic instincts aforesaid. So they induced some of the leading mechanics of Boston to hold a meeting at the 'Green Dragon Inn' in Union Street, their private gathering place, and pass resolutions in favor of the Constitution, and send a committee to present them to him. He was surprised at the news of the meeting, and the nature of the resolutions, and asked who was there. They were just the men, or the class of men, whom he confided in. He inquired why they had not called him to attend the meeting. 'Oh, we wanted the voice of the people,' was the answer. Mr. Adams was still more surprised, and, after long consideration, concluded to accept the Constitution with the amendments."

Daniel Webster gave in 1833 a graphic account of the same incident, in which Paul Revere, whose attributes, as he goes on in life, become rather those of Vulcan than Mercury, is made to play the leading part: —

"He received the resolutions from the hands of Paul Revere, a brass founder by occupation, a man of sense and character and of high public spirit, whom the mechanics of Boston ought never to forget. 'How many mechanics,' said Mr. Adams, 'were at the Green Dragon when the resolutions were passed?' 'More, sir,' was the reply, 'than the Green Dragon could hold.' 'And where were the rest, Mr. Revere?' 'In the streets, sir.' 'And how many were in the streets?' 'More, sir, than there are stars in the sky.'"

In the "conciliatory propositions" all powers not expressly delegated to Congress were reserved to the several States; the basis of representation was altered; the powers of taxation and the granting of commercial monopolies by Congress were restricted; grand jury indictments in capital trials were provided for; the jurisdiction of federal

courts in cases between the citizens of different
States was limited, and the right of trial by jury
was given in such cases. Upon the introduction of
these amendments, Mr. Adams urged the ratification of the Constitution, upon the understanding
that they were to be recommended. Still another
speech followed, in which he became a strong
advocate of the instrument, and dwelt upon the
amendments one by one; and it is a curious feature
of the speech that, though he well knew where the
amendments really came from, yet with some of
his old-time cunning his evident desire is to encourage the general impression that Hancock originated them. It was a matter of great importance
that the popular governor should be supposed to
have presented his own views; and the admiring
Mr. Wells, unconscious, as we have found him before, of any devious trickery, takes pains to show
how Adams strove hard to produce in his hearers
a false impression. It is not edifying, but it is
certainly droll, to see how the young foxes successfully manage to outwit the old fox, who then, all
unconscious that he has himself been a victim, goes
on with his wily expedient to inveigle the convention into doing right.

The debate proceeded, the eloquence of Fisher
Ames making a powerful impression in favor of
the Constitution. Massachusetts had instructed
her delegates to insist on an annual election of congressmen; Samuel Adams, always believing that
power delegated should return as soon as possible

to the people, from whom alone it could come, and willing, no doubt, to subscribe to Jefferson's phrase, " Where annual election ends, tyranny begins," asked why congressmen were to be chosen for two years. Caleb Strong explained that it was a necessary compromise, at which Adams answered, "I am satisfied." The concession seemed so important to the convention that he was asked to repeat it, which he did. At length he suggested certain other amendments. These were rejected by the convention, though afterward accepted by the nation. They now form the 1st, 2d, 3d, and 4th articles in amendment; the clauses of the conciliatory propositions were also in part adopted as amendments.

We need not follow more particularly the episodes of the convention, which at last ratified the Constitution by a narrow majority, the vote standing one hundred and eighty-seven to one hundred and sixty-eight. Probably there were few men in the convention, as there were few in the country, who did not feel that there were defects in the form proposed. The only real difference apparently between Samuel Adams and those who were held to be special advocates of the Constitution was that, while all felt there were defects, the latter wished to accept the instrument at once and unconditionally, and to run the risk of future amendments; whereas Mr. Adams felt that the ratification should be accompanied by a recommendation of amendments. The first conciliatory proposition in particular, expressly reserving to the States the rights not delegated to the federal government, Adams regarded as "a summary of a bill of rights," and therefore of great importance. Jefferson also declared that the proposition supplied the vital omission of a bill of rights, which was what "the people were entitled to against every government on earth, general or particular, and what no just government should refuse or rest on inference." Bancroft is careful to point out that Adams by no means makes the acceptance of the amendments *a condition* of ratification, but would have them simply *recommended* at the same time with the ratification.

Letters of Mr. Adams soon after this express very earnestly his desire to have the amendments adopted. He wished "to see a line drawn as clearly as may be between the federal powers vested in Congress and the distinct sovereignty of the several States, upon which the private and personal rights of the citizens depend." His fear was lest "the Constitution, in the administration of it, would gradually, but swiftly and imperceptibly, run into a consolidated government, pervading and legislating through all the States; not for federal purposes only, as it professes, but in all cases whatsoever. . . . Should a strong Federalist see what has now dropped from my pen, he would say that I am an 'Anti-Fed,' an amendment monger, etc." [1] Mr. Bancroft sums up well Samuel Adams's posi-

[1] To R. H. Lee, July 14, 1789, from the autograph.

tion when he speaks of " the error that many have made in saying that he was at first opposed to the Constitution. He never was opposed to the Constitution; he only waited to make up his mind." [1] His contemporaries indeed declared that his influence *saved* the Constitution in Massachusetts. His position is quite different from that not only of Patrick Henry, but also from that of R. H. Lee and Elbridge Gerry, who opposed with all their power.

As the year 1788 drew to a close, the federal Constitution being now in force, though two States still withheld their assent, an effort was made to send Samuel Adams again to Congress. In the newspapers of the time the most earnest tributes are paid to him. He is set side by side with Washington. Says the " Independent Chronicle " of December, 1788 : " While we are careful to introduce to our federal legislature the American Fabius, let us not be unmindful of the American Cato." "America," says another, " in her darkest periods ever found him forward and near the helm, and for her sake he with cheerfulness seven years served her with a halter round his neck. Naked he went into her employ, and naked he came out of it." Says another : " It has been said, he is old and anti-federal. His age and experience are the very qualifications you want. His influence caused the Constitution to be adopted in this State."

[1] From a private letter to the writer.

Mr. Adams, however, lost the election, which was won by Fisher Ames, a young lawyer of thirty-one, who by his eloquence in the Constitutional Convention had raised to the highest a reputation before becoming brilliant. The virulence of party spirit was excessive. To have advocated amendments to the Constitution, however reasonable and proper, was enough to condemn the most respected man, as far as the Federalists were concerned. There was danger even from other weapons than sharp tongues and pens. A note is still preserved, written rudely on coarse paper, with the words blurred by the moisture of the wet grass of Samuel Adams's garden, into which it had been thrown, in which he is warned against assassination. In April following, however, Adams became lieutenant-governor, Hancock being governor. He had already been in Hancock's council, and the reconciliation had now become cordial. Adams, indeed, had always been magnanimous. In Hancock's case, the lapse of years and increasing infirmities mitigated animosities, and gave opportunity to the better nature which he certainly had. Their supporters, rejoicing to see the old patriots once more friends and again in the foreground together, printed the ticket in letters of gold.

The following year the venerable pair were again chosen, and in a speech to the legislature, made by Adams upon entering on his second term of office, one finds expressions so cool and wise concerning the great constitutional question, that it is hard to see how even the smoke of partisan battle could have blinded men to their justice : —

"I shall presently be called upon by you, sir, as it is enjoined by the Constitution, to make a declaration upon oath, (and shall do it with cheerfulness, because the injunction accords with my own judgment and conscience,) that *the Commonwealth of Massachusetts is, and of right ought to be, a free, sovereign, and independent State.* I shall also be called upon to make another declaration, with the same solemnity, *to support the Constitution of the United States.* I see the consistency of this, for it cannot have been intended but that these constitutions should mutually aid and support each other. It is my humble opinion that, while the Commonwealth of Massachusetts maintains her own just authority, weight, and dignity, she will be among the firmest pillars of the federal Union.

"May the administration of the federal government and those of the several States in the Union, be guided by the unerring finger of heaven! Each of them and all of them united will then, if the people are wise, be as prosperous as the wisdom of human institutions and the circumstances of human society will admit."

A conflict which seems to have aroused the old energy of Adams more than any other that occurred during his declining years was that as to whether theatrical representations should be allowed in Boston. In 1790 the legislature was petitioned for authority to open a theatre in Boston, which was promptly refused. In the following year a town meeting instructed the representatives to obtain, if possible, a repeal of the prohibitory act. It was carried, over the protest of Samuel Adams and the old-fashioned citizens. When Harrison Gray Otis made a vigorous demonstration on the same side, Samuel Adams "thanked God that there was one young man willing to step forth in the good old cause of morality and religion." He himself fought the Philistines on the floor of Faneuil Hall until his weak voice was drowned in roars of disapproval. The prohibitory act was not repealed, but a theatre was opened in spite of it, upon which Hancock vindicated the law by causing the whole company to be arrested on the stage. A new application from the town for a repeal of the act brought the legislature to compliance. Samuel Adams had now become governor, for we are anticipating somewhat. His theory was that the governor was simply an executive officer, whose only proper function was to carry out the popular will as expressed in the legislative enactments. He says in one of his inaugurals: "It is yours, fellow citizens, to legislate, and mine only to revise your bills under limited and qualified powers; and I rejoice that they are thus limited. These are features which belong to a free government alone." But desperate circumstances demanded desperate expedients. His dear Boston, so far from becoming the "Christian Sparta" of his dreams, was fast going to the dogs of depravity. Under the circumstances consistency was a jewel not at all too precious to be sacrificed. He set himself stub-

bornly against the popular will and vetoed the repeal. So long as he sat in the chair of the chief
magistrate the prohibitory law remained on the
statute books, though the scandalous play-actors
dodged through their performances after a fashion in spite of the constables, to the delight of
the graceless generation which had come into the
places of the fathers.

Though his natural force was suffering some
abatement, Adams could yet defend with power
still great the old, oft-threatened positions, in front
of which, all his life, he had fought so faithful
a battle. John Adams returned from Europe in
1788, after an absence of nine years. In the earlier
time the kinsmen had been of one mind, but the
younger had imbibed aristocratic notions during
his life in courts, which divided him from his
friend. A correspondence between John Adams,
then vice-president of the United States, and Samuel Adams, then lieutenant-governor of Massachusetts, which, although courteous, illustrates the difference of their ideas, was a notable controversy of
the time. Of the democratic ideas Jefferson became the leading exponent. Although at present
not dominant, these were soon to become the prevailing ideas of America. Of the holders of these,
" Republicans," as they were at first called, Samuel
Adams was recognized as the head in Massachusetts.

With the approach of the fall in 1793, Hancock's infirmities perceptibly increased, and his end

was plainly near. The two men had come to stand once more hand in hand, as in the bygone days, when Gage had outlawed them together, and they had fled before the regulars with the volleys of Lexington filling the April morning. What though Hancock had trimmed and played the fool? Again and again he had risked wealth and life, as he stood chivalrously in the thick of peril. What though he had insulted and calumniated his old associate? His heart had turned tenderly to him once more in old age, and Samuel Adams, as tenderly, held him once more in a brotherly clasp. Here is his last letter to Hancock: [1] —

BOSTON, Sept. 3d, 1793.

MY VERY DEAR SIR, — I received your letter on Saturday evening last. It cheered the spirit and caused the blood to thrill through the veins of an old man. I was sorry for the injunction you laid me under. I hope you will relax it, and give me leave to keep it. I shall then read it often, and when I leave it, it will be read to your honor after you and I shall be laid in the dust. I am rejoiced to discover by it that your mind is firm and your speech good. Shall I venture to conjure you, as your friend, strictly to comply with the advice of your physicians? I have seen Drs. Jarvis and Warren; they tell me that they were all united in opinion, and say that they are in hopes, under Providence, to bring you to such a state of health as to enable you to perform the duties of a station with which the people have honored you, which I pray God you may continue in many years

[1] From the autograph.

after I am no more here. Mrs. Adams joins me in best regards to you and Madam.

> Your sincere friend,
>
> S. ADAMS.

Hancock died at last on the 8th of October. He was honored with a most solemn funeral, and Samuel Adams followed the coffin as chief mourner. The strength of the septuagenarian failed to sustain him under the emotions that overwhelmed him. He withdrew from his place as the train wound past the Old State House, and it went on to the Granary Burying Ground without the man of the gray head and the trembling hands, who through Hancock's death had become chief magistrate of Massachusetts.

On January 17, 1794, Samuel Adams delivered his first speech, as governor, to the Senate and House. He thought it worth while to recapitulate to some extent the ultimate grounds of freedom which he had so often asserted, and it was perhaps well, in the widespread doubt that had come to exist as to the expediency of trusting government to the hands of the people.

In 1794, 1795, and 1796 Mr. Adams was elected governor by heavy majorities, although the Federalists made efforts to defeat him. In his addresses to the two houses he occupied the reasonable mean between the extreme Federalists and the extreme Republicans, insisting upon the necessity of a just concession of power to the Union, while urging at the same time a maintenance of the rights of the States. He approved thoroughly the policy of Washington as regards European entanglements, acknowledging the wisdom of his proclamation of neutrality, issued soon after the arrival of Citizen Genet.

The Jay treaty proclaimed in 1796, favored by ·Hamilton and Fisher Ames, Adams opposed, in company with Madison, Gallatin, and Brockholst Livingston, and made no effort to stop the expressions of popular disapproval which, in Boston, became riotous. His position drew down upon him unmeasured wrath from the Federalists, though few at the present time will maintain that the provisions of that treaty were altogether wise.

As the year 1797 opened, Samuel Adams, now seventy-five, gave notice, in a speech to the legislature, of his retirement from public life. That he had honor in this hour elsewhere than at home had been shown in the presidential election which had just taken place, when, in the electoral college, Virginia had thrown for Thomas Jefferson twenty votes, and for Samuel Adams fifteen. Both houses of the Massachusetts General Court addressed him in terms of great respect, and in May the toil-worn servant of the people laid down his responsibilities.

His appearance in age is thus described by Wells:—

"He always walked with his family to and from church, until his failing strength prevented. His stature was a little above the medium height. He wore a tie-wig, cocked hat, buckled shoes, knee-breeches, and a red cloak, and held himself very erect, with the ease and address of a polite gentleman. On stopping to speak with any person in the street his salutation was formal yet cordial. His gestures were animated, and in conversation there was a slight tremulous motion of the head. He never wore glasses in public, except when engaged in his official duties at the State House. His complexion was florid and his eyes dark blue. The eyebrows were heavy, almost to bushiness, and contrasted remarkably with the clear forehead, which, at the age of seventy, had but few wrinkles. The face had a benignant but careworn expression, blended with a native dignity (some have said majesty) of countenance, which never failed to impress strangers."

Henceforth he lived in his house in Winter Street (the Purchase Street home he had been forced to resign), his wife at his side, cared for by his daughter and her children. In cap and gown he walked in his garden or sat in the doorway. As age grew upon him his nearer life receded, and the great figures and deeds of the Revolution were oftener in his thoughts. Once more he walked with Otis and Warren and Quincy; once more, in mind, he rallied into closest battle-order the scattered Massachusetts towns, put to flight, unweaponed, the Fourteenth and Twenty-ninth regiments, and barred out Gage in the great crisis of the throe when "the child Independence was born." In mixed companies, and among strangers, he was reserved and silent; among friends he was companionable, abounding in anecdote, and keenly alive to wit. His grandchildren read to him, or were his amanuenses. To the last he was interested in the common schools. In 1795, while rejoicing over the establishment of academies, he had, as governor, expressed to the legislature the fear that a large increase of these institutions might lessen "the ancient and beneficial mode of education in grammar schools," whose peculiar advantage is "that the poor and the rich may derive equal benefit from them, while none, excepting the more wealthy, generally speaking, can avail themselves of the benefits of the academies." His form now was familiar in the schoolrooms, and he was known as a friend by troops of children.

It is pleasant to record that in the storm of party fury, now hotter than ever, there were some Federalists broad-minded enough to do him honor. When, in 1800, Governor Caleb Strong was advancing through Winter Street, in a great procession, probably at the time of his inauguration, Mr. Adams was observed in his house looking out upon the pageant. The governor called a halt, and ordered the music to cease. Alighting from his carriage, he greeted the old man at the door, grasped the paralytic hands, and expressed, with head bared, his reverence for Samuel Adams. The soldiers presented arms, and the people stood uncovered and silent.

Could he have lived a second life, a brilliant

recognition would probably have fallen to him.
The forces of federalism were becoming exhausted;
the incoming wave of democracy would certainly
have lifted him into a place of power. Already, as
we have seen, Virginia, in 1796, cast fifteen votes
in the electoral college for him as president; her
great son, Jefferson, as he came at last into the
supreme position, recalled with enthusiasm their
association and sympathy in the first Congresses,
and could hardly find language strong enough to
express his regret that old age must have its dues.

"A government by representatives elected by the
people, at *short* periods, was our object; and our maxim
at that day was, ' Where annual election ends, tyranny
begins.' Nor have our departures from it been sanctioned by the happiness of their effects." " How much
I lament that time has deprived me of your aid ! It
would have been a day of glory which should have called
you to the first office of my administration. But give us
your counsel, my friend, and give us your blessing, and
be assured that there exists not in the heart of man a
more faithful esteem than mine to you, and that I shall
ever bear you the most affectionate veneration and respect." [1]

His work was done, and Adams calmly awaited
the end. As his friends were obliged to buy
clothes for him that he might make a respectable
appearance at the first Continental Congress, in
1774, so at the last it would have been necessary
to support and bury him at the public expense,

[1] February 26, 1800 ; March 29, 1801 ; from the manuscripts.

had he not inherited from his son, the army surgeon, claims against the government which yielded about six thousand dollars. This sum, fortunately invested, sufficed for the simple wants of himself and his admirable wife.

Tudor, in his " Life of James Otis," gives the following often-quoted description of the political character of Samuel Adams : —

"He attached an exclusive value to the habits and principles in which he had been educated, and wished to adjust wide concerns too closely after a particular model. One of his colleagues who knew him well, and estimated him highly, described him, with good-natured exaggeration, in the following manner : ' Samuel Adams would have the State of Massachusetts govern the Union, the town of Boston govern Massachusetts, and that he should govern the town of Boston, and then the whole would not be intentionally ill-governed.' "

It is not a good description of Samuel Adams's limitation. He believed, to be sure, in the town first, then the State, then the Union ; but he had no such overweening confidence in himself as is here denoted. From the voice of the plain people there could be, in his idea, no appeal. In town meeting assembled, their mandate would be wise, and must be authoritative. To that he deferred submissively in important crises, postponing his own judgment. His comrades knew it, and sometimes shrewdly played upon him, as when they overcame his hesitation before the federal Constitution. Even when he himself was far in the foreground, acting with all energy from his own inspirations, it is probable he often fancied that he represented and was pushed by the popular impulse. He was submissive before "instructions," as if in some way he were really hearkening to the voice of God. He was slow in recognizing the ways through which, in a vast republic like ours, all large affairs must be administered. A nation of fifty millions cannot be run upon the town meeting plan. There is a perilous decentralization, toward which, in the great forming days, Samuel Adams tended, as others rushed toward peril in the opposite extreme. Into the feeble Congress of 1781 he could not bear that there should be any introduction of "one-man power," which alone could give it efficiency; he favored terms of office too short for the suitable training of the official; he thought power must ever return speedily to the people who gave it, so that the representative might never forget that he was the creature of his constituents. The cases are few, however, in which his advocacy was unreasonable; when all has been said that can be said, America has had but few public men so devoted, so wise, so magnificently serviceable as he.

He grew feeble during the summer of 1803, and was conscious, as was every one, that the end was at hand. Early on the morning of Sunday, October 2, the tolling bells made known to the town that he was dead. The "Independent Chronicle" did him honor the next day in a fine specimen of dignified, old-fashioned obituary.

There was embarrassment, through political enmity, in procuring a suitable escort for his funeral. But at length difficulties were overcome, and an impressive train, headed by the Independent Cadets, and consisting of many dignitaries and private friends, accompanied the plain coffin through the streets, during the firing of minute-guns from the Castle. He was borne past the doors of the Old South, which in his age had become his place of worship; at length the muffled drums reverberated from Faneuil Hall, but before reaching it, at the Old State House, the funeral turned. Had no occult sympathy established itself between the heart that had grown still and the pile that rose so venerable in the twilight of the autumn day? No other voice had sounded so often in its chambers; its thresholds had felt the lightness of his youth and the feebleness of his age. Beneath its roof had gathered the scattered Massachusetts towns in the great old days, and, submissive to his controlling mind, had there wrought out a work that must sanctify the spot forever. Had there been a poet in the crowd, one fancies the blank windows of the council chamber and the assembly-room might have been seen to become suffused, and the quaint belfry to make some obeisance. There is no record that any sign was given. The train moved up Court Street into Tremont Street : in the Granary Burying Ground at last Samuel Adams found his

grave. In what is now Adams Square, the town
he loved has commemorated him worthily in imposing bronze. His dust lies almost beneath the
feet of the passers in the great thoroughfare, close
to that of the victims of the Boston Massacre.

CHAPTER XXIII

THE TOWN MEETING TO-DAY

Have New Englanders preserved the town meeting of Samuel Adams? Fifteen million, scarcely one quarter, of the inhabitants of the United States, are believed to be descendants of the twenty-one thousand who, in the dark days of Stuart domination, came from among the friends of Cromwell and Hampden to people the Northeast. In large proportion they have forsaken the old seats, following the parallels of latitude into the great Northwest, and now at length across the continent to California and Oregon. At the beginning of the century Grayson wrote to Madison that " New Englanders are amazingly attached to their custom of planting by townships." So it has always been; wherever New Englanders have had power to decide as to the constitution of a forming state, it has had the township as the basis. But in the immense dilution which this element of population has constantly undergone, through the human flood from all lands, which, side by side with it, has poured into the new territories, its influence has of necessity been often greatly weakened, and the form of the township has been changed from

the original pattern, seldom advantageously.[1]   In
New England itself, moreover, a similar cause has
modified somewhat the old circumstances.   While
multitudes of the ancient stock have forsaken the
granite hills, their places have been supplied by a
Celtic race, energetic and prolific, whose teeming
families throng city and village, threatening to outnumber the Yankee element, depleted as it has
been by the emigration of so many of its most vigorous children.   To these new-comers must be
added now the French Canadians, who, following
the track of their warlike ancestors down the river-
valleys, have come by thousands into the manufacturing towns and into the woods, an industrious
but unprogressive race, good hands in the mills,
and marvelously dexterous at wielding the axe.
Whatever may be said of the virtues of these new-
comers, and of course a long list could be made
out for them, they have not been trained to Anglo-
Saxon self-government.   We have seen the origin
of the folk-mote far back in Teutonic antiquity.
As established in New England, it is a revival of a
very ancient thing.   The institution is not congenial to all; the Irishman and Frenchman are not at
home in it, and cannot accustom themselves to it,

[1] George E. Howard, Introd. to *The Local Constitutional Hist.
of the U. S.*   S. A. Galpin, *Walker's Statistical Atlas of U. S.* ii.
10.   Johns Hopkins Univ. Studies, as follows : Albert Shaw, *Local Government in Illinois;* E. W. Bemis, *Local Government in
Michigan and the North-West*; E. R. L. Gould, *Local Government
in Pennsylvania;* J. Macy, *Institutional Beginnings of a Western
State* (Iowa).

until, as the new generations come forward, they take on the characteristics of the people among whom they have come to cast their lot. At present, in most old New England towns, we find an element of the population numbering hundreds, often thousands, who are sometimes quite inert, allowing others to decide all things for them; sometimes voting in droves in an unintelligent way as some whipper-in may direct; sometimes in unreasoning partisanship following through thick and thin a cunning demagogue, quite careless how the public welfare may suffer by his coming to the front.

Still another circumstance which threatens the folk-mote is the multiplication of cities. When a community of moderate size, which has gone forward under its town meeting, at length increases so far as to be entitled to a city charter, the day is commonly hailed by ringing of bells and salutes of cannon. But the assuming of a city charter has been declared to be " an almost complete abnegation of practical democracy. The people cease to govern themselves; once a year they choose those who are to govern for them. Instead of the town meeting discussions and votes, one needs now to spend only ten minutes, perhaps, in a year. No more listening to long debates about schools, roads, and bridges. One has only to drop a slip of paper, containing a list which some one has been kind enough to prepare for him, into a box, and he has done his duty as a citizen." [1] In the

[1] *New York Nation*, May 29, 1866.

most favorable circumstances, the mayor and common council, representing the citizens, do the work for them, while individuals are discharged from the somewhat burdensome but educating and quickening duties of the folk-mote. As yet the way has not been discovered through which, in an American city, the primordial cell of our liberty may be preserved from atrophy.

Though the town meeting of the New England of to-day rarely presents all the features of the town meeting of Samuel Adams, yet wherever the population has remained tolerably pure from foreign admixture, and wherever the numbers at the same time have not become so large as to embarrass the transaction of business, the institution retains much of its old vigor. The writer recalls the life, as it was twenty-five years ago, of a most venerable and uncontaminated old town, whose origin dates back more than two hundred years. At first it realized almost perfectly the idea of the Teutonic " tun." For a long time it was the frontier settlement, with nothing to the west but woods until the fierce Mohawks were reached, and nothing but woods to the north until one came to the hostile French of Canada. About the houses, therefore, was drawn the protection of a palisade to inclose them (*tynan*) against attack. Though not without some foreign intermixture, the old stock was, twenty-five years ago, so far unchanged that in the various " deestricks " the dialect was often unmistakably nasal; the very bobolinks in the meadow-grass, and the bumblebees in the hollyhocks, might have been imagined to chitter and hum with a Yankee twang; and "Zekle" squired "Huldy," as of yore, to singing-school or apple-paring, to quilting or sugaring-off, as each season brought its appropriate festival. The same names stood for the most part on tax, voting, and parish lists that stood there in the time of Philip's war, when for a space the people were driven out by the Indian pressure; and the fathers had handed down to the modern day, with their names and blood, the venerable methods by which they regulated their lives. On the northern boundary a factory village had sprung up about a water-power; at the south, too, five miles off, there was some rattle of mills and sound of hammers. Generally, however, the people were farmers, like their ancestors, reaping great hay-crops in June with which to fat in the stall long rows of sleek cattle for market in December; or, by farmer's alchemy, transmuting the clover of the rocky hills into golden butter.

From far and near, on the first Monday of March, the men gathered to the central village, whose people made great preparations for the entertainment of the people of the outskirts. What old Yankee, wherever he may have strayed, will not remember the "town meeting gingerbread," and the great roasts that smoked hospitably for all comers! The sheds of the meeting house close by were crowded with horses and sleighs; for, in the intermediate slush between ice and the spring

mud, the runner was likely to be better than the
wheel. The floor of the town-hall grew wet and
heavy in the trampling; not in England alone is
the land represented; a full representation of the
soil comes to a New England town meeting, — on
the boots of the freemen. On a platform at the
end of the plain room sat the five selectmen in a
row; at their left was the venerable town clerk,
with the ample volume of records before him. His
memory went back to the men who were old in
Washington's administration, who in their turn remembered men in whose childhood the French and
Indians burned the infant settlement. Three lives,
the town clerk's being the third, spanned the whole
history of the town. He was full of traditions,
precedents, minutiæ of town history, and was an
authority in all disputed points of procedure from
whom there was no appeal. In front of the row
of selectmen with their brown, solid farmer faces,
stood the moderator, a vigorous man in the forties,
six straight feet in height, colonel of the county
regiment of militia, of a term's experience in the
General Court, and therefore conversant with parliamentary law, a quick and energetic presiding
officer.

It was indeed an arena. The south village
was growing faster than the "street," and there
were rumors of efforts to be made to move the
town-hall from its old place, which aroused great
wrath; and both south village and "street" took
it hard that part of the men of the districts to the

north had favored a proposition to be set off to an
adjoining town. The weak side of human nature
came out as well as the strong in the numerous
jealousies and bickerings. Following the carefully
arranged programme or warrant, from which there
could be no departure, because ample warning
must be given of every measure proposed, item
after item was considered, — a change here in the
course of the highway to the shire town, how much
should be raised by taxes, the apportionment of
money among the school districts, what bounty the
town would pay its quota of troops for the war, a
new wing for the poor-house, whether there should
be a bridge at the west ford. Now and then came
a touch of humor, as when the young husbands,
married within the year, were elected field-drivers,
officers taking the place of the ancient hog-reeves.
Once the moderator for the time being displeased
the meeting by his rulings upon certain points of
order. "Mr. Moderator," cried out an ancient
citizen with a twang in his voice like that of a
well-played jewsharp, "ef it's in awrder, I'd jest
like to inquire the price of cawn at Cheapside."
It was an effective *reductio ad absurdum*. Another rustic Cicero, whom for some reason the
physicians of the village had displeased, once filled
up a lull in proceedings with: "Mr. Moderator, I
move that a dwelling be erected in the centre of
the graveyard, in which the doctors of the town
be required to reside, that they may have always
under their eyes the fruits of their labors."

The talkers were sometimes fluent, sometimes stumbling and awkward. The richest man in town, at the same time town treasurer, was usually a silent looker-on. His son, however, president of the county agricultural society, an enterprising farmer, whose team was the handsomest, whose oxen were the fattest, whose crops were the heaviest, was in speech forceful and eloquent, with an energetic word to say on every question. But he was scarcely more prominent in the discussions than a poor cultivator of broom-corn, whose tax was only a few dollars. There was the intrigue of certain free-thinkers to oust the ministers from the school committee, — the manœuvring of the factions to get hold of the German colony, a body of immigrants lately imported into the factory village to the north. These sat in a solid mass at one side while the proceedings went on in an unknown tongue, without previous training for such a work, voting this way or that, according to the direction of two or three leaders.

Watching it all, one could see how perfect a democracy it was. Things were often done far enough from the best way. Unwise or doubtful men were put in office, important projects were stinted by niggardly appropriations, unworthy prejudices were allowed to interfere with wise enterprises. Yet in the main the result was good. This was especially to be noted, — how thoroughly the public spirit of those who took part was stimulated, and how well they were trained to self-reliance, intelligence of various kinds, and love for freedom. The rough blacksmith or shoemaker, who had his say as to what should be the restriction about the keeping of dogs, or the pasturing of sheep on the western hills, spoke his mind in homely fashion enough, and possibly recommended some course not the wisest. That he could do so, however, helped his self-respect, and caused him to take a deeper interest in affairs beyond himself than if things were managed without a right on his part to interfere; and this gain in self-respect, public spirit, self-reliance, to the blacksmith and shoemaker, is worth far more than a mere smooth or cheap carrying on of affairs.

Is there anything more valuable among Anglo-Saxon institutions than this same ancient folkmote, this old-fashioned New England town meeting? What a list of important men can be cited who have declared, in the strongest terms that tongue can utter, their conviction of its preciousness![1] It has been alleged that to this more than anything else was due the supremacy of England in America, the successful colonization out of which

[1] John Stuart Mill, *Representative Government*, p. 64, etc.; De Tocqueville, *De la Démocratie en Amérique*, i. 96, etc.; J. Toulmin Smith, *Local Self-Government and Centralization*, p. 29, etc.; May, *Constitutional History of England*, ii. 460; Bluntschli, quoted by H. B. Adams, *Germanic Origin of N. E. Towns*; Jefferson to Kercheval, July 12, 1816, and to Cabell, February 2, 1816; John Adams, Letter to his wife, October 29, 1775; Samuel Adams, Letter to Noah Webster, April 30, 1784; R. W. Emerson, *Concord Bicentennial Discourse*, 1835, etc.; Bryce, *American Commonwealth*, ii. p. 246.

grew at last the United States. France failed precisely for want of this.[1] England prevailed precisely because "nations which are accustomed to township institutions and municipal government are better able than any other to found prosperous colonies. The habit of thinking and governing for one's self is indispensable in a new country." So says De Tocqueville, seeking an explanation for the failure of his own race, and the victory of its great rival.[2] None have admired this thorough New England democracy more heartily than those living under a very different polity. Richard Henry Lee of Virginia wrote in admiration of Massachusetts[3] as the place "where yet I hope to finish the remainder of my days. The hasty, unpersevering, aristocratic genius of the South suits not my disposition, and is inconsistent with my views of what must constitute social happiness and security." Jefferson becomes almost fierce in the earnestness with which he urges Virginia to adopt the township. "Those wards, called townships in New England, are the vital principle of their governments, and have proved themselves the wisest invention ever devised by the wit of man for the perfect exercise of self-government and for its preservation. . . . As Cato, then, concluded every speech with the words 'Carthago delenda est,' so

[1] Lecky, *Hist. XVIIIth Century*, i. 387.

[2] *De la Dém. en Am.* i. 423.

[3] *Life of R. H. Lee*, Letter to John Adams, October 7, 1779, i. 226.

do I every opinion with the injunction: 'Divide the counties into wards!'"[1]

The town meeting has been called "the primordial cell of our body politic." Is its condition such as to satisfy us? As we have seen, even in New England, it is only here and there that it can be said to be well maintained. At the South, Anglo-Saxon freedom, like the enchanted prince of the "Arabian Nights," whose body below the waist the evil witch had fixed in black marble, had been fixed in African slavery. The spell is destroyed; the prince has his limbs again, but they are weak and wasted from the hideous trammel. The traces of the folk-mote in the South are sadly few. Nor elsewhere is the prospect encouraging. The influx of alien tides to whom our precious heirlooms are as nothing, the growth of cities and the inextricable perplexities of their government, the vast inequality of condition between man and man — what room is there for the little primary council of freemen, homogeneous in stock, holding the same faith, on the same level as to wealth and station, not too few in number for the kindling of interest, not so many as to become unmanageable — what room is there for it, or how can it be revivified or created? It is, perhaps, hopeless to think of it. Mr. Freeman remarks that in some of the American colonies "representation has supplanted the primitive Teutonic democracy, which had sprung into life in the institutions of the first settlers." Over vast

[1] *Works*, vi. 544; vii. 13.

areas of our country to-day, representation has supplanted democracy. It is an admirable, an indispensable expedient, of course. Yet that a representative system may be thoroughly well man-. aged, we need below it the primary assemblies of the individual citizens, "regular, fixed, frequent, and accessible," discussing affairs and deciding for themselves. De Tocqueville seems to have thought that Anglo-Saxon America owes its existence to the town meeting. It would be hard, at any rate, to show that the town meeting was not a main source of our freedom. Certainly it is well to hold it in memory; to give it new life, if possible, wherever it exists; to reproduce some semblance of it, however faint, in the regions to which it is unknown. It is well to brush the dust off the half-forgotten historic figure who, of all men, is its best type and representative.

INDEX

INDEX

"No taxation without representation," made a popular phrase by Otis, 40.

OGDEN, ——, of New Jersey, a loyalist at Stamp Act Congress, 65.

Old South Church, 13, 100, 151, 152, 223, 227, 292, 293, 373.

Old State House, associated with Adams, 53, 54, 317, 334, 348, 373; description of, 54; connection with town meetings, 55; at time of Massacre, 152, 154.

Oliver, Andrew, stamp distributer, hanged in effigy, 47; refused reelection to Council by Assembly, 85; advises Hutchinson to request removal of soldiers, 156; becomes lieutenant-governor, 168; his letters obtained by Franklin, 199; their character, 202; used to blacken Hutchinson, 205, 209; his removal requested, 205; death, 236; his character, 250; unseemly scene at his funeral, 250.

Oliver, Peter, refused reelection to Council by Assembly, 85; refuses compliance with Assembly's order to decline payment from king, 234; impeached, 235; prevented by fear from attending his brother's funeral, 250.

Otis, Harrison Gray, applauded by Adams for opposing repeal of law prohibiting theatres, 363.

Otis, James, senior, promised chief justiceship by Governor Shirley, 38; passed over in favor of Hutchinson, 38.

Otis, James, advocate-general, 38; resigns position and assails British government in writs of assistance case, 38; accused by Hutchinson of low motives, 39; success of his oratory described by John Adams, 40; prepares memorial against parliamentary taxation, 45; contrast with Adams, 56; popularity, 57, 81; willing to submit to Stamp Act, 57; favors colonial representation in Parliament, 58; at Stamp Act Congress, 64, 65; representative for Boston in 1766, 83; secures opening of debates of the Assembly to the public, 84; compliments Hawley on his boldness, 86; admits parliamentary right to lay customs duties, 91; increasing eccentricity, 92; leads town meeting in "Romney" and "Liberty" affair, 100; quarrels with Adams over publication of Assembly's letter to Hillsborough, 102; less democratic than Adams, 104; chosen Boston representative at conven-

tion of towns, 110; hinders action by failure to attend, 110; frequenter of Edes & Gill's office, 120; reelected Boston representative in Assembly, 121; enraged at accusations of disloyalty, 133; assaulted by English officers, 133; his violence and arrogance, 134; managed by Adams, 134; probable self-seeking, 135; an embarrassment to colonial cause, 135, 136; expresses loathing of soldiers, 144; supports Hutchinson on question of validity of royal instructions to override charter, 168; becomes insane, 168; chairman of the Committee of Correspondence, 179; his power as a leader, 319; really a danger to patriot side, 320; how made use of by Adams, 327.

PAINE, ROBERT TREAT, prosecutes soldiers after Boston Massacre, 165; elected delegate to Continental Congress, 265, 267; his journey thither, 277; arrival at second Continental Congress, 300; favors conciliation, 307; loses popularity in Massachusetts, 309.

Paine, Thomas, effect of his pamphlets, "Common Sense" and "The Crisis," testified to by Adams, 309; his ability as a writer, 324.

Parker, Jonas, his share in battle of Lexington, 297.

Parliament, its supremacy over colonies, denied in colonies and by Franklin, 28; admitted frequently by Massachusetts, 28; question debated in Parliament, 72-75; still maintained in England, 76; asserted by Declaratory Act, 82; denied by Hawley, 86; growth of opposition to, in colonies, 88; debate opened by Hutchinson, 187, 188; reply of the Assembly, 189, 190.

Parsons, Theophilus, writes a speech for Hancock to deliver in favor of the federal Constitution, 354.

Paxton, Charles, customs officer at Boston, applies for a writ of assistance, 38; returns as customs commissioner under Townshend Acts, 91; his letters obtained by Franklin, 199; their character, 202; used to discredit Hutchinson, 205, 209.

Pemberton, Thomas, selectman, on Boston committee to demand removal of soldiers, 153.

Pennsylvania, Assembly of, instructs delegates to oppose independence, 311.

Pepperell, Sir William, his success in taking Louisburg, 17.

Born to an old Concord, Massachusetts, family, educated at Harvard College and the Harvard Divinity School, JAMES KENDALL HOSMER (1834-1927) served briefly as a Unitarian minister in Deerfield, Massachusetts, then moved west to become a professor at Antioch College, the University of Missouri, and Washington University in St. Louis. At retirement he was librarian of the Minneapolis Public Library. Though he wrote on a wide range of subjects, Hosmer was primarily a historian, and his biography of Samuel Adams (1885) was perhaps the best known of his many books.

PAULINE MAIER is Professor of History at the Massachusetts Institute of Technology. She has written widely on America's Revolutionary period, her most recent work being *The Old Revolutionaries; Political Lives in the Age of Samuel Adams.*